FIRST IN HIS CLASS

A Biography of Bill Clinton

DAVID MARANISS

SIMON & SCHUSTER

New York   London   Toronto   Sydney   Tokyo   Singapore

SIMON & SCHUSTER
Rockefeller Center
1230 Avenue of the Americas
New York, NY 10020

Designed by Irving Perkins Associates, Inc.

Manufactured in the United States of America

5   7   9   10   8   6   4

Library of Congress Cataloging-in-Publication Data
Maraniss, David.
First in his class : a biography of Bill Clinton / David Maraniss.
p.   cm.
Includes index.
1. Clinton, Bill, 1946–   .   2. Presidents—United States—Biography.   I. Title.
E886.M29   1995
973.929′092—dc20
[B]   94-48245
CIP
ISBN 0-671-87109-9

Photo Credits
1, 2, 4: Family photos acquired by *The Washington Post* and David Maraniss. With permission. 3, 24: *Arkansas Democrat-Gazette.* 5: Old Gold Yearbook. 6, 7: American Legion. 8: Protocol. With permission from Georgetown University. 9, 10: Tom Campbell. 11, 12: Lyda Holt. 13. Jacques M. Chenet/The Gamma Liaison Network. 14: Brooke Shearer. 15: *The Washington Post.* 16, 18: *The Southwest Times Record.* 17: The Doug Wallace Papers, University of Arkansas/Little Rock. 19, 20, 25: AP/Wide World Photos. 21, 22, 27: Arkansas Governor's Office. 23. Reuters/Bettmann. 26: Harry Truman Moore. 28. Mark Duncan, AP/Wide World Photos. 29. Glenda Cooper.

To Linda, Andrew, and Sarah

CONTENTS

8   *Contents*

PREFACE

THE TITLE OF this book is meant to evoke its central theme: how Bill Clinton, out of the thousands of bright, ambitious people from the postwar baby boom generation, became the first to reach the White House. He never was first in his class except in the broadest sense of the phrase, though he finished near the top in high school and college. The title also embraces the school years that were so pivotal in the lives of our generation, a period loosely known as the sixties, which in this book runs from the summer day in 1963 when Clinton shook President Kennedy's hand to the fall day in 1971 when one of his best friends, a former Vietnam war resister, killed himself.

Time and again as I worked on this book, people asked me a simple question: Do you like Bill Clinton? As a newspaperman for the last twenty years, I had trained myself to avoid answering that sort of bias-establishing inquiry. As a biographer, I realized that I had to confront it, if only in my own mind. Yet I also saw the paradox: the very reason I wanted to write the book was to get beyond the narrow dimensions of a political world in which, increasingly, superficial judgments are being made about people. My natural inclination goes the other way, toward trying to understand people's actions within the circumstances of their time and place. That is what I sought to do with Bill Clinton. Midway through the writing process, I began to frame the question differently. Clinton became not a politician but a character. Whether he was doing something admirable or questionable, I would say the same thing to myself: Well, that's Clinton. In that sense, I came to like him even when I disliked him and dislike him even when I liked him. Perhaps that is another way of avoiding the question, but it is the only honest answer I can give. He is a big character, whether he is acting big-hearted or small.

Any book inevitably defines itself, but I feel compelled to alert the reader to what this book is not. It is not intended to be a book preoccupied with Clinton's sex life, nor is it an investigation of the Whitewater controversy. Both subjects appear in modest proportions. Those hungering for more of either will have to do their dining elsewhere. My goal was for this book to be neither pathography nor hagiography, but a fair-minded examination of a complicated human being and the forces that shaped him and his generation. It is not an authorized biography. Clinton and his wife, Hillary Rodham Clinton, declined to be interviewed for this book. Some White House aides, especially those attached to Hillary Clinton, were unhelpful. I did interview Bill Clinton five times, and Hillary Clinton once, during the presidential campaign. The White House in any case was not an essential place to find sources for a biography that ends on the night Clinton announced for president. Nearly four hundred people were interviewed for this book. Among them were scores of Clinton's closest friends, colleagues, and relatives, who eagerly shared recollections and documents.

There is, of course, always room for dispute about anyone's life, especially the interpretation of events in a life as full and complex as Clinton's. To fortify the narrative, I have relied on documents whenever possible. Virtually every interview for the book was on the record, and every event and quotation is sourced and cited in the chapter notes at the end.

PROLOGUE: WASHINGTON, D.C., 1963

THE BOYS RODE down to the White House in two air-conditioned buses, fifty scrubbed faces per coach, hair clipped, shoes polished, slacks creased, young chests fairly busting from white short-sleeve knit shirts inscribed over the left breast with the seal of the American Legion. They were high school seniors-to-be, a proud collection of eager-beaver class leaders born in the first year of the postwar boom, groomed for success in the backwater redoubts of service club America, towns named Hardaway and Sylvester and Midland and Lititz and Westfield and Hot Springs. Some of these boys were so provincial that they had never before traveled by overnight train or flown by commercial airliner. Now, for five days in Washington as senators at Boys Nation, they had been playing the roles of powerful actors on the political stage, their schedules crammed with mock debates, speeches, and elections, as well as lunches in the Senate Dining Room and briefings at the Department of State. Boys Nation was an educational exercise, mostly, and partly a reward for academic achievement, but it also offered a hint of something grander. Hour after hour the boys heard older men call them the future leaders of the free world, and while some only dimly envisioned such a prospect, others accepted it as their fate. For them this week was a coming-out party and dress rehearsal.

The capital region was caught in a midsummer snare of high heat and humidity that July of 1963, particularly stifling to the one hundred teenage senators each night out at the University of Maryland campus where their closet-sized dormitory rooms lacked not only air conditioners but even electric fans. But on Wednesday the 24th as the buses rolled south from College Park toward the White House, the morning sky opened blue and gentle, graced by a soft breeze, as though the weather acknowledged its own assignment for an event that, decades later, would resurface as a national icon of political fate and ambition.

The boys were on their way to meet President John F. Kennedy in the Rose Garden. Though young, stylish, and witty, Kennedy was hardly a mythic figure two and a half years into his term. Many in the Boys Nation enclave looked upon him with ideological caution, reflecting the conservative views of their sponsors in the American Legion's division of National Americanism. They made no secret of their admiration for Republican Senator Barry Goldwater of Arizona, an apostle of antifederalism then building a national movement that made Kennedy nervous about a second term. Still, JFK was a war hero and the leader of the free world. He represented the archetype of what Boys Nation alumni were supposed to become. The boys were excited to meet him. For most of the half-hour trip down from the Maryland campus, their buses resounded with nervous, anticipatory chatter.

Daniel J. O'Connor, a New York lawyer and director of National Americanism for the Legion, led the contingent on the first bus. He and his staff assistants, veterans of World War II or Korea, carefully briefed their charges on proper behavior in the Rose Garden: *Security will be tight. If you wander off, the Secret Service will stop you. Stay together. Stay in rows. If the president comes down to greet you, do not crowd around. If you do, he'll withdraw.* O'Connor knew that his boys were well mannered. He had encountered little trouble from them in Washington beyond a few curfew violations and the time when some of them disturbed Secretary Rusk by snapping flashbulb cameras as he delivered a solemn address on world affairs at the State Department auditorium. Minor stuff. But O'Connor wanted to be certain that the Legion boys would not replay a recent Rose Garden embarrassment when foreign exchange students had mobbed the president and somehow liberated his cuff links and tie clasp, walking off with his accessories as unsolicited souvenirs.

On the bus, O'Connor chatted with several boys. He asked each one where he was from and what he thought of Washington so far. One lad lingered in his presence longer than the others, leaving an impression that O'Connor could call to mind years later. It was Bill Clinton of Hot Springs, Arkansas. He was only sixteen, but one of the bigger boys physically at six foot three and two hundred pounds, with a wave of brown hair and a good-natured manner. Clinton was curious about what lay in store for the boys that morning. His own intentions were clear. He asked O'Connor whether he could have his picture taken with President Kennedy. "Sure," O'Connor said. "But I'm not sure what the Secret Service regulations are. We'll have to see when we get there." Clinton pressed the issue. It sure would be great, he said, if he could get his picture taken with the president. The boy from Arkansas, O'Connor recalled, "certainly seemed bound and determined."

WHATEVER little encouragement Clinton needed to confront the political whirl of Washington that summer came from two strong women: his mother, Virginia, and his high school principal, Johnnie Mae Mackey. They were opposites in many respects: Virginia Clinton, a nurse anesthetist, layered her face with makeup, dyed her hair black with a bold white racing stripe, painted thick, sweeping eyebrows high above their original position, smoked two packs of Pall Mall cigarettes a day, bathed in a sunken tub, drank liquor, was an irrepressible flirt, and enjoyed the underbelly of her resort town, with its racetrack and gaming parlors and nightclubs. Johnnie Mae Mackey strode through town as a tall and imposing enforcer of moral rectitude whose interests were God, country, flag, politics, church, and Hot Springs High. Yet they were both optimists, and they saw one bright boy as the embodiment of their hopes. They had lost husbands already, each of them. Billy Clinton was their manchild.

Mackey, whose husband, a World War II veteran, had died of diabetes, belonged to the American Legion auxiliary at Warren Townsend Post No. 13 in Hot Springs. Through that club and her position at the school she became an influential force in student government programs sponsored by the Legion each summer. She had a deep interest in Arkansas politics and played a prominent role in Governor Orval Faubus's network of women supporters around the state. She instilled in her students the conviction that the political life was noble and that there was no higher calling than public service. One of her favorite tasks during the final week of class each spring was to announce over the public address system the names of junior boys and girls who had been selected by the faculty to attend Arkansas Boys State at Camp Robinson in North Little Rock in June. Hot Springs traditionally sent a large and powerful state delegation under Mrs. Mackey's leadership. In the class ahead of Clinton's, a Hot Springs student had been elected Boys State governor.

To be elected governor was the ultimate accomplishment at the state level of this political prepping ground. It was the contest that attracted the most gossip, speculation, and excitement, the one that carried heady prestige within the peer group. Many states did not even elect the two senators who attended Boys Nation; they were chosen instead by adult supervisors, who often simply rewarded the governor and lieutenant governor by sending them to Washington. Arkansas elected its senators, but the senate vote came at the end of the week, almost as an afterthought to the contest for governor. When Clinton arrived at Camp Robinson, he had little chance at the governorship. For one thing, it would be difficult for Hot Springs to grab the top post two years in a row. But even more important, the most respected and well-connected student leader in Arkansas was running for governor that year—Mack McLarty of Hope.

Mack and Billy, acquaintances since they attended kindergarten together, presented a classic small-town contrast. They had been born months apart in Hope, a modest railroad hub in southwest Arkansas. McLarty's mother came from the landed gentry and his daddy ran the most prosperous Ford dealership in that corner of the state. Clinton's mother was the daughter of the town iceman. His biological father was dead and his stepfather was an abusive alcoholic. In the stratified southern culture, McLarty was expected to excel; Clinton's abilities were viewed as a freak of nature. When the Clintons left Hope for Hot Springs in 1952, when Billy was six, the wave of their departure left barely a ripple. Only his mother and grandmother harbored grand notions of what might be in store for him.

Thomas Franklin McLarty III, cocksure, snappy, and athletic, a natural leader who became student council president and all-district quarterback for a powerhouse 11–1 football team, Number 12, as quick as a hiccup on the option—Mack was Hope's favorite son. Governor of Boys State was thought to be merely the first step in his march to prominence. As a campaigner, Mack was sweet and syrupy. In his speeches at Camp Robinson he talked mostly about how glad he was to get to know so many good people in such a fine state in such a wonderful country. His slogan was candy-coated: If You Can Remember M&Ms, Remember Mack McLarty. He built a campaign coalition drawing largely from athletic contacts and trounced his articulate but rather bookish opponent. There seemed to be a conspiracy of quarterbacks that year: the boys elected lieutenant governor and attorney general were also signal callers.

But none of the quarterbacks worked the field quite like clumsy Bill Clinton when he ran for senate at the end of the week. He studied each barracks at Camp Robinson, learning which schools were staying where, what the likes and dislikes of the students in each section might be, who they might know in common. The other boys from Hot Springs had seen Clinton switch into campaign mode before but never with this intensity. Ron Cecil was amazed by his friend's political savvy and the urgency with which he shook the hands of strangers. Phil Jamison, another classmate, noticed that Clinton was thoroughly familiar with the camp culture before he arrived and had plotted his senate race while other boys were still finding their way around. There were hundreds of boys there, Clinton told Jamison, and if he could meet every one of them they would like him and he would win. He formed a campaign team that canvassed the cabins at night and posted himself outside the cafeteria at six-thirty each morning, working the breakfast crowd like a factory gate.

McLarty, elected governor, maintained his status as the top boy in Arkansas. But Clinton, elected senator, was the one now going somewhere. He prepared for his trip to Washington. "It's the biggest thrill and honor of my life," he said after winning. "I hope I can do the tremendous job required of me as a representative of the state. I hope I can live up to the task."

ON the morning of July 19, 1963, two young senators from Arkansas met at Adams Field in Little Rock for the flight to Boys Nation, the first venture to the East Coast for either Clinton or his colleague, Larry Taunton of El Dorado. Amid the excitement and anxiety, Taunton took special note of the relationship between the other boy and his mother. He had rarely seen anything like it. Mrs. Clinton radiated such an intense interest in her son that she seemed almost to be hovering over and around him.

Every week, it seemed, her boy Billy was doing something else to make her proud, to relieve her mind of her own troubles. Virginia Clinton had convinced herself that he had a rendezvous with fame. She loved to tell the story of how a second-grade teacher had predicted that he would be president someday. Now he was flying to Washington. Maybe, she told friends, Billy would meet the handsome young president. The Clintons were Democrats in a resort town overtaken by conservative northern retirees who had come to Hot Springs for its mild climate and restorative waters. In his ninth-grade civics class, when the teacher organized a Nixon-Kennedy election debate, Clinton was the lone Kennedy supporter.

The eighteenth annual American Legion Boys Nation was meticulously regulated. Reveille at seven each morning, lights out at ten at night. The boys marched in straight lines to the dining hall and waited in lines for the buses that carried them down to the federal district each day. They were organized into four sections—Adams, Jefferson, Washington, and Madison —each section with its own counselors and living quarters. The two senators from each state shared a dormitory room, but they were placed arbitrarily in separate political parties, one a Federalist, one a Nationalist. Clinton was assigned to Adams Section, Nationalist party. The official politicking began Sunday night, after a day trip to the Tomb of the Unknown Soldier at National Cemetery, when the Nationalists and Federalists convened to draft their party platforms and the senators began considering their two major bills for the week, one that called for the creation of a department of Housing and Urban Affairs and included a public accommodations civil rights measure, and another that would institute federal funding of campaigns. There was little dispute about foreign policy. Southeast

Asia, a growing trouble spot for the Kennedy administration, was not yet the preoccupation that it would soon become for these boys. The looming danger, the Federalists declared, was "the Communistic threat." Clinton's Nationalist party agreed, adding that the Communists must be stopped wherever they attempt to impose their will through force because "appeasement leads to aggression."

The most contentious issue was civil rights. Voices rose as both parties debated planks in their platforms and the full Boys Nation senate deliberated over S-1. The argument was played out during one of the pivotal years in the American civil rights saga. Months earlier, Governor George Corley Wallace of Alabama, who had taken office promising "segregation now, segregation tomorrow, segregation forever," stood in front of the schoolhouse door as federal marshals enrolled the first black students at the University of Alabama. And one month after the boys left Washington, Martin Luther King, Jr., would stand before a massive throng at the Lincoln Memorial and deliver his "I Have a Dream" speech.

Race was still largely viewed as a North-South issue, but the lines were not so clear at Boys Nation. Three of the leading civil rights proponents were southern youths—the two boys from Louisiana, Fred Kammer of New Orleans and Alston Johnson of Shreveport, and Bill Clinton of Arkansas—all of whom were questioning their southern heritage of racial separation and inequality. Clinton could not be called a civil rights activist. He had not publicly protested the patterns of racism he grew up with in Hot Springs, where the schools, swimming pools, clubs, and motels had been segregated, where "Dixie" was the high school fight song until his junior year, and where the local Lions club recruited members of the high school choir to appear in blackface for the annual minstrel show. But long before Clinton reached Washington that summer he had rejected the legacy of racism. His mother would later remember how frustrated he seemed as a boy of eleven watching Governor Faubus defy federal orders during the integration of Little Rock Central High School in 1957.

Most of the boys were not that far along. Orson L. (Pete) Johnson of Alabama came to Washington determined to push through a resolution heralding the constitutional primacy of states' rights, the rhetorical banner behind which southern states protected their segregated policies. It passed 48 to 46. Johnson and his Boys Nation sidekick, Tommy Lawhorne of Georgia, tried to mold the southern senators into a voting bloc. One morning at breakfast they confronted Clinton. Johnson thought he had Clinton cornered. He told the Arkansan that he "didn't need to be voting for these civil rights resolutions." The argument got emotional, but Clinton would not budge.

With both parties divided on the issue, civil rights advocates came out of the Boys Nation session with a modest victory. The bill establishing the urban affairs department and a public accommodations law was defeated. Both party platforms declared that education, not government enforcement, offered the surest means of eliminating racism. The Federalists, dominated by a group of northern conservatives who held segregation and government activism in equal disfavor, stated: "Ideals cannot be forced upon a person by sheer physical force. The thought of this turns many against such an ideal; prejudice and hate must be removed from the hearts and minds of people where it really exists." Clinton's Nationalists took a slightly more determined position. "Racial discrimination is a cancerous disease and must be eliminated," they declared. "But legislation alone cannot change the minds and hearts of men. Education is the primary tool which we must employ . . . it must begin in the home, in the church and in the schools."

On Monday morning, the boys ventured to Capitol Hill to visit the Supreme Court and the Library of Congress. Many of them were invited to lunch with the U.S. senators from their state. The Senate Dining Room was quite a sight: hordes of boys in white knit shirts hobnobbing with white men in summer suits. The Arkansas luncheon quartet consisted of Bill Clinton and Larry Taunton at the sides of Democratic senators John L. McClellan and J. William Fulbright. Taunton, with his mellifluous radio voice and self-assured style, had considered himself his roommate's equal until that day. His mind swirled with possible questions to ask the older men. They seemed so wise and dignified. What could he say? He knew that Senator Fulbright was intensely interested in U.S. foreign policy. Taunton combed through his mind for some interesting way to catch Fulbright's attention, but could not draw the senator from his conversation with Clinton. He noticed an "instant affinity between Senator Fulbright and Bill," who seemed "so at ease with the situation." Clinton had already studied Fulbright's life and career, and considered the intellectual Arkansan his first political role model. That day, Clinton would say later, he thought he was "the cat's meow. Fulbright I admired no end. . . . He had a real impact on my wanting to be a citizen of the world."

First, though, Clinton wanted to be vice president of Boys Nation. He offered himself as a candidate that night at the Nationalist Party Convention with an odd boast, noting that he came from Arkansas, the state with the governor who now had the longest continuous string in office in the country. There he was showcasing Orval Faubus, the very symbol of old-school Arkansas racial politics that he disdained. By Clinton's normal standards, everything about his vice-presidential campaign was a bit halfhearted. It was a race that he would refrain from mentioning later in life. John E. Mills of New York was the Nationalist Party recording secretary, who kept unofficial voting records. They show that Clinton was among seven candidates for the vice-presidential nomination at the start of the evening. He drew six votes on the first ballot, fourth highest. Jack Hanks, Jr., of Texas led the field with eleven. On the second ballot Clinton had fallen to fifth place. He worked the convention hall and picked up another vote on the third ballot, but that was all he could muster. He withdrew after the fourth ballot, throwing his votes to Hanks, who won the nomination and ultimately the vice-presidency.

Over at the Federalist Convention, Fred Kammer squirmed in his seat as his party nominated Richard Stratton, a conservative delegate from Illinois, a boy who seemed to be popping up every few minutes to utter another quote from his favorite ideological tract, *A Nation of Sheep* by Senator Goldwater. At one point Kammer turned to a nearby senator and muttered a Latin aphorism from Virgil: "I fear the man of one book." A year later, Stratton would reach the same conclusion. As a youth delegate to the Republican Convention at the Cow Palace in San Francisco, he looked on with alarm as Goldwater announced that "extremism in the name of liberty is no vice." The scene in the Cow Palace would frighten Stratton, revealing to him the rougher side of rugged individualism. To most of his colleagues at Boys Nation, however, Stratton seemed mature. He won the nomination and trounced his opponent from Kansas in the general election.

IT got quiet inside the Boys Nation buses as they pulled through the White House gate from the south. You could hear the motors idling and the pneumatic whoosh when the driver opened the door to talk to a guard. In his seat, Richard Stratton, a bundle of nerves, whispered to himself the words he would say to President Kennedy: "... Mr. President, we're all grateful to you for having us here." Bill Clinton was at the front of the first bus. He wanted a prime spot in the Rose Garden. Stay in lines, the counselors reminded them. Walk directly to the lawn below the speaker's podium. Do not throw elbows. Don't run. You represent your states and Boys Nation and the American Legion. Do us proud.

With that the buses unloaded and a most awkward, comic sort of race began. Without running, without pushing, several of the boys moved as quickly as they could to outpace the others, speed-walking while attempting to go unnoticed. "There was a barely controlled eagerness," according to Larry Taunton. "You don't want to push and shove, yet move with extreme rapidity to get to the front." With his long strides, Clinton took the lead and placed himself in the front row, just to the right of the outdoor podium, perhaps fifteen feet or so from where the president would stand. Only a few dignitaries, counselors, and protective agents would get between him and President Kennedy.

At quarter to ten, Kennedy stepped out from the back portico. Behind him were the four chiefs of staff of the uniformed services, in the middle of an Oval Office discussion with the president, who was trying to persuade them to support a nuclear test ban treaty. Kennedy strode to the podium, looked out at the boys in a semicircle below him, and introduced General Curtis LeMay of the Air Force, Admiral George Anderson of the Navy, General Earle Wheeler of the Army, and General David Shoup of the Marine Corps. (Decades later, one of the most vivid memories of many of the boys would be that of Curtis LeMay standing behind Kennedy with an unlit stogie in his mouth.)

"I read about your meeting last night," Kennedy said—referring to an article in *The Washington Post* that put the boys' treatment of the civil rights issue in the most positive light, taking note only of their statement that "racism is a cancerous disease" and must be eliminated. "It seemed to me that you showed more initiative in some ways than the Governors' Conference down in Miami, and we are impressed by it."

Richard Stratton was still whispering his lines to himself when the president said something that cleared his mind and put him at ease. "And I want to congratulate Mr. Stratton on his overwhelming majority," Kennedy said, smiling. "Those of us who just skim by are properly admiring."

The White House and its grounds, Kennedy told the boys, were constant reminders of the best in American history. Eyes turned as he pointed south. "These trees which are just behind you were planted by Andrew Jackson when he was here in the White House. The tallest tree over there was planted by the first President who came to the White House, John Adams. So all around you is the story of the United States and I think all of us have a pride in our country." He had recently returned from a trip to Europe, the president went on, "and was impressed once again by the strong feelings most people have, even though they may on occasions be critical of our policies . . . that without the United States they would not be free and with the United States they are free, and it is the United States which stands guard all the way from Berlin to Saigon." Kennedy concluded by praising the American Legion for looking to the future as well as the past, a future represented by the boys, of whom he said: "No group could be more appropriately visiting here now. We want you to feel very much at home."

When the applause receded, Stratton approached the podium, uttered his few lines of thanks from the boys, and handed Kennedy a Boys Nation polo shirt, which the president said he would wear that weekend at Hyannis Port. Kennedy shook hands with a few Legion officials at his side and turned as though he might head back to the Oval Office, but he did not. As the president walked toward them, the boys surged forward. Clinton was the first to shake his hand. The sixteen-year-old from Hot Springs lost his breath, his face contorted in what he would later call "my arthritis of the face." The Boys Nation photographer was nearby, snapping away. Kennedy suddenly retreated, smiling, and headed back to the White House, his cuff links and tie clasp intact.

Most of the boys were riding an adrenaline high when they left the Rose Garden. After an early lunch at American Legion headquarters, they visited the Pentagon, the Lincoln Memorial, and the Washington Monument. Visitors were still allowed to climb the stairs to the top of the monument in those days, and the boys took to the stairwell with glee—running all the way to the top in a wild, noisy race. Benny Galloway, an all-state football player from South Carolina, easily outran the field on the way up. On the ride back to the Maryland campus, the boys joked about the race and boasted about the morning at the Rose Garden. Where were you? Did you get to shake his hand? I touched his suit! He looked right at me! They spent the rest of the evening calling collect to their folks back home.

The next morning, their last in Washington, they returned from a day at the FBI and the Capitol to find a bulletin board at Harford Hall cluttered with photographs taken during the week by a Legion photographer. Each picture was numbered so that the boys could order copies. They mobbed the board, writing down their selections. Along with an overwhelming feeling that in Washington he had seen the career he longed for, Bill Clinton brought home a captured moment bonding his joyous present with his imagined future, a photograph he had been bound and determined to get—the picture that his mother wanted.

CHAPTER ONE

HOPE AND CHANCE

WILLIAM JEFFERSON BLYTHE III arrived in the world one month ahead of schedule. He was lifted from his mother's womb in a Caesarian section performed at Julia Chester Hospital in Hope, Arkansas, at an hour past dawn on August 19, 1946, weighing six pounds and eight ounces. The birth of this fatherless son in a place called Hope did not go unheralded. There had been record heat the day before, exceeding a hundred degrees, followed by a ferocious thunderstorm that cracked and boomed all night, igniting three fires in town. The local moviehouse happened to be showing a film that captured his twenty-three-year-old mother's predicament: *The Young Widow,* starring Jane Russell.

His mother, the young widow, Virginia Dell Blythe, took him home to Hervey Street, to a big white house with hardwood floors and French doors where she lived with her parents, Edith and Eldridge Cassidy, who from then on were known to him in the southern vernacular as "Mammaw" and "Pappaw." His first gifts were a rocking horse and a pair of sandals, followed by a silver spoon and napkin holder. The first word he later uttered, as recorded in his baby book, was "Pappaw." This was, if true, also his first political decision, the safest choice, for if Billy had babbled something resembling "Mama," his mother and grandmother might have argued over which one of them he meant. It is central to understanding the man he would become that he began life in Hope with no father and, in essence, two mothers who competed for his love and attention. Virginia carried him and bore him, but once he was home, Edith assumed that she was in control. Virginia might escape to walk him in the stroller or rock with him on the front porch swing, but when he was in the house, Edith ordered his life. She had him eating and drinking at assigned times, pushing food in his mouth if necessary, and his sleep was regulated to the minute, napping and waking with metronomic discipline.

This was Mammaw's way. Edith Grisham Cassidy was forty-five when her grandson was born. She was one of Hope's dazzling characters, an imposing figure: short, wide, and intense, with penetrating eyes and high cheek-bones, her hair cropped and dyed a licorice black, her face a daily creation, framed by spit curls, heavily powdered in bright white, with circles of rouge on her cheeks and deep red lipstick, looking somewhat like a stylized character in a Japanese kabuki show. She was a respected private nurse in her small town, and loved to wear the uniform: the white headpiece, the white starched dress and white stockings, the flowing navy blue cape inscribed in golden initials. She got around Hope in a big Buick, her face barely visible over the steering wheel, and it seemed to one of her nieces that whenever Aunt Edith drove by, the car was tilting noticeably to the driver's side.

Most things tended to tilt in her direction. She was ambitious and tem-peramental, unsatisfied with her lot in life as the wife of a good-natured man who excelled at making friends but not at making money. She taught herself nursing through a correspondence course after growing restless as a housewife and frustrated by a style of life beneath her expectations. Sometimes it appeared that she was kinder to outsiders than to her own family, with the exception of grandson Billy once he came along. She was devoted to her patients, ministering to them with tender care, if necessary staying overnight to treat the sickest among them, occasionally traveling to Arizona in winter and Wisconsin in summer to nurse convalescents. When she was off regular duty, she often drove up to the black section of Hope and cared for the children of domestics and orderlies.

Edith had a mercurial nature, a rollicking sense of humor coupled with a mean streak most often directed at her daughter or husband. She had taken out the whip to punish Virginia for childhood indiscretions, and even when the daughter became a mother of her own and had outgrown the switch, she could not escape Edith's criticisms and orders. Nor could Edith's husband, who had known her since their early childhoods spent on neighboring cotton farms near the hamlet of Bodcaw ten miles east of Hope. Her temper grew fiercer over the years. She was a yeller and a thrower: Eldridge became adept at ducking flying objects. Her relatives would later talk openly about relationships they thought she had had with a few doctors, yet she constantly accused her husband of being too friendly with some of the ladies in town.

James Eldridge Cassidy, with his soft, easy voice and soothing smile, was irrepressibly friendly. He came off the farm with a fifth-grade education, raised by relatives after his father died, inclined to treat friends and strang-ers as part of an affectionate extended clan. When he moved to town in the twenties, he found his niche as the deliveryman for Southern Ice, first riding a horse-drawn wagon along the oiled dirt roads and later driving a refrigerated truck down the paved streets. By either means of transportation, he was proud of being the iceman of Hope, a job that allowed him to greet scores of people each day, entering their houses as though he were a member of the family, hauling slabs of ice on his back in a big black leather strap, his clothes dripping in sweat from the effort of carrying fifty- and seventy-five-pound blocks from the street to oak ice boxes in his customers' kitchens. Hope, the seat of Hempstead County, with a population of eight thousand, was the sort of place where everyone knew everyone else, but to know is not necessarily to like. Eldridge Cassidy was universally liked, a salt-of-the-earth fellow who let boys ride along with him as helpers and who invariably stopped to assist anyone who needed a tire fixed or an appliance repaired.

Eldridge doted on his only child Virginia, whom he called "Ginger." He insisted on buying her new books for school rather than used ones so that she would not be embarrassed in front of her girlfriends, most of whom came from wealthier families. He was reduced to tears once, apologizing profusely, when he lacked the money to buy her an Easter dress. Sometimes at night, when Edith was shrieking at him, he would slip out to the front porch with his daughter and tell stories and watch the cars go up and down Hervey Street and listen to the screech and whistle of trains rolling into the depot two blocks away. By the time Virginia was twelve, Eldridge would offer her a swig or two of his whiskey. He was an antiprohibitionist, brought up among bootleg distillers, and believed that keeping things from people would only make them want them more. Virginia worshiped her daddy, while fearing her mother, but she took parts of her personality from each of them: Edith's task-oriented determination, and occasional temper, along with Eldridge's congeniality.

Virginia worked during her teenage years as a waitress at the Checkered Café at the corner of South Main and Third Street downtown, and immersed herself in activities at Hope High School: National Honor Society, press club, library club, music club, science club, freshman class secretary, student council member. Yet she was also regarded as a lighthearted, unaffected girl who loved to laugh and to flirt. Her self-defining quote under her picture in the senior class yearbook was: "I'd like to be serious but everything is so funny." In a section entitled "Just Imagine," where graduates assumed opposite personalities, she was teased with the line, "Just imagine Virginia Cassidy with a sophisticated nature." And in a "Last Will and Testament" in which seniors passed along a character trait, she wrote: "I, Virginia Cassidy, will to Mary Jo Monroe my magnetic attraction for boys." As a young girl, she scoffed at her mother's penchant for bold makeup, but by the end of high school she was practicing the first brush strokes of the painted face that would become her adult trademark: her dresser upstairs on Hervey Street was cluttered with mascara, lipstick, eyeliner, and eye shadow.

Virginia's senior yearbook was not a traditional leatherbound book with glossy paper, but a special edition of the local newspaper, the *Hope Star*. It was published on May 28, 1941, and the entire front page of the broadsheet was taken up by a staged photograph portraying the unpredictability of the world the seniors would enter after high school. Two students were shown standing on the stage of the school auditorium, gazing with earnestness and fear at an oversized die that they had tossed into the air, wondering whether it would land on the side that said "War" or the side that said "Peace." Only a few days later, the federal government procured tens of thousands of acres of prime farmland on the outskirts of town for the construction of the Southwest Proving Ground, where the Army would test rifle shells, small bombs, and flares for use in the coming war. The proving ground became a metaphor for the Hope High graduates. They felt explosive, ready to prove something, recalled Jack Hendrix, one of Virginia's classmates. "There was a sense of getting on, getting away, getting out of Hope."

VIRGINIA got away to the nearest big city, Shreveport, fifty miles south in Louisiana, to study nursing at Tri-State Hospital. It was there, two years later, on a midsummer night in 1943, when she was working the late shift, that she met Bill Blythe. At least he called himself Bill in Shreveport. His family back in Texas knew him as W.J., the initials for William Jefferson. He went by other names with other people who had various claims on his affection. He could not be stuck with one identity, or even one birth date. His family placed his date of birth as February 27, 1918, but in his military records he said that he was one year and six days older, born on February 21, 1917. Vital statistics, in any case, were of no interest to Virginia Dell Cassidy on the night she caught sight of Bill Blythe. Whether he was twenty-six or twenty-five, his history did not matter, nor did hers. The moment she saw him, with his confident, fun-loving demeanor, sparkling blue eyes, broad shoulders, and sandy-brown hair, she forgot about an old boyfriend from Hope whose ring she had worn for four years. Blythe was "a handsome man," she would say later. "But you see handsome all the time. This was some strange and powerful attraction. Love at first sight."

Blythe had arrived at the hospital with a female companion, but if that was a forewarning, it was lost on the student nurse. While the woman, who had complained of sharp abdominal pains, ended up in the operating room for an emergency appendectomy, all Virginia could think about was whether Blythe was married or engaged to the patient and, if not, how she could snare his attention. She flirted through eye contact, and as Blythe was leaving, halfway out the door, he turned around, came up, looked at the ring on Virginia's finger, and asked what it signified. "Nothing," she said, and their romance began. In later recollections of the episode, Virginia never explained who the other woman was or what happened to her. She said Blythe portrayed himself as a traveling salesman who had made a brief stop in Shreveport on his way back to Sherman, Texas, his home town, to enlist in the Army. He was so struck by her, Virginia recounted later, that he decided to stay in town, find an apartment, and take a job selling Oldsmobiles.

There is a contradiction at the center of that version of events. Blythe's military records show that he already had been in the Army for two months by the time Virginia said she first saw him. He was inducted by Selective Service System Board 2 in Caddo Parish, Louisiana, on April 24, 1943, and entered the service in Shreveport ten days later, on May 3. That means that rather than just passing through Shreveport, as he had implied to Virginia, he must have been there already for several months. There would have been no need for him to return to Sherman to enlist since he had already done so in Shreveport. It remains a mystery how he simultaneously managed to be in the Army and work at a car dealership, just as it is curious how Virginia, who by her account was with him almost every day during their courtship, could be unaware of his military status. But everything about Bill Blythe was contradictory and mysterious. He constantly reinvented himself, starting over every day, the familiar stranger and ultimate traveling salesman, surviving off charm and affability. Anyone doubting his persuasive powers need know only this: When Virginia brought her parents down to Shreveport to get their blessing for her to marry him, it took him only minutes to win over the skeptical, tough-minded Edith.

They were married in Texarkana on September 3, 1943, less than two months after they had met and five weeks before he would be shipped overseas. It was a classic wartime wedding, performed in private by a justice of the peace, bonding two people who knew little about each other's past and less about their future except that they would soon be separated. Virginia assumed that the man she was marrying had never been married before. She never asked, and Blythe never told. She knew that he had grown up on a forty-acre corn, cotton, and chicken farm on the road between Denison and Sherman on the north Texas plain; that he was the sixth of nine children of Willie Blythe and Lou Birchie Ayers; that the Blythes and Ayers came out of Corinth and Ripley, Mississippi; and that he began working at a dairy at age thirteen when his daddy got sick. She knew that he got a job as a mechanic when his daddy died, and that he eventually left home for the life of a traveling salesman, determined to become rich, roaming Texas, Oklahoma, Louisiana, Arkansas, Tennessee, and all the way out to California, selling heavy equipment for the Manbee Equipment Company. She knew that much and she knew that when she looked at him, she "became weak-kneed"—and that was all she knew.

She did not know about the December 1935 marriage license filed across the state line in Medill, Oklahoma, recording the marriage of W. J. Blythe and Virginia Adele Gash, a seventeen-year-old daughter of a Sherman tavern owner; or about the divorce papers filed in Dallas a year later, after Adele had left the Sherman farmhouse and W.J. had sent her clothes on in a suitcase.

She did not know about the birth certificate filed in Austin, Texas, on January 17, 1938, two years after the divorce, listing W. J. Blythe as the father of Adele Gash's baby boy, Henry Leon Blythe.

Nor did she know about the marriage license filed in Ardmore, Oklahoma, on August 11, 1938, recording the marriage of W. J. Blythe and twenty-year-old Maxine Hamilton, or about Maxine's divorce from Blythe nine months later, in which the judge ruled that W.J. was "guilty of extreme cruelty and gross neglect of duty . . . in that he refused to provide for her a place to live, and within two weeks after their marriage he refused to recognize her as his wife, that he abandoned and deserted her in Los Angeles, California, and refused to furnish her transportation to her parents in Oklahoma City, Oklahoma."

Virginia did not know that in 1940, W.J. married Adele Gash's little sister, Faye, and divorced her after a few months, though his motivation in that arrangement seemed to be not love but a desire to avoid marrying another young woman who claimed to be pregnant with his baby.

She did not know about the birth certificate filed in Kansas City in May 1941 listing W. J. Blythe as the father of a baby girl born to a Missouri waitress to whom he also might have been briefly married.

Bill Blythe married Virginia Cassidy without telling her any of that, and within weeks he was gone off to war, sailing away on a troopship headed for the Mediterranean as a technician third grade with the 3030th Company, 125th Ordnance Base Auto Maintenance Battalion. For several months, he was stationed in Egypt at a base in the desert outside Cairo, repairing engines and heavy equipment used in the North Africa campaign. On May 1, 1944, his battalion boarded Transport No. 640 in Alexandria and sailed across to Naples, then marched thirty miles inland and set up shop near the town of Caserta. The technicians and mechanics of the 125th kept the war machine in motion, rebuilding engines, reconditioning transmissions, retooling trucks and tanks, and salvaging junked vehicles for usable parts. Their base looked like a piece of transplanted industrial Detroit.

They were a long way from the fighting. They worked ten-hour days, with Sunday afternoons off, and were able to pass off the worst assignments to Italian civilians and prisoners of war. They had two base theaters, one open-air and one enclosed, where they watched movies five nights a week. There were softball games and boxing matches. Joe Louis came by one night to referee the bouts. A USO baseball tour brought in Leo Durocher of the Brooklyn Dodgers. Every night during the summer, groups of soldiers went into town to swim at the Royal Palace swimming pool. There were weekend trips to Naples, Anzio, Florence, Rome, and the beach at Capua. They encountered social diseases, malaria, and occasional food poisoning.

By the time Blythe reached Italy, Virginia had graduated from nursing school and was back in Hope, living with her parents on Hervey Street and working as a nurse. Bill Blythe had never lived in Hope; he barely knew it, but he listed it as his place of residence on his military papers. Virginia wrote him daily letters about her life there, and put him on the mailing list for *Hometown News*—a folksy mimeographed letter written by "Mister Roy" Anderson, an unreconstructed Confederate who mixed news of the town with state and national events, describing blackberry blossoms "white as drifted snow," the G.I. Bill of Rights, Masons taking the Degree, crappie biting in the lake, the ammunition tests out at the Southwest Proving Ground rattling windows five miles away. In one letter, old Mister Roy contrasted his life in Hope with that of a G.I. from New York:

He has seen the tall Empire State Building and Radio Center with million-aires in 'em and I have seen tall pecan and scaly bark hickory nut trees with squirrels in 'em. He has seen Central Park with swans on the lagoon —I've seen Grassy Lake with wild ducks on it. He got watermelons from a Dago fruit stand, I got mine from a melon patch in the moonlight. He pays a florist $1.50 each for gardenias; I get em in Vera's garden. When he dies, he will have paid pallbearers, I will have six friends to tote my weary wornout body.

All of which brings me to say this: I got a letter from a homesick kid the other day addressed to: Roy Anderson, Hope, Arkansas, God's Country. Ain't it true?

Bill Blythe had no plans to stay in God's country when he got home from the war. He had a job waiting for him in Chicago, selling heavy equipment for a company that he had worked for before the war, and he intended to pick up Virginia and take her up there. Virginia, in her later recollections, said that she reunited with him in Shreveport in November 1945, after he had already made a stop in Sherman. But his military records indicate that Blythe did not arrive home from Italy until December 1 and was honorably discharged at Camp Shelby, Mississippi, on December 7, mustered out with $203.29 in his pocket after serving two years, seven months, and fourteen days. If he then visited Sherman before his rendez-vous with her in Shreveport, it is unlikely, given travel times in those days, that they could have seen each other until December 10. This is inconsequential except for one thing: the timing of the conception of William Jefferson Blythe III. For years afterward, there were whispers in Hope about who little Billy's father was, rumors spawned by Virginia's flirtatious nature as a young nurse and by the inevitable temptation of people to count backwards nine months from the birth date to see who was where doing what.

Nine months before August 19, 1946, Tech 3 Bill Blythe was still in Italy. Virginia heard the talk. Her answer was that Billy was born a month early. He had been induced weeks ahead of schedule because she had taken a fall and the doctor was concerned about her condition.

VIRGINIA Blythe had little time to get to know her husband. Two months in 1943 before he shipped out. One week in Hope at the end of 1945. Three months in Chicago in early 1946, living high up in an old hotel. And of those Chicago days, subtract the many nights that he was out on his sales route, driving around Illinois and Indiana in his dark blue 1942 Buick Sedan. By May 1946, Virginia was back in Hope. She and Bill were waiting for a house to open up in suburban Forest Park so they could move in, and until it was ready it made more sense for her to live with her parents than in the hotel, pregnant and alone. Altogether, she was with him less than six months.

May 17 was a Friday afternoon, the end of Blythe's work week on the road. The house in the suburbs was ready. He turned his dark sedan south and drove toward Hope to pick up his wife and to bring her back. He headed diagonally through the flat farmlands of Illinois, past Effingham and Salem and down to the tip at Cairo, where he drove west across the Mississippi River into Missouri. At ten-thirty he pulled into a service station in Sikeston and refilled the tank. Then he sped into the night mist along Route 60, determined to make it to Hope before dawn. It seemed that everyone was out on the road that night, moving too slowly for Blythe's taste. He passed Elmer Greenlee, who was on his way home after closing his roller rink. He passed Roscoe Gist, who was driving home with his wife after a night at the movies. He passed both men so fast that they took note of the big, dark Buick as it went by. Three miles west of town, one of Blythe's front tires blew out. The car swerved across the oncoming lane and cut through the corner of a field, rolling over twice and landing upside down near the service ditch of a farm road intersecting the highway. Greenlee arrived at the scene a few minutes later. The doors to the Buick were closed. The radio was still playing. The headlights shone into a nearby field. The car was empty.

Soon a crowd gathered. Several men turned the Buick over, fearing they might find someone crushed below. Two hours later, Chester Odum and John Lett were wading in a nearby drainage ditch when they spotted a hand. They pulled Blythe's body out of a shallow pool of stagnant rainwater. Coroner Orville Taylor, who was at the scene, determined that Blythe had probably crawled out the driver's side window and staggered toward the highway, only to fall into the ditch. The only bruise on his body was a bump on the back of his head. "Salesman Drowns in Ditch After Car Turns Over," read the headline in the Sikeston newspaper the next day. In the *Hope Star,* it was front-page news: "Husband of Hope Girl Is Auto Victim."

Eldridge Cassidy drove up to Sikeston to recover the body. The funeral for William Jefferson Blythe was held that Sunday at one o'clock at the First Baptist Church of Hope. He was buried in Rose Hill Cemetery in a plot that Eldridge had already bought for himself, his wife, his daughter, and his daughter's husband. Billy was born three months later.

ON the day that Billy Blythe was born, the latest edition of *National Geographic* arrived in the mail with a pictorial feature on the new Arkansas: "Louder than hounds or fiddles are the challenging voices of this born-again Arkansas as it shouts to make itself heard above the roar of new paper mills and aluminum factories." But not everything was new in the New South in the summer of 1946. On that same August day, baying bloodhounds and a rifle-toting posse surrounded a swampy hollow on the edge of Magee, Mississippi, flushing out two black World War II veterans who had been falsely accused in an ambush shooting. In Georgia that day, a series of lynchings of black men inspired Governor Eugene Talmadge to declare that, while he ran the state, "such atrocities will be held to a minimum"—a promise that, according to a wry editorial writer in the *Arkansas Gazette,* would "not mean much to the person or persons so unfortunate as to constitute the minimum." On that day in Columbia, Tennessee, a jury was being chosen for a race riot trial, and in Athens, Alabama, a probe had begun into the beating of several blacks.

The last lynching in Hope had been in the 1920s, when a black man accused of raping a white woman was tied to a rope and dragged down Main Street behind a horse and then hanged from an oak tree. But the race issue still defined Hope, as it did most southern communities. Tension between blacks and whites had increased in the months after the war.

Some white G.I.s were upset to come home and find black men working in the factories, making decent wages and holding jobs that the whites felt belonged to them. Black veterans came home to find that they were still denied their civil rights and had to live in houses that lacked indoor plumbing, confined to several blocks in the fourth ward on the northeast side of town in a sector known to whites as "Colored Town." Most of the black women in the fourth ward crossed the railroad tracks to work as cleaning ladies and nannies for the white families. There was a black-owned funeral parlor and hotel, but the grocery store on the edge of the black neighborhood was run by a white proprietor: Eldridge Cassidy.

His days as the iceman had ended a few years earlier, cut short by bronchial problems. He gave up his ice truck reluctantly, and searched for another job that suited his personality. He worked at a liquor store for a few years during the war until Hempstead County voted to go dry, then borrowed some money and opened the grocery on Hazel Street across from Rose Hill Cemetery. The store was one of the most integrated establishments in Hope, with black and white customers who bought the same canned goods from one counter and sodas from the ice box, along with illegal whiskey from a cabinet below the register. It was through credit that Eldridge Cassidy got the money for the store, and he was equally free with credit for his customers—and reluctant to collect. If the store was not a profitable proposition, it served a function that he cared about more, offering a place away from home where he could see people and tell stories and boast about his grandson Billy.

Mammaw, Pappaw, Virginia, and Billy lived together in the house on Hervey Street for less than a year before Virginia left for New Orleans, alone, to train at Charity Hospital as a nurse anesthetist. It was the only occupation that interested her. She never liked just being a nurse, following the orders of imperious male doctors, and she certainly did not like following in her mother's footsteps as a practical nurse in Hope. She told her friends that it was difficult for her to leave her baby son for months at a time. But she had decided that learning anesthesia would allow her to make more money to support him. And she was eager to get away from her mother, who acted as if she were in charge of Billy anyway and was longing to care for him. And she loved New Orleans, a city that she had got to know during her nursing school days. Virginia left in the fall of 1947, when Billy was one, and was gone for most of the next two years. One of his earliest memories, Bill would say decades later, was visiting his mother in New Orleans, then getting back on the train with Mammaw and looking out the window and seeing his mother on her knees, crying, as she waved good-bye.

Edith kept him occupied in Hope. When he was two, she began preparing homemade flash cards with letters and numbers on them and taught him the rudiments of reading while he sat in his high chair. It was not, he would say later, "like John Stuart Mill reading Milton at age five or anything like that—but it was reading." She dressed him in knickers and fine pin-striped outfits. She introduced him to church at age three, enrolling him in the Sunbeam program at First Baptist. Often, when she was busy, Eldridge would take Billy over to the country store, where he would play with little black kids from the neighborhood. Billy came to respect Edith, but it was Pappaw who won his heart, "the kindest person" he ever knew. Yet it was gentle old Pappaw who unintentionally brought another man into Billy's life, someone with a decidedly different manner and temperament, a free-wheeling sharpie from Hot Springs named Roger Clinton who ran a car dealership in town and on the side occasionally supplied the Cassidy grocery store with bootleg whiskey.

Virginia had met Clinton at her father's store before she left Hope, and saw him occasionally in New Orleans or during her trips home, which he usually paid for. She knew nothing about him except that he ran the Buick agency in Hope, that he came from Hot Springs, and that he lived up to his nickname, "Dude." He loved to drink and gamble and have a good time. He was a natty dresser, his face splashed with cologne, who always went to work "looking like he was freshly out of the bathtub." Virginia was unaware when they began dating that Clinton had a wife and two stepsons back in Hot Springs. She did not know that when his wife, Ina Mae Murphy Clinton, filed for divorce in August 1948, she charged in court papers that he had abused her, once taking her pump shoes and smashing her in the face, leaving her with a black eye and a bloody scalp. She did not know that he was not as adept with money as he seemed to be, that he was often bailed out of financial scrapes by one of his older brothers, Raymond, who owned the successful Buick dealership in Hot Springs and had set Roger up in business in Hope.

She did discover, soon enough, that he was a philanderer, once busting into his apartment on Elm Street across from the Episcopal church manse after being tipped off by a friend that he had been entertaining a stewardess there. She found the room empty but strewn with lingerie, which she took outside and hung on the clothesline. Still, she decided to marry Roger Clinton, to the dismay of her family.

"I'm fixin' to marry Roger Clinton," she told her favorite uncle, Edith's brother Buddy Grisham. Grisham later remembered the rest of the conversation this way: "I told her, 'No,'—I said, 'You're not fixin' to do that.' Roger was in the Buick business, so I said, 'You're fixin' to marry a bunch of Buick cars!' She could have a new car to drive whenever she wanted— these women give in to that . . . I told her she'd have hell from then on."

According to Virginia's later recollections, her mother threatened to seek custody of Billy and even consulted a lawyer about how she could do it. The custody threat never made it into court, but it did divide the family more than ever. When Virginia Blythe became Virginia Clinton on June 19, 1950, her parents and her four-year-old son were not at the ceremony.

Billy lived with his mother and Roger Clinton in a boxy one-story wooden house at the corner of Thirteenth Street and South Walker, in a neighborhood bustling with young families. Mosley the welder lived nearby, and Smith the grocer and Osteen the bank clerk and Polk the lumberman and Taylor the car salesman, along with Williams, the retired railroadman next door. Hope was in the midst of its postwar boom. Young couples were having children, settling down to jobs, finding their way back to church in a revivalist mood, happy to be alive. The little family at 321 Thirteenth Street did not seem out of the ordinary. The husband ran the Roger Clinton Buick Company at 207 East Third Street. The wife worked as a nurse anesthetist. The little boy loved to wear his Hopalong Cassidy outfit with black pants, black coat and hat, and a T-shirt with the cowboy star's picture on it. He went to kindergarten with Donna Taylor, the neighbor girl who kissed him behind a tree one day, and with Mack McLarty, the son of the other auto dealer in town, the rich one, and Georgie Wright, the son of a doctor. He was a talkative, sensitive, chubby little boy. The only blue jeans that fit him at the waist were so long that he had to roll them up halfway to his knees.

Billy would "light up" when he was around other children, Donna Taylor later recalled. "Some people like to be with other children. He was like that. He was always right there. Almost obnoxious. He was in the center of everything. One time we were scuffling around in my house and he kicked out the glass of a cabinet." Another time, while he was jumping rope during recess at school, Billy caught his cowboy boot in the rope and fell and broke his leg. The other children gathered around their bawling classmate and chanted: "Billy's a sissy! Billy's a sissy!" He was in a cast for weeks. His playmates noticed that he liked the attention the cast brought him.

By first grade Billy Blythe was known as Billy Clinton, though his name was still officially William Jefferson Blythe III. He called Roger Clinton "Daddy," but Roger Clinton did not legally adopt the boy and rarely spent time with him. Roger usually had had several drinks by the time Billy saw him at night. Roger was gone a lot, and when he was home, he often sat alone in a room or argued with Virginia. One night Virginia dressed Billy up to take him to the hospital in Hope to visit her maternal grandmother, who was dying. Roger did not want them to leave. When she said she was going anyway, he hauled out a gun and fired a shot over her head into the wall. Virginia went across the street to the Taylors' and called the police. Billy slept at a neighbor's house. Roger spent the night in jail.

. . .

IN September 1952, Roger Clinton sold the Buick agency to Sid Rogers. A few months later he moved his family to Hot Springs, an hour up the road. They spent several uneasy months living on a farm on the edge of town, as Roger made a halfhearted effort to change his way of life. Virginia hated the farm, she later said, and especially disliked the thought of Billy being out there alone with Roger while she was working miles away at the hospital in Hot Springs. By the next summer they had settled into a comfortable two-story frame house high on a ridge above Park Avenue, one of the main thoroughfares in Hot Springs. Virginia thought that Roger had bought the house with money from selling his car agency. In fact, it belonged to big brother Raymond. Roger had left the Hope car dealership in financial disrepair and had gambled away the money he had got for it. His brother was helping him start over again.

The house at 1011 Park Avenue was nestled between two worlds. The backyard and long rear gravel driveway led back to Circle Drive, with spacious brick homes and graceful lawns shaded with oaks and magnolias, where the lawyers and city officials lived. The front windows looked across to the pine-covered North Mountain of Hot Springs National Park, and the tiered front lawn led down to the avenue of middle American carefree vacation glitz, starting with the swimming pool at the Plaza Motel next door, followed by the Settle Inn, the Lynwood, the Parkway, the Wheatley, the Town House, the Tower, and the Ina Motel. A half-mile down, the string of motels was interrupted by the neocolonial red brick and white column sterility of Park Place Baptist Church, then resumed with the Bellair, the Cottage, the Swan Song, and the Park Avenue, ending with the exotic Vapors nightclub, a former drive-in turned into a Vegas-style crystal palace, replete with bar, casino, and roll-out stage offering big-name entertainers like Tony Bennett and Liberace.

A left turn past the Vapors led down to the center of town, with the Arlington Hotel standing gaudy sentinel over bathhouse row. The baths' restorative waters gave the town its name. Most Hot Springs residents knew the baths in order running down from the Arlington along Central Avenue: Superior, Hale, Maurice, Fordyce, Quapaw, Ozark, Buckstaff, and Lamar.

Hope was flat and understated; Hot Springs was all hills and excess. While every town has its juxtaposition of virtue and sin, in Hope and most other southern communities it was well beneath the surface. In Hot Springs, more of it was out in the open. The biggest illegal yet blatantly obvious gambling operation in the South flourished side by side with dozens of churches, some of them funded with gambling money. It was poetic to be born in Hope, but it meant more to grow up in Hot Springs. Hot

Springs was a vaporous city of ancient corruption mingling with purely American idealism.

The Clintons had arrived in Hot Springs in 1919 from Dardanelle, a small town along the Arkansas River about forty miles to the north. They were drawn by the restorative waters sought by Roger's ailing mother, Eula Cornwell Clinton. The four Clinton boys, Raymond, Roy, Robert, and Roger, and their sister Ilaree, grew up in the city during the heyday of gambling and prostitution, both controlled by gangsters and protected by city officials. At the end of each month, officers rounded up the prostitutes and marched them over to the courthouse, where they paid five-dollar fines and went back to business. The telephone operators in town had the whorehouse numbers memorized. The gamblers, it was said, had to bribe a string of thirteen public officials from Hot Springs to Little Rock, the state capital. When the Clinton boys were teenagers, they took note of the gangsters who came to town as other boys might pay attention to baseball stars. Al Capone had a corner suite on the fourth floor of the Arlington, looking across Central Avenue to the Southern Club gambling house. He sat on a chartreuse couch and kept a machine gun in the closet. Raymond and Roger were especially impressed by the way Capone walked down the street with his hat tipped down, shielded by two bodyguards in front, two behind, and two on each side.

From late Prohibition days through World War II, the town was run by a colorful little dictator named Leo P. McLaughlin who wore spats and a lapel carnation and paraded down Central Avenue in a buggy pulled by his show horses, Scotch and Soda. His theory of politics, as once described by his partner in power, Judge Verne Ledgerwood, was: You rub my back and I'll rub yours. His definition of integrity was summarized in what he once said about his police chief: "He was honest. He did exactly what we told him to do." McLaughlin was eventually deposed by a band of reform-minded World War II veterans, but they turned out to be more interested in a share of the power than true reform, and soon made their peace with a new generation of gamblers.

Raymond Clinton, originally one of the reformers, rose to affluence as a Buick dealer who sold cars to the gamblers and politicians, and had a fine house on Knollwood Drive out on Lake Hamilton, one of the three artificial lakes that surrounded the city. Roy Clinton, who ran a feed store and antique shop, was less of a political operator than Raymond, yet he was the one who entered politics, serving in the Arkansas legislature for two terms in the early 1950s. Roger Clinton was more drawn to whiskey and gambling and nightlife. He spent much of his time drinking and playing around with two of his running buddies, Van Hampton Lyell, who operated the Coca-Cola plant, and Gabe Crawford, who ran a drugstore chain and developed a shopping center. For a time, Crawford was married to Roger's niece. When he was drunk, he would beat her. Drinking and wife abuse seemed to be part of the culture of Hot Springs in those days, according to Judy Ellsworth, whose husband later became mayor. The city, Ellsworth said, was "full of a lot of angry, repressed women" who had been mistreated by their husbands. The men "got away with anything they wanted to. They had no respect for women. They all had mistresses. They all beat their wives. It was the tradition of this city. The men had a way of compartmentalizing their lives. Honesty was never a trait with them. It was never-never-land."

Virginia was not immune to those troubles. She struggled with her roustabout husband and with some doctors in town who did not like dealing with a female professional. But she had a duality in her own nature that led her to find the flashy side of Hot Springs irresistible. She enjoyed the shows at the Vapors, liked to drink and gamble at the Belvedere Country Club, and became a regular at Oaklawn race track. She drove around town with the top down on her Buick convertible, and made dozens of close friends, women and men. Billy spent much of his time under the care of an older white woman named Mrs. Walters. At night, he would hear his parents fighting. Daddy, as he called Roger, drank too much. And Mother would make Daddy go into fits of jealous rage because, he said, she was too friendly with other men. As a nurse anesthetist, Virginia's hours were irregular: she could be called out for an operation at any time of day or night. But even with her job and her hobbies drawing so much of her time, the psychological center of her life seemed to be her son Billy. She talked constantly about how bright he was and what a promising future he had. She made it clear that she expected him to achieve.

Billy tried to carve out a separate life in Hot Springs. He spent two years in a Catholic grade school and raised his hand in class so much that one of the nuns gave him a C for being a busybody. In 1955, when he was eight, he dressed himself in a suit on Sunday mornings and walked alone the half-mile down Park Avenue to Park Place Baptist Church, carrying his old leatherbound Bible. Mrs. Walters, his nanny, who was more religious than his mother or daddy, told him that he might be a minister like Billy Graham some day. It seemed to the pastor, Reverend Dexter Blevins, that Billy was there "every time the door opened." Even though his parents were not churchgoers, Clinton said later, he was a believer and felt the need to be there every Sunday. He thought it was important "to try to be a good person."

When he switched to public school for the start of fourth grade, Billy walked up the side of the hill to Ramble School with his new best friend David Leopoulos, and within days he seemed to be running the place. An expression that he had brought with him—"Hot dog!"—became part of the Ramble lexicon. He stuck out his big right hand and introduced himself to everyone in the school as Billy Clinton. None of his friends knew that his name was Billy Blythe and that Roger Clinton was not his father. "He just took over the school," recalled Ronnie Cecil, whose parents ran a hamburger stand on Park Avenue. "He didn't mean to, but he just took the place over." Cecil and Leopoulos quickly learned that Billy was the smartest kid in the class, and that he could help them, sometimes unwittingly. When they were given simple yes-no tests, Billy knew the answers and he would write them out in capital letters—Y-E-S or N-O—pressing his pencil down so loudly on the crisp paper that Cecil could hear and copy his friend's responses, all of which were correct.

Every boy in the school had a crush on the music teacher, who was sweet, young, and perfumed. She taught them once a week, and during her class the students would clamor for her to let them act out the folk song "Froggie Went A-Courtin'." The boys always wanted their teacher to play the part of Miss Mousie so that they could fantasize courting her. When she played that part, she picked Billy to be Froggie.

"Miss Mousie, will you marry me? Uh-huh, uh-huh," Billy Clinton sang.

"Without my Uncle Rat's consent, Uh-huh, uh-huh," the teacher sang back. "Without my Uncle Rat's consent, I would not marry the president. Uh-huh. Uh-huh."

CHAPTER TWO

IN ALL HIS GLORY

To OPEN THE side door and enter the tan brick ranch house near the corner of Scully and Wheatley streets where the Clinton family lived during Bill's high school days was to visit a shrine to the oldest son. He was, at seventeen, during his final year at home, if not the master of his house at least the central force within it. One wall in the living room displayed his teenage accomplishments: a studio portrait of him from the year before, when he was junior class president, circled by a solar system of scholastic awards, Boys Nation mementos, and framed band contest medals. The refrigerator was stocked to his taste. An easy push on the foot pedal and the freezer would spring open to a half-gallon supply of his favorite peach ice cream; without asking, he would scoop it out in two huge mounds, one for himself, one for a visitor. Jars of peanut butter were always in the cupboard, with fruit on the counter so that he could satisfy his desire for peanut butter and banana sandwiches. Friends marveled at the speed with which he knifed banana slices into neat rows atop the bread. His bedroom was the largest in the house, the master bedroom really, with its own bath. In the carport sat the black four-door finned Buick that he drove to Hot Springs High School, along with the family's cream yellow Henry J coupe that he took out on special weekends.

The primacy of the senior son within the Clinton nuclear family—Bill, mother Virginia, stepfather Roger Clinton, and seven-year-old half brother Roger Cassidy Clinton—was in one sense not so unusual. It reflected the middle American cultural inclinations of that time and place, where towns gilded their teenagers with the status of golden youth, destined to better fortunes than the generation before, demigods of the classroom and playing field, their daily lives primed for competition and rewards. David Leopoulos, Clinton's closest childhood friend, thought of Hot Springs circa 1963 as an olfactory sensation, a sweet pine scent of innocent pleasure

evoking a time when "it seemed to us that the whole town was made
specially for teenagers." It was an aroma so powerful and lingering that it
could overwhelm Leopoulos decades later as it took him back down the
streets of his teenage years, to Cook's ice cream parlor and the A&W Drive-
In along Albert Pike, to the forest lookout and parking hideaways on the
mountain ridge above downtown, to the pep rallies, concerts, dances, and
festivals at the Gothic red brick high school. The feel of the town and the
generational aspirations of middle-class parents convinced the high school
seniors that they owned the world. Members of their class, according to
Bobby Haness, who competed with Clinton for top math scores, were
treated as "the Chosen Ones—we were made to feel different and better."

But that explains only part of what was happening on Scully Street,
where the household was struggling with Roger Clinton's alcoholism. In
the literature on children of alcoholics, there is a type sometimes referred
to as the Family Hero, who plays one of two well-defined roles, either as
caretaker and protector of the family or as its redeemer to the outside
world. As protector, the Family Hero, usually the oldest child, assumes
adult responsibilities and provides an anchor of coherence to siblings and
parents, leading to an attitude that things are always better, the family
safer, when this person is in charge. As redeemer, the Family Hero is often
excused from the family's inner burdens and dispatched into the world to
excel and to return with praise and rewards that will make the entire unit
feel worthy. In this role, the Family Hero becomes a vessel of ambition and
the repository of hope. Bill Clinton, during his high school years, was the
prototype of the Family Hero in both definitions.

The Scully Street house itself represented Virginia Clinton's best effort
to escape her marriage. It was a solid but modest dwelling hidden away in
a hodgepodge neighborhood of working-class shacks and brick ramblers in
the lowlands across the south side railroad tracks. It seemed like a step
down socially from the large frame house high on the hill above Park
Avenue that the family had lived in during their first six years in Hot
Springs, but it was nonetheless a haven from Roger's long-term abuse. After
secretly saving money for several years in anticipation of escape, Virginia
had fled to Scully Street, away from Roger, in the spring of 1962 and filed
for divorce, arriving with her boys not long before a vacant field across the
street exploded in a brilliant show of magenta, white, and pink peonies, a
luxuriant one-acre bouquet that seemed specially arranged for Virginia, a
woman as flamboyant and resilient as the blooms. But even as the escape
eased their fears, the divorce process was painful, revealing the roles taken
within a dysfunctional family: Roger's drinking and fits of jealousy, Virginia's perseverance and forgiveness, and the elder son's burden of responsibility.

In seeking to end the marriage on grounds of mental cruelty and abuse, Virginia testified in April 1962 that Roger's drinking, a problem since the start of their marriage, had worsened in recent years. She said there had been two violent eruptions three years earlier, first at a dance when he became drunk and kicked her and struck her, then at home on March 27, 1959, when "he threw me to the floor and began to stomp me, pulled my shoe off and hit me on the head several times." Virginia separated from Roger briefly after that incident, but took him back when "he promised to quit drinking and treat me with love." Bill not only comforted his mother during these troubles, he offered her strong testimonial support during the divorce. In his own affidavit, he stated that he was familiar with his step-father's habitual drinking and had witnessed the second assault on his mother. "I was present March 27, 1959," he said, "and it was I who called my mother's attorney who in turn had to get the police to come to the house to arrest the defendant."

Roger soon enough broke his promise to quit drinking, and Bill was called in for help again two years later, at a Christmas party in 1961 at the house of a family friend. Virginia said Roger humiliated her that night with verbal abuse. "He was so intoxicated I was unable to get him home," she said. "I was finally able to get my oldest son Billy to help me with the car and finally able to get him home." Roger's explosions were most often jealous rages fueled by alcohol. Although a notorious womanizer himself, he constantly accused his wife of being unfaithful. Virginia was a naturally affectionate woman who loved to hug and schmooze and flirt. As a nurse anesthetist on call whenever the doctors needed her for surgery, her odd hours made Roger suspicious. His distrust was exacerbated by reports he would get from friends that they had seen Virginia drinking coffee with this doctor or that medical supplies dealer.

"He is very jealous, continually calling to check on my whereabouts, which is causing me considerable embarrassment with the people with whom I have to work," Virginia testified. His jealousy had shut her off from friends, she said. "He doesn't want me to go anywhere myself and has refused to let me associate or to have many friends." His behavior was not only embarrassing her at work, it was also causing her performance to suffer. When she came home at night after work and found him drinking and upset, she would have to stay up so late reasoning with him that she would have a difficult time the following day.

The oldest son seemed emotionally distraught, not by the physical threats of his stepfather—he loomed over the man—but by the onus the family turmoil placed on him. He had come to understand that if the violence and abuse were to end, he had to be the one to stop them. He was an adolescent put in the position of reversing roles so that, as he later said, "I was the father." Decades later, Clinton and his mother would re-count what they described as a pivotal confrontation between Billy and Roger when Billy was fourteen. According to that later story, Billy stormed into his parents' bedroom one evening when he heard his stepfather yelling at his mother, demanded that Roger stand and face him, and ordered Roger never to strike his mother again. Virginia claimed afterward that this confrontation put an end to the physical abuse, though the divorce transcripts indicate that Roger continued to torment and threaten her and Billy in the following months. In Bill's affidavit, taken a few weeks before the divorce but several months after the night when he dressed down his stepfather, he recounted more fights.

"On one occasion last month I again had to call my mother's attorney because of the defendant's conduct causing physical abuse to my mother and the police again had to be summoned to the house," he stated. "He has threatened my mother on a number of occasions and because of his nagging, arguing with my mother I can tell that she is very unhappy and it is impossible in my opinion for them to continue to live together as hus-band and wife. The last occasion in which I went to my mother's aid when he was abusing my mother he threatened to mash my face in if I took her part."

Days after the divorce was granted on May 15, 1962, Virginia began reconsidering. Her love for Roger was gone, yet she felt sorry for him. He pleaded with her once again to take him back and again promised that he would reform. For days at a time he would park his car near the peony field across the street from the house and sit out there for hours, patheti-cally watching the family that had turned away from him. Whatever fears lingered in Virginia were overtaken by a nurturing sense that he could not make it alone. Billy was upset when he learned of the possible reconcilia-tion. He had already told the court that he did not believe his parents could live together any longer as man and wife, and now he had to convince his mother. "Mother," he said, instructing her in how to live her life for the first time, "you're making a mistake to take him back."

The only Roger Clinton that Bill cared about then was Roger Cassidy Clinton, who called the big brother he adored "Bubba." Bill felt so protec-tive and responsible for little Roger that he did something that on the surface seemed contrary to his expressed feelings about the old man, un-less considered in the light of brotherly love and maternal pressure. De-spite the fact that his mother had just divorced Roger Clinton, Bill went to the Garland County Courthouse and officially changed his name from Wil-liam Jefferson Blythe to William Jefferson Clinton. Why would he take the surname of an alcoholic stepfather who threatened him, a man who had never formally adopted him and who he hoped never would be part of the family again? He explained later that it was because he wanted to share the same last name with his little brother: "I decided it was something I ought to do. I thought it would be a gesture of family solidarity. And I thought it would be good for my brother, who was coming up." His mother encouraged the change. He had always been known in school records as William J. Clinton, she told the court, and there were "no pleasant associations connected with the name of Blythe as he never did know his father."

Within two months, Virginia took Roger Clinton back. They remarried in August 1962. Roger was ensconced in the house on Scully Street and everyone there legally carried his name, even the boy he had never adopted. But it was not his castle. He lived there more now as a tolerated guest, a boarder. By the time Bill began his senior year in the fall of 1963, everything in the house revolved around the golden son. Roger Clinton would sit for hours at night in a swivel chair in the rec room on the far side of the dinette in the back of the house, a tumbler of liquor at his side, watching television through trifocal eyeglasses or listening to his collection of jazz records: Benny Goodman, Glenn Miller, and the Dorsey Brothers. In his younger days, when he was cool and handsome and his nickname was "Dude," he had spent most of his after hours partying at downtown clubs. Now his drinking was more private. He stashed liquor miniatures around the house and in tool bins at the auto parts shop he ran at his older brother's Buick dealership. His history of verbal and physical abuse, while known among the adults of Hot Springs, was largely shielded from Bill's friends. Carolyn Yeldell, a schoolmate who lived next door, was in and out of the Clinton house every week for the final two years of high school without learning the depth of the Clinton family's duress.

CLINTON held no elective office at school his senior year. He had planned to run for student body president, the logical progression from junior class president, but the principal, Mrs. Mackey, called him in after school one day, along with his friend Phil (Jet) Jamison, who had also filed to run, and told them that they were spreading themselves too thin. She said she needed someone who could give the council full attention, not just do it with one hand while also playing football or running track or leading the band. She had decided to institute a point system for extracurricular activities. No student could exceed ten points per year. Bill, as band major, and Phil, as a football player, already had six points each, and the six points of being student body president would push them over the limit.

Jamison and Clinton argued vehemently with the principal. They said her plan was unfair, arguing in the abstract so that it would not look as if they only cared about themselves. They respected and feared Mrs. Mackey;

she was like a God to the students. Yet now, as they made their points, she started crying. Jamison realized that "she was crying because she believed in the principle of what she had decided to do and was not directing it against us. She thought Bill was the greatest. It hurt her to know we were taking it personally."

Mrs. Mackey did not back down. The only office Clinton could hold without going over the point barrier was class secretary, a position that usually went to a girl. He ran for it, challenging Carolyn Yeldell, who was not only his neighbor but a close friend. They ended up in a runoff, standing out in the hallway together as their classmates cast ballots in the auditorium. Billy had a sense that he would lose: Carolyn was his equal as a student leader, a Baptist minister's daughter who had courted friendships and club memberships with as much intensity as Clinton during their high school years. Whatever he could do, she could do as well, if not better. If he made Boys State, she made Girls State. If he went to Boys Nation in Washington, she went to Girls Nation. If he won a medal for sight-reading on tenor saxophone, she won a medal for singing or piano performance. As they lingered in the hallway, he turned to her. "Carolyn," he said, "so help me, if you beat me for this, I'll never forget it." She won.

Even without elected office, Clinton was the school's golden boy. Mrs. Mackey would let him out of class to speak to the Optimists or Elks or the Heart Association about his experiences in Washington at Boys Nation and the desire he felt to do something for his country. The speaking engagements grew so frequent that Mrs. Mackey turned down some requests, fearful that his grades might suffer. Such fears were probably unnecessary. Clinton excelled in class without appearing to study much. David Leopoulos, who struggled through school, later could not remember Clinton studying in all the time they spent together. Paul Root, who taught world history, recalled that Clinton seemed more at ease than other students. When Root assigned outside readings, Clinton chose George Orwell's *Animal Farm,* an allegorical study of totalitarianism. It seemed to Root that Clinton's interest had nothing to do with what grade he might get for the report. He was totally absorbed in the theme within the book: power, how one gains and holds power. "Bill loved to argue, to debate, but he never appeared worried about the subject matter. He just played with it."

That is not to say that Bill Clinton was noncompetitive. He always wanted to win. During his sophomore year when the students from different junior highs joined together for the first day of intermediate Latin, their teacher, Elizabeth Buck, asked them to translate a speech of Julius Caesar's. Clinton zipped through three-quarters of the material, far more than anyone before him, and sat back proudly at his desk. Then along came Phil Jamison, who at a different junior high had had a more demanding Latin teacher. Jamison recited the entire text fluently. Although Clinton graciously congratulated Jamison at the time, he brought it up for weeks thereafter, and Jamison could tell that behind the smiles his friend was upset.

Hot Springs High was the coveted public school among the seven whites-only secondary schools in Garland County, the local equivalent of a top private institution: rich and academically driven, with a cadre of teachers who had devoted their lives to the school. Mrs. Buck, who taught Latin for four decades, was exacting and inspirational. When students entered her classroom, they first contemplated her Thought for the Day, taken from classical texts. Her favorite was from *Hamlet,* Polonius's advice to his son Laertes. She would write it in chalk in her perfect blackboard style: "To thine own self be true, and it must follow as the night the day, thou canst not then be false to any man."

The students enjoyed the way she brought a dead language to life, dressing them in togas as they performed plays and readings from ancient Rome. One day they were reading from Cicero and Mrs. Buck decided that they should put Cicero's arch enemy, Catiline, on trial. Catiline was the Huey Long of the first century B.C., covering his reckless ambition in the rhetoric of populism, inciting the oppressed masses in his plots for power, which included plans to kill Cicero and take over the imperial city. As Mrs. Buck was about to assign roles, she later recalled, "Billy Clinton raised his hand and said, 'Let me be the lawyer,' defending Catiline."

"I said, 'Don't you know you have a lost case before you start?' "

"And he said, 'I really want to try it.' And so he did."

He put up a vigorous defense and became enraptured with the courtroom, where he had a captive audience susceptible to his powers of persuasion, a focus group for his budding rhetorical and political skills. Defending Catiline, he told Mrs. Buck, made him realize that someday he would study law.

On the other end of the spectrum was the senior physics class, taught by a well-meaning man who came straight from the hills. Billy and his friends took advantage of Thural Youngblood from the first day of class, when they decided that he was not their intellectual equal. They spent much of the class talking to each other in a juvenile code language: "E-Ga" meant a girl had a "good bod." Youngblood tried to discipline the students —Carolyn Yeldell could mimic him chewing out Clinton: "Ah, hey, yum, Bale Clane-ton, you don't get set down, I'm gun lower your grade from an F to a G, huh." But physics was a free-for-all. One day Clinton, Jamison, and Ronnie Cecil escorted their teacher to the equipment closet in the back of the room and locked him inside. He banged and pleaded to be let out, but they pretended that the lock was stuck, and studied other subjects and talked among themselves until the bell rang.

The calculus teacher, Mr. Cole, was a serious man who was also the assistant principal. His advanced class had only eight students, and was held in an annex a block down the street from the red brick high school. Clinton and Jamison were there on the afternoon of November 22 that fall when the telephone rang. Cole walked to the back of the room to answer it, listened but said nothing, then walked back to his desk and put his head down. He sat there, stunned, until finally he looked up and said, "The president has been shot in Dallas."

Moments later the phone rang again, and the teacher walked slowly back to answer it, and was informed that Kennedy was dead. Clinton would never forget the look on his teacher's face when he returned that second time. "He was totally ashen-faced. I had never seen such a desolate look on a man's face." Jamison looked over at his friend, the budding politician who only four months before had enjoyed the thrill of his life when he shook Kennedy's hand in the Rose Garden. "He was motionless. Not even a twitch on his face. Yet you could feel the anger building up inside him."

In the weeks after the assassination, Bill Clinton was in great demand at the club luncheons around town. His speech to the Civitan Club on December 3 focused on his memories as one of the last people in Hot Springs to see JFK alive. The handshake on that July morning in 1963 had begun its transformation—from personal exploit to community myth.

WITH his real father long dead, his stepfather diminished, his political hero slain, Clinton was eager for a father figure. Band teacher Virgil Spurlin came closest to filling that role. Spurlin was a big, warm-hearted man, an ex-Marine and Baptist deacon who created an extended family out of his group of musical disciples. The band room was on the side of the field house behind the school, and many students treated it as their separate world, hanging out there before and after school and between classes. John Hilliard, one of Clinton's schoolmates, who played the trumpet and later became a composer, thought of the band room as "almost like a hideaway. It was even kind of underground. It was the home spot for all of us. It had a warm atmosphere. We'd leave the band room to venture out."

The culture in most American towns revolved around high school athletics. In Hot Springs, music competed with sports for top billing. The Trojan football team was often hapless—at pep rallies, students mockingly practiced their most common cheer, "Block that kick!"—but the band and chorus brought home medals every year. The chorus was a massive Wagnerian throng of more than four hundred. And band was something that Hot Springs children prepared for from an early age. A special band teacher worked in all eight elementary schools, roaming from school to school during the week and bringing the citywide group of elementary school musicians together every Saturday. They played in the Christmas parade each winter and in the Miss Arkansas pageant parade held in Hot Springs each summer, one of the town's favorite events where beauty contestants glided through the shaded streets in convertibles donated by Clinton Buick.

Clinton took up the tenor saxophone. He practiced every night, using it to fill up the lonely, uncertain hours of childhood. He had always hated to be alone, and playing the sax was one of the few ways he could tolerate it. Within a troubled home, Clinton once said, the saxophone gave him "the opportunity to create something that was beautiful, something that I could channel my sensitivity, my feelings into." And it taught him that it took work and discipline to turn his jumble of feelings into notes that were clear and melodic. Every summer he went up to band camp in Fayetteville. By the time he arrived in high school, he was the best saxophone player in the city and soon would compete as the best in the state. Often at night he would go next door to Carolyn Yeldell's to rehearse for contests: she would accompany him on piano. He toted his saxophone around as a prized possession. For Christmas during his junior year, his mother bought him a new case, but on the first day back at school Carolyn dropped it as she was getting out of his car, bending the handle in a way that could not be fixed. Clinton yelled at her with an intensity that made her realize how important that instrument was to him.

At Hot Springs High, Virgil Spurlin saw in young Clinton something more valuable than a proficient sight reader and deft improviser; he saw a natural leader who could help him keep the group in order during the year and serve as a lieutenant when Hot Springs hosted the statewide band festival each spring. There were three top student positions in the band: student director, drum major, and band major. The band major was the teacher's administrative assistant. It was the perfect assignment for a young politician. The logistics that went into the state band festival were as intricate as plotting out a season's schedule for major league baseball, a mathematical equation that required patience and precision. Thousands of students representing 140 bands around the state would descend on Hot Springs for three days in April. All played in a wide variety of judged venues—solos, accompanied solos, ensembles, sight-reading, marching bands, orchestras. Spurlin, the band director at the host high school, was responsible for putting it all together: hiring scores of judges from out of state and finding rooms for them at the Arlington Hotel, renting forty pianos, and arranging the thousands of performances.

After the schools sent in lists of their performers, Spurlin would take out three-foot poster boards, staple several together, and tack them to a wall. Then he and Bill Clinton would start drawing grids and filling in the names,

places, and judges. They would start with one school and carry it all the
way across the board, from marching band to solos, then move on to the
next. The schedule called for ten performances an hour, one every six
minutes. Each band director was given a pocket-sized timetable, a miniature version of the poster board schedule, and was held responsible for
making sure his students were at the right place at the right time, not an
easy task, since competitions were staged not only at Hot Springs High but
also at music stores downtown and at private studios. While competing in
the festival themselves, Clinton and his classmates recorded the results on
a huge board in the band room and served as escorts and runners.

In a cosmopolitan resort town with big bands featured in all the top
hotels and nightclubs, it was no embarrassment to play tenor sax for the
award-winning high school dance band, the Stardusters; or to lead the Pep
Band with its white overall uniforms during basketball season, pounding
out the driving, sexy theme to "Peter Gunn"; or to form a jazz trio known
as the Kingsmen and play Dave Brubeck riffs in the auditorium during the
lunch hour, wearing dark shades so that the other kids called you the
Three Blind Mice. Billy Clinton did those things, and while he was not
as smooth and popular in the highest circles as Jim French, the football
quarterback, he had a sexual aura of his own. One family picture of him
that year captures his playful persona: Billy in his living room, bedecked in
his band major coat weighted with medals, but below that wearing shorts,
white socks, and black low-top tennis shoes, holding a putter and crouched
over a golf ball on the rug.

Although the teachers looked upon him as a model youth, Billy Clinton
and his compatriots in the band were more like fraternity brothers who
knew how to impress elders with their manners and then have a good time
out of view. John Hilliard, the trumpeter, a year behind Clinton, roomed
with Clinton and four other seniors on his first overnight trip to Blytheville.
Hilliard, who thought of himself as a "goody two-shoes," stayed in the
motel room while Clinton and his pals were out past midnight and came
back in a rowdy mood. On another trip when the band was at a festival
at Robinson Auditorium in Little Rock, Clinton was leading a gang of boys
up the stairs when they encountered some girls going down. He pulled
out his hotel room key and said, "Here it is, girls! Room 157. See you
later!"

Carolyn Yeldell, who watched Billy from the parsonage next door to his
Scully Street house, and had a crush on him, thought that he was always
finding a new girl through music. "He'd go to band camp in Fayetteville
and there'd be this sort of be-still-my-beating-heart if he saw a good-looking
clarinetist. Bill always had this sense about him that he collected girls. Like
the Ricky Nelson song, he had a girl in every band. He had the eye for girls

everywhere. He had global vision even then." They had vision for him as well. Yeldell noticed that when her girlfriends visited her, they parked their cars near the hedge that separated her house from Clinton's so that if he looked out his picture window he could see them.

The band culture played to Clinton's personality. He never wanted to be alone. He enjoyed working a crowd, whether old friends or new. He made many close friends in high school, but he seemed more comfortable in crowds. It seemed to Carolyn that he would "make crowds happen. He had a psychological drive for it, a need for happy and nonconfrontational associations." When the action was too slow moving, even if people were around, he might simply tune out. Sometimes when David Leopoulos was over at the house on a rainy day, when they were sitting in the dining room playing a game, he would look over at Clinton and realize that he was somewhere far away. He would talk, Leopoulos later said, and Clinton would not hear a word he said.

GRADUATION for the Hot Springs High class of 1964 was a week-long extravaganza. It began with a commencement sermon by Carolyn Yeldell's father, the Reverend Walter Yeldell, at his Second Baptist Church. His sermon was entitled "Missing One's Destiny." A "Silver Tea" was held the next day at the home of Mr. and Mrs. Don Dierks, a timber family whose son Joe was elected student council president after Billy Clinton and Phil Jamison could not run. The house was festooned in red and white, from the bunting to the mints. Seniors were escorted inside to a receiving line of parents, class officers, and school officials, and served tea and cake. Mrs. Mackey was there that night, and at one point gathered a group around her, Billy Clinton and Joe Dierks and David Leopoulos and Phil Jamison and Carolyn Yeldell and a few others. The stern and upright principal's face softened as she spoke. "I've never said this to anyone before, but there is something special about the class of '64," she said. "This is going to be a very great class. It's going to accomplish a lot."

The class picnic was held at Lake Hamilton, followed by Senior Assembly Day in the auditorium. Seniors walked around the halls of the old school getting their Old Gold Yearbooks signed for the last time. Clinton was in the book nearly thirty times. "Billy, I am honored to have known a gentleman who has courage, ambition and determination," his guidance counselor, Edith Irons, wrote in his book. "God has richly blessed you. I know in a few years I shall 'read' about you—please don't get too 'big and busy' to drop by and see your old counselor." When friends and teachers handed him their yearbooks, he often turned to the page with the picture of him shaking hands with President Kennedy and signed below the photograph.

His longest message, and his most humble, was to the band director, Virgil Spurlin:

Dear Mr. Spurlin,

Ever since before I could play the C scale—I've been overwhelmed in the presence of your huge hulk of manhood. I know of no finer man anywhere, and I've been fortunate enough to meet many. You've had such a great effect on me—I'll never be able to say what I feel . . . how much I love and respect you and how much I appreciate everything you've done for me. I honestly tried to do a good job for you, I think I almost made it. Now it's time for me to leave and make the best I can of myself, and I know that no matter how I do, I'll be better because of my association with one of the great Christian men that the Lord ever gave life.

God Bless you,
Bill Clinton

The class banquet was held May 28, and the next day, finally, came the seventy-eighth annual commencement at Hot Springs High School. Clinton and several of his friends spent the afternoon climbing magnolia trees near the school to cut blossoms that they scattered around the grass at Rix Field, where the ceremonies would be held that night. The skies turned dark gray and it rained before the eight o'clock exercises began, but the seniors voted to keep the ceremony outside. After the processional, band members tried to keep their instruments dry under the grandstands, where the rainfall was so heavy that a few drums ended up floating in water. In the class of 363, there were 50 honors graduates who wore gold tassels. The caps and gowns were light gray. They entered the stadium from both ends along a fence decorated with red and white satin ribbons. There were three student speakers: Letha Ann Wooldridge, the valedictorian; Ricky Lee Silverman, the salutatorian; and William Jefferson Clinton, whose grades placed him fourth in the class. He had the last word: the benediction. Part prayer, it became the first political speech he gave to a sizable audience:

Dear Lord, as we leave this place and this era of our lives, we ask your blessing on us while we stand together for the last time as the Hot Springs High School class of 1964. Our high school days are no more. Now we must prepare to live only by the guide of our own faith and character. We pray to keep a high sense of values while wandering through the complex maze which is our society. Direct us to know and care what is right and wrong, so that we will be victorious in this life and rewarded in the next. Lord give us the strength to do these things. Leave within us the youthful idealism and moralism which have made our people strong. Sicken us at the sight of apathy, ignorance and rejection so that our generation will remove complacency, poverty and prejudice from the hearts of free men.

And Lord, once more, make us care so that we will never know the misery and muddle of a life without purpose, and so that when we die, others will still have the opportunity to live in a free land. Take our hands, Dear God, and lead us from this place, into the future, into Eternity, and we will be together again. Amen.

At home on Scully Street that weekend, Virginia Clinton wrote a note to her mother. Edith Cassidy was in many ways Billy's first mother, the one who took care of him for two years as a toddler while Virginia, the young widow, was in New Orleans learning her trade. It was Mammaw who first thought Billy was special, who taught him how to read before he turned three. The two women had competed for his love and respect ever since, but now they could share in his growing success. Virginia wrote her mother a letter bursting with pride in the boy they sometimes called "Bubba."

"Dear Mother," she wrote. "Here are some of the clippings and activities of Bubba lately. I typed out the beautiful prayer that Bill wrote and recited at the place of graduation. His voice was magnificent as it sounded over the microphone in the football stadium. Of course, I was so proud of him I nearly died. He was truly in all his glory that night."

CHAPTER THREE

THE ROAD AHEAD

THERE WAS NO shortage of useful advice offered to freshmen entering Georgetown University's School of Foreign Service in the fall of 1964. The head of the orientation committee enlightened the newcomers on the grading quirks of various professors and pointed out the favored pubs in a city where eighteen-year-olds were allowed to drink beer. The Jesuit fathers warned them of curfews and dress codes: in the rooms by eight-thirty, with only a half-hour break for snacks and socializing before lights out at eleven from Sunday through Thursday. Coats and ties required in class and at the dining hall. No females in the dorm. No public displays of affection, known as PDAs. A columnist for the school magazine, *The Courier,* placed those rules in the context of administration hypocrisy: "Remember, at Georgetown you will be addressed as 'Gentlemen' and treated as children." Another writer offered a sardonic guide to conformist behavior: "The basic rule for survival on campus is to be tough, think tough, act tough. Wear tight chinos to prove your masculinity; wear madras shirts and shoes without socks, just like the 50 guys standing outside the 1789 to prove you can look exactly like another 50, or 500, or 5,000 Happy Hoyas."

Georgetown in that era was divided into two distinct worlds. The college of arts and sciences, known as the Yard, was all-male and 96 percent Catholic, a homogeneous bundling of parochial school boys from the East Coast who were the quintessential Happy Hoyas. The School of Foreign Service was part of what was known as the East Campus (a few blocks east of the Yard), a consortium that also included the School of Business Administration and the Institute of Languages and Linguistics. The East Campus was a diverse melting pot compared with the Yard: there were women around, first of all, most of them in languages, but 148 in foreign service and a handful in business. The East Campus also enrolled scores of wealthy foreign students: the sons and daughters of ruling elites, including a band of polo-playing Cuban exiles who wore their coats like capes, inhaled nonfilter cigarettes, cruised the Hilltop in their convertible sports cars, and got most of the glamorous girls. The School of Foreign Service was the least Catholic part of Georgetown, almost evenly divided between parochial and public school graduates and including a few hundred Protestants and forty-one Jewish students.

Bill Clinton matched none of the Hoya profiles when he arrived at the East Campus for freshman orientation. Going sockless was a bit advanced for someone just making the transition from white socks to dark ones. He might decide to follow the crowds to the campus pubs, but once inside he would guzzle soft drinks or water, not beer: his family turmoil scared him away from alcohol, which he considered a dangerous indulgence. As diverse as the School of Foreign Service was compared to the rest of the university, a drawling Arkansan apparently was enough of an oddity that when Clinton stopped by the administration office on the first day, the freshman dean mused aloud whether Georgetown had made a mistake admitting a Southern Baptist whose only foreign language was Latin. Clinton knew it was no mistake: Georgetown was the only school he had applied to during his senior year in Hot Springs, after hearing about it from his guidance counselor, Edith Irons. He wanted to be in Washington, near the center of politics. As he walked out of the admissions office with his mother, he assured her that the dean's sarcasm would soon be overtaken. "Don't worry, Mother," he told her. "By the time I leave here they'll know why they let me in."

Clinton's roommate reached Room 225 Loyola Hall while Bill and his mother were out. Tom Campbell was more nearly the Hoya prototype, an Irish Catholic boy from Long Island who had attended a Jesuit military high school. He had driven to Washington with his father, a conservative judge, and when he got to the dorm and saw his roommate's name, he worried about how his old man would react to his sharing a room with a black classmate. Campbell, who had never associated with black people or Southern Baptists, assumed that his roommate was black because of the name: William Jefferson Clinton. His father was helping him unpack when Bill and Virginia returned and overwhelmed the Long Islanders with southern charm. The moment they walked through the doorway, they immediately made the place theirs. As a pair, Campbell said later, "they just filled the room."

Loyola Hall had once been a hospital wing, an aging brick building with a scattered assortment of single, double, and even four-bedded rooms that were assigned in alphabetical order. Most boys on the second floor had last names beginning with C, a few with B or D. John Dagnon of New

Castle, Pennsylvania, had the biggest room across the hall from Clinton and Campbell, and he hosted a corridor meeting on that first night. There was inevitable posturing and politicking as the freshmen went through the ritual of establishing a pecking order. At the start of the evening, the group seemed to revolve around Dagnon and an urbane, witty midwesterner who let it be known that he was heir to a life insurance fortune. But it did not take long for Clinton to become a dominant force, sticking out his over-sized right hand, asking his classmates where they were from, what they were interested in, then working the conversation around to his roots, the giant watermelons grown in Hope, Arkansas, and inquiring, gently, as to whether they had given thought to running for any student office.

Although many of the boys tried to play it cool, Clinton showed little reserve. He was eager and friendly. There was something about him that left the more refined budding Hoyas puzzled. Here they were, ready to start anew, shedding their past lives, and there was Clinton boasting about where he came from and using his background as the setting for self-effacing jokes. Thomas Mark Caplan, a jeweler's son from Baltimore, thought that Clinton "stood out immediately for his sense and evocation of place. He was not from homogenized, suburban America." Only later would some friends appreciate that Clinton used Arkansas as a foil for his vulnerability.

Clinton adjusted quickly to his surroundings. While another southern freshman at Loyola Hall, Kit Ashby of Dallas, struggled with his identity, hauling out a book his mother had sent him—*What Presbyterians Believe* —so that he could argue with his Catholic hallmates about the Trinity and original sin, Clinton felt comfortable enough with his Baptist heritage that he could worship among the Catholics at the campus chapel. He bought stationery with the Georgetown seal and postcards depicting the Gothic spires, and sent a passel of letters and notes to old friends and relatives. To his grandmother, Edith Cassidy, in Hope, he wrote: "Dear Mammaw, I love it here. It is very beautiful. . . . My roommate is a very nice boy from New York. We're going to have to study very hard. But it will be worth it. Love, Billy."

He and roommate Campbell turned out to be a harmonious pairing. They were moderate in behavior; no all-night drinking binges in Room 225. Campbell was a straight-shooter, no hard edges, no fakery, solicitous of Clinton in all things political, yet good-naturedly alert to his ambitions and foibles. Clinton tried to assist Campbell with his classwork, and Campbell tried to teach Clinton how to march straight after they signed up for the optional Air Force ROTC program that met every Tuesday morning at quarter to eight for an hour of drilling. (Neither effort was very effective. Campbell struggled with his classes, and Clinton, in Campbell's opinion, "just didn't look good in a uniform, and despite having been in a band, he simply could not figure out left face from about face.") With his military school background, Campbell was fairly neat, and Clinton obliged on his side of the room, keeping his laundry off the brown linoleum floor. They enjoyed much of the same music: Dave Brubeck, Nancy Wilson, Glen Yarborough. The southern boy's teenage obsession with Elvis Presley was in temporary recession. Clinton brought an old pop-down phonograph with him from Hot Springs, which Campbell enjoyed, and an oversized wind-up alarm clock, which drove him crazy.

The alarm clock—"this god-awful ticking alarm clock," Campbell called it—seemed to get louder every night. Soon it came to symbolize their differing attitudes toward time and achievement. Campbell had bent to enough discipline in his life, imposed by father and school, and was enjoying the relative freedom of the university. He worried little about apportioning his time and less about studying. Clinton's discipline had been largely self-imposed. From his early years he had tried to fit more hours into a day, and now as his aspirations grew, so did his need to find more time to realize them. The freshman year was only a few weeks old when his Development of Civilization professor, Carroll Quigley, inspired him to make his days even longer. In a lecture on great men, Quigley noted that many of them required less sleep than other mortals. The greatest leaders, he said, often slept no more than five hours and refreshed themselves during the day with brief catnaps. Clinton returned to the dorm room after that morning lecture and immediately set his alarm clock for a twenty-minute nap. And he began sleeping five hours a night, the big clock resounding with the urgency of his mission.

CLINTON needed to walk no further than three doors down the hall to be reminded of his vision of greatness. Tommy Caplan was an ebullient fellow more interested in literature than politics, yet his connection to John F. Kennedy made Clinton's handshake with his hero seem trivial. Clinton told his grandmother about his floormate. "One thing I really want to do is go see President Kennedy's grave," he wrote. "There is a boy down the hall from me who worked for Kennedy in the White House. He knows all the Kennedy family and John Kennedy Jr. is supposed to visit him at Georgetown sometime this year. He is only three years old, but this boy says he is a really smart boy and just like his daddy."

Tommy Caplan had met Kennedy in 1960, when the Massachusetts senator was campaigning for president and Caplan was an eighth-grade reporter for his school newspaper in Baltimore. Of all the prospective presidential candidates in both parties, Kennedy had been the only one to respond

affirmatively to young Caplan's request for an interview, and they had met
briefly during Kennedy's visit to Baltimore before the Maryland primary in
May. That summer, Caplan had organized the Teen Democrats of Maryland,
volunteering at the Democratic party offices in the old Emerson Hotel in
downtown Baltimore and occasionally running errands, by train, to the
national headquarters in Washington.

After Kennedy reached the White House, Caplan, by then a sophomore
at Gilman, an Episcopal prep school in Baltimore, developed the idea of
creating a junior peace corps, in which teenagers from the United States
would correspond with their contemporaries in developing countries. He
began a lobbying campaign for his idea, telephoning and writing officials
inside the White House, until eventually Ted Sorensen, Kennedy's special
assistant and speechwriter, Evelyn Lincoln, his personal secretary, and Robert Kennedy, the U.S. Attorney General, all responded. By 1963, the Youth-
to-Youth pilot project was a reality and Caplan spent much of the summer
commuting to Washington, recruiting young Americans to join his program and acquiring the names of foreign students through the United
States Information Agency. Caplan was also a regular and welcome visitor
at the White House, often loitering at Mrs. Lincoln's desk until the president appeared.

One year after Kennedy's assassination, Georgetown was still in the
Camelot shadow. Ads in *The Hoya* honored JFK as the "ideal embodiment
of noblest manhood of our time." The Jesuit school announced plans to
honor the nation's first Catholic president with a posthumous honorary
degree at Georgetown's 175th anniversary program, and Robert F. Kennedy had agreed to accept it. There was a feeling too that Lyndon Johnson,
as different as he was from Kennedy, was nonetheless his legitimate inheri-
tor, carrying forward and even expanding Kennedy's sense of optimism.
Johnson had pushed through the Civil Rights Act of 1964, whose public
accommodations provisions signaled a massive federal assault on racial
segregation in America. He had also persuaded Congress, including Clinton's home-state role model, Senate Foreign Relations Committee Chairman J. William Fulbright, to approve the Gulf of Tonkin resolution that laid
the legislative groundwork for further intervention in Vietnam, but few
among the students realized how the Vietnam War would cloud their
futures. In that fall of 1964 there was a sense of great progress.

It was in that effervescent environment that the two Kennedy worshipers, Caplan and Clinton, became sidekicks. One day Caplan took Clinton
over to the National Archives, where Kennedy's former secretary, Evelyn
Lincoln, was cataloguing the late president's personal effects for future
display. Mrs. Lincoln showed them Kennedy's famous rocking chair, and
his desks, and in an annex behind her office, they walked down row after

row of metal stacks holding the artifacts of JFK's life. Caplan had seen some of these very items when he was padding around the Kennedy White House. Now he would become the backstage adviser to a Kennedy acolyte.

Clinton had lost two elections in a row—to Jack Hanks, Jr., of Texas for the Nationalist party vice-presidential nomination at Boys Nation, and to Carolyn Yeldell for senior class secretary at Hot Springs High. In both cases he had run for offices below his aspirations and therefore had done so halfheartedly. Now he would run as hard as he could. Within a few days of settling in Room 225 he had been off and running for president of the freshman class. Campbell helped him distribute leaflets and Caplan advised him on speeches, but Clinton ran his own show. His candidacy was non-ideological, and he developed a platform of dry moderation. He called for better communications through a campus government newsletter and referendum powers for the student body. "I believe this is a possible platform," he assured potential voters. "The feasibility of every plank has been carefully examined."

Every voting bloc in the East Campus electorate was carefully examined as well. In surveying the political landscape, Clinton learned that student politicians from Long Island tended to dominate. Another Long Island power play was taking shape, with a slate of freshman candidates that included Glen Pallen of Garden City for president, Judi Baiocchi of Manhasset for secretary, and Paul Maloy of Manhasset for treasurer. Campbell could help Clinton cut into Pallen's Long Island vote. Clinton saw great potential support among the women at the language institute, especially after he talked one of them out of running against him. He mimeographed his platform and signed copies by hand while eating breakfast. And then he set out to meet every voter on the East Campus. John Dagnon across the hall, another non–Long Islander, was running for treasurer against Maloy, and formed an informal alliance with Clinton, accompanying him around the dorms at night, going door to door. On the way back they would pay respects to the Second Loyola prefect, a graduate student who encouraged their political efforts.

The nominations were officially posted October 23 in the Palms Lounge of the Walsh Building, where Clinton and his opponents had brought in their own cheering sections replete with guitars, a trombone, and even an English horn. Clinton and Pallen delivered back-to-back speeches. Clinton's performance was lost to history, but Pallen's address was unforgettable. He delivered an overwrought oration written by his hallmate, David Matter, burdened with world-is-ending rhetoric, warning that society was falling into "a bottomless abyss of perdition." No one in the room knew what got into Pallen or what he was talking about. Matter thought he had written something profound until he noticed all the snickering. From then on, all

Matter or Clinton had to do to produce a laugh was to evoke the "bottomless abyss of perdition."

On Halloween Eve, Clinton was elected president of the freshman class. He took office with a phalanx of Long Islanders, who were somewhat surprised to find him in their midst. "Bill Clinton—who looks and sounds like an amiable farm boy, is the latest to ascend to that position of status supremacy known as freshman class president," the next issue of *The Courier* proclaimed. If anyone on campus was thirsting for bold action from the new student leader, they would be disappointed. "The freshman year is not the time for crusading, but the building of a strong unit for the future," Clinton told the student magazine. "You must know the rules before you can change them."

Clinton copied the stories about his victory and sent them to his mother in Hot Springs and his grandmother in Hope. Virginia Clinton had followed the campaign closely, writing her son every two or three days with news from home and getting back about one letter and one phone call per week. On the evening of Saturday, November 8, he sat at his desk in Room 225 and wrote a short note to his mammaw, explaining that his birthday greeting to her was late because of the election contest:

> I know I'm late, but I've had so much to do lately, as the article will show. I'm staying home tonight and trying to study. Next week our class has to build a float for the football homecoming and I have lots of tests. I'm making pretty good grades so far, all A's and B's except for English. I've got a C, but so does everyone else in the class. I'll just keep working and hope to bring the grade up. Must study . . . love you, Billy.

SINCE its founding in 1919, the School of Foreign Service at Georgetown had maintained its own professors and courses, but in a larger sense it was shaped by the theories of education of the Jesuit founder, Ignatius Loyola, based on sequential core courses. Some of the professors were priests, some laymen, all colorful characters. Robert Irving, the English professor in whose class freshman Bill Clinton was getting a C, was a trim and caustically witty man who often lectured while seated, legs crossed beneath him, until some theme especially excited him and he would lift his body from the chair much like a gymnast working the sawhorse, then recross his legs from right over left to left over right. His students knew that he loved writing and literature, and they soon discovered that he had zero tolerance for lazy formulations. Tommy Caplan wrote an essay in which he described the emotions he felt emerging from the Capitol at night. "All these things and more go through your mind," he wrote. The paper was returned with the phrase circled and the rejoinder—"If you are a capricious little bilge pump, that is."

Non-Catholic students were not required to take theology classes, but instead studied comparative cultures under Father Joseph S. Sebes, a Hungarian-born China scholar who spoke Spanish, Italian, German, French, two dialects of Chinese, and English, all in a thick Hungarian accent. Sebes was a thin, pale aesthete, cigarette drooping from his mouth, who loved nothing more than to eat, drink, and philosophize with like-minded souls. Late in the afternoon, after his teaching was done, he would trudge up the hill from the East Campus to drink scotch and smoke a half-pack of cigarettes while unwinding in the office of a Jesuit compatriot, admissions dean Joe Sweeney. As the evening wore on, he might be found deep in conversation with students treating him to dinner upstairs at the 1789. He had arrived at Georgetown in 1958 with one kidney, saying that he came there to die; he drank and smoked as though he considered death imminent, and stayed around for another generation.

The course Sebes taught freshmen non-Catholics in 1964 was known around campus by its nickname, "Buddhism for Baptists," and it seemed especially designed for the young Baptist from Hot Springs. Sebes, according to one of his disciples, Father James Walsh, "devised the course to present world religions from within. When he taught Buddhism, he laid out the beliefs and practices as though he were a devout Buddhist. He taught Islam as a convinced Muslim. Taoism was second nature to him. He never said 'they,' but always 'we'—'we Hindus,' 'we Buddhists.' It was sympathetic imagination—the ability to put yourself into the world view of other people." To the extent that Sebes's approach to learning took hold, Walsh believed, "students came away with the instinct to look at issues from various angles—that instinct eschews polarizing tendencies and values the ability to find common ground. This is not congenial to everybody, of course. People who tend to be literal-minded might label those who try to practice it as duplicitous, even slick."

Otto Hentz, then a twenty-four-year-old Jesuit not yet ordained, who taught Clinton's introductory philosophy course, picked up where Sebes left off. Hentz championed the philosophy of analogical imagination. Drawing on the work of the Jesuit theologian William Lynch, Hentz presented his students with three perspectives on the world around them: the univocal, where everything is clear and distinct, black and white, if you say "chair," all it means is chair; the equivocal, where everything is differences and uncertainty; and the analogical, where clarity is found within complexity, not despite it. People who are analogical tend to be misunderstood by univocalists, who need to make everything absolute, Hentz would say, but the analogical thinkers more often make their way successfully through the world. He saw an analogical mind at work in the essays of eighteen-year-old Bill Clinton.

One day after class Hentz invited Clinton out for dinner, an invitation no hungry freshman would turn down, and as they sat across from each other in a booth, Hentz sipping a beer, Clinton engulfing a hamburger, the teacher began making a sales pitch for the Jesuit order. He talked about how Jesuits got an exemption from the Pope to be active in politics, retelling his favorite joke that Jesuits say the missing line in Creation is "then God created politics and saw that politics is good."

"I think you should seriously consider becoming a Jesuit," he said to Clinton. "I've been impressed with your papers."

Clinton laughed and asked, "Don't you think I oughta become a Catholic first?"

"You're not?" Hentz replied.

"No, I'm not. I'm a Southern Baptist."

Hentz had not considered that possibility. "I saw all the Jesuit traits in him—serious, political, empathetic. I just assumed he was Catholic," he said.

If there was one subject on the East Campus that brought everyone together, it was the class on the development of Western civilization taught by Carroll Quigley, a layman. As Clinton later said, "Half the people at Georgetown thought he was a bit crazy and the other half thought he was a genius and they were both right." But Quigley unified the campus because his course was mandatory—and legendary. Freshmen inevitably heard upperclassmen tell them strange and wonderful stories about the man—his quirks and his intimidating tests.

Quigley grew up on the edge of the Irish ghetto in Boston, went on to Harvard and, with his nasal accent and dropped r's here and added r's there, sounded rather like John Kennedy. He was a tall, slender man with graying hair, a bald patch in the back, a sharp nose, and dark, penetrating eyes, and when he was lecturing in his classroom in White-Grabener, strolling back and forth, his voice rising and falling, he gave the impression of a crazed bald eagle. He seemed intimidating and arrogant offstage, yet he was master of the classroom lecture, full of drama and sweep, determined to teach his students how to think and what to think. "You've never met anyone else in your lives," he would tell them, "whose mission was trying to save Western civilization." His approach to history was broad. His life's work, a thousand-page tome entitled *Tragedy and Hope*, was to be the culmination of two decades of lectures, presenting a systematic vision of history, placing events and trends into categories to find order in chaos. It was then on the verge of publication.

His exams were notorious, with questions as sweeping as his theories.

Days before each exam, Quigley would write out the questions and his own preferred answers in fountain pen with a long, looping hand inside a blue book, so that his grading assistants could measure the student efforts against perfection. On exam day, students were not allowed to ask questions about his questions. Jim Moore, who was in Clinton's class and competed with him for top grades, would never forget one question that "caused most of the class to tank." It concerned Anatolia, although Quigley had never used that term before when talking about the area that became modern Turkey. "People were saying, holy shit, where the hell is Anatolia? Some would write about Greece, Mesopotamia, the Hittites, they had no idea what they were writing about." Which was fine with Quigley, who regularly flunked one-fifth of the class. In Clinton's day there were few vocal complaints. Jon R. Reynolds, who took the course a few years before Clinton, found Quigley "capricious and arbitrary—but on the other hand there were many gas-bags with facile pens who were accustomed to BS-ing their way through who were quite properly skewered."

Clinton never had to dip too deeply into the gas bag. While most students were afraid to approach Quigley, Clinton often strolled up to the front after class and engaged the professor in conversation. He seemed to emerge from those huddles feeling a bit more confident about the next test, amazing his friends by guessing what two questions would be asked, and pleasing Quigley by framing his answers within Quigley's well-defined system.

Quigley's lectures were packed with students anticipating great theatrics. The best attended lecture on campus was Quigley's discourse on Plato. He reviled Plato as a precursor of the Nazis and dismissed *The Republic* as a fascist tract. He was especially repelled by Plato's Principle of Specialization: that individuals have one and only one proper function, a function to which they are born, and can only be happy if they accept that role and do not try to change their place in society. Quigley's contempt for Plato would reach its climax with an amazing display of classroom showmanship. He would rip pages from the book as he tore it apart verbally, and finally conclude by heaving it out his second-floor window. One year he gave the lecture while construction crews were at work outside. He opened his window, let the book fly, turned to the class, shouted: *"Sieg Heil!"*—and at that moment there was a detonation on the construction site. Even Professor Quigley was stunned.

At the very least, Quigley got his students thinking. They would go back to their dorms and debate his attack on Plato late into the night. And at the most, Quigley left some lifelong lessons with his students, none more than Clinton. As much as Clinton and his classmates enjoyed the Plato lecture, it was Quigley's lecture on future preference that stuck with them. "The thing that got you into this classroom today is belief in the future, belief that the future can be better than the present and that people will and should sacrifice in the present to get to that better future," Quigley would say. "That belief has taken man out of the chaos and deprivation that most human beings toiled in for most of history to the point we are at today. One thing will kill our civilization and way of life—when people no longer have the will to undergo the pain required to prefer the future to the present. That's what got your parents to pay this expensive tuition. That's what got us through two wars and the Depression. Future preference. Don't ever forget that."

Over the ensuing decades, Clinton rarely delivered a major political speech that did not include a paraphrase of that lecture from the crazy genius who taught him Western civilization.

FROM the nursing home in Hope, located in what once was Julia Chester Hospital, the place where she used to work as a nurse, in the same room where her grandson was born, Edith Cassidy marked off the days until Billy would come back to Arkansas for Christmas. She was sixty-three and lived alone in a single room. She kept a stack of envelopes at her nightstand already stamped and addressed to William J. Clinton at Box 232 Hoya Station. Next to the envelopes were his letters and postcards to her— wishing her a happy Thanksgiving and thanking her for sending a picture of Mack McLarty and his cousin Phil; telling her that he had caught his first cold and gone to the infirmary to get some penicillin tablets ("the handkerchiefs you always taught me to carry have really come in handy"); bubbling with the news that the daughter of the president of the Philippines was in his philosophy class. Age and illness had reduced Edith's handwriting to a nervous scrawl. She documented her life in a palm-sized blue-green address book that contained the names and addresses of patients she had treated in her nursing trips to Wisconsin and Arizona, as well as the comings and goings of her college boy. "Billy came home from Washington DC Friday Dec. 18 1964," she wrote to herself in an open page near the back of the book. "He was here Dec. 24."

Aside from the trip down the highway from Hot Springs to Hope to see his mammaw, Clinton spent most of the Christmas break on Scully Street, shooting baskets in the driveway, reading books, working crossword puzzles, playing with his pudgy little brother Roger, now and then going out to a party at night with his high school friends. He went to a dance near the high school and ran into Phil Jamison, who was suffering as a first-year cadet at Texas A&M and trying to transfer to the Naval Academy. Jamison was stunned to hear that Clinton had been elected president of the Georgetown freshman class. "How could the only guy from Arkansas show up there and within a few months win an election like that?" Jamison wondered. Before that, Jamison's feelings about Clinton's political ambitions were "maybe yes, maybe no." But from then on, nothing Clinton accomplished surprised him. The party near the high school lingered in Jamison's memory for another reason. The senior class behind theirs was a bit wilder, readier to party and to challenge authority than they had been. Several of the boys in that class brought alcohol to the dance and got in trouble for it. They accused Clinton of turning them in for drinking. Jamison later vouched that they had nothing to do with it: "I can safely say that I didn't turn them in and Bill didn't either. But they considered us prudes and jumped to that conclusion."

In high school at Hot Springs or in college at Georgetown, Clinton seemed oblivious of how he was perceived. He always had people who resented him, who thought he was a phony. A number of his classmates at Georgetown, including some who would later be among his best friends, were at first put off by his irrepressible glad-handing. One fellow freshman, Jim Moore, bonded quickly with Clinton's roommate, Tom Campbell, but could barely tolerate Clinton for most of the first semester. He thought Clinton was too smooth: "Everybody else has moods, especially in college, where you have dramatic swings, study hard, party hard, you have the issues of growing up." Clinton by contrast always seemed positive, upbeat, enthusiastic. Nobody, Moore thought, could maintain that attitude and be for real. He seemed to Moore like the career student body president, more surface than depth.

It was only after the Christmas break, when Carroll Quigley posted first semester grades for his Western civilization class, that Moore began to reconsider those early impressions. Out of 230 students in his freshman course, Quigley had given two A's. Moore got one. Clinton the other. Moore was shocked: here this young pol from Arkansas was as smart as he was. He decided that he should get to know Clinton better.

Among his fellow student politicians, Clinton stood out as well. Some admired him, some felt a bit overwhelmed by him, and some disliked him and took pleasure in getting under his skin. As president of the junior class when Clinton led the freshmen, Phil Verveer, a liberal activist who was perhaps the most admired undergraduate on the East Campus, worked with Clinton at council meetings once a week. He found Clinton to be deferential to the upperclassmen yet already in a class by himself. All student pols thought they were special, yet knew who among them truly had the skills to go further. Clinton was the one, Verveer decided. He might have been jealous, but Clinton's "disarming style" somehow took the tinge off envy. David Kammer, the freshman vice president, a young

man from southern New Jersey with his own political ambitions, found
Clinton disarming in another way. He reminded Kammer of President Johnson. "Johnson would say, 'Let us reason together,' then surround you to
the point where you were not reasoning so much as being coerced. There
was that contradiction at the center of my perceptions of Bill. He had a
smile and a big body and that body language of embracing and getting
close and getting done what his goals were."

To freshman treasurer Paul Maloy, mastermind of the Long Island slate
that Clinton had foiled, Clinton was 90 percent bluff and 10 percent blus-
ter. They were political and cultural opposites. Maloy was a leader of the
campus Young Republicans, Clinton a lifelong Democrat. Maloy was a
young man of a few concise words, Clinton a flowery storyteller. Maloy
thought the purpose of student life was to have a good time. Clinton took
it a bit more seriously. Maloy appreciated the college skill of doing nothing,
wasting time, sleeping, drinking after hours at The Tombs. His friends were
of the same type. One was known as "The Rack King," not for his skills
with the other sex but for his ability to sleep fifteen to twenty hours at a
stretch. And there was Bill Clinton, his big alarm clock tick-ticking away,
teaching himself how to live without sleep, moving on to the next thing
and the next thing, talking to his buddies while writing a platform, sending
notes to Arkansas friends while his college mates were watching Perry
Mason, napping only so that he could get up extra early to get a jump on
all the Maloys out there. They grated on each other's nerves. Maloy could
not stand the way Clinton, a superior student, would feign such deep
interest in other people's scholastic standing; it seemed, Maloy thought,
that Clinton's first words of greeting were always, "How ya doin? What's
your QPI?" (QPI was the grade point average known at Georgetown as the
Quality Points Index). Since his QPI was lower than Clinton's, Maloy took
the greeting as a pointed jab.

But he knew how to rile Clinton. "We would fight all the time as student
officers, and I knew how to get him to lose his temper," Maloy later
recalled. "Everyone thought he was unflappable, but I figured out how to
do it. I'd accuse him of being insincere. I'd say, 'You goddamn southern
phony!' His face would get red and he'd lose it a bit. He was a bit of a
choirboy, but flim-flamming you."

It was a contentious year for the East Campus Council. They drew up a
student bill of rights which gave students an expanded role at the university, placing undergraduate members on the discipline committee and athletic board. They took a stand in support of an outspoken teacher, Francis
Kearns, who claimed he was denied tenure because of his radical beliefs.
In mid-March 1965 they debated an issue that extended beyond the
boundaries of Georgetown: whether to provide funding for students who

wanted to participate in the civil rights march from Selma to Montgomery in Alabama. The demonstrators in Selma had already been tear-gassed and beaten as they attempted to walk across the Edmund Pettus Bridge, and a young clergyman from Boston had been murdered by angry whites. Father Richard McSorley, Georgetown's leading activist priest, organized a delegation to make the trip south as a show of support. He had a dozen or so student followers, including Phil Verveer, the junior class president, and Walter Draude, president of the senior class, who went before the council seeking a statement of support and financial backing. The council was split: some thought the southern civil rights crusade was beyond the purview of Georgetown students. Verveer and Draude called upon their fellow students to awaken to the world around them.

Their side eventually won, supported by Clinton, who first tried to take the middle ground. He agreed with the civil rights marchers in principle and endorsed their mission, though he said he also appreciated the conservatives' argument that it should not be underwritten with student funds. Verveer accepted the fact that Clinton was more moderate than him. "He was still learning. He was trying to get the lay of the land. He was staying pretty close to the center."

The center was precisely where Georgetown as a whole seemed situated in the spring of 1965. The sociocultural phenomenon that would come to be known as the sixties lapped at the edges of the hilltop. There were few drugs on campus. The social scene was closer to the boola-boola era, with enormous crowds lining up outside The Tombs on Wednesday nights to drink beer and listen to the old-fashioned a cappella college songs sung by the Chimes. Although Peter, Paul and Mary drew an appreciative audience at McDonough Gym, the new music was still competing with the old: Clinton would join Tommy Caplan in Caplan's room to listen to the soundtrack from *Gone With the Wind.*

The student council's Selma debate was played out in a one-dimensional context. The handful of black students at Georgetown were Africans. A letter to the editor of *The Hoya* asked plaintively: "Why are there not any Negro basketball players at Georgetown?" The best known black on campus was the gym custodian, Pebbles, who was patronizingly accepted by the Georgetown Gentlemen. The only other blacks made the beds and served the meals. Women were slightly more visible, but they were not immune to old-school perceptions and traditions. Since the nursing school was also in the East Campus area, most males assumed that a female student was a nurse unless she proved otherwise. *The Courier* offered a regular photographic display of monthly nominees for Miss Foreign Service, a tame version of *Playboy*'s playmate of the month. One edition in Clinton's freshman year featured a special layout on "The Girls of Portugal." Georgetown women also had to overcome a widespread impression that they were less fun to date than their competitors from Immaculata, Mount Vernon, Marymount, Dunbarton, Marjorie Webster, and Trinity, the local women's colleges that virtually cleared out on weekends as their students headed over to the action on the hilltop. In Loyola Hall, the word was that Web girls, from Marjorie Webster, were the hottest.

The debate on Vietnam had only just begun at Georgetown, sparked by word that the first alumnus had been killed in the war. Prowar and antiwar voices seemed about evenly matched in the student journals. Columnist Gary Wasserman supported the war, quoting JFK's inaugural vow to "pay any price, bear any burden, meet any hardship, support any friend, oppose any foe to assure the survival and the success of liberty." But freshman Jim Regan countered with an article entitled "Vietnam: Let's Get Out!" that said of the war: "It is unprincipled. It is unjustified. And it is hopelessly futile." Claiborne Pell, the Democratic senator from Rhode Island who lived in a Georgetown townhouse visible from Clinton's second-floor dorm window, drew a ripple of interest when he spoke on the East Campus and raised questions about U.S. bombing in North Vietnam. Clinton, who had spent a weekend that year at the Campbell house on Long Island defending Lyndon Johnson against his roommate's father's attacks from the right, was still supportive of the president.

DENISE Hyland left her British Literature class one day in February of that freshman year and encountered Bill Clinton waiting in the hallway. He wondered whether he could walk her to the next class. As they stepped outside, he asked her out on a date. They went to an Italian restaurant for dinner. As they were walking back along Reservoir Road toward Hyland's dorm, St. Mary's Hall, he asked her out again—this time for an occasion that was months away, the Diplomats Ball. "He flabbergasted me, I didn't know what to say," Hyland remembered. "He said he hoped I didn't think he was too forward, and that I didn't have to answer him right away." He gave her a peck on the cheek, and strolled through the night back to Loyola. Taken by his earnestness, charmed by his southernness, she said yes the next day, and the first serious romance of Bill Clinton's life began.

Hyland was one of six children in an easygoing, upper-middle-class Irish Catholic family from Upper Montclair, a leafy suburb in northern New Jersey. Her father was an orthopedic surgeon and her mother was a dietitian. She was only seventeen when she arrived at Georgetown to study French at the language institute, tall and poised, as reserved as Clinton was outgoing. As a schoolgirl she had studied maps, history books, and *National Geographic* magazines. Their mutual friends noticed that she had a grace about her that brought out the better side of Clinton's nature. She was innocent, though not naive, and her unthreatening manner allowed Clinton to express his self-doubt and vulnerability. They went everywhere together. On warm spring nights they would often end up at the Capitol. They would sit on the west steps and look out at the Mall, out into the quiet darkness to the beacons of the Washington Monument and Lincoln Memorial, and talk about the nation and its problems. When he ran for sophomore class president near the end of the freshman year, Hyland helped pass out leaflets and type his platform. She organized the women in her dorm into a potent campaign operation that helped Clinton win again.

At the end of the semester she took him home to New Jersey to meet her family. He charmed the Hyland brood, wrestling in the living room with Denise's two little brothers, teaching her little sister how to make peanut butter and banana sandwiches, chatting late into the night with her mother in the kitchen as she washed the dishes and he dried. It was as though he wanted to lose himself in this functional and secure family. Then Denise went to France for the summer and Clinton to Hot Springs. Every day he drove to Mount Pine to work as a counselor at Camp Yorktown Bay. At night he read books and wrote letters to his girlfriend in France, letters that revealed a sentimental young man.

"I meet some awfully cute kids at camp," he wrote in his first letter to Hyland.

> Some really make you realize how lucky you are. One flunked seventh grade last year and has always been in trouble.... One had his way paid by the Houston Boys Club and his mother, the mother of six more, didn't give him a cent to take with him.... When they get back to Houston he has to call an aunt to find out where he lives. They were giving swimming tests tonight and one little scrapper tried even though he couldn't swim a lick. When one of the counselors pulled him out he was so pale and shivering. Later I was walking with him to the gym and he told me he was really a lucky boy—his experience in the lake was nothing—he swallowed his tongue, he'd been poisoned, and been in a bad wreck. His father died three months ago. The little guy was so cute telling me how he was going to take care of his mother and sister—kinda hard though— cause they are all bigger than he. Camp is really good for these boys— good for this one too I guess.

Soon after Clinton arrived in Arkansas, his grandfather Allen W. Clinton took deathly ill. "My grandfather is dying tonight, Denise," he wrote Hyland on June 10. "Mother and Daddy just left and all the family is beginning to congregate. He is a fine old gentleman of 85 and until two years ago he produced some of the best vegetables you ever saw in his acre garden. Worked at the garage until the very end. He was never much of a church-goer, but I have a hunch he is going to have a good trip." Clinton had always admired people like this grandfather, uneducated Arkansans whose lives seemed simple and honest. They appealed to him almost as characters out of the Old Testament. After the funeral, Clinton wrote about him again: "He was really amazing to have lived so long—but I guess more amazing is he lived so well. He was really quite a man, especially for one who lived so simply, and the greatest in the world might have been a carpenter."

In his letters, Clinton rarely mentioned the man he called "Daddy"—his stepfather Roger Clinton—but went on about his mother's gardening and her carbohydrate diets and gave constant progress reports on his eight-year-old brother Roger. His care for Roger seemed almost maternal. Hyland would open the letters to discover what the boy looked like, how his shoulders were broadening, how "he weighs 90 pounds now." Clinton's preoccupation with his own weight was transferred to his little brother. They were eating too many sweets, he lamented: "Sometimes I think the whole house will sink into a heap of sugar."

Time was another constant in his letters: he was always taking note of it and trying to find more of it. "It's 1:30 a.m. and I have to get up at six." When he could not sleep at night, he said, he would turn on the light and read. One night he woke up at three-thirty and read until five. "I wish I could wake up and read in the middle of every night."

His reading interests ranged from the dense and furious southern prose of William Faulkner to the corny poetry of Edgar Guest, which he de-scribed to Hyland as "very simple, kinda southern, kinda negro, very beau-tiful poetry." Guest was neither southern nor black. He was a London-born journalist whose homespun verse for the *Detroit Free Press* was syndicated to an adoring national audience. But when Clinton read Guest's work he thought it was written expressly for his idealized vision of his childhood in Hope and Hot Springs, not the private torment that alcohol visited upon his family but the sheltering of his mammaw and pappaw in Hope and the free and easy days roaming the streets of Hot Springs with his adolescent friends. "David Leopoulos and I agreed today—no one ever enjoyed being kids more than we did—it would be pretty hard to crowd more living in," he wrote.

Nothing pleased Clinton more than to show off his homeland to friends from other places. His first visitor was Tom Campbell, who came down from Long Island for a week that summer. Campbell arrived in Little Rock late at night and was struck first by its smallness. "I remember the black-ness," he recalled. "On the East Coast, it was all lights. Out there it was blackness, lights, blackness again. The whole feeling was something I'd never experienced before. It was exotic: the heavy southern air, the warmth, the darkness. I felt like I was in another country on the drive from Little Rock to Hot Springs." They goofed around with Leopoulos, shot baskets in the driveway, went water-skiing out at Uncle Raymond's place on Lake Hamilton, and had a little party on Scully Street.

Carolyn Yeldell was home that summer from Ouachita Baptist University. She had read Emily Post, and "learned the whole business of entertaining," preparing for a future where she might be the wife of a politician. She and Clinton went to the grocery store and bought crackers, cheese spreads, vegetables, and sodas. When she got home with the party food, her mother was upset that she had used her hard-earned money, money that was supposed to go toward a tonsils operation, for a party next door. "Who do you think you are," she snapped at Carolyn, "Mrs. Astor?" Carolyn "cried and cried," she later remembered. "I was making my mark as an entertainer or practice bride. I wanted to be the perfect hostess. That I would spend my money on it horrified my parents. I don't remember Bill chipping any money in. But I remember Roger Clinton, Sr., was impressed. He said, 'You are going to make some man so lucky.' "

When his roommate went back to Long Island, Clinton began concentrating on the year ahead. He had already been elected sophomore class president, and he drafted plans for an orientation committee that would greet every freshman at the Main Gate and help them move into their dorms. He also began plotting his future beyond that. "What feedback are you getting from the French regarding Vietnam?" he asked Hyland in an August letter. Then he added: "I've been meaning to ask you, does the Institute of Language and Linguistics offer a course in Vietnamese? I really want to know. If I go to summer school next summer, I can take it in my junior year. Someone has to be there after—and during—the war to speak and help the people—probably not over one or two people in our embassy can converse fluently. Let's hope there'll come a time when guns won't have to win our battles for us and we can begin to win battles in the cold war again." Hyland wrote back that she was uncertain about the language question but could tell him that there was "a real negative feeling about America" since the Johnson administration had escalated the war.

From his letters that summer it was clear that Clinton was struggling with the competing impulses of humility and ambition. He was looking wistfully at his past, seeing it only in its innocence. And of his future, he wrote: "Just searching, I guess, for a road ahead. Maybe I am beginning to realize that I am almost grown, and will soon have to choose that one final motive in life which I hope will put a little asterisk by my name in the billion pages of the book of life."

Denise Hyland sensed what that little asterisk might denote. When she reached Nice after studying in Dijon, she met a group of college students from France and America, including some Texans. "This one tall proud Texas boy was talking on and on about his political future," Hyland later recalled. "And I turned to him and I said, 'Remember this name—Bill Clinton—because someday he will be president.' "

CHAPTER FOUR

HE WAS ON FIRE

FOR THE START of his sophomore year at Georgetown, Clinton made the return trip east by car, the first time that he had covered the distance on the ground. Kit Ashby, his classmate from Dallas, came up to Hot Springs and joined him for the 1,200-mile drive. Their plan was to go nonstop, four hours on, four hours off for each driver; but in those days before the completion of the East-West interstate system, the journey was an arduous succession of narrow twists and turns. Ashby was shocked and awed by "how many miles, how many hours, how much land" there was between where they grew up and where they went to school. He was at the wheel as they drove through the hills of Tennessee, and he saw, for the first time in his life, the makeshift memorials to accident victims that were becoming commonplace along American highways: seven white wooden crosses lined the embankment as he negotiated the sharpest bends in the road. Clinton understood all too well the real-life consequences of those symbolic markers: a highway in southern Missouri had taken away the father he never knew. In the middle of the night, overtaken by drowsiness, they pulled over at a rest stop in Virginia and slept for a few hours. They drove across the Potomac and up to Georgetown the next day, two college boys on top of the world, big men on campus, Clinton possessing everything he might want at nineteen: the white Buick convertible with its red interior, the affection of Denise Hyland, and the presidency of the sophomore class.

As the student officer responsible for making the incoming freshmen feel welcome, Clinton had the opportunity to make new friends and build his constituency at the same time. He seemed to be everywhere at once: at the Main Gate shaking hands with anxious parents and students as they pulled up; at Loyola Hall, hauling luggage up the stairs. No one knew how to navigate the campus more skillfully. As polished as Clinton had become at Georgetown politics, appealing to students by calling for lower cafeteria

prices and to Jesuit administrators by stressing student moderation and
civility, he was even more adept in the classroom, where it seemed that he
studied the teachers with as much diligence as he applied to the subject
matter. His coziness with professors was a source of constant razzing from
his friends. Tom Campbell, once again his roommate, this time in Harbin
Hall, would tease Clinton by placing his hand on his nose in an obscene
gesture and saying, "Bill, you've got your nose up their ass all the time."
Clinton would deny it, claiming that he was "trying to clear up an inconsis-
tency." But Campbell knew better. He marveled at how Clinton could
figure out what was important to a professor and pick his brain, raising
points of special interest to the teacher. Clinton was doing what came
naturally to him, Campbell concluded. He was working the room.

Although Campbell, Moore, and Ashby chided Clinton about his solicitous approach to teachers, they also had enough sense to try to get into
classes with him and pick his brain in study groups. Clinton's ability to
anticipate test questions by studying the professors was what set him apart
from the rest of them, Ashby believed. A medical student had once told
Ashby that the great doctors were not those most interested in helping
people but those who were most fascinated by the human body and how
it works. "Bill had that same intense fascination with people and how they
work. That was the thrust of his intellectual curiosity."

That curiosity was put to full use in the most exacting course in the
sophomore curriculum, U.S. Constitution and Law, taught by Walter I.
Giles. The course was modeled after a law school seminar. Undergraduates
formed study groups to survive, parceling out the heavy reading load.
Clinton was in a study group with Moore and Ashby. When they gathered
to go over law cases, the others were struck by Clinton's clarity and sense
of humor about coursework that could otherwise seem intimidating. He
would tell stories to relax the others, and "better than anyone I had seen,"
Moore observed, "he could absorb a lot of information and come right to
the point." He was a meticulous notetaker. John Spotila, a freshman friend,
missed classes one week and borrowed Clinton's notes. Clinton had not
only outlined with Roman numerals and subheadings, but cross-referenced
the material. From then on, Spotila copied Clinton's notebook every day.

The Giles course, much like Quigley's, was one of the shared experiences of School of Foreign Service students. Some agreed with Phil Verveer's description of Walter Giles as a "somewhat imperious character."
He was definitely a man of traditions. All classroom exchanges were conducted formally as "Mister" and "Sir," and students stood when answering
questions. It was highly embarrassing to be called upon and not have an
answer; the only way to avert that humiliation was to come to Giles before
class started and plead *nolo contendere.* What Giles imparted to his disci-

ples was respect for the founding documents of American law and their application in the twentieth century. He had a liberal outlook toward human rights, an expansive interpretation of the Constitution and the Bill of Rights, and what Tommy Caplan regarded as "a great sense of the genius of our founding fathers and of the majesty of their document."

The Warren Court was in its heyday then, interpreting civil liberties and civil rights in ways that Giles generally favored. Landmark cases emerging from the Warren Court would quickly become part of Giles's course, providing new material for his rigorous exams. Two weeks before each test, he would distribute a syllabus of cases and readings that his students should be familiar with in order to handle the essay questions. Everything that was going to be on the exam would be somewhere in that stapled syllabus, but there was so much that it was virtually impossible to read it all. Clinton, knowing how to read the professor, knew how to read the syllabus, and the study group the week before an exam would focus intently on what Clinton picked out as the essential material. Although his exams were difficult, Giles stressed that they were the least important part of his class. It was the learning process that he loved. On the first page of every syllabus, Giles would present his philosophy of learning, a quotation from Justice Benjamin Cardozo: "In the end the great truth will have been learned, that the quest is greater than what is sought, the effort finer than the prize, or rather that the effort is the prize, the victory cheap and hollow were it not for the rigor of the game."

Giles lived near campus in a carriage house with a felicitous history: it was originally part of the estate of the Marbury who lent his name to the landmark 1803 U.S. Supreme Court decision, *Marbury* v. *Madison,* which established the judicial branch's right to review the constitutionality of legislation. It seemed to David Kammer that Giles "was wedded to the institution" of teaching, much in the manner of an Oxford don. He socialized with students outside the classroom, especially during football season. Football Sundays were a Giles ritual. He held four tickets for Washington Redskins home games and would invite students to accompany him. Clinton was among those invited, though he was of no help downing the cooler full of martinis that the professor and his brood toted into D.C. Stadium. For away games, Giles invited a group of six or eight who gathered at his carriage house and watched the game on television while downing Heinekens, martinis, and Bloody Marys, and sharing his Triscuits topped with Cheddar cheese and bacon. It was partly a performance, and those who performed well would find a second invitation in their mailbox.

Those who stood out in class and at the carriage house were tapped for a peculiar and colorful drama. It was called the James Madison Martini Lecture. Giles would walk into class that day and open a portable bar—

Tanqueray gin, Martini & Rossi, olives—and launch into a discourse on the role of olives in American constitutional history. As he spoke, he would mix a pitcher of martinis. As the lecture concluded, he would call a group of students up to the front, hand each a martini glass, and propose a toast. "Gentlemen, to the republic!" They would toss down their martinis and the glasses would be filled again, followed by a second Giles toast: "Gentlemen, may confusion reign among enemies of the republic!" Confusion certainly reigned in the heads of the classroom leaders as they stumbled out in a two-martini daze.

Clinton thrived in this environment without being a drinker or much of a Redskins fan. He was, in the football realm as most everything else, still an Arkansas chauvinist. His high school friend Phil Jamison, who had transferred from Texas A&M to the Naval Academy that year, came to Washington on October 16 to attend Navy's contest against Pitt, and after the game he and two fellow plebes from Arkansas made their way up to the Georgetown campus to spend the afternoon and evening. Clinton took them over to the lounge in Denise Hyland's dorm where they watched Arkansas beat Texas in a Southwest Conference showdown, 27–24. The women of Georgetown had never witnessed anything quite like that late afternoon when Clinton and his buddies filled the dorm lobby with ear-splitting howls of "Whooo-pig-sooey!" That night, Clinton and Denise got Jamison and his friends dates for the dance at McDonough Gym featuring the Four Tops.

That was Bill Clinton at Georgetown, a curious mix, calling the hogs in support of an all-white college football team one hour, singing the lyrics to the soulful Motown tunes of the Four Tops the next. He was of both worlds. The progressive Clinton would make the case for the Johnson civil rights initiatives. The traditional Clinton revered his southern roots and the people back home so much that he tried to shy away from confrontations on issues of race. When his grandmother mailed him a pouch of postcards from Hope with an overtly racist image, a Sambo-styled black boy polishing enormous watermelons, Clinton mailed one back to her with the message: "Dear Mammaw, Thought I would send you one of your cards just to prove I'm using them."

Denise Hyland enjoyed watching her boyfriend portray himself as "a simple southern guy coming to the brave new world of the East Coast." She knew that part of it was true: he was enough of a hokey razorback to walk around campus wearing a bright red V-neck vest hand-knitted for him by a relative. But it was also partly a ruse, a way for him to lure people into underestimating him. He would play that just-a-humble-southern-boy game, teasingly, even with Denise's mother. He sent her a note that year after a visit thanking her for letting Denise drive him to the airport in New

York—"A small price to pay," he wrote with mock self-ridicule, "to get rid of the southern plague." Later, when he learned that Denise would be working as an intern at an export-import firm in the financial district the next summer, he wrote Mrs. Hyland another self-effacing, pun-filled note: "Take care of Miss Financial District. Make sure she doesn't become an 'export' to someone of 'import.' I wouldn't have a prayer—oh yes, even Baptists have those."

THE times were changing rapidly on college campuses by the spring of 1966, but still not at Georgetown, which remained decidedly mainstream, all beer and no drugs. War protests on campus amounted to fifteen or twenty peaceful souls holding vigils near the statue of Georgetown founder John Carroll. The editorialists in *The Courier* maintained their prowar position, arguing: "American withdrawal at the present time is absurd. We are a world power engaged in a world struggle and the liberal neo-isolationists among us should realize the need for effective use of this power if our position and their liberties are to be maintained." Some students were starting to worry about the military draft, however, as the troop numbers in Vietnam increased. "All males harbor fears over the Armed Forces Qualification Test," one *Hoya* columnist wrote. "Fear not, we have the solutions: Poke out right ear drum; kiss your Army recruiter; shave your legs during the physical; burn your best friend's draft card; become one of George Hamilton's buddies; get religious convictions, or for that matter criminal ones will do; finally, if all else fails, enlist. Patriots never pass physicals."

Clinton and Tom Campbell enlisted that spring of their sophomore year in a fraternity, Alpha Phi Omega, which served as both social club and service organization and was especially valuable for a Georgetown politician in that its members were charged with overseeing student elections. There was a modest amount of hazing of pledges, although hazing was officially banned by the administration. Don Pattee, who was Clinton's "big brother" for the initiation period, made Clinton report to him every day for six weeks and do whatever he ordered: shine his shoes, run errands, craft a fraternity paddle, and run the gauntlet. The initiation rite on Hell Night was held at Pattee's parents' house across the Potomac in Arlington. Clinton, Campbell, Shullaw, and the other pledges were blindfolded and herded down to the basement, where they were forced to kneel in the darkness. One by one they were brought upstairs and questioned about their fraternal worthiness. At five in the morning, when Tom Campbell's turn arrived, he started laughing and could not stop for thirty minutes.

For Easter break, Clinton brought Tommy Caplan home to Hot Springs. Caplan had spent much of that year holed up in his dorm room in Harbin

Hall reading Hemingway and Fitzgerald, and writing short stories of his own, determined that someday he would write the great American novel. They flew out to Little Rock on a garish pink Braniff jet, an appropriately colorful means of transporting the easterner to Arkansas. Caplan had long been impressed by Clinton's novelistic sense of place, not just his ability to bring Arkansas characters to life through his storytelling, but his eagerness to be part of that story while so many of his classmates were breaking away from their pasts. From here, Clinton's attachment seemed less odd. Caplan was overwhelmed by the embrace that he, a stranger, felt on that cool but ripe southern evening when they rolled into Hot Springs, the top down on the convertible they had driven from the airport. It was an embrace that made him understand more about his friend than anything he had witnessed at Georgetown. They were on Central Avenue in downtown Hot Springs, waiting at a stoplight, when from the crowd on the sidewalk came the call of welcome to a favorite son: "Hey, Billy Clinton's home!" All week long, they would turn other corners and the cry would go out: "Hey, Billy Clinton's home!" To Caplan, it seemed like a film—"the best of an almost vanished America. You had the feeling of real affection and coherent, small-town life."

The sophomore year ended quietly for Clinton. When the election for junior class offices was held after Easter break, he decided not to run. His friend David Matter entered the race and was elected class president. In temporarily withdrawing from the student political scene, Clinton was following a well-worn political track. Most of the ablest student leaders at Georgetown had served as freshmen and sophomores and then sat out the third year as they prepared for the top job, student council president, as seniors. Furthermore, Bill Clinton was ready to take his first step into the real world of politics back home.

DURING election years in the 1960s, the center of Arkansas politics was the Marion Hotel, long since demolished, which stood on the banks of the Arkansas River just to the east of the Old State House in Little Rock. It was a musty old place, with thick carpets and painted pipes exposed in the hallways, and no air conditioning. Tradition demanded that serious candidates for state offices set up their headquarters there, an address of such prestige that competitors often found themselves on different wings of the same floor or directly above and below each other. One of the ways in which political journalists measured the strength of candidates was to count the number of rooms each had rented at the Marion. When he launched his campaign for the Democratic nomination for governor in 1966, Judge Frank Holt took six rooms on the third floor, twice as many as anyone else.

One sultry morning in early June, Lyda Holt was seated at a desk in the campaign headquarters near an open window in the corner room facing the Old State House, typing a speech she intended to give on her father's behalf. Lyda was the older of the judge's two charming daughters, just back from her freshman year at Mary Baldwin College in Virginia. She hated to type and was not having a very successful go of it as she worked on the speech. Then "a nice looking young man appeared in front of me, leaned against the window ledge, and said, 'Would you like me to type that for you?' And I said, 'Yes.' That was my introduction to Bill Clinton. . . . He just kind of waltzed through. He just showed up. He typed the speech—and it came out edited, better than what I wrote."

In signing up with the Frank Holt campaign that summer, the first full-time campaign adventure of his life, Clinton had relied on family connections. His uncle Raymond Clinton was known as a player in Garland County politics, someone to whom state Democrats would turn for votes and favors. Young Bill was first introduced to the Holt people as "Raymond Clinton's nephew—a bright boy who goes to school up east." Holt, the unassuming brother in a powerful political family led by Jack Holt, Sr., who had twice run for governor himself, was the favorite of the Democratic party establishment. Although he was more progressive on civil rights than Orval Faubus, the man he sought to succeed, Holt nonetheless represented the safe choice. People who thought Arkansas was in need of urgent change had a variety of other candidates from whom to choose. There was Republican Winthrop Rockefeller, who had moved to Arkansas in 1953 to repair his personal life in a place where he was unknown. By 1968, fifteen years later, he was leading a GOP resurgence in the traditionally one-party state, promising to sweep away every remnant of the Faubus machine and modernize Arkansas. There was Brooks Hays, the former congressman, who had made a courageous if politically suicidal stand in support of the federal government's desegregation of Little Rock Central High School. And for rebels on the segregationist side, Jim Johnson, the razorback version of Alabama's George Wallace, who attacked the Faubus machine from the populist right.

Holt was immediately put on the defensive as the machine candidate. Jim Johnson accused him of being "hand-picked by the big boys," and in a phrase that could not be forgotten, belittled the judge as nothing more than a "pleasant vegetable." Another conservative opponent, orthodontist Dale Alford, said Holt was a passenger on the "Faubus steamroller" driven by the retiring governor's political enforcer, William J. Smith, who was said to wield the sort of raw power that made legislators straighten up a little when he came into view. If the supposed links to Faubus were not enough, reporters were tipped off that Holt had met privately with the state's most powerful financier, bond broker W. R. (Witt) Stephens, only hours before entering the race, implying that he was Stephens's puppet as well. Rumors spread that he had been promised a federal judgeship if he lost.

These broadsides against Holt were for the most part bogus. Although he arose from the party establishment, he was not beholden to Faubus or Stephens, but suffered from his own becalmed nature. He demonstrated passion once, at the start of the campaign, when he paid his filing fee, banged his fist on the desk, and bellowed, "I am completely free and unobligated." That done, he assumed naively that the attacks against him would end.

In his own fashion, Holt thought that his campaign offered the most important symbol of change. He surrounded himself with young people, a coterie of college student leaders, and called them "the Holt Generation." It was an adaptation of the popular television commercials heralding "the Pepsi Generation," with a jingle and red, white, and blue buttons evoking the soft-drink imagery. Lyda Holt, president of the freshman class at Mary Baldwin, was one officer in Holt's generational brigade, which also included Paul Fray, president of the Young Democrats at Ouachita Baptist University; Leslie Smith of Vanderbilt University, a former Arkansas Junior Miss; Dick King, president of the Arkansas State Teachers College student body; David (Mac) Glover, past president of the University of Arkansas student body; Bill Allen, a former Arkansas Boys State governor and student leader at Memphis State; and Bill Clinton, former Boys Nation senator and sophomore class president at Georgetown.

The young recruits worked sixteen-hour days, often sleeping at the Marion Hotel or on a spare couch at the Holts' house on Reservoir Road. The college boys wore khaki pants and blue knit shirts or white shirts and ties. Clinton was the youngest member of the group, aside from the judge's daughter. In larger gatherings of the Holt Generation crowd and in correspondence to his Georgetown friends, Clinton assumed a modest posture —"and warming the bench, me," he wrote to Denise Hyland when describing the powerhouse lineup of student leaders. But he came off the bench at the first opportunity, offering to be the chauffeur when the campaign brain trust decided that Holt's wife, Mary, and two daughters, Lyda and Melissa, should barnstorm the state. Holt toured the state in one car; his family, with Bill Clinton driving them, toured in another. They would head out during the week and return to Little Rock on weekends to do their laundry.

For a young man who wanted to make his name in Arkansas politics, that might have been one of the two best jobs in the Holt campaign. Bill Allen had the other: he was Holt's travel aide. But traveling the state with the Holt women offered certain advantages. ("Bill was no dummy," Lyda Holt would joke later.) They were more interesting company, for one thing, and they sometimes turned to their driver for advice, or even invited him now and then to be a stand-in.

They were quite a quartet, Clinton and the Holt women, driving around the state in a Ford sedan with a banner proclaiming "FRANK HOLT FAMILY" on the side door, Bill and Mrs. Holt in the front seat, talking politics or literature, Lyda and Melissa in the back, practicing the speech they might give at the next town square. "I never took orders from three women before," Clinton wrote with mock displeasure to Denise Hyland in Manhattan. This comment was a bit disingenuous, as a triumvirate of women—his grandmother, his mother, and his high school principal—had been the only ones to order him around his entire life, and it could not mask the pleasure he was getting from the assignment. He was thrilled to tell his East Coast girlfriend of all the exotic places they had visited—"Marmaduke and Piggott (some names, huh?)"—and to send her postcards from such landmarks as Burks Café and Steakhouse in Conway—"Here I come, broke and loaded with bull."

His letters to Denise often lavished praise on Mrs. Holt, who stayed up several hours past midnight one night in a small-town motel talking politics with him. One day they were driving along a rural highway and noticed that a house was on fire. They helped evacuate the residents, along with a batch of puppies.

As the fire engines arrived, Mrs. Holt said, "Get in the car, we've got to get out of here!"

"Why?" implored Clinton. "This is good press!"

But they left.

Near the end of June, the Holt Generation group gathered in Little Rock to tape a fifteen-minute campaign program. It offered Clinton a chance to shine among his peers, and to save face for his colleague, Dick King. King could not remember what he wanted to say, so he wrote his speech on his hand. But his hand started to sweat from the television lights. "The joke was when my hand started running I couldn't remember what I believed in any more. Bill had to rescue me by whispering my lines to me," King would later recall. Clinton wrote Denise about the show, diminishing his own role ("I looked ugly") while boasting about the results: "Many people called in and said they thought it was the best political program they had ever seen."

The day after the show aired, he sent a letter to his grandmother at her nursing home in Hope. "Dear Mammaw—I hope you saw me on TV last night. Mother said she called you and told you I'd be on," he wrote. "The program was pretty good, I thought, and I sure hope it gets Judge Holt some votes. Last night I was at the little town of Alread, near Clinton, at the same time the TV program was on. I had to speak to a small group of people there. This job is great. I really feel like I'm doing something worthwhile." Clinton closed the note by saying he would be in Hope for a rally on July 7.

Lyda Holt later remembered that she was scheduled to give the speech in downtown Hope that night, but Clinton made a special plea. "Bill came up to Mother and said, 'I know Lyda's supposed to speak, but my grandmother is going to be in the audience, so is it okay if I did it?' I thought, 'Great,' since I didn't like speaking that much anyway. So Bill spoke. And if we had any doubts about his future, they were erased. He had that ability to take feelings and emotions and match them to words. It was a gift from God. He gave a warm, true gutty vision of my dad. He talked about how honest Dad was. How he could bring Arkansas forward and move it out of the past. How he had a vision for young people, a vision for Arkansas. And he talked about family and roots."

In recounting the scene to Denise in a letter the next day, Clinton presented a different account, making it seem as though he had been forced to give a speech that he was not prepared to deliver. "Last night I spoke for Judge Holt on the courthouse square," he wrote. "His daughter Lyda was supposed to give the address but Mrs. Holt made me do it when she found out my grandmother was in the audience. You would have been proud of me. I didn't think I did so well, but some of the prejudiced home folks were really giving me the big head—plus saying—'Why I haven't seen you since you were this high' or 'I remember your mother used to wheel you down Main Street in your baby buggy.' It was great to be home."

Hope was an ancestral home for Mary Holt as well. Her uncle, a former congressman, had once been the town's leading politician. The day after the speech, she took Clinton and her daughters out to Rose Hill Cemetery to clear the family grave sites and grace them with fresh flowers. When they were done, Clinton asked Lyda Holt if she wanted to walk in the cemetery. They took a long walk around. Finally, Clinton stopped and said, "This is my dad." He pointed to a flat marble gravestone about fifteen feet from the path on the northern edge of the cemetery. It read:

WILLIAM JEFFERSON BLYTHE
FEB. 27, 1918
MAY 17, 1946

"Oh, my Lord," Lyda Holt gasped. She had always thought that Mr. Clinton was his dad. They stood there quietly as Clinton told them the story of how his father had been killed in a car accident before Bill was born. Blythe's grave rested next to an identical marker for Clinton's maternal grandfather, Eldridge Cassidy, the Hope iceman, who died at age fifty-six.

The visit, he told Denise in a letter, was "a good reminder that I have a lot of living to do for two other fine fellows who never even got close to the average lifespan. . . . If I had to die tomorrow I guess I'd feel in a way that I've lived a long time—and a full time. But should I live to be old I know I'll feel as if I just started on this journey of life and hardly be ready to leave."

From the cemetery, Clinton took the Holts over to see Mack McLarty, who was home for the summer working at his father's Ford dealership. Seeing Mack and his family, the symbols of success in Hope, always reassured Clinton, he later told a friend, yet served to remind him of how much work there was ahead for him to get where he wanted to go, far beyond the life of a small-town hero.

A few days later, the foursome spent an afternoon campaigning in Arkadelphia in the Fourth Congressional District where Democrat David Pryor was on his way to winning a seat in the U.S. House of Representatives. It was a scorching day, and Pryor was dripping with sweat as he walked toward the Arkadelphia fire station to start shaking hands. As he approached, a young man came strolling out and struck up an intense conversation. When Pryor got back to his car, his wife asked, 'Who was that you were talking to?' Pryor said it was young Bill Clinton from Hot Springs. "You're gonna hear a lot about him," Pryor said. He could tell. When Clinton asked a question, he listened to the response. He was, said Pryor, "on fire."

Temperatures soared near the century mark as the Holt family caravan rolled east toward the Mississippi Delta. "I think the heat has burned GU out of my system," Clinton wrote to Denise, referring to Georgetown by its initials. Hot, flat, and poor, the Delta was by any measure a long way from the hilltop, and had more of the feel of rural black poverty than Hope, Hot Springs, and Little Rock, the Arkansas towns with which he was most familiar. Clinton's reactions to what he was seeing in the Delta alternated between awe and embarrassment.

"Boy, you meet all kinds on a trip like this," he told Denise in a July 14 letter. "I would give anything if you could see all the tiny towns we've been through—Altheimer, Wabbaseka, Ulm, McGehee, Lake Village, Arkansas City. The populations are mostly Negroes and the towns are either just a square or only one street for a couple of blocks. The buildings are the same as those erected at the town's birth." But in another section of that same letter he described his dismay at encountering Deep South racism at its most blatant. "Now we are campaigning in the heart of cotton country, south and east Arkansas, where Negroes are still niggers—and I couldn't believe my eyes when I saw restrooms and waiting rooms still marked in Colored and White. It made me so sick to my stomach."

When they reached McGehee, the Holt women attracted the notice of a feature writer from the *Memphis Commercial-Appeal,* who wrote an article about what he considered the novelty of finding a candidate's wife and daughters out on the trail. The story detailed the scene inside the car. One can see Clinton's presence everywhere, though he is mentioned only at the end in an offbeat way:

> The Holts travel in an air-conditioned Ford in an attempt to save themselves from the unbearable heat—but it doesn't help much. They jump in and out of the auto time and again all day.
>
> "We're constantly debating whether it's better to run the air-conditioning when we're in the car or just roll the windows down and stay in one temperature all the time," Mrs. Holt said.
>
> Between towns the two girls do some reading and Mrs. Holt looks over a typical itinerary provided a week at a time by campaign headquarters in Little Rock. . . . In the back seat Wednesday were two paperback books, one on Kennedy and a novel—Khartoum. The car, loaned for the campaign, came equipped with a stereo tape player which Wednesday appropriately was playing a tape of the Norman Luboff choir titled "On the Country Side."
>
> And there's a convenient safety device. College student Bill Clinton of Hot Springs, the Holt family driver, can lock all four car doors instantly with a flick of the switch on the dash.

Those books in the back seat did not belong to the Holt girls, but to Clinton. In his letters he faithfully reported to Denise what he was reading and suggested readings for her. "Never finished '1000 Days' [Arthur Schlesinger's account of the Kennedy presidency] but did read Khartoum, the Loved One by Evelyn Waugh and Who's Afraid of Virginia Woolf," he told her. "Have dabbled in five or six others." In response to Denise's latest review of a book he had recommended, he added: "I knew you would like The Making of the President '60. White is a great writer and a perceptive politico." He also noted that he had recently received a letter from his favorite professor, Walter Giles, "wishing good luck in the campaign, but expressing hopes it hasn't interfered with my reading." If anything, the campaign widened Clinton's perspective, presenting him with characters straight out of many of the books he was reading. After encountering one provincial tycoon, Clinton described him to Denise with a literary reference. "Just like a Jonas Cord of 'The Carpetbaggers' or Will Long of 'A Long Hot Summer,' he wrote, "he hasn't learned to gracefully exercise the power that goes with his money."

. . .

EVERY week, Frank Holt's opponents attacked him with unsubstantiated charges, and every week Holt chose to ignore the attacks. Clinton admired Holt's attitude and thought that it was strategically sound. "Denise, he's never lost an election and I see why," he told his girlfriend. "He really lives by his religious and ethical convictions without being self-righteous or pious. He refuses to attack his opponents as they attack him. He wants to win on his own merits or not at all. He thinks he can't build Arkansas unless he can win in this way." Then came the shock of primary night. Holt barely survived, finishing second in a six-way race to Jim Johnson, his despised former colleague on the state Supreme Court, the self-described "Justice Jim" who appealed to people's fears and prejudices in his backward state. Johnson finished with 25 percent of the vote to 22 percent for Holt and 15 percent for the third-place finisher, Brooks Hays. Holt's showing was more of a surprise to his followers than it should have been. In retrospect they could see how little room to maneuver he had, with Johnson on his right, Hays on his left, and scores of Republicans taking advantage of the open primary system to vote for Johnson, the man they thought would be easiest for Rockefeller to beat.

Holt tried to shape the runoff race as New South versus Old South, but to little effect. To whatever extent Arkansans were looking to become part of a New South, those who did had now decided that Winthrop Rockefeller, not Holt, would be the one to take them there. And in a year when many of the state's schools were just facing desegregation, there was plenty of sentiment around for Justice Jim's Old South.

Three days before the runoff, Clinton wrote Denise that he thought Holt had finally taken the offensive in the campaign. "All I can do is pray for reason and real courage to come to our voters Tuesday." On election eve: "I think I'm sure victory will come, but you can never tell. And after the shock of the 26th I'm so worried. . . . Cross your fingers and hold tight— he's just got to get in there." But the family already knew better. Lyda Holt sensed on election morning that they had lost. "We went to church that morning and let go." That night, Clinton was assigned to accompany Lyda. She later remembered "how reassuring" he was. "He stayed sweet and nice. When you lose an election, it's like a death. And Bill that night said to me, 'Now remember, the outcome of an election is not the measure of a man.' "

Clinton made his next important political move as Judge Holt was playing out his last one. He told Jack Holt, Jr., that he needed some money to help pay for his college tuition and wondered whether there was any way he could work for Senator Fulbright's office in Washington. Holt called Lee Williams, Fulbright's administrative assistant. "Lee, I've got one you shouldn't overlook," he said. "There's a young man down here who's just the kind the senator likes to have around him."

Lee Williams was always looking to help aspiring young men, just as he had been helped when Fulbright called the University of Arkansas Law School a generation earlier and asked if there were any bright graduates around who could work on his staff. Clinton was at home on Scully Street a week later when he got a morning call from Williams. "You've been recommended to me by someone in whom I have implicit faith," Williams said. "Tell me about yourself and what your aims are." Clinton talked about his interest in government and politics and said he needed money to complete his education at Georgetown. He brought up the time he had come to Washington for Boys Nation and had lunch with Senator Fulbright.

"Well," said Williams, "we've got two jobs up here—one part time that pays about thirty-five hundred a year and another that is full time that pays about five thousand."

"Well, how about two part-time jobs?" asked Clinton.

Williams chuckled.

The job offer brought with it only one disappointment. All summer long Denise Hyland had been planning to visit Clinton and his family in Hot Springs. She had arranged to come near the end of August. But Clinton would be gone by then. Williams wanted him right away. Virginia Clinton wrote Denise a note of apology. "We're all so disappointed you're not coming. The prospect of your coming even brightened Mr. Holt's defeat. You know my dear this door is always open to you. So this time you set the date. Bill's Daddy and brother both feel cheated." But Clinton would see Denise soon enough in Washington. Nothing could get him down now. On August 19, the day he turned twenty years old, he declared it "one of my happiest birthdays ever." He had just gone up to Little Rock to pick out a new suit, a pair of shoes, and luggage. He was "okay on the clothes end," he told Denise. "But I'm still awful nervous about going to D.C."

CHAPTER FIVE

THE BACK ROOM BOYS

ON THE AFTERNOON of September 26, 1966, Bill Clinton dashed off a letter to his grandmother at her nursing home in Hope extolling his new life as a Georgetown junior and clerk on Capitol Hill. "Dear Mammaw," he wrote in his backward-tilting left-handed scrawl,

> I am well settled in school and at work. I attend class in the morning and at night and work in the afternoon. It is of course exciting to be here around all the senators and already this year I've seen the president, the vice president and senators Fulbright, Robert and Edward Kennedy, Javits, Long of Louisiana, Smathers of Florida, Yarborough of Texas, Anderson of New Mexico, McClellan, Thurmond of South Carolina, Church of Idaho, Williams of New Jersey, Boggs of Delaware, McCarthy of Minnesota, Murphy of California, Stennis of Mississippi and others. There's not much time to do anything but study and work, but I love being busy and hard work is good for people.

Clinton wrote the note from a desk in the documents room of the Senate Foreign Relations Committee, a cramped annex on the far side of the committee's fourth-floor public hearing chamber in the new Senate Office Building. The annex was a cross between a mailroom and a library, its walls lined with filing cabinets containing reports, newspaper articles, and committee publications. Three college students clerked there: Alabaman Charles Parks, who attended American University and got his job through the patronage of his home-state senator, John D. Sparkman; and Arkansans Phil Dozier of the University of Maryland and Bill Clinton of Georgetown, both hired by Lee Williams, the top personal aide to the committee chairman, Senator Fulbright. The fourth junior clerk was Bertie Bowman, the only black on the staff, a Washingtonian who had worked his way up from

janitor. By their elders on the Senate Foreign Relations Committee staff
these four were known as "the back room boys."

They sorted the mail, filled the hundreds of requests for committee
reports that came in each week, combed a half-dozen daily newspapers
and clipped them for stories related to foreign affairs, and ran errands
between the Senate Office Building and the main committee room in the
Capitol. The back room, as with everything on Capitol Hill, had its own
seniority system. Parks, the oldest of the three college boys, relegated
the messenger role to Dozier, who in turn passed it along to Clinton. It
was the equivalent, for Clinton, of winning a free pass to his favorite amusement park. It allowed him to roam the corridors of power and schmooze
with secretaries and congressional aides, and also offered him more opportunities to study the senators he had listed in the note to his grandmother, often stopping to listen to their pronouncements at committee
hearings.

Fulbright and his chief of staff generally frowned upon aides loitering in
the back of the room when the committee was in session, but "they
granted dispensation to the boys who were working their way through
school," according to Norvill Jones, then the staff expert on Southeast Asia.
Buddy Kendricks, the documents room supervisor, made a special effort
to get the boys to the hearings as part of their Capitol Hill education. The
tutor for that education was not Fulbright, who was formal and usually too
preoccupied for small talk, but Lee Williams, who kept close watch on the
young Arkansans he had placed in the Capitol Hill patronage system. Phil
Dozier regarded Williams as "a surrogate father to Bill Clinton and me—
he took us under his wing and watched over us." He also constantly reminded them how lucky they were to witness the great foreign policy
debates of their time. Williams viewed the back room assignment as "the
kind of thing that if you were a student you'd pray for, a once in a lifetime
opportunity for someone with the ambitions of Bill Clinton. Everything in
the international arena came through that committee. It had a tremendous
influence on those boys."

Clinton had long considered the committee chairman his role model. At
age sixty-one, James William Fulbright, a Rhodes Scholar, former president
of the University of Arkansas, and scion of a wealthy Fayetteville family,
was seen as a dignified statesman of superior intellect whose presence in
Washington countered the mocking stereotypes of unsophisticated Arkansas. "People dumped on our state and said we were all a bunch of back
country hayseeds, and we had a guy in the Senate who doubled the IQ
of any room he entered," Clinton once said of Fulbright. "It was pretty
encouraging. It made us feel pretty good, like we might amount to something."

Fulbright's public persona had changed considerably in the three years since he and Clinton first met for lunch in the Senate Dining Room during the Boys Nation visit. Back then, he was considered an insider whose mission was to help guide the Kennedy administration's foreign policy through Congress. When Lyndon Johnson ascended to the presidency after Kennedy's assassination, Fulbright assumed a similar function. "You're my secretary of state," Johnson once said to him. He played a reluctant but essential supporting role in passage of the Gulf of Tonkin resolution, which the administration took as congressional acquiescence to its plans to send more American soldiers to fight in Vietnam. But by 1965 Fulbright had split with Johnson when the president sent troops to the Dominican Republic to quell a leftist rebellion. He thought the administration was panicking over communism for no reason.

Soon the fissure separating Johnson and Fulbright over the Dominican Republic expanded into a profound ideological divide on Vietnam. By the time Clinton arrived on Capitol Hill in 1966, his Arkansas role model had concluded that the Vietnam War was a tragic mistake waged by an administration that had deceived Congress and deluded itself with what Fulbright called "the arrogance of power." He was becoming the administration's most pointed critic, and the foreign relations committee which he headed was perceived as the center of dissent to Johnson and the war. Johnson boasted in private that he would destroy Fulbright and other Senate doves within six months. Fulbright wrote a letter to Johnson trying to explain the historical limits of superpower force. "Greece, Rome, Spain, England, Germany and others lost their pre-eminence because of failure to recognize their limitations, or, as I called it, the arrogance of their power," he stressed, "and my hope is that this country, presently the greatest and the most powerful in the world, may learn by the mistakes of its predecessors."

Clinton, who held a student deferment and was two years away from the threat of being drafted, at first viewed the personal and ideological conflict between his boss and President Johnson with mixed feelings. He was "for the war—or at least not against it," when he began work that fall. It did not take long for him to change. Clinton admired Johnson for his support of civil rights, an issue where he had shown more courage than Fulbright, but in foreign relations Fulbright held sway.

It was difficult to work on the foreign relations committee staff and not be influenced by the pervasive antiwar environment. There "wasn't anyone on that staff who felt otherwise," according to Norvill Jones. "There was not a hawk on that staff." Jones, who had come to Washington to work as Fulbright's messenger boy when he was only fourteen in 1944, had become "the main Vietnam man" on the committee staff by the mid-1960s.

Clinton, as he made the rounds as messenger, expressed a deep interest in the committee's Vietnam work. Jones recalled later that Clinton "was always picking my brain—trying to learn more about it."

When not quizzing Jones, Clinton would turn to Lee Williams for his analysis. Williams, a crafty political operative, had at first cautioned Fulbright against breaking publicly with Johnson, arguing that it would cost the senator dearly in terms of federal projects in Arkansas. But once the break was made, Williams was as blunt in his opposition to the war as anyone on Capitol Hill. He and Clinton spent hours discussing America's role in Vietnam. He told Clinton that he was not a peacenik, but that the last good war U.S. soldiers fought in was World War II. He was ashamed that his country was involved in Vietnam, where he felt it had no business.

Clinton and Dozier, southerners who had grown up in environments where the military was revered, where most boys longed to become Marines, often debated whether they could fight in a war they opposed. Dozier told Clinton that he wanted to serve his country but was against the war. Clinton said he felt the same way. On rare occasions, they received special invitations to share their concerns with Fulbright. One day Clara Buchanan, Fulbright's secretary, came up to Room 4225, the back room, and said that the senator wanted to take Bill and Phil to lunch in the Senate Dining Room. Both boys were excited by the invitation, but Dozier was also nervous. He wanted to impress the senator that he was keeping up with events in Vietnam, so he asked him over lunch about the role the Laotian mountain tribes were playing. "What impact if any are the Montagnards having on the Vietnam War?" Dozier asked. Fulbright said, "I have no idea what impact the Montagnards are having on the war." Dozier felt as though Fulbright thought he was "missing an oar."

Dozier was struck by how sure of himself Clinton seemed. One day they were sitting at their desks in the back room, stuffing committee reports into envelopes, when Clinton turned to him and said, "Someday, this is going to be my office." It was unclear whether Clinton meant it literally or simply as a way of saying he intended to be in public service, Dozier said later, but he had no doubts that the prediction would be fulfilled or exceeded in either case. Dozier had shared an apartment on E Street with a young Capitol Hill elevator operator who dated Luci Baines Johnson, the president's younger daughter. He had visited the White House several times over the years—even after his boss and the president had their falling out—listening to records and doing the frug with the Johnson girls in the living quarters solarium. Clinton was fascinated. He would often ask Dozier, "What's it like inside the White House?"

· · ·

CLINTON and his friend Tom Campbell had planned to live in a house with several of their buddies in their junior year, but Campbell's father killed the idea, saying his son's grades were too precarious for the off-campus lifestyle. If Campbell carried a B average for the year, he could live in a house as a senior. Clinton decided that he could not abandon his longtime roommate, so for their third year at Georgetown they shared a dormitory suite in Copley Hall, and once again Campbell was treated to the buzz of an alarm clock waking Clinton in the dark so that he could study before breakfast, the only free time he had in an eighteen-hour day of classes and work.

The busy roommates rarely spent time together except on weekends. One Saturday morning in early October, they drove through the fall foliage of Virginia's Shenandoah Valley to visit Lyda Holt at Mary Baldwin College in Staunton. Denise Hyland was still Clinton's steady girlfriend at Georgetown, but he had grown close to Lyda during the summer campaign back in Arkansas, and they saw quite a bit of each other that fall. In Staunton, Lyda and one of her friends took Clinton and Campbell on a long walk around town and showed them the birthplace of Woodrow Wilson.

Frank Holt had been depressed in the months after his loss in the gubernatorial race. Lyda encouraged him to come east to cheer his spirits. "Daddy needed a boost and I thought Bill could help give it to him. So he came to Washington and we all went out to dinner at Blackie's House of Beef and talked politics and told stories and laughed." Holt returned to Washington several times that school year and often called Clinton when he was in town. The veteran judge and the ambitious collegian had a positive effect on each other. Holt knew important people in Washington and introduced them to Clinton, whose esteem for his political elders and enthusiastic plans for a career in Arkansas politics made Holt feel better about the future of his state. "Last week Frank Holt was in Washington and we had a fine time," Clinton wrote to his grandmother after one visit. "We went to see Congressman Jim Trimble who was our congressman from Hot Springs before he lost the last election. He was in Congress for 22 years and really told some good stories."

That Thanksgiving, Clinton traveled to New Jersey with Denise and spent the holiday in the warm embrace of the Hyland family. They headed back to school on Sunday with Tom Campbell and his younger sister. Clinton was driving his white Buick. Mary Lou sat in front and Tom and Denise were in the back, sleeping. As they approached Baltimore, there was a pileup and a car smashed into Clinton's from the rear. Denise was the only one hurt—a minor whiplash injury to her neck that was later treated at Georgetown University Hospital. Clinton apparently bore no fault for the accident, but none of his friends placed much trust in his driving ability.

. . .

CLINTON'S work on Capitol Hill did not seem to harm his studies, or his beloved Quality Points Index, as he had once feared. "My grades for the first semester came out pretty good, made a 3.52, that's about an A – average, and my name will go on the Dean's List," he wrote his grandmother. As planned, he entered the race for student council president in the spring of 1967. David Matter, the junior class president, filed to challenge him for the post, the pinnacle of student power on the East Campus, but soon changed his mind. Matter realized that he was elected junior class president only because Clinton had decided not to run that year. He did not feel he could beat Clinton this time, so he withdrew and instead signed on as Clinton's campaign manager.

Matter had reason to believe this race was a sure thing. Clinton had won easily in his two previous races for freshman and sophomore class president, and by his junior year was perhaps the most prominent member of his class, better known than any sports figure at a college that did not emphasize athletics. Not only was Clinton a strong presence on campus, but his opponent, Terry Modglin, a working-class kid from St. Louis, seemed to shrink in contrast. Modglin was short, wiry, and bespectacled, and neither a stellar student nor an adept speaker. But the very characteristics that seemed to make Clinton the favorite worked against him in the council president campaign. His political skills, his ability to think on his feet, to build coalitions and networks, were unrivaled on campus; but perhaps they were a bit too much, and he was too smooth. People were wary of him. "Bill," said Tom Campbell, "was a little too slick for some people."

Modglin ran the campaign of his life. He had begun preparing for it a year ahead of time, late in his sophomore year, when he lined his desk with strategy cards reminding him what he had to do to build support. His obsession was so great that one day Phil Verveer, a student government leader two years ahead of Modglin and Clinton, walked into Modglin's dormitory room, took one look at the note cards on his desk, shook his head, and muttered, "Don't do it, Terry, it'll ruin your grades and you'll never get into law school." Modglin was not to be deterred. His organization was meticulous. If someone asked him who his first one hundred supporters were, he could list them in order. He recruited the best communicators to his side, realizing that he could not compete with Clinton as an orator. He developed a Madison Avenue–style campaign theme. In imitation of the "Dodge Rebellion" commercials on television, he blanketed Georgetown with banners urging students to "Join the Modge Rebellion!" The campaign trademark became the white cowboy hat, and

Modglin supporters played the roles of good guys in a Wild West shootout with Bill Clinton.

Clinton played into Modglin's hand by building his campaign around a nineteen-point document whose title revealed its sober attitude: "A Realistic Approach to Student Government." One page listed his achievements at Georgetown—president of freshman and sophomore classes, chairman of freshman orientation committee, chairman of Sports Week, chairman of the unification campaign to merge the student councils of East Campus and the Yard, listed in *Who's Who in American Colleges and Universities,* Dean's List, chairman of Interdenominational Services, editor of the first-ever collegewide student directory—a list that seemed more impressive to parents than to most college students in 1967. His specific proposals were moderate, from asking for lower parking costs and student-written course critiques to demanding less dictatorial advisers in the Institute of Languages and Linguistics and better courses in the junior year abroad program.

But Clinton not only misread the way his college résumé might be perceived by his peers, he underestimated the mood of rebellion against the school administration and its paternalistic rules. According to Jim Moore, Clinton related to the Jesuit management "in a positive way—as usual. He wanted to co-opt the management and convince them they were wrong and turn them around. Some people felt Bill wouldn't be tough enough to get the administration to loosen up in its control of our lives and curricula. Georgetown students were just discovering that they could sometimes get authority figures to bend and change. Bill's approach was too slow for them."

Clinton understood what was happening to him, and Kit Ashby chided him for his reluctance to criticize Modglin, even in private. "Bill never wanted to say, 'That guy's an asshole!' " He would say, 'That's an interesting guy,' or whatever. We used to kid him about that—'Come on, Bill,' we'd say, 'Form the mouth, ass . . . hole'—but his basic instinct was to find, even with the most obvious asshole, something good. We wanted him to get angry in that campaign but he would not do it." Clinton was still keeping faith with the philosophy that Judge Holt ingrained in him the previous summer: Never stoop to the level of the opposition. He told Jim Moore that he felt his approach was reasonable and that in the end the majority of students would understand his message. He would not pander, he said, to "the radical segment of the student body."

To call Modglin and his supporters radical is a stretch. The extent of Modglin's political activism was that he had prayed for peace during an antiwar vigil on campus and had participated, as Clinton had, in the school's volunteer program in the inner city. In many ways he was to the

right of Clinton, and showed no qualms about bargaining for votes anywhere he could find them. He struck an alliance with the conservative
Delta Phi fraternity, the arch rival of Clinton's Alpha Phi Omega, by promising them the coveted chairmanship of the Diplomats Ball. (On election
day, Modglin recalled later, "guys emerged from the frat house in a
drunken stupor and were led to the polls" to vote against Clinton.)

Clinton's allies worked tirelessly for him. Denise Hyland had become so
attuned to Bill's political needs that she carefully selected a dorm room
that year in Darnell Hall on the side near the busiest walking path so that
she could stick Clinton signs in her window to the best effect. She and her
friends made hundreds of yellow and red cardboard campaign buttons and
distributed "This Is Clinton Country" signs in all the dorms. They went
around on a door-to-door canvass, only to discover that their candidate
was now turning people off who had once admired him. The election was
painful. Kit Ashby later said he did not realize "the depth of negative
feelings until near the end," when many of his friends told him they were
going with Modglin.

Whatever chance Clinton had of overcoming the perception that he was
the machine candidate was wiped out in the final week when his campaign
was involved in two dirty tricks. The first misdeed was a mild one—a
newsletter supporting Clinton called "The Spirit of '67" was censured by
the East Campus Election Committee for claiming endorsements of seniors
without their permission. The second episode involved an overreaction by
campaign manager David Matter. There were campaign posters plastered
all over campus, but Clinton's seemed to be disappearing. After a week of
what he took to be sign-stealing by the opposition, Matter decided to
retaliate. "We stayed up all night and went through the entire campus and
tore down every single Modglin poster. Bill was not involved. But I was
using his car, the white Buick convertible. I piled the Modglin posters in
the car and drove to an overlook over the George Washington Parkway
and threw them over the hillside. And I got caught."

The election was on a Friday. Clinton's fraternity brothers in Alpha Phi,
wearing blue and gold armbands symbolizing their impartiality, counted
the votes that night in the Hall of Nations in the Walsh Building, the scene
of two previous Clinton victory celebrations. Both candidates were there
along with dozens of their supporters. As the vote tabulations were placed
on a chalkboard, dorm by dorm, it became clear quite early that "the
Modge Rebellion" had carried the day. The final vote was 717 for Modglin
and 570 for Clinton. The rebels in white hats shouted: "Modglin! Modglin!
Modglin!" and lifted their unlikely champion on their shoulders to carry
him out of the room. "I was completely euphoric," Modglin recalls. "And
Bill looked like he was in shock." Clinton stayed behind to deliver a con-

cession speech in which he thanked his campaign workers and wished Modglin the best of luck. Then he and his friends went over to what was supposed to be a victory party organized by Denise Hyland at the house Jim Moore and Kit Ashby were living in on Potomac Avenue.

Lyda Holt, who had taken a deep interest in Clinton's campaign from her long-distance perch down at Mary Baldwin College, forsook any social activities that weekend night and stood by a pay telephone booth outside her dormitory making calls every thirty minutes trying to get the results. She never got through to Clinton and he never called her back. "As the night wore on I thought, Oh, Lord, that's not a good sign. I never heard from him, so I figured he lost."

Matter, who took personal responsibility for his candidate's demise, was inconsolable at the party, feeling so bad that he started crying. Clinton hugged him again. "Bill was as strong as can be, hugging me," Matter said later. "He was concerned about my welfare that evening and thereafter. I took it far harder than he." On the outside, perhaps; but inside, Clinton suffered a deep pain that he shared with a few close friends. Kit Ashby knew that his friend "really felt burned. He learned in later years how to take punches, but that one really hurt because it was so personal. He hurts very badly when someone says, 'I don't like you, you're no damn good.' He thought his heart was in the right place. But there were more than twelve hundred and fifty people who knew him and more than half voted against him. It hurt."

The lesson, Clinton told Jim Moore that night, was that he had not been listening to people hard enough. "His response was, 'If I do it again, I'll just have to work harder. Instead of handbills under every door, I'll have to talk to everybody in person. I'll have to find out the people I thought would be with me who voted for the other guy and go out and talk to those people.' It was all a matter of working harder."

Yet life moves on quickly for the young. The very night that he cried on Clinton's shoulder, Matter ended in bliss with a girl he met at the party. Modglin went on to a senior year of leadership that was marked more by chaos than rebellion—he flunked two courses and nearly got booted out of school. And Clinton, relieved of student politics, was free to concentrate on a competition of a different sort, a campaign for a prestigious graduate school scholarship that he might not have had a chance to win had the majority of his peers at Georgetown not considered him a shade too smooth to lead their student council.

AT the same time that he struggled with political rejection, Clinton sought personal redemption of a sort, a final resolution of his relationship with his stepfather. Roger Clinton's physical decline, obvious for years, was now taking a life-threatening turn. Two years earlier, back on Scully Street, he had been sitting at the dinette when Virginia looked over at him and said, "Roger, your neck is swollen!" One of Virginia's close friends in the Hot Springs medical community suggested that Roger check into the Duke Medical Center in North Carolina for tests and treatment. There they discovered that he had cancer in a gland behind his ear and recommended surgery. Roger would not agree to anything that altered his appearance. He agreed to have the biopsy, but told her that he would never have a disfiguring operation. The cancer was fought with radiation instead. Roger made the long trip to Durham four times for treatment.

Bill visited Roger Clinton several times that spring of his junior year. He took Denise Hyland with him once. She remembers that she wore a navy blue suit and Bill a coat and tie, and that the weekend evoked a feeling of overwhelming sadness. But at no time during the drive down to Durham and back and never during their three-year relationship did Clinton confide in Denise about his stepfather's drinking and abuse. She was not alone in that regard. Despite the trauma that Roger had put the family through over the years, Bill hid much of the animosity he might have felt. As confessional as Clinton was about other subjects, he never told his friends in high school or in college about his stepfather's darker side, though they might have seen it accidentally during visits to Scully Street. Lyda Holt visited the house one summer and saw Roger stagger and throw up violently into a wastebasket. But to Clinton's friends, he seemed like a vague figure. Clinton did not mention him often, and when he did it was with formal respect.

During his years at Georgetown, Clinton was distanced from the family turmoil but could not rid himself of the guilt he felt about Roger's troubles and his inability to resolve them. "... I know I have never been much help to you—never had the courage to come and talk about it," he wrote that spring in a letter to Roger in which he sought, finally, to get his stepfather to turn to him for help. "You ought to look everywhere for help, Daddy," Clinton wrote. "You ought to write me more—people—even some of my political enemies—confide in me...." But now that Roger was weak and ill, the need was not so much for reform as for reconciliation. The same son who at age fourteen had ordered his stepfather to stand up and listen carefully as he told him never to strike his mother again, now at age twenty-one felt sympathy for a defeated man struggling to stay alive.

"Daddy has been so sick," he wrote to Denise. "But there's something wonderful now—he knows for sure—as much for sure as can be—that he has post-radiation sickness, which will endure for a long time but is not a recurrence of the malignancy we feared. The prospect of getting well boosts his spirit. He has fought so hard, so bravely—maybe the only battle he's ever really faced. Surely he'll be allowed to win."

. . .

WHEN the school year was out, Clinton did not return home to Arkansas. He kept working in the back room at the foreign relations committee in the mornings and had signed up for two summer school courses at George-town for the afternoons. Before classes started, he and Tommy Caplan took a vacation up the coast. In New York City, they toured the Metropolitan Museum of Art and the Frick Collection, where they saw a self-portrait of Rembrandt, a painting, Clinton told Denise later, that left him "truly en-tranced for the first time in my life by an artist's work." When they were together, this voluble duo—the writer from Baltimore and his big-handed political buddy—knew how to have a good time. That night, on Caplan's tab, they took rooms at the Carlyle Hotel and "in a fit of gluttony had dinner at the restaurant and then ordered room service."

The binge left Clinton wallowing in the guilt that often enveloped him when it came to food and willpower. When he returned to Washington, he told Denise that he was looking forward to the discipline that his summer schedule would impose on him, a routine that would "reintroduce me to sleep, exercise and good food." When he started jogging that summer, his friends were surprised. He had not been much of an athlete and certainly never seemed the running type. So why did he start running now? Perhaps a hint came in a letter to Denise. "This running is a great deal," he con-cluded a bit prematurely. "You can run for 30 minutes or so and then eat all you want and put on no weight."

A more likely reason was that Clinton had been encouraged by Senator Fulbright to begin the process of seeking a Rhodes Scholarship, an honor then awarded yearly to thirty-two American men who were sent off to Oxford University in England for further academic training. Fulbright had won a Rhodes Scholarship while at the University of Arkansas and sailed for England in the fall of 1924 as an American innocent, returning as a pipe-smoking, tweeded intellectual who had enjoyed what he called the best years of his life at Oxford. The scholarship had always been associated with athleticism—Fulbright had played tennis at Arkansas, and Bill Bradley, the Princeton University basketball star, had just won one—but superior physical skills were not mandatory. Cecil Rhodes, the imperialist industrial-ist who founded the scholarship, said that he was looking for neither the pure intellectual nor the pure athlete, but "the best man for the world's fight—an all-rounder, but of a special kind: an all-rounder with a bulge; some outstanding quality, be it of character, personality or ability." Clinton had some bulges of the sort Rhodes discussed, but to be certain, he wanted to minimize any that might appear at his waist.

It was a summer of uncertainty. In his philosophy class he read the works of Kierkegaard, Camus, and Sartre. For a graduate-level class on U.S.

relations in the Far East, he prepared a twenty-eight-page paper with ninety-two footnotes on the events in August 1964 that led to congressional approval of the Gulf of Tonkin resolution—"the one that gave LBJ his blank check in Vietnam," as Clinton told Denise in a letter. The material he needed for that report was available in the back room of the Senate Foreign Relations Committee, which was in the midst of historic hearings on the subject. Chairman Fulbright was by then convinced that he and other senators had been lied to by President Johnson about the events in the Gulf of Tonkin three years earlier—reports of aggression against U.S. vessels by North Vietnamese gunboats had been exaggerated. The administration, Fulbright said, "had already set its policy intentions and used the attack to implement them, while misrepresenting the actual event." He also now believed that the congressional resolution resulting from that deception did not authorize the administration to wage full-scale war. Clinton's paper reached the same conclusions.

For the first time, Clinton was overtaken by feelings of disillusionment. Not only did he disagree with his party's policies in Vietnam, policies that had escalated the war to the point where thirty thousand young men were being drafted each month, but he was worried that the nation's commitment to civil rights was diminishing. In a letter to Denise, he fretted that the status of race relations "and the good Americans who want to bomb North Vietnam into the Stone Age" made him wonder "if our nation has any shared values."

In the middle of the Gulf of Tonkin hearings, Clinton was assigned a rather odd diversion. Sharon Ann Evans, who had just been named Miss Arkansas, came to Washington for a day on her way to the Miss America contest in Atlantic City. Fulbright's office had been asked to provide her with an escort. Clinton got the job. He told Denise that it was because Evans was a six-footer and "I was the only one in Fulbright's office over six feet." It turned out that they had several things in common. Both had lived in Hope as youngsters. Evans's roommate at Ouachita Baptist University was Linda Yeldell, the younger sister of Clinton's friend and neighbor, Carolyn Yeldell. But they were political opposites. When Evans was asked which dignitary she would like to meet during her visit, she chose FBI director J. Edgar Hoover. Clinton cooled his heels in the lobby of the FBI building as Evans disappeared into Hoover's inner chamber, shook the director's hand, and chatted for five minutes, overcome, she said, by "the power, the mystique." When she emerged, it was obvious from the look on Clinton's face that he disapproved. She thought that he did not like her because she would rather meet Hoover than Fulbright.

In fact Clinton was infatuated with Evans, as he was with many young women that summer. He and Denise Hyland had slowly broken off the romantic side of their relationship, though not their friendship. As their college years were nearing an end, they came to a mutual understanding that neither one of them had an interest in marriage and that it was time for them to see what else was out there. Clinton saw a lot out there. He was dating several times a week, according to one friend, "like a guy getting out of prison." He stayed that summer at the house on Potomac Avenue with Kit Ashby and Jim Moore, and constantly seemed to show up with a new date he had met on Capitol Hill. Moore thought it was "a revelation" to Clinton that "there was a whole culture of people in Washington just there for a few years to have a good time and not focused on long-term relationships. He had met women on the Hill before but never followed up on the opportunities. Then he became a free agent, and young ladies figured it out, and it was, 'Holy shit, Bill Clinton is free and available and looking forward to having a good time!' "

Only the summer before, Clinton had said that the Arkansas heat was burning Washington out of his system. Now it seemed that the swirl of Washington was distancing him some from his Arkansas roots. He got home for a brief visit in early September before the start of his senior year. Several boys from his high school class had quit college or dropped out and joined the Marines. Duke Watts was about to leave for boot camp when Clinton arrived back in town. All summer, Watts and Joe Newman, one of Clinton's close friends from band, had been "chasin' girls" in bars and restaurants. One Friday night, as Watts later remembered it, "I was all set to go, duded up real nice, when the phone rang and it was Joe, and Joe said, 'Clinton's in town and he wants to go with us.' I kind of winced a little but said all right and he tagged along."

They went to Coy's Steakhouse on the edge of Hot Springs. Watts looked at Clinton and saw an alien being. He could not imagine how this fellow, the same guy who was so coveted by young women in Washington, could ever get to first base. Clinton was wearing sandals. His hair had grown out a little. Watts thought that he and Joe "knew how to dress for the women," whereas Clinton "wasn't well groomed, to put it mildly; I don't know if he had any money or even ate there at Coy's. His demeanor wasn't equal to ours." Watts had joined the Marine Corps and was proud of what he had done. He had it in his mind that he had chosen a path of honor. He was "thinking all these noble thoughts." And then Clinton started talking about the war and how strongly he opposed it. There were, Watts thought, "some anxious moments there. I know I was glad when the night was over."

CHAPTER SIX

ALL HELL
BROKE
LOOSE

THE FIVE YOUNG men who shared the white house on Potomac Avenue for their senior year in college were "boringly respectable," according to Tommy Caplan. This was the fall of 1967, the season that followed the summer of love in San Francisco's Haight-Ashbury district, the time when college campuses across the nation became theaters of protest, scented by tear gas and the sweet smell of pot, echoing with the chants of "One, two, three, four, we don't want your fucking war!" Even the moderate young men and women of Georgetown were encountering the culture of the sixties. Allen Ginsberg, a veteran guerrilla fighter in the battle against boring respectability, visited Gaston Hall that school year and asked how many happy Hoyas in the crowd had ever smoked marijuana. He smiled beatifically when fifty hands rose. Perhaps to some of his high school classmates back in Hot Springs, Bill Clinton seemed a shade on the rabble-rousing and unkempt hippie side, but within the wider spectrum of sixties behavior, Clinton and his housemates were trim and tame.

These were five collegians, after all, who celebrated Caplan's twenty-first birthday that fall by flying up to New York City with their dates to dine at the fashionable "21"—not exactly an alternative food co-op. It was an elegant affair, staged in an upstairs room. Ashby sat across the table from one of Caplan's high society friends, Jamie Auchincloss, Jacqueline Kennedy's younger stepbrother, watching in wonderment as the son of the ruling class ate an artichoke with his hands, something the Texan had never seen. A trip to Manhattan with Caplan, the bon vivant of the housemates, was always a grand and potentially awkward step into the high life for his college pals: this time Caplan underwrote the entire feast, with bottles all-around of Dom Pérignon, and then booked rooms at the Carlyle.

In a moment of frustration that month, someone had scrawled "Georgetown Gentlemen Are Lapdogs of the Establishment" on a plywood fence surrounding the site for a new library on campus. Few on the hilltop felt compelled to dispute the insult or respond with graffiti. While one poll indicated that a majority of Georgetown students opposed the war in Vietnam, for the most part they had not yet soured on the system. One of the magnets that drew them to the School of Foreign Service was its ready access to the power establishment: Congress, the White House, Washington society, the Department of State, the Pentagon. The Potomac Avenue house was typical in that sense. Two of the five senior friends worked on Capitol Hill: Clinton for Senator Fulbright and Ashby for Senator Henry Jackson of Washington. Caplan volunteered in the office of Senator Robert Kennedy. The other housemates had military attachments: Campbell was preparing to fly planes for the Marines after graduation, and Moore, an Army brat, was buying food for the group at the commissary at Fort Myer across the Key Bridge in northern Virginia.

Lapdogs or not, none of the Potomac five were among the fifty thousand "shaggy doves" who gathered in front of the Lincoln Memorial on October 21 in the first mass demonstration against the Vietnam War, the March on the Pentagon later celebrated in prose in Norman Mailer's *Armies of the Night* and in poetry in Robert Lowell's "October and November" ("... then to step off like green Union recruits for the first Bull Run, sped by photographers, the notables, the girls ... fear, glory, chaos, rout ... our green army staggered out on the miles-long green fields, met by the other army, the Martian, the ape, the hero, his new-fangled rifle, his green new steel helmet"). Clinton shared the conviction of many of those peace recruits that the war in Vietnam was wrong, but his opposition remained a conviction, not activist, rooted in the documents he read at the foreign relations committee and in the arguments of Chairman Fulbright.

Fulbright, in his book *The Arrogance of Power,* presented a clear philosophy on political dissent, both its vital role in a democracy and its most effective means of expression, and his views played powerfully on the mind of his clerk, who cherished his autographed copy of the treatise. "To criticize one's country is to do it a service and pay it a compliment," Fulbright wrote there. "It is a service because it may spur the country to do better than it is doing; it is a compliment because it evidences that the country can do better than it is doing. ... In a democracy, dissent is an act of faith." But for dissent to be persuasive, Fulbright argued, it had to be presented in less raucous ways than the street demonstrators were deploying. "The most effective dissent is dissent expressed in an orderly, which is to say a conservative, manner," he added. "The student, like the politician, must consider not only how to say what he means but also how to say it persuasively. The answer, I think, is that to speak persuasively one must speak in the idiom of the society in which one lives."

Speaking the idiom, wherever he was, ranked among Clinton's greatest talents. By his second year in Fulbright's shop he was a certified Hill rat who knew the lingo of the place, the tunnels and subway shortcuts, the lore, all the latest rumors and inside stories about LBJ and the frailties of senators who only a year earlier he had viewed as gods. He loved nothing more than to talk politics, and often on Fridays he would find his way over to the House office of freshman congressman David Pryor for late afternoon bull sessions. "Sometimes he'd bring a friend over and we'd just sit around and talk politics for an hour or so," Pryor says. "He was inquisitive. He wanted to know why people did things and how the system worked."

Clinton's manner with congressmen was similar in many respects to the way he dealt with professors: by showing a keen interest in their stories and special concerns, he gained insight and scored brownie points at the same time. But this was not necessarily the manipulation of a sycophant or social climber. His interest in people seemed egalitarian. His closest friend at work was Bertie Bowman, the fellow back room boy and former Senate janitor who was the only black on the foreign relations committee staff. They would talk all the time and sing duets together in the back room while they were working. Sometimes they would be walking down the hall together, running errands, singing "Blue Suede Shoes" or "Return to Sender" in harmony. They both liked Elvis. Bowman was sixteen years Clinton's senior, yet their relationship transcended age and race. "He would say, 'Come on, go here with me,' and I'd say I had to check with my wife, and he'd say she can come, too," Bowman later recalled. "Sometimes white folks invite you only to certain things, other things they don't think of you. Bill would introduce me to whites as an equal, not as 'Bertie' and 'Mister.' "

His housemates on Potomac Avenue noticed another way in which Clinton had adapted to the Capitol Hill environment. He started being chronically late. Time in the world of Congress was a free-form concept: hearings started late, congressmen came and left and schmoozed as they pleased, only occasionally disciplined by the buzzer attached to their office clocks alerting them that a vote was imminent. The atmosphere was built around the notion that the rest of the world could wait. And so it became with Clinton. His friends would plan a dinner or dance and wait for Clinton to show up, and after an hour or two had gone by, he would arrive and say, "Oh, sorry, I was talking to somebody." Usually, Tom Campbell would discover, Clinton had been talking to "some nincompoop about nothing."

Campbell, who had lived with Clinton for four years and knew his idiosyncrasies, finally stopped expecting Clinton anywhere on time. "We would just say, 'Here's where we're going, come when you get there.' You could see him change during his time on the Hill where he met all those diverse people. He was always gone, always talking to people, always late."

Even as Clinton's comings and goings grew tardy and unpredictable, his mind sought order in other ways. Rudiger Lowe, a German studying at Wesleyan College in Connecticut under a Fulbright scholarship, was taken aback by the preciseness of a letter he received from Clinton assigning him a topic at a Georgetown-sponsored student conference on the Atlantic Community. Clinton not only informed Lowe what his topic was and the specific length of his paper, but went on to suggest how it might be organized. Lowe's topic was the U.S. role in unification efforts with Eastern Europe. Clinton outlined it with Roman numerals and a's and b's. It was the way Clinton took notes in class, and prefigured his style as a politician later, when he would respond to questions by breaking answers into points one, two, and three, or a, b, and c.

On the eve of the conference, the Georgetown sponsors held a party for the European students in attendance. Clinton, who had studied German to fulfill his language requirement in the School of Foreign Service, approached Lowe and inquired, in German, "Are you the student from Germany?" They spent the rest of the party chatting in German. The next day Clinton asked Lowe whether he would like to meet Senator Fulbright. Lowe knew that "Fulbright was this great senator challenging LBJ," and thought there would be little chance of getting to meet him. "But Clinton went out and made a phone call and came back and said, 'We're having breakfast with him tomorrow morning.'" Who is this fellow Clinton? Lowe began thinking to himself. Later in his tour of America, Lowe met Robert F. Kennedy and Chicago mayor Richard J. Daley ("How do you stay in power so long?" Lowe asked the big-city boss, to which Daley offered a chuckle), but for all the famous people he met in America that fall, he was most struck by the young organizer of the conference at Georgetown. He left the United States with an old German adage flashing in his mind about Bill Clinton: From this wood great politicians are carved.

EVERY morning that November, Virginia Clinton asked the same question of her gravely ill husband: "Don't you think we ought to call Bill?" The treatments had not worked. It was not radiation sickness but cancer that was ravaging his body. The fight that had finally won him the respect of his stepson was surely lost. Roger Clinton was dying fast. "Not yet," he kept saying to his wife, until finally the morning came when he emerged from the bathroom and said, "It's time"—and Virginia called her son Bill at Georgetown and had him fly home to Hot Springs.

They had known each other for seventeen years now, Roger and Bill, since the boy was a four-year-old named Billy Blythe, then and always the prize of his mother's life in a way that no other man could be. What Roger gave him other than a new last name and years of fear and anguish he was only now able to comprehend. He had seen the old man drink too much and beat his mother, and he had once wanted him gone; but now that the leavetaking would be forever, he started to understand why his mother had ignored his advice six years earlier when he had pleaded with her not to take Roger back. He came to realize that "somewhere deep down inside," Roger "could never understand what was good about himself," and that when he drank too much, "all of his darkest fears would come out." But Roger had always adored Bill. It had been apparent several times when Bill visited him at the hospital at Duke. Next to Bill, Roger felt inadequate. He was just an auto parts clerk with a drinking problem and cancer eating away at his face. He could not see any good in himself. But in his wife's first son, who bore his name, he saw the promise of the world.

The house at 213 Scully Street seemed like a hospital wing when Bill got home. Roger looked pitiful, his weight forty pounds below normal, his mouth constantly drooling. He was attended to day and night by volunteer nurses, Virginia's friends and colleagues pulling eight-hour shifts. Doctors who had worked with Virginia shuttled in and out, reading charts, prescribing drugs, advising the family on how little time was left. Virginia would not enter the sick room to see her husband at the end. She did not want to because "it was not a pretty sight to see."

Mary Jo Nelson, Bill's friend from high school, was with him when Roger died. She had gone to the house to deliver pain-killing drugs from the pharmacy where she worked. She watched Bill follow the stretcher out to the driveway and stand there, wordless, as the ambulance conveying his stepfather's body rolled down the street, the wagon's red taillights brightening in the distance as it braked at the corner, turned left, and disappeared. Bill stood there, shoulders slumped, staring through the November mist. Two fathers dead—and in a sense he knew neither of them. He put his big left arm around Mary Jo and walked back into the house.

THE notion that Bill Clinton might be selected as a Rhodes Scholar was the subject of a running joke among his housemates, who assumed that Rhodes winners had to be not only A students and campus leaders (categories where Clinton fit the bill) but also athletes of some sort. These good friends knew Clinton's athletic prowess, or lack thereof, all too well. He had started running the previous summer but was still somewhat out of shape. He had never played a varsity sport in high school or college. Even his mother called him "gawky and not quite coordinated enough." As a touch football player, his best talent was winning arguments about whether someone had been touched. As a basketball player, he was lumbering, his feet seemingly glued to the gym floor. In golf, he was a mid-handicap hacker. He was a decent bowler, but bowling shirts seemed a bit unstylish for the Rhodes scene.

But Clinton always had a plan. This time he decided that he could best demonstrate his sporting manner by employing his greatest skill: politics. He maneuvered his way into a slot as chairman of the Student Athletic Commission in time for the Rhodes interviews. The Rhodes selection process had two levels, state and regional. Clinton survived the Arkansas competition in Little Rock and reached the regional finals in New Orleans. By then, he and his counterparts in the regionals across the country came to realize that they had harbored a misconception about the athletic skill requirement. Although the Rhodes questionnaire asked applicants to list activities that demonstrated their "fondness for and success in sports," track stars and quarterbacks fell away while debaters and Shakespeare scholars advanced. George Butte in the Southwest region said playing the concert piano was his sport. Robert Reich in the New England region was a self-described "anti-athlete who vigorously avoided athletic events." Compared to these fellows, Clinton seemed less the clumsy ham loaf and more like Jim Thorpe.

The interview process for Rhodes candidates ranks among the most peculiar enterprises in academia, equal parts dissertation defense, locker-room sizing up, television quiz show, cocktail party bull session, debating society, and drawing of straws. Some of the young men were the proverbial big fish from smaller ponds, who felt intimidated the moment they walked into the traditional interview eve cocktail parties where candidates and their judges—the Rhodes secretaries from the states in their region— sipped sherry and chatted. Darryl Gless out of tiny Schuyler, Nebraska, felt so nauseated after the cocktail party that he went back to his room, called his sponsoring professor at the University of Nebraska, and said he wanted to go home. The whole scene, he said, made him angry. "A lot of the guys were using the occasion to show off and members of the selection committee were provoking confrontations. They'd pick up a point from one person and turn to me and say, 'Do you agree with that?' "

Some candidates, especially those recruited by the Rhodes networks at Harvard and Yale, which in those years supplied as many as one-third of the thirty-two scholars, seemed to be sure things and sprinted through the process with nary a worry. Nelson Strobridge Talbott III was one such sure bet—a squash-playing scholar of Russian and chairman of the *Yale Daily News,* who had spent the previous summer in London as a *Time* magazine intern and was hand-picked for a go at the Rhodes by his Yale mentors. During Talbott's final interview, one lawyer on the selection committee decided that the young man was having it too easy, and so started asking him a series of arcane questions about the oil depletion allowance about which, Talbott later confessed, "I didn't know shit from shinola." But just as Talbott was struggling with an answer, the chairman of the committee interrupted. "I have a question, too," said the chairman. "How in the Midwest did you learn how to play classical guitar?" The lawyer now stewed in his seat. It was as if he had broken an unwritten rule: the chosen recognize the chosen.

Everyone got an odd question or nasty challenge from someone on his selection committee. Mike Shea, a psychology major from the University of Iowa, encountered a professor from Luther College who badgered him mercilessly for not having read a certain psychohistory of Martin Luther. Keith Marshall was asked, "As an Episcopalian, how do you feel about that issue?" To which Marshall responded, "I am not an Episcopalian." Certainly the strangest scene that year unfolded at the interviews in New York, where Daniel Singer and one other candidate competed for the last of four regional slots. Singer waited in the hallway as the selection committee grilled the other student. The fellow finally emerged, ashen-faced. "They asked me the craziest stuff," he muttered. Singer was called forward and took his seat. "We've about run out of ways to settle this, you're such good candidates," the chairman said. "So we want you to debate this point: Why should the cow jump over the moon?"

So often in his adult career as a medical researcher, Singer recalled decades later, he had hoped that some sort of divine inspiration would strike him and he would say "aha" and have a mystery of life solved or a question answered—so often he had hoped for that and so often it had not happened. But it did happen once, back then in that stuffy room in Manhattan with the somber selection committee members staring at him and his Rhodes on the line and a nursery rhyme clanging around in his head. All of a sudden he was loose. He found an answer out of nowhere.

"It's pretty obvious that the cow should jump over the moon," he said, "because the purpose of having cows is to produce more milk and you need heat on the udders for effective milk production so at night instead of wasting time if you could get the cows to jump over the moon they'll get warm from the refracted light and keep the udders heated and the milk flowing."

Daniel Singer made Rhodes Scholar.

Good fortune came to Bill Clinton in other ways. The first was that he was competing for a scholarship from Arkansas and the South, which many then considered the least competitive of the eight Rhodes regions—not that the scholars selected from the South were any less outstanding, but that there were fewer of them. Tom Ward, a Rhodes Scholar in the class of 1967 from Meridian, Mississippi, considered the South, "candidly, the easiest region to get in." From his area, Clinton was competing against a relative handful of equally talented candidates, according to Kit Ashby, "whereas if he were trying for a Rhodes from New York he would have faced hundreds."

Here was another situation in which Clinton's provincial roots worked to his advantage. East Coast contemporaries often seemed puzzled by his rise. How could someone come out of Hope, out of Hot Springs, out of Arkansas, and move up so surely and quickly? The answer may rest in the presumption of the question. Hope and Hot Springs nourished Clinton as few larger communities could have done. And Arkansas, unpretentious, slow moving, relatively uneducated, inordinately proud and possessive of its favorite sons, was the land of opportunity for a young man on the rise.

At the South regional in New Orleans, Clinton told Arkansas stories with gusto and made it known that he intended to return to his home state after his academic training and embark on a career in government service. Keith Marshall, a candidate from Louisiana and Yale, who was an artist, stood on the balcony of the Royal Orleans Hotel in the French Quarter with Clinton that Friday night in December. They waved down at the jubilant crowds moving along the narrow street below. People waved back. Clinton turned to Marshall with a smile and said, "This is just like being president of the United States." During his appearance before the selection committee the next day, Clinton was asked several questions concerning politics and a few related to medicine. One interviewer asked him about heart transplants—something he had known nothing about until the day before, when on the flight to New Orleans he had read a magazine article on the subject.

Clinton survived the cut, along with Marshall, Paul Parish, a diminutive English major from the University of Mississippi, and Walter Pratt, another student from Mississippi who attended Vanderbilt. The four selected scholars were separated from the eight who had been rejected and led to a small room, where they were interviewed one by one by a local newspaper reporter. Clinton was the first to be interviewed. Parish listened intently to the young man from Arkansas and at first was angered by what he heard. Clinton was talking about "how proud his mother would be, how excited she would be, how she was looking forward to this so much and all her faith in him was going to be worth it." Listening to Clinton, Parish thought about his own mother, and how he would not dare say how much he wanted to please her, even though he did. When it was Parish's turn to be interviewed, he said he did not want to be a human interest story.

Some young men were rendered speechless, ecstatic, the moment they learned they had been chosen as Rhodes Scholars, a prize that would rank them first in their generational class. Walter Pratt was so overwhelmed that when his plane arrived back in Jackson, "they opened the door and I was about to step out without the stairs being there. It was euphoria of that kind." Up at the New England regional in Boston, when Dartmouth friends Robert Reich and John Isaacson were driving back to school after being selected, they were stunned silent until they got about thirty miles north of Boston and then, according to Reich, "we just howled and howled with laughter." Willie Fletcher of Seattle and his colleague from Washington State, Frank Aller, rode a Greyhound bus back from Portland up through western Washington, shocked that they had both been selected. Fletcher would never forget the moment when they got off the bus in Centralia, where he was going to spend the night at his girlfriend's house. "Frank got off for a moment to meet her, and we were standing there next to the bus in the Northwest drizzle and I suddenly felt overwhelmed. It was the best moment of all. We had been anointed. We were awed and bewildered. It seemed that the whole world was in front of us."

In New Orleans, after leaving the interview with the local reporter, Clinton turned to Marshall with tears in his eyes. Sobbing, he spoke lovingly of Roger Clinton, and said he was sorry his father had not lived long enough to see this day. Virginia Clinton had stayed home on Scully Street that Saturday. She would not leave the house until she had heard from her son. He finally called, and his first words to her were: "Well, Mother, how do you think I'll look in English tweeds?"

THE house on Potomac Avenue was a two-story white stucco cottage with brown wood trim, nestled beside a vacant lot on a shaded slope high above the river. It had five bedrooms, one for each senior, with several bathrooms, two upstairs sun porches, and a picture window in the living room that offered a magnificent view of the Potomac. The entrance led directly into the kitchen, which served as the house's gathering place. Though the five friends had hectic schedules, on many evenings they managed to get home for supper. Moore was the principal chef. He was, according to Kit Ashby, "big on pork chops and minute steak. Never got into sauces or stuffed trout." They ate at the kitchen table, close enough to the stove so that they could reach back and grab a pan from the stove for second helpings.

Supper at the kitchen table promised not only a well-rounded meal but often an engaging debate on civil rights or the war in Vietnam. Clinton was the house liberal on civil rights—"a Martin Luther King man, through and through," Jim Moore called him. He had memorized King's famous "I Have a Dream" speech and when the mood struck he might recite whole stanzas right there during dessert. He chided Tom Campbell for growing up in a suburb with a covenant prohibiting Jews—as prejudiced, he would say, as anything back in Arkansas—and argued vehemently with Ashby over the federal civil rights laws, which Clinton considered historic and necessary but Ashby thought unfairly superseded the doctrine of states' rights. But the civil rights movement had shifted its attention by 1968 away from the ideal of integration and toward the concerns of poverty and black nationalism and economic power. As the larger debate grew more contentious, Clinton struggled to find his footing. Race had always been the issue with which he defined himself, as a progressive son of the New South, but now it was more complicated. The housemates talked a lot about black power and King's move toward economic power. They were difficult issues and Clinton, Moore thought, "did not seem clear in his own mind about them."

On the war in Vietnam, the ideological spectrum again ranged from Clinton, as a moderate dove, to Ashby, the Scoop Jackson protégé, as a moderate hawk. Moore usually sided with Clinton, while Campbell and sometimes Caplan joined in with Ashby. Their dinner conversations, perhaps mirroring debates in homes across the country, grew intense in late January and early February 1968 when the North Vietnamese and Viet Cong launched their heaviest attack of the war, the Tet Offensive, which started on the first day of cease-fire marking the lunar new year. By the old standards of body counts and positions lost and taken, U.S. and South Vietnamese troops prevailed during the Tet Offensive; but what the American public saw was a graphic picture of bloodshed and vulnerability, one that led a majority of people to think that the war had gone on too long at too great a cost. A Viet Cong squad attacking the U.S. Embassy compound in Saigon, U.S. troops getting wiped out in the inner city of Hué, the Saigon police chief summarily executing a Viet Cong prisoner on the street, plugging a bullet into his brain—these became symbols of a faraway war spinning out of control. Public confidence in President Johnson's handling of the war dropped to a new low, with only 41 percent in a Gallup Poll saying they approved of his policies in Vietnam.

Ashby argued that Tet showed that the U.S. military was losing not to the enemy but to its own media. The media, he said, were trying to interpret Tet as negatively as possible. But to Clinton, what happened on the battlefield was in one sense beside the point. He shared the opinion of Senator Fulbright, who in a speech the month before had proclaimed that even if the United States won in Vietnam, it still would have been fighting an immoral and unnecessary war. "All that we are demonstrating in Vietnam," Fulbright had said, "is America's willingness to use B-52s, its napalm and all other ingenious weapons of counterinsurgency to turn a small country into a charnelhouse." One night they argued for hours about whether U.S. troops should be able to follow the enemy into Cambodia. "If it was me," Ashby said, "I wouldn't stop at the border." Clinton looked at it from a risk point of view, trying to limit the scope of the war.

Two weeks after Tet came "Black Friday," perhaps the single most important day of the Vietnam era for Bill Clinton and the estimated 226,000 young men who were then college seniors or in their first year of graduate school. On February 16, President Johnson and the National Security Council (NSC) abolished draft deferments for graduate students except those in various fields of medicine. The NSC declared that keeping nonmedical graduate students in school was no longer essential to the national interest. In a letter to his state directors, Lieutenant General Lewis B. Hershey, director of the Selective Service System, said the graduate school deferments were being eliminated because they represented one of the obvious inequities of the draft system, allowing the educated elite to avoid military service altogether while sons of the working class fought the war. "Many of those deferments," Hershey said, "can be pyramided into exemption from military service."

Now, suddenly, the pyramid scheme was gone and the college seniors of 1968 stood exposed as the most vulnerable group in the draft. When a plan for eliminating graduate school deferments was first proposed by a national advisory commission on selective service, part of the concept was also to change the chronological order in which men were drafted, replacing the oldest-first policy with one in which nineteen-year-olds were drafted first and twenty-six-year-olds last. But Johnson administration officials decided not to change the oldest-first policy, meaning that not only would Clinton and his cohorts lose their possible deferments but they would be ahead of younger men who had no college plans. For those who thought that educational deferments had placed an unfair burden on poor men who did not go to college, the new policy seemed to address the inequity with a vengeance. Early reports indicated that some local draft boards had so many college-educated men becoming available that they might not have to draft any nineteen-year-olds at all. The year before, only 14,000 college graduates had been drafted. With the deferments gone, that number would rise to 150,000, officials predicted, with another 75,000 college graduates enlisting voluntarily.

For the young men in the class of 1968, the draft now became an obsession. It had been an occasional subject at the Potomac Avenue dinner table before; now it came up constantly. "What are you going to do?" was the essential question.

Tom Campbell had resolved it the previous year by signing up to train as a pilot for the Marines. To learn to fly, he was willing to risk being sent to Vietnam.

Tommy Caplan had been knocked out of the college ROTC program after four years because of an injury and was undraftable as a 4-F.

Kit Ashby, though supportive of the war, was determined to go to graduate school and "fight off the draft" for as long as he could. Figuring that the military would find him sooner rather than later, he applied to the University of Texas graduate business school in his home state, at least in part because it was less expensive than an Ivy League program.

Jim Moore, who had been accepted into the Foreign Service, thought the best course was to volunteer rather than take his chances with the draft. He soon signed on with an officer training program in the Army, hoping that he would never see combat: either the war would end or he would get called back for a slot in the Foreign Service.

The housemates agreed that the student deferments that had been sheltering them were inherently unfair. Clinton frequently mentioned all the boys from Hot Springs who were fighting in Vietnam already. But he also wondered whether it was right to force talented young men to fight a war they did not believe in when they would be willing to serve their country in other ways. He often spoke of a high school friend, a math genius who had dropped out of MIT, who was now cleaning rifles. "Is this the right way to do it?" Clinton's friends remember him asking. In a paper he had written for a law seminar that year, Clinton had concluded that the draft system was "illegitimate" because of its inflexibility. His paper explored the legal arguments "for and against allowing, within the Selective Service System, the classification of selective conscientious objector, for those opposed to participation in a particular war, not simply to participation in war in any form."

If there had been such a category, Clinton would have fit within it. He had devoted all his energies that year to winning the Rhodes Scholarship. Would he have to participate in a war he did not believe in rather than go to Oxford, where they were training "the best men for the world's fight"?

ON the first day of March the five seniors held the last grand party of their college careers. They lined the walkway and steps outside with miniature French flags for what they called The Hundred Days party, a double-theme affair honoring Napoleon's one-hundred-day return from exile on the isle of Elba as well as the class of 1968's final one hundred days of student life on the hilltop. There was nothing particularly rebellious at the party, yet that night somehow marked the ushering in of a new and uncertain time for the Potomac Avenue friends. Back in September when they flew up to Manhattan for Tommy Caplan's lavish birthday celebration, they were still clinging to an age of innocence. Now the sixties seemed to be coming at them hard and furious. Campbell felt a sense of doom.

Within two weeks of the party, Senator Eugene McCarthy, carrying the antiwar banner, almost defeated President Johnson in the New Hampshire primary, and four days later Senator Robert Kennedy joined the Democratic presidential contest, quickening the political pulse at Georgetown, an institution that still carried the memory of Camelot. "I run to seek new policies," Robert Kennedy said. "Policies to end the bloodshed in Vietnam and in our cities, policies to close the gap between black and white, between rich and poor, between young and old in this country and around the rest of the world." McCarthy, the laconic poet from Minnesota, reacted with hostility to this fiery new arrival on the presidential scene. He said he alone had challenged Johnson at a time when others "were willing to stay up on the mountain and light signal fires and dance in the light of the moon. But none of them came down, and I tell you it was a little lonely in New Hampshire. I walked alone." Kennedy's move provoked another debate at the Potomac Avenue dinner table. Kit Ashby derided his announcement as opportunistic. Clinton, who preferred Kennedy to McCarthy, argued that timing is everything in politics and that Kennedy was smart to seize the moment.

When Johnson announced later that month that he would not seek or accept renomination for a second term, it seemed that change might come swiftly and peacefully. Then, on April 4, the Reverend Martin Luther King, Jr., was shot and killed in Memphis, and some sectors of Washington went up in flames. From their protected place high on the hilltop above the city, Georgetown students were in no physical danger during the riots that week. Tom Campbell thought of it as "a sort of never-never-land up there. Everyone felt the authorities would form a skirmish line at the edge of Georgetown" if looters and arsonists ever got that far. Still, some merchants who normally catered to the Georgetown Gentlemen made absurd efforts to shield themselves from the fury. One pricey shop specializing in preppy sports jackets placed a Soul Brother sign of solidarity in its window.

There was nonetheless a wartime feel to the campus. A curfew was imposed from dusk to dawn. Hundreds of National Guard troops spent their nights sleeping on the floor of McDonough Gym. Every afternoon, students clambered up to the Gothic rooftops and watched smoke drift to the eastern horizon. Some students, including Clinton, signed up to help the Red Cross deliver food and supplies into the inner city.

One Sunday morning, Clinton drove his white Buick convertible to National Airport to pick up Carolyn Yeldell, his friend from Hot Springs. Their relationship had changed in the past year. The girl next door used to be Clinton's musical accompanist, virtuous and naive. But that Christmas of their senior year when Clinton had flown home, Carolyn had gone to the Little Rock airport to meet him and gave him a welcome home kiss that was decidedly unsisterly. "My God, where did you learn how to kiss like that?" he had said to her on the way home from the airport. "No wonder everyone wants to marry you." That kiss, according to Yeldell, "put a whole new spin" on their relationship. Their letters back and forth over the next few months were more intimate, and when she flew to Washington for spring break at his suggestion, she arrived with a prospect of romance on her mind.

As she looked out her airplane window on the approach to Washington, she saw a city smoldering in flames and smoke.

"I've signed us up for some volunteer work," Clinton said as they walked to his car in the airport lot. She said okay, not knowing quite what he meant but nervous about the possibilities. They drove to a relief agency, loaded the trunk and back seat of his car with food and first aid equipment, and pasted a Red Cross insignia on the door. Their mission was to drive the goods to an inner-city church where people who had been burned out of their homes were living in the basement. Imagine the rush of adrenaline that the classmates from Hot Springs High felt as they sped through Washington in Clinton's white convertible, both trying to mask their whiteness by pulling porkpie hats over their foreheads, Clinton chanting, "Go! Go! Yes! Yes!" as they rolled through red lights, never stopping until the delivery point was reached. And this was on Sunday morning, when the streets were empty and calm.

After they had delivered the first aid supplies and food without incident, Clinton did not want to go back to the Potomac Avenue house yet. "Let's go downtown and take a better look," he said. They drove past blocks of charred storefronts and parked on a side street near the 14th Street corridor. They got out of the car and walked down the street, looking at the rubble and broken glass.

"I wish I had a camera," Carolyn said.

Clinton turned to her with a look of reproval and said, "You will never forget this as long as you live."

As they rounded a corner on the way back to the car, they saw six black men walking abreast, moving slowly toward them from a half-block away. The college seniors from Hot Springs scurried back to their white Buick and drove away.

The scene at Potomac Avenue was unforgettable, too, in a less momentous way. Clinton had another girlfriend at Georgetown by then, a bold, brainy senior named Ann Markesun. He had not told Carolyn about her. It was quite a balancing act, talking on the phone with Markesun while Yeldell was in the house. Yeldell knew that something was up because "the guys at the house were furious with Bill for not being honest. I would be in the house and he was on the phone with Ann. He seemed kind of distant."

A few days later Clinton took Yeldell over to Annapolis to visit their high school friend Phil Jamison at the Naval Academy. Jamison remembers the trio watching the Wednesday parade on the academy grounds as well as a ceremony honoring veterans who had returned from Vietnam. They did not discuss the war, but if they had, Clinton and Jamison would have found that their views were not so far apart. Jamison and his classmates at the Naval Academy "weren't so thrilled about the war, either," Jamison said later. "We had a picture memorial in our rotunda with yearbook pictures of grads killed in Vietnam. And by then it was starting to stretch all the way around the rotunda. Vietnam was not looking all that good to any of us."

The great unraveling reached surrealistic levels as the school year neared its end. Early on the morning of June 5, two Marine Corps officers were killed and two companions injured when a man pulled out a gun and fired, after a racially tinged incident at the Little Tavern hamburger joint on M Street near Key Bridge. The assailant, who said he had been called racist names, had come to Washington to participate in the Poor People's Campaign's Resurrection City, the economic empowerment protest organized by followers of the slain Martin Luther King. After the shooting, he fled in a car up Prospect Street toward the Georgetown campus and passed a group of fraternity brothers. Another senior, who had just learned that he had flunked a course and would not graduate on time, was drunk in the street and got hit by the escape car. His friends took him to Georgetown University Hospital.

John Dagnon, one of the friends, went to the emergency room. He was checking on his injured buddy when the door opened and in came the dead and wounded from the Little Tavern shooting. Dagnon looked over to the television set in the waiting room. Bobby Kennedy had been assassinated following his victory in the California primary. There was, it seemed, blood and death everywhere.

The Potomac Avenue housemates were asleep by then. They had turned off the television set moments after Kennedy had been declared the victor —and before he was shot. It was not until early the next morning that Tommy Caplan learned the news in a telephone call from his friend John Lacey. He went downstairs and shook Clinton awake, and they sat on the edge of Clinton's bed in shock. Two Kennedys dead: one killed during their senior year in high school, another at the end of their senior year in college.

Caplan was invited to New York for the memorial service at St. Patrick's Cathedral and the long funeral train ride down to Washington. He arrived at the church an hour early and ended up taking a twenty-block walk around Manhattan with Walt Rostow, a member of JFK's East Coast brain trust who helped Lyndon Johnson prosecute the Vietnam War that Robert

Kennedy had entered the presidential race to try to stop. The funeral train moved slowly from New York to Washington. Every few miles it slowed as throngs of onlookers saluted the coffin. Tommy Caplan, rarely at a loss for words, rode in silence much of the route, staring out the window, engulfed by a sense of "how lost our country seemed." He had operated on the assumption that Robert Kennedy would win. Like Clinton, he had harbored an image of the future in which Robert Kennedy would be president. That made the assassination more shattering. "One's vision had to be radically revised. It made me despair. It seemed the triumph of hopelessness."

The following day was graduation day. Nobody was up for it. All the normal parties had been canceled that week, including the luau and senior dance with rock and roller Chuck Berry, and many students thought even the commencement itself should be shelved. As parents and relatives walked through the Main Gate, they were encountered by a group of seniors holding signs protesting the business-as-usual approach. But the morning had dawned clear and bright. It was a beautiful day as they walked onto the lawn at Healy and took their seats and a swing camera took a grand panoramic shot of the class. As the program began, clouds started to roll in and the scene was enveloped in darkness. Just as Mayor Walter Washington was about to give his commencement address, a hard rainstorm began and the Georgetown graduates of 1968, as Ashby later put it, "ran for our lives."

So much for ceremony. The thunderstorm did what the administration would not do. It forced the cancelation of graduation exercises. Mayor Washington's unspoken address was instead mailed to every senior. The trauma of the riot, the deaths of King and Kennedy, the bloody war and the gathering storm of the draft, the terrible rain—it was all part of the same mess. The black dye from their commencement gowns had stained the white shirts the boys were required to wear beneath, leaving dark splotches that seemed all too appropriate. Their generation had been inflated with possibilities, Tommy Caplan lamented, and now for most people it all became impossible. Some members of the class of 1968 would spend decades trying to shake that despair.

But one member of the class was indomitable and ready for more action. Bill Clinton had a plan. He had persuaded Jim Moore, who had some free time before basic training started at Fort Benning, to travel back to Arkansas with him to work on the reelection campaign of Senator Fulbright. Their job for a week or so would be to return cars that had been loaned to the campaign by auto dealers around the state. "This is going to be great," Clinton said to Moore. "We'll drive around the most beautiful state on the planet and talk to judges during the day and date their daughters at night. You'll be this great guy from Washington I'm importing. We'll say you were a youth coordinator for Robert Kennedy or something, and people will just die to have you as their house guest and you'll be able to go out with all these good-looking girls."

"I can deal with that," Moore said.

WHAT should be said in summary about Clinton's first four-year experience in Washington? It is clear that these were not years of rebellion for him. If the overwhelmingly white, bourgeois Hilltop milieu was too narrow and homogeneous, it also protected him from the excesses of his generation. It allowed him to follow a moderate course during an increasingly immoderate period. Although one of the slogans of the day warned that no one over thirty should be trusted, Clinton drew heavily from four old-fashioned liberal mentors: Carroll Quigley, who emphasized the philosophy of future preference; Joseph Sebes, who offered an empathetic way of looking at other cultures and points of view; Walter Giles, with his reverence for the Constitution as a living document; and J. William Fulbright, who preached the limitations of power and laid out the intellectual arguments against the war in Vietnam.

Clinton began college as a grind, studying diligently and comparing his grades with classmates. By his senior year he had developed a different style, in which he could find twenty things to do other than study, until the final moment, when he would somehow absorb weeks' worth of material in a few hours of intense cramming. Perhaps that is the metaphor for a politician's life, and in Washington as an undergraduate he began to master it. His two years on Capitol Hill gave him an invaluable lesson in practical politics: from his unobtrusive, almost invisible station as one of Fulbright's back room boys, he observed the real world of the Senate, examining the vanities and foibles of supposedly great men and learning how public policy turns on personal relationships as well as substance. His experience as a student politician at Georgetown was noteworthy not because it transformed him in any significant way but because it set a pattern for the rest of his career. The Georgetown years established that Clinton was first in his class in terms of political will and skill, and yet people could sometimes tire of him. Still, even losing would not derail him from his political course. Nothing could.

CLINTON and Moore used Little Rock as their hub, driving out from the capital city to every corner of the state. To Moore, Bill Clinton's homeland seemed dense and exotic. One night they stayed at a plantation house along the Mississippi Delta, a place straight out of *Gone With the Wind,*

Moore thought, with magnolia trees shading the mansion and black servants offering iced tea to visitors—and pretty southern belles, literally the
judge's daughters, ready to be taken out at night to the local drive-in
movie. Another day they drove down to Hope, Clinton's birthplace in
southwest Arkansas, a world away from the Delta, where everyone seemed
different degrees of poor. Then they headed north to Fayetteville and spent
the night with a university official who was as enlightened as anyone in
Washington.

The trip became a political science class for Moore, with Clinton as the
professor. Clinton told him that to win an election in Arkansas and at the
same time bring about social change, you first had to win over the courthouse crowd. You had to be able to walk into any courthouse in Arkansas
and know the county clerk, know the whole power structure and what
was important to those people. Moore realized that "that was part of the
reason Clinton was driving the cars around and dating the judges' daughters." As they drove through the Arkansas river valleys, Clinton told Moore
that the power job in Arkansas, the one he coveted, was governor. It was
the place where you could really do things to change people's lives, he
said. And the surest stepping stone for that was the attorney general's
office because that job gave you the access you needed to those county
courthouses. Moore was impressed by how familiar and comfortable Clinton seemed with that courthouse network when he was only twenty-one
and had spent most of the past four years far away in Washington. His
friend was no carpetbagger.

Clinton talked about the ways he would try to emulate Senator Fulbright
and the ways he would have to break from him. Fulbright had two radically
different personas, he told Moore. In Washington, the senator was the
patrician intellectual and internationalist. He was J. William Fulbright. For
a long time this style worked well for Fulbright back home, especially in
the rural areas. It made the backwoods people feel better about themselves
to see this nattily dressed, professorial statesman who would address them
without condescension, using big words and talking about global issues.
But it only worked as long as Fulbright came home often enough to sustain
the connection with the folks and to show an interest in their workaday
concerns. Once that connection was lost, nothing could restore it. Fulbright could start wearing red flannel shirts and suspenders and go by just
plain Bill Fulbright, but that might not be enough. It is the burden of a
good politician, Clinton said, to learn how to reconcile these seeming
contradictions. In Fulbright they were becoming too stark, leaving him
vulnerable. The people in Arkansas were starting to feel distant from
J. William and leery of just plain Bill.

On the issue closest to Clinton's heart, civil rights, he saw Fulbright as a relic from another era. He told Moore that he respected the senator enormously but felt that he had compartmentalized international and local morality. His unwillingness to step out on the race issue was something that Clinton could not justify. He told Moore that the time for that style of southern politician was over. When he got elected, he would do so without forfeiting his personal moral views. The central question Clinton was dealing with, Moore concluded, was "how you move into the new world and hold on to power at the same time."

There it was, in the summer of his twenty-first year—an essential question of Bill Clinton's career for all the decades to come.

Fulbright's toughest primary opponent that year was someone all too familiar to Clinton, "Justice Jim" Johnson. Two years earlier Johnson had defeated Clinton's candidate, Judge Frank Holt, in the Democratic gubernatorial primary, but then lost to Republican Winthrop Rockefeller in the general election. Johnson was a fiery racist in the George Wallace mold, and now he was running side by side with the Alabama governor, who was campaigning for president and "moving through the South faster than Sherman did," as Clinton once put it. Johnson attacked Fulbright for his opposition to the war, calling the senator the "pinup boy of Hanoi." Had Fulbright not spent more time than usual the year before traveling around Arkansas trying to explain his position on the war, he might have been more vulnerable to Johnson's overheated challenge.

After Moore left, Clinton went to work full time for Fulbright's reelection campaign. It operated out of familiar territory, the old Marion Hotel, which had served as headquarters for Frank Holt two years earlier. Lee Williams, Fulbright's top aide, was down from Washington to run the campaign, with help from several other Fulbright aides, including James McDougal, the director of his Little Rock office. Though only twenty-eight, McDougal was a colorful veteran of Arkansas and Washington politics. He had been elected to the Democratic state central committee as a teenage political prodigy from Bradford in rural White County, and at age twenty helped run John Kennedy's state presidential campaign. Senator McClellan rewarded McDougal with a patronage job on Capitol Hill, where he worked as the assistant bill clerk in the Secretary of the Senate's office before Fulbright hired him to run his home office. By the time Clinton met him that summer, McDougal was a reformed alcoholic and an unreconstructed populist hustler and storyteller. They hit it off, trading notes on women and regaling each other with stories from the backwoods of Arkansas and the back rooms of Congress.

When Lee Williams asked Clinton what he wanted to do for the campaign that summer, he said he wanted to be as close to the candidate as possible. He was made Fulbright's driver—not the easiest assignment.

Fulbright was an odd mixture: shy and aloof, scholarly and formal in appearance, yet jocklike and profane in private. When being driven around Arkansas, he preferred to talk rather than listen. The time that Clinton and Fulbright spent on the road was brief and calamitous. One afternoon shortly after the candidate and his young disciple drove off together, McDougal and Williams were sitting in the office back in Little Rock and took a phone call from the road. It was Fulbright calling from southwest Arkansas, utterly perplexed, saying that the floorboard of their light blue Ford Torino was ankle deep in water. After asking a few questions, McDougal determined that Clinton had caused the crisis by running the air conditioner constantly with the vents closed. "Two goddamn Rhodes Scholars in one car out there and they can't figure out why they're making rain!" McDougal said to Williams. That was only the beginning. Another day Clinton drove one hundred miles in the wrong direction before Fulbright realized the mistake and ordered him to turn around. Another day he left the car for valet parking at the Arlington Hotel in Hot Springs, but took the keys with him, creating a traffic jam in the garage for a half-hour until he was found inside embroiled in a debate over the Vietnam War with a local veteran.

They exasperated each other. Fulbright exasperated Clinton because he could never win an argument with the old man. Clinton exasperated Fulbright because the young buck would never shut up. Finally, they came off the road and Fulbright stormed into the office at the Marion Hotel and announced, "Jim will be going out with me Monday!" McDougal had never seen Fulbright so distraught. McDougal thought he was "out of control. He couldn't bear any more. He couldn't bear another minute of it." Williams still wanted McDougal in the office, and ignored the senator's request to change drivers. Early the next Monday morning, Fulbright chose the only course of action left to him. He took the wheel himself and drove quietly out of town alone.

Clinton put the best face on his adventure. If he ended up doing other things, he said in a letter to Denise Hyland, it was because he had more important matters on his mind. "Lately I have returned to my speechmaking," he wrote. "And I've attacked more fiercely than ever before the distorted ideas which find their fruition in Wallace's candidacy but linger in varying degrees in the minds of so many here and throughout the country."

Clinton split his time between his mother's house in Hot Springs and apartment 9-G at Quapaw Towers in Little Rock, which belonged to Paul Fray and his wife Mary Lee Saunders Fray. The Frays had known Clinton since 1966 when Paul and Bill were part of the Holt Generation team. Mary Lee, who grew up in a conservative Baptist military family from northern Virginia, had been the president of the Young Republicans at Ouachita Baptist in Arkadelphia, where she knew many of Clinton's girlfriends, including Sharon Ann Evans, the reigning Miss Arkansas, and Carolyn Yeldell, the girl next door on Scully Street. Mary Lee had worked on Republican Winthrop Rockefeller's campaigns, but switched parties after marrying Paul, and now was employed in Fulbright's Little Rock office. Clinton paid no rent at the Frays' apartment, but there, as in so many other cases during his life, he found ways to fit in as part of the family, and earned his keep by making life interesting for his hosts and vacuuming the rugs and washing the dishes. Fray had no second thoughts about letting him stay in the apartment alone with his wife. Clinton, he believed, "knew how to keep his private life separate."

Late in the summer, Tom Campbell drove up from Navy flight school in Pensacola, Florida, on a weekend leave to visit his college roommate. They met halfway, on the square of a small town in Louisiana. Clinton had persuaded Sharon Ann Evans to accompany him down to the meeting point. She drove back alone in his car while Clinton rode with Campbell. As Miss Arkansas, Evans was a celebrity in Little Rock that year, far better known than Clinton. She knew the governor and took Clinton and Campbell to meet Winthrop Rockefeller. It was the first time Clinton had stepped inside the Governor's Mansion. The deepest impression Campbell took from the visit came when Clinton drove him to a rural village to watch Justice Jim speak to a crowd of farmers wearing bib overalls. Clinton, fuming, waited in line after the speech, shook Johnson's hand, then said to him, "You make me ashamed to be from Arkansas." Johnson reacted calmly to his young critic, saying, "Well, son, if you disagree with me, put it in a letter." Clinton told Campbell that even though he despised Justice Jim, he learned something from the way Johnson had responded without getting angry. Campbell could see Clinton "filing that away."

Clinton was a cool customer himself in other respects, especially when it came to women. He was writing letters to his first Georgetown girlfriend, Denise Hyland, and to a later Georgetown girlfriend, Ann Markesun. In Hot Springs, Carolyn Yeldell thought she and Bill had something special going, and in Little Rock he was spending considerable time with beauty queen Sharon Ann Evans. Clinton had friends everywhere, it seemed, male and female, and he loved and cared about them all. Evans was especially curious about Markesun—"the blond-headed girl from Georgetown"—and would often ask Clinton's friends about her. "I don't know if I thought of us as an item," Evans recalled later. "If I did, it was fleeting. There were so many other people in Bill's life. Maybe deep down I had a sense that I knew where his life was headed."

Carolyn Yeldell could see only too well how Clinton's friendship with

Evans had developed. Evans was bridesmaid that summer at the wedding of Carolyn's little sister and Clinton had attended the wedding. "From then on Sharon picked up in Bill's eye. That was hard. All of a sudden her Volkswagen was in his driveway all the time." Still, Yeldell did not want to think that her own relationship with Clinton was on the skids. Then, one Sunday morning, "it hit me over the head and I came to my senses. It was a question of what to do after church. I walked out my back door and up the front walk to Bill's front door—and saw Bill and Sharon through the window. They were standing embraced in a major kiss near the table. It was that classic moment, right before I was going to ring the bell. I turned around and went back home." Her dreams of being the politician's wife started to fade. "I needed honesty. He hadn't ever said to me, 'I'm going to start dating Sharon now, so you're not my girlfriend anymore.' He would sort of play the field."

If Clinton never directly addressed their own situation, he felt free to share with Carolyn his thoughts about his future. One day after that incident they were standing in his kitchen and he blurted out, "Carolyn, did you ever think about who you're going to marry?" Once she had thought it could be someone just like Bill Clinton. But she would never say that now. It was a rhetorical question anyway. He wanted to tell her the type of woman he would marry. "The woman I marry is going to be very independent," he said. "She's going to work outside the house. She needs to have her own interests and her own life and not be wrapped up entirely in my life."

Ann Markesun might have fit those requirements. She was attractive, more forceful and aggressive than Hyland, Yeldell, or Evans—and hipper than Clinton, certainly not the type to be wrapped up in his life. Markesun came out to visit him near the end of the summer, around Labor Day, accompanied by Richard Shullaw, one of Clinton's fraternity friends, who was on his way to Texas. When they reached Hot Springs, they stayed at the house at 213 Scully Street. They went water-skiing on Lake Hamilton, with Markesun, tan and muscular, tacking a sailboat around the lake while sporting a bikini that later became the stuff of local legend.

Shullaw caught a fever in the Arkansas sun and was bedridden at the Clinton house the next day. Virginia Clinton, he said, "took very sweet care" of him. The next day the three Georgetown friends went rambling about the countryside in Clinton's convertible. Shullaw was in the back seat, only partially protected from the sparks that were flying around up front. "Bill and Ann got in all these heated arguments, these political disputes. She was on her way to becoming a real radical and had been totally turned off to mainstream politics after the Democratic Convention in Chicago. As I recall, she was deeply against the war and was to the left of Bill, who was trying to be pragmatic and explain why he would support Hubert Humphrey." Clinton and Markesun also spent a few days at the Frays' apartment in Little Rock. Paul Fray enjoyed watching Markesun "getting in Clinton's face" during a dispute over monetary policy.

BILL was the pride of Hot Springs that summer. They were sending their brightest son off to Oxford as a Rhodes Scholar—unless, that is, he got drafted and shipped to Vietnam. The Rhodes Scholarship provided Clinton no legal protection from Garland County Draft Board No. 26, which had reclassified him 1-A, eminently draftable, back on March 20, one month after graduate school deferments were abolished. Most draftable young men were being called for pre-induction physicals within two months of getting classified 1-A. The draft board was inducting Hot Springs boys by date of birth at a rate that would reach Clinton's August 19 number before he finished his first term overseas.

Raymond Clinton took it upon himself to find his nephew some time. Even when Roger Clinton was alive, Raymond, the older brother with money and influence as a successful car agency owner, was paternalistic in his handling of family matters. "Manipulative" is the word Virginia chose to describe him. He would help his family and maintain his grip over it at the same time. "That was Raymond's method of operation," Henry Britt, a Hot Springs lawyer and former judge, said later. "He would assist relatives whether they wanted help or not."

Although he was not a military man, Raymond Clinton had important connections to the military power structure in Hot Springs, including the Garland County Draft Board. He belonged to the local chapter of the U.S. Navy League, a social club that met once a month in different area restaurants for a night of food, drink, and conversation. Henry Britt was also in the Navy League, as were Trice Ellis, commanding officer of the local Naval Reserve unit, and William S. Armstrong, who ran a bulk oil plant in town and served as chairman of the draft board.

Britt had performed legal work for Raymond Clinton over the years, once bailing out another Clinton relative who had been jailed for nonsupport after a divorce. At Raymond's request, he had also written a number of letters of recommendation for Bill Clinton's college and Rhodes Scholar applications. He would draft the letters and other prominent citizens in town would sign them. They were unlikely associates: Britt was a conservative Republican and noted opponent of the gambling rackets, while Raymond Clinton had longstanding ties to the Democratic party and did business with the gamblers. But Raymond Clinton was known around town for his ability to ingratiate himself with powerful people of all sorts. Ray

Smith, Jr., a lawyer and populist Democrat who represented Hot Springs in the Arkansas House for three decades, knew that "Raymond and Britt were extremely close," and always suspected that Raymond Clinton took pains to let people know that he was close to Judge Britt as a means of lending himself more authority in the community.

One day that summer, as Britt remembered it later, Raymond paid a visit to his Central Avenue storefront office and said, "Well, we've got to keep Bill out of the draft so he can take advantage of his schooling." Britt undertook two efforts to delay Clinton's induction so that he could go to Oxford for at least one year. There is no clear and documented evidence that Clinton knew about the lobbying that his uncle and the lawyer were doing on his behalf. Britt thought that "Bill must have known." Clinton has said that he did not. Given Raymond Clinton's history of meddling in other people's affairs without asking, and given Bill Clinton's propensity to be acutely aware of everything going on around him in his home town, either conclusion seems possible. But later letters that Clinton wrote to friends in which he seemed to have a measure of inside knowledge of his draft fate make it more probable that the nephew did know what his uncle and others were doing for him.

The first relief Raymond Clinton and Britt found for Bill was a naval billet. This would not only give him more time—he would not have to fill it until after the school year ended in June—but it also would more likely keep him out of harm's way in the war. Trice Ellis, the local naval commander, said he was only too happy to accommodate the request, which he did not consider out of the ordinary, and was "impressed by the chance to enlist someone with a college education." He called the Navy command in New Orleans and secured a two-year active duty billet for young Clinton. Ellis assumed that Clinton would stop by that summer for an interview, but Clinton never did. When he asked Raymond Clinton what happened, Raymond told him not to worry, Bill would not be coming, he had been taken care of in another way.

That other way was more direct, providing Clinton with only temporary relief but not obligating him to military service. Britt called draft board chairman Armstrong, his close friend, and asked him, as he later recalled, to "put Bill Clinton's draft notice in a drawer someplace and leave it for a while. Give the boy a chance." This is apparently what Armstrong did for several months. Another member of the Garland County Draft Board, Robert Corrado, later remembered Armstrong holding back Clinton's file and saying that they had to give him time to go to Oxford. According to Opal Ellis, the board secretary, the board "kind of leaned over backwards to let him go to Oxford."

Special consideration for Rhodes Scholars was not unusual around the country. The draft board in Alameda County, California, was so impressed by the achievements of the only black Rhodes winner that year, Tom Williamson of Harvard, that they granted him a graduate school deferment even though such deferments supposedly no longer existed. Darryl Gless, whose small home town in Nebraska was so proud of him that they strung a banner across the Main Street bank welcoming him back from his successful Rhodes interview, also was given a special deferment. Dartmouth scholar John Isaacson visited his draft board in Lewiston, Maine, and pleaded with them to let him go to Oxford, which they did. University of Iowa scholar Mike Shea went to England "happily but erroneously 2-S" for the first year. Paul Parish's mother in Port Gibson, Mississippi, received a letter from the governor telling her that Paul should go to England because they were trying to get an exemption for Rhodes Scholars. For virtually every member of the Rhodes class of 1968 there was a similar story.

Willie Fletcher, a Harvard graduate from Washington State, was a year older than most of his classmates and feared that he would be drafted immediately. He cut a deal with the Navy, signing up for a four-month officer candidate school that summer on the condition that when he finished in October they would defer his commission for two years and let him go to Oxford. The only reason he enlisted was to avoid service during the time when the war was being fought. He considered the war "deeply immoral," did not want to fight in it, and hoped that by the time he earned his commission it would all be over.

Vanderbilt's Walter Pratt had won one of the four Rhodes slots from the South region with Clinton and was so awed by his accomplishment at the time that he seemed ready to fly home without an airplane. Members of his draft board in Jackson were equally proud of their native son and left him with the impression that they would let him go to Oxford without drafting him, even after the deferments for graduate students were abolished. Many of the scholars, including Clinton, had acknowledged during their undergraduate years that the draft system gave unfair protection to the wealthy and educated. Pratt was the first one to act on that sense of guilt. As he got closer to going to England, he felt that he could not "in good conscience claim a deferment that nobody else was going to get." He had friends who were graduating and not receiving deferments. Subconsciously, he said later, he was comparing himself to them. "I did not see myself as special. So I went to the local Army recruiter and signed up for officer training school." While his colleagues prepared to set sail for the British Isles, Pratt reported for basic training at Fort Polk in Louisiana.

Clinton was less certain about his obligations. His life seemed unsettled. He wrote Denise Hyland on September 23, ten days before he was to leave, that he had not figured out how to get his trunk to New York for the

Atlantic crossing. "I still know nothing about the draft," he added. "I am resolved to go and enjoy whatever time I have." Denise was working that fall in the marketing research department of Chase Manhattan and was having second thoughts about the career she had chosen. She felt somewhat adrift, she wrote in a letter to Clinton. The corporate world seemed unfulfilling to her. She wanted something more. He told her he knew the feeling. It seemed as though their whole generation, their country, had lost its bearings. "To be adrift in a stormy sea is no sin," he wrote. "Perhaps it is essential to really knowing yourself and seeking your future."

CHAPTER SEVEN

THE GREAT
ESCAPE

ON A BRIGHT and crisp early October noon, "the best men for the world's fight" assembled at the foot of West 46th Street in Manhattan for a most curious passage. There, at Pier 86 on the Hudson River waterfront along what once was known as "luxury liner row," Bill Clinton embarked on a great adventure, certainly, yet one that found him advancing, retreating, escaping and searching all at once, sailing away from the fiery tumult of America in an opulent vessel from a bygone age bound for the sheltering, silent libraries of medieval England.

He arrived wearing a gray suit and was seen off by Denise Hyland, who boarded the liner with him and stood on deck for a few minutes. When she looked into his eyes one last time to bid him bon voyage, she was struck by his expression of awe—a sense of "Oh, my God, I'm the luckiest guy in the world!" The anxiety he felt about his uncertain draft status gave way to the thrill of the moment: here he was, the first from any branch of his family to graduate from college, now standing amid the academic gold medalists of his generation, headed overseas for the first time, carrying not a rifle but a sack of books and a saxophone case, graced with a mark of prestige that would brighten his résumé forever, retracing the path to Oxford and worldly sophistication that Senator Fulbright had followed nearly half a century earlier.

The S.S. *United States* with her razor-sharp bow and two massive funnels was an impressive sight as she edged down the river out past the Statue of Liberty to the broad ocean beyond. She was known as "The Big U," an affectionate nickname for the biggest, sleekest American luxury liner plying the North Atlantic, a quadruple-screw turbine steamship that since her maiden voyage in 1952 had proudly retained the Blue Riband as the world's fastest liner, averaging more than thirty-two knots and surpassing forty knots in occasional bursts of record speed. Fast and elegant she was, but also obsolete, destined for drydock within a year. The group voyage to England by sea had been a cherished Rhodes tradition, a rite of bonding, a decompression chamber of sorts from the New World to the Old, but it seemed out of date if not vulgar by now, when airplanes could reach the same destination in hours rather than days, and the world moved to a more urgent rhythm. The great ship and the elite young men sailed off together facing the same paradox. They were molded to succeed in a way of life that was vanishing.

There were dozens of other students sailing The Big U to England that month, including a sizable number of undergraduate women in junior year abroad programs whose presence greatly enlivened the trip. But as the voyage got under way, the first-year Rhodes Scholars spent much of their time among themselves, erasing and redrawing the invisible but palpable lines of highbrow versus middlebrow, Ivy League versus Land Grant, cool versus uncool. A historian among them once said of the American Rhodes Scholars that they go through several stages of self-realization. First, hearing the accomplishments of the others, they wonder, How did I get here? After spending five days together on the boat, the question becomes, How did they get here?

This might seem to be a hard crowd to intimidate. When "How Gentle Is the Rain" played over the sound system in the restaurant bar and Paul Parish blurted out assuredly, "Anybody know what this song is based on?" it seemed that the answer—"A Bach cantata!"—arrived from thirty voices at once. But beneath their surface composure many of the young men were struggling with a measure of self-doubt. George Butte, an English major from the University of Arizona, the son of Phoenix schoolteachers, looked around at the group of intellectuals and "felt like an outsider amid the mandarins." Darryl Gless from the University of Nebraska suddenly assessed himself as "something of the provincial hick. I was really from the bushes compared to a lot of those guys." The women on board seemed equally imposing to him. "A woman would say she was from Vassar or Barnard and I'd say, 'Where's that?' and they'd look at me as if I were teasing them."

Butte and Gless might not have realized that many of the fellows they considered mandarins were sizing up the competition and feeling deficient themselves. Robert Reich of Dartmouth, who made everyone else's list of the most impressive figures in the brood, was "overwhelmed by the intellectual firepower and felt grossly inadequate" during the first round of mingling aboard ship. The others, to Reich, "seemed ready to launch their careers in the direction of ambassadors or presidents or university professors." He felt that "a great mistake had been made by the selection committee in picking me." Reich's Dartmouth friend John Isaacson, a college debate champion, felt as unsure of himself as anyone, though he was certain that he intimidated some of the others. "At that age you don't really know how to know about somebody, so you just try to talk your way through."

Clinton was different. While others looked for one or two compatriots, he ignored the hierarchy that was developing and looked for friendships everywhere. He had an ability to walk into any conversation on the deck and immediately place himself at the center of it. Some of his fellow scholars took to him quickly. Darryl Gless thought that Clinton was "down to earth and altogether lacking in pretense. Aside from the self-deprecating humor, he was also an extraordinary listener. Others were good at self-presentation with a script to impress you with." Others found him a bit too manipulative. Daniel Singer's first impression was that Clinton "sought out everybody that he thought was informative or valuable and debriefed them. He picked brains." Douglas Eakeley of Yale classified him as "a classic southern glad-handing politician." Was he open about his political aspirations? Rick Stearns of Stanford certainly found him to be. "I remember meeting Clinton and him telling me within forty-five minutes that he planned to go back to Arkansas to be governor or senator and would like to be a national leader someday." Then and always, these contradictions co-existed in Clinton—considerate and calculating, easygoing and ambitious, mediator and predator.

THE first day at sea was smooth and sunny. George Butte, virtually penniless but for the Rhodes stipend, in a burst of optimism rented a deck chair for the full five days. Bob Reich basked in the afternoon warmth, his feelings of inadequacy melting along with larger burdens. The assassinations, the war, the draft, the raging cities—they were sailing away from all that. "What a relief!" Reich sighed. After four years of college activism, he was feeling "a little burnt out," and now, as they left America, he felt as though a weight was being lifted from his shoulders.

Reich was a formidable character, with his piercing blue eyes, his curly black hair, his quizzical, hectoring nature—"What are you saying there?" he would ask, never at a loss for words himself. He was a physical runt, only four foot ten, his growth stunted by Fairbanks Disease, a rare genetic illness in which the hip joints fail to grow fully. Yet he was an overpowering theatrical presence. Tom Williamson, like everyone else encountering Reich, discovered that "you put his size aside within minutes of meeting him. He was totally smooth in engaging you, and he did it without a chip on his shoulder." John Isaacson, his Dartmouth classmate, was impressed by Reich's sheer competence at everything but athletics. "He was a cartoonist, funny, quick, actor, director, academic. He could come into the newspaper office and type at eighty words per minute an articulate essay on something. I felt like an awkward child in comparison."

At Dartmouth, Reich acted as though he were a peer to the administrators and sometimes as if he were their boss. John Sloane Dickey, the college president, relied on him for advice on how to accommodate the contentious forces of youth, from the antiwar radicals to the black power advocates pushing for their own studies program and union. They were quite a pair, the talkative little Reich and the six-foot-six Dickey, a graceful Dartmouth scholar who would lope across campus with his golden retriever. Isaacson thought that Dickey had "begun listening to Reich out of sheer amusement and later listened out of sheer necessity." It might not have been entirely coincidental that Dartmouth devolved into chaos soon after Reich departed for England.

Reich made several forays into the larger world of politics during his Dartmouth days, working in Robert Kennedy's Senate office the summer after his junior year, and returning to Washington the following October to participate in the March on the Pentagon, the one Clinton and his housemates had skipped. He served as a student coordinator for Senator McCarthy's antiwar presidential campaign in five states and ended his college days by being selected from the multitudes for a *Time* magazine cover story on the class of 1968, placed on the cutting edge of a collection of 630,000 seniors that *Time* said included a fair share of draft dodgers and pot smokers but also "the most conscience-stricken, moralistic, and perhaps, the most promising graduates in U.S. academic history."

At the time, Reich not only seemed more imposing than the six-foot-three Clinton, he also more clearly personified the agitated, rebellious mood of his comfortably born generation. Clinton brought with him the values of lower-middle-class Arkansas, not yet ready to reject an established order that he and his kinfolk were striving to become part of; not so eager to denounce American materialism when his family had never enjoyed it. Reich, who came out of the wealth and conservatism of suburban Westchester County, New York, fretted that his generation was being seduced by status and the accumulation of goods. He was rebelling against "status quo-ism," he informed *Time,* and was promoting a new humanist ethic that allowed for self-initiative and creativity. "Destruction is the choice when creation is impossible," he said, as a means of explaining the violence seeping into protest movements in 1968.

By the second morning aboard The Big U., a North Atlantic storm pushing twenty-foot swells sent Reich back to his cabin where he remained thereafter, immobilized by seasickness, "vomiting quietly and wondering how [my] forefathers made it across." He was by no means the only scholar turning green. The *United States* was a rough-riding ship, designed with speed in mind at a time when the government thought it might be needed for troop transport. It rode light, fast, and high in the water, rather like a duck, rolling with the waves, undulating rather than chopping, its stern yawing.

Daniel Singer was also sick the rest of the trip: "It was horrible. I remember watching food slide around on the table. I spent most of my time in the hold." George Butte never used his paid-for deck chair again. To Darryl Gless, a student of Shakespeare accustomed to losing himself in literary landscapes and castles dim and dank, the remainder of the trip evoked a familiar image, "one of extraordinary grayness." Often penned indoors by the nasty ocean wind, the scholars and their friends set up camp in the bar and drank, smoked, and talked the days and nights away. It was in mid-ocean aboard The Big U, his stepfather dead and the memories of his abusive bouts of drunken rage buried with him, that Bill Clinton broke his long vow of alcoholic abstinence. Someone offered him a drink, and rather than automatically declining, he said to himself, "It's wrong for me to be scared of this," and he accepted. No longer "terrified of indulgence," he became an occasional beer and wine drinker.

Clinton excused himself from the bar scene once and knocked on Reich's cabin door holding a tray of crackers and ginger ale. "I thought you might be needing these—heard you weren't feeling so well," he said. As the story was retold and embroidered over the years, it seemed that Clinton devoted hours to nursing Reich back to health, forgoing all pleasure for the sake of a sequestered friend. In fact, Reich had several concerned visitors, and his wretched condition was one of the regular topics of discussion in the lounge, along with the draft and the war and the Democratic Convention in Chicago that August and the attractiveness of various young women aboard the ship.

Most conversations returned to each young man's draft status and how long he expected to last at Oxford before the fateful induction notice arrived. "A lot of us whose futures were uncertain were going to Oxford by the grace of God and weren't sure how long we would stay over," Doug Eakeley said later. Hannah Achtenberg, a Smith College graduate on her way to St. Anne's to study economics, spent hours chatting with the Rhodes Scholars in the ship lounge. She thought that "all the boys were scared stiff because of the draft. Some didn't know whether they would last a month. Some were tortured about whether they should have left at all. Some were wondering whether they should ever go back. Everyone was trying to figure out how to manage the dilemma." One scholar, Frank Aller from Washington, intimated that his inclination was to resist rather than accept induction.

Aller was at the center of the draft discussions, along with Strobe Talbott, who perhaps more than any other member of his Rhodes class captured the crosscurrents of the moment. Talbott was the cautious, correct, accomplished son of a liberal Republican investment banker from Cleveland, a straight arrow who, following in the tradition of his grandfather and father, was registered at birth for admission to Yale, and who would later become such an old blue that he would sing the Whiffenpoof song in the shower. Talbott had been trained at elite private schools for leadership by the establishment that was now unsettled because of the Vietnam War. At Yale he was Mr. Inside, close to campus officials and chairman of the *Yale Daily News,* at a time when the inside was in chaos, rebelling against itself. Disheveled and earnest in a prep school way, he was in the conservative wing of the antiwar movement and could never be a revolutionary. Unlike Reich, who painted his world with bold brush strokes, Talbott was precise and incremental. John Isaacson compared them by saying that "Reich saw nothing but forests, one forest after another, while Talbott saw every single tree in the forest."

But Talbott was to Yale what Reich was to Dartmouth, a link to the administration and a student leader. He and his best friend at Yale, Derek Shearer, the son of the journalist Lloyd Shearer, met every month with Yale's president, Kingman Brewster, to talk about student social issues, including their proposal to make the institution coeducational. They also spent hours talking to Brewster about the war. Yale was one of the intellectual battlegrounds of the time. At Shearer's invitation, James Reston of the *New York Times* visited the campus and, after having lunch with Talbott, wrote a column saying that the Washington establishment was in trouble if it had lost the trust of responsible young men like Talbott.

Talbott's voice against the war in Vietnam turned out to be a surprisingly loud one. At the Yale class of 1968 commencement, he publicized a petition drive signed by four hundred of the one thousand seniors declaring that their opposition was so strong they would not accept conscription into the military. "Many of us simply could not, if ordered, pledge ourselves to kill or be killed on behalf of a policy which offends our deepest sense of what is wise and right," Talbott said then. "We could not do so unless we were to betray our obligation to decide what is humanely permissible and morally possible for ourselves."

Chosen to give one of two student speeches on Class Day during graduation week, Talbott directed his comments to the special circumstances of the young men in his class—the draft and the elimination of graduate school deferments. His class faced a paradox, Talbott said, for though it was "now no longer deferred and now faced with an order to report for induction, [it] is also the seat of the most intensive outrage against the war which it is being ordered to fight. This generation, after graduating from studenthood to soldierhood, harbors the most deepseated opposition to the policies it is being ordered to defend." Few members of his class had experience with the military, Talbott continued, but "all of us, the entire class of 1968, are in a sense already veterans of the war in Vietnam. We are certainly veterans of that dimension of the war which has brought such frustration and intellectual if not literal violence into our country, into our homes and into our lives."

Now Vietnam reached them even in the darkest recesses of The Big U. When Talbott and his friends ducked inside the ship's cinema to watch a movie, they found themselves confronted by John Wayne starring in the Vietnam glory film, *The Green Berets.*

There was another aspect to the voyage that seemed even more incongruous—in retrospect, deliciously so. Also aboard the luxury liner, making his own escape of sorts to Europe, was Bobby Baker, the ultimate Washington wheeler-dealer, a longtime LBJ crony who had been convicted in a splashy 1967 corruption trial of income-tax evasion, theft, and conspiracy to defraud the federal government. Baker knew that he was bound for prison sooner or later, whenever his defense lawyer, Edward Bennett Williams, emptied his ample briefcase of appeals. In the meantime he would continue living the high life. Baker's set of first-class cabins lodged a traveling entourage that included some slick-haired sharpies in sharkskin suits and a few platinum blond escorts. "The whole scene was bizarre. Here were these bright academics slipping across the Atlantic to flee thoughts of the draft and Vietnam and *The Green Berets* is playing in the boat theater, and Baker and his boys are in the bar every time we go in there, trying to instruct us on the ways of the world," recalled John Isaacson. "The whole crowd of us were appalled. They were racist and jingoistic and stupid. Here we were heading off as idealists and they persuasively convinced us that there was something sleazy and corrupt in the government."

If the Rhodes boys were appalled by Baker, he was enthralled by them. Near the end of the voyage, Baker emerged at the center of a reception held in their honor. Rick Stearns, who was already active in the reform wing of the Democratic party, refused to attend "as a matter of principle." But Clinton was there, standing at Baker's side, soaking in tales of power and intrigue. Robert Gene Baker of South Carolina had worked on Capitol Hill since he was a twenty-year-old page. When Lyndon Johnson became Senate Majority Leader, he tapped Baker for his staff and relied on him thereafter as a vote-counter, schmoozer, gossip, and bill collector. The other senators called him "Lyndon Jr." or "Little Lyndon." Clinton, a connoisseur of practical politics, loved to hear Baker's stories about Johnson and the Senate and the way things really worked. It was while watching his performance with Bobby Baker that Strobe Talbott said he first understood Clinton's "raw political talent."

THEY reached Europe on the fifth day, first making a short stop early in the morning at Le Havre across the English Channel in France. Bob Reich stayed on deck, looking out at the port with a sense of awe, thinking to himself, "This is actually France!" He had never been overseas before. "I remember hearing people shout at each other in French. It seemed remarkable." Ten of his fellow travelers skipped off the ship and roamed the dock, absorbing the foreign sounds and smells, but soon grew afraid that The Big U would leave without them. Hannah Achtenberg, who had become a little sister to the Rhodes crew, later remembered how they linked arms and started running wildly back to the boat together. As they clambered across the wharf, arm in arm, Strobe Talbott cried out, "What a motley group of Christian gentlemen!"

Late that afternoon they steamed past the Isle of Wight and landed at Southampton on the South English coast. The passengers lined the deck as The Big U eased up to the pier. Darryl Gless stood next to Clinton at the rail. They looked down and saw a slender man in big glasses, wearing a bowler and a long black raincoat, and holding an umbrella. "Look at him!" Clinton said, and they both laughed. He seemed to fit the upper-crust stereotype so perfectly that Clinton thought he might be an entertainer in period costume. In fact he was Sir Edgar Williams, who had served as chief of intelligence for British Field Marshal Bernard Montgomery during World War II. Sir Edgar, the warden of Rhodes House, was a man of tradition who drank sherry every afternoon and quite enjoyed his annual trek to Southampton to meet the boat from America and escort the Yanks to their colleges at Oxford.

He rounded up his class of 1968 and directed them to a waiting bus for the ride north to Oxford. Two of the Rhodes group had shipped cars. Daniel Singer followed the bus in his old Volvo. It was a strange, disorienting ride through the dark English countryside that chilly October night. Singer lost the caravan at the first roundabout. The boys on the bus could see little but slanting rain pounding against the windows. When the bus reached Oxford, it deposited the scholars in clumps at each of the colleges to which they had been assigned. Four of them—Doug Eakeley of Yale, Reich and Isaacson of Dartmouth, and Bill Clinton of Georgetown—were dropped off at University College on High Street, a curving thoroughfare lined with the dark stone fronts of several medieval Oxford colleges.

At the front gate they were met by Douglas Millin, the college porter who was every bit as much an English character as Sir Edgar. Where the warden came out of the officer corps, the porter was the veteran enlisted man—crusty, foul-mouthed, cynical, all-knowing, protective of his turf, scornful of his superiors. He took one look at the quartet and muttered, "They told me I was getting four Yanks and here they send me three and a half!" Then, turning directly to Reich, he bellowed: "You're the goddamn bloody shortest freaking American I've ever seen in my life! I didn't know it was possible for America to produce someone that freakin' small." He assaulted each of the Americans in turn and intimidated them so thoroughly that they rarely dared venture too far into his cloistered world thereafter. All of them but one, that is. To Bill Clinton, this ornery porter was just another skeptical voter to swing his way.

CHAPTER EIGHT

THE DREAMING SPIRES

THE FIRST ROOMS that Bill Clinton occupied at Oxford were on the second floor of an old stone almshouse, ornamented with honeysuckle, which faced Helen's Court in the right rear corner of University College. He had a sitting room and a bedroom. Doug Eakeley lived across the opposite stairwell in similar quarters. There was a toilet on the first floor and a cold-running shower on the second. The only warmth came from coin-operated electric heaters. No shillings in the pocket, no heat at night. The Americans at Helen's Court were cared for by a "scout" named Arch, a chubby-cheeked servant who according to college lore once waited upon Feliks Yusupov, the Russian prince who had assassinated Rasputin. Bob Reich and John Isaacson, the other two Rhodes Scholars at Univ, were housed on the far side of the college in a modern red brick building with central heating that disappointed them with its featureless twentieth-century efficiency.

Even in the gray gloom of that Oxford autumn, University College was a museum of enchanting colors. The gold-yellow stone walls streaked with black-brown dirt from ages past. The green Front Quad, different somehow from the green of Arkansas and other verdant plots in the New World: richer, sublime, as though every blade of grass had been hand-colored in deep green day after day, century after century. The white marble statue of Percy Bysshe Shelley, Muse of Poetry, a Univ man himself once, long ago, before he was sent down, expelled in 1811 for publishing an atheist tract, but now honored in his own mausoleum, a drowned romantic figure in Carrara marble the white of white chocolate. The soft reds and greens of portraits in the Hall above red-brown oak paneling and below a warm brown hammer-beam roof. The luminous blues and yellows of painted glass in the chapel depicting the Fall and expulsion of Adam and Eve from Eden.

Every morning during his first week, Clinton bounded down the cold stairwell of the almshouse out onto the brick courtyard, weaved through the Gothic maze of Univ past the porter's lodge, and stepped out into the mist of the High Street to explore his new surroundings. He visited most of the nearly thirty colleges that comprised Oxford University, separate academic fortresses with their own personalities and traditions, walled off and imposing from the street, entered through heavy oak doors opening onto brilliant lawns framed by ancient stone buildings. He loped across the street to inspect the classic beauty of Queens College and the new digs of Frank Aller, the tall, brilliant Asia scholar from Washington. He traipsed past the Bodleian Library and under the Bridge of Sighs along dark and narrow Catte Street, and turned left on Broad to Blackwell's bookshop, a bibliophile's paradise that he would revisit countless times, then on to Balliol College, new home of eight Rhodes Scholars, including Rick Stearns and Tom Williamson. He made his way north to Rhodes House with its squared rubble front, where Sir Edgar resided and occasionally invited his Rhodes charges to dinner. He ventured east to the slender, meandering River Cherwell and the deer park in the forest grove of Magdalen College, where Strobe Talbott was staying. To the west he absorbed the bustle of the covered market and the hustle of shops along Cornmarket. South down St. Aldate's he found Pembroke College, where J. William Fulbright learned to smoke a pipe and wear tweed knickers.

He walked fourteen hours a day that first week or so, returning in the dark to his room to plop down "sore and exhilarated." Reich was his frequent companion and fellow explorer. They talked nonstop, gesticulating as they roamed the ancient streets. "We were suddenly within ruins! We were in seventeenth-century and eighteenth-century ruins! I can't describe the feelings we shared," Reich said later. "The architecture, the customs, the manners, the strange ways the English talked. We were constantly comparing notes." For centuries, their college, affectionately known as Univ, had laid claim to being the first of the Oxford colleges, going back to King Alfred in the year 872. It turned out that this boast was spurious and that the founding of Univ was more accurately placed in the thirteenth century, slightly after Merton and Balliol. Such ancient quibbles were of some importance in a place where an institution called New College was indeed new in 1379.

Clinton was so excited by his daily excursions through Oxford that he could not sleep much at night. In an October 14 letter to Denise Hyland, he reflected on how beautiful he found it all, even with the miserable weather. "I am happy if lonely," he wrote. "And I'm convinced I was right to come even if I'm drafted out soon."

America seemed very far away. In the Weir Common Room, he and Reich, Eakeley, and Isaacson sipped tea, ate Cadbury biscuits, and read the London newspapers for political news from home. Through a foreign lens, the United States often appeared chaotic, a land troubled by assassinations and wars. Londoners complained of the Americanization of their city every time another cement slab rose on the skyline. The *Sunday Times* ran articles on the obesity and violence of Americans, quoting one as saying, "We are the most terrifying people on earth." Oxford, in contrast, seemed insular and quaint, if not irrelevant, to many of the Americans. Perhaps that was always the case—Ralph Waldo Emerson once said that "the wind that blows in Oxford blows out of the past"—but it seemed especially so that year. Tom Williamson, removed from a country where "our cities were burning and our campuses were in turmoil," found life in Oxford "like being put in a crypt and awakened one hundred years before." There were no telephones in their rooms. The scholars communicated through notes or by showing up at one another's quarters and hoping someone was there. They ate at fixed times, dining in college halls wearing fashionably shabby black waist-length academic gowns, listening to fellows recite grace in Latin and Greek in dialogues that were part prayer, part witty repartee with the college master.

At times it seemed that Clinton stood out like a multicolored plaid sports coat in this atmosphere of subdued tweeds. He was, thought Doug Paschal, a scholar at Christ Church, "always the character who wanted to do one more thing, go one more place, stay up one more hour, have one more drink. He came across as somebody with a great appetite for life . . . a bit clumsy physically and verbally, making waves." To Paschal, Clinton seemed unguarded. "He would say things others might have said if they weren't so worried about it. The Oxford of that time was a very complicated place, and we could not escape the sense of the brash and loutish and insensitive American presence, always slightly aware of not fitting in exactly. On the other hand, there were lots of people who responded quickly to the robustness and good nature of people like Bill, though there would always be some class-conscious Englishmen who would bristle at someone like him crashing around in the china shop."

The cultural gap led to some measure of tension in the relationship between the Americans and certain Oxford dons. George Butte, studying literature at New College, encountered one tutor who, while gazing out his office window as he sipped his sherry, said with a chuckle that he was amazed to read Faulkner and discover that he was a good novelist. Tom Williamson's dons gave a cool reception to his proposal to write about slavery, dismissing the topic as too American and parochial, but were far more enthusiastic when he switched his interest to Ethiopian politics. John Isaacson found his philosophy dons disdainful of the attempts by American students to relate philosophy to the ethical dilemmas of the age.

That is not to say that the ancient town of dreaming spires was devoid of the confrontational politics of the sixties. Emboldened by the student uprisings that had swept through the capitals of Europe, the young men and women of Oxford were pushing up against the walls of tradition. "People were starting to question all kinds of assumptions about how the place should be run, the extent students should be involved," recalled Nick Browne, an Englishman in his third year at Univ when Clinton arrived. "It was a time when the Rolling Stones were extolling the street fighting man and you could hear The Who on campus. The revolution in dress had reached Oxford: hair down to your shoulders, bright yellow satin shirts, an affected scruffiness." Wilf Stevenson, a Scottish undergraduate at Univ, noted that students then were catching a wave of generational energy from the street revolt in Paris the previous spring and were looking for ways to ride it. "We knew about the barricades of Paris. But we were absolutely naive and hopeless. We didn't know how to turn into action everything we were feeling. It was evanescent, with nothing at the end of the day to show for it."

The protests at Oxford did not match the bold student actions in Paris, but they did offer a decidedly British satiric touch. Dozens of agitated junior fellows disrupted the matriculation ceremony outside the Sheldonian Theatre, complaining that the formal rite accepting new students to Oxford was anachronistic. The protest gave birth to a memorable picket sign: "Matriculation Makes You Blind." Another satirical protest was launched against the stuffiest college, All Souls, which had no undergraduate or graduate students, only fellows for life, and was derided as a haven for reactionaries. Of an All Souls master by the name of Sparrow, one sign proclaimed: "Sparrow Is a Tit." Humorous radicals led by Christopher Hitchens of Balliol College, who went on to become a rambunctious British journalist, seemed to enjoy nothing more than lampooning Master Sparrow. They adopted the albatross as their logo of the left, a sarcastic symbol of intimidation. "Albatross Eats Sparrow" was one of their signs.

On broader issues, the student body leaned leftward. The most ferocious Oxford Union debate of the term addressed the question of whether American democracy had failed. Arguing the negative, Clive Stitt declared that "had it not been for one major boob in Vietnam, the Johnson-Humphrey administration would have gone down as one of America's greatest." Arguing the affirmative, a purple-shirted young aristocrat named Viscount Lewisham "poured scorn" on the American presidential candidates, Vice President Hubert H. Humphrey and Republican Richard M. Nixon. The motion that American democracy had failed carried 266 to 233. All this denunciation of America unsettled the Rhodes Scholars during their first term at Oxford. Many of them were harshly critical of American foreign policy and disappointed in the choice offered in the 1968 presidential election, but they were not ready to give up on American democracy, and certainly not to hear it blasted by class-conscious Englishmen. Darryl Gless was often angry with the Brits. "They assumed that because we were Rhodes Scholars we were prowar and rich. They were so critical of America, I often found myself defending my country."

Clinton's reaction was similar. Martin Walker, a British student at Oxford, sat near Clinton at a party that year where the dissolution of the United States was the primary topic of discussion. "One guy was going on about how democracy had failed and the country was in a prerevolutionary situation, and Clinton countered that. He said, no, the system was able to work. And he cited civil rights. At the time that was not a fashionable position to take. Everyone else in the room was taking the fashionable position that America was hopeless."

In early November, the Americans stayed up all night at the Rhodes House watching the stateside elections, and returned gloomily to their rooms the next morning after learning that Nixon had won the presidency. One of the few bright moments of the long night was when word came that Senator Fulbright had won reelection. The next day Clinton sent a telegram to Fulbright in Little Rock:

> GOT RESULTS AT RHODES HOUSE ELECTION PARTY
> YOU RECEIVED A GREAT CHEER EVERYTHING FINE HERE
> HAPPY FOR YOU AND MRS FULBRIGHT CONGRATULATIONS
>   BILL

Fulbright sent back a short note.

> Dear Bill: I appreciate so much your warm telegram. It was thoughtful of you to wire me at such a busy time. I am looking forward to seeing you on your return. Merry Christmas.
> With all good wishes, I am sincerely yours,
> J. W. Fulbright.

Fulbright seemed to have a soft spot for Clinton, despite the disastrous driving episodes of the previous summer and his disdain for Clinton's ever curlier locks. Long hair was selfish and counterproductive in the fight against the war, Fulbright would constantly tell his young charges.

The Vietnam War was another point of contrast between the Americans and the British. Most of the Rhodes Scholars opposed the war; yet during their first months overseas, they were slow to immerse themselves in the antiwar movement. Many of them did not want to jeopardize their scholarships. There had been reports from back home that Lieutenant General Hershey, director of the Selective Service System, was attempting to punish dissenters by ordering the drafting of known war protesters. Others were still relishing the sense of escape that had overwhelmed them as they sailed away from America. None took roles in the large antiwar march in London on October 27 where there was a confrontation at the American Embassy in Grosvenor Square. British students at Oxford, some marching under the banner of the Oxford Revolutionary Socialist Society, had gone to London proclaiming that the protest was "a rehearsal for the Revolution," and returned frustrated that they had not stirred up more of a fuss. Chris Hitchens, who was also a prominent Oxford Union debater, one of those who argued that American democracy had failed, said the student socialists were "building up an important mass Marxist movement in the country," but that the legion that went to London was somewhat thin because "nobody wants to get sent to jail at this stage of term."

At times the fire was aimed at Rhodes Scholars, which frustrated them. They thought their British counterparts were grandstanding. "It was easy for us to say all these things," recalled Martin Walker, then a correspondent for *Cherwell.* "But the Americans were the ones who really had to deal with it. For them, it was a deeply private grief. They had this threat of conscription hanging over them. They faced the draft. We did not." Walker's college, Balliol, which housed the most Rhodes Scholars, was the intellectual center of Oxford radicalism, the walls of its Junior Common Room lined with posters of black power leaders and burning inner cities. "People there were always shouting, 'Enough talk, it's time for action!' " recalled Daniel Singer. "It was an effete, supercilious characteristic of the Brits, when only the Americans faced a real problem."

LATER in his life, when recounting his academic efforts at Oxford, Clinton would say that during his first year there he read for a degree in PPE— politics, philosophy, and economics—an undergraduate program requiring a series of tutorials and examinations in the three broad subjects. PPE was a popular choice at Oxford among Rhodes Scholars, including Bob Reich. But the archival records show that Clinton was never in the program. Uncertain about what he wanted to pursue at first, he began in what was called B. Litt. politics probational. The probational meant it was a tentative choice, the B. Litt. denoted a research degree program that required no tutorials or lectures but a massive fifty-thousand-word dissertation at the end of two years. The politics don at Univ was on sabbatical that term, so

Clinton was assigned a supervisor from Balliol. Such cross-college moves occurred frequently as students discovered that their college did not specialize in their field or that the dons in that subject were not available. Clinton was supervised by the Balliol don only in the loosest sense. The topic he chose for his dissertation was Imperialism. He checked out dozens of books on the subject from the college library and the larger Bodleian Library and read them in late October and early November.

In the middle of that first eight-week term, Clinton changed his mind and transferred to a B. Phil. program in politics, which called for more interaction with college dons: weekly tutorials, fortnightly essays, a shorter dissertation at the end of the two years, and examinations in four subjects —political theory, comparative government, and two electives. He also changed supervisors, switching to Zbigniew Pelczynski at Pembroke College, Senator Fulbright's old haunt. Students in the Oxford system are not necessarily supervised and tutored by the same don, but Pelczynski took on both tasks with Clinton. He was a soft-spoken intellectual of forty-three whose genteel life as an Oxford don was not something that had come to him as a birthright. Pelczynski grew up in Grodzisk, Poland, and as a teenager during World War II joined the Polish resistance. He was captured by the Germans but liberated by the British, and finished the war fighting in the Polish armed forces under British command. He came to Oxford in 1946 at age twenty-one to study political theory and never left.

During the fall and early winter of 1968, Pelczynski was lecturing on Soviet politics. He was an anti-Communist with leftist tendencies that were diminishing year by year. Although radical students regularly attended his lectures, they had begun to strain his patience. He thought that they "were always posing. They weren't genuine. They were always painting America as the bad guy, the bogey, and they gave me hell on political theory. They would get up and quote Marx. Once I'd had enough and I said, 'Well, you're not going to give me this Marxist shit again!' " During his lectures on the Soviet Union, Pelczynski explored the totalitarian model and questioned whether it was still valid. Splits in the Soviet ruling elite suggested to him that it was no longer the totalitarian monolith of Stalin's day.

For his weekly tutorials, Clinton visited the Polish don in his old bachelor rooms in the North Quad at Pembroke. Pelczynski swiveled pensively in "the Egg," his tomato red modernistic chair, as Clinton discussed readings and essays with him. They went through a mix of political theory and comparative government subjects: the presidential versus cabinet systems of government in the United States and Britain, the separation of powers, notions of democracy, and totalitarianism and pluralism in Eastern Europe. The tutor found his young Rhodes pupil engaging and sharp if not academically brilliant. Clinton was not the ablest American graduate Pelczynski taught at Oxford, "at least not in a purely academic sense," he would note later. "But he had a sharp analytical mind and an impressive power to master and synthesize complex material." It was clear to Pelczynski that Clinton "had the mind of a politician, trying to figure things out, rather than the patience of an academic." He was also "a rather effective arguer, on paper and verbally."

Clinton wrote a number of essays for Pelczynski. He struggled somewhat with the short subjective essay form at which British students excelled. "What suited Clinton was the longer form, laying out all the different lines of thought and synthesizing them rather than independently developing his own line of thought," according to Pelczynski. The essay that most impressed Pelczynski was entitled "Political Pluralism in the USSR." Clinton had been given two weeks to write it, during which he read or looked through some thirty books and articles on the subject. Pelczynski considered Clinton's eighteen-page essay a model of clarity. He kept it in his files and used it later as a teaching tool.

In an essay that was virtually all synthesis, Clinton divided the writings on Soviet pluralism into three schools. First was the Totalitarian school, which came into prominence before Stalin's death. "This group does not accept the viability of factional disputes over policy issues or vested interests of long standing," Clinton wrote. "Any divisions within the leadership are attributed to personal struggles for power, which inevitably will end in the triumph of one man, who, by his victory, returns absolutism and stability to the system."

Then came the Kremlinology school, whose proponents argued that the Soviet system featured a continual power struggle among various factions who, if they could not achieve absolute power for themselves, sought to make sure that no other faction gained a dominant position. This theory was applied to the troubles Khrushchev had with his opponents in the Presidium in the early 1960s and his eventual ouster. "Kremlinologists go beyond the Totalitarian school in acknowledging a very limited but persistent kind of political pluralism in the existence of factions within the party leadership, factions which, in turn, are related to divisions within the bureaucracy and society as a whole," Clinton wrote. But this theory was not without its weaknesses, he said, and was especially vulnerable to the charge that it was bogged down in micro-history.

Clinton gave no name to a third school of Soviet scholarship, which, he said, "begins with the assumption that industrialization and urbanization lead to the differentiation of society and the multiplication of interest groups. In short, a pluralistic society emerges, and with it, the demand and the necessity for more political pluralism." In this theory, the Soviet Union might be compared to "a large Western corporation, with all the inbred resistance of bureaucracies to change, plus the additional albatross of a past marked by the use of terror and the dominance of ideology, a past which lingers on into the present and could re-emerge full blown in the future." There were both optimists and pessimists in this third school. Some believed the Soviet Union would evolve into a parliamentary democracy; others predicted that it would either move gradually to more pluralistic politics or disintegrate.

In his summary, Clinton stayed on moderate ground, agreeing with Pelczynski that political pluralism did exist in the Soviet Union to a certain degree, and that many social forces—the intelligentsia, the youth, the peasants, the churches, the consumers, the nationalities, and the bureaucrats—had developed agendas "more or less independent of the priorities of the rulers." This could lead to any one of six futures for the Soviet Union: oscillation between liberalization and repression as the dictators deem necessary; immobilism and degeneration; continued domination by conservative bureaucrats seeking to maintain their positions within the system; rule by a coalition of elites; evolution toward pluralism within a one-party system; or evolution to a multiparty parliamentary democracy. Although Clinton did not pick his favorite among the six alternatives, he implied by listing his favorite authors on the subject that he inclined toward the theory that the Soviet Union would either move toward parliamentary democracy or collapse.

"One final warning in closing," Clinton wrote. "Any conclusions herein must be hypothetical and no more. Certainty is precluded by the volatility of Soviet politics, fragmentary evidence, questionable reliability and variety of plausible interpretations of available evidence, and this writer's very limited background and competence in this field."

THE scholar's life at Oxford was unlike anything the Americans had experienced. They had oceans of time and virtually no responsibilities that first year beyond the tutorials and occasional papers. The lectures were not tied to the courses and did not have to be attended. Even some British students were disoriented by this freedom. Martin Amis thought it could lead to feelings of isolation. Oxford, he later wrote, "is for the most part a collection of people sitting alone in their rooms, one of which turns out to be you."

But for Clinton, who hated to be alone, there were plenty of diversions. Here he was, after all, surrounded by people who loved to talk as much as he did. Doug Eakeley's strongest memory of Clinton at Univ is a lunchtime scene: Clinton lingering at the long table in the Hall, surrounded by undergraduates long after the noontime meal is finished, chatting away. The younger English students, Eakeley noticed, "were in constant fascination with Bill and he with them. They were so verbally facile. It was expected that you would not just eat and run but eat and talk and debate the great issues of the day until you were thrown out of the dining hall. Bill was always in the thick of it." Clinton also joined a dining club run by George Calkwell, a Greek history don at Univ. The informal club consisted of six dons and fourteen junior fellows. They met in the Senior Common Room to eat, drink, and talk away the night.

There was another club that met more often, a floating seminar that gathered late at night in Clinton's rooms on Helen's Court, or over at Reich's on the other side of Univ in the modern Goodhart Building, or across the street at Frank Aller's place at Queen's College, or over at the Taj Mahal, a cheap Indian restaurant near Balliol College favored by Rick Stearns, who challenged the cooks to find a dish too hot for his palate. This club had no name and a flexible membership of Rhodes Scholars and friends. They would sit in the corner of the restaurant or in the shadows of their rooms, slumped on the floor, leaning against beds, warmed by a heater and some wine, and talk politics for hours. The floating seminar, thought Univ politics don Maurice Shock, "introduced Clinton to a central thing—that politics consists of making use of people you can trust who really are very clever." The topics ranged widely, from the Soviet invasion of Czechoslovakia to the sorry state of American politics to the ideology of Mao Zedong to the British influence in nineteenth-century Crimea, but always, weaving in and out of the conversation, came their feelings about a war they hated and a draft they did not want to face. They were all "quite fanatically political," thought Doug Paschal, and none more so than Clinton, who came to the discussions "with his antennae absolutely alerted and trained."

But Clinton could never cast himself in only one role. He could play the expatriate at night with his American friends, yet move from there to an entirely different level of discourse as he befriended the ultimate source of power at Univ—Douglas, the college porter who had greeted the four Americans on arrival with such disdain. Douglas was a hard-liner on the war and most everything else. He intimidated everyone, even the master and fellows at the college, whom he might order to get a haircut or tell to go to hell. Wilf Stevenson considered Douglas "a true martinet, an old-school guy. He was terrifying. His stern upbraiding shot like a bullet through you. But he was the guy who ran the college and he knew every-thing." He knew, for instance, where to get formal attire or contraceptives and what rooms were available for guests. But it took some nerve to ask him about such matters. The first year, noted Nick Browne, "he might ignore you completely. The second year he might start talking to you.

Douglas was a classic of his time, the old staff sergeant. He had a way of seeing through people." John Isaacson, after experiencing Douglas's hazing on the day they arrived, decided that befriending the porter was not on his must-do list. "I checked him out for thirty seconds and decided it was too much for me. I said the hell with it. I wasn't capable of dealing with him."

The porter's lodge was a twenty-by-eight-foot room on the left side of the main gate. Two paned windows faced High Street and two tall windows looked back toward the college and the Front Quad. A small black door on the far side led into a hideaway bedroom. The T-shaped counter inside the lodge was crammed with keys, notes, mail, and card indexes. There were two telephones on the wall, and two chairs and a coin-operated heater behind the counter. This was the domain of Douglas—and, soon enough, of his buddy from Arkansas. Not long after the Rhodes Scholars arrived, Clinton entered the porter's turf and adopted it as his own. He spent hours in the lodge, answering the phone, passing out keys, spreading and gathering gossip. Isaacson would never forget the odd image of the two of them. "They'd be sitting there, their feet up on the counter, two bull-shitters swapping stories. Douglas would tell stories about the war and Bill would tell stories about Arkansas. Anyone who entered had to pay homage to them. It reminded me of the stores up in Maine where we'd go fishing when I was a kid. You'd walk in and there'd be the proprietor and a friend, and they'd look at you like you were an alien entering their world. That was the porter and Bill."

Several more hours of Clinton's week were applied to another aspect of English life previously unknown to him: rugby. He was more successful at conquering the porter's lodge than at mastering this sport, but he gained some measure of esteem from his British mates for exuberance. The Univ squad practiced on the pitch off Folly Bridge Road every Tuesday and Thursday afternoon and played matches against other colleges on Wednesdays. Univ was in the first division of Oxford colleges and supported two teams. Clinton played on the second fifteen. Chris McCooey, the Univ star and club secretary who played on both teams, thought that Clinton "wasn't very good, but it didn't matter because what he contributed was wonderfully American enthusiasm. Actually, a bit much enthusiasm. He flattened a guy in the first lineup who didn't have the ball. When the ref said you don't do that I had to explain, 'Sorry, he's from America, where you can flatten anyone.' " Clinton was flattened himself more than once after getting his feet crossed while participating in the crablike formation known as a scrum. He played in the second row of the scrum, where his job was to push hard and try to make the ball go back to his side.

After the rugby matches, the players would repair to the clubhouse for

beers or go down to the buttery, the wine cellar at Univ, for wine and
cheese served up by the college bartender. The cellar was located under
the dining hall, about fifty yards from Helen's Court, convenient and
cheaper than the nearby pubs. The pub favored by Clinton and his Rhodes
friends was the Bear, whose old walls displayed the colorful ties of every
school at Oxford. Clinton was a modest drinker by now. Two drinks and
his face would turn bright red. He was partial to the shandy, a concoction
of lemonade and beer. He and some of his pals took rather well to the
uncelebrated British fare, especially steak and kidney pie and shepherd's
pie. To further clog their arteries, they spent many mornings at another
favorite hangout, George's, a sawdust-floored breakfast nook, consuming
mountains of grease: eggs, bacon, and bread all fried in the same pan. Rick
Stearns had a soft spot for the famously unhealthy dish known as Scotch
Eggs, hard-boiled eggs wrapped in minced pork and fried in breadcrumbs.
But some British food was scorned by the Americans, most notably the
kippers that the scouts would occasionally bring around at breakfast. James
Shellar, a Univ-based Rhodes Scholar in the class ahead of Clinton's, would
"look at that fish-eye staring up from oil and say, 'Oh, no thank you.' " He
was not alone. "It was like the miracle of the loaves and fishes when they
came around with the kippers—six kippers could feed the whole hall. The
rest of us would settle for cornflakes."

While Clinton engaged his British mates playing rugby, Bob Reich delighted them on stage. He was an actor and director who took part in every
Univ production. That fall, outside an audition room, he caught sight of a
seventeen-year-old girl who took his breath away. He was "too timid to ask
her name at the time," and when she left, he feared that he would never
see her again. So he decided to direct his own play, *The Fantasticks,* and
when the girl showed up for auditions, he cast her in the leading role.
Claire Dalton later became his wife. Reich was more widely known around
Univ than his big southern sidekick. It was an artsy college whose master
was Sir John Maud, later to be known as Lord Redcliffe-Maud, a tall and
distinguished statesman, after-dinner speaker, and actor. His wife was a
pianist who brought fine concerts to the college. The Mauds and all the
senior fellows at Univ enjoyed Reich for his dash and wit and theatrical
talent. John Albery, then a chemistry don, thought of him as "small and
twinkly, and very clever, very clever indeed."

By the undergraduates at Univ, Reich and Clinton were viewed almost
as an American tag team. It seemed to Chris McCooey that they "were kind
of a double act, those two—Bill was big and lumpy and overweight, and
Reich I guess was kind of a certified dwarf. It was like Laurel and Hardy.
And they were very good value. They added a lot of fun to the college."
Wilf Stevenson also described Clinton and Reich as a team. "They were

quite a sight, swaggering around side by side. They were always deeply into some argument and you'd hear a snippet as they passed by. 'No, you're completely wrong about that,' one would be saying about some political theoretician. 'He was saying something else in that part of the book!' "

When he had surveyed Oxford to his satisfaction, Clinton began taking road trips with his friends. They called themselves the "Roads Scholars." Clinton was known for his wanderlust: anyone who wanted to leave could call him and be fairly sure of landing a traveling companion. They hitch-hiked everywhere, and used their college ties—or scarves, literally—to help them along. Each school at Oxford had a tie and a scarf, with the college colors. According to Mike Shea, "You'd put your scarf around your neck and get some interesting rides and conversations. It worked better during the daylight, when the striped scarves were clearly visible. One weekend Shea and Clinton hitchhiked to Nottingham for the weekend and headed back later than they had intended on Sunday night. It was raining and miserable and they stood by the side of the darkened road for hours before anyone stopped. Looming in the gloom in his long coat late at night, Clinton was not too inviting to pick up." At the time, Shea thought he might be "a lot better off out there with Bob Reich."

Clinton's frequent companion on the road was Tom Williamson, with whom he hitchhiked to London and back several times, and all across the United Kingdom, including a trip to Dublin to see the woman Williamson had been romancing since they met on The Big U crossing the Atlantic. The picturesqueness of the blossoming friendship between Williamson and Clinton, the only black Rhodes Scholar and the aspiring Arkansas pol, was not lost on them. At Clinton's suggestion one day, to break up the tedium on the road, they reversed roles of the worst black and white stereotypes. When cars stopped to pick them up, Williamson sat in the front with the driver and ordered Clinton to the back, Williamson assuming the haughty airs of a southern master, Clinton the shuffling humility of a servant-slave. They enjoyed each other's sense of humor. Williamson would poke fun at Clinton, saying, "You know, Bill, it's really nice that you are progressive and open-minded here in England, but if you want to go back to Arkansas and make a political career, you'll have to make compromises. You'll have to be a Dixiecrat."

Thoughts of Arkansas and his political future were never far from Clinton's mind. That fall a large group of Rhodes Scholars took a bus up to Stratford from Oxford to see a production of *King Lear*. Darryl Gless, the Shakespeare student, sat next to Clinton on the ride back. Clinton talked to him about the play all the way back, relating it to his life in different ways. He told Gless that he was moved by the scene in Act III when Lear is turned out of Gloucester Castle onto the heath and takes shelter in a hovel where he encounters the poor for the first time. "That scene," Gless recalled later, "prompted Bill to talk about his eagerness to go back to Arkansas—to give something back to the place that gave him opportunities that his family could not have bought. As we were riding home that night, Bill talked about his mother, a nurse like mine. He told me about his father and his stepfather, who had died, like mine. We were both from small towns in rural states. We talked a lot about our lives, but he kept coming back to his aspirations and the play. He was struck that Lear had been on the throne for decades before he learned the first thing about how his subjects lived."

Clinton had a fascination with how other people lived. Curiosity about the people around him was one of his strongest traits, the main intersection of his gregarious, empathetic personality and his political ambition. Some people watched Clinton in action and marveled at his big heart. Paul Parish could see it "any time you were with him and you met a third person, a friend of yours who Bill did not know. That friend would end up telling Bill things about himself. The kinds of things Bill brought out in people were the kinds of things you wanted to be around. People's souls shined in their faces when they were talking to Bill." There was another dimension to it. Clinton had already heard the stories about how Lyndon Johnson could tell whether someone was for him or against him with one look into the person's eyes.

He was always searching out more eyes to practice on. After watching him operate that fall at Oxford, John Isaacson, the Dartmouth debater who had political dreams of his own, was intrigued by Clinton's political aptitude in artful conversation. Isaacson concluded that Clinton "had two moves, the Sponge move and the Radar move. The Sponge move was to soak information and give it back. The Radar move was Clintonesque. He was not so much a talker as a bouncer. He would try out different versions of what he thought and bounce them off you while looking at your eyes. That was his radar system. When the radar hit the eyes, he knew it. I remember feeling like he was throwing stuff at you and you had to react to it. It was charming and yet slightly annoying, like, what is this? People would say he was a great listener, and he was in a way, but you were on Bill's topics when you were with Bill. Not that he didn't have a lot of topics, but you were working in Bill's territory. Big territory, but his territory. He was capable of keeping it that way. I was frustrated and awed by it. I was aware of it as a source of power. He was smart and morally earnest, and also a bullshitter who told stories."

How long could this leisurely life of nonstop bull sessions last? Clinton pondered that question one night in December, at the end of the Michaelmas term, as he walked the streets of London. He had listened to the symphony that night at "the majestically royal Festival Hall on the Thames," he wrote in a letter to Denise Hyland in New York. Then he had crossed the river and followed the lights of the city to Westminster. He stopped, he said, "for a brief conversation with Abe Lincoln, who stands in the square," then walked on to Trafalgar Square, then to the tube station and back to the Chelsea apartment of a friend. "It was a beautiful night," Clinton wrote. "One good for putting the pieces of life together and threading the past through today to tomorrow." Too soon, he feared, the Oxford idyll would be his past and the U.S. armed forces would be his present and perhaps Vietnam his future. He told Denise that the Selective Service System wanted him to take his draft physical in London in January. He expected to be called for the draft by March 1, 1969.

FOR two months at Oxford it had been damp and cold, and it seemed to the Rhodes Scholars that it was as chilly inside as out. A forty-degree temperature there felt to them like twenty degrees back in the States. Even U.K. students from the north felt colder in Oxford than in their native realms. Wilf Stevenson, who had grown up in Glasgow, thought Oxford was worse than Scotland. "There's a cold edge that comes off the Thames and hits Oxford, making it at times enormously cold and wet and horrid and dark." Oxford was a fine place from which to flee when term ended and a six-week break began. The Rhodes Scholars scrambled across the continent looking for sun. Darryl Gless headed for Italy, "descending from the Alps out of the mist and fog and rain and snow and ending up in this sunny land where the people were sunny, too." Daniel Singer went "assrunning . . . to Alicante in search of the warmest spot on the European continent, ruminating on consciousness all the while."

Strobe Talbott ventured the other way, to where it was colder still. He was the first of his Rhodes group to visit Moscow. The forty-eight-hour train ride began in Holland and carried him across the continent into Russia. He spent almost a month there, living at Moscow's Metropol Hotel. At Yale, Talbott had concentrated on nineteenth-century Russian literature and poetry. He was so earnest about it that in his first-year Russian literature class he bought two copies of the textbook on the Russian short story and cut and pasted them into large notebooks so that he could annotate every page. But his prep school literalness concealed a poet's soul. He loved to read Russian poetry and tried to write his own.

At Oxford, Talbott took an interest in the modern Soviet poet Vladimir Mayakovsky, a lyric writer who became known as the poet of the Revolution, the Bolshevik darling who had a falling out with Stalin and shot himself in 1930. Talbott was in Moscow to learn more about Mayakovsky, and while there was granted an audience with the poet's mistress, Lillia Brik. He also connected with some passive dissidents, who quietly shared their sense of despair with him. They took him to a Polish Catholic church and to a synagogue. "It was the depths of the Brezhnev period, with the intelligentsia on trial, the invasion of Czechoslovakia had occurred earlier in the year, the depths of the Cold War with really bad cultural politics," Talbott recalled later. "Moscow was grim, grim, grim." In the midst of the grimness, Talbott started a tradition that all his friends who followed him there over the next two years continued. He bought as much Stolichnaya vodka as he could afford and brought it back to Oxford.

Clinton made the longest journey during that school break. He went home to Arkansas. He had not planned to go, but Virginia was getting married again, to her third husband, Jeff Dwire, and Dwire had contacted him at Oxford and made arrangements for Bill to come back to surprise his mother. "Mother's marrying a man who runs a beauty parlor," is how Hannah Achtenberg recalled Clinton breaking the news to his Oxford friends. Achtenberg was touched by Clinton's utter lack of self-consciousness about it. He did not say businessman or entrepreneur—"he just said the man ran a beauty parlor."

Dwire, in fact, had once run the most popular beauty parlor in Hot Springs, where he charmed Virginia and scores of devoted clients and traded gossip with them. He was responsible for creating Virginia's trademark coiffure, persuading her to keep the white racing-stripe streak in her hair by dyeing the hair around it. Dwire was a divorced handyman with a decidedly checkered past. In the early 1960s, he had been convicted in a stock-swindling case and served nine months in prison. Some of Virginia's friends were shocked and disappointed that she would consider marrying an ex-con. Many of Dwire's former clients were surprised that he would choose Virginia from among the many women he had charmed. With his swept-back slick hair, long sideburns, and soft, charming demeanor, Dwire embodied the contradictions of Hot Springs, the town of secrets and vapors and ancient corruption, and the two sides of Virginia, who worshiped her high-achieving son, yet was attracted to horse racing, gambling, and fast-talking men.

In a letter to Denise Hyland, Clinton said his mother had never seemed so happy as when she walked in her front door and saw him. "The surprise came off," he wrote. "She cried and cried." Virginia had thought it would be her first Christmas without her son. "I had no earthly idea he was coming back. Jeff had arranged it. I walked in the door and dropped the mail, and stooped down to pick it up, and there were these two big feet by the door. It was Bill. They were lucky I didn't die!"

There were plenty of friends eager to see Clinton when he got home, including Carolyn Yeldell, who was back from Indiana University for the holidays. Since she had inadvertently seen Clinton kissing Miss Arkansas the previous summer, Yeldell had tried to quell her longtime affection for him. Now that Bill was home, she decided to give it one last try. Clinton invited her to a reception for his mother and new stepfather at the lakefront home of Marge Mitchell, Virginia's close friend. As they were driving along, Yeldell turned to him and said, "Bill, you are still really interested in Sharon, aren't you? You really do care about Sharon, don't you?" Clinton said nothing. He would not look at Yeldell. He was not only interested in Sharon Evans but also in Ann Markesun from Georgetown and several other young women he had met overseas. "There was no answer there," Yeldell says. "So I had to read the silence."

That night, back at her bedroom in the parsonage across the shrubs from the Clinton home on Scully Street, Yeldell sought out one final counsel. She fell to her knees and asked, "God, am I supposed to marry Bill Clinton?" The answer that screamed inside her was a resounding: " 'No! He'll never be faithful!' "

To young Bill Clinton, friends were links in an ever-expanding network. Sharon Ann Evans, for instance, had introduced Clinton to Governor Winthrop Rockefeller the previous summer, and now, on a Saturday during his winter break, he managed to get himself invited up to Winrock, the Rockefeller estate. Although Rockefeller was a Republican, Clinton admired his progressive views on race. If Clinton broached the subject of his precarious draft situation with Rockefeller, there is no documentation of it. He does not mention the subject in a thank-you letter that he wrote to the governor a few days later. He was thinking farther into the future, past the draft and the Vietnam War to a time when he might have Rockefeller's job. "Thank you for having me at Winrock last Saturday and for taking the time to talk with me about your work," Clinton wrote. "Now I have a better understanding of where we are in Arkansas and what we should be doing. Now I have more sympathy for you. But I have envy too, because your hard won chair, for all its frustrations, is full of possibilities."

Few of the boys Clinton grew up with were in Arkansas that winter. Two of his oldest friends, David Leopoulos and Ronnie Cecil, had gone through the ROTC program at Henderson College in Arkadelphia and were now serving in the Army overseas—Leopoulos near Pisa, Italy, and Cecil in Korea. Phil Jamison was completing his training at the U.S. Naval Academy, none too excited by the prospect of flying helicopters in Vietnam but ready to go when the time came. Jim French, the handsome high school quarterback whose father was a respected physician in Hot Springs, was at the Marine Corps officer training school at Quantico. French's neighbor and friend, little Mike Thomas, a kid who kept getting cut from the high school football team but never gave up, had just arrived in Vietnam to lead a long-range reconnaissance platoon for the 1st Cavalry after being trained in jungle warfare in Panama. Bert Jeffries, the son of Clinton's Sunday school teacher at Park Place Baptist Church, was up near the demilitarized zone with a Marine Corps recoilless rifle platoon. Duke Watts and Ira Stone were also with the Marines near the DMZ.

Two soldiers from the Hot Springs High School class of 1964 were already back from Vietnam. Tony Fuller and Tommy Young had come home in caskets.

CHAPTER NINE

FEELING THE DRAFT

THE DAY WHEN Bill Clinton would have to confront his military obligation was looming. Sometimes it appeared close at hand, sometimes further away. Almost every month his expectations shifted. During his surprise trip home to Hot Springs for Christmas, he must have had contact with the Garland County Draft Board or picked up a hint of inside information from his new stepfather, Jeff Dwire, who was in frequent contact with the board secretary, because he would return to Oxford believing that his induction might be delayed several more months. "Time to get back to my other newer life for whatever time I have left," he wrote to Denise Hyland after watching the New Year's Day bowl games on television at his mother's house. "Looks like I will finish the year now."

But not long after he arrived back at Oxford for the second eight-week term, it seemed less likely that he would finish the year. On January 13, 1969, eight months after his draft board first reclassified him 1-A, Clinton finally took his preinduction armed forces physical examination at a U.S. air base near London. In a letter to Hyland, he noted that he had passed the physical and now "qualified as one of the healthiest men in the western world." The order to take the preinduction physical was a signal that his draft board considered Clinton's induction imminent. Draft regulations allowed graduate students who received induction notices to finish the term they were in, but there was some confusion as to how that would be interpreted at Oxford, which worked on a three-term system. It remained unclear what Clinton would do. If only, he told one friend, the draft system had been reformed in the way he once proposed in a paper written at Georgetown, so that young men could seek alternative service in the Peace Corps or Vista rather than fight in wars that they did not believe in. There was no such choice for him now if and when the draft board called his name.

Still, the decision was not yet upon him. For Frank Aller, the Rhodes Scholar from Washington State, the time for action had arrived. Aller, an aspiring journalist, had received a notice from his home-town draft board in Spokane ordering him to report for induction into the Army. He could not claim to be a conscientious objector, Aller told friends, because he believed that some wars were worth fighting, though not the war in Vietnam. His friends sensed Aller's turmoil. They stayed up late at night with him and took long walks through the Magdalen deer park talking about the options of resisting and maybe going to Sweden or Canada. Aller chose to stay in Oxford and fight the U.S. Selective Service System. On January 20, he mailed a letter to his draft board saying that he could not in good conscience report for military service. "I believe there are times," Aller wrote, "when concerned men can no longer remain obedient." He later explained his motivations in a letter to Brooke Shearer, Derek Shearer's sister and Strobe Talbott's girlfriend and future wife:

> When I decided to refuse induction . . . there were really two considerations which were foremost in my mind. One was the hope, expressed by the resistance movement on the west coast and elsewhere, that the spectacle of young men refusing to fight in a war they opposed would "move the conscience of America" and have some kind of tangible impact on American politics. The other consideration was more personal: an expression of the horror and revulsion we have all felt about the war, and the belief that a person should try to take action in accordance with his convictions.

Of all the Americans at Oxford, Aller presented the most interesting juxtaposition with Clinton. They seemed alike in some ways: two bright young men out of the middle class, tall and engaging, gentle and empathetic, consumed by politics and world affairs, readers, talkers, listeners, always at the center of things. All of this they had in common, yet they were very different. Aller was thin, resolute, and fragile-seeming; Clinton was lumpy and unbreakable. Aller was sweet and ironic, shaped by the reserve and skepticism of Pacific Northwest Presbyterianism, prone to quiet mood shifts. Clinton was warm, temperamental, and sappy, shaped by the gregariousness and face-value Baptist piety of his Arkansas roots and freewheeling Hot Springs. For Aller, every moment presented a moral choice. Clinton confronted life as an optimist: each moment offered an opportunity.

Aller was in Oxford on the day that he was supposed to report for induction in Spokane. His friends held a party for him that night at Isaacson's place at Univ. Willie Fletcher, who had shared that moment of joy with Aller when they got off the Greyhound bus and stood in the drizzle in western Washington, freshly anointed Rhodes Scholars, the whole world in front of them, felt awkward at the party. He was as opposed to the war as his buddy, yet he had slipped around it by joining the Navy, and Aller had met it head-on and was resisting. Fletcher was experiencing "not only great admiration and love for Frank" but a feeling of doubt about himself and the course he had chosen. Aller was quiet throughout the night. Reich, who kept making toasts, later wrote that the evening was one of his most vivid memories of the Oxford years:

> I remember it was drizzling. . . . John Isaacson's room was bedecked with flowers and champagne. We played Judy Collins and Leonard Cohen albums late into the night. At midnight we toasted Frank. He said a few words in response, something about the war, and friends, and America. By one o'clock most of us were slightly tipsy or beyond. I can vaguely see Strobe and John, gently guiding Frank out the door toward the bathroom. Hannah Achtenberg was in the corner, a bemused expression crossing her face. There was a sense of triumph, somehow. America and the war seemed sinister at that moment, and so foreign, and we so helpless to do anything about it, that Frank's decision seemed to fortify us against it. Within that tiny room . . . amidst the pillows and champagne, I felt that we all had triumphed.

Aller was the first one out of the foxhole. "We all knew how to work the system," recalled Daniel Singer. "We knew what to do in the foxhole—to keep our heads down. We were going for a lot of ludicrous 4-Fs." One American at Oxford was trying to eat his way out of military service. A former Yale classmate of Singer and Talbott's had starved himself into a 4-F. It was not uncommon for Americans at Oxford to check into the Warneford Hospital in pursuit of psychiatric deferments. Sara Maitland, then the girlfriend of Paul Parish, noted that "there was very much the feeling that no one was going to go and anything you could do was legitimate. But there was also the feeling at bottom that Frank was right and everybody else was cheating." Fletcher thought Aller was idolized because he had done something the others had only talked about. "All of us in some form talked literally or metaphorically about resisting—'What if I go to Canada or Sweden,' that type of thing, the options. And yet we knew at the time that Frank was one of the few who would really do it."

Aller's resistance marked a turning point for the Rhodes crew. Perhaps the change was under way in any case, but it became more ominous around then. Richard Nixon had campaigned on the promise of a secret plan that would bring the war to an end, but now he was president and his presence in the White House brought no prospect of peace. The hope that the war would be over in 1969, the year of greatest vulnerability for the scholars, appeared dim. The war was going on. There were more than a half-million American troops in Vietnam. The quotas of fresh inductees filled by local draft boards were rising month by month. Among the young men who had sailed away on the S.S. *United States* four months ago, the war and the draft were wiping out earlier sensations of awe and escape.

Not long after Clinton took his preinduction physical, Paul Parish went to the military base at South Ruislip outside London for the same examination. Parish was so frail that many of his friends thought he would flunk the physical. But, he "failed to fail." He returned to Oxford and began a grueling process seeking a conscientious objector exemption on the grounds that serving in the military violated his moral beliefs. One other member of their Rhodes class, George Butte, had applied for conscientious objector status even before he left for Oxford the previous summer and was granted it with virtually no challenge from his Phoenix draft board. Butte even got permission from a draft board in Maine, where he was scheduled to perform his alternative service by teaching at a school, to go off to Oxford instead and fulfill his conscientious objector responsibilities upon his return. But every local board operated differently, using wide discretion within the same national rules. One of the top draft officials in Mississippi seemed a difficult obstacle for Parish to get around. He had declared that no Mississippi boy was going to disgrace the state and that where conscientious objectors belonged was on the front line.

As soon as Parish decided to apply for the exemption, he found himself struggling to maintain his equilibrium. He needed someone to talk to, and the person he found most available was Bill Clinton. It was not just that Clinton was sympathetic and enjoyed helping other people with their burdens; he was also the easiest one to impose on because he never seemed to sleep. Late at night, Parish would slip out the back gate of Christ Church, across the alley to the back of Univ on Helen's Court, and up the almshouse steps to confer with his southern compatriot. Once, when they talked all night, Parish got locked out of Christ Church and crashed on Clinton's floor. Their talks were filled with self-doubt. Clinton, according to Parish, would express his concerns that the draft system was unfair, "that poor people didn't have the same access to networks of people who knew the ropes, to help them make the cases they needed or to pull strings for them." Parish's qualms were on a less political level, that he "might just be shimmying out of it." Each of them wondered whether they would be able to live with themselves whatever happened.

Parish covered his insecurities, the chill of Oxford, and the heat of the war, by transforming his exterior. He was the first in his class of scholars to affect a British accent and English mannerisms. With his wit and refined artistic sensibilities, Parish charmed the ruling-class Oxford set that circled around Sir Edgar Williams, the warden of Rhodes House. He fell in love with Sara Maitland, a delightful young woman who was four years younger, in her first year at St. Anne's College, one of the handful of women's schools at Oxford. Maitland had grown up in a generous mansion in southwest Scotland, but at Oxford she began rebelling against her aristocratic roots and found Americans refreshing. She immediately took to Paul and Bill, Frank and Rick and Strobe, and their friends, and began inviting them over to her rooms at St. Anne's for Tuesday afternoon tea parties.

If it is possible that a big-fisted, southern-accented, politically ambitious American was nonetheless born for a British tea party, that unlikely person would be Bill Clinton. His first tea party, with "young men and women talking about this and that, just being clever about something," left him greatly impressed "by how well they all spoke and what an emphasis there was on it." Maitland was equally charmed by the talkative chap from Arkansas. She considered Clinton "quite easily the most gregarious human being" she had ever encountered.

Maitland lived in the attic of a Georgian terrace house at No. 9 Park Town, with a sloped-ceiling parlor where a dozen students might gather for tea. The sessions organized by "The Lady Sara," as Aller and Clinton called her, and her college roommate, Katherine Vereker, were especially popular with the Rhodes boys. "It was a very good way to meet English people and especially English women," according to Maitland. "The Rhodes guys kind of missed the sociability of women: Oxford was such a male-dominated society. But here it was free house. It was tea in the afternoon. It was talk. Lots of politics. Lots of literature. Bits of philosophy. How ghastly our parents were. Who was sleeping with whom." They often discussed books. Clinton introduced Maitland and the others to the southern writers William Faulkner, Reynolds Price, Flannery O'Connor, and Carson McCullers. And they were all reading Montaigne and Rousseau— looking for what Maitland called "the modern lessons in those essays." Clinton took an immediate interest in Vereker, a stunningly good-looking student of politics whose father was a senior professor of philosophy. They were a couple on and off, though never together for very long stretches of time. Vereker was not as taken with Clinton as he was with her. What people remember most about them is that they loved to dance together. Maitland remembered Clinton as "a very enthusiastic dancer."

This was hardly a wild crowd, considering what wild implied in 1969. There was some casual sex, quite a bit of drinking, and the sweet smell of marijuana and hashish clung to their clothing as they gathered in cloistered rooms for late night parties. *Cherwell* declared that year that students were smoking more pot than ever. Cannabis was "incredibly easy to lay your hands on," according to the report, which said that most pot was smoked by small groups of friends gathering in their flats. It cost between four and six pounds per half-ounce. Maitland places the Rhodes circle on the tame edge of the drug culture. "Nothing beyond dope, nobody using acid. Somebody may have tried mescaline. Some pot and hash in the evenings."

Martin Walker, the Balliol College journalist who was dating one of Maitland's friends, said that hashish was even more readily available than marijuana. "We would scramble it into tobacco cigarettes. We'd take out the tobacco from a standard English cigarette, hold a match up to a lump of hashish, put it in, and smoke that." Clinton was at many of the parties. He was with a group that went to a rock concert in London and smoked marijuana beforehand at a London apartment. Paul Parish, experimenting with dope for the first time, blacked out on the way down the steps, and Clinton carried him back inside. Decades later, Clinton would be ridiculed for grudgingly acknowledging that he had smoked marijuana overseas and then quickly adding the caveat that he did not inhale. Was it true? "We spent enormous amounts of time trying to teach him to inhale," Maitland recalled. "He absolutely could not inhale." The problem with Clinton was that he did not know how to smoke and could not take the tobacco, according to Walker, whose lasting image of Clinton at those parties is of the big southerner leaning his head out an open window gasping for fresh air. "He was technically correct to say that he did not inhale."

ONE day that winter, Charlene Prickett got a call from "this delightful, cheery young man who announced himself as Bill Clinton." He had never met or talked to Prickett before, but told her that he had compiled a list of the names, addresses, and telephone numbers of every Arkansan studying in England. She was on his list. She had grown up in Batesville and graduated from the Presbyterian-sponsored liberal arts school there, Arkansas College, before heading off to Europe on a one-year Rotary International scholarship to study at Leicester University. Not surprisingly, Clinton and Prickett had a few friends in common. One was Sharon Ann Evans, the former Miss Arkansas, one of Clinton's down-home girlfriends. Prickett had been Miss Batesville and had become friendly with Evans on the Arkansas beauty pageant circuit. Their other mutual acquaintance was Cliff Jackson, who was studying at St. John's at Oxford on a Fulbright fellowship and before that had attended Arkansas College with Prickett. Jackson was now dating Prickett's best friend at Leicester and had in turn introduced Prickett to her boyfriend and future husband, a Canadian Rhodes Scholar named

Jim Waugh who was also studying at St. John's. Jackson knew Clinton because they were teammates on Oxford's subvarsity basketball squad, although no doubt Clinton would have hunted him down anyway in his pursuit of every young Arkansan in the British Isles.

Clinton told Prickett that he wanted to visit that weekend. Fine, Prickett said, but she would not be there because she was heading in the opposite direction, down to Oxford, to see her boyfriend. Arrangements were made for Clinton to take the train to Leicester and sleep in Prickett's bed. "I was toddling to the train station with my suitcase and here came this tall, gorgeous man with his suitcase the other way," Prickett later recalled. "We met on the street between my place and the train station. He said, 'You must be Charlene,' and I said 'You must be Bill.'" Her flatmates, three British women, were expecting the Rhodes Scholar. He charmed them all and started dating one of them, an undergraduate from the Midlands. All three British women, according to Prickett "kind of went ga-ga" over Clinton. "There was a little tension in the household. I wanted to stay right out of that. I wasn't about to play favorites. I was aware that Bill had lots of friends."

As a way of returning the generosity, Clinton encouraged Prickett to stay at his place at the old almshouse whenever she traveled to Oxford to see Jim Waugh. Oxford rules then still prohibited overnight stays by members of the opposite sex, but the rules did not seem to apply to Clinton. Douglas the porter did not simply look the other way when it came to Clinton's friends; he looked out for them and provided them with extra pillows and blankets and keys if necessary, such was the bond in the Douglas-and-Bill club. Prickett visited frequently as her romance with Waugh intensified.

Waugh was in a singular position to witness the birth of an Arkansas rivalry that reverberated down through the decades, a one-sided rivalry, in truth, that existed virtually without Clinton's awareness yet in some ways became among the most revealing of his career—his relationship with Cliff Jackson.

Jackson had sailed to England on the S.S. *United States* with the Fulbright fellows in September, one month before Clinton and the Rhodes crew made the same voyage. He suffered from seasickness on the way over and spent most of the first term at St. John's College at Oxford cold and lonely, taking some small comfort in hot soup he cooked up in a crock every afternoon, unsettled by the darkness of the medieval atmosphere compared with bright Arkansas. He met Clinton in October when they joined the same universitywide subvarsity basketball team. They were both on the clumsy side, glued to the ground, yet as twin towers over six feet tall and more than two hundred pounds, they brought some height and bulk to the lineup. As aspiring young Arkansas pols, they were opposite sides of the same coin. At college, they had each been class president, Clinton at Georgetown, Jackson at Arkansas College. In the summers they had worked in Arkansas political campaigns. Clinton was a Democrat, whose heroes were Fulbright and the Kennedys. Jackson was a Republican, who admired Winthrop Rockefeller and Barry Goldwater. They shared a yearning for accomplishment and a do-good urge of the sort that can grow in bright and hungry children from modest homes in middle America. "I am an ambitious person, wanting to reach the heights of success, and yet wanting to do something meaningful with my life," Jackson wrote to a college mentor during his year at Oxford.

There is no evidence that Clinton thought more of Jackson at the time than that he was one among scores of new acquaintances. But to Jackson, Clinton loomed larger. The more he saw of Clinton, the more he brooded. He realized that he and Clinton both wanted to go the same places in Arkansas and in the world. Clinton seemed so ambitious, so eager to please, so elusive to Jackson. When he watched Clinton in action, was he seeing a bolder image of himself, or what he would have to become if he wanted to make it? Did Clinton have something that he lacked? Did he want whatever it was that Clinton had? Those were the questions Jackson later said he was contemplating after a dinner party in Leicester that both he and Clinton had attended. After Clinton left, a few Brits at the table took out their verbal swords and began slicing him to pieces as a glad-handing phony.

When Jackson got back to Oxford, he wrote his American girlfriend a letter ruminating on the dinner and the struggle between keeping one's integrity and aggressively pursuing one's political ambitions. His girlfriend offered the opinion that Clinton's extroverted personality might be an attempt "to overcome fears of rejection and of insecurity." The number of girls Clinton had dated while at Oxford led her to the conclusion that he needed constant reinforcement from the opposite sex. "Maybe he is indeed a 'politico.' That is something that he must needs ponder about," she said. "You must find the happy medium, Cliff, where control of a crowd is through sincere attention and not cold manipulation. Won't be at all easy."

Jim Waugh, who took neither side in the rivalry, looked at those same Clinton character traits and interpreted them differently. He found Clinton not so much manipulative as flexible, while Jackson was rigid. "Cliff had a personality that didn't deal well with adversity, and I knew it well because it was similar to mine; where the people side of things is going wrong, the tendency is to pull back and wonder why people don't like me. Cliff responded that way. Bill didn't. Bill came forward, and if he saw something wrong, he tried harder. Cliff pulled back when things were not working out in a human sense. He was a control freak. There was a sense that if there weren't people involved, he would be the one at the top of the totem pole. But he had trouble dealing with the multitudes of variety of people. Not everyone is going to like you, so what do you do about that? Treat it as though someone shot you in the heart or as an opportunity to learn more about people? Clinton used it as an opportunity to broaden himself. Cliff tended to narrow down, and ultimately that led to wanting to get even."

For all their sharp differences, Clinton and Jackson shared one preoccupation: the war in Vietnam. Jackson supported President Nixon and hoped that he could fulfill his promise of peace with honor. But his intellectual endorsement of the war was not different in one respect from Clinton's opposition. Neither young man was eager to fight. Waugh spent many evenings with Jackson in the Junior Common Room at St. John's watching reports from the war on television. Jackson was always quiet and somber on those occasions, according to Waugh. "He didn't say a lot when he watched the war. He was imagining: 'What if that were me?' rather than a Canadian like me saying, 'Shit, what are they doing there? Why not get out?' He was torn between his right-wing views and the fact that he could be the next guy shipped off, a concern not atypical of most other Americans at Oxford." Jackson talked to Waugh about the draft. "It certainly was a big issue with him. He was scared of it. My sense was that he was doing everything possible with his connections back home to avoid it. It was something that would come up in our conversation almost every time we met. He would say he called so-and-so or had written so-and-so."

Jackson later denied that he had tried to pull any strings on his own behalf, but acknowledged that he was preoccupied and anxious about the draft—even though he was in less jeopardy than many of his American classmates. Unlike Clinton, Jackson had gone to Oxford with some protection from being ordered back to Arkansas for induction. He was classified 1-Y, a physical deferment that meant he would be called up only in times of national emergency. He had received the deferment after presenting officials with letters from his doctors attesting to his allergies and vascular headaches. But he was a self-described worrier who constantly fretted that his draft board would reclassify him or that the war would escalate to the point where 1-Y's became vulnerable. "I was scared and anxious, yes, like most young men of that period," Jackson recalled later.

ALTHOUGH being in England could not rid the Rhodes Scholars of their anxieties and concerns, it did remove them from the chaos and excesses of 1969 student activism in the United States. Their histories make it probable that the most active scholars would have steered clear of violence had they been in American graduate schools that year. They were on the moderate side of the youth rebellion. But the rage of the times might have placed them in more precarious situations than they encountered in Oxford and London. It was partly a matter of numbers. According to the sociologist Todd Gitlin, the first year that Clinton and the Rhodes Scholars were in England marked a dramatic turn toward violent confrontation on American campuses, with "over a hundred politically inspired campus bombings, attempted bombings, and incidents of arson nationwide, aimed at ROTC buildings, other campus and government buildings. In the spring of 1969 alone, three hundred colleges and universities, holding a third of American students, saw sizable demonstrations, a quarter of them marked by strikes or building takeovers, a quarter more by disruption of classes and administration, a fifth accompanied by bombs, arson, or the trashing of property."

The increasing violence of the American protest movement was a debate topic that spring at the Oxford Union when Allard Lowenstein made an appearance. Lowenstein—the demanding, charismatic leader of the "Dump Johnson" movement, the early Pied Piper of student antiwar activism—was as articulate in his opposition to the Vietnam War as ever, but had become equally vehement in his denunciation of movement violence. By the spring of 1969, his campus speeches were often attacked by student radicals who derided him for still believing in an electoral system. Everywhere he went that spring, Lowenstein encountered a sense of despair among onetime allies in the student movement that led them either to become more confrontational and sectarian or to drop out altogether. Many of the same students who earlier had shorn their hair for Eugene McCarthy or Robert Kennedy's presidential campaigns had now, in the wake of the assassinations of Kennedy and Martin Luther King, the violence of the 1968 Democratic Convention in Chicago, the election of Richard Nixon, and the continuation of the war, concluded that democracy was nothing more than a racket.

When Lowenstein spoke at Oxford, Clinton went with Darryl Gless to hear him. They were both taken by Lowenstein's combination of passion and reason, but the intensity of their reactions differed in one significant respect. When Gless listened to Lowenstein, he heard only the ideas. When Clinton listened to him, those ideas became a part of a political calculus. "I was naive, effusive, extremely enthusiastic about Lowenstein," Gless recalled later. "Bill brought me up short by saying, 'Well, he's good for the times.' I said, 'What do you mean? He's good, period!' But Bill said he was a good politician, and politicians must invariably compromise. I was making him out to be a flawless hero and Bill wanted me to rethink it." Gless got irritated at Clinton for being less enthusiastic, but later concluded that Clinton was right. "Bill's little lecture was: Don't be naive in your hero worship. You must qualify such views by understanding what politicians must do. Bill several times tried to teach me to be a little less naive about the way the world works."

The inner circle of Rhodes politicos, which included Clinton, Rick Stearns, Strobe Talbott, Bob Reich, John Isaacson, and Frank Aller, prided themselves on their sophisticated understanding of the world. They searched for historical connections, eager for the next book that might put their political and personal unease in the sharpest intellectual context. One day that term, Talbott and Isaacson were playing squash on the Univ court when Isaacson took a swing at the ball and thwacked Talbott in the right eye. Talbott was wearing protective glasses, but they were cheap ones that he had bought in New Haven the year before, and they shattered, severely cutting his cornea. His friends took him to Radcliffe Infirmary, where he underwent surgery. Clinton visited Talbott almost every day during his recovery, and since Talbott's vision was temporarily impaired, he sat at his friend's bedside and read to him. After passing along the Rhodes gossip of the day, Clinton would open *Pax Americana* by Ronald Steel, a Democratic foreign policy analyst, which explored the interventionist impulses that had led the United States into Vietnam, and argued that intervention could become "an end in itself, dragging the nation down a path it never intended to follow, toward a goal it may find repugnant."

"What we need are fewer historical compulsions, less Manifest Destiny, more skepticism about the ideals we are promulgating, and a greater realism about the causes in which we have become involved," was Steel's conclusion. "Above all, we need to develop a sense of proportion about our place in the world, and particularly about ourselves as the pathfinders to the New Jerusalem. America has little to fear from the world, although perhaps a good deal to fear from herself—her obsession with an obsolete ideological struggle, her well-meaning desire to enforce her own conception of virtue upon others, her euphoria of power, and perhaps most dangerous of all, the unmet, and often unacknowledged, inadequacies of her own society. . . . It is now time for us to turn away from global fantasies and begin our perfection of the human race within our own frontiers." What Clinton was reading echoed in many respects the work of his mentor, Senator Fulbright.

Another scholar at Oxford who would play a key role in developing that theme in years to come was Richard Stearns of Stanford, perhaps the most accomplished political mind in the Rhodes crowd. Stearns was a year older than most of the other scholars and had arrived in Oxford after a hectic student political career that included a year as vice president of the National Student Association and another working in the McCarthy campaign. At the time they met, Stearns was well ahead of Clinton on the national Democratic stage, though he was the insider type, more comfortable dealing with party functionaries than with constituencies. He seemed outwardly as dour and sarcastic as Clinton was irrepressibly eager. At Balliol College, the incubator of British politicians, he enjoyed leaving the impression with avid Marxists that he worked for the Central Intelligence Agency. Where Clinton was open and obvious, Stearns moved about shrouded in mystery. But he was smart and slyly funny, and he and Clinton hit it off. Stearns later noted that they both "came from middle-class backgrounds and were not embarrassed by it." "And we were the two most interested in electoral politics in the entire group. The fact that I had worked on a presidential campaign fascinated Bill."

When the middle term at Oxford ended in late March, Clinton and Stearns traveled together to Germany, arriving at 9:26 on the morning of March 23, according to the records of Rudiger Lowe, who picked them up at the station. Lowe, the former Fulbright fellow from Germany who had met Clinton during a conference at Georgetown in their senior year, had by then developed a pen-pal relationship with Clinton that would continue through the decades. Also waiting for them in Munich were Ann Markesun, Clinton's last Georgetown girlfriend, and a friend of Markesun's who was already there working as an au pair. The group roamed Bavaria together, exploring Munich and the Bavarian castles. In a postcard to Denise Hyland on March 27, Clinton wrote: "Have been in Bavaria in snow for week seeing churches, castles, landmarks. Staying in a little village outside Munich. Sunday I went ice skating for the first time in my life.... In the shadow of the Alps with beautiful light snow falling."

The brief note to Hyland left out an adventure at a rink in Garmisch, where Stearns got ordered off the ice by local authorities. He had been speed-skating around the oval in Olympic style, his arms pumping long and smooth, one fist occasionally placed with casual grace behind his back, feeling free and easy, obviously impressing the awkwardly slip-sliding Clinton and the young women, when rink officials told him to knock it off because he was digging ruts too deep in the ice for the figure skaters. It seemed always thus with Stearns and women in those days: trying too hard for his own good. His friend Clinton would have much advice for him on that subject in later months, but not now. Right now Clinton was having enough trouble of his own.

Clinton and Markesun were quarreling again, much as they had been the previous September when Markesun had visited him in Hot Springs before he left for Oxford. "She was very attractive and fiery and they were always fighting," Stearns recalled. "If the trip was an effort to get them back together, it didn't succeed." They stayed together long enough to travel with Stearns to Vienna, where they spent much of their time at the opera house, standing in the rafter area to watch *La Bohème* and *Don Giovanni.* Then the tempestuous relationship exploded. Clinton and Markesun not only parted ways, but they threw Stearns into the middle of the dispute. He had been planning to travel on to Italy alone. Instead, suddenly, he was hitting the road for Graz and Venice with Ann Markesun at his side.

On March 29, traveling alone, Clinton headed north to reunite with Rudi Lowe at the family home in Bamberg. Clinton, who had been studying Eastern Europe in his work with Zbigniew Pelczynski, was eager to see the border. He and Lowe drove to the village of Blankenstein in Upper Franconia, a town that was divided east from west by a small stream and a fence guarded by East German troops. Clinton was "very taken by the physical manifestation of repression and animosity," Lowe recalled, and asked his host to take pictures of him at the border. He stepped two meters across the line to pose. "I told him to be careful, they are watching," Lowe recalled later. "He said they wouldn't shoot an American."

No sooner had Clinton arrived back in England than he went off to meet Sharon Ann Evans. She landed at Heathrow for a whirlwind ten-day tour in which Clinton served as her escort, host, and tour guide. That Clinton could move in such quick succession from the brilliant, assertive Markesun to the beauty queen Evans showed that his tastes were as eclectic in women as in everything else.

Evans felt that she was "running with the herd" in England. That was how it always seemed with Clinton, she thought. Back in Arkansas the previous summer, they were together amid a larger crowd of friends. Now it was the same with this new herd: Paul Parish and his girlfriend; Frank Aller and his; Strobe Talbott, Bob Reich, Tom Williamson, Rick Stearns, sometimes Jim Waugh and Charlene Prickett—there was always some combination of interesting new people with them wherever they went. They spent the first five days in London, according to a record of the trip that Clinton kept and later gave to Evans. On Friday the 4th of April they saw Westminster Abbey, Big Ben, the Lincoln Statue, No. 10 Downing Street, Trafalgar Square, St. Martin's-in-the-Fields, Piccadilly Circus, the parade of the Horse Guards, and London Bridge. The following day they toured the Houses of Parliament and watched a national band festival at the Royal Festival Hall. On Easter Sunday, they went to Speaker's Corner in Hyde Park and listened to black power advocates from the West Indies, observed an Irish Republican Army rally in Trafalgar Square, and returned to Westminster Abbey for evensong services.

The next day they toured the National Gallery. When they came outside, they noticed a peace demonstration in Trafalgar Square. The speaker's platform was set up near the statue of Lord Nelson; banners proclaiming "Americans Go Home" were draped across the dais. Evans and Clinton and that day's herd of friends watched the scene for an hour or so from the steps of the gallery. It was the first antiwar demonstration Clinton had witnessed during his time overseas. His presence there could not have been more innocuous, although decades later Republican operatives would attempt to give it a sinister meaning. Later that day Clinton wrote a note to Denise Hyland, relating that he had gone to the antiwar rally and "sat for hours" watching it. "Times are getting tough," he said, referring to the way he and his friends were struggling with the draft and the war. Although he had been playing tourist and tour guide for nearly three weeks and had given hardly a glance at his studies, he felt compelled to give Hyland a report on his academic progress at Oxford. "My work is going well," he wrote. "I might even become an educated man here."

He also gave an optimistic draft update in the April 7 letter. "For now," he wrote, "I hope to finish two years here before being drafted." Why he would write this remains a mystery. Perhaps he had received an inside report from his uncle Raymond Clinton or his stepfather Jeff Dwire. Or perhaps he was just acting out of his innate need to please and to avoid unpleasant thoughts. In any case, it is difficult to imagine why Clinton, three months after passing his preinduction physical and classified 1-A, would think he could avert the draft for more than another year.

One moment when they were alone, Clinton talked to Evans about the draft and the war. In that conversation, he told Evans that he sometimes felt misplaced among the cynical expatriates at Oxford. "My friends," he said, "just don't understand my need to serve."

BERT Jeffries was killed in Vietnam. The word from his mother reached Clinton the day after he and Evans got back to Oxford. James Herbert Jeffries was one of Clinton's oldest friends in Hot Springs, a neighborhood pal from the carefree preadolescent days up on Park Avenue, the son of A. B. (Sonny) Jeffries, Clinton's favorite Sunday school teacher at Park Place Baptist Church. They had stayed in touch through the years with letters and occasional visits home on holidays. Clinton kept up with Jeffries even in Vietnam, and had received a letter from him the previous December. On the morning after hearing of his friend's death, Clinton wrote a note to Jeffries's parents:

Dear Mr. and Mrs. Jeffries,

I heard about Bert just yesterday when I returned to Oxford. Since then I have thought of him so much, remembering backyard football and dreaded band rehearsals and throwing knives in the floor in Sunday school. I remember too that we were baptized on the same night and playfully argued over who would be the last one into the water . . .

Bert had lived a different life from his friend Bill in the years since high school. While Clinton was at Georgetown, Jeffries struggled to find himself. He attended the University of Arkansas for a few years, but never felt comfortable there and dropped out. He fell in love, got married, fell out of love, and got divorced. He moved to Dallas and worked for a printing company. He learned that two of his high school friends had been killed in Vietnam, and decided with two buddies, Duke Watts and Ira Stone, to join the Marines and go over to Vietnam, at least in part to avenge their deaths. "I didn't want him to go," his father said later. "He was only twenty-one, and I was worried about him." But Jeffries signed up and was sent to Vietnam in the summer of 1968—at the time Clinton was hoping he could delay being drafted long enough to sail for England and Oxford.

On March 20, 1969, Jeffries and his squad in the 106th recoilless rifle platoon of the 9th Marines went out on routine patrol ten miles north of Khe Sanh in Quang Tri Province near the demilitarized zone. At just after ten that morning, a member of his squad stepped on an enemy land mine. Jeffries was only a few feet away. The explosion sent shrapnel into his body: his face, head, neck, chest, abdomen, back, right leg and both arms, amputating his left hand. He died instantly. A. B. Jeffries was working out of town when the Marine Corps officers came to his house to break the news. His wife answered the door and knew that her son was dead. The Western Union telegram arrived the next day: "Please accept on behalf of the United States Marine Corps our continued sympathy in your bereavement." More than four hundred friends mourned Bert Jeffries's death at the funeral services at Gross Mortuary on the morning of April 4. He was buried in a graveyard on the edge of town. Duke Watts and Ira Stone came back from Vietnam to serve as honorary pallbearers.

"The thing about Vietnam was that either you wanted to go or you did not want to go," Watts reflected decades later. Jeffries wanted to go. So did he. Watts was proud of the fact that he went to Vietnam, even though he later decided that he hadn't accomplished anything there and he left feeling that "it never amounted to a hill of beans." But he would never want to say that to Mr. Jeffries.

·   ·   ·

THE final term of the Oxford school year started out a mess and deteriorated from there. The tutor Clinton thought so much of, Zbigniew Pelczynski, took an academic leave to work on a book on Polish communism in a
palazzo on Lake Varese in Lombardy. Clinton's supervision was transferred
to a sociologist at Hertford College, but it was never the same. He stopped
attending tutorials, and though he continued reading a lot, he essentially
stopped working toward his degree. Most of the books he read had nothing
to do with his studies. One week his reading list included *True Grit,* a
western written by Charles Portis, a native Arkansan; *The Moon Is Down,*
by John Steinbeck; *Soul on Ice,* by Eldridge Cleaver; and *Progress, Coexis-
tence and Intellectual Freedom,* by Andrey Sakharov. He also reread *North
Toward Home* by Willie Morris, the autobiographical account of a Missis-
sippi-bred writer dealing with his roots and the disorientation he felt when
he left the South. Senator Fulbright had helped Clinton meet Morris in
New York City back in October on the day before Clinton sailed for England. They had toured Manhattan in a taxi, lunched at Elaine's, a writers'
hangout, and talked about the South and watermelons and Oxford, where
Morris had been a Rhodes Scholar twelve years earlier.

In letters to friends back home, Clinton talked constantly about how
much he was hurting and how "heavy" the situation was for him and his
friends at Oxford. He said that he could not shake the feeling that he
should return to America and fulfill his military obligation. But he hated
the war and did not want to fight in it. The war was all around him. Bert
Jeffries was dead. Frank Aller was resisting. Paul Parish was going for a
conscientious objector exemption; he had asked five people to write letters to the Claiborne County Draft Board in Mississippi attesting to his
character: Bill Clinton; his mother and father; Lucy Turnbull, his professor
of classics at Ole Miss; and Sir Edgar Williams, the warden of Rhodes House.

Sir Edgar Williams might seem like an unlikely ally, given his military
bearing and his distinguished wartime service, but he had taken to this
Rhodes class in all of its intense and anxious brilliance. When Strobe Talbott had injured his eye in the squash match, the Williams family invited
him to their house to convalesce after his release from the infirmary. Sir
Edgar took delight in the practical jokes that his wife and daughter played
on young Talbott, who was, he said, "utterly sober-minded." Parish was an
even more frequent guest at the Williams manse. That spring he came by
most days for an hour or so at teatime. "I needed company and they gave
it to me."

The Rhodes boys called Sir Edgar "The Rhodent," though never to his
face. Some were so intimidated by his presence and his circumlocutions
that they never tried to get to know him. But those who did, like Parish
and Talbott, appreciated his dry, amusing soul. He would sit in his leather

chair and smoke his pipe and soon disappear in a cloud of smoke. He was not much for dispensing wisdom to Parish or any of the other troubled scholars, and when he did talk, he was not always reassuring. "He was such a prig about the war," recalled Willie Fletcher, who opposed the war despite his status as a Navy ensign during his Rhodes years. "He once said to me, 'Could you look yourself in the mirror in the morning if you didn't fight in it?'" Yet Williams willingly wrote letters to draft boards in the United States "explaining what it was they were doing at Oxford."

Clinton spent days drafting his letter for Parish, using it as a means of bringing coherence to his own thoughts. He had thoroughly researched the issue, and cited several Supreme Court cases that he argued had broadened the scope of the conscientious objection statute. He later said that he thought it was the best paper he had written all of his first year at Oxford. Parish agreed. He said it made his case.

On April 30, 1969, the number of U.S. military personnel in Vietnam reached its all-time peak of 534,000. The next day, May morning, was a holiday in Oxford. Parish and Sara Maitland, Clinton and several friends went down to the Cherwell for a breakfast picnic, cooking eggs and sausages on a little outdoor stove. It was a glorious spring morning, and the Rhodes group watched with delight as the daughters of Oxford townsfolk, following an ancient tradition, covered themselves in daffodils, jonquils, and hyacinths, and got tossed into the slender river—clothes, hats, flowers, and all. The Lady Sara covered her pink corduroys and flowing silk shirt in flowers and got thrown in with the rest. The choir sang madrigals at 6:00 A.M. from Magdalen Tower and the church bells rang with joy. The days before and after might be clouded by anxiety, but here, briefly, was one perfect day.

Clinton's own May Day of a very different sort had arrived that week in the form of a letter from the Garland County Draft Board. It was the five-page SSS Form 252, the Order to Report for Induction. Decades later, when recounting his dealings with the draft, Clinton would fail to mention that he had received this draft notice. He would claim that in the midst of everything else that happened in the months before and after, the draft notice slipped his mind. But it did not seem insignificant at the time. He called his mother and stepfather right away to tell them the news and to see what could be done. Somehow the letter had been sent by surface mail and had arrived in Oxford after the assigned reporting date. By the time the induction notice arrived, Clinton had begun another school term, and according to draft regulations that meant he was allowed to finish out the term before reporting. He was by no means alone in that regard. A study by the Scientific Manpower Commission released that spring indicated that between 16,000 and 25,000 young men received their draft notices while in graduate school that year and had their induction dates postponed until the end of the term. But there was no getting around the fact that Clinton had been drafted. He wrote letters to many friends back in the United States telling them the news. "You may have heard that I've been drafted," he said in the letter to Hyland.

Clinton talked about the induction notice with Cliff Jackson, who was heading home May 22 to work for the Arkansas Republican party in Little Rock. Jackson wrote letters to his mother and his college mentor in which he mentioned his classmate's plight. "I really hate to come back to Arkansas and start paying those expensive prices for everything," he wrote his mother. "But I'm glad I'm coming back like I am and not like Bill Clinton from Hot Springs, who is a Rhodes Scholar here at Oxford. Bill has been drafted and will have to enter the Army probably in July. It is such a shame!"

Some of his closer friends at Oxford said later that they could not recall Clinton receiving a draft notice, although they remembered him under great duress during his final days in Oxford that spring. Paul Parish carried one image with him, but when he called it up in his mind's eye he could not say for certain whether it happened in real life or in a dream. The memory was that one night Clinton knocked on his door at Christ Church. Parish and Sara Maitland "were really involved in something" at that moment, so Parish did not answer. The knocking persisted for a long time before it stopped. The next day Clinton found Parish and said that he had gone to his room the night before to tell him that he had been drafted. When no one answered, Clinton said, he sat on the steps leading down from the fourth floor of the hall, alone in the dark, put his head in his hands, and cried.

CHAPTER TEN

THE
TORMENT

CLINTON STRETCHED HIS elastic personality almost to the snapping point during his final month at Oxford in the spring of 1969. An erratic sleeper, he slept less. A voracious eater, he ate more. A frenetic chatterer and letterwriter, his communications grew more intense. He spent much of his time alone jotting down his thoughts in a leatherbound diary that Denise Hyland had given him the year before. "The diary you gave me has become one of my most valued possessions," he wrote her. "It is both an escape and an outlet, a staff to lean on and a mountain that defies conquest. I have written on almost all the pages." An accumulator of friends, he found more time to cultivate young women who would listen patiently and with grave concern as he struggled with his conscience. He internalized the fragility of his friend Paul Parish, the conscientious objector, and the moral anguish of the soulful Rhodes resister, Frank Aller. In those ways he had become an exaggerated version of his own flexible character. Yet in spirit he was diminished. His lifelong sense of optimism had reached an all-time low. There seemed to be no larger purpose to his self-absorption. If only, he told his friends, the war would go away so that he could get back to thinking on a nobler plane.

"I do hope you are finding some purpose to living," he lamented in one letter to Hyland. "Peace of mind is not always necessary, perhaps not even beneficial at this time."

The tardy induction notice did not save Clinton from the draft, but only gave him a pocket of time. His future seemed limited to three options. He could submit to the draft and enter the Army that summer as a private. He could join Frank Aller as a resister. Or he could find a way to void the induction notice in exchange for enlistment in a military alternative—the National Guard or a Reserve Officer Training Corps program—that might allow him to continue his education and shield him. The discussions he had with friends about those options were the most difficult of his life, Clinton said later. But his friends knew that he had invested too much time, hope, and ambition in his political future to abandon it by resisting. "Maintaining viability within the system was very important to him. Right from the start we all took his aspirations with real proper seriousness," recalled Sara Maitland. "His wish to be viable within the system was never treated as him copping out. It was clear Bill had a job to do within the system." Resisting, according to Strobe Talbott, was "completely inconsistent in Bill's case with what everybody knew to be Bill's ambition. Bill was going back to the United States to go into public service. There was never any doubt." Their classmates considered Talbott and Clinton the two members of their crowd most sympathetic to the establishment against which they were mildly rebelling. Daniel Singer thought that "Clinton and Talbott wanted to solve problems by established solutions. This whole choice of whether to play by the rules or overthrow the system was not difficult for Clinton. He believed in the rules and he succeeded with them."

Of the options which remained, then, the one Clinton said he wanted to take or expected to take fluctuated depending on the people he was with and the circumstances of the encounter, but most of his effort went into finding a military alternative.

In telephone conversations with his stepfather, Jeff Dwire, Clinton compiled a list of officials he should talk to when he got back to Hot Springs who might help him get into a National Guard or ROTC program. He contacted John Spotila, the friend from Georgetown who was attending Yale Law School, and asked what it would take for him to get into that school and enroll in the graduate ROTC program there. He telephoned Paul Fray, his political ally from the Holt Generation days. According to Fray, Clinton called collect and asked him for help getting into the Air National Guard. Fray, who was studying law in Little Rock and serving in the Arkansas National Guard, came from a politically connected family and had several contacts in the state's military establishment. He arranged for Clinton to take an Air Force physical when he got back to the States.

Clinton also had a conversation in Oxford with Cliff Jackson, who was now about to depart for Little Rock to work for the state Republican party. As Jackson later recollected their meeting, Clinton told him that he had researched his situation and determined that since he had already received an induction notice, the only way he could enlist in an ROTC program or the National Guard was with the approval of the state Selective Service System director in Little Rock, an appointee of Republican Governor Winthrop Rockefeller. "He wanted my assistance getting the draft notice killed," Jackson said later. On May 26, four days after Jackson, back in Little Rock, began work for the state GOP, he received a letter from Clinton. "I got a letter from Bill Clinton on Monday, indicating that he is coming home around July 1 to join the National Guard," Jackson wrote to his girlfriend at Leicester University. "Although quite frankly, it was, I thought, somewhat excessive and politically oriented in that I'm a good person to be on amiable grounds with. Methinks he could have waited awhile in writing."

Why would Jackson act as though he were Clinton's ally and make himself available for assistance if he was as ill-disposed to Clinton as he appeared to be in his letters? "I was ambivalent," Jackson said later. "But he was my friend. He was leaning on me." An alternative explanation is that Cliff Jackson in 1969 was as torn as Clinton, and as manipulative, ready to trade favors with his Arkansas rival. Although there is little documented evidence other than Jackson's letters that Clinton turned to him for help, there is also no evidence to the contrary. Jackson's version of events demands caution but not outright rejection. The broad outline of his story matches a reasonable reconstruction of Clinton's actions, except that he seems to have exaggerated his own role. His recollections possibly are colored by the competitive jealousy he felt toward Clinton during their Oxford days, an animosity that would become inflamed over the years in proportion to Clinton's fame.

If Clinton was scheming with Jackson to void his draft notice, he gave little hint of that to some friends. One of his newfound British girlfriends that spring, Tamara Kennerley, later noted that in their conversations about the war, Clinton always "thought he was going to Vietnam." The way that different people interpreted Clinton's intentions so differently during this period can be explained at two levels. To a certain extent, the contrasting views of outsiders mirrored Clinton's internal ambivalence. At a deeper level, though, it was an indication of his habit of adapting to the people around him and trying to present to them the version of himself he thought each would most admire.

In any case, Clinton's friends bade farewell to him assuming that he would not be coming back. The party lasted three days. It began in the Univ courtyard with Arch the scout serving as bartender, offering the guests Black Velvets—Guinness and champagne. Eakeley presented Clinton with a walking stick and a two-way touring cap, with brims facing both directions. The stick and cap, he joked, were to help Clinton find his way through the jungles of Vietnam. At times the party winnowed down to a few stragglers. Darryl Gless sat in the candlelight with Clinton, "reflecting gloomily over the state of the world." At other times it erupted into a noisy, convivial, let-your-hair-down affair. Rudiger Lowe, Clinton's German friend, who was visiting Oxford, remembered it as the longest party he had ever attended. The highlights were a barbecue picnic on the roof of Univ

and a punting adventure on the Cherwell with a less-than-steady Clinton
working the pole and Lowe certain that "any second we would be taking
an unwelcome bath." To Sara Maitland, the party was another occasion in
which every college rule was flouted without consequence. "Bill had this
room at Univ that was easily accessible and the college porter adored him.
All was waived for Bill at Univ. It was just, 'Oh, yes, go on in!' " It was all
sort of looking the other way. Bill was to have all the rules broken. It was
dead impressive."

On June 26, the farewell party moved to London's Heathrow Airport,
where Clinton boarded a plane for New York. Maitland drove to the airport
in her sports car with Paul Parish. It was, she said later, "just a mess. . . . We
had this tearful departure at the airport. It had all become an enormous
sort of emotional drama. Bill had decided to go. Was it the right thing
to do? The wrong thing to do? It was all very stressful, going back to
Arkansas."

When Clinton arrived in America, it all seemed very different. He stayed
for two nights at Denise Hyland's home in Upper Montclair. His relationship with Denise was changing again. When he appeared at the front door,
Clinton found a suitor already there, Denise's future husband, who was
gracious if perplexed about sharing space with this fellow who was so
burly and full of hugs. Clinton encountered another change when he ventured into Manhattan for a reunion with Willie Morris, the editor of *Harper's* magazine and former Rhodes Scholar from Mississippi. Morris had
impressed Clinton with his charm and wit the first time they met, eight
months earlier, on the afternoon before Clinton sailed for England. But
their meeting this time left him disillusioned. Morris did not seem the
same man. "All the light is out of his eyes," Clinton later wrote. "All the
life is out of his stories."

On his way to Arkansas, Clinton stopped in Washington. Rick Stearns,
who was there that summer helping the McGovern Commission reform
the Democratic party, introduced him to the network of political activists
who still believed in the system and were trying to end the war through
public pressure. And on Capitol Hill he visited the offices of Senator Fulbright. Lee Williams, the Senate aide who had hired Clinton to work in
Fulbright's shop three years earlier, was now one of the busiest unofficial
draft counselors in Washington, advising hundreds of young men who
sought alternatives to fighting in Vietnam. Clinton was by no means alone
when at last he turned to the office of the influential committee chairman
for guidance and help.

"They came to us in droves. I had so many young people to see, I
couldn't do my job. We talked about the alternatives. What could one do?
I tried to help every young person who came to me do what their con-

science dictated," Williams said later. "You would never hear us, Fulbright or me, advocate violation of the law. That was not the way to go. But other than that we would offer to help them any way we could. We would call and find out where they were looking for people in the National Guard, where there might be an ROTC slot." Williams, a proud veteran of World War II, thought the immorality of the war in Vietnam justified any effort within the law to avoid participating in it. He often said that he would not have gone to fight in Vietnam himself, but would have found some other way to serve. Williams later could not recall much about his discussions with Clinton beyond the sense that Clinton was going through "a terrible emotional struggle"—tugged in different directions by his hunger for public service and his disdain for the war and the draft. Williams offered to help him search for alternatives. If Clinton learned anything in Washington that made him optimistic about finding an alternative, he did not share it with friends. In a thank-you note to Denise Hyland that he sent from Washington, he wrote merely: "No new developments in the service."

WHEN his airplane touched down in Little Rock, Clinton's mother was in the lobby, radiating excitement and concern. Standing nearby was Sharon Ann Evans's mother, Honey Evans. Sharon had planned to greet Clinton at the airport but could not make it because Clinton had changed flights. She had sent her mother out to apologize. Virginia ignored Honey Evans. She had had a falling out with Sharon Ann earlier that summer when word got back to her that Miss Arkansas had delivered a speech in Hot Springs in which she implied that she might make her home in Hot Springs as Mrs. Bill Clinton some day. Evans had not really said that, though she did mention her friendship with Clinton in a lighthearted fashion; but whatever she said was too much for Virginia, who rarely found any of her son's girlfriends satisfactory. This talkative beauty queen was not good enough for her boy, she thought.

Jeff and Virginia Dwire and thirteen-year-old Roger Clinton now lived in the house on Scully Street. Even though Clinton always talked fondly of home when he was away from it, he now seemed out of place. David Leopoulos was with the Army in Italy. Carolyn Yeldell was spending the summer away and would not be home for a few weeks. It seemed that hardly anyone his age was in town. His mother thought he seemed to have an emotional wall around him: "Bill and Jeff had a lot of conversations about the draft. But I didn't really know the agony that he was going through. I just knew he played a lot of basketball in the driveway. He shot baskets hour after hour. Shooting off the frustration." Clinton wrote letters of anguish to his Rhodes friend Paul Parish, who was spending the summer at Sara Maitland's country mansion in Scotland and working on his appeal for conscientious objector status. The letters, Parish later recalled, "were all, 'I could do this or I could do that.' The tenor was: It is almost impossible to see anything that appeals to the moral sensibility. If good has a taste to it, didn't any of his options have it. All the choices he saw were corrupt."

In his first days home it appears that Clinton saw no choice but to submit to the draft. There was little time left. In a letter he wrote to Denise Hyland, he revealed that he had been given a new induction date: July 28. The local National Guard and Reserve units, which had been checked out by his stepfather, Jeff Dwire, and his uncle, Raymond Clinton, were full. "I am home now and every day it becomes clearer the draft is the only way," he wrote to Hyland on July 8. Later in the same letter he was more emphatic: "I'm going to be drafted. There isn't much else to say. I am not happy, but neither was anyone else who was called before me, I guess."

But the mood of resignation Clinton expressed in that letter was swiftly replaced by a determination to beat the July 28 deadline and find a military alternative. Sometime during that period he tried to take the first step toward enlisting in officer candidate school by taking physicals for the Air Force and Navy officer programs, but he failed them both. "I was just under the maximum size, so I could have got in," Clinton later said of the Air Force examination. "But I didn't have fusion vision so I couldn't live in a plane." He apparently failed the Navy officer examination because of faulty hearing.

On July 10, he drove to Little Rock and met with Cliff Jackson. A letter Jackson wrote to his girlfriend in England the next day described the meeting. "Bill Clinton visited with me most of yesterday and night," Jackson wrote.

> He is feverishly trying to find a way to avoid entering the army as a drafted private. At this moment, though he is still pursuing several leads, all avenues seem closed to him. The Army Reserve and National Guard units are seemingly full completely, and there is a law prohibiting a draftee from enlisting in one of those anyway. The director of the state selective service is willing to ignore this law, but there are simply no vacancies. I have had several of my friends in influential positions trying to pull strings on Bill's behalf, but we don't have any results yet. I have also arranged for Bill to be admitted to U of A law school at Fayetteville, where there is a ROTC unit which is affiliated with the law school. But Bill is too late to enter this year's class unit and would have to wait until next April. Possibly Colonel Holmes, the commander, will grant Bill a special ROTC "deferment" which would commit him to the program next April, but the draft board would have to approve such an arrangement. They have already refused to permit him to teach, join the Peace Corps or Vista etc.,

so Bill has only until July 28 to find some alternative military service. I feel so sorry for him in this predicament—it could have easily been me!

Jackson asked his boss, Van Rush, who was then head of the Arkansas Republican party, to arrange a meeting for Jackson and Clinton with Willard A. (Lefty) Hawkins, the head of the state Selective Service System, who had been appointed to that post by Governor Winthrop Rockefeller. It would take Hawkins's approval to kill the draft notice in exchange for alternative military service, a common practice during that era. Rush made the call, urging Hawkins to meet with Jackson and an unidentified friend who was having a draft problem.

Jackson's claim that he "arranged for Bill to be admitted to the U of A law school" was an exaggeration, but it correctly focused on Clinton's ultimate course of action. The advanced ROTC program at the University of Arkansas did not have quotas and was open to law students. It had grown rapidly in size in the year since graduate deferments were eliminated, becoming a safe haven for students looking for a way around the draft. "We were used to guys with long hair and beards enrolling," recalled Ed Howard, then the master sergeant and drill instructor for the Arkansas program. "I remember one law student saying to me, 'I'm doing it because I don't want to be drafted, but I'll do my best while I'm in.' Another law student in ROTC marched in peace marches. The marches would come by our building and I would look out my second-floor window and see him waving up at me." Fayetteville, then, seemed the best available option for Clinton.

Lee Williams, Fulbright's chief aide, a graduate of the University of Arkansas Law School, had several contacts there and worked the telephone from his Capitol Hill office trying to arrange Clinton's enrollment. His papers indicate that he contacted the director of the ROTC program, Colonel Eugene J. Holmes, on July 16, after discussing the specifics of Clinton's situation earlier with one of Holmes's assistants. A page of notes Williams took while talking by telephone with the ROTC staff indicates that Clinton was hoping to delay his enrollment in the program until he finished his second year at Oxford. The precise though abbreviated notation relating to that call reads: "Must have first year ROTC def[erred]." Another abbreviated notation indicates that Clinton would not undertake the required basic training for the program until the following summer: "Comb[ine] Basic—6 weeks, Fort Benning, Ga. Summer [1970]."

At about the time Williams made his phone call, at least one inquiry came from the office of Governor Rockefeller, according to Holmes's top assistant, Lieutenant Colonel Clint Jones. Jones later recalled that both Fulbright's office and Rockefeller's office asked him essentially the same question—"Could we do anything to help young Bill Clinton?" His reply was: "Probably, have him come in and see us." Clinton, his hair now trimmed, traveled up to Fayetteville that week to make his case. He met with Colonel Holmes at his home and with Lieutenant Colonel Jones at the ROTC headquarters on campus in the old business administration building. Holmes later said that his meeting with Clinton involved "an extensive, approximately two-hour interview." Clinton did not tell Holmes during that interview that he was an opponent of the Vietnam War and of the draft. The next day, according to Holmes, he took several calls from members of the Garland County Draft Board telling him that Senator Fulbright's office was putting pressure on them and that they needed the colonel to relieve it by enrolling Clinton in the program.

Whether Holmes felt unduly pressured is a question that he answered in widely different ways in later years when Clinton's draft history became of political interest. In any case, he enrolled Clinton in the program and the July 28 induction notice was nullified. His draft board soon granted Clinton a 1-D deferment as a reservist.

"On the 17th, eleven days before my induction date, I was admitted to a two-year, two-summer camp ROTC program at the University of Arkansas for graduates and junior college transfers," Clinton wrote to Denise Hyland on July 20. "I will have a two-year obligation just as if I've been drafted, but I'll go in as an officer three years from now. It's all too good to be true, I think. There is still the doubt that maybe I should have said to hell with it, done this thing and been free!" Clinton's sense of being out of place in Arkansas permeated the letter. "It seemed really strange going back to Fayetteville, like going back to my boyhood," referring to the few weeks he had spent at band camp in Fayetteville during the summers of his adolescence. Of Hot Springs he said: "At least I have my hair cut a little . . . and will not be run out of the hometown on appearance. But I will have a month in which I will try to get involved with some interesting and fairly forthright activities of the local blacks and kids of both races. . . . If this letter is a bit disjointed and rambling," he concluded, "it is because I am not yet fully adjusted to the new circumstances and my apparent future."

The letter leaves the clear impression that Clinton thought he would be going to the University of Arkansas Law School that fall, even if he could not begin the ROTC program until he completed the basic training camp the following summer. One clue is the line ". . . but I'll go in as an officer three years from now." If he were to return to Oxford for a year and then attend law school, which takes three years to complete, he would not finish until four years later. Another clue is the line in which he says that he will "have a month" in Hot Springs to work with children. Law school began in a month. Oxford's first term was not until October.

Before working out the ROTC deal, Clinton had vacillated between being resigned to going into the Army and working to prevent it. Now that he was protected from the draft, he seemed as troubled as before. In a letter to Tamara Kennerley in England, Clinton said that the idea "of not being in the Army now and going to Arkansas law school is almost more than I can handle—just having a hard time adjusting." But in that same letter, he also emphasized the antiwar sentiments that had driven him to fight the draft notice in the first place. Looking ahead to the time when he would be done with law school and enter the service as a commissioned officer, he wrote, "Hopefully, there will be no Vietnam then."

One weekend during that period, Clinton drove to Houston for a reunion with three of his Georgetown housemates. Kit Ashby had just finished a year of graduate business school at the University of Texas at Austin. He, too, had been drafted the previous spring and had tried to find an alternative that would allow him to complete his schooling. He had finally struck a deal to sign up with the Marines if they allowed him to finish his program at Texas. It was a deal much like Clinton's agreement in Arkansas, with one major difference: Ashby had a time certain for reporting to active duty and knew that he might end up in Vietnam. The other two housemates at the Houston reunion, Tom Campbell and Jim Moore, were already in the service. Campbell, a Marine Corps pilot, was stationed at Beeville, Texas, and Moore, an Army intelligence officer, was between points on a path that would take him to Vietnam. Although Clinton did not dwell on his own circumstances, his buddies came away with the impression that soon enough he, too, would be in the military. But they also found him having a hard time accepting the likelihood that he would not be going back to Oxford. "His basic desire," according to Ashby, "was to be able to go back."

Strobe Talbott traveled to Arkansas in early August and stayed at the Clinton house in Hot Springs for several days. Attempting to recollect that visit decades later, Talbott remembered hanging out at Jeff Dwire's beauty parlor, playing basketball in the driveway with Bill and his little brother Roger, and waiting for what seemed like an hour or more for Virginia Dwire to put on her makeup in the bathroom. He also recalled taking a tour of graveyards, one where Roger Clinton was buried in Hot Springs, and another where William Jefferson Blythe rested in Hope. He was certain that he and Clinton talked about the war and draft deferments, but he could remember no specifics. Cliff Jackson later claimed that Talbott was "one of the chief architects of Bill Clinton's scheme to void his draft notice" and avoid reporting for the scheduled July 28 induction. Jackson said he had a "crystal-clear recollection" of Talbott and Clinton visiting him at Republican party headquarters in Little Rock and discussing their plan of action. His memory in this is counter to the facts. It places Talbott in two places at once. Talbott was in the Soviet Union in July when Clinton got his deferment. It is possible that Clinton and Talbott, during their time together in August, talked about whether Clinton could find a way to go back to Oxford and delay his enrollment at law school in Fayetteville; but whether any discussions of that sort were held in front of Jackson is based on Jackson's testimony alone. Talbott could not remember meeting Jackson.

WHEN he visited Clinton in Hot Springs in August, Talbott already knew that he could return unfettered to Oxford for a second year. He had obtained a 1-Y physical deferment for a lateral cartilage injury he had suffered while playing football at the Hotchkiss School as a teenager. His "gimpy knee," Talbott later wrote, "was enough to keep me out of the Mekong Delta but not off the squash courts and playing fields of Oxford."

And so it was with many Rhodes Scholars. Boisfeuillet (Bo) Jones, studying at Exeter College, received his induction notice at about the same time that Clinton did and went home that summer resigned to the fact that he would soon be in the Army. He reported to the Atlanta induction center on Ponce de Leon Street at eight o'clock one morning carrying a bag of paperback books and clean underwear, expecting to be a soldier before the day was out, but failed the physical because of high blood pressure and by two that afternoon was free to continue his life of academics and top-flight tennis. In the University College quartet alone, all but Clinton were saved by their own bodies. When Bob Reich took his Army physical, he was greeted by a sergeant who barked out, "Hallelujah! We got ourselves a tunnel rat." Reich gave him a puzzled look. "What'd you say?" he asked. "A tunnel rat," repeated the sergeant. "We need short guys like you to flush the VC out of tunnels with hand grenades." As Reich later remembered the scene, his life flashed before his eyes. Then, in the physical, when he reached the height-measuring station, another sergeant put his hand on Reich's shoulder and said, "I'm sorry, son." Sorry about what? Reich wondered to himself. Sorry I'm going or sorry I'm not going? But the sergeant relieved him with the words, "You're just too short." Reich was an inch and a half under the five-foot minimum. The other roommates had less dramatic draft adventures. John Isaacson, another squash player, suffered migraines, and Doug Eakeley had a shoulder that dislocated enough to get him out of the Army but not enough to keep him off the Univ tennis team.

And so it was with millions of privileged and lucky young men. The student deferment, the gimpy knee, the bad back—most of those who did not want to be in the military found a way out. Of the 26.8 million men of draft age during the Vietnam era, 8.7 million enlisted and 2.2 million were drafted. The ranks were filled with the poor and undereducated. High school graduates were twice as likely to serve as college graduates. The great majority of young men, nearly 16 million, avoided military service altogether through deferment, exemption, disqualification, or resistance. Those like Frank Aller were by far the smallest group: 209,000 were accused of resisting or dodging the draft; of whom 8,750 were convicted.

Many young men who could not get physical exemptions sought refuge in the National Guard or ROTC. The extent to which these were viewed as last-ditch choices for potential draftees was documented by a Department of Defense study, which found that nearly half of all officers who came up through ROTC programs said they would not have enlisted had they not faced the draft. Clinton was one of several Rhodes Scholars who received an induction notice during the spring term at Oxford and came home looking for a way out through the Reserves or the National Guard. The manner in which two of those scholars, Mike Shea and Tom Ward, handled their situations lends perspective to Clinton's behavior.

Mike Shea spent his first year at Balliol College at Oxford protected by a graduate deferment that was no longer supposed to exist. Finally, near the end of the spring term, his draft board in Iowa realized that it had made a classification error and sent him a notice of induction. Shea was not the sort to spend his time "pondering the true correctness and morality" of the war and how best to respond. "I did not have a serious conscience about this. I was not at the same level of introspection and analysis that Aller and Clinton were at. I merely thought this is a really stupid war and I don't think I can stop it but I have no desire to cooperate." So he went home and enrolled in the ROTC program at the University of Iowa Law School. "I did exactly what Clinton almost did. But Clinton had all these conscience problems." Shea went off to basic training at Fort Benning without worrying about whether he had sold out to the military even though he opposed the war. "My feeling was the system was totally fucked. It was just a thousand clowns. I was not making a grand political statement, loved by all—'Oh, okay, I'll go to Fort Benning and learn how to shoot flamethrowers.' My decision was viewed as being an expedient gesture devoid of any moral input at all—which it was."

Shea's casual attitude led to a casual conclusion. He developed bad knees, got a medical discharge, and returned to Oxford after one year in the States.

Tom Ward, in the Rhodes class ahead of Clinton's, also received an induction notice near the end of the 1969 spring term and returned to Meridian, Mississippi, looking for a way out. His position on the Vietnam War was that it was a faraway conflict and that he would just as soon it stayed that way. He acknowledged that his opposition was "in direct proportion" to the closeness of his draft notice. The contrast between his life in England and his upbringing in Mississippi confused Ward even more. The Rhodes crowd had been the most political group he had ever associated with in his life. Now he was trying to find his roots again, to figure out what had happened to him in England. He had been thinking about staying in England, he said later, or "whether to go to Sweden, Canada. Or go to jail. All of that was part of the context of the conversation. I was overwhelmed, frankly. I knew I was in over my head. I had a hard time distinguishing in my own life how much craziness I was going through and how much was just the growing political reality."

His father, an influential Republican lawyer in Meridian, told Ward that he would be making a grave mistake if he went to jail or sought a conscientious objector exemption. He convinced his son that he had only been talking to alienated Americans. But although Ward's father supported President Nixon, he did not want his son getting shipped off to Vietnam as a drafted private. They found a slot in a National Guard unit where he could also coach basketball at a junior college. "It was easy for me to get help. Mississippi is like Arkansas—with the good ole boy network." But Ward, who eventually became an Episcopalian minister in Nashville, felt empty and distressed by the ease with which he escaped the draft. The realization that young men who lacked his connections were fighting a war that he could so easily avoid haunted Ward for years. Yet he also came to believe that even the limited vulnerability that Rhodes Scholars faced in that summer of 1969 hastened the end of the war. "I just think historically the war broke down when we started drafting the Bill Clintons and the Tom Wards. People like my father were not going to have their sons dying in that war and were politically influential enough to stop it. That is the moral ambiguity of the situation."

IT was not until Clinton had offered himself to the military establishment, not until he had signed up for the University of Arkansas ROTC, that he started to become actively involved in the antiwar movement. In mid-August he traveled to Washington and spent several days with Rick Stearns at the McGovern rules staff and visited the Vietnam Moratorium Committee headquarters on Vermont Avenue, where activists were planning a one-day nationwide protest against the war, scheduled for October 15. Clinton had a few friends who were well connected in the movement, including Stearns, but he was virtually unknown himself. He was on the outer edge of the antiwar subculture, according to David Mixner, one of the principal organizers. With his affable manner and expressions of guilt about avoiding the draft, Clinton was regarded as "somewhat of a suspicious character."

But he was not without value. No one in the movement had better connections to Fulbright and the Senate Foreign Relations Committee.

The brief visit to Washington restored Clinton's spirits, but it also reminded him how out of place he now felt in Arkansas. In an August 20 letter, he thanked Stearns for a "wonderful week" that he said was "therapy for a sick man." Stearns, who was more circumspect, took Clinton's anxieties seriously, but not too seriously. "Bill was a lot more revealing about himself and more willing to talk in that vocabulary than I would be. Some of it was a bit tongue in cheek. Some of it was florid expression." The August 20 letter went on to display both of those qualities. "I am home now, still full of the life that your friends and my friends and the city pumped into me. Before I forget, let me tell you how grateful I am to you for introducing me to all those people. Arkansas is barren of that kind, or at least I've found few of them. Maybe they have better sense than to traffic with such a naive, sloppy minded romantic." Clinton added that he hoped he could go with Stearns to a September gathering in Martha's Vineyard planned by young leaders of the antiwar movement. "I need and would like like hell to be doing something like that."

On the evening of September 8, Stearns called Clinton from Washington and they talked about Oxford and the draft. He felt guilty and hypocritical for having the ROTC deferment, Clinton said. Stearns was among the scholars who had managed to get graduate school deferments for the first year, but he had recently been reclassified 1-A by his draft board in California and expected to be drafted any week. Still, he said he was going back to Oxford for his second year. "I told Bill that the only fair thing for me to do was to take my chances," Stearns later recalled. "If I get drafted, I get drafted, but I wasn't going to worry about it. If the day came, it came. I felt that was more honorable than trying to connive a way of avoiding the whole thing." The next day, Clinton wrote Stearns, saying that he had heard from Ann Markesun, who "seems far saner than I am." The draft board in Mississippi, Clinton reported in that letter, was about to meet on Paul Parish's appeal. He had just heard from Parish's mother. "The feeling is he'll get out, but will be called home at the end of the first term to do alternative service."

Clinton then described his own state of mind, a subject he and Stearns had been discussing on the telephone the night before. "My mind is every day more confused than it was before; and countless hours doing nothing save waiting for the phone to ring are driving me out of my head," he wrote.

Nothing could be worse than this torment. . . . And if I cannot rid myself of it, I will just have to go into the service and begin to root out the cause. I wish I could describe to you the quandary I am in, so you could counter with some helpful advice—I have been here all summer in a place where everyone else's children seem to be in the military, most of them in Vietnam. I look forward to going to the U of A, the thing for aspiring politicos to do, and going to ROTC to become a second lieutenant at 26—in between then and now I have this thing hanging over me like a pall. I can't justify putting it off. You see, I haven't explained it very well—the anguish is not that apparent—I am running away from something maybe for the first time in my life—and I just hope I have made the correct decision, if there is such a thing. I know one of the worst side effects of this whole thing is the way it's ravaged my own image of myself, taken my mind off the higher things, restricted my ability to become involved in good causes or with other people—I honestly feel so screwed up tight that I am incapable, I think, of giving myself, of really loving. I told you I was losing my mind. Anyway—I'm anxious to hear from you. I want so much to tell you we're going back to England.

Three days later, on September 12, Clinton stayed up all night writing a letter to William Armstrong, the chairman of the Garland County Draft Board, saying that he never had any real interest in ROTC and wanted to be reclassified 1-A and drafted as soon as possible. But if writing that letter was a cathartic moment for Clinton, it did not resolve his ambivalence. He carried the letter around with him every day for several weeks. But he never mailed it.

The series of events that led Clinton on a path back to Oxford are in dispute. By Clinton's account, he talked to Colonel Holmes and gained permission to return to Oxford for the second year since the basic training that he was required to attend before beginning advanced ROTC would not start until the following summer. Holmes said later that he allowed Clinton to return to Oxford for "a month or two," but expected him to enroll in the law school as soon as possible. But a letter that Clinton wrote Holmes from Oxford in December 1969 in which he apologized for not writing more often—"I know I promised to let you hear from me at least once a month"—is the strongest evidence that Holmes was aware of and approved Clinton's plan to go back to Oxford. It may be that Holmes made a private agreement with Clinton in 1969 that he was embarrassed to acknowledge years later. But if he did, he apparently never told his subordinates about it. The rest of the ROTC staff was expecting Clinton to enroll that fall. Ed Howard, the drill sergeant, later recalled that there was great anger when word spread through the ROTC office that Clinton was not on campus. "A lot of people in the unit were kind of mad about it, angry that he didn't show up," Howard said. "We did not know where he was. All we knew is that Bill Clinton did not show up. We didn't normally have people promise to do something and not do it. He was supposed to enroll come enrollment time that fall. When he didn't show up there was some disappointment."

Cliff Jackson was among those angered by Clinton's decision. He said in a letter to his girlfriend that he was starting to suspect that Clinton's friendship with him was mere convenience. "Bill Clinton is still trying to wiggle his way out of the 'disreputable' Arkansas law school," Jackson wrote in one letter. "P.S.," Jackson added in a letter on September 14, "Bill has succeeded in wiggling his way back to Oxford."

THAT was the day that Mike Thomas was killed in Vietnam. Thomas had been in Bill's class at Hot Springs High, where they had served as class officers together. He was the class mascot, a scrappy little fellow who "wanted to be a jock in a big way," according to Jim French, one of his closest high school friends and the quarterback of the football team. Mike tried out for the football team every fall, and was brought into games only to hold for extra points. Defensive nose guard Bill High, the biggest player on the team, was stunned one day during the offseason when Coach C. B. Haney ordered the boys to pair off and wrestle each other and Thomas immediately challenged High. High later described him as "a fearless little tiger." Thomas went off to the University of Arkansas but did not finish. His father, Herman Thomas, had been a captain in World War II, a veteran of the Battle of the Bulge, who lectured his son on the meaning of patriotism. "Mike was in a fraternity at the University of Arkansas," Herman Thomas later recalled. "All the boys in it were figuring out ways to get out of service. In his second year, Mike got all teed off at those guys. He joined the Army as a buck-ass private. He enlisted, went through basic training, then was held back so he could go to officer training school. He was the smallest man in his class, but made it all right." He went through jungle warfare training in Panama and got his orders for Vietnam. When he stopped at home on his way out, his father thought he seemed "gung-ho, ready to go."

In Vietnam he was a platoon leader in Company E of the 1st Cavalry Division (Airmobile), performing long-range reconnaissance in free-fire zones. His platoon loved Mike Thomas. "He had this kind of charming way of talking, this southern drawl," remembered one of his men, Greg Schlieve from Washington State. "I had never been around anyone like that. He was matter-of-fact—'If this happens, here's the contingency plan.' If we'd say, 'Mike, that's not a good trail to go down, we're hitting contact,' he had our concerns foremost. He wouldn't ask anyone to go where he wouldn't go. During battles and firefights, he was able to direct men and go around and check on your ammo, your water, and somehow by putting his hand on a man's shoulder that was maybe terrified, he had the capacity to calm a man down, more or less say, 'Hang in there, buddy, we're going to make it.' I despised most of the officers. They pissed me off. But Mike never forgot the number-one goal is for you all to come walking back. I just absolutely thought without a shadow of a doubt that Mike was the most courageous man I ever met. He was little—five foot five—but carried the heaviest pack in our platoon—one hundred and twenty pounds. No one could come up and say he needed a break, his pack was getting him down. Every time we took a break, Mike would scooch his pack against a tree and two of us would grab his arms and lift him up. It was too big for him to put on his back alone."

The war was undergoing a subtle transformation on September 14, the day Mike Thomas died. In Saigon that morning, General Creighton W. Abrams, the United States commander in Vietnam, paid an unusual visit to the residence of South Vietnamese President Nguyen Van Thieu to discuss President Nixon's intention to withdraw 35,000 troops from Vietnam and to revise the military draft system back home. Some sixty-five miles from Saigon in the Vietnamese countryside, Lieutenant Thomas put on his pack and led his troops back from a mountain peak they had been guarding. A relief platoon had just arrived. Thomas was driving through a jungle trail in the second vehicle on the way back, with his radio operator at his side, when they were ambushed by Viet Cong. Everyone jumped for cover. The radio operator, who was overweight, got caught in his wires. Thomas crawled back from the brush and was untangling him when a mortar shell hit the hood and killed them both.

Their deaths brought the American toll in Vietnam to 38,953. The Army posthumously awarded Thomas a Silver Star, a Bronze Star, a Purple Heart, and a Good Conduct Medal. The mortar shell that killed Mike Thomas took other casualties as well. For a long time his father grieved that perhaps he had spent too much time glorifying war by talking so much about his own exploits in World War II. Greg Schlieve went through decades of psychological distress after returning from Vietnam. "I have always thought that I should have died, and not Mike. I am the one who was an asshole," Schlieve said later. "I did not like God's plan to take Mike and leave me."

Schlieve eventually came to believe that Vietnam led his entire generation into denial—soldiers and nonsoldiers alike. No one wanted to talk about the real reasons why he and Mike Thomas went to war or the reasons why Bill Clinton and his Rhodes friends did not. "I believe it is hard for a soldier to admit that he went to Vietnam and killed human beings just for the glory of it, or because he had nothing better to do," Schlieve concluded. "But I also believe there is another truth to be told by the students, that they were protesting the war because they were deathly afraid of dying, which is what they should have felt if they were human. Approval and acceptance are of such importance to human beings. Antiwar protesters had smokescreens. They would get enormous approval from peers to be against it. And vets had their own smokescreens. We couldn't see the truth about ourselves, either. We would say we were patriotic, responsible young men. That's bullshit. Maybe ten percent of the true story. For a lot of us who went, we were going after the same thing—approval. We were trying to get it from our peers, from our father who had been in World War II. We were striving to get our father's love. It's hard to see the truth, and many will deny the truth before accepting it. And it doesn't matter if you were a soldier fighting the war or a student fighting against it. We all had our reasons for taking up our battle cries, and I believe our battle cries very cleverly fooled us all."

BATTLE cries. They could be heard one weekend that September at the fashionable Martha's Vineyard estate of John O'Sullivan, the antiwar son of an investment lawyer. Clinton and Stearns were there along with a few dozen former student leaders in the presidential campaigns of Eugene McCarthy and Robert Kennedy. The Vineyard conclave was a reunion one year after the chaos of Chicago. It was a long weekend of touch football, antiwar rhetoric, congressional vote counting, and posturing among a fraternity of ambitious young politicos. Like the teenagers who traveled to Washington for Boys Nation in 1963, like the Rhodes Scholars who sailed across the Atlantic in 1968, many in the crowd at O'Sullivan's estate thought of themselves as future leaders of the free world. One of those in attendance, Taylor Branch, who had just arrived from Georgia where he had worked on a voter registration project, referred to the group as "The Executive Committee of the Future." He said it with a touch of irony.

In Georgia, Branch had seen an old black man dip inside his overalls and show him a hernia the size of a squash. Now he was surrounded by earnest young men in their early twenties sitting around calling senators by their first names. There was Frank (Church) and Harold (Hughes) and Gene (McCarthy) and George (McGovern). "The whole antiwar scene seemed inflated, unreal, compared with the experience in Georgia," Branch recalled. "It was my first realization that people you thought were on the inside really are not so much inside or superior. There is a real nervousness for political people who feel important to get together and be together. This intense awareness of who was there and who had done what. It was the end of the sixties up there, but all those people had their tickets punched for the future."

Clinton took a long walk along the beach with David Mixner that weekend. They talked about their common roots from small-town America. Mixner had grown up in Elmer, New Jersey, a place not unlike Hot Springs in its patriotic fervor. Behind his tough facade as a movement leader whose name was constantly in the papers, Mixner confided to Clinton, he was just a rural kid who felt inadequate in this high-powered intellectual crowd and torn between his hatred for the war and his sense of duty. He felt more comfortable at a picnic in Elmer than at a dinner party hosted by a wealthy liberal. He did not even know how to eat an artichoke. Clinton reassured Mixner by telling stories about his life in Arkansas and how he felt torn between two worlds as well.

"Are you embarrassed," Clinton asked Mixner, "when you go home and meet someone who's in the service?"

"Yeah," Mixner said. "I try to avoid them."

CHAPTER ELEVEN

THE LUCKY
NUMBER

RHODES SCHOLARS WERE provided rooms at their colleges only during their first year at Oxford. For the second year, they were expected to find their own digs. Rick Stearns rented a spacious, rectangular second-floor room at Holywell Manor overlooking a twelfth-century church and graveyard. The apartment had two appliances of note: a short-wave radio from which Stearns learned French and listened to the music of Berlioz, Schubert, and Mahler; and a space heater that created a warm comfort zone of perhaps ten feet. Anything on the far end of the room was apt to freeze. That included the tapwater in the sink as well as Stearns's unanticipated lodger for the first month, his worried pal from Arkansas, Bill Clinton.

No one had expected Clinton back for a second year. He slept on a rollaway bed. He was rootless, moving through Oxford with scruffy hair and a grubby Army coat, the preferred cold-weather garb of the student set. He seemed less connected to the establishment than at any other time in his life.

When the *American Oxonian,* official journal of the Rhodes Association in the United States, published its list of scholars studying at Oxford in the fall of 1969, Clinton's name was not on the roll. He was, in fact, in school that year, but his unexpected last-minute arrival had kept him off the *Oxonian* list. Whether he was a scholar in spirit as well as fact is an altogether different question. The Michaelmas term of his second year was much like the Trinity term of his first—he had little or no interaction with Oxford dons. Zbigniew Pelczynski, who had struck up a harmonious relationship with him the first year before taking a sabbatical, returned to Oxford that fall unaware that Clinton was there. "I was under the impression that Clinton had left and been drafted," Pelczynski recalled. "It was extraordinary and tragic. I might have been able to help him in a difficult time. I have a feeling he felt his future was so uncertain, his Oxford life was so hanging on a thread, that he simply stopped attending tutorials regularly." Pelczynski later examined Clinton's file to determine what had happened to him, and found that during the first term of the second year, Clinton's relationship with another tutor was "very, very tenuous." Or perhaps it was nonexistent. One contemporaneous account indicated that the politics don who was supposed to oversee Clinton was on sabbatical that fall.

So Clinton was freeloading at Holywell Manor and paying little attention to his studies. But he was, finally, something that he had never been before, not at Georgetown during his Fulbright days, not at Oxford in his first year. He was now, briefly, a full-blown antiwar organizer. Through his work with the Vietnam Moratorium Committee, Clinton became a key contact for American students who wanted to lend overseas support to the October 15 protest. Randall Scott, an American student attending the London School of Economics that fall, called moratorium headquarters in Washington before leaving for England to see if there would be a London version of the U.S. demonstrations. He was told to contact Bill Clinton at Oxford. Once he reached London, Scott called Oxford and after some difficulty found Clinton, who said the Rhodes Scholars might take some action related to the moratorium. "Many of us are quite concerned," he later remembered Clinton telling him. Scott talked with Clinton again during the second week of October and was told that dozens of Americans at Oxford planned to travel to London to join a teach-in at the London School of Economics and march to the American Embassy in Grosvenor Square, where they would present officials with a petition against the war signed by Rhodes Scholars.

The American Oxonians held several meetings to plan their London actions. Steve Engstrom, a Little Rock native spending his college junior year abroad, was in Oxford then visiting friends and was taken to an antiwar meeting where, he was told in advance, he would meet a future governor of Arkansas. "My friend said the guy's name was Bill Clinton, and I laughed because I thought I knew all the up-and-comers in Arkansas. I had been a student politician. I knew Mack McLarty. But I had never heard of Clinton." He found that many of the Rhodes Scholars were stridently antiwar and furious with the American government. Clinton, who ran the meeting, struck Engstrom as a voice of relative moderation. "I noticed that Clinton had already gathered the respect of the people in the room. He played the role of moderator. He was standing there listening to people asking questions and people making comments, and he facilitated the dialogue. I was amazed by how he handled an intense situation so calmly. I told my friend later, 'You're right, the guy probably will be governor some day.' "

That Engstrom could look at an antiwar organizer and see a future governor of Arkansas says as much about the time as it does about Clinton.
Opposition to the war was a mainstream sentiment that fall. A Gallup
Poll conducted in late September showed that "disillusionment over the
Vietnam war" had reached a new peak, "with six persons in ten now of the
opinion that the U.S. made a mistake getting involved in Vietnam." The
moratorium, though organized by student leaders, was drawing a broad
range of support from moderate politicians. The presidents of seventy-nine
colleges and universities endorsed the moratorium. Secretary of Defense
Melvin Laird's son announced that he would participate in the protest at
the University of Wisconsin-Eau Claire. Students at President Nixon's alma
mater, Whittier College, said they would light an antiwar "flame of life"
and keep it burning until the war ended.

Amid the panoply of protest on Moratorium Day, the London demonstrators barely gained notice. In a letter to his parents in Wisconsin, Randall
Scott described the scene: "And I can express the feelings of several hundred happy Americans standing in front of their embassy at night with
candles blazing—each one concerned for and not against their country.
This was not a bunch of wild-eyed radicals. To give some indication, nearly
all of the Rhodes scholars currently at Oxford signed a petition which was
presented that afternoon." Another peace petition, signed by forty Labour
members of Parliament and presented to embassy officials by six MPs
who attended the demonstration, was the only petition that made press
accounts. The largest headline in the British newspapers about the protest
was in *The Guardian.* "Mr. Newman Supports Students," it announced,
over a story revealing that the actors Paul Newman and his wife, Joanne
Woodward, vacationing in London, had joined the students outside the
embassy. It was a solemn, peaceful demonstration by all accounts. No one
there was shouting for the defeat of the U.S. armed forces or victory for
the NLF, the National Liberation Front of Vietnamese Communists and
Nationalists often adopted as the home team in football-style chants. Clinton led a teach-in discussion and served as a marshal outside the embassy.
Tom Williamson, who traveled to London with Clinton and was also a
marshal, thought they were "soulmates in opposition to the war," and felt
strongly about what they were doing, but noted that they were also typical
young men who had other things on their minds. "If you were a marshal
you got to stand in one place and watch a lot of people walk by. A lot of
girls. That was one of the fringe benefits."

The fall of 1969 was an odd, rushed, condensed time back in America.
The antiwar movement was constantly splintering, one faction trying to
outdo another. By November, the movement was larger but more fractious
than ever. Another protest was held in Washington one month after the

moratorium, this one organized by the more confrontational but still peaceful wing of the antiwar movement, known as the New Mobilization Committee, or Mobe. On the eve of the demonstration, William Ayers, a leader of the Weathermen, the most provocative of several radical groups, tried to blackmail the organizers by saying that for $20,000 his band of predominantly upper-middle-class suburban white revolutionary nihilists would not trash the November 15 event. Ayers said the Weathermen needed the money to pay for legal bills they had piled up after their arrests for a violent demonstration in Chicago. The organizers refused to pay. A Mobe leader asked Ayers what the ultimate goal of the Weathermen was. "To kill all rich people," came the response. When it was noted that Ayers's father was a wealthy financier, he replied, "You know what Abbie Hoffman says, 'Bring the war home. Kill your parents.' "

The day of the Mobe brought the biggest demonstration in the history of Washington. A crowd estimated by police at 250,000 and by organizers as more than half a million marched down Pennsylvania Avenue and assembled at the Washington Monument. As the event ended, a few thousand young militants scrambled across to the Justice Department and incited a rocks-and-bottles versus tear-gas melee with police. Attorney General John N. Mitchell and his top deputy, Richard G. Kleindienst, looked down on the confrontation from their offices on the fifth floor and seized on the opportunity to portray the antiwar movement as anarchistic, even though all but a fraction of the demonstrators were peaceful and the organizers had fielded more than two thousand marshals to try to keep matters under control.

In London that day the same drama was played out on a miniature scale. Clinton and his American friends at Oxford attended the protest outside the U.S. Embassy in Grosvenor Square. This demonstration was larger than the October 15 event, drawing more than five hundred American and British protesters who gathered at midafternoon and spent several hours marching around the square four abreast. Each marcher wore a black armband and carried a card bearing the name of an American soldier killed in Vietnam. One at a time, hour after hour, marchers stepped before a microphone and read the name of a dead soldier before placing the card in a small coffin. Late in the afternoon, a small band of young Communists came marching down the street, chanting anti-imperialist slogans and taunting the police. Father Richard McSorley, a Georgetown University professor active in the world peace movement, happened to be in London that day, taking part in the peaceful protest. He encountered a young Communist who was yelling "Down with imperialism!" through a bullhorn. "You know, peace activists organized this event and people came to act peacefully. If you had tried to organize it on the theme of down with imperialism, no one would have come," McSorley told him. "You have no right to interrupt what we're doing." Rick Stearns and Clinton "ended up on the sidelines watching various Trotskyites pitching coins at horses" in Grosvenor Square. "There was an ugly mood in that crowd," Stearns said later, adding that he and Clinton "were both offended by anti-American taunts and the aura of violence the groups projected."

At the end of the evening, they announced over a loudspeaker that they would hold a prayer service at St. Mark's Church across from the embassy the following day. Clinton arrived in a suit and tie. He recognized Father McSorley from his Georgetown days and asked the priest to open the prayers. McSorley recited St. Francis's prayer for peace. "After my prayer we had hymns, peace songs led by two women with guitars, and the reading of poetry by a native white South American woman," McSorley later wrote. Stearns recited John Donne's sermon—"Any man's death diminishes me, because I am involved in Mankinde; And therefore never send to know for whom the bell tolls; It tolls for thee." McSorley wrote that he found all the poems moving. "Mixed with the reading were more peace songs. All the readers were young people. Although it was a sad day, it was encouraging and comforting to see the determination of these young people who would stand against the evils of war." And, McSorley noted, he was "glad to see a Georgetown student leading in the religious service of peace."

After the service, Clinton introduced McSorley to Stearns and his other friends, and they again marched over to Grosvenor Square, this time carrying small white crosses, which they placed on the steps of the embassy. There were no confrontations with police.

Decades later, Republican partisans would attempt to portray Clinton as an unpatriotic if not seditious radical for helping to organize the London protests and criticizing his government while overseas. Weighed in the context of the times, the charge loses gravity. Opposition to the war was so strong in Clinton's age group that among the Rhodes Scholars who came to London to protest that fall were Willie Fletcher, who was an ensign in the Navy, and two graduates of the U.S. Naval Academy, J. Michael Kirchberg and Robert Earl. (Earl was nervous about getting his picture taken.) Kirchberg eventually became a conscientious objector; Earl later ended up in the White House during the Reagan years serving as a top assistant to Lieutenant Colonel Oliver North. Another American student at the London School of Economics was more prominently mentioned than Clinton in the local press accounts of the October 15 demonstration. Michael Boskin, identified as a student from Berkeley, California, was quoted in *The Guardian* as saying that the demonstrators had asked the American Embassy to close for the day so that employees could join the protest. This same

Michael Boskin would later serve as chairman of Republican President George Bush's Council of Economic Advisers.

ALONGSIDE Clinton's role in the London antiwar protests was another story —his decision to give up the 1-D deferment, scrap the University of Arkansas Law School and ROTC altogether, and resubmit himself to the draft. It is a difficult episode to sort out, muddled by Clinton's various accounts, which tend to be incomplete or contradictory, and by a scarcity of documentary evidence. The essential question is not so much what Clinton did as why he did it. Was it a decision driven by guilt and honor that should be accepted at face value? Or was it the end-game maneuver of a draft-wise young man playing every angle to avoid military service without appearing unpatriotic or duplicitous? Was Clinton unaware of all the draft news coming out during the time he made his decision? Or was he aware at the time he relinquished the ROTC deferment that actions taken during that period by the Nixon administration had considerably narrowed the odds of his getting drafted again? There is a temptation to choose one or the other explanation, yes or no, rule out anything in between. But with Clinton it is rarely that simple. A civil war raged inside him between his conscience and his political will to survive. It seems that he tried to appease both impulses. At times he might have been guided by virtue. Other times he deceived the world, if not himself.

The question of when Clinton decided to give up the deferment is important as it relates to his truthfulness in later accounts and to what he would have known about his vulnerability to the draft on the day he made the decision. His draft records show that he held the 1-D deferment from August 7 to October 30, 1969. Those two dates mark the days when the Garland County Draft Board met, considered Clinton's case, and reclassified him, first from 1-A to 1-D, then back from 1-D to 1-A. They are not the dates, however, when Clinton took the actions that led to the reclassifications. According to a letter he wrote to Denise Hyland, Clinton struck his ROTC deal with Colonel Holmes on July 17—three weeks before the draft board officially reclassified him. Similarly, it seems certain that Clinton notified the draft board that he wanted to give up his deferment and be reclassified 1-A some time before the official October 30 draft board action. There are no documents substantiating this. The draft official with whom Clinton and his family dealt in giving up the deferment, William S. Armstrong, then the chairman, died before anyone had reason to ask him.

Clinton's first public response to questions surrounding the deferment came nine years later, in 1978, when he was back in Arkansas running for office. His answer was largely accepted as reasonable at the time, though in retrospect it does not hold up. According to the *Arkansas Gazette* edition of October 28, 1978, Clinton, responding to a charge that he had used the ROTC to dodge the draft, stated that "the accusation was baseless because he never received a draft deferment." The central paragraph in that article reads:

Clinton explained Friday that while at Oxford he had decided to take advantage of the ROTC opportunity and had made the agreement in the summer of 1969. The ROTC unit was to mail the agreement to Washington at the end of the year and the deferment would start in 1970. On returning to Oxford, however, he decided against the deferment and wrote to Col. Holmes, the ROTC commander, saying he would prefer to go ahead and subject himself to the draft and get it over with although he would proceed with the ROTC training if Holmes desired. A relative of Clinton's talked to Holmes and was told the agreement would be cancelled, Clinton said.

The most obvious problem with Clinton's 1978 response is his claim that he never received the deferment. It was later established that he had been deferred and that it was the deferment that saved him from being inducted on July 28. His induction deadline was not part of the dispute in 1978 because neither his accusers nor the press were aware that he had been drafted and Clinton did not volunteer that fact. As to the concluding thought in the paragraph, that Clinton said he told Colonel Holmes he would go ahead with the ROTC training anyway if Holmes so desired, there is no mention of this in the only letter Clinton wrote Holmes later, and Clinton never raised the matter again in his subsequent statements on the issue.

Clinton offered a different narrative thirteen years later, during a December 1991 interview with Dan Balz, a political reporter for *The Washington Post.* In that interview, he again failed to mention that he had been drafted in the spring of 1969, and in fact left the impression that he had never received a draft notice. ". . . I expected to be called while I was over there the first year," Clinton said, "but they never did." He then told how he had arranged to get into law school and the ROTC but decided at the end of the summer that "that was not a good thing to do, you know?" He went on: "I'd already had one good year at Oxford, but by then four of my classmates had died in Vietnam, including a boy that was one of my closest friends when I was a child. And so I asked to be put back in the draft. . . . And the guy that was head of the ROTC unit really tried to talk me out of it. He said, 'You don't need to do this.' I said, 'Yeah, I just can't put it off. Call me. Let's go.' I told my draft board. They said okay, if that's what you want, we'll do it. The guy at the draft board then said they were going to call me in January."

There is no evidence that either of the conversations Clinton related to the *Post* in that account took place in the manner he described. Months after the interview, in fact, Clinton acknowledged that he did not directly make the arrangements to be placed back in the draft, since he was already in Oxford by then, but rather used an intermediary in Arkansas, his stepfather Jeff Dwire. Another important revelation came after Clinton's interview with the *Post*—the letter Clinton wrote to Colonel Holmes in December 1969 explaining why he had given up his deferment. The text of that letter, which will be examined in detail later, leaves the impression that Clinton was explaining his actions to Holmes for the first time, making it less plausible that the student and the colonel had an earlier conversation of the sort Clinton related to the *Post.*

The best estimate of when Clinton gave up his deferment can be deduced from statements made by Randall Scott, the graduate student at the London School of Economics who dealt with Clinton while organizing the October 15 teach-in and protest at the American Embassy. According to Scott, when he first called Clinton at the end of September or beginning of October to find out whether the Rhodes Scholars would participate on Moratorium Day, Clinton told him that he was "very uncomfortable being involved in the moratorium with [my] 1-D." Clinton indicated that some of his high school friends had been killed in Vietnam and that he did not feel right protesting while he remained in what might be viewed as a safe haven. He told Scott that he "intended to drop it." On the day of the protest, according to Scott, he met Clinton and told him that carrying the petition to the U.S. Embassy was a courageous act by the Rhodes Scholars. Clinton's response was, "And I told my draft board to make me 1-A."

From Scott's reconstruction of his conversations with Clinton, then, it seems that Clinton, acting through his stepfather, asked the draft board to drop his deferment and reclassify him 1-A sometime between October 1 and October 15.

The fact that Clinton felt uneasy about his deferment and thought about giving it up is documented in the July 20 letter to Denise Hyland and the September 10 letter to Rick Stearns. "There is still the doubt that maybe I should have said to hell with it, done this thing [submit to the draft] and been free!" Clinton wrote in the Hyland letter. To Stearns, he wrote: "Nothing could be worse than this torment . . . and if I cannot rid myself of it, I will just have to go into the service and root out the cause." If Clinton sincerely wanted to ease his torment by entering the service, however, he could have given his draft board chairman the letter he said he stayed up all night on September 12 writing—the one revealing that he did not have his heart in the ROTC program and wanted to be drafted as soon as possible—instead of keeping it in his back pocket for weeks and leaving for Oxford without mailing it. Or, surer yet, he could have simply enlisted. The reason he took neither of those routes is explained in the letter he wrote to Colonel Holmes a few months later, in December 1969, in which he said, ". . . I didn't see, in the end, how my going in the army and maybe going to Vietnam would achieve anything except a feeling that I had punished myself and gotten what I deserved."

If Clinton did not mail the letter while he was in Hot Springs or enlist while he was there because at the time, even though he was feeling guilty about the deferment, he did not really want to be in the Army or go to Vietnam, what compelled him finally to give up his deferment once he reached Oxford? The preponderance of evidence leads in one direction: to the notion that with each passing week there were more signs that he might not get drafted even if he abandoned the deferment. If Clinton, acting through his stepfather, arranged to have the local draft board reclassify him 1-A after October 1 (as seems most probable based on Randall Scott's recollections), he would have known that it was largely a symbolic act providing him the best of both worlds—the ability to say that he had given up a deferment, and the knowledge that even though he was 1-A again, he would not be drafted that year. This became possible because on October 1, President Nixon, seeking to defuse the antiwar clamor on campuses, ordered the Selective Service System to change its policy for graduate students. From that day on, graduate students who received draft notices would be allowed to finish the entire school year rather than just the term they were in. Clinton was safe at least until the following July.

In the weeks before the October 1 policy change for graduate students, the Nixon administration had taken several other actions that eased the pressure on students facing the draft. On September 14, newspapers in New York, Washington, and Arkansas carried articles quoting sources as saying that the Nixon administration would soon withdraw 35,000 troops from Vietnam and suspend the draft temporarily later that fall. The stories also said that there was a possibility that once the draft was resumed, only nineteen-year-olds would be called, and that the Army would send to Vietnam "only . . . those draftees who volunteered for service there." On September 17, Nixon confirmed the troop cuts in Vietnam and said that he would soon announce a major policy change concerning the draft. On September 19, the president announced that the October draft call of 29,000 men would be spread out over three months—essentially canceling the call for November and December—while the administration pushed for a draft lottery system. Nixon said he would impose draft reform by executive order if Congress did not act on its own. Under the lottery system discussed in stories that day, young men would be vulnerable to the draft for only one year. Their vulnerability would be determined by a random selection of numbers from 1 to 365. Each day of the year would get a number, which would be the number for all young men born on that day. The lower your number, the more likely you were to get drafted. Those with high numbers would probably get through the year and never have to worry about the draft again.

In his December 1991 interview with the *Post,* Clinton said, "I didn't know anything about any lottery and I sure as hell didn't know what my number was" at the time that he was reclassified 1-A. The second half of that statement is true. There was no way he could have known his lottery number in October because the lottery had not yet been implemented. The first half of the statement, however, seems unlikely. Clinton and his contemporaries had a consuming interest in the draft and followed every nuance of draft policy. Studying the draft was as important to them as any graduate school course. The possibility of a lottery was a major story around the time Clinton made his decision to drop the deferment. It was not even a new idea: the lottery had been part of the public debate about draft reform since the previous May.

It was, in summary, a mixed bag of certainties, probabilities, and un-knowns that Clinton was dealing with that October. He had to be aware that the revised graduate student policy protected him from induction that school year. He knew that the Selective Service System was cutting back on draft calls. The word was out that a lottery was coming. The Nixon administration had already announced two troop withdrawals starting what came to be known as the Vietnamization of the war. All of those signs were encouraging for a young man who did not want a deferment yet was not eager to fight in Vietnam. But it was not clear that Clinton had avoided the draft completely. He had, whatever his motivations, exposed himself to some degree of risk by asking to be reclassified. If the lottery came, his draft fate would depend on a number. Luck would help determine the fate of a gambling town's favorite son.

ONE Friday afternoon, Clinton and Stearns got into a discussion about poetry and discovered that they both loved Dylan Thomas, the lyrical Welsh poet. As a lark, they decided that they should make a pilgrimage to his birthplace. They grabbed their coats and Stearns's orange-covered edition of Thomas's poems and walked down to the rotary on the edge of Oxford and started hitch-hiking west. The weather was rainy and bitterly cold. They made it to Cardiff on the first day, and then caught a ride from a spelunker who was scrambling off to a cave exploration near a little village in the middle of Wales where no one had heard of Dylan Thomas. They sensed that they should be heading west, toward Swansea, but found it much easier to hitch rides north and south, and never got within range of Thomas's birthplace. They finally retreated to Bristol, back across the border in England, where they walked into a pub just as Tom Jones's "Green, Green Grass of Home" was playing on the jukebox. Any friend who had ever been with Clinton during the playing of that sentimental melody was left with the same memory: Clinton overtaken by feelings of homesickness. And so it was on that rainy night in Bristol. The song brought tears to his eyes.

They spent another miserable night in a bone-cold tourist lodge with "thin little blankets and a heater that only worked ten minutes at a time." By Sunday morning they were ready to concede defeat and began walking toward the motorway back to Oxford. On the way they passed a grocery where fresh bread, still steaming hot, had just been delivered. They bought a big loaf and a quart of milk with the money they had left and went out and sat on the curb and devoured it. The grocerywoman saw the two Americans through the store window. Concerned that they might get indigestion, she provided them butter to go along with the bread. Clinton charmed her, leaving Stearns once again in awe of his friend's adaptability. "The woman was so taken with Bill that she and her husband shut their store and invited us upstairs to the living quarters for their English Sunday dinner. After dinner they showed us sites in Bristol and took us to the bus station and bought our tickets back to Oxford. The grocers had two small children, and when we got back to Oxford, Clinton bought them gifts and sent them notes," Stearns recalled decades later. "He probably still does."

The makeshift living arrangements at Holywell Manor did not seem to bother Clinton or Stearns, but they were not acceptable to one and all. Having the big Arkansan over there on the other side of the room put a crimp in Stearns's romantic life, and tenants in the room directly below complained about the noise. At one point they delivered a note under the door which said that it seemed "a reasonable request" that the occupants should not shift furniture or hammer nails after midnight. "If this is not heeded," the threatening note went on, they might feel compelled to "tell the landlord why a bed is wheeled out every night, which would have serious repercussions." Clinton took the note in good humor, and joked to Stearns that the complainants did not know "that you and I are queer." He also said that "if I weren't your guest, and basically nonviolent and a little chicken, I'd go down and wipe [the note writer's] body over the floor." Those comments reflected a risqué, macho, satirical side to Clinton's humor, well known only to his close male friends.

In the third week of November, Stearns, who had finished his readings for the term, traveled back to Washington to continue his work on the McGovern Commission. It was also a chance for him to pursue a woman Clinton had introduced him to the previous summer—a former classmate of Clinton's at Georgetown who was working on the staff of Democratic Senator Thomas J. Dodd of Connecticut. Stearns was infatuated with the young woman, but he was having little success with her. Clinton tried to explain the problem. "He basically said that she hated my guts," Stearns later noted in his deadpan style. "Bill tried to explain to me why he was successful with girls and I was not. He said, 'Have you ever thought about listening to someone else?' I tried to impress girls by telling them everything I knew. Bill said, 'If you let them do the talking, they'll be far more interested in you. To have someone listening to you is flattering.' " In his letter to Stearns, Clinton said that he was having a hard time working at night because he could not keep his mind off Peggy. Stearns had never heard of Peggy. Clinton had flattered so many women that his friends could not keep up with them.

In another letter, Clinton thanked Stearns for "taking me in and making the time bearable and then happy when I was so low down." His uncertain existence in Oxford seemed to be stabilizing. He had been invited to share a flat at 46 Leckford Road with two other Rhodes friends, Strobe Talbott, the Russia scholar, and Frank Aller, the China scholar and draft resister. A room at the Leckford Road house became available when another American student left and they needed someone to pick up the share of the rent. The cost per housemate was three pounds a week plus a share of utility bills, easily affordable for even the poorest Rhodes Scholars, who along with free tuition were provided with $1,700 a year by the Rhodes trust. The narrow brick townhouse on the northern edge of the university had three floors, with a bedroom on each floor. There was a toilet on the first, a full bath on the third, and a telephone on the second.

Sara Maitland, a frequent visitor, thought of the house as being "particularly shambolic—an absolute slum." Her characterization of Leckford Road rings true. It was, she thought, "a bit of a joke because it was poshed up years later, but back then it was a mess. It belonged to a college and was rented by someone who sublet it illegally. No one paid much rent and no repairs were done. It was sort of a standoff. No one ever scrubbed the kitchen floor." The kitchen, with its peeled green linoleum flooring, was the largest room in the drafty house, warmed by a gas-fire heater beneath a wooden mantelpiece, and it served as the common room. There were usually a few people in there clustered around the fire, chatting and brewing tea on the nearby stove. Talbott considered the atmosphere "graduate student bohemian," meaning it was serious though sloppy and free form. There was no lock on the front door, and friends constantly came calling.

Visitors from London and Cambridge often spent the night. "It was rather hippieish. People were kind of in and out of it a lot," said Maitland. "You never knew who was going to sleep quite where. All the mattresses were on the floor and there were books everywhere."

Brooke Shearer, then a sophomore at Stanford, came to Oxford that Thanksgiving and stayed at the Leckford Road house with Talbott. Jan Brenning, Aller's girlfriend, was also there, leaving Clinton as the only one without a live-in mate. Shearer, a California dynamo, was taken aback by the easygoing house style, and quickly organized the holiday activities. She and Talbott rode bicycles to the covered market in downtown Oxford, bought a fresh turkey and hauled it back the mile and a half to the house, the fowl's head still on and its legs dangling from the basket. Shearer cut off the head and organized a cooking routine in which the friends would baste in fifteen-minute shifts while she read *Mrs. Dalloway,* Virginia Woolf's novel about an English society woman reflecting on her life as she prepares for a dinner party.

"Frank and Bill shared what was supposed to be the first shift and ended up so deep in conversation that they did the whole job," Talbott later wrote. "Perhaps because it was such an American holiday and they felt so far from home in so many ways, they talked on and on about whether real patriotism required submitting to the draft or resisting it." Their turkey-basting conversation came in the context of what had happened the day before. On November 26, President Nixon had signed H.R. 14001 enacting a draft lottery, which was to be held the following week, on December 1. The dinner conversation veered in a different direction, toward Russia and literature. Yasha Jacob Zaguskin, a Russian émigré and translator living in Oxford, was among the guests at the makeshift banquet table.

That night, Clinton wrote to Denise Hyland. He was reflective and a little blue. He suggested that he could send her a flight schedule and she should come over for a visit—an unlikely prospect now that she had fallen in love with someone else and was thinking of marriage. In earlier letters to Hyland, Clinton had made it seem as though he were studying hard even when he was not. No more. "I may never pick up a parchment," he wrote. "Of course that's not the value of the place for me, but a degree would be nice to have and Mother would love it." He said he had just talked to his family over the telephone, and he gave Denise his usual update on his little brother Roger, now thirteen. "Roger is selling magazines through a school project and has sold twice as many as anyone else. He won a Polaroid camera, a turkey and is sure to get the grand prize of a TV or stereo. At least one of us has practical ability."

.   .   .

THE first draft lottery since World War II began at 8:02 P.M. on the first day of the final month of 1969 in a small conference room at the Selective Service System headquarters in Washington. Lieutenant General Lewis B. Hershey presided over the event, which was witnessed by a pack of cameramen and reporters and fifty-six youth representatives. In the middle of the room, resting on a stool, sat a big glass bowl containing 366 plastic blue capsules that looked like the containers for charms sold in candy-store machines. Each capsule contained a gummed sticker with a date on it. One by one, the capsules were plucked from the bowl and opened, and the stickers were posted on a light blue tote board. Representative Alexander Pirnie from Utica, New York, ranking Republican on the House subcommittee overseeing the draft, was asked to pick the first capsule. He fished around in the bowl and emerged with September 14—a date with chilling symbolic meaning to Bill Clinton. September 14 was the day on which his high school classmate Mike Thomas had died in Vietnam.

Clinton's birthday brought him luck that night. August 19 was the 311th day picked.

When details of the lottery drawing reached Oxford the next day, it seemed as though Clinton's apparent draft gambit had worked. The lottery that year was the largest it would ever be, with a pool of 850,000 young men—400,000 nineteen-year-olds and 450,000 others of ages ranging from twenty to twenty-six who previously had held deferments. Clinton now rested near the bottom of an enormous pool. The last big monthly draft, in September, had taken 29,000 men. It was highly unlikely, given the administration's Vietnamization policy, and the staged withdrawals of troops from Vietnam, that the monthly numbers would reach that magnitude again. Even if they did, the yearly quota for 1970 would be about 350,000 men, which would be filled at least one hundred numbers short of Clinton's No. 311. Although he was theoretically draftable for another year, and at times he told friends that his draft board still thought it might get to him, he was, in reality, free.

In a situation where Clinton once thought all his options were bad, he had avoided everything he did not want to do. He did not want to resist the draft, and thereby imperil his political dreams. He did not want to get drafted and fight in Vietnam. He did not want to spend three years in the safe haven of ROTC, and two years after that as a commissioned lieutenant, even if the war had ended long before then. He did not want to go to the University of Arkansas Law School, when so many of his Rhodes friends were heading to Yale. And he did not want to feel guilty about his deferment. "It was just a fluke," Clinton would say decades later, when first asked how he had made it through this period without serving in the military. But of course it was not a fluke. A fluke is a wholly accidental stroke of good luck. What happened to Clinton during that fateful year did not happen by accident. He fretted and planned every move, he got help from others when needed, he resorted to some deception or manipulation when necessary, and he was ultimately lucky. In the end, by not serving in the military, he did what 16 million other young American men did during that tumultuous era.

All that was left for Clinton after he won No. 311 in the draft lottery was to explain his actions to one of the men who had helped him at a crucial moment, Colonel Holmes of the University of Arkansas ROTC. On December 3, Clinton belatedly wrote Holmes a letter explaining why he had decided not to enroll in the ROTC after all. This letter would later emerge as the best known essay of Bill Clinton's life, the testament of a bright, troubled, manipulative young man struggling with his conscience and his ambition. It is a remarkable letter, classic Bill Clinton, sincere and deceptive at the same time, requiring a careful reading between the lines, paragraph by paragraph.

> Dear Col. Holmes,
>
> I am sorry to be so long in writing. I know I promised to let you hear from me at least once a month, and from now on you will, but I have had to have some time to think about this first letter. Almost daily since my return to England I have thought about writing, about what I want to and ought to say.

(It was, in fact, the only such letter. Clinton wrote no more to the colonel. He had every reason to know that Holmes would have little interest in hearing from him after this.)

> First, I want to thank you, not just for saving me from the draft, but for being so kind and decent to me last summer, when I was as low as I have ever been. One thing which made the bond we struck in good faith somewhat palatable to me was my high regard for you personally. In retrospect, it seems that the admiration might not have been mutual had you known a little more about me, about my political beliefs and activities. At least you might have thought me more fit for the draft than for the ROTC.

Holmes did save Clinton from the draft by working out the ROTC deferment before the July 28 induction deadline. Though Clinton did not know him very well, Holmes was a straightforward, gentle father figure of the sort Clinton had long cherished, going back to his high school days with band director Virgil Spurlin. When in the presence of such men, Clinton was inclined not to say or do anything that would disappoint them.

Let me try to explain. As you know, I worked for two years in a very minor position on the Senate Foreign Relations Committee. I did it for the experience and the salary but also for the opportunity, however small, of working every day against a war I opposed and despised with a depth of feeling I had reserved solely for racism in America before Vietnam. I did not take the matter lightly but studied it carefully, and there was a time when not many people had more information about Vietnam at hand than I did.

Clinton rewrites his own history here. When he began working in the documents room at the foreign relations committee in the fall of 1966, he had no strong feelings about the war and leaned toward support of President Johnson's position. There is no doubt that he studied the issue while he was there and dramatically changed his position over two years, but his opposition to the war was fairly quiet. No one at Georgetown University considered him an antiwar activist. Father McSorley, the leading peace activist on campus, had never met Clinton during his undergraduate years; their first encounter was at the London demonstrations that fall.

I have written and spoken and marched against the war. One of the national organizers of the Vietnam Moratorium is a close friend of mine. After I left Arkansas last summer, I went to Washington to work in the national headquarters of the Moratorium, then to England to organize the Americans here for demonstrations Oct. 15 and Nov. 16.

Again, apparently for dramatic effect, Clinton overstates his role. He did not travel to England primarily to organize for the October and November demonstrations, but he did help organize the Americans at Oxford once he was there. The "close friend of mine" he refers to as a national organizer of the moratorium apparently was David Mixner. Clinton had met Mixner only that summer. But Rick Stearns, when asked whether that qualified Mixner as a close friend of Clinton's, commented, "It doesn't take more than a day for Clinton to consider someone a close friend."

Interlocked with the war is the draft issue, which I did not begin to consider separately until early 1968. For a law seminar at Georgetown I wrote a paper on the legal arguments for and against allowing, within the Selective Service System, the classification of selective conscientious objection, for those opposed to participation in a particular war, not simply to "participation in war in any form." From my work I came to believe that the draft system itself is illegitimate. No government really rooted in limited, parliamentary democracy should have the power to make its citizens fight and kill and die in a war they may oppose, a war which even possibly may be wrong, a war which, in any case, does not involve immediately the peace and freedom of the nation. The draft was justified in World War II because the life of the people collectively was at stake. Individuals had to fight, if the nation was to survive, for the lives of their countrymen and their way of life. Vietnam is no such case. Nor was Korea—an example where, in my opinion, certain military action was justified but the draft was not, for the reasons stated above.

This paragraph is a crystallization of countless conversations and debates Clinton had had with his Rhodes friends over the previous year. The most revealing sentence is not his explanation of why he considered the draft illegitimate then, but why it was legitimate in World War II. Clinton and his classmates could not dismiss the memories of their fathers and what was considered the last good war. In claiming their moral ground on Vietnam, it was important for them to think that they would have been eager to fight in World War II. They felt mistreated by fate that they had reached adulthood at a time when their country was fighting a war they did not believe in.

Because of my opposition to the draft and the war, I am in great sympathy with those who are not willing to fight, kill, and maybe die for their country (i.e. the particular policy of a particular government) right or wrong. Two of my friends at Oxford are conscientious objectors. I wrote a letter of recommendation for one of them to his Mississippi draft board, a letter which I am more proud of than anything else I wrote at Oxford last year. One of my roommates is a draft resister who is possibly under indictment and may never be able to go home again. He is one of the bravest, best men I know. His country needs men like him more than they know. That he is considered a criminal is an obscenity.

(George Butte and Paul Parish in Clinton's class had filed as conscientious objectors. Several members of the class ahead of theirs were in the process of seeking C.O. status, including one commissioned lieutenant in the U.S. Navy. The letter of recommendation was for Parish. Aller, the roommate resister, was both a source of inspiration and guilt for Clinton.)

The decision not to be a resister and related subsequent decisions were the most difficult of my life. I decided to accept the draft in spite of my beliefs for one reason: to maintain my political viability within the system. For years I have worked to prepare myself for a political life characterized by both practical political ability and concern for rapid social progress. It is a life I still feel compelled to try to lead. I do not think our system of government is by definition corrupt, however dangerous and inadequate it has been in recent years. The society may be corrupt, but that is not the same thing, and if that is true we are all finished anyway.

When Clinton says he decided to accept the draft, he means accepting it in the sense of not being a resister. Some critics have focused on his desire to maintain his political viability as a sign of overbearing ambition. In the context of Clinton's life to that point, it seems less raw, rather an honest reflection of who he was and where he was going. The final sentence reads more like Aller than Clinton, and was no doubt influenced by their long discussions during the week before Clinton wrote the letter.

When the draft came, despite political convictions, I was having a hard time facing the prospect of fighting a war I had been fighting against, and that is why I contacted you. ROTC was the one way left in which I could possibly, but not positively, avoid both Vietnam and resistance. Going on with my education, even coming back to England, played no part in my decision to join ROTC. I am back here, and would have been at Arkansas Law School because there is nothing else I can do. In fact, I would like to have been able to take a year out perhaps to teach in a small college or work on some community action project and in the process to decide whether to attend law school or graduate school and how to begin putting what I have learned to use.

The first line here is a basic admission that he had been drafted in the spring of 1969, a line that somehow was ignored decades later when the letter surfaced at a time when Clinton was not acknowledging that he had received a draft notice. The rest of the paragraph seems somewhat disingenuous. When Clinton met with his Georgetown housemates the previous July, he left the impression with them that he wanted nothing more than to return to Oxford for his second year. His September 9 letter to Stearns underscored that notion as well, ending with the line, "I want so much to tell you we're going back to England."

But the particulars of my personal life are not nearly as important to me as the principles involved. After I signed the ROTC letter of intent I began to wonder whether the compromise I had made with myself was not more objectionable than the draft would have been, because I had no interest in the ROTC program in itself and all I seemed to have done was to protect myself from physical harm. Also, I began to think I had deceived you, not by lies—there were none—but by failing to tell you all the things I'm writing now. I doubt that I had the mental coherence to articulate them then.

Clinton here reveals that he understands that deception can involve more than lies. In dealing with the draft issue over the ensuing years, he would be plagued more than anything else by what he did not say— omissions in his story.

At that time, after we had made our agreement and you had sent my 1-D deferment to my draft board, the anguish and loss of my self regard and self confidence really set in. I hardly slept for weeks and kept going by eating compulsively and reading until exhaustion brought sleep. Finally, on September 12 I stayed up all night writing a letter to the chairman of my draft board, saying basically what is in the preceding paragraph, thanking him for trying to help in a case where he really couldn't, and stating that I couldn't do the ROTC after all and would he please draft me as soon as possible. I never mailed the letter, but I did carry it on me every day until I got on the plane to return to England. I didn't mail the letter because I didn't see, in the end, how my going in the army and maybe going to Vietnam would achieve anything except a feeling that I had punished myself and gotten what I deserved. So I came back to England to try to make something of this second year of my Rhodes scholarship.

This paragraph presents the basic contradiction in Clinton's explanation of why he gave up his deferment. On the one hand, he wants the moral high ground of making himself 1-A, but on the other hand, he still does not want to be drafted or go into the Army and fight in Vietnam. It also again suggests that Clinton played the draft like a chess player and withdrew his deferment only when he thought it safe to do so.

And that is where I am now, writing to you because you have been good to me and have a right to know what I think and feel. I am writing too in the hope that my telling this one story will help you understand more clearly how so many fine people have come to find themselves still loving their country but loathing the military, to which you and other good men have devoted years, lifetimes, of the best service you could give. To many of us, it is no longer clear what is service and what is disservice, or if it is clear, the conclusion is likely to be illegal. Forgive the length of this letter. There was much to say. There is still a lot to be said, but it can wait. Please say hello to Col. Jones for me.

    Merry Christmas

    Sincerely,

    Bill Clinton

That same week, Clinton sent another letter to the United States. It was his application to Yale Law School.

His lengthy writ of conscience did not find an especially receptive audience when it reached Colonel Holmes in Fayetteville. "The letter was the talk of the unit," according to Ed Howard, the drill instructor. "We all knew about it. Lieutenant Colonel Jones advised us of the letter. He was more upset than the average instructor." Howard, who went on to become a real estate broker in Malvern, Arkansas, in later years supported Clinton's political endeavors in the state, but he harbored ill feelings about Clinton's handling of the ROTC episode. The letter, he said later, only intensified the anger the ROTC staff had felt toward Clinton since he had failed to enroll at the law school. "There was anger again. Our feeling was that his conscience bothered him." According to Howard, no one on the staff believed Clinton's explanation that he abandoned ROTC because he wanted to be drafted. "I don't think anybody ever took it serious. It was apparent to us that he used the dodger routine."

Another effect of the letter was the creation of a Bill Clinton heading in the Dissidents File at the ROTC headquarters in Fayetteville. The military during that era maintained files on anyone associated with the program who opposed the war. Howard said there was an intelligence network linking all the units around the nation. "If we had a guy from Houston or Austin demonstrating against the war, we'd clip the story and send it to Fort Sam Houston, Fifth Army Headquarters for the ROTC, and then on to the pertinent unit. A dissident file was kept on Bill Clinton after he wrote the letter to Col. Holmes." The letter was the main document in Clinton's file.

As one who worked in the ROTC unit and later supported Clinton, Howard was a witness without any apparent hostile motive. Holmes's reactions fluctuated over the years, ranging from benign to neutral and finally, near the end of the 1992 election, to openly hostile. When asked in 1978 to comment on Clinton's behavior during the ROTC episode, he claimed that he could not remember any specifics. In 1991, his recollection was that he had treated Clinton "just like any other kid." Early in the 1992 presidential campaign, he began to speak out, telling the *Wall Street Journal* that he felt that he had been manipulated by Clinton. Late in the campaign, on September 16, 1992, he issued a lengthy statement questioning Clinton's "patriotism and his integrity," and saying that he came to believe that Clinton deceived him to avoid the draft.

The Holmes statement was written with the help of his daughter, Linda Burnett of Fort Smith, a Republican activist, and released with guidance from the office of the former Republican congressman from that district, John Paul Hammerschmidt. According to David Tell, a member of President Bush's opposition research staff, he and several other Bush campaign officials reviewed the letter before it was made public. Although it might have honestly conveyed Holmes's long-repressed antipathy toward Clinton, there was much in it that was illogical. Tell, in fact, was disappointed when he first read the letter because it was "full of rhetoric and precious few facts." Most of the letter expressed Holmes's outrage over Clinton's participation in antiwar rallies. Recalling now in detail a conversation that he said he could not remember at all when he was first asked about it in 1978, Holmes said that Clinton failed to reveal his history of antiwar protest during their initial meeting in July 1969. "At no time during this long conversation about his desire to join the program did he inform me of his involvement, participation and actually organizing protests against the United States involvement in Southeast Asia," Holmes stated. "He was shrewed [sic] enough to realize that had I been aware of his activities, he would not have been accepted into the ROTC program as a potential officer in the United States Army."

What Holmes failed to take into account was that Clinton's antiwar activities came *after* their July meeting: Clinton could not tell him about events that had not yet occurred. Holmes certainly knew that Clinton had worked for Senator Fulbright, a staunch opponent of the war. And as drill instructor Ed Howard pointed out, Holmes's ROTC unit was not above enrolling law students who were seeking a way around Vietnam. His unit, in fact, had grown considerably in 1969 precisely for that reason.

CHAPTER TWELVE

THE GRAND TOUR

IT WAS TRADITIONAL in the eighteenth century for young English noblemen to embark on grand tours of Europe before they got on with their futures. Sir Edgar Williams, the longtime warden of Rhodes House, a man of traditional tastes, thought of the Rhodes mission as "a modern version of the old Grand Tour" for the American scholars under his supervision at Oxford. During long breaks between terms, the scholars were expected to explore the continent on their Rhodes stipend. Whatever academic skills they acquired at Oxford seemed almost secondary to this notion of introducing the best men for the world's fight to the Old World for which they would do intellectual battle. Clinton had traveled to Scotland, Ireland, Wales, France, Germany, and Austria during previous breaks and long weekends; but now, for the Christmas holiday of his second year, he was ready to undertake one of the full-length grand tours, to Russia and back —five weeks by train moving in a circle north, east, and then west, with extended stops in Oslo, Helsinki, Moscow, Prague, and Munich.

Clinton's was not a nobleman's holiday. There were no servants at his command, he slept at youth hostels more often than hotels, and he lacked the trunkful of formal attire, instead lugging a bag that held denim jeans and cigarettes to sell, trade, or give away as thank-you presents. He traveled solo, which was rare for him, though part of the Rhodes tradition—most scholars went off by themselves at least once during their Oxford years. But he was never alone for long: he rode the chuckwagon line, to use an idiom of the American West, finding friends, relatives of friends, or friends of friends at every stop along the route.

The first stop on his forty-day journey was in Oslo. As he was ambling down the stairs of the Oslo train station, Clinton noticed that Father McSorley was in the crowd directly ahead of him. Clinton's strides carried him abreast of McSorley and he caught the priest's eye. They had met only one month earlier at the antiwar prayer service at St. Mark's Church in London. " 'What are you doing here?' " McSorley remembers that Clinton asked him, to which he answered that he was there to visit several peace groups in the Norwegian capital. Clinton, with no immediate plans, asked if he could come along. McSorley was delighted to have a companion. "I said, 'Sure,' and off we went." In place of a tourist guidebook, McSorley carried a calendar from the War Resisters League listing the important peace groups in each European community. He had annotated his copy with advice from Quaker peace activists in London. Their first stop was an old Victorian mansion near the University of Oslo that housed the Institute for Peace Research, where they met several young Norwegians who were conscientious objectors opposed to Norway's role in the North Atlantic Treaty Organization.

McSorley and Clinton strolled through the university, lunched with a professor teaching the New Testament, visited another peace center founded by two actors, and drank tea at a chalet near the train station before parting. " 'This is a great way to see a country!' " Clinton said as they sipped tea. " 'You see as much as a tourist, you have an important subject to talk about with the people you meet, and you learn something of the process of working toward peace.' " Clinton's comment stuck in McSorley's mind so firmly that he considered using 'A Great Way to See a Country' as the title for a book he would later write about his peace travels around the world. That book, which McSorley published himself under the title *Peace Eyes,* offers a brief account of his afternoon with Clinton in Oslo. It was from McSorley's account that Republican partisans during the 1992 presidential campaign began painting a distorted picture of Clinton's trip to Moscow. Was it an accident, they asked, that McSorley and Clinton toured the peace institutes of Oslo, or were they in fact traveling together across the continent on what was called "the Peace Train"? The answer is that Clinton and McSorley were not traveling together. They met by coincidence. Clinton tagged along with McSorley because he was an insatiably curious fellow who liked companionship. From Oslo, McSorley traveled south and west, through Sweden to Copenhagen. Clinton headed the other direction, toward Finland.

While still in Oslo, Clinton had another innocuous encounter that later became the subject of a joke that in turn fueled a rumor that was exaggerated down through the years. The meeting was with James Durham, an old acquaintance from Hot Springs. The false rumor was that during their meeting, Clinton broached the subject of staying in Scandinavia and renouncing his American citizenship. Apparently it was that bogus rumor that excited certain Republican officials so much during the 1992 campaign that they searched Clinton's passport files in a State Department warehouse to see if any documents there offered clues to his alleged flirtation with apostasy.

James Durham was another Hot Springs golden boy, a brilliant student and track star in the class ahead of Clinton's who was studying biophysics at the University of Oslo on a Fulbright fellowship. During his time in Norway, he had gone native. He had joined the Norwegian national rowing team. He dreamt every night in Norwegian. He became enchanted with Scandinavian socialism and for a time embraced pacifism. He attempted, he said later, to become "a flaming radical—I was in Europe longer and immersed in those processes longer than Bill. I experimented in radicalism." He told his parents he planned to marry a Norwegian and stay there. There would, of course, be a military consequence to any such decision. Durham had a low lottery number and was protected from the draft only because the Garland County Draft Board gave him even more preferential treatment than Clinton had received. He was still classified 2-S, protected by a graduate deferment for more than a year and a half after such deferments were eliminated.

When Clinton arrived in Oslo, he had Durham's address in his pocket, and went to see him at his closet-sized room in the student housing complex. "So Bill knocks on the door and I was surprised," Durham later remembered. "He hadn't called. I wasn't expecting him." They talked for a few hours, mostly about the draft and Vietnam. Durham said that he still had a deferment and was not sure what he would do next. Clinton said he was 1-A but had a high lottery number and was planning to return to the United States to attend law school at Yale. It seemed to Durham that Clinton was looking for support and encouragement that he was "doing the right thing by going back." The two young men from Hot Springs agreed on most points, but got into an argument when Clinton talked about antiwar demonstrations. Durham opposed the war but did not like demonstrations. The argument did not dominate the discussion, and when Clinton left the apartment, they parted on friendly terms.

Over the years, the argument between Durham and Clinton, which Durham had passed along to his father, a staunch Republican and Hot Springs physician, ballooned into an impassioned exchange during which Clinton said he was about to renounce his citizenship and Durham talked him out of it. That version became more popular in the 1980s when Clinton was governor of Arkansas and Durham jokingly evoked the Oslo meeting to members of his family who were complaining about Clinton's actions in Little Rock. "Well," Durham told them sarcastically, "I did what you wanted—I sent Billy home!" By 1992, the rumor spread through the GOP gossip circuit that Clinton had once tried to renounce his American citizenship and someone had a letter to prove it. And Jim Durham, who had once talked of staying in Norway and marrying a Norwegian, which he never did, was now Colonel James Durham of the United States Marine Corps, with an office at the Pentagon, and quietly bewildered by it all.

Clinton's grand tour moved on from Oslo to Helsinki. Again he had no schedule or place to stay, only the name of a friend's family and a telephone number. The friend was Richard Shullaw, a classmate from Georgetown whose father was deputy chief of mission at the U.S. Embassy in the Finnish capital. Richard happened to be visiting his family for Christmas when Clinton called and announced that he had just arrived in town after running into Father McSorley in Oslo. It was, Shullaw thought, as though Clinton "was just dropping out of the sky." He was taken aback when Clinton arrived at the family's small apartment down the hill from the elegant Georgian-style embassy. He had not seen Clinton since the summer after their senior year in college. This was a new counterculture version of his old friend standing at the doorstep in Helsinki. "He had a beard and curly long hair. He looked quite different from Mr. Cleancut America." The Shullaws did not have room for Clinton so they made arrangements for him to stay at a youth hostel downtown. But he ate most of his meals, including a quiet Christmas dinner, at the Shullaw apartment, and Shullaw's father paid his hostel bill, about five dollars a day.

Finland was freezing, dark and wet. "I have found the world's winter," Clinton wrote Denise Hyland on a postcard depicting an icy Helsinki scene. But the tourist from Oxford was bundled up for the weather, warmed by his healthy beard, heavy boots, and a thick, oversized coat, and he and Shullaw spent several days touring the city. "We did not meet with a lot of people. We did not meet with peace groups," Shullaw recalled later. "Bill was very much the tourist. We talked a lot about his experiences at Oxford and about our mutual friends. Bill always adjusted himself to the person he was dealing with. We had a pleasant, relaxed time." Clinton said that he was going on to law school. He charmed the Shullaw family, especially Mari, the little sister, who suffered from a heart murmur, but met his match in Pelle, the Shullaws' beagle. "Pelle did not care for Bill. He took one look at Bill and set off the most ungodly racket," Shullaw later remembered. "The beagle wouldn't shut up. Bill tried to make friends with the dog, but Pelle would have none of it. We have a picture of Bill sitting on a sofa at the house talking to us and reaching out a tentative hand to pet the dog on the head, and the dog making a move as if to say, 'I'll have none of this fellow!' Mother was quite embarrassed about it. Pelle was one friend Bill could not make."

Two men who decades later would run against each other for president of the United States were trying, separately, to enter the Soviet Union on December 31, 1969, the final day of the sixties decade. One was H. Ross

Perot, then a thirty-nine-year-old Texas industrialist, who had spent most of December attempting to fly twenty-five tons of supplies to American prisoners of war held in North Vietnam. Perot had been rebuffed in Southeast Asia and now sat in Copenhagen, his chartered Boeing 707 loaded and ready to go, waiting to hear whether the Soviets would grant him a visa so that he could carry out his alternative plan—to fly to Moscow and have the supplies delivered to the POWs by Soviet postal authorities. On the evening of the 31st, the U.S. ambassador to the Soviet Union passed the word: no visa for Perot. That same day, Bill Clinton reached the Soviet border on the train from Helsinki. He already had a visa, easily obtained in London, where the Soviet Union was advertising for tourists. In the year since Strobe Talbott had visited Moscow, nearly a dozen Rhodes Scholars had made the trip, and more would follow in the spring and summer, making Moscow, even in the deep freeze of the Cold War, one of the most popular stops on the grand tour.

Not that the Soviet government received the Oxford boys graciously. As Clinton later told the story, Soviet authorities searched the bearded young American at the border, perhaps suspecting that he was smuggling dope. "Upon entering Russia, he was requested to strip down to the bare skin," one American who was in Moscow then recalls Clinton telling him. "The seams of his clothing were examined, and every single item of his personal effects was searched. They even examined his teeth."

Clinton was less sophisticated than Talbott in his understanding of Soviet communism, and of Russian literature and history, but he was not naive. He had read under the tutelage of Zbigniew Pelczynski, the Pembroke College don, and more recently undergone a cram course with Talbott and David Satter, the other Rhodes Scholar Sovietologist. Talbott and Satter engaged in a running commentary on Soviet affairs that tended to go over the heads of their classmates, but Clinton jumped into the discussions in the weeks before his trip and absorbed as much as he could. Their view of the Soviet Union hardened in later years, but even then it could not have been described as "soft." "There was still a kind of residual leftism at Oxford at the time that viewed the Soviet Union benignly, but Americans on the whole did not have a benign view," Talbott said later. "My own view was that the Soviet Union was a monstrosity made up of an extraordinary number of fine people." Clinton approached the Soviet Union with much the same perspective as he had Vietnam, as a place that was diverting America's attention from solving its domestic problems, as "this giant country which was so completely absorbing all of America's energy."

Moscow was dark when Clinton arrived, bitterly cold and drearily gray. He told his friends later that he was struck as much as anything by all the gray—gray skies and gray military uniforms everywhere he looked. He had one friend of a friend in Moscow, Anik (Nicki) Alexis, a young West Indian woman who had studied at Oxford and was close to Tom Williamson. Alexis was an intriguing international character. Born in Martinique, the daughter of a diplomat working in Paris, she was fluent in several languages, including Russian, and was studying at Moscow University. Clinton called on her at her university dormitory, got her to take him around the city, and saw her several times during his time in Moscow. Alexis complained to him that the Soviets discriminated against her and other black students, mostly Africans, at Moscow University, more than any other people she had encountered in her life.

The National Hotel off Red Square was host to a colorful menagerie of Americans in the opening days of 1970. Late one night Clinton went into the hotel bar and encountered Charlie Daniels, a plumbing contractor from Norton, a small town in southwestern Virginia. Daniels was in Moscow seeking information on American servicemen missing in action in North Vietnam and Laos. He invited Clinton to have a drink with him and one of his associates, Henry Fors, a chicken farmer and the father of a missing pilot. Daniels later wrote in his diary: "We were joined at our table by Bill Clinton, a young giant of a man sporting a full beard, who introduced himself as a Rhodes scholar whose home was in Hot Springs, Arkansas. Bill was majoring in political science at Oxford, and had decided to visit Russia to get first-hand knowledge of Communism. Bill's knowledge and ability to explain the inner workings of Communism kept Henry and I avid listeners until the bar closed at 2:00 A.M. Our 'one for the road' turned into a whole bevy. I'm sure glad we had only a few stairs to climb to reach our rooms and a spinning bed."

Before they fell asleep, Daniels and Fors spent a minute talking about Clinton. "We thought he might be a spy—this big fellow, friendly, constantly jabbering," Daniels says. "I'm just a dumb plumber. Henry's a chicken farmer. Bill could talk about anything. When we left him and were alone in our room, I said, 'Henry, this guy, I don't know what to think of him, do you?' He fascinated all of us."

They were equally interesting to Clinton, with their down-home folksy ways and fantastic stories of international derring-do. It turned out that Norton was the home town of the famed CIA pilot Francis Gary Powers, who had been shot down while flying his U-2 spy plane over the Soviet Union in May 1960. Powers's father ran a shoe store in Norton in the same building that housed the offices of attorney Carl McAfee. "I got a son flying over Russia," Powers told McAfee while sizing up a foot. "Hell, nobody flies over Russia but Russians," McAfee responded. But when the U-2 plane was shot down and Francis Gary Powers was paraded in front of the world by the Soviets, McAfee flew to Moscow and helped defend him and arrange his release in a prisoner exchange. Daniels, the self-described dumb plumber, sponsored a grand parade for Powers when he came back to Norton. From then on, McAfee and Daniels were up for missions of intrigue together. McAfee was with Daniels and Henry Fors now in Moscow in the effort to track down some MIAs. They had planned the trip for a year, working through their contacts in Lions International and gaining support from the State Department. They had met with H. Ross Perot in Dallas earlier in the fall, and now found it ironic that they were in Moscow with their visas and Perot was stuck in Copenhagen with no way in.

Clinton attached himself to the Daniels entourage. This bushy, bearded antiwar protester, this adaptable character who could make himself at home anywhere from the porter's lodge at Oxford to his stepfather's beauty parlor in Hot Springs, was now just one of the gang with the plumber and the chicken farmer and the small-town attorney looking for miracles in Moscow. "You wonder why Bill gravitated to us? He's twenty-three and we're on top of the best story in the world," Daniels said later. "We're driving the Russians crazy, the North Vietnamese crazy. So when he finds us, he stays with us. He's found a home." He also found a setting at the table. As far as Daniels could tell, Clinton had no money and was hungry. When Daniels, Fors, and a Parisian couple assisting them, Jean and Pelly Sureau, returned from the French Embassy at noon on January 5, according to Daniels's diary, they found Clinton back at their hotel room, chatting with McAfee, ready and waiting to join them for lunch. For the next two days he was sure to appear whenever it was time to eat or when he knew the group would gather to discuss the day's events. There were, said Daniels, "no big secrets, we let it all hang out. We knew our vehicle was bugged. We knew our rooms were bugged. So when someone wanted to say something private, we'd give a signal and go for a walk outside. Bill was part of the action. If I went out, most of the time when I came back, Bill would be there. If we went outside to eat, he went with us."

The only thing Clinton had to offer the group was his understanding of the Soviet system. As limited as his knowledge was, he was not reluctant to share it. On the second day of their time together, Daniels again wrote in his diary about Clinton's lectures. "Henry and I led Bill into another interesting account of his study of Communism," Daniels wrote. "He talked of his studies of Marxism, the revolution engineered by Lenin, and the Purge by Stalin which led to his downfall. Henry and I listened with the avid interest of children hearing the fantasy of Walt Disney." That conversation, according to Daniels's diary, was followed by a hearty lunch. Soon Clinton brought his friend Anik Alexis into the entourage, and she proved to be of more practical help, serving as an interpreter in French, English, and Russian. The group arranged a meeting with North Vietnamese officials in Moscow, but failed to learn anything about Henry Fors's son or twenty-nine other missing servicemen on their list.

Senator Eugene McCarthy arrived at the National Hotel on January 6, another intriguing fellow on this curious stage. The antiwar senator from Minnesota, only two years removed from his campaign against Lyndon Johnson, was entertaining thoughts of running for president again, and joked about his ambitions with some Americans he met during an impromptu lunch on his first day in the Soviet Union. "I have to be careful what I say so that it's not publicized that I'm starting a campaign in Moscow," he said. His daughter Mary, a senior at Radcliffe, had accompanied McCarthy to Moscow. He said he hoped to meet with Premier Aleksei N. Kosygin to talk about trade issues. Kosygin left the senator cooling his heels, but McCarthy did get to meet Charlie Daniels and his gang. He came to their room in the hotel, listened for hours to their story, and agreed to try to help them by meeting again with North Vietnamese Embassy officials. Not much came of that meeting either, although the North Vietnamese were said to have received McCarthy more cordially than they did Henry Fors the chicken farmer. "That figures," Fors said later that day, when told of McCarthy's reception. "McCarthy has the reputation of being the biggest God-damn peacenik in the United States!"

Clinton bade farewell to his newfound friends the next day and boarded the train for Prague. He entered the elegant capital city of Czechoslovakia less than fifteen months after the Soviet-led Warsaw Pact tanks had crushed the Communist reform movement led by Alexander Dubček, who had been seeking to create "socialism with a human face." Clinton's college at Oxford, University College, had a special connection to the freedom movement in Prague. Univ's administration protected two Czech students who had been traveling in England and did not want to return to their country after the Soviet invasion. "We were all very moved by the Prague Spring," noted John Albery, a distinguished professor of chemistry who later became the college master. "I was particularly moved because my field is strong in Prague and I knew a lot of Czech scientists. It was happening in a beautiful European city. It was appalling—the sight of those tanks. We wanted to do something, so we set up a fund to raise money to bring in the two students to Univ College as the Russians were moving in. We raised money in the Junior Common Room and the Senior Common Room. The response was remarkable." Tom Lampl and Jan Kopold started their studies at Univ the same fall that Clinton arrived. Kopold and Clinton became friends. Before Clinton left for his trip to Moscow, Kopold had written his parents in Prague to advise them that a friend would be stopping there in early January. "My friend Bill Clinton will come to Prague,"

Kopold wrote. "If he cannot find an affordable hotel, he may stay with you. He has a wide knowledge of political systems and will come from Moscow."

Clinton stayed with the Kopolds for several days, saving whatever money he had to buy trinkets and glass jewelry for friends back in England. His hosts lived in a glass, chrome, and glazed white brick building in the Dejvice neighborhood. Their five-room apartment on the sixth story had high ceilings and a parquet floor and was filled with books. A balcony ran across the front of the building. Clinton had a room to himself with a window facing Freedom Square. He ate breakfast in the breakfast nook just inside the front door with Jan's grandmother, Marie Smermova, and dinner with Jan's parents, Bedrich Kopold and Jirina Kopoldova. Jirina served him pork, cabbage, and bread dumplings. He drank plenty of beer, as they all did. He toured the city during the day, according to Jirina Kopoldova, and stayed home with the family in the evenings. Bedrich Kopold took Clinton up to the roof to look out on the city. He also took a memorable stroll with the young American. "One time we were coming back from the Old Town and we passed by the U.S. ambassador's residence and we walked and talked about the political situation of 1968, and he was very interested in it, and when we walked past the embassy residence I said, 'It would be very nice if you came back as cultural attaché,' and he said, 'Why not?' " It would have been impolite for Clinton to say that he had far greater ambitions than that. Jirina Kopoldova raised the stakes and got a different response. "We told Bill Clinton one day he would be a senator and he laughed very much."

The stories of what happened in Prague in 1968 captivated Clinton. One of the Czech heroes in the face of the Soviet invasion lived in the same building, across the landing. He was General Bohumir Lomsky, a Czech general who had faced down the Russians by ordering them, in perfect Russian, to leave the Czechoslovak Parliament building. Apparently they thought he was Russian, and obeyed. Clinton's hosts were well known in Czech political circles, and their story reflected the tragedy and intrigue of their nation's Communist era. Jan Sverma, Jan Kopold's grandfather, had been the editor-in-chief of the Communist party daily *Rude Pravo*. He died fighting as a partisan in World War II and had a bridge named for him in Prague at the bottom of Revolucni Street. Marie Svermova, the grandmother, was a member of the Politburo of the Communist party of Czechoslovakia from 1945 to 1951. She was purged from the party in the 1950s and spent six years in Communist prisons. Her brother, Karel Svab, once headed the secret police and refused to come to her aid when she was on trial. Jan's father, Bedrich Kopold, was also purged, tried and imprisoned in the 1950s, and forced to work in the uranium mines. While he was in jail his wife Jirina says she was forced to sign papers for the Communist secret police, which later left the false impression that she was an informer. By 1968, all three—Marie Smermova, her daughter Jirina Kopoldova, and Bedrich Kopold—were strong supporters of Dubček and what came to be known as the Prague Spring.

When Clinton paid his visit, Jirina was working as a chemical researcher at the Academy of Sciences and Bedrich taught sociology at a technical university. The grandmother was home and had more time to spend with their guest. On Clinton's final day in Prague, she took him on a long stroll through the old city, chatting as they made their way along the cobbled streets. She later wrote in her calendar: "I went with Bill to the Strahov Library and the Loretta [monastery]." Marie Smermova knew no English, so she and Clinton communicated as best they could in German, the language he had studied at Georgetown. Not long after he left, she was interrogated by the state security agents.

Clinton's final stop before returning to London was Munich, where he stayed again with Rudi Lowe and his family. There was more partying than politics as the grand tour neared an end. Munich's six-week carnival had begun, and Lowe remembered taking Clinton to several masquerade parties and balls. "I still have a picture of Bill in his mask," Lowe says. "What we mostly did was drink beer and have a good time."

THE trip to Moscow revealed nothing about Clinton's loyalty, or alleged disloyalty, to his country, but it did reveal his loyalty to his mother, and hers to him. They were an effective political team, even then. The first telephone call Charlie Daniels made when he arrived back home in Norton was to Hot Springs. Clinton had asked Daniels to call his mother to tell her that her boy was all right. And within ten days of Clinton's visit to Prague, the Kopolds received a handwritten thank-you letter from his mother. "My dear Mr. and Mrs. Kopold," she wrote:

> I would like to take this opportunity to thank you for your many kindnesses to my son, Bill Clinton. You made his stay in Czechoslovakia such a pleasure. I'm so appreciative. I guess children no matter how old or what size they are never outgrow their parents fret and concern for them when they are traveling in a foreign country. Bill is safely back at Oxford. We spoke with him Sunday. He had a most enjoyable journey but was tired from it and ready to settle down academically. If ever you are in the United States please favor us with a visit. We would be delighted to have you. Thank you again for your hospitality to one that is so dear to me
> —Sincerely, Virginia Dwire.

· · ·

THE cast of Rhodes Scholars housemates and friends whose lives revolved around 46 Leckford Road early in 1970 was as eccentric in its way as the National Hotel crew to which Clinton had attached himself in Moscow. Here was Strobe Talbott, the studious Yalie, with his baggy tweed jackets and frayed collars and his thick black mustache, looking a little like a young Sean Connery, holed up in his room with an old typewriter, a Russian-English dictionary, and piles of transcripts that had been delivered to him in London by *Time* magazine, for which he had been an intern in Moscow the previous summer. *Time* wanted Talbott to study the transcripts, translate them, and write a preface for a book it was preparing. This was hardly the typical graduate student enterprise. There was an air of mystery around the papers, which had great historical weight—the private recollections of ousted Soviet leader Nikita Khrushchev. To assist with the translation, Talbott brought in Yasha Zaguskin, who was part of Oxford's small but vibrant Russian émigré community that included Boris Pasternak's sisters. Clinton was in the tight circle of friends who kept Talbott's secret.

If Talbott threatened to transform the Leckford Road apartment into a Russia House, Frank Aller counterbalanced that with his fascination for all things Chinese. Aller was researching a thesis on the Long March of 1934–35 in which Mao and thousands of Communist revolutionaries undertook a year-long survival trek north across the vast Chinese countryside to escape Chiang Kai-shek's Nationalist forces and establish a stronghold in northern Shensi. In search of intellectual mentors, Aller had developed a correspondence with Edgar Snow, then living in Europe, who was the first Western journalist to interview Mao and his comrades after the Long March and to tell their story in *Red Star Over China.* Aller, angular and red-bearded, had a manner that was part West Coast hippie, part Asian mystic: the way he padded around without shoes, the way he sipped tea, the way he sat on the floor leaning against a pillow, smoking a cigarette or marijuana in the darkness, listening to Pink Floyd with his girlfriend. He seemed to merge his gentle orientalism with the intense moral demeanor of a draft resister. Visitors occasionally encountered Aller sitting on the floor, using an ancient Chinese art of reading sticks to divine his future.

Then there was the third Rhodes man in the house, Clinton, who "looked like a lumberjack" to Brooke Shearer, Talbott's girlfriend. "He was big and burly and had wonderfully thick curly hair and a beard. But it became him. His appearance suggested that he was rougher than he was." Shearer described him as a nocturnal creature who would read late into the night. Mandy Merck, another friend, thought Clinton's face appeared older then than it would a decade later when he was again fresh-scrubbed. At Leckford

Road, he "looked old and heavy-lidded, kind of tired and seedy. And he had problems. I took him to have a plantar wart removed from his foot and he threw up on me on the way home. He was not exactly Mister Suave."

Nor was he on the rhythm of someone studying hard, according to Merck. "You didn't get the feeling that he was pushing himself to prepare for a course. He was reading and tootling the sax." With his draft crisis behind him because of his lucky lottery number, Clinton was slowly easing his way back into the B. Phil. program he had been reading for sporadically since his days with Zbigniew Pelczynski. But there are no indications that he worked with a tutor during the middle term of his second year, and his attitude toward receiving a degree from Oxford seemed unchanged since November, when he had written to Denise Hyland that it was unlikely he would ever "pick up a parchment."

Perhaps Clinton's field of study, unlike Talbott's Russia or Aller's China, was not one that Oxford could help him with very much. He was interested in political science primarily as he could apply it to his future. Throughout his two years at Oxford he maintained and honed his excellent political instincts, which alternately impressed and amused his friends. Sara Maitland, who later became a feminist writer, credited Clinton with helping her shed her political naivete. It happened one night when she sat in a pub near Leckford Road with Clinton and Aller and talked about Vietnam. "Frank was describing the effect that napalm had on people and I burst into tears. And Bill turned to me and said, 'Bursting into tears is being liberal. Doing something about it is being political!' I remember that as something profoundly instrumental in my life."

It was taken for granted among Clinton's Oxford friends that his political style had a larger purpose. They teased him about his future much as his Georgetown roommates had done years earlier. When the Khrushchev transcripts were published in the United States as a book entitled *Khrushchev Remembers,* Talbott sent a copy to Clinton's old Georgetown roommate, Tom Campbell, in which he joked about his Arkansas friend's covert role in the enterprise. "As you know there is some mystery about the origin of these memoirs," Talbott wrote. "In point of fact they were dictated to me by William Clinton, hence the tone and spirit of two shrewd peasants. The editors decided I should change all references to Orval Faubus into Stalin and disguise the real narrator Clinton into Khrushchev. The reason for this I promise was commercial and in no way political. Keep the secret." The reason the joke worked was that even then, when they were all in their early twenties, Talbott from the Oxford years and Campbell from the Georgetown years both imagined a future in which their friend Bill Clinton would be as well known on the world stage as a former leader of the Soviet Union. The least they expected for him was a seat in the U.S.

Senate. During a holiday visit to Italy, Merck sent Clinton a postcard depicting a bulbous, naked Bacchus, the Roman god of wine, astride a giant tortoise. "Senator Clinton will see you now," she wrote on the back.

The postcard, in a lighthearted but fitting manner, connected politics to sex. Did a hunger for the former correspond to an insatiable appetite for the latter? One night at Leckford Road, Clinton and Merck delved into a long discussion on that topic. The conversation at first focused on the tragedy of the previous summer involving Ted Kennedy and a young campaign worker, Mary Jo Kopechne, who had drowned after a car in which she was a passenger, driven by the Massachusetts senator, veered off a narrow bridge on Chappaquiddick Island and plunged into the water. Clinton said he had been around Capitol Hill and had studied that culture. "Politics gives guys so much power and such big egos they tend to behave badly toward women," he told Merck. "And I hope I never get into that."

There was more to the shaping of Clinton's sexual persona than his irrepressible political ambition. He had been reared by a mother who loved to flirt, who walked around in a tube top and short shorts and spent considerable time each day trying to make herself sexually alluring, and he left home just as the country was entering a new age of sexual freedom. All of this went into the making of the unbashful young Clinton. The cherub-faced, saxophone-playing boy of sixteen who had jokingly jangled his hotel room key at girl clarinetists he encountered at a band contest in Little Rock was now the lumberjack-bearded scholar of twenty-three playing strip poker in Oxford one night with four friends, three of them women. "Five of us were in the game and I knew that whoever didn't win the game could be staying the night," Mandy Merck later recalled. Merck won, but before she left, the other four players, Clinton included, were undressed. "I don't know if the others were purposely losing hands or what," she said. "But there was a sexual atmosphere to it."

In the sexual realm, as in most other aspects of life, Clinton was adept at employing self-deprecating humor and easygoing charm to take the edge off situations that might have turned disastrous for a clumsier fellow. One night he invited Merck and Sara Maitland to accompany him to a lecture at Ruskin Hall by Germaine Greer, the flamboyant feminist author who was writing *The Female Eunuch*. He told Maitland that he wanted to see Greer because he had heard that "she had great legs," but that he would not go without women escorts. They came late and sat in the back of the cavernous hall. Greer arrived, tall and glamorous with a mane of long hair, wearing a close-fitting rawhide midiskirt.

The highlight of her lecture was her contention that intellectual men were hapless as sexual partners and that women should go to bed with working-class men. Her thesis on class and sex "left everybody a bit jaw-dropped," as Maitland recalled. Everybody except Clinton, apparently, who in the spirit of the moment asked Greer if he could have her telephone number in case she ever changed her mind about intellectual men. Maitland and Merck later disagreed on when and how Clinton offered this tantalizing proposition. Maitland thought it was in front of the entire audience during a question and answer period; Merck thought it was afterwards, when Greer had left the podium. But they agreed on the classic Clinton moment. "It was very Bill-like, that exuberance of what a good time he was having, and it was so much what every man was feeling at the meeting, and Bill was so unembarrassed about it," Maitland recalled. "Mandy and Bill and I were all very pleased with ourselves walking home that night."

Merck felt so comfortable around Clinton that she turned to him when she was having trouble with her love life. He was, she later said, the first man to whom she came out as a lesbian. She had fallen in love with another woman but was devastated when the relationship started to fall apart. "I thought I was going to lose this person. The woman involved wasn't in town, so I went over to see Bill and in the course of talking to him I said, 'I'm involved with this woman and I'm afraid it's not going to work and I'm feeling rather wretched.' I was tearful, and Bill was all, 'There, there—I didn't know you were. . . .' " Clinton soothed her. He was neither disapproving nor shocked.

David Mixner, one of the moratorium leaders in Washington, visited Leckford Road early in 1970 and almost went through a similar confessional with Clinton. Mixner was gay but keeping his sexual orientation deep in the closet. He was fearful that if his homosexuality became public it would embarrass his family and get him "quickly shunted to the side" of the antiwar movement. Once when he thought he was being blackmailed, he went on a three-day binge of drinking and drugs. He contemplated killing himself. His friends, thinking that he had suffered a nervous breakdown, sent him to Europe on a speaking tour. During that trip, he stayed for several days at Leckford Road at Clinton's invitation. He rarely saw Talbott, who spent most of his time behind his locked door. Aller was in and out. But Clinton was always around and spoke to Mixner for hours each day.

They talked about dating women. Mixner told Clinton about his first lover at Arizona State University, who had died in an auto accident. It was a male lover, but Mixner feminized him when talking to Clinton. Clinton, whose father had died in an auto accident, wanted to know everything about the accident: how it happened, how Mixner felt, what it was like to see someone killed, what Mixner felt happened to people after they died.

Clinton, Mixner recalled, "had a way of making you feel you were the most important friend in his life and what happened to you was the most important thing that ever happened." At one point, talking to Clinton, Mixner felt tempted to reveal his homosexuality, to tell the whole story. He wanted to tell Clinton, Mixner said later, but was "afraid I'd lose him as a friend."

Clinton's final months at Oxford offered him more than enough opportunity to play the role of comforting friend. The breakup of the relationship between Paul Parish and Sara Maitland was so tumultuous and life-changing that it sent first Maitland and then Parish to psychiatric wards. Parish was dealing with several tensions in his life: his relationship with his mother, his latent homosexuality, his efforts to become a conscientious objector, his loneliness in the solitary academic corridors of Oxford. One of the unfortunate manifestations of his illness was that he could not stand to be in the same room with Maitland. The Parish-Maitland drama received mixed reviews at Leckford Road. Talbott, in the midst of his Khrushchev project, showed little patience with the couple. As Maitland later put it, "He didn't want roving nutcases around, and I can't blame him." Aller and Clinton were more tolerant. Maitland was treated at a hospital on the edge of Oxford, and Aller and Clinton rode the No. 1 bus out to see her several times. With each visit, they brought the Lady Sara, hostess of the most popular tea parties in town, a small pot of exotic tea. After Maitland was released from the hospital, Clinton decided that a visit to a hair salon would help calm her nerves. He arranged the appointment without consulting Maitland, who had gorgeous long hair which she really did not want cut. Although the visit did nothing to help her relax, she was heartened by Clinton's concern.

When the Hilary term ended in April, Clinton and Rick Stearns rode the train to Spain, the final leg of their grand tour of the European continent. Stearns, ever earnest, had compiled a reading list and suggested that he and Clinton study the Spanish Civil War as they traveled. They shared copies of George Orwell's *Homage to Catalonia*, André Malraux's *Man's Hope*, Ernest Hemingway's *The Sun Also Rises*, Franz Borkenau's *The Spanish Cockpit*, and Hugh Thomas's *The Spanish Civil War.* The journey invigorated Clinton intellectually much as the trip to Moscow had done months before. But there was another purpose. Waiting to see them in Madrid were two young women, Lyda Holt and Jill Thrift, both of whom had recently graduated from Southern Methodist University and were studying art at the Prado. Lyda and Clinton had remained friends since they had met in her father's campaign for governor in 1966. Now they were trying to fix each other up with their friends: Lyda with Stearns, Clinton with Thrift.

Lyda had not seen Clinton recently and gasped at the sight of him, with his sloppy work clothes, scruffy beard, and bushy brown hairdo. His side-kick Stearns was equally grubby, sporting stringy hair and a Fu Manchu mustache that he hoped gave him the flair of Pancho Villa. Not that Clinton had lost his Arkansas charm. One night in Madrid the four had dinner with Lyda's aunt and uncle, who were visiting their daughter, Peggy Freeman, who was also living there that season. Jack Holt, known as Poppa Jack, was the political operator in the Holt family, and Clinton spent hours after dinner debriefing him on events back home. Clinton thoroughly delighted Lyda's Aunt Marge Holt as well, though not enough to make her overlook his appearance. When he left, she turned to her daughter and sighed, "My goodness, I just don't know, Lyda dating someone with that long hair and beard!" Lyda Holt thought her aunt "was of a mind to grab some scissors and cut that beard off!"

The quartet spent hours touring the Prado, the world-class art museum that so enthralled Lyda that she visited it every day. She was surprised by Clinton's taste in artists. "I thought he would go for Velázquez, who was humanistic and painted his subjects so craftily they didn't realize they were being psychoanalyzed for history. Wrong. He loved El Greco. Then I took him to the Goya room and he loved that. El Greco I thought would be too contemporary for him, but he wasn't. And he was enthralled with Goya. Goya didn't pull any punches. He was graphic about how the world was ripping apart." Clinton also liked the work of Hieronymus Bosch and spent several minutes analyzing Bosch's *Table Top with the Seven Deadly Sins.*

When they went off to tour the rest of Spain, the matchmaking effort devolved into a picaresque farce. Stearns thought the women were too clothes-conscious. "The girls had a preposterous amount of clothes—one suitcase was just full of shoes!" Stearns recalls. And Lyda found Stearns deadly earnest and uptight. The lessons Clinton had tried to give him on how to make friends and woo women were not paying dividends here. "I was trying to get poor Rick to loosen up. Relax. This is Spain," Lyda said later. "He very seriously asked me what I intended to do with my life. I said I would like to go into retail, run a gift shop someday. That might have horrified him. It seemed like the harder he tried, the worse it got." And try Stearns did. When they reached Seville, he felt so guilty about the way he and Clinton looked compared with their dates—"they were showing up at dinner every night like fashion plates!"—that he shaved off his mustache. But he sensed that by that time all was lost. While Holt and Thrift went shopping, he and Clinton traipsed off to the Mexican pavilion at Seville's fair and started drinking what looked like orangeade at five centavos a cup. It was a sweltering day on the Spanish plain, and the beverage seemed especially refreshing to the American lads. They assumed that it could not have much alcohol. Soon enough they were tipsy. They were sitting on a curb, giggling, when the young women found them—one of the few times in Clinton's life when he appeared drunk.

SOON after he returned to Oxford, Clinton again assumed one of his favorite roles, playing tour guide for an Arkansas friend visiting England. David Leopoulos, mourning the recent murder of his mother, who had been stabbed to death at her antique shop in Hot Springs, rode the train north from Camp Darby near Pisa with his Army buddy Steve Gorman. Clinton hoped that the holiday in England might ease the grief of his closest friend from his childhood. They had not seen each other for more than a year, the longest they had been apart since they were eight years old. Leopoulos was always hungering to spend time with Clinton, who represented to him not only the sweet memories of their childhood in Hot Springs but also an imagined future of unlimited promise. He boasted to Gorman of the Rhodes Scholar they were traveling to Oxford to see: "This guy's going to be president someday."

But the trip to England proved anything but relaxing. The thumping, screeching, rumbling, and lurching of the train as it twisted through the Alps kept them up all night. When the clean-cut Army computer specialists, sleepless and exhausted, dragged their heavy canvas bags through the station in London, Gorman turned to Leopoulos and muttered, "Where the hell is he?"

Leopoulos looked down the corridor and saw "this guy with long hair, a bushy beard, blue jeans" walking toward them, accompanied by a young woman. "There's Bill," he said.

"He's going to be president?" Gorman asked, incredulous.

"Yeah," said Leopoulos. "He'll clean up okay."

Throughout the visit, Leopoulos's mother's death was never mentioned, a polite avoidance that David not only appreciated but thought was typical of Clinton. "Bill will not talk about awful, negative things with his old friends," Leopoulos said later. "He would rather avoid them. Shut them out. But I knew that the feeling was there."

IN the final term of his second year at Oxford, Clinton showed signs of becoming a serious student. He attended special cram courses, known as revision courses, that were intended to prepare students for degree examinations. Alan Ryan, a politics don at New College, ran the revision courses in politics. "It was a sort of two-year polishing-up session so that people could come and revise like mad for the actual examinations—a sort of thirty-three things you need to know in thirty-five minutes type thing." Though Ryan could not remember Clinton being in his class, university records indicate that he was. Univ politics don Maurice Shock, who had returned from a leave, became Clinton's supervisor for his final term. Shock filed a report stating that Clinton was working hard but that his effort to fulfill the B. Phil. requirements was a race against time which he would most likely lose. In the month before the June examinations, Shock suggested that Clinton was not ready and should instead return for a third year, switching from a two-year B. Phil. to a three-year D. Phil., which required a dissertation of as much as 100,000 words.

Most Rhodes Scholars stayed at Oxford for two years, though there was money available for a third year for students who needed the extra time. Clinton considered the third-year option, which several of his friends, including Talbott, were taking, but decided that getting the Oxford degree was not worth the delay it would cause in his long-range plans to run for public office. He had already been accepted into Yale Law School, as had several other Oxford friends, including Bob Reich and Doug Eakeley. Yale Law seemed like the place to be—both an important establishment credential and a gathering place for many of the most politically astute members of his generation.

When Clinton appeared at Shock's rooms at Univ College one day that spring, accompanied by Reich, and announced that he would not be staying for a third year, the don was neither surprised nor disappointed. "I didn't take any kind of dim view that he decided not to take a degree," Shock recalled. "It was clear that he had gotten a lot out of it." Although Sir Edgar Williams, the warden of Rhodes House, took pride in the academic accomplishments of his foreign charges at Oxford, he nonetheless had a subtle appreciation for what the scholarship really meant to the Americans. "If you were an American and entirely on the make, you would do well in college, try for the Rhodes, get your name in the newspapers for winning one, and then resign it and go to Harvard or Yale Law School," Williams noted. "The motivation is to get it. What you do here doesn't really matter so long as you enjoy yourself. Don't fail to take notice that it's a free trip to Europe. Make friends. And, we hope, don't grow to dislike the English."

In the end, nine out of the thirty-two members of the American Rhodes class of 1968 never received Oxford degrees, the highest percentage in the post–World War II period. Among Clinton's closest friends, only Reich and Eakeley took their Oxford degrees in two years. Although each scholar had his own story, the larger trend seems obviously related to the times. To some extent it had to do with a cultural shift in which the new generation was challenging traditional totems of academic achievement. But the complications arising from the war and the draft were more important in their thinking. Many of those who eventually left without degrees, including Clinton, later expressed regret and wished that they could go back and complete that unfinished period of their lives. Although later in his career Clinton never spoke bitterly about his Oxford experience, he rarely extolled those years, either. One reason was a touch of embarrassment: Oxford represented unfinished business. Perhaps that sense of mild regret and ambiguity served as the fitting metaphor for an extraordinary, unrepeatable era.

When the Trinity term ended, Frank Aller headed for Spain to work on an autobiographical novel. Strobe Talbott traveled to Boston, where he continued his translation of the Khrushchev memoirs before returning to Oxford, where he and several members of the class, including Paul Parish and Frank Aller, would study for a third year. And Clinton flew to Washington, where he would spend the summer as a low-level organizer in Project Pursestrings, an effort to persuade Congress to cut off funding for the Vietnam War. In mid-July, he drove to Springfield, Massachusetts, for the wedding of college roommate Kit Ashby, who was then a Marine Corps officer on his way to Vietnam. Clinton, who had no money, slept in the basement at the house of the parents of the bride. Early on the wedding morning, the prospective bride tiptoed down to the basement where the ironing board was stored, to iron the train of her wedding gown. "I was trying to hold the dress so it wouldn't fall on the floor; doing it quietly but with great difficulty," Amy Ashby later recalled. "All of a sudden this voice says, 'Why don't you let me hold it.' Bill had taken the white sheet he had slept on and wrapped it around himself. I was shocked. He looked like Jesus. I said, 'God, Bill, you look like Jesus Christ!' He helped me hold down the train."

The wedding at Sacred Heart Church reflected the crosscurrents of the era. The six ushers were Marines in dress uniform. The six groomsmen included the brothers of the bride and groom as well as the Potomac Avenue housemates from Georgetown, except for Tom Campbell, who was flying Navy planes in Japan. Ashby and many of his Marine buddies were on their way to Vietnam. The lasting memory that Amy Ashby had of the wedding reception in her parents' backyard was of Clinton, bearded and shaggy, standing face to face with a crewcut soldier, arguing one more time about the war that defined their generation.

William Jefferson Blythe III. Hope, Arkansas, 1950.

Virginia Kelley and William Jefferson Blythe.

Roger Clinton and Bill Clinton.

Bill Clinton, with his mother and half-brother, Roger.

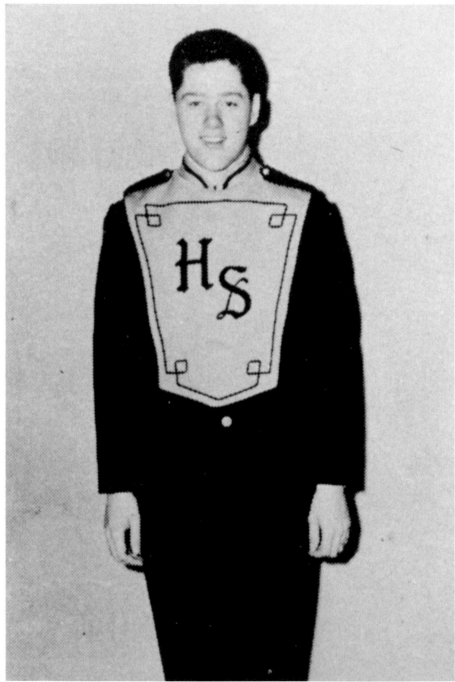

5

In a cosmopolitan resort town with big bands featured in all the top hotels and nightclubs, it was no embarrassment to play tenor sax for the award-winning high school dance band; or to lead the Pep Band during basketball season; or to form a jazz band and play riffs in the auditorium during lunch hour.

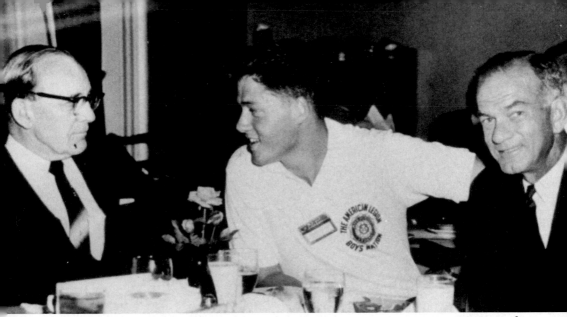

6

The young men of Boys Nation were invited to lunch with the senators from their state in the Senate Dining Room. Bill Clinton sat between Senator John McClellan (left) and Senator J. William Fulbright. Clinton had already studied Fulbright's life and career and considered the intellectual Arkansan his first political role model.

The highlight of Boys Nation was a visit to the Rose Garden. After a brief speech, President Kennedy greeted the boys, and Clinton made sure he was the first to shake his hand. Later, at graduation, when friends and teachers gave him their yearbooks, Clinton often turned to the page with this picture on it and signed below the photograph, which has subsequently become famous.

7

Georgetown, 1965. As the student officer responsible for making the incoming freshmen feel welcome, Clinton had the opportunity to make new friends and build his constituency at the same time. No one knew how to navigate the campus more skillfully.

8

The five seniors who shared a house on Potomac Avenue were "boringly respectable." Within the wider spectrum of sixties behavior, Clinton and his housemates were trim and tame. Despite the war in Vietnam and the rioting following the assassination of Martin Luther King, Jr., Tom Campbell (right) thought of it as "a sort of never-never-land up there."

9

Clinton with Denise Hyland (center couple), his steady girlfriend at Georgetown, at a black tie ball with friends—Kit Ashby (far left), Jim Moore (fourth from left), and Tom Campbell (fourth from right).

10

For his first full-time campaign adventure, Clinton worked on Judge Frank Holt's run for the Democratic nomination for governor of Arkansas. Holt lost the election but helped Clinton land a job on Senator Fulbright's staff.

11

The young recruits, a coterie of college student leaders who became known as "the Holt Generation,"often worked sixteen-hour days. Clinton eventually became a chauffeur for the judge's wife and two daughters, who barnstormed the state. When the route took them to Hope, Clinton asked if he could give the speech, since his grandmother would be in the audience.

12

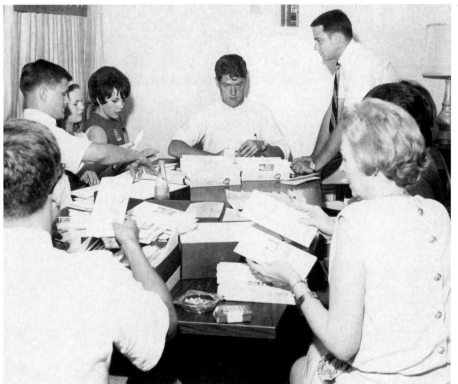

13 For the Rhodes Scholars in the class of 1968, being in England may have removed them from the chaos and excesses of student activism back home, but it could not rid them of their anxieties and concerns about the draft.

14

No one had expected Clinton back for his second year at Oxford—his draft status had seemed so hopeless. So Clinton freeloaded for a while with friends before being invited to share a flat at 46 Leckford Road with Strobe Talbott (left), the Russia scholar, and Frank Aller (right), the China scholar and draft resister. Aller's suicide in 1971 marked an end to the sixties for their Rhodes group. Clinton maintained a strong relationship with Talbott, and chose him to be ambassador at large for Russia and the other former Soviet republics and later appointed him deputy secretary of state.

15

In 1986, eighteen years after the Rhodes Scholars of the class of 1968 sailed across the Atlantic, Robert Reich, who was teaching politics and economics at the Kennedy School of Government at Harvard, wrote in the *American Oxonian:* "Rumor has it that Bill will be the Democratic candidate for president in 1988. I just made up that rumor, but by the time you read this, the rumor will have spread to the ends of the nation." Reich's work on industrial policy and world trade became a cornerstone of Clinton's economic thinking, and Reich was appointed secretary of labor.

16

Clinton was never more in his element than on the campaign trail. Every hand he shook, every corner store he stopped in, every pie supper he attended, helped him transform his image from the long-haired Rhodes Scholar and law professor into a young man of the people.

After working on the staff of the House Judiciary Committee's impeachment inquiry against President Nixon, Hillary Rodham joined Clinton in Arkansas and took a teaching position at the law school. While Clinton was a diffuse and easygoing professor, Rodham was precise and demanding.

17

Clinton and his chief campaign aide, Paul Fray (left), standing by the tally board [18] on election night in 1974. Clinton lost his race for Congress. The following morning, Clinton was back in downtown Fayetteville shaking hands. He was warming up. The next race had already begun.

With his own election for Arkansas attorney general locked up, Clinton signed on to work on the presidential campaign of fellow southerner Jimmy Carter. Three years later, President Carter sent Governor-elect Clinton a congratulatory note: "You and I will succeed in meeting the goals for our country by working closely together to serve those whom we represent." [19]

20

In January 1979, Bill Clinton was sworn in as the youngest governor in the United States in four decades. For the friends of Clinton and Rodham, this first inaugural had the aura of a generational rite of passage. For Virginia Kelley, it was a moment she had been waiting for—and guiding her son toward—his whole life.

21

Governor Clinton meeting with Brigadier General James (Bulldog) Drummond (right) at Fort Chaffee after the Cuban refugee riot. Clinton was given high marks for his performance under pressure, but his close friendship with President Carter became increasingly strained and was then held against him by Arkansas voters.

The governor at the Hope Watermelon Festival. Since his college days, Clinton had been at ease sticking out his oversize right hand and working conversations back to his humble roots—and the giant watermelons of Hope.

22

23

With Clinton in the governor's office, Hillary Rodham seemed to have little difficulty embracing the acquisitive and competitive corporate life she had once repudiated. Her decision to join the Rose Law Firm, which represented, among others,
the holy trinity of Arkansas business and industry—Stephens Inc., Tyson Foods,
and Wal-Mart—later provoked questions of conflict of interest.

Vincent Foster, Jr. (below), and
Webster Hubbell (right) were
Hillary's partners at the Rose Law
Firm and business associates. They
would both join President Clinton's
administration in high positions.

24

25

The 1988 Democratic Convention in Atlanta was the third consecutive convention at which Clinton had made the coveted list of speakers. After the first sentence, the speech went downhill. After a few minutes, Clinton could see that he had lost the audience. At the twenty-one-minute mark, ABC cut away and people could be heard shouting, "Get the hook!"

26

By the time Clinton began his campaign for a fifth term, he was such a large, familiar figure in the state that he faced the ultimate political paradox. His self-image had always been one of action and change, yet now he had come to represent permanence and the status quo.

27

Clinton and Al Gore at the national meeting of the Democratic Leadership Council in May 1991. The buzz among journalists and political opinion makers was that Clinton's keynote speech established him as a serious national figure who seemed to have a clear idea of what he wanted to do as president.

28

²⁹ On October 3, 1991, with his wife, Hillary, and their daughter, Chelsea, at his side, and with many of the key figures in his life—including his mother, Virginia Kelley, and friends Carolyn Staley, David Leopoulos, Tommy Caplan, and Bob Reich—in attendance, Clinton announced his candidacy for president.

CHAPTER THIRTEEN

LAW AND POLITICS AT YALE

LUCK AND FATE always seem to appear at the edge of the road as Bill Clinton drives along his highway of ambition, two friendly hitchhikers, thumbs out, ready to be picked up for stretches here and there when other passengers appear less attractive. Usually there are less mysterious ways to explain how he got to where he wanted to go. But in the fall of 1970, luck and fate not only went along for the ride, they crowded him out of the driver's seat and took over the steering wheel. How else to explain the combination of circumstances that awaited him when he moved to Connecticut to begin law school?

After his adventuresome and enlightening, though officially unfulfilled, academic spell at Oxford, Clinton returned to the United States anxious to launch his political career, yet reluctant to head back to Arkansas without the imprimatur of an advanced degree from an elite institution. He rejected the option of staying at University College for a third year and earning his degree there, as Oxford officials had invited him to do, largely because his political itch, his need to get on with his life, made another year at Oxford seem indulgent if not irrelevant. He had already discarded the idea of attending law school back at the University of Arkansas at Fayetteville for a number of reasons, not least his desire to remain in the company of the brightest of his generation. Yale Law School offered the answers to his every need—political, academic, social, and personal.

But if luck and fate played their crucial roles for Clinton at Yale, they had little to do with his getting in. He earned his place by distinction of his Rhodes Scholarship and by scoring high on the law boards. That said, there could not have been a better setting for him. Clinton, impatient, wanted to attend a prestigious law school and to immerse himself in American politics at the same time. Nowhere could this be done more surely than at Yale, which was not only elite and distinguished but also experimental and adaptable to the free-form culture of the era. The stereotype of an Ivy League law school's first year as a rigorous boot camp where crusty old professors did their brutal best to exhaust and demoralize students was turned on its head at Yale Law. Grades had been all but eliminated before Clinton arrived, replaced by a more egalitarian pass—fail system that freed students to devote more time to the issues of the day, or whatever diversions caught their fancy, than to grinding out four-point averages on the way toward slots on the *Yale Law Journal* and partnerships at Wall Street firms.

The prevailing sentiment at Yale Law was that you truly had to put your mind to it to flunk out. It was, as one professor said, a very tough country club to get into, but once you were in, you were in. With that surplus of academic freedom, Clinton needed only a political campaign to round out his days. As luck would have it, one was ready and waiting for him when he arrived, and not just any campaign but perhaps the nation's most compelling Senate race. One of the candidates, Joseph D. Duffey, a thirty-eight-year-old peace and civil rights activist and ethics professor at Hartford Seminary, had emerged as a successor of sorts to Eugene McCarthy and Robert Kennedy, leading the antiwar legions on another long march for peace two years after the crusades of 1968. Fate would reappear before the school year ended, when Clinton encountered a young woman who was to bring order and clarity to his life's ambition.

BUSLOADS of student volunteers rumbled into Connecticut in 1970 for the "New Politics" campaign of Joe Duffey. The pilgrimage had started during the first week in May, when college political activism, which had been faltering, returned after the invasion of Cambodia and the shooting of four young protesters by National Guardsmen at Kent State University in Ohio. Suddenly the old mill towns of Connecticut were the places to be for the mobile young masses of the antiwar movement. The movement's ambitious young leaders came to Connecticut in force, too, some of them the same aspiring activists who had met on Martha's Vineyard a year earlier at the gathering that was half-jokingly dubbed " The Executive Committee of the Future." They were drawn by a sense that the war in Vietnam would only be ended by changing votes in Congress, one election at a time, and because they saw the Connecticut campaign as a rehearsal theater for the big show, the struggle for the future of the Democratic party that was sure to come in 1972.

Tony Podesta, a McCarthy campaign veteran who then qualified as the living definition of a political junkie, brought Clinton into the Duffey organization. They had worked together that summer for several weeks at Project Pursestrings. Of all the antiwar groups and projects in Washington during that era, Pursestrings was among the most conventional. It had been funded with help from several establishment figures and several young liberal Republicans were recruited to give it a bipartisan flavor. The Pursestrings office on K Street served as a meeting place for the mainstream of the young antiwar activists, including several from the Vineyard crowd, who would organize during the day and at night gather at taverns or apartments to talk and drink and play poker and impress young women. Clinton was clean-shaven again. (The beard appeared and disappeared depending on where Clinton was and what was expected of him. His mother, who never liked the beard, believed that Clinton grew it because "he had a baby face and decided it would look better for him," and that he was encouraged to keep it by people who would "come along and say he looked like Jesus—well, he thought that was wonderful!")

By the summer of 1970, Clinton was beginning to build a reputation within this network of high-achieving peers. There was an unspoken understanding in the group that most of them were skilled organizers and strategists but only a few had the aptitude and ambition to run for office themselves. According to Podesta, there "were two guys at Pursestrings we all thought would someday end up in a primary running against each other. One was Jim Johnson and the other was Bill Clinton." Johnson was several steps ahead of Clinton on the political ladder at that point. He ran Pursestrings while Clinton was among the assistants. And Johnson thought big: looking around the K Street office one day, he remarked: "This would be a great place to run a presidential campaign!" He considered running for office, but never did. He assisted other politicians instead, including Edmund Muskie and Vice President Walter Mondale, and eventually became a corporate executive.

Many from the Pursestrings contingent ventured up to Connecticut before the three-way August 19 Democratic primary, which Duffey won. The political rush that Podesta felt after that victory—which took him by surprise; he had already sent out a press statement with Duffey's concession before the votes were counted—caused him, he said later, to lose his senses and contract his first case of Potomac fever. He agreed to coordinate the Duffey forces in the general election, which promised to be another colorful three-way contest involving Duffey, Republican Lowell P. Weicker, Jr., and the incumbent, Thomas J. Dodd, who was running as an independent after being dumped by the Democrats when the Senate censured him for misusing campaign funds. Podesta served as Duffey's number-two aide, known to the troops as "Deputy Dog," behind Anne Wexler, a party activist and McCarthy campaign veteran from Westport who was Duffey's campaign manager and future wife.

They had "the pick of the best young organizers around," including Podesta's younger brother John; Steve Robbins, another Pursestrings veteran; occasional help from the moratorium leaders Sam Brown, David Mixner, and John Shattuck; Lawrence Kudlow and Michael Medved (antiwar activists who later undertook the ideological transformation to neoconservatism); a crackerjack all-women advance team consisting largely of students from Smith College; and Bill Clinton, who was recruited to run the Third Congressional District based in New Haven. For someone with Clinton's personality, a political explorer always searching for exotic places to discover and fresh faces to charm, Connecticut's tough old Third Congressional District presented itself like a bright new world. New Haven and the inner ring of towns around it, with their mixture of Italian and Irish ethnics, their police club and parochial school cultures, their ward captain style of old-fashioned politics, challenged Clinton's resourcefulness. So too, in their own way, did the fashionable outer suburbs dominated by patrician Republicans, another breed virtually unknown in Arkansas. The district was Democratic in those days, but barely so, and there were enough Dodd loyalists in the ethnic neighborhoods and Republicans in the suburbs to make the antiwar theology professor from Hartford less than an easy sell.

First, Clinton had to sell himself, both to the Duffey partisans and to other Democrats who had supported either of Duffey's primary opponents, zipper manufacturer Alphonsus J. Donahue, the choice of longtime party boss John Bailey, and state senator Ed Marcus, who had positioned himself as the law-and-order candidate. "There was a little bit of reaction at first: Why are you sending this law student from Arkansas here? How could anyone who doesn't have the water of New Haven in his blood know what to do?" Podesta recalled. "Bill Clinton was an unusual choice as our ambassador to the Donahue and Marcus people, but he did very well. He won them over and brought them to our campaign. He became the guy the staff liked the most and the volunteers liked the most. He had the most friends by the end." He was also the candidate's favorite organizer. Duffey's strongest memory of Clinton during the campaign was of the young Arkansan waiting for him at the curb in New Haven, ready to brief him on where they were going, the issues they would emphasize that day, and the various factions they would have to deal with. "Bill knew what he was doing," Duffey said later. "He could talk to anyone."

When Clinton first called Mickey Donenfeld, a registered nurse and the Duffey coordinator in conservative Milford along Long Island Sound, and said, in a soft, southern drawl, "Hah, Ahm Bill Clinton and ahm the third congressional coordinator," Donenfeld muttered to herself, "Oh, my God!" She conjured up an unpleasant image of what it would be like dealing with this sleepy, laid-back character. Irv Stolberg, a leader of the reform Democrats in New Haven who had been fired from his teaching position at Southern Connecticut University for his antiwar activism and was running for the state legislature that fall, found Clinton "one of the few Yalies who had any depth of political interest." Clinton "spoke funny," Stolberg thought, "but aside from that he was easygoing and bright, and it didn't take him very long to figure out the area." It was part of Clinton's peripatetic campaign style to spend most of his time trying to master the area and its people. He would visit the storefront headquarters at the New Politics Center near the corner of Elm and Church in New Haven most mornings, but it was hard to keep him there for long. "Bill," according to Stolberg, "was running around the district more than running the office. He spent a lot of time in the outlying towns."

Chuca Meyer, one of the Smith College recruits, spent several days traveling the roads of the district with Clinton, who would either follow her or ride along in her Volkswagen bug. "I was told the new guy needed to be taken around the district to meet the local coordinators so I said I wouldn't mind showing him around," Meyer said later. "Every day we'd hit a few new places—Milford, Stratford, Hamden, Wallingford, all the towns around New Haven. Those of us who had joined the campaign had this feeling about Joe—almost this proprietary feeling. New people kept coming in after he made it through the convention and won the primary, and they had to go through this test: 'Do you really care about Joe or are you just along for the ride?' " Duffey's original staff members referred derisively to the talented newcomers as "Hessians." But what struck Meyer about Clinton was that she never went through that testing phase with him. "I felt I knew him the whole time."

As in the first campaign in which he had worked, Frank Holt's race for governor of Arkansas in 1966, when he spent his extra hours over at the Holt house in Little Rock eating and chatting and napping, Clinton used the Duffey campaign to develop family-style ties with colleagues. It seemed that he had a surrogate mother in every town. On his way home at night he would often stop at Mickey Donenfeld's in Milford. "He'd come over, Chuca would come over, with their friends, and we'd talk and I would feed them. Bill ate quite healthily. Whatever we had, he'd eat. He'd come over for breakfast, too. Bacon and eggs. And he took a lot of naps at my house. In the living room, on the couch, he'd be snoozing."

They were mostly catnaps. Clinton was always on the move. He shared a four-bedroom beach house on Long Island Sound near Milford with three law school classmates: Doug Eakeley, his Rhodes Scholar friend from Uni-

versity College; Donald Pogue, who had been the Dartmouth debate part-
ner of John Isaacson; and Bill Coleman, one of ten black students in
Clinton's class. The drive to New Haven, where the law school and Third
District campaign headquarters were located, took about twenty minutes
up Route 1. When not cruising the district checking on local coordinators,
Clinton was often traveling an hour up the highway to the state headquarters in Hartford. Anyone looking for him that semester knew that the Yale
Law library was probably the last place to find him. Although his
housemates and campaign co-workers were amazed by how Clinton
seemed to find extra hours in his day, he devoted few of them to Yale Law.

The Senate race was the toughest course he took that semester, and it
left the most lasting impression on him. The two central dilemmas Joe
Duffey and his supporters faced in 1970 were the same ones Clinton would
struggle with over the next two decades during his rise in Arkansas and on
the national scene: first, how to hold together the competing forces within
the Democratic party; and second, the related question of how to champion social change without alienating the vast American middle class.
These questions were still relatively new for the Democrats in 1970 after
a decade in which the party and country at large had been ripping apart
over issues of peace and race.

The cultural fissure was widened in Connecticut by Dodd's presence on
the ballot as a third-party candidate. Although the Democratic machine
ostensibly supported Duffey once he won the primary, Dodd, despite his
difficulties, retained many of his ties to old-line elements of the party.
Wexler realized that in many of the blue-collar districts where the Duffey
forces canvassed, there was "a longstanding devotion to Tom Dodd based
on the many years of help he had given families during hard times." Organized labor was split. Some union leaders still held grudges against Wexler
for her prominence in the McCarthy campaign and reluctance in the fall of
1968 to endorse their favorite son, Hubert Humphrey. With Dodd and
Weicker, a moderate Republican, positioned to Duffey's right, and with
Duffey's public identity shaped by his activism on civil rights and Vietnam,
it was difficult for the campaign to articulate broader themes and avoid
being tagged as too far to the left.

Duffey and his campaign leaders understood the dilemma intellectually.
From the moment that students started flooding into the state after the
invasion of Cambodia, Duffey viewed their presence as a mixed blessing.
Many of the students came out of wealthy suburbs and had no skills at
communicating with working-class voters, whose sons tended to be the
ones getting killed in Vietnam. "We had a lot of students who had never
talked to a union member in their life and who had no idea what a factory
was like inside," Duffey recalled. He said he became so fearful of how the

youth brigades might hurt his effort to build a broad-based coalition that he established a rule that students could canvas only when accompanied by people from the neighborhood.

In the Duffey campaign, as in the antiwar movement and the Democratic party, there was a tension between the middle and the left, between purists and realists. Duffey and his top aides considered themselves realists who, in Podesta's words, sought to build "a broad-based, new kind of redefined Democratic coalition that was post-Great Society and accepted the notion that government couldn't solve everything." Clinton, with his adaptability and his ability to talk to opposing factions, "embodied the campaign's efforts to appeal to diverse elements," according to Wexler. Some believed that Clinton was better at that effort than the candidate himself. Duffey, earnest and intelligent, was admired by his troops, but he was not charismatic or especially adept at the mix-and-mingle aspects of politics. John Spotila, the Georgetown classmate of Clinton's, who was also attending Yale Law School, was recruited by Clinton to run the West Haven operation, which was regarded as Archie Bunker territory. Duffey, Spotila thought, "could never bridge the gap there. I'm not sure that he really tried. I never saw him in West Haven. Bill was better at bridging the gap than Joe was."

The irony here was that Duffey, more than most of his followers, was a product of blue-collar America. He had grown up in West Virginia, the son of a coal miner who had lost a leg in the mines. But by the time he made the Senate race, many people thought of him as the darling of Connecticut's cocktail party liberal elite. "You're too god-damn nice" to run, one friend told Duffey, who had been ordained as a Congregationalist minister. That Duffey was an antiwar college professor and chairman of the liberal Americans for Democratic Action "made it harder with blue-collar voters," according to Podesta. Larry Kudlow, coordinator for the First Congressional District based in Hartford, said the campaign could see the working-class white voters splitting away—the same voters who a decade later would be called Reagan Democrats—"but we couldn't get to them. We could not deal with what was then called the hard-hat vote. There was a lot of hostility."

In the campaign's final month, construction workers wearing hard hats as badges of patriotism often confronted Duffey along the campaign trail, carrying signs that read "Duffey the Radical" and "SDS, Pot and Duffey Go Together" and "A Vote for Duffey Is a Vote for Khrushchev." When one critic rushed up to Duffey at a Knights of Columbus picnic in New Haven and called him a Communist, one of his key labor supporters, Vincent Sirabella, a leader of the blue-collar workers at Yale, stepped in, assumed a fighting stance, and proclaimed, "Nobody calls my friend Duffey a Communist in front of me!" Duffey himself finally lost his temper in October when he heard that Vice President Spiro Agnew had delivered a speech labeling the Americans for Democratic Action a "nest of radicals" and its chairman, Duffey, a "revisionist Marxist." (Duffey was once quoted saying that of himself in a sarcastic manner, attempting to contrast his views with those of hard-line leftists. Now he denounced Agnew as a "cowardly liar.")

The Duffey crew worked hard to the end. The issues staff put in long hours developing positions on everything from military conversion to recycling. Duffey would privately joke that his campaign had "more positions than the Kama Sutra." The canvassers eventually reached nearly every Democratic and independent household in the state. Chuca Meyer, who spent election day getting out the vote in the industrial city of Waterbury, was "naive enough to believe in miracles. We'd had miracles in the convention and at the primary, so why not another one?" But at campaign headquarters there was less optimism. "No one there thought Duffey could win —not even Duffey," according to Podesta. Weicker prevailed in the three-way contest with 41.7 percent of the vote. Duffey finished second, with 33.8 percent. Dodd was the spoiler, with 24.5 percent. Podesta viewed it as "a tidal wave of rejection. It wasn't close. There was no thought of a recount." Duffey lost every congressional district, including Clinton's. He carried heavily Democratic New Haven, but not by as much as expected.

Losing elections was nothing new for Bill Clinton, but he rarely seemed to suffer for losing. He emerged from the Duffey campaign with an expanded circle of friends and allies who would come to his assistance in later years. He found another political mentor in Anne Wexler, who shared his reverence for the system, a practical reformer who had the instincts of an old-fashioned pol, loved the political game and its rules, and who played to win. And in Duffey's defeat he caught the first glimpses of what he might have to do later to bring elements of the party together.

Perhaps the lesson of Connecticut was best expressed by Duffey himself in a campaign postscript which he later wrote:

> It is always tempting to blame our defeat on those people who never understood what we were trying to say or who rejected our efforts to lead them. But the fact is that the search for a new politics in America is still at a very primitive stage. . . . Many of our policies have been formulated as if the nation were composed of only two major groups—the affluent and the welfare poor. But somewhere between affluence and grinding poverty stand the majority of American families, living on the margins of social and economic insecurity. The new politics has thus far

not spoken to the needs and interests of those Americans. We have forgotten that they, too, feel the victims of decisions in which they have no voice.

Clinton had spent many days and nights talking to Duffey and Anne Wexler about how the new politics might someday figure out ways not to alienate middle America. Duffey's words were stored away.

ONCE during the campaign, Anne Wexler, overtaken by curiosity, asked Clinton whether he ever went to class. "He kind of laughed and I never asked him again. I never asked him again because I needed him. And he seemed very relaxed about it."

In the middle of November, a few weeks after the election, a first-year student at the law school was walking from class one afternoon when she was approached by "this tall guy with a huge head of hair and a beard" (apparently the beard was back).

"Hi, I'm Bill Clinton. Can I borrow your notes?" the young man said to Nancy Bekavac.

"For what?" Bekavac asked.

"For everything," he said.

"Are you in our class?"

"Yes ma'am."

"Well, where the hell've you been?" she asked. "We've been here since September!"

"Running the Joe Duffey campaign. We just lost," he said.

"Well, why borrow my notes? Borrow Reich's. He's your friend, isn't he?"

"He writes too much," Clinton said. "I want to borrow yours."

"Okay, but I've got to take some stuff out of the notebooks."

"What've you got in there, love letters?" he asked.

"Worse. Poems."

Bekavac relented and gave Clinton all her notes for four courses. He copied them and gave them back. No one saw him devote much time to reading them. One of his housemates, Bill Coleman, worried about Clinton in the weeks before final exams when it seemed that he had not opened a book. But Clinton was "as nonchalant about it as can be. He almost made fun of my worry for him." Late at night, in the back of the house, Coleman would sometimes stumble across Clinton reading and gasp: "Oh, God, you're finally reading your procedures book!" But it would turn out to be a novel. Once it was Proust's *Remembrance of Things Past.* In the morning, Coleman would find Clinton in the same place, reading another novel. It was not that Clinton never studied. He studied at odd hours, briefly, with great intensity, according to another housemate, Don Pogue. "He was very quick. I would love to know how fast he could read. He would get through more in an hour of concentrated effort than just about anybody I've ever seen. And he never slept much. If he slept more than four and a half hours a night, I'd be surprised."

Clinton rarely attending class, working day and night on the Duffey campaign for months, was not particularly out of the ordinary at Yale Law. One student worked full time for the mayor's office in New York City for the three years that he was in law school—and got his degree. Steve Cohen, a political activist in the class two years ahead of Clinton's, entered Yale Law in 1968 so exhausted from several political campaigns that he never went to class during his first year and a half in New Haven. It was not simply the relaxed grading system that made Yale Law a haven for political activists. Yale Law was considered a center of progressive thought, especially in comparison with Harvard Law, which was three times as large and more rigid and conservative. Relating the law to society was at the core of Yale's academic mission. Faculty and students were involved in storefront legal clinics and model cities programs dealing with welfare and poverty in New Haven. Students were encouraged to take courses at the university outside the law curriculum, and members of the law faculty were noted for their expertise in other areas ranging from economics to psychology.

Rather than demanding memorization and legal exactitude, many professors emphasized interpreting broad concepts. "In exams the concern was more whether you could get the policy argument right than get the right citations in a case," recalled Robert Borosage, then a leading radical student at Yale Law. "So for people with conceptual minds, like Clinton, it was pretty easy." James Blair, an Arkansas attorney who became a close friend years later, remembered Clinton telling him about his experience in a corporate law course. "He never went to class and studied for the final at the last minute. When he got there, he learned that it was an open book test. The first thing Bill had to do was go get the book. So he started thirty minutes late. And somehow he still did well on the test. So the professor called him in and asked, 'How did you do this?' And Bill said, 'Corporate law is a lot like politics and I understand politics. It's just a case of making sure each employer gets something out of it.' "

Because of his nonchalant attitude, Clinton at times could be underestimated. Pogue, though impressed by Clinton's seeming indefatigability, was skeptical about whether his housemate could "get into the deeper meaning" of his law studies. He was "flabbergasted" when he discovered that Clinton could. The revelation came when they decided to write a paper together for constitutional law. After spending hours talking out the themes with Clinton, Pogue offered to write the first draft. He "worked

and worked and worked on it," but in the end Clinton "got totally exasperated" and decided that they should write separate papers. Pogue had been
a championship debater in college and considered himself no slouch when
it came to presenting and defending positions. But Clinton "produced
something of such remarkable subtlety and fluidity" that it made Pogue
feel dense and fuzzy-headed by comparison.

THE Yale Law School sits grandly on the north side of campus, an imposing
golden-stone Gothic fortress occupying the entire block enclosed by Wall,
York, Grove, and High streets. Set off by a moat of ivy, it is a self-contained
attachment of buildings known as the Sterling Law Buildings, with its own
dormitory, dining hall, and library, graced everywhere by wood-paneled
walls, vaulted hallways, brick floors, and bay windows. Carved into the
Gothic stone arches leading in from Wall Street are symbolic scenes from
the courtroom, including a goat-headed client holding a money bag and a
lawyer as parrot. Above the inner doorway are more carvings, including
one classroom scene that is perhaps less symbolic, showing a professor
gesticulating as he lectures students dozing with their heads on their desks.
The architecture of the school was as solid and distinct as its pedagogical
reputation: select, activist, and clinically oriented. But its faculty in the
early 1970s was harder to characterize.

Here was a brilliant, eclectic gallery of professors. Fleming James, Jr.,
was the tweedy, gravel-voiced authority on civil procedure. Alexander
Bickel, a curmudgeonly, old-fashioned moderate in the mold of his mentor
Felix Frankfurter, advocated judicial restraint and disdained many of the
sweeping decisions of the Warren Court. Charles Reich had emerged that
year as a shy, ethereal counterculture guru with his best-selling book *The
Greening of America*, which heralded a generational revolution that he
predicted would transform America's corporate mind-set so that beauty
and humanity were more revered than status and achievement. He taught
a course that students called Kindergarten II, in which they could read
virtually anything they wanted and were required to write papers only if
they sought honors. Tom Emerson was a devoted First Amendment scholar
and champion of free speech who sympathized with the student protesters.
Charles L. Black, Jr., a liberal constitutional law expert, saved his passion
for writing poetry. Boris Bittker, a federal income-tax specialist, took a
keen interest in black slave reparations. Guido Calabresi was beloved as the
bright, twinkling-eyed magician of torts. Burke Marshall, a former assistant
attorney general under Robert Kennedy, was widely admired by the activist students and was of particular interest to Clinton because of his Kennedy connections.

Somewhat less popular was Eugene Victor Debs Rostow, one of the intellectual architects of the Johnson administration's Vietnam policies. Rostow had served as the law school's dean during the late 1950s and early 1960s, and was regarded as a first-rate dean, but when he returned in 1969 after his stint in Washington he discovered that the climate had changed. He would stroll into the student cafeteria in his three-piece suit and launch into lunchtime discussions with students in which he would tell them that if only they were privy to the secret knowledge he possessed they too would support the Vietnam War. Sometimes the students argued with him; more often they shunned him or satirized him. One weekend they held a Rostow Brothers Film Festival on the effects of American bombing in Vietnam.

One of the giants of the faculty was J. William Moore, known in the legal world as a god of procedure. "J. Willie," as the students called him, was short, rotund, and crusty, a cigar-chomping conservative Montanan who demanded that his students stand when they addressed him—all good lawyers have to talk on their feet, he would say. The women students considered Moore a male chauvinist who was reluctant to call on them. But he was respected nonetheless, a powerful figure who knew all the rules of procedure because he had literally written the book on them. It is hardly surprising that Clinton considered Moore one of his favorite teachers and spent a great deal of time picking his brain. Always drawn to esteemed older men, especially ones who appeared intimidating, Clinton worked Moore just as he had courted his toughest professors at Georgetown, Quigley and Sebes and Giles. They were not father figures in any traditional sense, yet in dealing with them Clinton surely explored aspects of a paternal relationship that he had never had.

Moore was, according to Pogue, "the kind of guy who, if you got into an argument on procedures with him, he would say, 'Okay, do you want to argue this on state principles or federal?' and whichever you chose he would take you apart on it. But Bill would get in there and mix it up with him—he had an ability to deal with teachers who intimidated everyone else." It was an early expression of Clinton as policy maven, a side of his personality that would become more apparent in later decades. Many of the arguments Clinton got into with Moore seemed esoteric. Pogue saw something deeper at work. "The thing is, Clinton understood that it was government. It was government in a real way. When you got into the issues, you realized that they involved the fundamental questions of what was in the public interest."

Finally there was Robert Bork, who taught first-year constitutional law to Clinton's section at eight in the morning. Bork enjoyed playing the role of contrarian, which in this case meant that he was a conservative strict constructionist who disparaged the concept of antitrust and most other forms of legal liberalism. A bulky, bearded chainsmoker, he marched into class with the demeanor of the former Marine that he was, his lecture notes scrawled on yellow pads, and strove to challenge and intimidate his students. One student naively tried to best Bork in an argument by stating, "Mr. Bork, Oliver Wendell Holmes said..." only to have Bork respond curtly, "Just because you quote Oliver Wendell Holmes, don't think it's checkmate!" Bork employed the Socratic method and would seek out the most radical members of his class as prospective targets of humiliation.

The law school was careening toward the end of a rebellious period when Clinton arrived, an era that Abraham Goldstein, who was named dean that year, called "the Dark Ages." The atmosphere of quiet diligence that traditionally enveloped the solemn corridors of the Gothic law building was overtaken by an anti-establishment mood. The year before Clinton enrolled, a troop of long-haired, tie-dyed, Frisbee-playing students set up tents and an inflated air trampoline in the Quadrangle, which they said they had liberated, and lived there for weeks, bouncing off the walls and boasting of their alternative lifestyle of sex and dope. Hippies, radicals, mainstream antiwar activists, and black power advocates co-existed, their various protests and controversies enlivening the daily grind. In the law school corridor, a chart was posted detailing the results of an anonymous poll on drug use among law students. At first it showed a typical bell curve, with some students claiming heavy use, a larger number saying they were moderate users, and a smaller number saying they rarely or never smoked dope. By the end of the term, the chart was full of deletions and revisions, with the numbers piling up on the heavy-use side.

Students ceaselessly challenged the relevance of the curriculum, and some professors in turn complained that their young charges had lost all semblance of civility, mouthing off in class and showing up in sloppy jeans and work shirts. Students who once would have coveted positions on the law journal instead conspired to put out an alternative social policy review. Bands of students gathered informally at their dorm rooms or apartments to discuss alternative readings on legal issues: one such study group included Pogue, Clinton, and Bob Reich. Black students, emboldened by the national black power movement, which was then at its peak, formed a black student alliance and a black table of solidarity in the cafeteria, and launched several protests against administration policies.

Clinton moved easily in this clamorous environment. During his occasional visits to the law school cafeteria, he found a seat for himself at the black table, a place rarely entered by other whites. Most of Clinton's friends felt that if the black students chose to sit together in solidarity, they should not interfere. Many of them would not have known how to enter that world anyway. But Clinton broke the self-imposed color barrier simply by sitting down and talking with Coleman, who was a regular at the table, and Coleman's friends, Eric Clay, Rufus Cormier, and Lani Guinier. At first some blacks stared at him as though he was an unwanted interloper, but he soon won them over. "It took him no time to penetrate the group," according to Coleman. "He disarmed people and eased whatever suspicions they might have had by using his sense of humor. He brought laughter with him. He was natural." Clinton would talk about whatever the black students were talking about, or tell his own tales about life in Arkansas, or joke about how he had not gone to class or read any of his law books. Part of Clinton's success might have been rooted in his southernness. Coleman developed a theory about southerners who had gotten beyond bigotry: "They feel some part of the soul that touches each other. There is something about the rhythm that creates a compatibility. Bill had it."

CLINTON used his southernness in other ways. He played with the country-bumpkin myth, as he had at Georgetown, taking delight in tales about the oversized watermelons of Hope. Nancy Bekavac, who befriended Clinton after he had borrowed her notes, would sit at his side at law school gatherings and watch him pose as a poor kid from Arkansas who could not be very smart. She would sit there and say to herself of whomever Clinton was debating, "Oh, you poor bastard, you are about to be rolled over." Occasionally she would intrude. "Now, Bill," she would say. "It wasn't Oxford, Mississippi, where you were a Rhodes Scholar, was it?"

Bekavac and Clinton went to movies together and sometimes stopped at an all-night diner on the highway between the law school and Milford, where they devoured french fries smothered in gravy and talked into the night. They shared an interest in the subject of lost fathers. Clinton had lost two fathers. Bekavac, an undertaker's daughter who grew up in the blue-collar town of Clairton, Pennsylvania, had lost her father during her senior year in high school. They both had younger brothers. Bekavac said she thought her brother Dan had become withdrawn since their father's death. He could talk about sports but nothing else. Clinton said his brother Roger also seemed to be taking the loss very hard. Clinton talked about the long process of his father's dying of cancer, about driving from Washington down to Duke to see him. He told Bekavac that by the time he realized that his stepfather was dying, he had very little time to make a relationship. "But at least you had time," Bekavac said. "I walked downstairs one day and my dad was dead of a heart attack and I didn't have any warning."

Even among the vivid array of characters at Yale, Bekavac stood out. Once, while listening to Robert Bork's attack on the legal foundations of the civil rights laws enacted during the previous decade, Nancy Bekavac, dressed in her daily uniform of blue jeans and a denim work shirt, guffawed loudly from the back of the room and yelled out, "You're joking!" She had spent the summer before law school in Vietnam, working as a stringer for journalists in Da Nang, and had returned fiercely antiwar and pro-soldier —a delicate balance. Bob Reich was intrigued by this woman in his constitutional law class who seemed even less afraid to challenge Professor Bork than he was and who wore the same clothes to class every day. "What is this," Reich asked, "some kind of uniform?" Bekavac replied, "Yes. That's what we had in the institution!" Wherever there was a loud discussion in the cafeteria, Bekavac could usually be found in the middle of it, which naturally interested Clinton. He would stop by and kibitz on her arguments, seeming bemused by the fury. Eventually, she would turn to Clinton and inquire, "Well, what do you care about?" To which Clinton would respond, " 'Lots of stuff. But you're doing fine.' "

What did Clinton care about? Sometimes Bekavac was not sure. "You could never view his performance in a totally positive way. You wondered, is it real? There were moments that were so genuine that there was no doubt about it, and moments when you wondered—is this posture?" The genuine moments usually involved civil rights and the Vietnam War. Clinton also cared about politics, of course, believed in it with an intensity that was unusual among his peers. "Politics," housemate Bill Coleman came to realize, "was a natural part of him, like does a frog croak." Yale Law was a political place in many respects, yet not political in the manner that Clinton was. "If you scratched the surface of any Yale Law student you would find a U.S. senator waiting to be appointed," said David Schulte, who edited the *Yale Law Journal* in Clinton's years there. "Very few were willing to do the work to get elected senator, but they all wanted to be there."

What sustained Clinton was his peculiar combination of realism and enthusiasm. When friends delved into political conversations with him, they understood that he was not naive or pollyannaish. He studied the weaknesses of various politicians as much as their strengths. The savvy, practical manner in which Clinton approached the political world was perhaps best illustrated by a letter he wrote to Cliff Jackson during his Yale years when Jackson, then at the University of Michigan Law School, sought a White House Fellowship and asked Clinton for advice on how to go about it. In his letter on Yale Law School stationery, Clinton wrote:

> About the White House Fellowships: the best story I know on them is that virtually the only non-conservative who ever got one was a quasi-radical woman who wound up in the White House sleeping with LBJ, who made her wear a peace symbol around her waist whenever they made love. You may go far, Cliff; I doubt you will ever go that far!
>
> You know as well as I do that past a certain point there is no such thing

as a non-partisan, objective selection process. Discretion and diplomacy aren't demanded so much by propriety as by the necessity not to get caught. I don't mind writing to Fulbright for you, if you'll tell me what you want me to ask him to do, but you ought to know that he won't give your politics a second thought. It would look good for Arkansas if you got the thing. . . . Wouldn't mind dropping David Pryor a line, either. He's in the favor-doing business now anyway, as you know.

With that acute sense of how the political game was played came the joy of playing it. Clinton thrived on what politics offered: endless opportunities to meet people and befriend them and make connections. Bekavac remembers how thrilled Clinton was when his mentor J. William Fulbright visited Yale. Clinton was invited to a private reception before the senator's speech and brought Bekavac along. Bekavac sensed that what seemed to excite Clinton most was the opportunity to introduce her to Fulbright. He planted her in a stairwell where she was sure to get a moment alone with him. "It wasn't that Bill wanted me to know that he knew this important person. He wanted me to share in the enjoyment of it. He had this great sense of occasion and pride and wanted me to have that experience." (That night in New Haven, Fulbright greeted Bekavac courteously and told Clinton to get his hair cut.)

After spending several weeks watching Clinton operate, Bekavac concluded that her friend, along with his obvious analytical skills, had a "novelistic sensibility about people." He would remember things about their lives. He thirsted for life stories. He remembered home towns and names of parents and brothers. "If he were a novelist, he would be like Tolstoy. Everyone has an epitaph—'the hulky Pierre.' He had that kind of impressionist sensibility. What he remembered about people was some human fact about their life not unrelated to sentimentality and emotionalism." That, says Bekavac, is how Clinton saw life: in thematic, recurrent, novelistic patterns.

His living quarters on Long Island Sound provided ample material for the novelist. It was a four-bedroom house with thin walls designed primarily for summer shore use, with a large glass-enclosed porch looking out on Fort Trumbull Beach. The tide would often go out hundreds of yards, providing a vast expanse of hard sand as a field for the young men and their friends to play touch football when the weather was suitable. On clear nights, the porch offered a spectacular view of the moon softly lighting the sand and the glistening Sound beyond. Clinton, Pogue, Eakeley, and Coleman shared the space with a stray dog that Pogue had found on the beach —a little mutt named Burt that chewed the furniture—and several women friends. Pogue's future wife was the most frequent guest. Clinton was interested in several women then. He had a capacity, Bekavac thought, for "fitting them all into one semester. Simultaneously." He had what his friends described as a brief and passionate love affair with a friend of Coleman's sister. Coleman would tell the story of this romance to class-mates as though he were describing a scene from *Gone With the Wind.* Clinton was also still writing letters to his many former girlfriends. When he learned that Denise Hyland, his Georgetown sweetheart, was to marry that winter, he wrote her a long good-bye letter.

Although no one was there much during the week, on weekends the beach house usually throbbed with friends escaping the grime of New Haven. With Carole King music playing in the background, Pogue would warm up huge batches of cider and grill chicken outside, satisfying his customers with "a pretty mean coq au vin." Clinton was reading novels that year. On Eakeley's birthday, he gave his housemate several of his favorite works by William Faulkner and Reynolds Price. He said that under-standing Faulkner was essential to appreciating human nature and the southern mind. According to a letter he sent Denise Hyland, he had also picked up a habit of the tweedy, literary set, a surprising one for someone who never smoked cigarettes. "I am," he wrote, "smoking away on my pipe."

Eakeley was the most responsible member of the household. He had found the house and he organized the living arrangements and the rent. He was the furthest along in his law studies, having begun his law work at Oxford. When his mother visited from New Jersey, he could pound the place into shape for an adult cocktail party. A Skull and Bones man from his days as a Yale undergrad, he was on his way to a certain Wall Street career. He looked as calm and placid as the waters of Long Island Sound on a still night, but he had insomnia. He would walk the beach at midnight and drink scotch to help him get to sleep.

Pogue was the house radical. He wore a leather jacket and drove a racy red Norton Commando motorcycle to school. When the beach house discussions strayed into the economic realm, Coleman remembers, "Don would accuse us of taking too superficial a look at it. He'd say, 'This is part of the capitalist system that needs to be changed.' "

Coleman was the son of William T. Coleman, Jr., a black Republican civil rights lawyer who later became Secretary of Transportation in the Ford administration. His family "believed in integration and the idea of blacks assimilating and becoming part of white society," and as part of his social-ization process Coleman went to predominantly white private schools, first Germantown Friends in Philadelphia, and then Williams College in Massachusetts. At Williams, his sense of pride in being part of the black bourgeoisie was "promptly dealt with and taken apart" and he discovered the concept of black pride. He and his black compatriots at Williams took over the administration building one night. One fellow called himself the minister of defense and tried to surround the building with electrical wires to shock anybody who came in. On the third day of the takeover, Coleman's mother obtained the telephone number inside the building, called him, and begged him to come out. "I said, 'Mother, I've got to do this, please don't embarrass me by calling anymore!' " By the time he reached Yale, Coleman had resolved the inner question of who he was. He could move between the black and white worlds comfortably by then, and in fact was known as an extremely friendly, laid-back student with a sardonic sense of humor and a tendency, like Clinton, to cram for exams.

"NEW HAVEN is the vile crotch of Connecticut," Bob Reich wrote to his fellow Class of 1968 Rhodes Scholars in his first annual letter that winter for the *American Oxonian* magazine. "Travelers avoid it, letters and telephone calls rarely penetrate its polluted periphery. Those of us who have braved it for a year find ourselves strangely out of touch with the rest of the world, even when we leave it. Maybe we smell. As a result, news of our Rhodes group must be based primarily on rumor, scandal, muck-raking, hearsay, Bill Clinton, gossip, and intuition—not the most reliable sources, I'm afraid, and I apologize in advance for borderline fiction."

The original plan was for Reich to live at the beach house with Clinton and Eakeley, his friends from Univ College, but he had decided that he wanted to stay in a dormitory to be closer to the Yale Law library. One semester in a dormitory proved enough even for him, however, and for the second semester he moved with Bekavac and two other students into a house on Crown Street that featured a front door painted bright orange. The landlord, a stranger to the cultural revolution exploding around him, was reluctant to rent to a mixed-sex group. He required his tenants to provide letters of approval from their mothers, but luckily for him, he rarely probed inside the orange door.

Reich was notable, wherever he went and whatever he was doing. *Time* magazine, which had featured him in a profile years earlier on the college seniors of 1968, sent a reporter up to Crown Street to file an update. The writer described Reich's house as "an urban commune"—a hyperbolic touch that did not reassure Bekavac's mother back in Clairton. And how had Reich changed since the fiery days of 1968? "Robert Reich is now less confident about how to achieve" social change, the reporter wrote. He noted that "life as a Rhodes scholar at Oxford's 700-year-old University College gave him his first serious look at democratic socialism, a system he thinks is inevitable for the U.S." Of his own future, Reich told *Time,* "I hope to be a kind of cross between a philosopher and a political hack."

The Rhodes Scholars had scattered, Reich noted in his alumni letter. Tom Williamson was in Ethiopia working as a consultant on public policy. Danny Singer was at medical school at Harvard. Keith Marshall was an art curator in New Orleans. George Butte was fulfilling his conscientious objector obligation in Dallas. Rick Stearns was commuting between Oxford and Washington, where he was working on the nascent presidential campaign of George McGovern. John Isaacson was "living it up in the netherworld of political hackery, and occasionally attending classes at Harvard Law School." A batch of scholars were still at Oxford, including Bo Jones, who was spending "an idyllic year in a cottage fifteen miles outside Oxford"; Mike Shea, who had been relieved from his Army obligation because of his bum knee; Paul Parish, who had returned from his nervous breakdown and was finishing his honors courses at Christ Church College, still unsure about when he might serve out his conscientious objector requirement; Darryl Gless, who missed getting drafted in the lottery by one number and was finishing his advanced degree in literature; and Strobe Talbott (*"Izvestia's* 'rising young CIA agent,' " Reich wrote), who was completing the Khrushchev memoirs and trying to get back into the Soviet Union.

And what had become of Frank Aller, the brilliant, troubled Rhodes draft resister? "Frank Aller made a traumatic reentry into the States, having missed his original induction day," Reich wrote. "Much to everyone's relief, a new induction day never came, and Frank spent the remainder of the year safely in Newton, Massachusetts, doing research into cable television. With the recent thaw in China's foreign policy, Frank hopes to be able to continue his Oxford studies on the Chinese mainland. He is now in Spokane, Washington."

Reich's account was incomplete. Aller traveled on a much more difficult journey that year than merely heading from Oxford to Newton to Spokane. When the Leckford Road gang parted company at the end of their second year at Oxford, Aller went to Spain to work on an autobiographical novel about a draft resister. It became his obsession and he continued writing it early that fall in Oxford and London. He wrote the novel twice through and never considered it done, yet the very act of writing it had a profound effect on him. "My whole experience with the book . . . was really the first time I tried to deal honestly with the questions of draft resistance and exile," he later confessed in a letter to Brooke Shearer, who was then studying at Stanford. "It was an exciting but also sobering experience, as I tried to assess what the decision meant after two years of living with it and what it was likely to mean in the long run. At the end of the period when I was actively revising the second draft . . . I realized that I was being led toward another decision just as difficult as the first one, if not more so."

Aller did not regret his decision to resist, nor consider it futile; but in grappling with its consequences while writing the book, he concluded that the symbolism of his action had outlived its usefulness. By early November 1970, he had come to believe that "the effect has ended, or nearly ended." With his effectiveness diminished, he and his "fellow criminals and conspirators," he wrote, could have "very little influence on what happens in the US in the future. Out of sight is out of mind. It's taken me some time to realize that." His positions on the war and the direction of American politics had not changed, but he was starting to feel irrelevant. He dreamed about going home. "To stay in this situation is to have my life defined by the war in Vietnam—sort of like being locked into a political time-capsule." Finally, the practical burdens of his decision were wearing him down as well—"the problems of passports, immigration requirements, citizenship regulations etc.—or my family."

Aller decided to come home. It was not an easy decision for someone who had been transformed into a martyr, a hero, by his Oxford friends. Brooke Shearer was but one of many friends Aller felt compelled to write to and warn about his decision, to "reassure them—when they hear about it—that I haven't suddenly lost control of what few mental faculties I originally had." Although he spent six weeks, after turning away from the second draft of his novel, trying to find another course of action, he could see "no other exit." It had become "a question of realizing when you're on a losing track—and doing something about it—or letting life pass you by."

When Aller finally arrived in Spokane, he was met by his family and a U.S. marshal, who was there to arrest him. As he walked off the plane, Aller made a gesture—hands up and bent at the elbows, fists closed, as though he expected to be handcuffed on the spot, but the marshal waited until they were in the car before he made the arrest. After his arraignment, Aller flew back to Boston, where he visited a draft lawyer who sent him to a psychiatrist. The psychiatrist concluded after one visit that Aller was severely depressed and unqualified for military service. With the psychiatrist's letter in hand, Aller flew back to Spokane. He finally took his draft physical, which he failed. He was reclassified 1-Y, a deferment that protected him from service except in case of a national emergency. The next day his indictment for draft resistance was dropped. It was a rather anticlimactic ending to a three-year drama. Now Aller was again faced with the prospect of what to do with the rest of his life. He bounced back and forth between Spokane and Los Angeles trying to line up work as a journalist.

Clinton went out to California for a brief gathering of the Leckford Road housemates late that spring. They gathered at Lloyd Shearer's house and at Brooke Shearer's on Arbor Road in Menlo Park: Clinton and Aller in their beards, Talbott in his fine mustache. Shearer, an English literature major who specialized in Virginia Woolf, was part of a feminist consciousness-raising group that met at her house. The boys were not invited, and in "a show of defiance, they went bowling, their feelings hurt." They also went to Santa Cruz, played football on the beach, walked the hills of San Francisco, and went to the movies. It was, for the boys from Leckford Road, their last fine time together.

CHAPTER FOURTEEN

RODHAM AND CLINTON

BILL CLINTON AND Hillary Rodham. From the opening round of courtship, here was an evenly matched romance and a fair fight. Two strong-willed personalities—ambitious, socially conscious, and political—they were introduced to each other in the cafeteria during the first week of law school by Bob Reich, who had known Rodham since her undergraduate days when she had traveled from Wellesley up to Dartmouth to attend a meeting Reich had organized of student leaders active in the academic reform movement. "I said, 'Bill, this is Hillary; Hillary, this is Bill,' but obviously it didn't take," Reich recalled. Not then, at least. In their later remembrances of their courtship, they both replaced his prosaic account with a more melodramatic scene. In their version, seemingly accurate except for its deletion of the Reich introduction, they circled each other for weeks before exchanging their first greetings. Clinton followed Rodham out of a civil liberties class, thought about an effective approach, then backed away. Rodham spotted Clinton in the law school lounge boasting about—yes, of course—the watermelons in Hope, and in her diligent fashion, unobtrusively, she began gathering information about him.

One day Rodham was sitting at a table piled with books, journals, and notepads in the library reading room, a peaceful wood-paneled chamber with high ceilings and light-flooded Gothic-arched windows on the third floor of the law school. Clinton loitered in the middle distance with a clear line of sight down the narrow-shafted room, pretending to study. Jeff Glekel, an editor of the *Yale Law Journal,* provided cover, hovering next to Clinton and trying to persuade him to try out for the prestigious journal. Struggling to hold Clinton's attention, Glekel laid it on thick: the best judicial clerkships, the most powerful law firms in Manhattan, the elite law school faculties—all of these awaited the *Journal*'s select editors. If he had said the State House, Congress, the White House, perhaps the sales pitch would have worked. As it was, Clinton said that he did not want to do it. His plan after law school was to go home to Arkansas and run for public office. Whether he wrote for the *Yale Law Journal,* he noted, did not matter to anyone down there. Clinton seemed inattentive in any case. He was looking across the room at Rodham. Soon enough she walked toward his table. "Look," she said. "If you're going to keep staring at me and I'm going to keep staring back, we should at least introduce ourselves. I'm Hillary Rodham." Clinton was knocked dumb by Rodham's bold approach, her classic pickup line, and scrambled to remember his own name.

On their first outing, Clinton and Rodham went together to sign up for second semester classes. When they reached the front of the line, the registrar was puzzled by Clinton's presence. "Bill, what are you doing here?" came the query. "You registered yesterday!" Clinton and Rodham then went for a walk and toured the college art museum, which happened to be closed, but which Clinton charmed his way into anyway by convincing a custodian to open it up for a private tour after he and Rodham picked up some trash. Clinton "locked in on" her after that. Rodham focused on him as well. He was that rare guy, she told friends, who did not seem afraid of her. It might have been that he was more adept at concealing his fear. Rodham's intellect, her reputation, her refusal to be cowed or wowed, seemed to attract him and scare him at the same time. He prepped his housemates before each of her visits to the beach house, hoping they could help impress her. It took a little time, Don Pogue said later, "before she decided he was going to be up to snuff. She had to be encouraged to see that point of view. She was brought out to the beach house to engage in lively conversation. We were all recruited to participate in it."

Rodham expressed mixed feelings about Clinton's style, especially the way he accentuated his Arkansas roots. Like so many contemporaries who had encountered him before her, she was taken by his sense of place, a rarity among students eager to shed their middle-class pasts. "He cared deeply about where he came from, which was unusual," Rodham said later. "He was rooted and most of us were disconnected." But she was not bamboozled by his down-home palaver. "They were funny together, very lively. Hillary would not take any of Bill's soft stories, his southern boy stuff," according to Pogue. "She would just puncture it, even while showing a real affection. She'd say, 'Spit it out, Clinton!' or, 'Get to the point, will you, Bill!'" Housemate Doug Eakeley remembered Rodham, in her sharp voice, interrupting Clinton in the middle of one of his Arkansas tales with the mocking reprimand, "Come off it, Bill!" Her midwestern directness, Eakeley thought, was "the perfect counterpoint to Bill's southern charm." Her focused intellect was also a perfect counterpoint to his restless, diffuse mind, and made her the superior law student. In one class they took together during the spring semester of 1971, Tom Emerson's Political and Civil Rights, Emerson kept private numerical grades even though the report cards were pass-fail. He gave Rodham a 78, one of the highest grades, and Clinton a mediocre 70.

There was, without stretching the point, a certain reversal of gender stereotypes in the Clinton-Rodham match. Steve Cohen, who was among Rodham's circle of friends from her first year at law school, concluded that "Clinton had the charm and the sex appeal whereas Hillary didn't so much. Hillary was straightforward, articulate, and self-possessed." Yet within a month of meeting Clinton, Rodham was talking about his depth. Some of her friends thought Clinton was interesting but too eager to be the focus of attention. Rodham decided there was more to him than that. "There's lots of layers to him," she told Cohen one day. "He's more complex than I thought. The more I see him, the more I discover new things about him." She also told Cohen about her new friend's determination to do something with his life, which was very much what she was about as well.

At the time they met, Rodham, though one year younger, had developed more of a reputation as a student leader. When Clinton was in the first year of his Oxford studies, she was at Wellesley College outside Boston, where her intellect helped her school win several matches on the College Bowl television quiz show. She also got her picture in *Life* magazine for delivering a commencement speech that was seen as a statement of purpose for her generation—philosophically curious, politically committed, and passionately antiwar. She arrived at Yale Law in the fall of 1969, one year ahead of Clinton, during the height of the hippie-radical period there, with an activist reputation. "The story of what she had done at Wellesley preceded her. We were awed by her courage," recalled Carolyn Ellis, one of her law school friends. "She arrived with many of us thinking of her as a leader already. We had seen her picture in the national magazine and here she was, three months later, in our class."

Rodham quickly befriended the antiwar activists in the class, including Cohen, Greg Craig, and Michael Medved, three leaders of the October 15 moratorium in New Haven, one of the largest regional demonstrations that day. Craig, who had delivered a class day speech at Harvard that had also gained national recognition, thought of Rodham as a "mainstream, conscientious, politically astute person who still believed in American institutions." In the context of Yale Law School, "that meant she was conservative." Craig exaggerated to make a point. Rodham more accurately was in the middle of the flux at Yale Law. She was, "like ninety-five percent of her classmates, passionately convinced that the war made no sense." She "looked like a hippie," according to Carolyn Ellis. She kept her hair long and flowing and came to class in sandals and blue jeans. Nothing about this attire made Rodham stand out from the other young women there. She wore thick glasses and was constantly changing the frames. Ellis regarded Rodham's frame-changing habit as "her whimsy—just the way she would change her hairstyle later, she changed her glasses all the time then."

What set Rodham apart was her combination of social commitment and pragmatism. During her first year, third-year students James Blumstein, Stanley Herr, and Jack Petranker founded the *Yale Review of Law and Social Action,* a leftist alternative to the *Yale Law Journal.* In the egalitarian ethic of the time, there was no hierarchy at the review. Rodham served as a commentator who critiqued articles before publication. The first volume featured an article written by Blumstein and Jim Phelan entitled "Jamestown 70." The authors, thinking that America was on the brink of insurrection, counseled against armed revolt on practical grounds, but suggested that their alienated generation should gain control of a state where they could experiment with different lifestyles, marital rules, and patterns of democracy: "What we advocate is the migration of large numbers of people to a single state for the express purpose of effecting the peaceful political take-over of that state through the elective process." They linked their proposal to the American frontier ethic, "where alienated or 'deviant' members of society can go to live by their new ideas; providing a living laboratory for social experiment through radical federalism."

Rodham read an early draft and told Blumstein that it was too abstract and theoretical, not practical enough. "This is mental masturbation," she said. "Get more specific. Get down to earth." She was particularly tough on the piece where she thought it would alienate people and hurt the cause. Her critique arose from her pragmatic sense of doability. While Blumstein and Phelan thought they were being serious, Rodham thought that they were just playing around. She took her politics more seriously than they did and she had no patience with their grandiose ideas.

IT ran in the family, the impatience for fuzzy thinking. Hugh Rodham, her father, was a tobacco-chewing, no-nonsense man, gruff and sarcastic. Dorothy Howell Rodham, her mother, declared that no daughter of hers— and Hillary was the only daughter, followed by two sons—would ever be afraid to say what was on her mind. "You weren't going to go into the Rodhams' house and say anything stupid," recalled Ernest (Rick) Ricketts, one of Hillary's closest childhood friends. "You couldn't get away with that with any of them. If you tried it with Hillary, she'd say, 'What? What'd you say?' " Dorothy Rodham often told a story about Hillary, which, even if it was embellished into a parable, nonetheless revealed the imprint the mother wanted to leave on the daughter. When Hillary was four, she was pushed around by a bigger girl who was the neighborhood bully. When she ran home and expressed her fear, her mother told her, "There's no room in this house for cowards." Dorothy Rodham instructed her daughter to hit back next time. Soon Hillary popped the bully in front of a group of boys, ran home, and exclaimed, "I can play with the boys now!"

The setting for this life lesson was a sturdy Georgian house on Wisner Street in the suburb of Park Ridge to the northwest of Chicago—deep in the placid, postwar soul of America. Hillary Diane Rodham was born at Edgewater Hospital on Chicago's North Side on October 26, 1947. Her father, a manufacturer who sold drapes to hotels and movie theaters, moved the family to Park Ridge when she was three. The suburb was her world until she was eighteen and left for college. Park Ridge was the upper middle of upwardly mobile middle America. It was old enough and sufficiently well off to avoid the conformity of tract housing developments: the elm-shaded side streets offered a pleasant mix of brown brick Georgian revivals, wood and stucco bungalows, and early twentieth-century two-story wood frame homes. Yet it lacked the pretense and exclusivity of North Shore suburbs like Wilmette and Lake Forest. Most of the women of Park Ridge, including Dorothy Rodham, stayed home: Hillary's childhood friends knew of only two mothers who held outside jobs. Most of the men worked in Chicago and, like Hugh Rodham, tended to be businessmen rather than doctors or lawyers. The town arose along the tracks of the Chicago & Northwestern commuter line, which carried tribes of dark-suited men into the city and back every day. The youngsters who lived along Wisner Street heard the distant rumble and whine of trains pulling into the station and saw plumes of smoke fill the horizon at rush hour.

There were no black or Asian families in Park Ridge at that time. Hispanics were seen only during the harvest season when migrant workers picked vegetable fields on the edge of town. The lone black student was a foster child. There were no Jewish residents either, though a few miles east along Dempster Street stood the kosher delicatessens of heavily Jewish Skokie. Park Ridge was an enclave of Methodists and Catholics. Divorces were virtually unheard of: when one marriage disintegrated in the Rodhams' neighborhood, it was the talk of the town. All communities have secrets and contradictions, and Park Ridge was no different. The town remained dry through the decades, but in name only. White panel trucks full of liquor would roll in on Saturday mornings and make back-alley deliveries. But for the most part the children of Park Ridge did not see this, just as they paid little attention to the fact that their town was segregated. They saw life being lived one way, remembered Rick Ricketts, "and we thought everyone else was like us."

The Rodhams voted Republican, as did most of the citizens of Park Ridge, many of whom had escaped the Democratic machine politics of Chicago. Hugh Rodham, who drove a Cadillac and railed against labor unions, instructed his children to watch the Republican national conventions on television every four years, but when the Democrats convened, the television was turned off. He taught his children how to read the stock market tables in the *Chicago Tribune.* Hillary once described the Park Ridge of her youth as "conservative but not paranoid," with "a strong support for education and a tolerant attitude about people." Dorothy Rodham held "a much more intellectual view than most moms in that neighborhood," according to Sherry Heiden, one of Hillary's friends. She had "a real love of beauty," recalled another friend, Betsy Johnson, and would return home from their annual summer trip to Pennsylvania with stained-glass windows, jeweled fobs, and other antiques she collected. Both parents encouraged Hillary to read and study world events and compete as an equal with boys. The basket on her bicycle was often filled with books. Even in grade school, she would talk about politics. "We'd get our *Weekly Reader* and discuss what was in it," recalled Rick Ricketts. "We'd talk about lots of things that you wouldn't expect fourth or fifth graders to think about." On summer afternoons, they sometimes sat on a low wooden fence at the corner of Wisner and Elm and solved all the world's problems.

When she was fourteen, entering the ninth grade, Hillary joined a Methodist church group for teenagers run by Don Jones, her congregation's youth minister. Jones sought to expose his students to the human condition outside their comfortable suburban world. He considered himself a liberal realist and called his class "The University of Life." "The name kind of fit what I was trying to do," Jones later recalled. "I felt knowing the human self, the limitations and the possibilities, was one of the most important concepts for any of us to grasp." His church group used secular art forms. They read the poetry of Wallace Stevens and e.e. cummings. On a retreat they watched one of Jones's favorite movies, *Requiem for a Heavyweight,* featuring Anthony Quinn as a burned-out fighter. Jones talked to his students about two characters in the heavyweight's entourage. One, played by Mickey Rooney, keeps trying to build up the fighter's esteem. The other, played by Jackie Gleason, seems less admirable because he knows the fighter is washed up and tells him so. But Jones offered a different perspective. The Rooney character, he said, was living an illusion. Deep down in the no of the Gleason character, on the other hand, was a theological yes. Before human beings can reach their potential, they have to get a realistic grasp of who they are. "In the midst of life, tragedy comes and it strips away our illusions," Jones told his students. "Those moments are times to realize our potential, our possibilities."

Rodham and her friends rode the old church bus to new worlds Jones wanted them to encounter. One Sunday night in April 1962 he took them to Orchestra Hall on Michigan Avenue for a lecture by Dr. Martin Luther King, Jr., entitled "Sleeping Through the Revolution." Jones arranged for them to go back stage after the speech and introduced each of them to King by name. Hillary Rodham's handshake with King was not as important in her life as young Clinton's handshake with Kennedy was in his, but there is a symmetry to the two events, one evoking a transference of politics, the other of social action. Jones also took his students to a recreation center on the South Side where they met with teenagers from the inner city. He used art to "level the playing field" between the kids from Park Ridge, who were better educated, and those from the city, who had tougher life experiences. Once he placed a print of Picasso's *Guernica* on a chair and asked them to describe what it meant. The Park Ridge students could speak of it only in abstract terms, while those from Chicago said that it reminded them of seeing people killed in their neighborhoods.

What Jones sought to accomplish in the trips to Chicago had nothing to do with a benevolent suburban church assisting the economically disadvantaged. Just the opposite: He was using the city as he used literature and film and art—as a means of prying open the minds of his comfortable students and introducing them to the pain, complexity, and alienation of the modern world. In a sense he was preparing them for the sixties.

After two years at Park Ridge, Jones left to teach in New Jersey, where he eventually became a theology professor at Drew University. He corresponded through the years with several of his former students, including Hillary. He had a powerful early influence on her social consciousness, yet he believed that in one sense his efforts to shock and disturb the children of Park Ridge had little effect on her. "I don't think my undersided stuff worked with Hillary. She was so secure in all of this. In part it had to do with her family. And in part the Methodist Church. Except for my brief interlude, Methodists there carried an almost sentimental belief in progress and a belief in people. They believed that if only we loved everyone, the world would be a better place. Hillary lived in this comfortable cocoon. And she had so many successes in her life. She withstood the sixties without losing hope."

THE high school experience in Park Ridge in the early 1960s "wasn't exactly *Happy Days,* but it was close," thought Sherry Heiden. There were greasers and jocks, some drinking, virtually no drug use. Girls wore skirts and dresses to school. Apathy and cynicism were not as prevalent as they would become later. Hillary and her classmates in Park Ridge, much like

Clinton and his peers in Hot Springs, Arkansas, were regarded as the chosen ones. There was little their parents would not do for their educational benefit. The baby boom was exploding in the northwest suburbs of Chicago. Hillary's class at Maine Township High bulged with fourteen hundred students out of a total enrollment of nearly five thousand. To accommodate the boom, a new school, Maine South, opened in her senior year. She was sent there along with half of her classmates, but it was a sterile new place with no traditions yet. Though Hillary's class would graduate from South, they would always think of their alma mater as the massive old three-story school at the corner of Dempster and Dee, with its green Art Nouveau designs inlaid in orange-tan brick topped by a red tile roof.

Hillary was perpetual motion in high school. Her picture pops up everywhere in the yearbooks: posing on the stairwell inside old Maine with the staff of *Ghost Writer,* the sophomore newspaper; seated in the auditorium as student council representative; at her classroom desk with the cultural values committee; standing under the flagpole as junior class vice president; on the end of the third row of the brotherhood society; among eight members of Maine South's "It's Academic" quiz show team; kneeling demurely in long checkered skirt and sleeveless black shirt as one of eleven National Merit Scholarship finalists. The picture that reveals the most about young Hillary Rodham shows her in the middle of seventy-two senior girls seated in the bleachers in their gym uniforms. Her face leaps from the anonymous mass of the photograph. Her straight dark-blond hair covers her right eye, giving her an almost piratical appearance; but even more than that, the lift of her jaw, the angle of her pose, the barely detectable smile, all add to a portrait of fire and self-confidence in an otherwise docile and awkward scene.

For the most part, the girls of Park Ridge felt discrimination in subtle ways. The most overt case for Hillary came long distance when she wrote to the National Aeronautics and Space Administration seeking guidance on how to become an astronaut. It was her childhood dream; she and her little brother Hughie would often go down to their basement and pretend they were flying a spaceship to Mars, with Hillary at the controls. But NASA tried to squash that dream. She received a letter back discouraging females from applying. Although she was not a gold medal candidate, she was a competent athlete who might have been on a varsity squad, but there were no girls' sports teams then. Her gender did not hold her back in school politics, which she loved. (She once invited Rick Ricketts to a girls' choice prom and "talked politics all through the dance.") She won more elections than she lost, and her only defeat was to another girl. At one point she decided that the school administration was not enthusiastic enough about student government. As chair of the committee in charge of elections, she drafted an elaborate proposal based on a mock national political convention—with nominating speeches, seconding speeches, candidate speeches, and floor demonstrations—and took it to the principal, who felt he had no choice but to let her implement it.

Near the end of her junior year, she wrote a long letter to her former youth minister detailing her many accomplishments. She had become a National Merit Scholar and had been invited to talk on a local television show about youth problems. She had been chosen chair of the organizations committee and was rewriting the student government constitution and reorganizing the committee. Student politics could get rough, she told Jones. In her last election, the opposition campaign manager started "slinging mud" at her, but she decided to respond with a "let's-keep-it-clean, flag, motherhood and apple pie campaign." And it worked. The spring prom was approaching, Hillary wrote, and her parents would serve as chaperones. She seemed embarrassed about the dress that her father let her buy. "Looking at it, I think everyone else next to me will think they are overdressed, it is so modest."

Hugh Rodham did not spoil his children. He taught them that rewards came only through hard work. His daughter earned her spending money as a baby-sitter. And if the scholastic rewards seemed to be coming too readily, he questioned whether the work was too easy. When she came home with perfect test scores or top grades, he would receive the news with a half-serious grunt that her school must not be very challenging. It was not that he was not proud of his daughter, just that he was not demonstrative. When guests came to the house, if he was at the television watching a sports event and drinking a beer, it was rare that he would budge from the chair or even grunt in acknowledgment.

Hillary Rodham was more talkative. In the rare instances when she got in trouble at school, it was because of that. She talked in class. Ricketts, her neighborhood pal, sat in front of her in a history class taught by Paul Carlson. Hillary kept up a running commentary during Carlson's lectures. "She would say something I had to respond to, so I would turn around, and Carlson would get mad at me," Ricketts recalled later. "One time Carlson was playing a recording of General MacArthur's 'Old Soldiers Never Die' speech and we both started laughing. Mr. Carlson took us out to the hall and read us the riot act."

In her politics, Hillary resembled her conservative father. She devoured Barry Goldwater's *The Conscience of a Conservative* and volunteered as a "Goldwater Girl" during the presidential campaign in the fall of 1964, her senior year. But starting with Don Jones's liberal realism, she felt the tug of other points of view. Most of her favorite teachers were young and socially conscious, including two women who persuaded her to apply to eastern women's colleges.

. . .

RODHAM finished high school in the top 5 percent of her class and was voted most likely to succeed. In the fall of 1965, she left suburban Chicago without looking back. Her mother, after dropping her off at Wellesley College on the edge of Boston, cried in the Cadillac all the way home as her unemotional husband drove silently along the turnpikes and toll roads back to the Midwest. Perhaps the mother realized that her daughter would never live in Park Ridge again save for a few weeks at a time during holidays and summer breaks. Though Rodham entered adulthood determined to forge a career in politics or social action, she felt no sentimental tug or practical reason to go home to do it. Bill Clinton always talked about heading back to Arkansas. No one heard Hillary Rodham speak the same way about Illinois.

Her politics changed semester by semester at Wellesley, which is to say that the college years from 1965 to 1969 transformed her as they did millions of other members of her generation. In the autumn of her first semester, she met Geoffrey Shields, a Harvard student who came from another Chicago suburb, Lake Forest, a wealthy community along Lake Michigan, where he had been a high school leader and all-state football player. They dated for three years and underwent similar evolutions from midwestern high school conservatives to northeastern campus liberals. Rodham was active in student government and Young Republicans in her first year, but Shields thought of her as largely nonideological, likening her mind to "a clean slate." She seemed "very interested in exploring political ideas, interested in the process as opposed to the ideology of politics." Her major focus was campus reform: making curriculum requirements more flexible and dormitory policies less restrictive.

By her sophomore year Rodham was writing to a friend that they could meet in New York, which she called a "saved city" because John Lindsay was elected mayor ("See how liberal I'm becoming!"). That summer she worked as a researcher, and baby-sitter, for a Wellesley professor who was writing a book on the Vietnam War from a beach house on Lake Michigan. Shields, who drove up to visit her at the Michigan resort several times, noted that by the end of the summer Rodham was a strong opponent of the war and no longer considered herself a Republican. By her junior year she was working with poor black children in Roxbury, taking part in protest marches in Boston and supporting Eugene McCarthy's antiwar presidential campaign. She had "grown up and out of the conservative materialistic mind-set which is typical of affluent suburbs," according to Shields. "She was not interested in making money or being affluent." During the summer after her junior year, she and her high school friend Betsy Johnson, who had just returned from a year studying in Madrid, ventured down to Chicago to see the tumult on the streets outside the Democratic National Convention. Both of their mothers had ordered them not to go, but the young women said that they were planning to see a movie, hopped in Johnson's car, and headed to the city. "We saw everything we wanted to look for," Johnson later recalled. "We saw police and large crowds of kids, chanting and yelling, and things being thrown out the windows at the Palmer House."

Rodham viewed the college years as a time when she could "try out different personalities and lifestyles," she explained in a letter to Don Jones. But it is an important aspect of her personality that even then there was a self-aware, moderate aspect to her experimentation. In another letter to Jones she talked about intentionally playing different roles at different times: now the social activist, now "sticking to the books," and occasionally "adopting a kind of party mode." She claimed that she even got outrageous at times, but immediately modified that assessment—"as outrageous as a moral Methodist can get." In her search for identity, she thought of herself now as "a progressive, an ethical Christian and a political activist." For those who are currently watching and judging her behavior later in life, when she seems to play contrasting roles at different times—here asserting her maiden name, there relinquishing it; here deferring to her husband, there instructing him on what to do; here posing like a model for the cover of traditional women's magazines, there emphasizing substance over style; here searching for the moral meaning of life, there playing the commodities markets to make a quick buck; here disparaging cookie-baking housewives, there peddling her chocolate chip recipe—it is instructive to know that she was, self-consciously, ever thus.

For a young person in the turbulent late sixties, Rodham was "personally pretty conservative," according to Shields. He said that she did not smoke marijuana during the years they were together, and that while she drank beer and liquor he never saw her drunk. She was disciplined about apportioning her time, though not obsessive. She preferred diving into political arguments or attending Harvard football games to studying in the Wellesley library, and while she had a sharp mind, she was not brilliant in every subject. Shields, an economics major, had to help her in that course because "she struggled some with numbers." After dates on weekends, they often ended up with a crowd at Winthrop House, where Shields lived, dancing or talking late into the night. Many of Shields's friends at Harvard also dated Wellesley women, who were considered more outgoing than Radcliffe women and more intellectual than those from the other women's schools in the Boston area.

As Rodham evolved into a liberal, she rarely seemed overtaken by dogma. She was a pragmatist above all. In the middle of intense political debates she would often say, "You can't accomplish anything in government unless you win!" Her focus was always on winning, according to Shields. "She was more interested in the process of achieving victory than in taking a philosophical position that could not lead anywhere." For her senior political science thesis, she analyzed community action programs and the effort to give poor people greater control of their own lives, including organizer Saul Alinsky's efforts in Chicago. According to Alan Schechter, her professor, Hillary "started out thinking community action programs would make a big difference," but eventually concluded that that view was "too idealistic and simplistic; that they might make a marginal but not a lasting difference" without outside money and help. She was also troubled by certain aspects of radical thought. Don Jones, her youth group mentor, wrote her a letter at Wellesley in which he questioned whether "someone can be a Burkean realist about history and human nature and at the same time have liberal sentiments and visions." She wrote back, "It is an interesting question you posed—can one be a mind conservative and a heart liberal?" She thought it was possible, but offered an example of the difficulty. She supported Martin Luther King, Jr., she wrote, but questioned some of the tactics of SNCC, the Student Non-violent Coordinating Committee, which was taking a radical black power position. "Some people think you can't be critical of the black power movement and still be for civil rights," she wrote. She did not think that her unwillingness to accept every radical idea meant that she was an enemy of the movement.

As their Wellesley days neared an end, Rodham and several classmates decided that a student should speak at commencement along with the traditional distinguished guest. There was an urgency to the generational pulse in the spring of 1969; students were either boycotting or refashioning commencements at schools across the country. Wellesley's president, Ruth M. Adams, disliked the idea of a senior speaker but reluctantly acquiesced on the condition that the address should reflect the sentiment of the entire graduating class. Rodham, as student government president, was chosen to give the speech. Her classmates were not shy about offering ideas and helping her draft what they took to be an important statement of purpose.

President Adams introduced Rodham after the commencement speech by Senator Edward Brooke, the liberal black Republican from Massachusetts, noting that among the four hundred graduating seniors, "there was no debate so far as I could ascertain as to who their spokesman was to be —Miss Hillary Rodham." Adams described her by saying, "She is cheerful, good humored, good company and a good friend to all of us."

But goodness was not what Hillary Rodham exuded on her graduation day. Before delivering her prepared remarks, she launched into an extem-

poraneous critique of Brooke's oration, which she found too full of compromises and statistics and empathy over action. Her words have a peculiar
resonance when considered in the light of how her future husband, a
man renowned for his empathy and tendency to compromise, would be
criticized decades later. "I find myself in a familiar position," Rodham
began, "that of reacting, something that our generation has been doing for
quite a while now. We're not in the positions yet of leadership and power,
but we do have that indispensable task of criticizing and constructive
protest and I find myself reacting just briefly to some of the things that
Senator Brooke said. . . . Part of the problem with empathy with professed
goals is that empathy doesn't do us anything. We've had lots of empathy;
we've had lots of sympathy, but we feel that for too long our leaders have
used politics as the art of the possible. And the challenge now is to practice
politics as the art of making what appears to be impossible, possible."

That Rodham would take on a United States senator, and not only a
senator but the highest-ranking black politician in the nation, sent mur-
murs of shock through the commencement audience. From that point on,
her listeners either loved or hated her message. Most of it was sixties
jargon, at times a cluttered mix of love-in piety and anticapitalist philosophy. "We are, all of us, exploring a world that none of us understands and
attempting to create within that uncertainty," she declared. "But there are
some things we feel—feelings that our prevailing acquisitive and competitive corporate life, including, tragically, universities, is not the way of life
for us. We're searching for more immediate, ecstatic and penetrating
modes of living."

Rodham the child of Park Ridge spoke of "a very strange conservative
strain that goes through a lot of New Left collegiate protests" which she
found "intriguing because it harkens back to a lot of the old virtues, to the
fulfillment of the original ideas." Rodham the activist of the sixties said her
generation was haunted by a disintegration of trust. "This is the one word
that when I asked the class at our rehearsal what it was they wanted me to
say for them, everyone came up to me and said, 'Talk about trust.'" But
what, Rodham asked rhetorically, was there to say about it? "What can you
say about a feeling that permeates a generation and that perhaps is not
even understood by those who are distrusted?" Rodham the moral Methodist spoke of respect—"that mutuality of respect where you don't see people as percentage points, where you don't manipulate people, where you're
not interested in social engineering for people." And Rodham the spokes-
woman for the Wellesley seniors closed by reading a poem from one of
her classmates, Nancy Scheibner, which began:

> My entrance into the world of so-called social problems
> Must be with quiet laughter, or not at all.

The Hollow Men of anger and bitterness
The bountiful ladies of righteous degradation
All must be left to a bygone age.

The speech, especially the challenge to Brooke, created a media stir, landing Rodham's portrait, with her long brown hair and striped bellbottoms and oversized glasses, in *Life* magazine. Geoffrey Shields, who by then was living in Vermont, got a call from her shortly after the commencement. "She said it had been hard for her to come around and make what was both a political statement and a personal attack. There was some exhilaration but also nervous questioning about whether it had really been the right thing to do. She realized what she had done was important. But when it was over she wondered about what she had said. She asked, 'Did I go too far?' "

IN the fall of 1971, Rodham and Clinton arranged to live in a small apartment at 21 Edgewood Avenue at the corner with Lynwood, within walking distance of the law school. It had been passed down from one class to the next. The previous tenant had been Rodham's friend Greg Craig. It was "a sweet little student apartment," according to Carolyn Ellis, with one bedroom, a built-in bed in the living room, and a small kitchen. The rent was seventy-five dollars a month. Neither tenant was there much. Rodham was spending most of her time in clinical work involving children's rights and legal aid for the indigent—the two principal interests of her career. Clinton held several part-time jobs, teaching law enforcement personnel at the community college, assisting an attorney in New Haven. He was attending class more regularly than at any other time in his Yale career. ("I am trying to at least learn the stuff this year," he wrote to a friend.) Classmates remember coming over for spaghetti dinners and marveling at how Clinton and Rodham could talk nonstop with great intensity about the issues of the day. But their first year together, while intellectually stimulating, could not be called an altogether joyous one.

On the morning of September 14, they were eating breakfast at the Blue Bell Café near the law school when a friend came in and said there was an emergency phone call. Clinton would later say that he was overwhelmed at that moment with a premonition of tragedy. He had a feeling that one of his friends was dead. The call was from Brooke Shearer, the girlfriend of Strobe Talbott. Shearer and Talbott were in Cleveland visiting Talbott's family. Talbott had dialed New Haven, but was so choked up he could not speak. He had given the phone to Shearer. She, like Clinton, had had a premonition. Hers came days earlier in Los Angeles as she boarded the plane for Cleveland and took one last look back at Frank Aller, who had driven them to the airport. Finally, it seemed, everything in Aller's life was together again. Not only had he flunked his military physical and had his indictment for resisting the draft dropped, but he had arranged, with help from Shearer's father, Lloyd Shearer, to get an interview with the *Los Angeles Times* foreign desk. That interview had led to an offer of work in the paper's Saigon bureau. He would write about the war in which he felt a moral obligation not to fight.

Aller seemed "hopeful and cheerful" at the airport when he said good-bye to "Strobovich" and "Brookechen"—his affectionate monickers for his friends. Yet as Shearer turned away and walked with Talbott toward the waiting jet, she had "a very distinct" reaction. "I remember thinking we should not get on that airplane. I could not say why. But it was a very strong feeling. But common sense or protocol tells you not to make a scene. It would have appeared ridiculous. I had these vague instincts. Something said to me, 'Something is not right here.' "

Now she was on the telephone saying what Talbott, silenced by grief, could not say. "Frank's dead," she told Clinton.

Aller had gone back to Spokane and put a bullet through his head. There was a suicide note, but it is long gone and no one claims to remember what it said. Some of his friends think Aller was a victim of Vietnam as surely as he would have been had he been killed on the battlefield. But most of them think that the notion that Vietnam killed him is simplistic. His torment was deep and personal. Talbott, who knew him as well as anyone, considered the suicide a "double shock"—a friend dead, and dead by his own hand. "Did I see anything in retrospect that was a progression to suicide? The answer is emphatically no." Yet in those final months, as the cloud of draft resistance and its consequences—exile or prison—finally lifted, it seemed that another darker cloud settled over Aller, Talbott thought, making him "seriously upset and depressed."

"Frank's dead." Clinton got the word from Brooke Shearer and passed it on. Clinton was the one who had the addresses and telephone numbers. He had a card file full of them, constantly revised and updated for letters and late night calls and future political solicitations. He notified friends in London and Oxford and Washington and Boston, who called friends, and soon everyone in the Rhodes crowd knew that Aller was gone. They all had their own perspectives along with the grief.

Aller's problems, thought Rick Stearns, "ran deeper than angst over how many bombs dropped on Hanoi that day." What did it mean, wondered John Isaacson, that Aller killed himself just at the moment when the major crisis in his life seemed to have lifted? To Isaacson it implied that Aller "needed the war to stay alive. He needed the external crisis to avoid the internal crisis." Brooke Shearer, too, concluded that the war might have kept Frank alive. His own "personal demons" finally killed him, she thought. Mike Shea thought perhaps Aller was the victim of an unanticipated sense of nothingness. He did something—resist—which he took very seriously, with the view that it was an important statement, "and in the end it had no effect on anything, it didn't even have an adverse effect on him, which depressed him." Willie Fletcher, the Rhodes Scholar who came out of Washington State with Aller, thought about the east-west tension that his home-state friend felt—not the tension between the United States and Vietnam but between the two sides of Washington. Aller was a boy from the east side of the mountains, the conservative side, but he crossed over and became a liberal and then a leftist when he went west to school in Seattle, and that tug between east and west was something that Fletcher saw Aller struggle with from the moment he met him.

But Fletcher, too, was stunned by word of Aller's suicide. He found out through a circuitous route, from a note sent to him by Sir Edgar Williams, the warden of Rhodes House in Oxford. He remembers sitting at his desk in the Office of Emergency Preparedness in Washington, D.C., where he was serving out his stint as a naval officer, and opening the letter and immediately calling Clinton in New Haven. "Hey, Bill, what happened?" he asked. They talked for an hour, a wandering conversation in which they tried to bring Aller back in their memories at least. "I didn't know Frank as well as I thought I did," Fletcher said at one point, to which Clinton responded, "Well, maybe none of us did."

But for Bill Clinton and Strobe Talbott and Willie Fletcher and the Rhodes Scholars of the class of 1968, the sixties ended that day in September 1971 when Frank Aller shot himself in the head.

THERE is some evidence that Clinton fell into another dark period after Aller's death, a time when he questioned the path he had chosen in life and the worthiness of the government and society he hoped to serve. The humor dropped out of his letters again, as it had during the days of his torment over the draft, replaced by weariness and doubt. A letter that he sent to Cliff Jackson, his competitor from Arkansas who was seeking a job in the Nixon White House, revealed a cynicism and tone of resignation. Of Senator Fulbright, his first political role model, Clinton told the conservative Jackson, "His politics are probably closer to yours than to mine." He was giving advice to Jackson, but he was also clearly writing to himself, wondering whether he still had the desire to reach his life's ambition as a world leader. "One final thing: It is a long way from Antioch to the White House, and it may not be a bad thing to make the leap," he wrote to Jackson, who had grown up in Antioch, Arkansas, not far from Hot Springs.

"Just always remember it's far more important what you're doing now than how far you've come. The White House is a long way from Whittier and the Pedernales too; and Khrushchev couldn't read until he was 24, but those facts leave a lot unsaid. If you can still aspire go on; I am having a lot of trouble getting my hunger back up, and someday I may be spent and bitter that I let the world pass me by. So do what you have to do, but be careful."

Jackson, in law school at the University of Michigan, was confounded by Clinton's advice. He had never before seen the disillusioned side of Clinton; he had always thought Clinton was too much the glad-hander and conniver. Jackson wrote back asking Clinton to explain himself. Clinton sent him a short note that again sounded as though it was meant more for the writer than the receiver: "As to the 'disturbing undercurrents' in my letter, they were not meant to sway you from your course, or to express disapproval at the kind of things you seem destined to do—only to say— these things too must be considered. You cannot turn from what you must do—it would for you be a kind of suicide. But you must try not to kill a part of yourself doing them either."

Clinton took a seminar that year taught by Jan Deutsch which focused on corporations and society. The ideas at issue included whether corporations could be compelled to treat workers fairly, deal honestly with consumers, and refrain from polluting the environment. Corporate responsibility was a vital topic in intellectual circles in the early 1970s, with academics churning out monographs on concepts ranging from worker ownership to placing executives under psychoanalysis. Each student was required to write a paper and read it to the class. Clinton went first. The question his paper addressed was whether the pluralist model of society, with its mix of corporations, regulatory agencies, labor unions, consumer groups, environmentalists, citizen advocates, chambers of commerce, could place enough pressure on corporations to make them responsible. Leftist intellectuals led by Herbert Marcuse believed that the answer was no. The pluralist model was a fraud in the final analysis, Marcuse argued, and freedom and democracy were illusions in the corporate capitalist system.

Greg Craig, who was Rodham's friend and another student in the seminar, remembers Clinton's presentation and how surprised he was by it. Everyone at Yale Law knew that Clinton wanted to be a politician and that he still believed strongly in the system. But "the whole thrust of his paper," Craig thought, was that "the pluralist model just didn't work. He said it didn't work because the money was out of whack. The corporations had all the money and they used it to defend themselves. Bill argued that the system was corrupted." Clinton seemed in "the depths of despair" then about the system to which he wanted to devote his life. "But if you had dreams, that was a terrible time," Craig said later. "If it was a tough time for him, an angry, hostile period of his life, it was consistent with what a lot of us felt."

What was the partnership of Clinton and Rodham like in those early days? The first public display came that spring, near the end of his second and her third year in law school. Rodham had decided to extend her studies at Yale Law to a four-year program. To look back on how they interacted then is to appreciate a dynamic that would change little through the years. Yale Law students were required to perform as lawyers either presenting appellate arguments in moot court or trying cases at mock trials. The trials, run by the Barristers Union, a student organization, were both major entertainment and serious competition. Cases were scripted like Broadway dramas. New Haven residents and Yale students were recruited to serve on the jury and enact the parts of witnesses. Student teams took the defense and prosecution cases and competed on two levels: the jury verdict was interesting but secondary. What counted was how each lawyer's performance was evaluated. At the end of the year there was a Prize Trial in which the top-ranked lawyers competed against each other, two to a side plus two alternates. A judge was brought in, usually one of national renown. The Prize Trial was an event in New Haven, drawing a packed house to a law school classroom transformed into a courtroom.

The Prize Trial for 1972 began at ten in the morning of April 29. Rodham and Clinton were the prosecution team. They had spent evenings and weekends for most of that month preparing their case, often working at the house of their alternate, Robert Alsdorf. Rodham ran the prep sessions. Alsdorf remembered at least one night when Clinton fell asleep—"he just nodded off"—while they were discussing the case. Michael Conway and Armistead Rood formed the defense team. Abe Fortas came to New Haven to preside as judge, a rather controversial choice in that he had only recently resigned from the U.S. Supreme Court in some disrepute. Elliot Brown, a first-year student, wrote the case, basing it on a recent trial in the South. Posters tacked up around campus before the trial summarized the case: "Herb Porter is a tough cop who doesn't like long-haired kids. But is that enough motivation to beat and kill someone? What did happen at the infamous road block on Rte. 34 last October? The newspapers called this the worst case of police brutality in Kentucky history. 'Maybe so,' says the defendant, 'But don't blame me.' "

Early in the trial, Clinton made the key prosecution argument on the admission of evidence. He argued vehemently, several people in the audience that day remember, and openly displayed his chagrin when the evidentiary ruling went against him. "Hillary was much calmer," according to Elliot Brown. "You could see her say, 'Okay, we lost it, let's move on.' "

Brown, as the scriptwriter, knew better than anyone that Rodham and
Clinton had a difficult case. He had to give both sides an argument, which
made it hard to write a scenario without a reasonable doubt, in essence
stacking the deck against the prosecution. And along with the tough case,
Rodham and Clinton were up against Michael Conway, perhaps the sharpest student in their class. Conway, who went on to become a top litigator
in Chicago, had arrived at Yale Law after serving as editor of the student
newspaper at Northwestern University. He had honed his skills like an ace
reporter and could deliver an oral argument as though he were dictating a
perfect story to the rewrite desk. The defense won the verdict and Fortas
gave Conway the top prize.

But what lingers in the minds of most of those who watched the trial is
the way the partnership of Clinton and Rodham operated. Clinton was soft
and engaging, eager to charm the judge and jury and make the witnesses
feel comfortable, pouting when a ruling went the other way. Rodham was
clear and all business. Alsdorf was struck by the contrasting styles, noting
that Rodham was never concerned about stepping on toes whereas Clinton
"would massage your toes." Nancy Bekavac, watching from the back of the
room, later said of the pair, "It was like Miss Inside and Mr. Outside. I
thought, 'What is this—Laurel and Hardy?' Hillary was very sharp and
Chicago and Bill was very *To Kill a Mockingbird*."

CHAPTER FIFTEEN

TEXAS DAYS

AFTER MEETING THE two state coordinators that the 1972 presidential campaign of South Dakota Senator George McGovern had dispatched to Texas for the general election, Houston political organizer Billie Carr lodged a sarcastic complaint with campaign manager Gary Hart. "You said you were sending some young men down to help us, but I didn't know they'd be this young!" Carr huffed. "One of them looks ten and the other twelve!"

The one who looked ten was the bushy-haired law student from Yale, Bill Clinton. Passing for twelve was a mustachioed political writer from Washington, D.C., named Taylor Branch. They were not only young but utterly unknown in Texas, which was how Hart wanted it. He realized that it was problematic to send out-of-state political operatives to a contentious place like Texas, where mortal enemies might conspire against an outsider who dared to tell them what to do. Yet he found it necessary. The historically sharp disputes between liberal, moderate, and conservative Democrats in Texas, to say nothing of the personality clashes within each of the factions, had intensified with the nomination of McGovern, a certified liberal. It would be virtually impossible to find native Texans who were not linked to one of the warring factions and thus unacceptable to others. Beyond that, Hart had established a policy of placing organizers in states other than their home states "so they would not be tempted to look after their own careers instead of McGovern's best interests."

Although unknown in Texas, Branch, who came from Georgia, and Clinton at least were southerners who knew the language and could adapt to the culture. Despite the admonition about their youthfulness, they apparently passed the test in a brief screening session with Carr, known as the Godmother of Texas liberals; Robert Hauge, an antiwar activist at Rice University; and Sissy Farenthold, a veteran Texas firebrand who was recovering from a disheartening loss in the Democratic primary for governor. Farenthold and Hauge, seeking to measure their ideological credentials, pressed Clinton and Branch about their positions on the Vietnam War and domestic issues, while Carr wanted to know about "the organizational stuff"—whether they had a feel for politics.

Clinton could cite his experience in the Duffey campaign in Connecticut, as well as his role as an antiwar organizer in England and his earlier work in Arkansas for Fulbright and Frank Holt. And unlike other veterans of the Duffey campaign, he qualified as someone who had supported McGovern from the beginning. At a reunion of Duffey workers at Anne Wexler's home in Westport during the summer of 1971, Wexler and other Duffey organizers had said that they were signing up to work for Maine Senator Edmund Muskie, then the frontrunner for the Democratic nomination. Clinton broke from the pack and said that he was for McGovern. His decision can be attributed to two factors. First, the intensity of his feelings about the Vietnam War: McGovern was the clearest antiwar candidate. And second, his friendship with Rick Stearns, his former Oxford classmate from California, who served as McGovern's deputy campaign manager and had been talking to Clinton about the South Dakota senator for several years, going back to his work on the McGovern Rules Commission. During the spring and early summer, Stearns had sent Clinton to Arkansas to work on his home-state delegation, which was committed to favorite son Wilbur Mills. Clinton also had operated close to Stearns at the Democratic Convention in Miami Beach. From a post in the main trailer, he had passed along instructions to a floor whip for several states. In the week before the disastrous withdrawal of Missouri Senator Thomas Eagleton as McGovern's runningmate because of his past use of electric shock therapy to treat depression was revealed, Clinton had polled southern delegates on the Eagleton affair. Along the way, he impressed Gary Hart, who thought he "combined a lot of southern charm with eastern sophistication." Hart also noted Clinton's hair. "He was one person in that period who had as much or more hair than I did."

Taylor Branch brought his own share of organizing experience to the Texas job. As an undergraduate at the University of North Carolina, he had been influenced by Allard Lowenstein, the charismatic antiwar leader and UNC alumnus who frequently visited the campus in search of disciples. During the summer of 1966, Branch trained under Lowenstein at a leadership camp at the University of Maryland, picketing the White House and listening in amazement as Lowenstein engaged Stokely Carmichael in a debate about black nationalism. Branch was engrossed in the issue of race relations. He had grown up in segregated Atlanta, where his father owned a dry-cleaning shop in the Buckhead section. All the workers were black. The lead cleaner, a man named Peter Mitchell, was also Taylor's father's workday pal. They would wager on Atlanta Crackers minor league baseball games and head off to Ponce de Leon park in an old white laundry truck.

Sometimes Taylor would tag along. When they entered the park, the trio would split up: Mitchell was required to sit in the blacks-only section of the bleachers.

By the end of his senior year in college, the volcanic 1968, which was also Clinton's senior year, Branch was dividing his time between civil rights and the war. That spring he traveled to Indiana to canvass for Eugene McCarthy's antiwar presidential campaign in the black wards of Indianapolis. On the night after the primary, which McCarthy lost to Robert Kennedy, Branch was at the Indianapolis airport. He was engaged to be married and had just received his draft notice and was flying home to take his physical. His mind was spinning with the possibilities awaiting him, one of which was jail. He had already decided that if he passed the physical, he would sooner go to prison than fight in Vietnam. Broke, dejected, and without a place to stay, he spent the night at the airport, sitting on his suitcase, waiting for a morning plane. In the middle of the night, someone tapped his shoulder. There stood Bobby Kennedy. He asked Branch and another bedraggled McCarthy volunteer if they would join him for breakfast at the cafeteria. Branch and his colleague squeezed into a booth across from Kennedy and talked politics. It struck Branch that while Kennedy should have been happy—he had just won a crucial primary, after all—he seemed as despondent as Branch, whose candidate had lost and who was facing an unwanted draft physical. It did not take Branch long to discover what was troubling Kennedy.

"I'm getting all the C students and McCarthy's getting all the A students," Kennedy lamented. "I don't like it." He asked the students why they were for McCarthy. They said that McCarthy was there first, challenging Johnson on the war, while Kennedy was holding back. But he wanted to end the war as much as McCarthy, Kennedy told them. "McCarthy can't end this war because he can't win," he said. "I can win." As the conversation went on, Branch thought to himself, "Here's a guy who might be president of the United States arguing with two college students in the middle of the night." After Kennedy left, Branch felt somewhat guilty. He wrote Kennedy a note explaining that he was still for McCarthy and hoped Kennedy didn't think he was a jerk. Then he flew home and flunked his draft physical. He was married on the day that Robert Kennedy was buried.

Branch's reputation within the movement was established that summer when he helped black activists Julian Bond and John Lewis organize the integrated Loyal National Democrats, who challenged the delegation that had been handpicked by Lester G. Maddox, Georgia's segregationist governor, for the Democratic Convention in Chicago. Over the next four years, he supplemented his graduate studies and journalism career with political forays. He helped organize the massive antiwar protests in Washington in

the fall of 1969. While working at *The Washington Monthly,* an icono-
clastic political journal, in early 1972, he polished a few speeches for
Senator McGovern and helped the campaign recruit delegates for the cau-
cuses in Georgia and Kentucky. When Rick Stearns broached the subject
of running the Texas campaign for the fall, Branch's marriage was falling
apart and he was eager for a change of scenery. The fact that he would be
working with Clinton made it easier for him to accept the job. He had felt
a rapport with his fellow southerner, and admired his political instincts,
since their first meeting three summers earlier at the summit of young
antiwar leaders on Martha's Vineyard. If Clinton and Branch were not a
subcommittee of Branch's satirical Executive Committee of the Future,
they were at least a compatible, energetic team.

THE McGovern headquarters that awaited them in Austin was located in a
one-story stucco shell on West Sixth Street noted for its creaky wooden
floors and peeled walls. Dust, which had settled on the floor and window-
sills for months when the building stood unoccupied, filled the air when
McGovern volunteers stampeded into the headquarters during that dry
summer of 1972, forcing staff members to drink water or coffee constantly
to wash out their throats. There is a measure of well-intentioned naivete
in every grass-roots campaign, and McGovern's Texas effort had its share.
Such embarrassing questions as "You are Commissioner who?" and "You
are Senator what?" echoed through the headquarters. After a few conversations with the local pols of Duval and Jim Wells County—a notorious
South Texas region where LBJ supporters provided the critical votes for
his first Senate election by stuffing ballot box 13—the McGovern campaign's boiler-room operators were told by a courthouse pol: "Look, we'll
carry it for you down here if you leave us alone. We don't need you and
we don't want you. Don't ever call us back again!"

Across from the boiler room was the radio room, run by Mark Blumenthal, who arrived in Austin not from Yale Law School but from a hippie
commune in New Mexico called Tree Frog, where he had lived for three
years. Blumenthal made only minimal lifestyle changes to accommodate
his new line of work. He now lived on a three-acre farm on the eastern rim
of Austin with his wife, an infant daughter, dairy goats, fig trees, a beehive,
and an ample supply of marijuana. He did not want to cut his hair, but
neither did he wish to embarrass the campaign, so he tucked his ponytail
atop his head and wore a wig on days when he might encounter the public.
He was also, like the rest of them, intensely devoted to the cause. Between
midnight and four in the morning, he would turn on the reel-to-reel tape
machine at his house and take feeds of McGovern's speeches from the
night before sent to him over the telephone by national staff technicians.

He would head into the office before dawn and start sending out McGovern actualities, or sound bites, to hundreds of radio stations around the Southwest.

Clinton and Branch entered this colorful scene in the midsummer heat just as the national campaign was struggling to recover from the Eagleton disaster. They shared a garden apartment in a complex across the Colorado River about two miles from headquarters and split their campaign duties along comfortable lines: Branch took finances, Clinton took politics. Everything seemed fresh and possible. In his first week in Austin, Branch was quoted in a San Antonio newspaper boasting, "We are going to win this thing." The Texans viewed the newcomers with curiosity. Blumenthal, whose office was across the hall from Clinton's, noticed that the big Arkansan was a curious mix of cultures. He kept his hair long and curly and sometimes wore cutoffs to work. Yet when he was alone in his room, leaning back in his chair with his feet up on the desk, jabbering on the telephone, occasionally chomping on an unlit cigar, Clinton looked to Blumenthal "like a real politician, a junior politician." Lisa Rogers, then a twenty-one-year-old college dropout who worked in the boiler room, was struck by "how big he was, and how calm, and how left-handed." Something about Clinton "belied the hippie image," according to Carrin Patman, the daughter-in-law of the venerable East Texas congressman Wright Patman, and the most establishment-type figure at McGovern headquarters. Not everyone was impressed. Anne McAfee, an early McGovern supporter whose husband ran Austin's union-label print shop, thought Clinton was "wet behind the ears and not likely to make much of a contribution."

Branch seemed more ideological than Clinton and was less extrovert. He occasionally flashed a temper, yet had a wonderful, high cackling laugh and was gracious in his dealings with the staff. He had "less patience treating assholes like nice people" than Clinton had, according to one former campaign worker, and because of his position as the keeper of the checkbook was more often placed in situations where he had to make tough decisions. "It was sort of a good cop–bad cop routine," recalled Billie Carr, who dealt with Clinton and Branch regularly. "Clinton was the good cop. He always thought your idea was good. He was always sweet. Taylor would have to say, 'No, you can't do it, we don't have the money for that project.' " There were parts of the pop culture that apparently had eluded Branch during the years in Washington when he was writing about bureaucrats and congressmen. When Lisa Rogers excitedly announced that Linda Ronstadt might hold a concert for McGovern, Branch asked, "Who's Linda Ronstadt?"

• • •

LESS than four years had passed since Lyndon Baines Johnson sat in the White House. In five more months he would be dead. But in the late summer of 1972, slowed by heart attacks, his rugged visage blurred by extra pounds and stringy long hair, LBJ played out his final days along the Pedernales as a phantasmagoric presence, not all there but not yet gone. At the Democratic Convention at Miami Beach, dominated by antiwar liberals to whom Johnson was anathema, it had seemed almost as though he had never existed. His portrait was absent from the floor gallery and his name unmentioned from the podium until the final night. But he remained an important symbol in Democratic politics, especially in Texas and especially during a general election. McGovern did not want to run for president without Johnson's blessing and endorsement. One of his first acts as the Democratic nominee was to telegraph the former president inquiring about his health and asking whether a visit to the ranch would be in order. Johnson was furious about the way he had been ignored at the convention and did not want to see McGovern, but wired back that he would be delighted to receive him.

The meeting was scheduled for August 22. Clinton and Branch helped the national staff arrange logistics for the visit and passed along whatever information they could gather on Johnson's mood. They also assisted in the advance work for several events scheduled in Austin surrounding the ranch meeting. There would be a rally at the airport when McGovern arrived with his new runningmate, Sargent Shriver, Bobby Kennedy's brother-in-law, and before and after the ranch trip there would be meetings with antiwar liberals, Chicanos, blacks, women, and labor.

From the isolated beauty of his ranch in the Texas Hill Country, Johnson ran one of the best political intelligence-gathering operations in the nation. He had been paying close attention to McGovern for months. His daily pouch of mail and documents included the literature of the campaign, which he not only read but annotated, sometimes with disdain. In early August, when McGovern had finally settled on Shriver as his replacement runningmate and when word got out about the imminent trip to Texas, Johnson was kept informed by telephone calls and memos from his network of former aides and cronies. An August 8 memo from former White House aide Horace Busby in Washington noted that McGovern's impending pilgrimage to the ranch "created quite a stir on Capitol Hill and downtown." Busby then offered a cold assessment of the ticket's chances: "Over the past ten days or so I have been traveling to different points of the compass talking with a broad assortment of organization Democrats about the campaign. While all are cautious in public statements about predicting the dimensions of McGovern's probable defeat in November, their private figures show those dimensions to be considerable."

Johnson requested that the meeting be closed to press and staff, a decision which greatly disappointed Clinton and Branch, who held grand notions about being in the room and serving as mediators between the nominee and the former president. Branch was "pissed that we couldn't go to the ranch." He thought he could mollify Johnson. Unlike many of their friends in the antiwar movement, Branch and Clinton professed no hatred for LBJ. Clinton considered him "a great man," who tragically allowed "his own paranoid aggression to consume him." Branch thought that even though he and Clinton "had no stature," as fellow southerners they might have "had more rapport with LBJ" than McGovern did.

One week before the meeting, Johnson made a political move that served his purposes while frustrating the McGovern campaign. He drove to Fredericksburg and dropped off a one-page endorsement of McGovern on the desk of Art Kowert, an old newspaper friend. He asked Kowert to publish it and then pass it along to the rest of the press. Longtime Johnson-watchers in the Texas McGovern camp concluded that LBJ did it to spite them. Many of Johnson's protégés, most notably John Connally, the former governor, and also former press secretary George Christian, had recently broken with their party and formed a national group known as "Democrats for Nixon." The hope was that Johnson's endorsement of McGovern at the ranch would be a strong counteraction to the Connally betrayal; but the peremptory announcement minimized that possibility.

The day after the announcement, Johnson received five pro-McGovern and fifteen anti-McGovern letters. The next day's pouch brought five pro-McGovern and eighteen anti-McGovern letters. Johnson's mail reflected public opinion. McGovern was trailing President Nixon in the polls by between 23 and 28 percent in mid-August.

The trip to Austin and the ranch marked the first time that McGovern and Shriver campaigned together. Waiting for them at Austin's municipal airport late on the night of August 21 was the largest crowd either of them had yet encountered along the campaign trail—more than ten thousand supporters waving banners that read "Jobs Not Bombs" and "Twenty Thousand More Americans Have Been Killed in Vietnam Since Nixon Took Office." The boisterous crowd reflected McGovern's popularity in the college town, the most liberal place in Texas. In his speech at the airport, McGovern promised that his campaign would bring the fractious state party together, but there was little evidence of that possibility. Dolph Briscoe, the Democratic candidate for governor, was absent from the welcoming party. Briscoe had not endorsed McGovern and would not say who he planned to vote for in November. Also missing were Senator Lloyd Bentsen, who had declined to serve as McGovern's state chairman; Lieutenant Governor-elect William Hobby; and Austin's mayor, Roy Butler, another conservative Democrat and LBJ partisan, who begged off, saying he had to interview a prospective city manager. The incumbent governor, Preston Smith, was at the airport, and in his speech he described himself as "a Democrat now and a Democrat in November," but that was not enough for some liberals in the crowd who booed him for past grievances. As the caravan carrying the campaign entourage left the airport after midnight and rolled toward the sprawling Villa Capri Motor Hotel near the University of Texas campus, it came to a sudden stop when the engine in the lead car carrying Secret Service agents conked out.

The next morning, McGovern and Shriver were flown out to the ranch in a small plane, and were met at the private landing strip by LBJ and Lady Bird, who were seated at the wheels of separate golf carts. McGovern was startled by the sight of the former president, dressed in a flannel shirt and khaki slacks. "He had hair down to his shoulders—longer than long hair, shoulder-length hair, he looked like General Custer," McGovern recalled. McGovern could not help thinking about the psychological implications of that shoulder-length hair. All those long-haired college kids raising hell with LBJ about the Vietnam War, and here he was with hair down to his shoulders. McGovern and Johnson bounced back to the ranch house in one golf cart and Lady Bird drove Shriver in the other. When they had settled outside under the shade trees, Johnson, according to McGovern's recollection, said that some of his friends were "in this thing called Democrats for Nixon—but they haven't got me. They haven't got me and they aren't going to get me." The quartet moved to a table for a noontime meal of small dinner steaks. "I remember vividly when Lady Bird served the steaks," McGovern later recalled, "Lyndon cut his into small pieces. He'd take a bite, one small little cube, then he'd light a cigarette and he'd smoke for a while. And Lady Bird would look at him. She had a faint smile. If there is such a thing as a sad smile, she had a sad smile. She watched him. She saw him reliving his campaigns. She knew about the heart attacks. She saw him smoking cigarettes. I think he smoked eight or ten cigarettes while Sarge and I were there." Everyone at the table knew the old man was dying.

At a press conference afterwards back in Austin, McGovern said that the Vietnam War came up "in passing" only two or three times during the three-hour discussion and that Johnson advised him to reach out to the elements in the party that did not support his nomination. He said that he would take LBJ's advice. "We are going to reach out needing all the help we can get."

It is doubtful that McGovern meant the sort of help that he received when he returned to his suite at the Villa Capri and met with a few dozen key Texas supporters and state campaign staff leaders, including Clinton.

This meeting was later charitably described by one veteran Texas political reporter as "a donnybrook of a family feud." Although Clinton and Branch had not been in Texas long enough to deserve much blame, the message of the meeting was that McGovern's Texas campaign was disorganized, directionless, and divided. Sissy Farenthold was vacationing in Europe with her family, but she was at the meeting in spirit, since much of the discussion was about the wide split in the party between her supporters and those of Dolph Briscoe. Briscoe's reluctance to join the McGovern team, some argued, was directly related to the fact that Farenthold was bitter about her loss to the conservative Briscoe in the Democratic gubernatorial runoff and would not endorse him for governor.

Not that it required an ideological divide to rile this Texas crowd. Several blacks were also upset about being excluded from the meeting and went to the local paper that afternoon to express their "ill feeling." Here was an example of the unintended consequences of political reform. George McGovern, who had chaired a commission that opened the Democratic party to groups that historically had been kept outside the system, was now constantly dealing with the frustrations of unrealized expectations. If everyone felt that they deserved a part of the action, they also were more easily aggrieved. The blacks who complained about McGovern's visit were university students who were unknown in Austin and had no connections to the campaign.

It is clear from a series of letters McGovern wrote a week later that Clinton and the Texas staff had made several unfortunate mistakes in dealing with the varied constituencies of the campaign. In a letter to Gonzalo Barrientos, a leading Chicano politician in Austin, McGovern apologized for not speaking to Barrientos during the trip and added: "I realize that my campaign in Texas has had many shortcomings, especially among Chicanos. However I think things have improved on all fronts in the last few days." A similar letter went to Leonel Castillo, the city comptroller in Houston. There was also an embarrassing omission involving Secretary of State Bob Bullock, who was among the handful of state officials willing to speak out for McGovern yet unable to get in to see him during the visit. "There is really no way to excuse or apologize for the mixup at the Villa Capri, but I do want you to know how sorry I am," McGovern wrote in a note to Bullock. "Perhaps these foolish errors are bound to occur occasionally, but it's especially painful when they involve someone like you, who has served us so long and so well."

ONE positive result of McGovern's trip to Austin was that he persuaded a colorful pair of Texas officials to serve as co-chairs of his Lone Star campaign and help Clinton and Branch find their way through the chaos of state politics. John C. White, the agriculture commissioner, and Bob Armstrong, the land commissioner, signed on at a time when most other elected officials in Texas were staying as far away from McGovern as possible. White had been a strong Hubert Humphrey supporter during the primaries and Armstrong had stayed neutral. But they finally decided, "Bullshit—we're Democrats and we'll run as Democrats," according to Armstrong. In the end the choice did not prove politically damaging to either of them, though Armstrong would later boast that his association with McGovern helped him make Richard Nixon's notorious enemies list "right there next to Bella Abzug," and White got "a damn good IRS audit out of it."

The Texans did not delude themselves about McGovern's chances in Texas. During the Austin visit, White told the senator, "I cannot see a win here. I think your ceiling is forty percent." Even so, the national staff promised them that Texas would be regarded as a key battleground state, targeted for at least one million dollars in campaign funds and frequent visits from McGovern and Shriver. Why would they spend so much time and money on a state that appeared to be a lost cause? Because to ignore Texas would amount to surrender. It was one of eight states that McGovern strategists believed they had to carry to win the election. They had already written off the Deep South. They had to try to win somewhere. To survive in that period, according to Gary Hart, the campaign manager, "you had to be an optimist." The optimists searched for signs of hope in the statistics of past campaigns. No Republican presidential candidate had carried Texas since Eisenhower in 1956. Humphrey had defeated Nixon in Texas in 1968, though by a mere 38,000 votes. The pessimists saw chilling similarities between 1972 and twenty years earlier, when Eisenhower trounced Adlai Stevenson in Texas with the help of a potent Democrats for Eisenhower organization led by a conservative governor, Allan Shivers, who assumed the role then that John Connally was playing now.

White and Armstrong lacked potent political organizations that they could lend to the McGovern effort, but they got along well with Clinton and Branch, and entertained and nourished the young coordinators. They were a generation older, but were more the good-natured uncles or big brothers than father figures. After a rough day on Sixth Street, Clinton and Branch were invited up to White's suite in the state office building, where the convivial agriculture commissioner dipped into his stock of confiscated whiskey. "He had this bootleg cellar and he'd bring out some of the best stuff and we'd drink it and talk," Branch recalled. Like most homegrown Texas pols, White and Armstrong loved to gossip about the characters they had dealt with over the years. Clinton was interested in stories about

Lyndon Johnson, and White, a storyteller who had known Johnson since 1950, had a supply of stories as deep and potent as his whiskey cabinet. Johnson, he told the young Arkansan, was an "exciting, dangerous man— it was dangerous to be his friend and worse to be his enemy." As he got to know Clinton, White came to think that in some respects he resembled LBJ, especially in the passion he felt for the process. In that respect White saw Clinton as a classic southern politician who viewed politics as "an art form, an entertainment, a story, a whole life."

Clinton took quickly to Armstrong. They were both southern moderate liberals who loved to shoot the bull, stay up late, flirt with women, and enjoy life. "They were right out front with the horseplay," recalled White. "They had a real buddy relationship." Armstrong would arrive at work at the General Land Office at about ten each morning, drink coffee and conduct business for a few hours, then slip out in the afternoon and head down to the Sixth Street headquarters with two six-packs of beer and his guitar. "I'm taking some sick leave," he would say on the way out the door. "I'm sick of all those Republicans." He had one foot in establishment politics and the other foot in the youth culture. "I was there at the dawn of the Age of Aquarius, at noon and at midnight," he said later. "It was exciting, a great time for newfound freedoms—that was what it was all about."

Most members of the campaign staff were under thirty. They worked long hours to try to elect McGovern while still enjoying life. Late at night, they would head over to Scholz's beer garden, the hangout for Texas liberals and unofficial McGovern headquarters, where Armstrong would be picking and strumming and holding forth. Sometimes the younger staffers would go bowling at an alley across the river on South Lamar Boulevard. The bowling crew included Clinton, Branch, and Texans Garry Mauro, Roy Spence, Judy Trabulsi, Nancy Williams, and Betsey Wright, all of whom would later become important political allies of Clinton's. Mauro, a University of Texas law student and former Aggie Yell Leader at Texas A&M, ran the Youth for McGovern operation. He shared Clinton's political obsession and thought he was on the fast track—working at headquarters and attending law school at the same time—until he realized that Clinton was running the state campaign while enrolled at Yale Law thousands of miles away. Mauro's girlfriend, Trabulsi, and her business partner, Spence, were fresh out of college and had just started an advertising firm that did some work for the campaign.

Perhaps the most resolutely ideological person in the crowd was Betsey Wright, an energetic political operative from the small West Texas town of Alpine, who had worked for the state Democratic committee. Wright lived two blocks from headquarters with Poppet, her Pomeranian. Although she was not yet thirty, she was considered a mentor and role model for some of the younger women in the office. Lisa Rogers called Wright "our moral pulse." Wright had a more difficult time with some of the men, especially Don O'Brien, an old-fashioned Kennedy-clan operative who had been sent to Texas to help Clinton and Branch deal with traditional Democrats who were leery of the long-haired McGovern crowd.

A former U.S. attorney from Sioux City, Iowa, O'Brien had worked with Bobby Kennedy, a connection that naturally impressed Clinton. Many of the women on the staff considered him a chauvinist. He called them "girls," until one day one of them, Ruthie Fischer, snapped at him, "We're not girls; if we're girls, then you're boys." Wright later said that O'Brien screamed at her about her hormones and depressed her so much that she turned into a "raging feminist."

Clinton and Branch led relatively moderate lives in Texas. They drank beer late into the night. There "was dope around, but not compared to beer—beer was the drug of choice," according to Lisa Rogers. Most of Clinton's other contemporaries, including Mauro, Trabulsi, Williams, and Spence, recalled smoking marijuana at late night parties and occasionally at the back picnic tables at Scholz's. They said they did not see Clinton smoke pot. The sexual atmosphere was free and easy. "Stories of who slept with whom among Texas Democrats have been a source of titillation for as long as I can remember: sex was always part of the game," recalled Bebe Champ, who worked on the campaign as an aide to Armstrong, the self-proclaimed Age of Aquarian. "All the women thought Bill was absolutely adorable and precious. I saw his attraction, the groupies around him, but he didn't seem to take it very seriously. As far as spending time with somebody, I didn't see him do a lot of womanizing." Commissioner White, who had seen his share of sex-hungry politicians during his days in Texas politics, noticed that "women were very attracted to Clinton" and that "he obviously liked women"—but that most women-chasers "would rather talk about women than politics and Bill would rather talk about politics."

Hillary Rodham, who got a job that summer and fall working in a voter registration drive in Texas for the Democratic National Committee, was in Austin with Clinton more than half the time. When she was away, usually in San Antonio, and occasionally back at Yale for her fourth year, the boiler-room women would come by Clinton's office and ask, "Where's Hillary? Where's Hillary?" to the point that Clinton, in exasperation one day, complained, "Gol dang, I couldn't do something if I wanted to!"

When she was around, Rodham sat at a desk next to Clinton's and left a vivid impression on the campaign staff. She wore jeans or brown corduroys to work, sported big square eyeglasses, and walked around carrying pads of yellow paper. Volunteers coordinator Joyce Sampson, then a housewife married to a University of Texas law professor, was "in awe of young women like Hillary who went to law school." Mark Blumenthal, the hippie-dippie radio man, found her to be aloof but intelligent. Bebe Champ thought Rodham was "not particularly warm but businesslike—she focused on what she was interested in and shut other things out." Rodham treated Ruthie Fischer "like a little sister—she worried that I wasn't going out enough and that I was putting too much into the election."

Taylor Branch welcomed Rodham's presence. He found it easier to talk to her than to Clinton about "more reflective things" such as the collapse of his marriage and the meaning of life. "Bill and I talked business. We laughed. We talked personalities, but we never sat down and philosophized. I was feeling rootless, unhinged, and it was easier to talk to Hillary about those things than to Bill." Betsey Wright also felt more comfortable with Rodham. The two women would sit under the blazing Texas sun at the massive limestone pool at Barton Springs, or across town at the airport waiting for a plane to come in, and talk for hours about the need for more women in politics. "It was a nascent feminist movement then. We had both read Simone de Beauvoir and Germaine Greer. And I'd just come off the heady experience of Sissy Farenthold's campaign in Texas," Wright recalled later. They reinforced each other's ambitions. Rodham thought that Wright's political experience in Texas would be valuable to other women around the country. Wright believed "that women were the ethical and pure force that American politics needed" and considered Rodham a perfect candidate to lead the movement. "I was less interested in Bill's political future than Hillary's. I was obsessed with how far Hillary might go, with her mixture of brilliance, ambition, and self-assuredness. There was an assumption about all the incredible things she could do in the world."

It was not at all certain during their Texas days that Rodham and Clinton would stay together. They did not see each other exclusively and appeared on the verge of splitting up at least once. San Antonio labor leader Franklin Garcia, a charismatic figure around McGovern headquarters, a fearless organizer and a soothing mystic, helped patch things up. "Franklin, I just want to thank you. You really saved our relationship," Clinton said to Garcia one night at Scholz's. The couple argued heatedly, yet they also shared a deep passion, according to Roy Spence. "They shared a passion for the dream—the dream of being in politics, of sharing the business of politics."

THE Watergate break-in, which had entered the political stage in 1972, seemed to have negligible effect on how the public viewed the presidential race. The public lack of interest in Watergate troubled Branch and Clinton, but it did not slow them down. One night at their apartment, they talked for hours about why they could not stop working. It was, according to Branch, the only concentrated philosophical discussion he and Clinton had during the months they worked together. "I thought it odd and curious that even though the polls showed very early it was over, we worked just as hard—we were obsessive. We decided that an awful lot of it had to do with the war. We thought the war would go on four more years, particularly the bombing, if Nixon won. Playing for those stakes made it important. Plus we always had this sense that a huge scandal might break at any moment, making the election close and Texas critical, so we couldn't relax."

There was no prospect of relaxation in any case. The Texas campaign was in constant turmoil as it tried to deal with historic political forces that it could not control. One such force was the growing disaffection of conservative southern Democrats with the national party, as symbolized by John Connally's embrace of Nixon. Connally's Democrats for Nixon group, funded largely by money from the Committee to Re-elect the President (CREEP), was running full-page advertisements attacking McGovern on defense, busing, taxes, and welfare. The dilemma for the McGovern forces was how to repudiate Connally and his crowd without alienating Texas Democrats who had not yet abandoned the ticket. It was a fine line.

When the Texas staff learned that Connally was planning to host a lavish fund-raiser for Nixon at his Floresville ranch, they saw it as a chance to mock the fat-cat ostentation of that event by staging a populist-style tamales-and-beans fiesta for McGovern on a nearby courthouse lawn. Branch and Clinton presented the counter-rally proposal to the Washington staff, which promptly rejected it. McGovern had absorbed too much criticism for his one-thousand-dollars-for-everyone welfare proposal, the Washington staff argued, and a scraggly tamales-and-beans affair might give the impression that they were engaging in class warfare. Gary Hart told them it was important for the campaign not to seem marginal. Clinton and Branch persisted, however, supported by their seasoned Texas advisers, White and Armstrong, who thought the tamale fiesta fell into the category of a classic Texas populist event. Since McGovern would not go, they tried Sargent Shriver. They pitched the idea to him during his next visit in the state. He "thought it was a great idea," and put it on his schedule.

Threats and counterthreats laced with obscenities flew between the Texas coordinators and the home office in the final stages of the Floresville advance work. The hostility was real but evanescent, the sort of profane give-and-take that seeps into most such relationships, where state coordinators demand more candidate time and money while the national staff tries to keep a larger strategy in force. Branch had worked out an agreement that expenses for the rally would be shared by Texas and Washington, but Washington's money was slow in arriving. The Texans were short of homegrown cash and often resorted to dramatic gestures to squeeze some out of the national office.

On the morning of the rally, Branch called Washington and said, "If your advance guy doesn't have your half when I get there, you might as well not send Shriver." Branch in fact had the necessary funds in his trunk. Steve Robbins and Tony Podesta, who had opposed the idea in the first place, exploded at the threat. "We're gonna have your ass, Taylor, you fucking incompetent! We're gonna get you fired for this!"

"You couldn't fire me," Branch screamed back. "You couldn't find anybody else to agree to take this goddamn job!"

Washington came up with the money.

On the night of September 22, Clinton watched Sargent Shriver, the patrician Democratic nominee for vice president, his coat off and shirtsleeves rolled up, mingle with fifteen hundred people, die-hard McGovern-Shriver supporters and hungry locals in search of a meal, who had assembled on the lawn of the Wilson County Courthouse at a people's party where the food and drinks were free: ten thousand tamales, three thousand pounds of beans, four thousand jalapeño peppers, trash cans full of peanuts, and two hundred and forty gallons of beer.

A few miles away, guests were arriving at John and Nellie Connally's contemporary stone frame and glass ranchhouse. Their long driveway was lined with limousines and a private airstrip hummed with helicopters and private jets. Among the wealthy Democrats for Nixon in attendance were oilmen, manufacturers, and university regents, even Johnson's former Air Force One pilot, sporting a "Nixon Now" button. Chrysanthemums floated in Big John's pool. On the front lawn, under an orange and yellow awning, outdoor tables shone with crystal and silver settings. President Nixon and his wife and four hundred guests dined on roast beef and black-eyed peas.

For every Texas Democrat who publicly followed Connally into the Nixon camp, there were more who remained silent. Ten members of the state Democratic executive committee refused to sign a petition endorsing the top of the ticket. In San Antonio, officials at Democratic party headquarters would not talk to local McGovern campaign officials. Clinton spent much of his time on the telephone sweet-talking reluctant party regulars or going out on the road to see them in person. He studied the politics of each county, paying careful attention to the various factions. "When he arrived there was a feeling that Texas was such a vast state that no outsider could possibly learn who was enemies of whom, but after a while, mention a name or an event and Bill knew more about it than you did," Bebe Champ said later. "If you went to this town you had to see so-and-so. He was so easy to talk to, people would tell him stuff, and he remembered it. He was so likable, people tried to help him not stub his toe."

Clinton got away from the Austin office whenever possible, often head-

ing south to the Rio Grande Valley and San Antonio, where he fell in love
with Tex-Mex food and became addicted to the mango ice cream at
Menger's Hotel, or east to Houston, where he studied political organizing
at the side of Billie Carr. Carr wore a "Liberal and Proud of It" button and
distributed "Billie Carr—Bitch" namecards. She first took sides when her
parents brought her to the 1928 Democratic Convention and pinned an Al
Smith button on her diaper. From the day in 1952 when Governor Allan
Shivers boasted to her, "Young lady, I have this state in the palm of my
hand," Carr had looked upon conservative Democrats as her mortal enemies and fought them at every opportunity. She had loyal followers, but
even among fellow liberals she had her share of enemies. Her detractors
complained that she was not a team player. Some people in the McGovern
campaign complained that she had the best mailing list of liberal activists
in the state but was reluctant to share it. Anne McAfee, one of Carr's liberal
antagonists in Austin, accused her of using the list to wield power. The
reason Clinton had to visit Houston so often, McAfee charged, was that he
was "courting Billie to try to get the list." That might have been part of it.
Clinton's dealings were usually played out on two or three levels at once.
Another reason could have been that he and Carr enjoyed each other's
company. Carr, a rugged, heavyset woman eighteen years older than Clinton, reminded him of some of the independent women of Hope and Hot
Springs, including his mother. She loved politics as a way to meet people,
and it was that interaction as much as ideology that drove her—a lot like
Clinton.

"Bill liked going out and shaking hands. He liked the meetings before
meetings and the meetings after meetings. He liked to eat and drink,"
Carr recalled. They would drive around in Carr's yellow Chevrolet to
organizational gatherings of only ten or twelve people, sometimes only the
host and a close friend or two. It was retail politics at its extreme. On many
nights as they drove back from a meeting, Clinton would tell her the life
stories of everyone who had been in the room. "I swear he would get
everybody's life story before he left. You couldn't get him away from
talking to people and listening to them even then." At larger party func-
tions Clinton would often be approached by Carr's enemies, who said it
was unwise to place her in a visible position. "Well, I understand you have
problems with Billie," Clinton said at one such confrontation. "But Billie is
working hard for us. We need you, too. What can you do for us?" Clinton
never demoted her or tried to hide her.

One day while they were eating lunch at a Mexican restaurant in Houston, Clinton told Carr about his future plans. "I'm gonna tell you something
and you're gonna laugh," Clinton said as he devoured a plate of enchiladas.
"As soon as I get out of school, I'm movin' back to Arkansas. I love Arkansas.

I'm goin' back there to live. I'm gonna run for office there. And someday I'm gonna be governor. And then one day I'll be callin' ya, Billie, and tellin' ya I'm runnin' for president and I need your help."

"Oh you are, are you?" Carr replied.

THE longer the campaign went on, the more it became obvious to Taylor Branch that he and Clinton had different political temperaments. To Branch, the campaign began to seem like "an endless fight over who got what." There was great sensitivity about which group or leader seemed to be getting preference. "We were always doing the wrong thing. If I did something for one group, others would complain." The low point for Branch came one afternoon in Houston when he was attending a black political event near the airport. Black leaders, led by state Senator Barbara Jordan, who was running for Congress and had just been named vice-chair of the state party, were upset that Chicanos had been granted a meeting with McGovern while blacks had only been able to meet with Shriver. "They were furious for pure status reasons," Branch recalled, "and told me that they would disendorse the ticket unless I diverted McGovern's plane and brought him to Houston." Branch told Jordan he would see what he could do. He excused himself from the gathering and called Steve Robbins and Tony Podesta, the schedulers. He explained the situation, but they told him the demand was ridiculous: there was no way they could divert the plane. Branch returned to the meeting and told Jordan that he had tried to persuade Washington to bring McGovern to Houston, but they had decided that diverting the plane was out of the question.

Jordan turned on Branch, he later recalled, and with her slow, precise, stern phrasing, she declared: "The *reason* that *you* did not get the *message* across with *sufficient clarity* so that they could *understand* the *message* is because *you . . . young man . . .* are a *racist!*"

Branch felt intimidated and upset. "I made your position as clear as possible," he said. Then he called Washington again. McGovern could not go to Houston immediately, but it was agreed that he would visit the black group soon—"and in the end," Branch remembered, "they had the meeting."

But if Branch asked himself, "Is this really worth it?," Clinton thrived. Branch concluded that "he was more interested in the game than I was, that's the heart of the matter. He liked what we were doing. He liked those meetings. He absorbed backbiting better than I did." Soon enough Clinton became renowned for his ability to settle factional disputes. Pat Robards, who worked at the Austin headquarters but came out of the fractious San Antonio region, saw that "every time a war broke out among ethnic groups, they would have certain demands and Bill would mediate between them all." The key to Clinton's success, according to Branch, was his ability to study the personalities of the people he was dealing with and determine what it took to get along with them, where their weak spots were, who was lazy, who was committed. "He was Johnsonian in that sense—knowing how to read personalities."

In the final month, the Texas campaign turned from mere chaos and clamor to outright farce. Clinton spent more time in the Rio Grande Valley, where the ticket at least had a chance of carrying a few counties. In Shriver's last visit to the valley, his plane could not leave: it was trapped on the runway for three hours as a pilot flying solo got disoriented in the foggy airspace above the airport, forcing the control tower to suspend operations as they tried to talk him down. Clinton knew that Shriver's delay could have serious consequences at his next destination, Texarkana, where Roy Spence had a television crew waiting amidst the crowd to film a final fund-raising commercial that they hoped might evoke John Kennedy's boisterous rally there at the end of his 1960 campaign. But the fiasco in the valley prevented Shriver's plane from arriving in Texarkana until well after midnight. By that time most of the crowd had gone home. Spence shot the commercial anyway, staying up all night to edit it so that the crowd appeared large and buoyant.

The spot was a rousing appeal for East Texans to stand tall with the party of Roosevelt, Wright Patman, Sam Rayburn, and LBJ. They were urged to send donations to a post office box in Austin. A few days after the spot aired, in a heady burst of optimism, Branch and Clinton walked to the downtown post office with a troop of colleagues from the headquarters, expecting to discover a stack of envelopes filled with checks. The post office box was empty. They returned the next day, and again it was empty. After that, an embarrassed Branch went alone. The following week, he discovered one envelope. He brought it back to the office and had the staff gather around for the ceremonial opening. "With great fanfare" and high expectations, Branch opened the package. Inside was a piece of toilet paper smeared with human excrement and a note declaring that the contents reflected what East Texans thought of George McGovern.

Yet paradoxically in those final weeks, as the evidence mounted that Nixon would be reelected in a landslide, the national McGovern campaign was awash in money. The direct-mail fund-raising operation was generating an astounding 25 percent return in a field where 3 percent was considered average. "We had this huge cadre of people who were desperately committed to George McGovern and thought he was the messiah who would end the war in Vietnam," recalled Tony Podesta. "It was like a Ponzi scheme in the end. We couldn't count the money fast enough." One night a McGovern adviser in the Washington office noticed thirty canvas bags in a back room amid various debris. "What's in those bags?" he asked. Trash, he was told. He opened a bag and found it stuffed with envelopes containing checks and cash—hundreds of thousands of dollars that might have gone straight from the hearts of true believers to the incinerators of the nation's capital. The money instead was sent out to targeted states, including Texas.

"It was unbelievable. It was not smart money, but emotional money," according to Roy Spence, who spent as much as he could on Texas media buys. Spence's partner, Judy Trabulsi, camped out at the Western Union office in Austin, a telephone in one hand, buying time on radio stations and simultaneously wiring them payments. Two nights before the election, Bebe Champ drove by the Sixth Street headquarters. The lights were off, but she stopped to see if anyone was inside and found the front door open. She walked past the reception area and down the hall to Clinton's office, where a small desk lamp provided the only light. Clinton seemed startled when Champ appeared at the doorway. She asked him what he was doing. The answer was in the dimness: Stacks of money were piled on his old wooden desk, cash that had come in from Washington for get-out-the-vote efforts on election day. Clinton was sorting it: this pile for San Antonio, this for Houston, this for the Valley. "I've got to get all this money out of here by tomorrow morning," he said.

It was of no use in the end—not the money, not the sixteen visits that McGovern and Shriver paid to the state, not the talents of Clinton and Branch. On November 7, Nixon crushed McGovern in Texas, winning 67 percent of the vote on his way to one of the most lopsided victories in American presidential history.

A few days after the election, Clinton and Branch and the rest of the Sixth Street gang drove out to Bob Armstrong's ranch near Liberty Hill on the outskirts of Austin and spent one long last evening together. They played touch football and sat around a campfire and sang to the accompaniment of Armstrong's guitar. Clinton crooned a few Elvis tunes and Branch sang "Rocky Raccoon." Most of the people there, according to Mark Blumenthal, were in "altered states of consciousness induced by the heavy disappointment that we lost so badly." Bottles of Jack Daniel's were passed around the campfire along with "a couple of joints."

Each one had a different way of dealing with loss. Franklin Garcia told Branch that he seemed to be in serious emotional distress. "You need to go hunting," Garcia told him. "Shoot a bird so that you don't think everything is so fragile." Branch would later head back to Washington and consider writing a book called "The Future of American Decadence," a title which, though it related to a wholly different subject, the underworld of agents and drug dealers in Miami, nonetheless seemed a perfect reflection of his mood in the aftermath of the campaign.

Betsey Wright was hired by Creekmore Fath, the liberal benefactor, to run an office whose purpose was to keep Sissy Farenthold's name politically alive. But soon, at Hillary Rodham's urging, Wright headed up to Washington to work for the National Women's Political Caucus, a point from which she dreamed of helping Rodham begin a long march to the White House.

Mark Blumenthal left for India in search of a six-year-old guru. "If America is going to buy Nixon again," he told friends before leaving. "I don't want anything to do with this."

Clinton lingered in Austin for several days after the election. He seemed to be in no hurry to return to Yale Law School, where he was enrolled as a third-year student but had not yet set foot in a classroom for his third year. "Aren't you worried about classes?" Bebe Champ asked him. "Nah, it's okay," he replied. One afternoon he was seen carefully going through all the mailing lists and files and letters, transferring names and telephone numbers to his growing personal file of index cards.

WHAT did his experience in Texas mean to Clinton? He certainly could have spent that summer and fall working for McGovern in Arkansas, where he was planning to begin his political career, or in Connecticut, where he was in law school. "Coming down to Texas had to be part of an agenda," thought Pat Robards. "It helped him enlarge his base. He made contacts here that he maintained. From then on, we'd all get postcards and fundraising newsletters from him." Even Mark Blumenthal, the hippie radioman, kept receiving postcards from Clinton after he left Texas. "When he was traveling, these postcards would come in the mail," Blumenthal recalled. "He'd send them to me, and I was a nobody. When I got one, I said to my wife, 'This guy's going somewhere.'"

Clinton learned an unforgettable lesson in the value of nurturing contacts, according to Roy Spence. "He learned from that race the power of a network; McGovern didn't have one, and it hurt him." Beyond Texas, the McGovern campaign proved invaluable to the Democratic party as an incubator for many of the party's finest organizers, strategists, and policy theorists over the following two decades, people who served as the support staff for the two McGovern aides who later entered the national electoral realm: first Gary Hart and then Clinton. Texas also provided Clinton a training ground to sharpen his skills dealing with contentious factions within the Democratic party, where he learned how difficult and petty politics could be, and what it took to survive. He came away with a stronger commitment to becoming involved.

As George McGovern watched his young protégé evolve over the ensuing decades, he would note another lesson that Clinton learned from the campaign, a reinforcement, actually, of a political reality that had first become clear to Clinton in Joe Duffey's campaign two years earlier. "He seemed to take away the lesson of not being caught too far out on the left on defense, welfare, crime. From then on he would take steps to make sure those were marketed in a way to appeal to conservatives and moderates." But in Clinton's heart of hearts, McGovern believed then and later, he would always remain "closer to where we were in '72 than the public thinks."

Not long after he got back to New Haven, Clinton wrote a letter to Creekmore Fath in Austin thanking him for his help and recalling the campaign with a certain wistfulness. "I wonder what's going on in Texas," he closed the November 25 letter. "I must confess I miss it and that lost, bumbling battle of ours." One night during that period he visited the house on Crown Street where Bob Reich and Nancy Bekavac lived and spent several hours delivering an emotional soliloquy on his Texas days. He sat in the living room on their soft, tattered couch, wearing his huge blue winter coat and a grungy white-knit sweater, and described how Lyndon Johnson had gotten fat and grown his hair out and almost looked like a hippie, and how the old LBJ and Roosevelt coalition was breaking up and there seemed to be a meanness in the country. Bekavac recalled that "there was this sense of identification Bill had with the passing of the Age of Titans. It wasn't a point-by-point analysis and refutation of what had happened in Texas, but more an evocation of what was no longer out there. He translated that into how difficult it would make his own rise in a southern state. He had been part of the largest, most lopsided defeat in American politics. The meaning of this was not lost on him."

For the second time in three years Clinton returned from a political campaign to Yale Law School, and once again he had no trouble passing his courses. The only grades came from final exams and papers, and Clinton managed to master them in a few intense weeks of cramming. His academic record at Yale was "very good but not outstanding," according to a summary that was later sent to the University of Arkansas Law School when he applied for a job there. Many Yale Law students felt that the third year of studies was excessive in any case; they had learned all they needed to know in the first two years. For Hillary Rodham, who had extended her law school career to four years, the final year was even less demanding, allowing her to focus first on the McGovern campaign and then on her work in children's rights.

As their law school years neared an end, the class of 1973 went through one final mood swing that spring. Now, at last, Watergate was the big story. At the end of each day the students would bunch together in the lounge and watch the unraveling of the Nixon administration on the nightly news. Bill Coleman felt "a sense of hope" just as they were leaving law school, "a harbinger of the possibility of change." The team of Rodham and Clinton served together that spring on the board of the Barristers Union, running the Prize Trials. One day Clinton showed up at a board meeting with his hair trimmed and wearing white bucks. He was, thought Robert Alsdorf, who also served on the board, rehearsing for his journey home, back to Arkansas and a life in politics. Alsdorf took one look at Clinton and said, "Let me know when you're running for president, Bill. I'll help you."

CHAPTER SIXTEEN

HOME AGAIN

CLINTON WENT OUT into the world as a favorite son, barely eighteen, and now, nine years later, a man of twenty-seven, he was back. He had survived the perilous journey through the sixties and come home with his mission accomplished. He had established his academic credentials at Georgetown, Oxford, and Yale. He had woven his way through the war years undamaged in body if not in soul. He had proved that he could compete with the brightest of his generation, and indeed had constructed a vast network of contemporaries who would stand by him for the rest of his career. He had discovered a wide world of women, including one who might help him get to where he wanted to go and who was, whether he always liked it or not, his match: bright, organized, ambitious, independent, sharp-tongued, unafraid of him and yet tolerant of his foibles. He had learned the ways of Capitol Hill and engaged in the rollicking and dirty business of electoral politics in Connecticut and Texas. He had visited the capitals of Europe and gazed upon Lenin's Tomb and Shelley's mausoleum and searched in the cold Welsh rain for the birthplace of Dylan Thomas. Now he was home in his green, green grassy place, his folk-tale Arkansas, here to begin Act Two: a political life.

The story of his return to Arkansas opens with a stretch, a peculiar exaggeration, a myth—harmless perhaps, but peculiarly Clintonian and revealing. The way Clinton would tell the story for years afterward, his hiring as an assistant professor at the University of Arkansas School of Law in the fall of 1973 was "a pure accident." The phrasing is reminiscent of his claim that his avoidance of the draft during the Vietnam War years was "a fluke"—which it most certainly was not, no more than his arrival at the law school in Fayetteville was an accident. In the tale as Clinton would tell it, he was driving home from Connecticut at the end of his Yale days and, acting on a tip from a friendly professor, stopped at a telephone booth along Interstate 40, placed a call to the Arkansas Law School dean, and talked his way into an interview and a job—simple as that, just a spur-of-the-moment bit of roadside serendipity. Wylie H. Davis, the law school dean at the time, would encounter the Clinton version of events years later and find it "amusingly inaccurate and somewhat melodramatic." And he would ask: "Why degrade a Horatio Alger-type story with a self-inflicted nuisance like the facts?"—to which he could only answer himself that he felt compelled by "neurotic lawyers and history buffs" to set the record straight.

Clinton began aggressively pursuing a teaching position at Arkansas several months before he got his law degree at Yale. He recruited a political friend from Fayetteville, Steve Smith, to serve as his intermediary. Smith was a liberal young state legislator who had become friendly with Clinton during the McGovern campaign, when he was the only Arkansas delegate at Miami Beach to vote for McGovern on the first ballot. He talked about Clinton to J. Steven Clark, an associate dean at the Arkansas Law School who was also part of the state's political network. In March 1973, during his spring break from Yale, Clinton contacted Dean Wylie Davis, who would later recall that from that point on, "the entire process was as deliberate and formalized as it was—and had to be—in every new hire case." The law school received glowing letters of recommendation for Clinton from several professors at Yale as well as a record of his grades, which Davis and his colleagues paid little attention to because they found the Yale grading system "a slightly arrogant and eccentric neo-British affectation"—a cutting but misdirected insult, since the pass-fail system was the product not of haughty academics but of rebellious students.

Clinton flew to Fayetteville in early May to appear before the Faculty Appointments Committee. David Newbern, who chaired the committee, had a curious first impression of the young applicant from Yale. On the morning of Clinton's first day in town, Newbern stopped at the Holiday Inn where Clinton was staying to pick him up and escort him to the law school for a day of interviews. He encountered Clinton in the coffee shop talking to Steve Smith. Newbern wondered how Clinton knew Smith and why he would be engaged in such an intense political conversation on the morning when he was interviewing to become a law teacher. Later, he escorted Clinton from one faculty office to another. Finally, in an exit interview, Newbern asked the question that had been troubling him all day.

"Bill, are you coming to Arkansas to teach with us, are you coming because you want to be a law professor, or is this just a stepping stone?"

"I have no plans at this time to run for public office," Clinton said.

It was, Newbern thought, the classic political response.

Whatever Clinton's intentions, the Arkansas law faculty was greatly impressed. "He charmed us all right out of our mortarboards," said Dean Davis, who thought that Clinton displayed "a wide range of interests and learning for a young person." Clinton talked politics incessantly during the interview, but it did not bother Davis much because "in Arkansas, politics is a hobby for everybody, so it didn't seem out of place." Newbern, Mort Gitelman, and a few other professors raised questions about Clinton before the faculty voted on him. They were impressed by his Rhodes Scholarship and the rest of his résumé, but wondered whether he would make a good scholar. "It was very clear even back then that Clinton's main goal was a political career," Gitelman recalled. "The faculty debated the appointment on the theory of whether he would make a legal scholar and do the publications." In the end they were convinced that he would excel as a classroom teacher, and was worth the gamble. The vote was unanimous. Clinton was offered the job on May 12 and accepted May 22.

He moved to Fayetteville in midsummer and rented a contemporary stone and glass one-bedroom house in the country about ten miles southeast of town along Route 16 on the road to Elkins and a route through the hills known as the Pig Trail. The mimosa-blossomed winding roads, rolling hills, lazy-looped rivers, thick pine forests, and green-gorge vistas of northwest Arkansas were hauntingly beautiful and familiar to him. He considered all of Arkansas his home, and Fayetteville in the Ozarks represented his carefree backyard, the place he had escaped to during the summers of his youth to attend band camp. But it also had another meaning that evoked profoundly different feelings in him. The university and its row of fraternity houses served as the social nexus and training ground of the Arkansas good ole boy establishment. Four years earlier, when he was contemplating attending the University of Arkansas Law School so that he could join the ROTC program there and avert the draft, the notion of returning to Fayetteville made Bill Clinton feel strange. Part of the equation that sent him back to Oxford for a second year instead of choosing the safe haven of the state university was the queasiness he felt about getting stuck in Arkansas, a place which seemed "barren" of global thinkers and intellectual stimulation, as he had written in a letter to Rick Stearns.

So his relocation in Fayetteville was not an entirely simple homecoming. His relationship with his state was shaped by a triangular internal contradiction that would stay with him from then on and is crucial to understanding Clinton's political evolution. At one point of the triangle was myth: the way he would romanticize the Arkansas of huge watermelons and simple country folk, especially when he was away from it. At a second point of the triangle was pragmatism: the realization that Arkansas was the easiest base, the only base, for his political rise. At the third point of the triangle was ambition: a powerful desire to move beyond his provincial roots. Clinton would make it seem that he came home to Arkansas and stayed there for two decades out of pure love and obligation—but events would soon prove otherwise.

On August 23, not long after he had settled, he appeared at a watermelon party of the Washington County Democratic Central Committee in the sprawling two-acre backyard behind the grand old house of Ann and Morriss Henry along Highway 45. The party regulars at the Henry house were local figures of the sort that any aspiring politician would need to know, hard-core committed Democratic loyalists who performed the drudge work of organization and were the primary sources of inside political gossip. Clinton swept through the crowd as though he were an honored guest. "He came in . . . he wasn't invited but somebody brought him . . . he had just got to town, he shook hands, he talked, and by the time he left he knew every single person there," Ann Henry recalled later. "It was a perfect way for him to leave an impression."

Clinton was eager to make an impression and quickly took on several projects outside the law school. He filed an amicus brief in support of his friend Steve Smith, who was a key figure in a voting-fraud case being heard in rural Madison County. Republicans charged that Smith had interfered in the 1972 election by helping elderly residents fill out their ballots at a nursing home. Smith said that he and two nursing-home employees merely helped distribute the ballots. Clinton, in his friend of the court brief, presented a legal argument placing Smith's assistance within the boundaries of laws relating to ballot delivery. The court eventually disallowed the twenty-five votes that Smith had garnered at the nursing home, not enough to change the election outcome. The case attracted the interest of political reporters in northwest Arkansas. "Clinton came up and sat in the jury box with us," recalled veteran political reporter Brenda Blagg of *The Morning News* in Springdale. "He was part of the crowd."

His first challenge to the local establishment came in Springdale, a comfortable middle-class community north of Fayetteville, where he formed a friendship with Rudy Moore, Jr., a progressive state legislator whose law firm had business and political connections to Senator Fulbright. Weeks before Clinton arrived, Fulbright had met with Moore and told him that a young man who had been on his staff was moving to the area to teach at the law school, and that he and Moore "ought to know about each other." Clinton called Moore when he got to town and they spent hours talking politics. "Right off the bat," Moore recalled later, Clinton became absorbed in a local issue involving doctors who were rejecting Medicaid patients. Medicaid was not a popular social program then among Springdale's doctors. Moore agreed to lend the clout of his legislative office to Clinton's informal poll, which found only one or two doctors in town who were willing to accept Medicaid patients. In his first political encounter with the health care issue, Clinton got nowhere. The Springdale doctors "crawled all over" Moore for "sending somebody to look into" their affairs. Moore and Clinton backed away, but not before Clinton had rung up one strike against him among the doctors.

There were no strangers in Fayetteville. Everyone seemed to know everyone else, and often it seemed they were all related and they all had political connections. During the last week in August, Clinton went to lunch at Wyatt's cafeteria with a group of professors and administrators, one of whom happened to be Rudy Moore's brother-in-law, Carl Whillock, a university vice president. Whillock had previously served as the administrative assistant to James W. Trimble, the former Democratic congressman from northwest Arkansas who had been defeated in 1966 by Republican John Paul Hammerschmidt. The talk among the group was almost exclusively about Watergate, the scandal that had become a daily television drama starring Chairman Sam Ervin and his colleagues on the Senate Watergate Committee. In the car on the way to lunch, Whillock, a dignified man who dressed conservatively, seemed unusually quiet. Finally, when they were all seated at the cafeteria, someone asked him what he thought of the scandal. "I think Richard Nixon would cause great bodily harm to close family members if it would help him politically," he said. Clinton was shocked. He had misjudged Whillock because of his appearance and his earlier silence. Now he wanted to know more about him, and the more they talked, the more fascinated Clinton became. If Clinton wanted to get anywhere politically up in these hills, he could not find a steadier guide.

THE University of Arkansas School of Law had never before encountered a faculty member quite like Clinton. With his boyish face and long curly hair, he looked like one of the students and he often acted like one as well. He was a student's law professor rather than a law professor's law professor. In part, his style reflected the contrasting philosophies of the school where he learned the law and the school where he was now teaching it. At Yale, the hard part was getting admitted: once you got in, you were part of an elite club, and it was virtually impossible to flunk out. Arkansas, the only law school in the state, was obliged to open its doors to a majority of applicants, four-fifths of whom came from within the state. The easy part was getting in. It was not unusual for 30 percent of the first-year students to receive failing grades. Several professors took pleasure in terrorizing first-year students. Clinton was the opposite.

Although Clinton wanted to teach the glamorous subjects, criminal law and constitutional law, he told the dean that he would be willing to take on whatever courses needed to be taught. In the fall of his first year that left him with agency and partnership, which he knew little about at the start, and trade regulation, an antitrust course that he had studied at Yale. He searched for ways to relate the material to the more lively world of politics. In the agency and partnership class, for instance, he often brought the class conversation around to Watergate. "We had long discussions about whether the people involved in Watergate were agents of the president," recalled Moril Harriman, a student in Clinton's first class.

It was difficult to distinguish Clinton's class period from the rest of his day. Before class he could usually be found at the student lounge eating breakfast and "shooting the breeze—about anything," according to another former student, Woody Bassett. If a subject caught his interest in the lounge and it had the vaguest relationship to the law, he might continue the discussion once class started. Clinton worked the aisle during class discussions and displayed an early variation of the town meeting or talk-show-host style he would later use with great effectiveness. Other Arkansas law professors tended to be more deliberate and sharp in their use of the Socratic method. They came in with notes and a set of concepts they wanted to cover. They asked pointed questions and called on students at random. Clinton often spoke without written notes and lectured in a conversational tone. Students were free to enter the discussion when they had something to say. In the end, this pressure-free approach led to lively discussions in which the whole class participated. "There was some grumbling by faculty members about the grades in Bill's courses," according to law professor Rafael Guzman. "There were always an abundance of A's and B's, D's were extremely rare, and I doubt very much that Bill ever gave an F. The inside joke was, 'Bill doesn't give D's and F's because he might someday need those votes.' " As the law school dean, Davis took note of Clinton's grading pattern and considered it "on the high side," but "not enough to take him to lunch about it—he just didn't want to give anybody anything below a C."

As word spread that he was an interesting teacher who gave high grades, his courses became increasingly popular. Even his admiralty class on maritime law, a subject of limited interest to most lawyers in Arkansas, bulged with seventy students. But Clinton's casualness sometimes drove even his students to distraction. He was slow in marking exams and posting final grades. One running story at the law school during Clinton's time there was about two law students catching sight of each other across a golf course fairway in late spring and one yelling across to the other, "Hey, I finally got my grade in Clinton's class"—pause—"from the fall semester!" Once he accidentally left the final exam blue books in his car and they disappeared. It was never clear whether he lost them or they were stolen, though Davis found it "mind-boggling that they could have been stolen." His students were given the option of retaking the exam or getting credit for the course without a grade—an unsatisfactory prospect for most of them since they were counting on Clinton's generosity to raise their grade point averages. Another semester on the morning of exam day, colleagues chortled knowingly at the sight of Clinton in a frenzy because he had waited until the last minute to prepare the exam. Students were answering the first question while Clinton was still writing the next. Clinton always seemed to be juggling too many things at the same time.

Mort Gitelman, as a senior faculty member, was asked to observe Clinton's classroom performance one semester to prepare a report for the tenure committee. Clinton was teaching constitutional law, Gitelman's specialty. His report "wasn't terribly kind to Bill," Gitelman recalled. "He was very good at engaging the students in the classroom, but a lot of times he was kind of off-the-cuff. I wouldn't say unprepared, but not terribly organized. He was not the kind of person who would prepare a class meticulously." On the positive side, Gitelman noted that Clinton possessed "qualities that went into the making of a good teacher. He wouldn't try to impose his views on people. He would draw people out." Had Clinton stayed in legal education, by Gitelman's account, "he would have been okay."

In the constitutional law class, Clinton devoted two weeks to a discussion of the seminal *Roe* v. *Wade* decision legalizing abortion. According to Woody Bassett, Clinton told the class that he believed *Roe* was "the most difficult of all court decisions" during that era, and that he thought "they made the right decision." The legal aspect of the case that he emphasized in class was how the Supreme Court devised a way to define a right of privacy not defined in the Constitution. He also spent time dealing with other women's rights issues related to abortion. When one state legislator proposed a measure criminalizing abortion, suggesting that women who had abortions should be prosecuted for murder, Clinton asked the class to consider the possibilities. "What would you do if a woman was sleeping and rolled over and accidentally killed her unborn child—would that be manslaughter?" he asked. "It was an intense discussion about how far it would go," recalled Jesse Kearney, a student in the class. "Bill was good at posing the questions."

Clinton reached Fayetteville at a crucial time for black students at the law school. They were part of the first wave of African Americans, ten to fifteen students per class. Many of them were on probation, on the verge of flunking out, and looking for a mentor on the all-white faculty. L. T. Simes, who came out of the Mississippi Delta town of West Helena, Arkansas, and Ouachita Baptist University, arrived at the law school in 1972, one year ahead of Clinton. "The first year we were there was the most difficult of my life," Simes said later. "Black students in law school were not faring too well as a whole. It was sink or swim." Among other concerns, many black students thought they were not being graded fairly.

Along came Clinton, who to the blacks seemed different from the rest of the faculty. He quickly became their friend and champion. He was young

and outspoken in renouncing racism and the black students naturally gravitated to him. In the classroom, his relaxed style was a special comfort to
the blacks. Outside the classroom, he became a tutor for many of the black
students, holding sessions at his house or at the law school lounge. "He
always had people around him, he was always holding court," Carol Willis,
a student from McGehee, another poor Delta town, recalled. "Most black
lawyers my age just about owe Bill Clinton for getting them out of law
school. He would take the time to make sure you understood the material."
Although his classroom style and tutoring helped the black students stay
in school, so too did the grades he would give them. They could get a B in
his class and a D in another and stay off academic probation.

The black law students eventually gave Clinton a nickname. They called
him "Wonder Boy." "In the South at that time, whites would say one thing,
but their deeds and words were often different," Simes said later. "So here
comes a person where no matter what your relationship with him was, he
was not prejudiced. He did not let race treat you different from anyone
else. That's why we called him Wonder Boy. It was a miracle the way he
was. He could have shunned black students politically. Fayetteville and
northwest Arkansas was a white enclave. Wonder Boy Bill did not waver
in respect to his conduct with African Americans."

YEARS later, perpetuating the myth that his life progressed in a series of
accidents and uncalculated events, Clinton would insist that he embarked
on his first political candidacy in Fayetteville reluctantly and only after he
had failed to persuade several other people to make the race. In fact, he
seemed eager, hungry—anything but reluctant. And he was especially
eager for a political office that, if he won it, would take him away from
Arkansas. He told Rudy Moore in the fall of 1973 that he wanted to run for
office but believed that a seat in the state legislature would not satisfy him:
"He felt he had to go bigger. He had his eye on a higher prize." At age
twenty-seven—twenty-eight by the time of the next round of fall elections
—there would be nothing extraordinary about Clinton serving in the state
legislature. In the realm of state politics, then, he was too old to be called
a boy wonder. Steve Smith, after all, had been elected when he was only
twenty-one, and Mack McLarty, Clinton's childhood friend from Hope,
went up to the state capitol as a representative when he was twenty-five.

The careers of Clinton and McLarty were rolling in different directions.
McLarty, even more than his ambitious kindergarten mate, carried great
expectations with him during his early life. People said that he was destined to be governor. They said it about him when he was the sixteen-
year-old governor of Arkansas Boys State, when he was the star quarterback

of Hope High, when he was the popular student body president at the University of Arkansas, and when he was elected to the legislature in 1971 as the presumed leader of an activist freshman class. Yet by the time Clinton returned to Arkansas ready to dive into electoral politics, McLarty had already climbed out of the pool. He served a single two-year term in the Arkansas House and then quit. He already had a wife and child when he entered the legislature, and there was pressure on him to go back to Hope and take control of the family's lucrative auto business, which he seemed far more eager to do than run for reelection. He yearned for stability, he was more comfortable in the business world and was troubled by the uncertainties of elective politics. Helping out behind the scenes, as a party chairman or fund-raiser, was more to his liking than being the center of attention, the target of opposition. It was hard for anyone to imagine McLarty losing an election in Hope, or in all of Arkansas—but he imagined it. "What if you don't win?" he asked himself. Politics, he would later confess, always seemed like "a high-stakes gamble." During his one term in the House, McLarty was uncomfortable and barely noticed.

Clinton was comfortable with everything about politics except the notion of being a small fish in a small pond. There was one obvious choice for him. As far back as February 1973, when he visited Arkansas from New Haven to take the state bar exam, friends remember him pounding them with questions that indicated he wanted to come home and run for Congress in the Third Congressional District, which included Hot Springs and Fayetteville. Now he was back in the state, and the moment had arrived. In early December, he drove to the Little Rock suburb of Sherwood and spent a long night talking with Paul Fray, his friend from the Holt Generation days who had been waiting eight years for the time when Clinton would run for Congress. As Clinton devoured a salty Virginia ham prepared by Mary Lee Fray's mother, he and Paul Fray analyzed the congressional district county by county.

They concluded that Hammerschmidt, the Republican incumbent, had a nearly unbreakable hold on the district's largest city, Fort Smith, because of the many retired military families in that area and Hammerschmidt's ability to satisfy their concerns through the House Veterans Affairs Committee. The key to giving Hammerschmidt a tough race was to concentrate on the other twenty counties, especially the rural ones in the hills. They had to go out into the hills, Fray said, "and hammer the hell out of them."

Not long after the session with Fray, on a bitterly cold evening that winter, Clinton walked over to Carl Whillock's comfortable seven-bedroom house in the shadows of Old Main near the law school in Fayetteville. He had been a regular visitor at the Whillock residence all school year. Whenever he had free time he would drop by to joke around and make

peanut butter and banana sandwiches with the Whillocks' three teenage
daughters, and then stay up late talking politics with Carl and his wife
Margaret. On this night they were chatting in the parlor room, warming by
a fire, when Clinton said, "I've been thinking about running for Congress.
What do you think about it?"

"Wait right here, I'll go get my card file," Whillock said. He came back
with a box that his wife had never seen before, brimming with names and
telephone numbers and key contacts all across the Third Congressional
District from his days as Trimble's aide. The two men sat in the kitchen
late into the night going over the names in Whillock's old file.

Hammerschmidt had not faced a serious challenge from a Democratic
opponent since he wrested the seat from Trimble in 1966, the year that
Republicans had first gained a foothold in Arkansas with the election of
Governor Winthrop Rockefeller. Hammerschmidt had won with two-thirds
of the vote in 1968 and 1970 and then a smothering 77 percent in 1972.
Over the course of his four terms in office he had become a popular
figure among voters and public officials from both parties through solid
constituency work and careful nurturing of the private interests in northwest Arkansas. As the only timberman in Congress, he was considered an
especially valuable ally of the heavily forested district's significant timber
industry. The odds were weighted against anyone seeking to oppose John
Paul, as Hammerschmidt was known, even though it was an off-year, when
the party out of power usually gained House seats and the Democrats
seemed especially ready to do so as President Nixon's popularity declined
with every new Watergate revelation.

Clinton solicited advice from other experienced political observers.
Most encouraged him to run while holding out little promise that he could
win. "I don't see how you can raise the money to make the race," said
attorney James Blair, a major political powerbroker in northwest Arkansas
who was managing Senator Fulbright's reelection campaign that year.
McLarty, the state party chairman, considered Hammerschmidt "a wonderful man" who was "well regarded and well respected," and not a top-
priority target for the Democrats. Blair's future wife, Diane Kincaid, a
political science professor at Arkansas who had met Clinton during the
1972 presidential campaign, noted the poor showing of previous chal-
lengers to Hammerschmidt but thought that Clinton was the first "plausible
candidate" to surface in eight years in that he "looked like a congressman"
and "understood national issues and the dynamics of the district."

Clinton was not easily discouraged. He told Blair that he would overcome his financial disadvantage by working harder. In Arkansas, that meant
traveling to every town in the district and meeting as many voters as
possible and asking them for their votes. The concept of retail politics was

a sacred political belief in Arkansas. The political folk wisdom included a statistical component: it was estimated that 60 percent of the people voted for the candidate who met them first and asked them for their vote. Clinton thought he could ask that many. He also assumed that the Watergate scandal would help.

Watergate influenced Clinton's career decision in more ways than one. In December 1973, just as he was attempting to gauge how the scandal would play in the hills of northwest Arkansas, Clinton was offered a position as a staff lawyer for the House impeachment inquiry staff. Under the direction of former Justice Department official John Doar, the inquiry staff was being formed as an adjunct to the House Judiciary Committee to sort out the Watergate evidence and make the legal case for Nixon's impeachment. In building his staff, Doar recruited heavily from Yale Law School, where graduates were recommended to him by Burke Marshall, his former colleague in Justice's civil rights division. Clinton and Hillary Rodham were on Marshall's list. Clinton would later say that he considered the offer "a great temptation" and "a great opportunity—one that just about any young attorney would've given anything for"—but there is no evidence that he spent much time debating his options. David Pryor, who was working as a lawyer in Little Rock and beginning a campaign for governor, later recalled Clinton visiting him one day and asking whether being associated with the impeachment staff would have any negative implications in Arkansas. Interestingly, according to Pryor, Clinton put the question in terms of his friend Rodham and his relationship with her. "He talked to me about Hillary going to work for the Watergate committee," Pryor recalled. "He asked, 'Is that a good idea?' It was a career consideration. He knew that his career would be in politics and the question was whether Hillary's connection with the Watergate committee might have political ramifications."

DURING his lunch hour one day in early January 1974, Clinton sat in his cramped third-floor office at Waterman Hall placing telephone calls. One call went to Ron Addington, a doctoral student and instructor in the school of education who was interested in politics and had told a mutual acquaintance that he wanted to meet Clinton. "Why don't you come over and let's visit," Clinton said when he reached him. They had common bonds. They were born within a month of each other in 1946 in the same area; Addington grew up in DeQueen some thirty-five miles from Hope. He was an Army reservist, conservative in dress, bearing and haircut. Clinton was wearing blue jeans, leather moccasin boots, a checkered shirt with a tie, and a corduroy sports jacket. His hair was long and curly. His appearance did not match Addington's expectations, which were closer to "the stereotype of a person who runs for office." But the two clicked, and Addington agreed to help Clinton prepare for his race for Congress.

Later that week, Clinton asked Addington to travel with him for a day of political meetings in Russellville, an important city in the congressional district some three hours away on the road to Little Rock. The journey ended in embarrassment. After meeting various political officials in town all day, Clinton and Addington were taken to dinner at the local country club as the guests of a wealthy attorney and political powerbroker whom Clinton was intent on recruiting to his side. As the dinner conversation dragged on, it became clear that Clinton was getting tipsy. Never much of a drinker, he was politely downing his drinks with everyone else at the table. His sentences became less and less understandable. It was clear to Addington that Clinton could not drink and remain coherent. In the car on the way back to Fayetteville, Addington scolded Clinton for his behavior. "I don't know whether you can drink while campaigning," he said. "Don't try it again." The lesson was brought home soon enough when the attorney endorsed another candidate.

Addington was in Little Rock, spending the weekend with his girlfriend, when Clinton called him from Fayetteville on the Sunday morning of February 24.

"I'm announcing tomorrow," Clinton said.

"Tomorrow?" Addington gasped.

"Yeah. We're setting up some press conferences."

"Okay, let's do it!" Addington said.

That was Clinton, he thought: impetuous, hungry, thinking that he could conquer the world in a day. And this was not even a normal day. It was a Sunday. And Clinton wanted press conferences in four cities—Hot Springs, his home town; Little Rock, the state capital and headquarters for the state political press corps; Fort Smith, the largest city in the Third District; and Fayetteville, Clinton's new base. Addington told Clinton that he would go to work on rounding up the press and meet Clinton in Russellville, a midpoint in the triangle between Little Rock, where Addington was staying, Fayetteville, where Clinton was, and Hot Springs, where they would both spend the night in preparation for the first press conference the next morning. They agreed to meet at the AQ Chicken House in Russellville that afternoon. First Addington called Doug Wallace, the editor of the University of Arkansas student newspaper, who was part of Clinton's team, and who had already spent Friday and Saturday preparing press packets. Then Addington got in the car with his girlfriend and headed north. When they reached the Chicken House, Addington hopped out and said goodbye to his girlfriend, who drove on to Fayetteville alone. From a telephone outside the restaurant, Addington began tracking down reporters to let them know the plans for the next day.

Clinton arrived in his Gremlin, late, and he and Addington headed out over the mountain from Russellville to Hot Springs, one of the most perilous, twisting drives in Arkansas. Halfway through the trip, Addington turned to Clinton and said, "If we survive, you are never going to drive again when I'm in the car!" Clinton was driving as he always drove, carelessly, talking and gesturing the whole time, his eyes often off the road, every now and then swerving wildly into the oncoming lane or running his right tires onto the shoulder. The car had no passing power, but Clinton would try to pass anyway, usually when he was chugging uphill heading into a blind curve.

At eight o'clock on Monday morning in frigid twenty-two-degree weather, sixty Clinton friends and relatives gathered at the Avanelle Motor Lodge in Hot Springs for the announcement. Ten relatives from the Clinton family were there, along with the parents of his high school friends: Phil Jamison's mother, Ronnie Cecil's father, Jim French's dad. Elizabeth Buck, Clinton's old Latin teacher, stood in the back near Virgil Spurlin, his high school band director. Here, at long last, was the opening moment of Bill Clinton's political career. He went after Hammerschmidt right away, ignoring the three other candidates for the Democratic nomination. He characterized Hammerschmidt as a close political ally of Nixon's and tried to link him to Watergate by saying, "Of all the men in Congress, he is one of those who has allowed the President to go as far as he has." If the people "demand more honest politics," Clinton declared, "they'll get more honest politics."

His mother Virginia was nearby. "All smiles," as Addington remembered her. "All smiles and laughing."

CARL Whillock's old card file was not the only valuable collection of names that Clinton turned to when he began his electoral career. He already had a file of his own, a cardboard box stuffed with alphabetized and annotated index cards listing the addresses and telephone numbers of classmates, professors, political organizers, and others he had encountered during his long apprenticeship. He spent time each night combing through the file, placing telephone calls, and writing notes to friends who might help his campaign.

Two years earlier, while working for McGovern in Texas, he had told Houston organizer Billie Carr that he was going home to Arkansas to begin a political career that would culminate with a run for president. Now he called her and said proudly, "Billie, I'm on my way!" He also called Bob

Armstrong and John C. White and Taylor Branch, who was back in Washington serving as the Washington editor of *Harper's* magazine. Though Branch by then had soured some on electoral politics and was hardly wealthy, he responded by contributing $250. It was, in a sense, a one-man phone bank and direct-mail operation. Most of Clinton's friends from Georgetown, Oxford, Yale, and Texas took note of the inevitable—their irrepressible pal Clinton had finally begun his lifetime race—and chuckled as they took his call or opened his letter. For the most part, they were charmed. Clinton was the master of the soft sell. He remembered the smallest details of people's lives, and his deftness at personalizing the notes tended to overcome whatever unseemliness might otherwise have tainted a blatantly political contact.

A letter he sent to Charlie Daniels, the plumbing contractor from Norton, Virginia, who had met Clinton four years earlier at the National Hotel in Moscow, stands as a perfect example of how Clinton would present himself: good-humored, humble, flattering, familiar: Dear Charlie," he began.

> I don't know if you'll remember me but this is the last day of the week we were together in Moscow four years ago now. I have been thinking of you, as I always do this time of year.... I am about to embark on a campaign for Congress against an entrenched GOP incumbent. I remember thinking when we were together what a campaigner you'd be— You're sure welcome here. Ha! My mother has never forgotten your thoughtful phone call upon your return from Russia. All the best, Bill Clinton.

Daniels was a registered Republican, but from then on, Clinton was his man. He visited Arkansas often, and even more often sent Clinton campaign checks.

The return rate on Clinton's personal direct-mail effort was uneven. Many of his young friends sent donations of between $10 and $50. "Sorry I couldn't send more," wrote Garry Mauro, who headed the Students for McGovern effort in Texas in 1972. Women friends old and new seemed to be reliable sources. Hillary Rodham wrote out two early checks for $400. Lyda Holt chipped in with $125. The Leckford Road connection was also fruitful. Strobe Talbott contributed $300, as did Brooke Shearer. The rest of the Shearer family, who served as Clinton's hosts when he visited California, also supported his congressional bid. Brooke's brothers, Derek and Cody, both journalists, gave a total of $450, and her mother, Marva Shearer, contributed $200. The first $10,000 of his campaign came from a source closer to home: a Hot Springs bank loan co-signed by his uncle Raymond Clinton and Gabe Crawford of the Oaklawn Pharmacy.

· · ·

THE Third District was more than Fayetteville, Fort Smith, and Hot Springs. Most of the twenty-one county district lay out in the northern hills, the region that Clinton and Paul Fray had targeted as the key to the election during their meeting in early December. It was a vast rural region steeped in country folkways. To get to Washington, Clinton would have to travel deep into the backwaters of his native state. At an organizational meeting of Clinton supporters in Fayetteville a few days after the announcement, Carl Whillock unfolded a map of Arkansas and traced the two-lane roads and highways leading from one county seat to another in the Third District. He knew the distances from town to town: with twists and turns through the hills, destinations were always far longer in minutes than in miles. Each time his hand stopped at a town, Whillock had a story to tell about a friend in the courthouse or at the weekly newspaper. He proposed that he and Clinton spend a day together driving through the hills from courthouse to courthouse.

They left at dawn on Wednesday, March 6. Whillock had not prearranged any meetings for the trip. He knew the daily patterns of the people he wanted Clinton to meet. They would be where they always were, and no matter what they were doing they would have time for an old friend. The political explorers headed north and east out of Fayetteville on Highway 62 until they reached Berryville, a town that Whillock knew intimately as the home town of his former boss, the late congressman Trimble. The rural essence of the district Clinton sought to represent was brought home to him at this first stop. Berryville was a county seat of Carroll County—not the county seat but a county seat. There were two county seats, with their own separate courthouses: Eureka Springs on the western side of the Kings River and Berryville on the eastern side—a vestige of the days, not so long ago in these parts of Arkansas, when rivers were difficult to cross. At the Berryville courthouse they met Eileen Harvey, the circuit court clerk and recorder of deeds, who cherished the memory of Trimble as her "dearest friend" and had once been a member of the same church as Whillock. "Carl tells me you know how to run in these hills," Clinton said to Harvey. He asked Harvey for her help. She gave it, not only offering to take him around the county, even across the Kings River, but also persuading her daughter to work in Clinton's county campaign. "We hit it off," Harvey said later. "He loved people and loved campaigning and I did too. Politics is nothing more than a selling game."

From the courthouse, Whillock and Clinton drove out to the Methodist parsonage in Berryville, where they met a young minister, Victor Nixon, and his wife, Freddie Nixon, who were leading peace and civil rights activists. "We sat around the front porch and visited for an hour or so," Whillock recalled. "And Freddie agreed to be Bill's Carroll County coordinator." That conversation on the porch began a long relationship between Clinton and the Nixons that was marked by deeply emotional moments. Victor Nixon would later serve as the minister at Clinton's wedding. Freddie Nixon would become one of Clinton's aides, and their friendship would bend but not break in a profound disagreement over the use of the death penalty.

The next stop was in the little town of Alpena on the border separating Carroll and Boone counties at a drive-in restaurant run by the wife of an old cattle farmer, Bo Forney, who served on the Democratic central committee. Forney was a rough-faced, gruff-talking, overweight character in bib overalls, seemingly a world apart from the young Rhodes Scholar with the curly hair and long sideburns. But again, Clinton knew how to talk Forney's language and won him over. The cattle farmer contributed $405 to Clinton's campaign before the year was through.

Driving east on Highway 65, Whillock and Clinton reached Harrison, the county seat of Boone County and the heart of enemy territory, Hammerschmidt's home. Harrison was a major hub in northwest Arkansas, large enough to have its own daily newspaper, the *Harrison Daily Times,* and Whillock knew the editor, J. E. Dunlap. Whillock realized that Dunlap, who wrote a column under his initials, J.E.D., was an ally of the incumbent congressman, JPH, but he took Clinton in to see him anyway, hoping to "soften J.E.D. up." It was a surprisingly productive visit. In that afternoon's paper, across page 2 from JPH's "Capitol Report" column opposing congressional pay increases, J.E.D. took note of his visitors from Fayetteville. "One candidate has already hit the ground running. He's running on the Democratic ticket for Congress in the 3rd District," J.E.D. wrote. "Bill Clinton, native of Hope, graduate of Hot Springs high school, a Rhodes Scholar and a graduate of Yale Law School, now a teacher in the U of A Law School, was in town this morning with a former aide of the late Cong. Jim Trimble, Carl Whillock. Clinton was shaking hands on a tour through the Harrison area."

Highway 62 took the travelers east out of Harrison and along the White River through Yellville and Flippin. It was Clinton's first glimpse of a scenic region where he would later, much to his eventual regret, invest in a vacation home development enterprise known as Whitewater. They reached the northeastern terminus of their trip in Mountain Home, where they met with Baxter County treasurer Vada Sheid at her family furniture shop. "These two men walk in," Sheid recalled later. "I knew Whillock from his days with Trimble. He introduced me to young Bill Clinton, a very personable young man. We found a place in the store to sit down and visit." Clinton cast his spell on another older woman. He was "the kind of person," Sheid thought, "who makes you want to be friendly with him." It quickly became clear that she and Clinton had much in common. They both loved politics—and more: "He said his birthday was August 19 when I asked him his age. I said, 'That's my birthday, too. That makes us both Leos!' I felt Leos had the same ideas about people. I agreed wholeheartedly to support him."

As Clinton rose to leave, Sheid noticed that a button had fallen off his shirt. "Now, Bill," she said, "you need a button sewn on your shirt if you're going to run for congressman." She had him sit still for a minute as she found a needle and thread and made him presentable again. It was the first of many times over the years when the friendly furniture store merchant would come to the aid of her ambitious young astrologically aligned friend. Two years after that first meeting in Mountain Home, she was elected to the Arkansas legislature, and a decade later she would cast a decisive vote that saved Clinton's reputation at the same time that it may have cost Sheid her career.

When they left Sheid Furniture, Whillock and Clinton temporarily split up. Clinton said he wanted to visit the newspaper office. "You do that," Whillock said, "and I'll go find Hugh and we'll meet at the drugstore at four." Hugh was Hugh Hackler, an old friend who had served in the Arkansas legislature with Whillock in the 1950s. At that point in the afternoon, Whillock guessed correctly that he would find the retired Hackler in the pool hall playing dominoes with his friends. Whillock took Hackler aside after the game.

"Hugh, I'm traveling with Bill Clinton, a fine young man running for Congress. I'd like you to meet him," Whillock said.

Hackler responded coolly. He said he had already promised people that he would support a candidate from Fort Smith, Gene Rainwater, in the Democratic primary.

"Well, I'm sorry you've done that, but Bill Clinton is going to be around a long time," Whillock responded. "One of these days he's gonna be governor or senator and you'll need to know him." That was enough to persuade Hackler to accompany Whillock over to the drugstore.

Whillock and Hackler found a spot in a red and tan booth with a black Formica table. They ordered coffee. Hackler was in his sixties and conservatively dressed. Clinton came in at four, sat down, and ordered a Coke. Whillock was not sure how his old friend would get along with his new one, but he need not have worried. The conversation began with a coincidence and only improved from there.

"Where'd you grow up?" Hackler asked.

"Hot Springs," Clinton said.

"I've got a good friend in Hot Springs. But I don't imagine you'd know him."

"Who is it?"

"Gabe Crawford. He runs some drugstores there."

Gabe Crawford was one of the closest friends of Clinton's mother and late stepfather. This was the same Gabe Crawford who had joined Raymond Clinton in co-signing the loan that gave Clinton the first $10,000 of his campaign. "We practically live at the Crawfords," Clinton said. "We're over at their house all the time."

After fifteen minutes of easy conversation, Hackler turned to Whillock and proclaimed: "Carl, I'm gonna call my friends and change this. I want to support Bill."

The last stops on the trip were in Marshall, the county seat of Searcy County, where they met with newspaper editors, and then the little town of St. Joe, where they visited Will Goggins, chairman of the county Democratic party. It was after nine when they reached St. Joe and Goggins was already in bed, with the lights out, but he answered the door, invited Whillock and Clinton in, and talked with them for an hour. Goggins was a Clinton man for the rest of his life. From St. Joe they retraced their path up and across Highway 65, weaving through the woods and river valleys in the darkness of an early Arkansas spring. It was after midnight when they got back to Fayetteville. Whillock was shocked to see that his wife and children were still up. "You really missed it!" one of his kids yelled excitedly. What had they missed? It seems that the latest campus fad had reached Fayetteville that night. For several hours, naked young men and women had been streaking up and down Maple Street past the Whillocks' house.

A few days later, candidate Clinton was asked to take a position on streaking. "It's a little extreme for my taste," he told an Associated Press reporter. "I find it offensive, but I think it's just a passing fad. Something quite similar went around when I was in high school. You may remember it. They called it 'Mooning' where you drop your drawers and stick your fat out the window in a passing car." The story was printed in the *Hope Star*, where Mack McLarty read it. He clipped the article and sent it to Clinton with a scrawled note: "Bill—Excellent press. Appears you handled yourself in your usual style. Trust you rec'd my $—Holler if additional help is needed. Mack McL."

IN the small world of Democratic politics in northwest Arkansas, the center of the action was Billie Schneider's little restaurant at Hillbilly Hollow on the road between Fayetteville and Springdale. At a long picnic table in her back room, Schneider's friends gathered several nights a week to drink beer and chew on large juicy steaks and even juicier politics. It was an eclectic crowd ranging from long-haired college students who called Billie "Momma" to wealthy lawyers who looked to her for the latest town gossip. One of the regulars was Don Tyson, the bantam rooster of the chicken-processing field, whose lucrative family enterprise was expanding into one of the state's most powerful companies. Momma was the Godmother of Washington County politics, a yellow dog Democrat who sometimes refused to serve diners whom she considered too Republican. She looked like a saloon owner from the Old West: her voice deep and raspy from too many cigarettes, her face craggy and shaped by the ups and downs of her life. She drank and swore and was not afraid to tell people what she thought about them. She had the outgoing personality of Clinton's mother, Virginia, and was not shy about offering the young law professor political advice.

One of the first press releases the campaign issued referred to William J. Clinton, which is how his name was printed in a local newspaper. Schneider saw it and called headquarters. "Ron," she screamed at Addington, who answered the phone. "You and Bill get your butts up here and I mean just as soon as you can!" Addington explained that Clinton was out campaigning and would not be back until later that night. "Well, when he gets in, get your butts up here!" Schneider said. Addington and Clinton walked into the restaurant just before closing. Schneider had some heated advice about what she had seen in the paper that day. The sight of Clinton's formal first name and middle initial sickened her populist soul. She wanted to make sure Clinton understood that he was back in Arkansas. This was not Georgetown, Oxford, or Yale.

"What is this William J. Clinton?" she asked. "You're not gonna run as William J. Clinton. You're Bill Clinton. And you're gonna run as Bill Clinton!"

CLINTON was a candidate now, but he still had to make it official. He had to travel from Fayetteville back to Little Rock to file. It was a four-hour drive each way, too long for him to make it down on the day he wanted to go and return in time for a big rally scheduled for that night on the University of Arkansas campus. A local nightclub owner offered the use of his airplane, a four-seat Cessna, but Addington had to recruit a pilot, which was a harder task than he expected. At the last hour, someone told him about a student at the university who had his pilot's license and could make the trip. They left on the morning of March 22. On the flight down to Little Rock, Addington told the pilot that he was taking flying lessons. The pilot said he had just earned his license a month earlier. It was a clear day and the trip down was free and easy.

They spent more time than planned in Little Rock—Clinton always found one more person to talk to. It was dark by the time they took off over the mountains on their way back to Fayetteville. Twenty minutes into the flight, Addington realized something was wrong. "I knew we weren't flying right, I could feel it in my bones. It was dark and this guy starts pulling out maps. Clinton was sitting up front with the pilot. He turned around and looked at me like, 'Where did we get this guy?' I said it would be all right." Addington noticed that they were flying over a town and told the pilot to dip lower so they could get a look at the water tower. It was the tower for Harrison. They were off course to the east. Addington told the pilot to set his compass due west for a flight path that would take them directly to Fayetteville. They arrived safely, though late, and with a furious, red-faced candidate on board.

On the drive from the airport to the campus rally, Clinton, sitting in the front seat, exploded. "God damn it!" he yelled, pounding his fist on the dashboard. "Don't you ever line up somebody like that again, Ron! I could have been killed up there. My political career would have been over before it began! I can't believe you jeopardized our lives like that!"

Addington wanted to point out that it was not easy for him to find a pilot, that Clinton had endangered them by being so late and making them fly at night, that Addington was as scared as Clinton and that they might still be flying somewhere toward Missouri if he hadn't had the sense to find the water tower and that Clinton, the worst car driver in the world, had little room to talk about endangering lives. But he could not get a word in. Clinton was fuming and would not stop for breath. Addington had never seen this side of Clinton before. It was a fierce, sudden temper tantrum. Pounding away on the dashboard. Madder than hell. The first eruption of his political life. For Addington and dozens of aides who worked at Clinton's side over the ensuing years, it would become a familiar sight.

CHAPTER SEVENTEEN

AND NOT TO YIELD

WHILE CLINTON DIVIDED his time between teaching law in Fayetteville and roaming the back highways of northwest Arkansas, Hillary Rodham was holed up in an office on Capitol Hill in Washington, surrounded by documents, protected by a double line of security, her movements circumscribed by the sensitivity of her mission as one of thirty-nine lawyers constructing a case for the removal of a president. More than twelve hours a day and seven days a week, Rodham worked at a desk in a mildewed suite on the second floor of the old Congressional Hotel. She rarely associated with anyone outside the closed circle of legal compatriots brought to Washington by John Doar, special counsel for the House Judiciary Committee's impeachment inquiry staff. She did not have her own apartment, but took an extra upstairs bedroom at the house of Sara Ehrman, a liberal Democrat whom she first met during the McGovern campaign in Texas. Ehrman, whose four-bedroom, four-bath house was a virtual youth hostel, rarely saw her industrious young boarder except around midnight when they might meet at the refrigerator in search of yogurt.

Rodham was twenty-six, less than a year out of law school, untested in the legal community, yet playing a coveted if minor role in the century's most gripping presidential drama. She did not arrive at the inquiry staff a complete stranger. She and Doar had met the previous spring, when Rodham and Clinton served on the board of directors of the Barristers Union at Yale Law and invited Doar to judge that year's student Prize Trial. After being selected by the Judiciary Committee to direct the impeachment inquiry, Doar built a staff quickly. Along with a few seasoned attorneys, his so-called chiefs, he needed a band of young legal warriors who could come to Washington for an indefinite period to work brutal hours for little pay. Rodham fit the job description, as did her classmate Michael Conway.

Prize recruits who showed the slightest hint of interest apparently were not given much choice by Doar, at least based on the way he hired Conway. After his luminous years as a student at Yale Law, where he had defeated Rodham and Clinton in the Prize Trial competition, Conway had joined a major Chicago law firm. He had barely settled in when he took a call in the first week of January from his former teacher and friend at Yale, Burke Marshall. They had a one-minute conversation during which Marshall asked Conway if he was interested in working for Doar on the impeachment staff and Conway responded that it was a "fascinating idea" and that he would have to think about it. An hour later Doar called. "Mike, I talked with Burke and he said you'll be here," Doar said. "I'll see you Sunday." Conway was in Washington that Sunday. Later that week he was given a tiny side office in a suite at the Congressional Hotel which he realized had once been a bathroom. Appropriate, he thought, since he was assigned to a task force looking into alleged misdeeds of the Watergate-related group known as "the plumbers."

Rodham arrived at about the same time and took a desk next to Tom Bell, a recent graduate of the University of Wisconsin Law School who had been recruited out of Doar's law firm in New Richmond, Wisconsin. Their windows looked out on a back alley. Rodham's first assignment was less intriguing than investigating the plumbers. Doar had organized the staff into two sections. Most of the lawyers were assigned to task forces in a section called Factual Investigation, which was to collect and examine evidence on activities that fell under the rubric of Watergate, including the break-in itself, the alleged coverup, the use of other dirty tricks in the 1972 campaign, as well as several non-Watergate concerns, including the secret bombing of Cambodia. Rodham was placed in a smaller section known as Constitutional and Legal Research. Its first major project was to research the constitutional grounds for impeachment: an important but scholarly task that not everyone was eager to do.

Rodham's section analyzed the constitutional intent of impeachment and its historical basis in four hundred years of English history. Virtually every word in their report delineating the grounds for impeachment carried weight. At one meeting they spent four hours arguing over whether to use the phrase "to the modern ear" in describing how high crimes and misdemeanors should be interpreted. Their report concluded that "to limit impeachable conduct to criminal offenses would be incompatible with the evidence concerning the constitutional meaning of the phrase . . . and would frustrate the purpose that the framers intended for impeachment." They found that in thirteen American impeachment cases, including ten of federal judges, less than one-third of the articles of impeachment explicitly charged the violation of a criminal statute.

The thoroughness of the report impressed Doar, who believed that the

precise wording of articles of impeachment would be of supreme importance. Rodham became one of his staff favorites. It did not matter that she
had a partisan past, that she had worked for McGovern, for she seemed
discreet in her demeanor, reverent of the process, and impartial about the
expected outcome of the endeavor, at least in front of the boss.

Doar was a seemingly nonpartisan figure: a moderate Republican who
had held a high-profile role in the Justice Department's civil rights division
during the 1960s and later served as president of the New York Board
of Education. From his impeachment staff, he demanded objectivity and
discretion. Fred Altshuler, a University of Chicago Law School graduate,
was nearly fired during his first week for making a political remark that he
thought was inconsequential but which Doar found injudicious. From then
on, he understood Doar's dictum: Just report the facts. Doar pounded into
his staff the notion that they had to show respect for the office of the
president. Even in private conversations they were to refer to Nixon as the
president.

Doar was solemn and complicated, variously eliciting frustration, exhaustion, and admiration from those who worked for him. His aides joked
that he was the type of person they would die for but did not want to live
with. He kept the door to his office closed. His obsession with organizational detail and neatness included a clean desk policy. A clean desk, he
told his troops, represented a thorough and methodical mind. Early on
Sunday mornings he roamed from office to office to reassure himself that
no one had taken a day off. His occasional pats on the back, known as
"Doar fixes," took on greater importance because of his belief in meritocracy. People were constantly being shifted up or down in the staff hierarchy depending on how Doar viewed their work, which gave the place a
measure of egalitarianism but also increased the anxiety level in an already
tense atmosphere.

The methodical approach that Doar took to the inquiry was in itself a
point of tension. He was so intent on avoiding the appearance of being out
to get Nixon that some partisan Democrats on the Judiciary Committee
referred to him as "the Republican counsel." They preferred the style of
one of his three senior associate special counsels, Richard Cates, a trial
attorney and professor from Madison, Wisconsin, who had been brought
in to help Chairman Rodino decide whether and how to proceed with the
impeachment inquiry before Doar arrived. Cates and Doar respected each
other, and years later became close friends, but at the time they held
sharply different ideas about how to conduct the investigation. Cates was
willing to draw conclusions about the evidence that had already been
accumulated from the Senate Watergate Committee hearings and earlier
investigative work. Doar started with a blank slate. Cates was a master of

the story line. He spent hours each day developing theories, placing details in their probable context. Doar, in the words of Tom Bell, "doesn't give a whit about" the story. "He is looking for detail after detail after detail, and when he's done, the story will take care of itself."

BOTH styles rubbed off on Hillary Rodham. Among the inquiry staff of ninety lawyers, researchers, and clerks, she seemed "the least perturbed by tensions inherent in Doar's meritocracy," according to Robin Johansen, who thought of Rodham as a self-contained person immune from the occasional backbiting. This image might have been both a symptom and a cause of Doar's regard for her. Bell, Rodham's office mate, noticed that Doar had more confidence in her than in most of the other rookie lawyers on the staff. "On occasion he would call her in and bounce something off her." One day Doar had Rodham stand by his side at a hallway press conference. (The way she would later tell the story, her presence inspired ABC News correspondent Sam Donaldson to yell out to her: "How does it feel to be the Jill Wine Volner of the impeachment committee?"—comparing Rodham with a young woman lawyer on the Watergate special prosecutor's staff. Donaldson has no such memory. "I don't mean this as a slam . . . but you've seen pictures of her in those days," Donaldson said later. "I don't think younger bucks like me paid any attention to her.")

Perhaps the television reporter did not pay much attention to Rodham, but her bosses on the impeachment staff certainly did. Bernard W. Nussbaum, another of Doar's top assistants, who came down to Washington from a Manhattan firm, drove Rodham home to Sara Ehrman's house many nights, striking up a paternal friendship and legal interdependence that would continue for decades. And Bell noticed that just as Doar took to Rodham, so too did Cates. "There were some tensions between Cates and Doar, and both confided in her. Hillary was in the middle." At the same time that she operated as one of Doar's favorites, she shared some of Cates's frustrations with the slow pace of the investigation. "This thing is going down in flames!" Tom Bell remembered Rodham fuming to him one day when one of the president's men was acquitted of perjury charges vaguely related to Watergate. She was "devastated with the verdict," according to Bell, fearful that things were moving so slowly that Nixon and his men might prevail in the courts and in Congress. Bell, who felt that his job was to be loyal to Doar, urged Rodham to be patient. "I said to her, 'This is how lawyers work.' "

Bell said that he and Rodham both "saw Nixon as evil," but in different ways. "Her opinion of him was more a result of the McGovern campaign and Vietnam and those kinds of issues. I saw him as evil because he was screwing with the Constitution. She came at it with more preconceived ideas than I did." Their perspectives on Nixon paralleled to some extent the way in which the two young lawyers viewed their assignments in Washington. "She saw the work as absolutely the most important thing in the world," Bell said. "I saw it as important but also as a job. To her it may have been more of a mission."

The more Bell got to know Rodham, the more it became apparent to him that "she wasn't as ideologically pure as the program for the players would indicate. Not that she made any false pretenses or anything. We were just two young lawyers who shared confidences." Their conversations were blunt and open. "She wasn't afraid to say that you were full of shit. And if you told her the same, she would take it."

It was natural for members of the impeachment staff to confide in each other so much because they had little time to interact with anyone outside their closed circle and were discouraged from doing so. "We're lawyers, not historians," Doar would tell them. "Don't keep a diary. Don't talk to anybody. Just do your work." When they left the office, it was usually in self-contained groups to eat lunch or dinner at their regular Greek and Italian restaurant hangouts on Capitol Hill. "We'd go out in groups and come back and work some more," recalled Fred Altshuler. This classic foxhole culture led to extreme familiarity and occasional explosions. Rodham was sometimes a consoling presence. Robert Sack, who had taken a leave of absence from a major New York law firm to serve on the inquiry staff, had "a small but nasty to-do" with one of the senior counsels and left the office one night feeling "very much put-down." As he was walking to his car several blocks away, he heard some voices behind him—"and there were Hillary and Fred Altshuler." Rodham wanted to buck him up and tell him that everything was fine.

Doar was obsessive about security. He instructed his staff never to talk in front of a window and to keep the shades drawn. He hired a retired Air Force colonel to arrange security in the office and develop methods of controlling sensitive information. Two types of wastebaskets were placed in each room, one for normal waste and the other for sensitive waste, meaning any papers or carbons related to the inquiry. Two clerks collected the sensitive waste each day, carried it to a van in the basement garage, and drove out to the District of Columbia waste-disposal site near RFK Stadium. Watergate reporters were hovering nearby at all hours of the day, especially columnist Jack Anderson's gumshoe assistants. One Anderson aide would camp out in the lobby and toss unanswered queries at staff members as they came off the elevator. Bell, who lived in an apartment building up the street from the Congressional Hotel, found notes slipped under his door by an Anderson assistant that said, "We know who you are and it is your constitutional duty to let the country know what is going on."

Unlike the Senate Watergate Committee, where different staff investigators had protected their own informational fiefdoms with safes full of documents, Doar created a research library that served as the central repository for material gathered by the inquiry staff. The computer age was dawning, but Doar felt uncomfortable with the security of computer systems, so his staff worked with original documents and transcripts catalogued by a team of researchers and librarians. They built a sophisticated chronology of the Watergate case on seven-ply index cards which were carefully typed and cross-indexed and in the end totaled more than a half million. The ever-expanding library became the symbol of the impeachment case and the representation of Doar's style. He was a documents man. He preferred the certainty of records to the fallibility of witnesses.

The library was also where most of the women on the staff worked. Rodham was among only three female lawyers, and though she was not treated as a token of her gender, there was an undercurrent of sexism in the office. At one point the women felt compelled to place a sign on the coffee machine that read: "The women in this office were not hired to make coffee. Make it yourself or call on one of these liberated men to do so"—followed by a list of male lawyers. Rodham was not shy about debating the roles that women should play in society. She once got into a debate with Albert Jenner, the Republican counsel for the committee, when Jenner commented that there were no famous women trial lawyers. "Hillary pointed out that the reason was because women generally did not have wives," recalled Terry Kirkpatrick, another of the women lawyers. "She said that the reason male trial lawyers could be famous was because their wives packed their bags and ironed their clothes and were supportive of them while they were doing their work." Jenner was "singularly unimpressed" with Rodham's argument, but Kirkpatrick never forgot it. It helped spark her own interest in the politics of gender.

With its unrelenting pressure and foxhole mentality, the impeachment staff experience was much like that of a political campaign. There was one notable difference, according to Bob Sack. "The most extraordinary thing is how little sex there was. It was so much of a fraternal experience. It had the characteristics of an intense political campaign but with much less sex." Rodham developed strong friendships with several men on the staff, but everyone knew that she had a boyfriend teaching law and running for Congress out in Arkansas. "I remember that she was dating Bill Clinton and her saying to me once, 'He wants to stay in Arkansas and get involved in politics'—and she kind of rolled her eyes a little bit," recalled Jeff Branchero, a staff clerk who had recently graduated from the University of California.

The Clinton and Rodham relationship during the months when they were apart was, as always, tempestuous. There were several young women clamoring for Clinton's attention, or he for theirs. Clinton's mother and younger brother thought that his bespectacled law school friend was not physically striking enough for him and tried to discourage him from getting too serious, but he would respond that in the long run it was Hillary or nobody. His physical attraction to other women would not diminish, but she was the only one he wanted to marry. Once, when he encountered a classmate from Georgetown, Melanne Verveer, who had married another Georgetown friend, Phil Verveer, Clinton blurted out—"I'm following Phil's example. I'm going for brains and ability rather than glamour." Melanne Verveer could have taken it as an insult of sorts. She accepted it as a compliment.

Rodham, for her part, seemed uncharacteristically passionate when it came to her Arkansas boyfriend. "She was absolutely, totally crazy about Bill Clinton," according to Kirkpatrick. " 'Besotted' is not a word I would normally apply to Hillary, but I think she was besotted. Bill came to visit her two or three times, and when he was coming to town her face would change. It would light up. It was very un-Hillaryesque." Rodham was circumspect in most matters, but did not suppress the highs and lows of her relationship with Clinton. The lows were provoked by his occasional inattention and self-absorption and indications that he might be seeing other women. The highs came with his overpowering personality and his future. "This is the honest-to-God truth," Bell later reflected. "She would come in some mornings mad because he wouldn't have called her. She would be cranky. But she would come in other mornings, hit me in the biceps, and say, 'You know, Tom Bell, Bill Clinton is going to be president of the United States someday!' "

Bernie Nussbaum heard the same audacious prophecy one night as he drove Rodham home from work in his Oldsmobile Toronado. It was enough to make him go "a little crazy." There they were, under great pressure handling a president's possible impeachment, and this young woman was boasting that her boyfriend was going to be president someday. Nussbaum, a thirty-seven-year-old New York City law partner, was only eleven years older than Rodham, but had an embracing nature that made him a father figure to her and many of the other young lawyers on the staff. He approached his impeachment assignment, like everything in life, with great intensity, what some of his colleagues called a "take-no-prisoners approach"—a style that was natural to him and had served him well in his previous jobs as an assistant prosecutor in the U.S. Attorney's Office in Manhattan and as a private litigator.

For Nussbaum and Bob Sack, any doubt about Nixon's impeachability was removed when they put on headphones and listened to White House tapes that the inquiry staff had obtained from the Watergate grand jury in late March. They spent one week playing and replaying the tapes at the side of former White House counsel John Dean, who had been present at many of the meetings with Nixon where the coverup was discussed. Dean now served as an expert translator of the disjointed and sometimes barely audible conversations that had been secretly tape-recorded. Sack thought to himself, "My God, in a hundred years people are going to sit around the National Archives and listen to these tapes. And they are going to wonder what the hell we and our clients, the members of Congress, were doing. How could people sit and listen to this and not do something about it? The evidence made it clear."

From the moment the secret tapes were delivered to the Congressional Hotel, they became the central focus of the inquiry. Doar stored them in a safe in his office and assigned Michael Conway to serve as the gatekeeper to control access to them. He brought in audio specialists to enhance the sound and held a competition to determine which staff members had the sharpest ears and could make the most sense of the conversations and accurately transcribe them. A special listening room was set up at the end of the hallway, not far from where Rodham and Bell worked. Staff members would file in, turn on the tape machine, put on headphones, turn off the lights, settle in on the couch, and listen to the president and his men. Sack felt "a sense of voyeurism—putting the earphones on and listening; like being a fly on the wall of the office of the president of the United States. We almost felt it was a little taboo."

Jeff Branchero proved to have the best hearing on the staff and, in keeping with Doar's meritocracy, spent the most time transcribing. He would take as long as an hour to work on one minute of tape, stopping, rewinding, and playing again and again until he knew instinctively the verbal habits of Nixon, John Mitchell, H. R. Haldeman, and John Dean. Rodham was in the room occasionally. She spent several hours listening to what they called "The Tape of Tapes"—"It was Nixon taping himself while he listened to his tapes, inventing rationales for what he said. At one point he asked Manuel Sanchez [his valet] 'Don't you think I meant this when I said that?' "

Rodham and Fred Altshuler, who became her closest male friend on the staff, worked together on an internal memorandum detailing the organization of Nixon's White House. By listening to the tapes and studying the presidential logs that listed the people Nixon met with each day, they reconstructed the daily decision-making process inside the Oval Office—who had access to the president, how decisions were communicated up and down. They developed case histories for various events: If Nixon meets with Haldeman and Haldeman talks about that meeting to Chuck Colson, what happens? Studying how the organization functioned, Altshuler said, "was important in terms of finding out whether the president in fact made decisions or underlings made decisions. If the chain of events is, X sees the president and comes out and does Y, you can draw an inference. We found that the president really ran an awful lot of details."

THE end came quickly. In historic sessions at the end of July, the Judiciary Committee voted for three articles of impeachment. Within two weeks, the president had resigned. The inquiry staff was still at work that day, preparing documents for the full House debate on impeachment. They gathered in the library and watched Nixon's farewell speech on an old black and white television set. People sat on the floor and leaned against the walls and the sides of desks. The room was somber and quiet. No cheers from Rodham or any of the other lawyers who had been taught to repress their personal feelings for so many months. "It was like a game ending in overtime—sudden death," recalled Michael Conway, who had already been recruited to work on the Senate staff for an impeachment trial that now would never be held.

As a remembrance of their unforgettable time together, Doar gave each member of his staff a framed picture of the group posed on the front steps of the Longworth House Office Building. It is, like so many snapshots of Hillary Rodham, a reflection of her will. Before the picture was taken, Doar had instructed the lawyers to stand together in the front. Rodham had defied his request, calling it elitist. She stood in the back with her friends on the support staff. Doar signed each picture with an inscription from the last quatrain of Tennyson's *Ulysses:* "To Strive, to Seek, to Find and not to Yield."

MUCH like her boyfriend Bill Clinton, Rodham always worked on at least two levels at once. During her months in Washington, she often expressed ambivalence about what direction to take in her life. Her professional interests seemed to be on the East Coast. She could go back to serving as a counsel for the Children's Defense Fund. She could go to work for a high-powered Washington law firm and learn more about the political world of the nation's capital. She could delve into politics herself. Or she could move to Arkansas to be with Clinton. Taylor Branch had several long talks with her about the future, continuing the confessional relationship that they shared in Texas. Branch could see that she was "at sea about whether she wanted to move to Arkansas." She told him that she did not know "how hard to be, how careerist to be." She believed in the feminist movement and in the freedom women were struggling to achieve. Would she be turning away from that by following her love to provincial Arkansas, a place that made her eyes roll when she talked about it?

And how would Arkansas receive her? That question inevitably arose in her conversations with Terry Kirkpatrick, who had grown up in Fort Smith and attended law school in Fayetteville when there were only a handful of women there. Rodham asked Kirkpatrick how the legal community would accept her in a state where women lawyers were still a rarity. It would be difficult, Kirkpatrick said. "You have to be three hundred percent better than any man to succeed. You have to pick your friends carefully. It's a very different culture. But the people when they accept you are loving and supportive and very willing to accept new ideas once they get past the initial shock." And there was something else attractive about Arkansas, Kirkpatrick told Rodham: "It's easy to make an impact there. You can be a big fish in a small pond."

Even on her final night in Washington, Rodham seemed uncertain. She went to dinner with Fred Altshuler and two of his friends, Marsha and Steve Berzon, who were just arriving in town as Rodham was leaving. At dinner, the others talked about the exciting legal work they were about to embark on, while Rodham reflected on the uncertain professional life that awaited her in Arkansas. "Hillary was showing personal affection for Bill, but she thought she would not face the same kinds of legal challenges," Altshuler said later. "She was somewhat uncertain. She had some ambivalence about it." The last thing on Rodham's radar screen, thought Altshuler, "was to head off to Arkansas."

But while on one level Rodham seemed ambivalent, on another level she had prepared for a move to Arkansas for more than a year in a quiet, careful fashion that made her decision all but inevitable. During her first visit to Arkansas in the summer of 1973, before Clinton began teaching in Fayetteville, she had joined him in taking the Arkansas state bar exam, just in case she would ever practice in the state. She and Clinton had even worried about whether it would hurt them in the future in Arkansas if they put the same New Haven address on the state bar applications. Clinton, during his first months at the law school, constantly talked about Rodham to Dean Davis and everyone else there. He told Davis that he and Rodham were "more or less informally engaged" and that he hoped that she would come out and teach with him at the law school. When Rodham visited Clinton in Fayetteville in early 1974, she was introduced to Dean Davis and other law faculty members at a reception. "I mentioned to her before she left that if she were ever interested in teaching here, she should give me a call," Davis recalled. "I talked to faculty people who had chatted with her and all were favorably impressed."

Rodham called Davis a month later to see if the offer still stood. When he said yes, she made arrangements to fly to Fayetteville to be interviewed for a teaching position. She had to leave her work on the inquiry staff for three days to make the trip, a departure that did not sit well with Doar. When she reached Fayetteville, some of the law professors she met had an odd first impression of her. "Hillary came in dressed as if she had been shopping in Bloomingdale's the day before," remembered Mort Gitelman. "It looked strange in Arkansas. She was wearing one of those long skirts and black stockings and horn-rimmed glasses. She did not look Arkansas." Gitelman could not know it, but except for the glasses she did not look like Hillary Rodham, either. She paid little attention to clothes except when she thought she had to impress people. This was one of those times. Terry Kirkpatrick had taken her shopping in Georgetown to buy the khaki suit that she wore to the interview. Her clothes, in the end, made little difference, according to Gitelman. "Once she opened her mouth, it didn't matter what she was wearing. We were impressed." Davis made her an offer, and she called him back on July 9 to accept it.

Why did she call on that day, before Doar had completed his summary and before it was certain when the impeachment work would be finished? Rodham knew that in essence the impeachment work was over the day she agreed to go to Arkansas. July 9 was the day that the impeachment staff released transcripts of its version of several key White House tapes. The Judiciary Committee transcripts differed dramatically from previously released and heavily sanitized White House transcripts of the same tapes. "Transcripts Link Nixon to Cover-Up" blared the headline in *The Washington Post.* The key quote came from a White House meeting on March 22, 1973, in which Nixon, according to the Judiciary Committee transcript, is heard to say: "I don't give a shit what happens. I want you all to stonewall it, let them plead the Fifth Amendment, cover-up or anything else, if it'll save it—save the plan. That's the whole point."

RODHAM left Washington on a humid mid-August morning in 1974. It was fitting that she was not driving herself, but being driven, yet going someplace that she wanted to go and that the owner of the car, Sara Ehrman, her friend and landlady in Washington, did not really want to take her. Ehrman was horrified at the thought of Rodham, who to her represented the promising future of the women's movement, abandoning the most powerful city in the world for a backwater law school in the Ozarks. But if Rodham was determined to go, Ehrman would at least help her get there. She came from a generation "where one follows one's man." She persuaded Alan Stone, a friend who had worked on McGovern's advance team in Texas, to come along as the driver. Rodham's life's belongings went with her—suitcases and a stereo in the trunk, a bicycle strapped to the roof. They drove through Virginia's lovely countryside, past Gainesville, Warrenton, Culpepper, on down to Charlottesville, stopping at Monticello, the home of Thomas Jefferson.

"You are crazy," Ehrman said to Rodham along the way, playing the role of surrogate mother. "What are you doing this for?" Rodham laughed. She was in a good mood. She said she loved Bill Clinton and wanted to take a chance. Stone defended her. He had been born in Arkansas and had fond memories of the state. The unspoken tension of the trip was that Rodham could not wait to get to Fayetteville and Ehrman, hoping to keep her, kept making detours to historical sites. To make up for the lost time of the side trips, Stone and Rodham drove late into the night. They passed through Nashville after midnight and encountered a surrealistic sight that kept them laughing halfway to Memphis—tipsy old men at a Shriners' convention tooting around on small white motor scooters. Finally, exhausted, they stopped at a roadside motel and all three shared a room. (Years later Stone would remember that night and laugh: he could tell the *National Enquirer* that he once slept with Hillary and another woman in a motel room in Tennessee.) On the way across Arkansas, Rodham ate her first catfish dinner. When they reached Fayetteville, they found their way out to Clinton's cottage and unloaded Rodham's possessions.

Clinton had just returned from a long stretch of campaigning in Bentonville. He was, as Stone remembered him that day, "kind of frantic."

CHAPTER EIGHTEEN

RUNNING WITH THE BOY

HILLARY RODHAM WAS not the first member of her family to reach Fayette-ville. One morning during the spring primary season, a fin-tailed Cadillac with Illinois license plates had pulled into the parking lot of the Clinton for Congress headquarters on College Avenue in Fayetteville. A short, burly man in his sixties emerged from the driver's side, limping as he walked toward the door, accompanied by a young fellow. "I'm Hugh Rodham, Hillary's dad," the older man said to Ron Addington. At his side was Tony Rodham, the younger of Hillary's two brothers. The names were, of course, familiar. Clinton had boasted to his campaign staff about Hillary Rodham: how smart she was; how she was a counsel for the House Judiciary Com-mittee staff; how he hoped that she would be warmly welcomed if she came to Arkansas. Once, at headquarters, he had read aloud from a letter she had written to him about her impeachment work.

Addington felt that he already knew Hillary. In the early stages of the campaign, he was constantly taking telephone calls from her. She would check on Clinton's schedule, then offer practical political suggestions. Even then, at the dawn of Clinton's electoral career, from halfway across the country, at a time when she and Clinton were uncertain about their rela-tionship and while she was working long days and nights on the impeach-ment inquiry, Rodham was pushing Clinton's political interests. "She started calling from day one, several times a day at first," Addington re-called. "She was telling me, you need to get this done, you need to get that done. What positions we had to fill."

But apparently Hillary never mentioned that her father and brother were driving down from Illinois. "Well, how long are you going to be here to visit?" Addington asked.

"Hell, I don't know," Hugh Rodham said. "Hillary told me I ought to come down here and help you out."

The Rodham men had met Clinton a few times during his Yale Law School days, when Hillary brought him home to Park Ridge. Although Hugh was conservative and had never voted for a Democrat, his family was leaning to the liberal side, not just Hillary but also the boys, and he was, above all, a Rodham loyalist. If Hillary urged him to work for Clinton, that was what he would do. It was a matter of family, not politics. Doug Wallace, the campaign press secretary, thought it seemed irrelevant to Rodham "why he was down there, besides the fact that his daughter told him to do it."

The Rodhams reported for work the next morning. What should they do? The office was overcrowded; there were not enough telephones and desks for the staff and volunteers. But there were stacks of "Clinton for Congress" signs that needed to be put up along the roadsides in the rural counties. And so the Rodham sign detail was born. Day after day, they would load signs into the trunk and roam the back roads in search of prime locations for cheap political advertising. Sometimes the campaign staff got inquiries from the field about the Yankees in the Cadillac. The calls prompted a discussion about whether they should smear the license plates with mud to obscure the fact that the car and its occupants were not from Arkansas. But the Rodhams were quickly embraced by the campaign staff and most of the people they encountered on the road. The old man seemed "rougher than a corn cob, as gruff as could be," in Addington's words, but he was a straight talker and a hard worker. In some respects, as a handyman who loved fly-fishing, he was more of a natural in the Ozarks than Clinton, whose main backwoods talent was storytelling. And young Tony seemed to be having the time of his life.

There was another aspect to the presence of Hillary's father and brother in Fayetteville while she was still in Washington. One of the worst-kept secrets at headquarters was that Clinton had become involved in an intense relationship with a young woman volunteer who was a student at the university. According to Doug Wallace, "the staff tried to ignore it as long as it didn't interfere with the campaign." Aside from the Fayetteville woman, the staff also knew that Clinton had girlfriends in several towns around the district and in Little Rock. Perhaps they could disregard his rambunctious private life, but could Hillary? There was some suspicion that one of the reasons she sent the men in her family to Arkansas was to put a check on her boyfriend's activities.

Paul Fray arrived in Fayetteville with his wife Mary Lee to work on the campaign shortly after the Rodhams appeared on the scene. He quickly surmised that "Hillary had put the hammer on her daddy to go down there and make sure everything was hunky-dory. It was her little spying mission."

One afternoon Fray was at Clinton's house in the country, going over the schedule for the next few weeks. "The phone rings and it's Hillary and she's raising hell" about Clinton's behavior, Fray recalled from what he heard of the conversation and from what Clinton told him after hanging up. Hillary, according to Fray, tried to make Clinton jealous by informing him that she was going to sleep with someone in Washington. Clinton "about broke down and cried" at that point, but rather than getting mad he launched into a long emotional appeal, saying that Hillary should not "go and do something that would make life miserable" for both of them.

In the May primary against three opponents and again in the June 11 runoff against Gene Rainwater, a state senator from Fort Smith, Clinton was a political whirlwind. He began with 12 percent name recognition and little money, and ended up easily prevailing in both races. The other candidates had regional power bases, but they were overmatched by Clinton's organizational skills and energy. The state AFL-CIO was ready to endorse Rainwater until Clinton appeared before the labor board's Committee on Political Education in Hot Springs. "Bill's knowledge and facility with words made our people fall in love with him," recalled J. Bill Becker, head of the state labor federation. "He just took it right away from Rainwater." Like so many of the people who were drawn into Clinton's orbit, the workers in his congressional campaign were alternately inspired and exhausted. College students accustomed to staying up late, but also sleeping late, had a hard time keeping pace with him.

He was always on the move from town to town, staying in the homes of old friends or newfound political allies, or at his mother's place if they ended the night near Hot Springs. His schedule was invariably on the remake, thrown off by his compulsion to stop and chat. He was, according to Jim Daugherty, a law student who was one of his drivers, "more interested in finishing the conversation than in finishing the schedule." Sometimes the Fayetteville staff lost touch with him. If he was working the southern stretch of the district, they would leave messages at the "Y" City Café, certain that he would stop at that tiny crossroads eatery on his way between Hot Springs and Fort Smith, lured by the gossip awaiting him there and the seductive coconut cream pie. A legion of law students served as his drivers and travel aides. On the road between stops, Clinton would take his Professor Quigley—inspired fifteen-minute catnaps, and scribble the outlines of his next speech. Chomping on a sandwich and talking at the same time, he would launch into a soliloquy about the ravages of inflation or of black lung disease, an issue in the mining towns of the Arkansas River valley.

For many politicians, the incessant demands of a campaign are the most

enervating aspects of public life. One face after another, one more plea for
money, one more speech where the words blur in dull repetition—at
some point it can become too much. Morriss Henry, a state legislator from
Fayetteville who along with his wife, Ann, befriended Clinton in 1974,
realized one night that he lacked the characteristic that he saw in Clinton,
the energy required to go the distance in politics. Henry, an eye doctor,
had worked all day performing cataract surgery and came home "totally
beat," but corraled the kids and his wife into the Dodge van to attend a pie
supper outside Fayetteville. On the way down, he suddenly blurted out,
"Do we really have to go?" Two-thirds of the way there, he answered
himself. "No! We don't." He had hit his political wall, and he turned around.

Clinton would never turn around. To him, the prospect of attending a
pie supper in "Y" City or Mount Ida seemed invigorating. Pie suppers rank
among the most cherished political folk rituals in western Arkansas. On
any Saturday night during an election season, communities gather for an
evening of entertainment as pies and cakes baked by local women are sold
at auction, with the money going to volunteer fire departments or other
civic institutions. One savory pecan pie can sell for three figures, especially
if the politicians in attendance try to buy some goodwill and end up in a
bidding war, as frequently happens. The candidates vie for microphone
time between pie sales and announcements. Homemade desserts, picnic
tables lined with voters, plenty of talking and raucous storytelling, usually
some barbecue at the rear counter—Clinton was never more in his element. He also realized that every pie supper he attended helped him transform his image from the long-haired Rhodes Scholar and law professor into
a young man of the people.

Before his eyes he saw what could happen to a politician who failed to
connect with ordinary people during that first spring of his electoral career
when the state's Democratic primary voters denied J. William Fulbright the
nomination, unsentimentally ending his thirty-year career in the Senate.
Fulbright had raised and spent more money than any previous candidate
in Arkansas and barely received one-third of the vote as he was overwhelmed by Dale Bumpers, the popular governor. Bumpers had an 85
percent approval rating while Fulbright's was in the low 30s. The polls
showed that voters no longer accepted Fulbright's stature in international
affairs as a sufficient trade-off for his indifference to local concerns. The
unease about Fulbright's distance from his constituents had increased year
by year. Now, finally, all efforts by his staff to make him seem like a regular
guy were futile. They presented him as plain old Bill and outfitted him in
flannel shirts, but the people had already decided that Fulbright was no
longer one of them.

Clinton intended to assist Fulbright during the primary, according to

James Blair, the senator's campaign manager, but became so involved in his own campaign that he never got around to helping his old boss. On the campaign trail, he more often found himself associating with Pryor and Bumpers when they stumped in the Third Congressional District. Arkansas political observers taking their first look at Clinton saw elements of Pryor and Bumpers in his style. He had Pryor's ability to work a room, and Bumpers's power to sway a crowd as an extemporaneous speaker. As the campaign wore on, the resemblances became more apparent: Clinton would study the two men, borrow a colloquialism from one, a hand gesture from the other, and incorporate them in his routine. It is not a contradiction to say that he was both a natural politician and an artful imitator, for those two types may in fact be one and the same; natural politicians are skilled actors, recreating reality, adjusting and ad-libbing, synthesizing the words, ideas, and feelings of others, slipping into different roles in different scenes, saying the same thing over and over again and making it seem like they are saying it for the first time. It can be at once a creative art yet wholly derivative, which is the best way to understand Bill Clinton's political persona as he reached the public stage.

In early July, after he had secured the Democratic nomination, Clinton went to Hot Springs for his ten-year high school reunion, the first time that the class of 1964 had reconvened. The theme of the reunion at the Velda Rose Hotel was "The Way We Were," the title song of that year's nostalgic film starring Barbra Streisand and Robert Redford. Photographs from the Old Gold yearbook lined the banquet-room walls. The *Hot Springs Sentinel-Record* described Clinton as "the most prominent graduate"—a Rhodes Scholar, University of Arkansas law professor, and Democratic candidate for Congress. He was seated at the front table along with his friend Phil Jamison, the class president, a naval lieutenant at Pensacola who had flown helicopters in Vietnam. The article noted that Carolyn Yeldell had now married and was teaching music in Indiana, and that Jim French, the quarterback, was in New Orleans training to be a doctor. David Leopoulos, Clinton's closest childhood friend, had begun a job at a community college in Florida. Of those present, there were twenty-one housewives, two lawyers, nine engineers, four secretaries, one minister, four bankers, and four doctors. "Lots of them," Clinton was quoted as saying of his classmates, "are doing impressive things I haven't done."

Clinton delivered a brief speech, but the crowd seemed to have little interest in politics. At the ten-year point, Jamison found that his classmates did not seem particularly interested in looking backward or forward, but were "caught in the here and now, trying to make their way." After the dinner, Clinton spent most of the night on the dance floor, enjoying himself with a string of old girlfriends. But not everyone was lost in the moment.

Jamison was cornered in the hallway by Rodney Wilson, a former Marine and Vietnam veteran. At first they traded war stories as though they were recalling old memories from high school, but the more Wilson talked, the more intense he became. He seemed depressed, and said he felt out of place and mistreated since his return from Vietnam.

Clinton, too, was still haunted by Vietnam that summer. The manner in which he had avoided military service in 1969 might be raised by John Paul Hammerschmidt's campaign. Hammerschmidt was a World War II Air Force pilot who strongly supported the war and had close ties to veterans' groups in the district. The documentary record of Clinton's actions after he received his draft notice at Oxford five years earlier, including the letter to Colonel Holmes in which he thanked Holmes for eventually saving him from the draft, rested in a file inside a fireproof half-ton vault at the University of Arkansas ROTC building a few blocks down the hill from the law school. Clinton's usual response to anyone who asked him about his military record was that he had received a high draft number in the lottery and was never called. He discussed the more complicated details of his draft history, and the letter to Holmes, with only a few friends. One was Paul Fray. "He told me what he said in the letter about the war," Fray said later. "I told him that he could get into a pickle if the Republicans got the letter and that he should try to get the original back."

Colonel Holmes had retired, and was living in northwest Arkansas. How Clinton contacted him and persuaded him to return the letter is unclear. Some members of the ROTC staff believe that Clinton relied on intermediaries from the university administration, where he had several friends and political supporters. Decades later, the colonel would label Clinton a draft dodger and claim that he had been deceived by the young man, but the evidence indicates that in 1974 he was still willing to help Clinton. ROTC drill instructor Ed Howard later recalled that Colonel Holmes called him one morning that summer and "said he wanted the Clinton letter out of the files." Howard, a noncommissioned officer, was alone in the office; most of the staff was at summer training at Fort Riley, Kansas. He called the unit commander, Colonel Guy Tutwiler, at Fort Riley and informed him of Holmes's request. Tutwiler instructed Howard to make a copy of the Clinton letter and give it to Holmes, but to keep the original. A member of Holmes's family stopped by the ROTC headquarters and picked up the letter.

Later that afternoon, Tutwiler called Howard again and told him to take the original letter and everything else in that file, which was among the records the ROTC had maintained on Vietnam War–era dissidents, and to send it to him at Fort Riley by certified mail. According to Howard, Tutwiler later explained that he had "destroyed the file, burned the file," because the military no longer maintained dissident files and he did not feel that Clinton's letter should ever "be used against him for political reasons." According to Fray, Clinton ended up with a copy of his letter to Holmes, and assumed that "the situation was done with." He did not know that Holmes's top aide, Lieutenant Colonel Clinton Jones, had already made a copy of the letter.

ON Friday, August 9, the day that President Nixon resigned, Clinton was campaigning in the northeastern end of the congressional district. He arrived in Mountain Home that evening for the third day of his stay with Mike and Suzanne Lee, who had made their home his regional headquarters. The Lees were old friends who had been in the class behind his at Hot Springs High. Mike had attended the Naval Academy with Phil Jamison, and he and Jamison had stayed at Clinton's Georgetown room whenever they could escape Annapolis for the weekend.

It was all part of the easy reciprocity of Clinton's world. He never had any money, he was always living off the grace of friends, yet his give-and-take spirit made it possible for him to sleep at other people's houses and clean out their refrigerators because he was bound to repay them with some act of generosity down the line. Now he was at the Lees' house in Mountain Home and the American political world was turning upside down. He sat in the living room and watched as Nixon announced that he was leaving the White House. Well after midnight, a reporter for the *Arkansas Gazette* called the house. Suzanne answered and went to the guest bedroom, awakening Clinton. He went to the kitchen to take the call, leaning against the wall, still half-asleep. It was, Suzanne said later, "amazing to listen to him. It was just like a rehearsed speech that he had been waiting to give. I couldn't believe he could do it right out of a deep sleep." But Clinton would not say publicly what he thought about Nixon's resignation: that it was good for the country but bad for him. "This is going to cost me the race," he confided to Mike Lee. The convulsions of Nixon's resignation, he said, would make the voters of northwest Arkansas less inclined to throw Hammerschmidt out.

Throughout that summer of the Watergate inquiry, Clinton had emphasized Hammerschmidt's friendship and support of Nixon. The Republican congressman tried to argue that "the people are tired of Watergate," but most evidence was to the contrary. Watergate filled up so much space in the political world that there was little room left for other questions, such as whether Clinton was too young and too liberal for the electorate. The more the public turned against Nixon, the more Clinton gained momentum. When Nixon resigned, as Clinton predicted, his campaign "went into a stall," according to press secretary Doug Wallace. "The voters stopped to catch their breath. Suddenly there was no Nixon to rail against."

Nixon's resignation was one of three major transitions for Clinton and his campaign late that summer. One afternoon, Clinton's mother came home from her hospital work with a carry-out dinner for her husband, Jeff Dwire, to discover him dead of heart failure brought on by diabetes. Dwire had been a soothing influence on Virginia during their five-year marriage. He was a charming dandy who enjoyed life and had had his own scrapes with the law, but he was kind to Virginia and her boys, and he made her happy in a way that no other man had since Bill Blythe. During his year in prison, he had become a jailhouse lawyer of sorts, acquiring enough knowledge to discuss legal subjects with Clinton and Rodham when they were at Yale. Dwire had been the one member of the family to accept Hillary warmly, a gesture that was reciprocated by Bill Clinton, who wrote a letter of support when Dwire unsuccessfully sought a pardon.

Everyone at campaign headquarters knew Dwire. Shortly before he died, he had spent several days in Fayetteville answering the telephones and offering advice. Paul Fray noticed the flashy rings on Dwire's fingers and worried about what the Hammerschmidt forces would do if they learned that he was assisting the campaign. "The last thing we needed was for word to get out about Clinton's stepfather with a prison record."

Dwire's death and Nixon's resignation were matters of consequence, yet in terms of their sustained effect on Clinton, they could not compare with the third event of late summer, the arrival of Hillary Rodham, who provoked a complicated set of reactions in her boyfriend and the people around him. On one level, Clinton feared that Rodham was too much of a potential political star to make the sacrifice of living in Arkansas. Once, earlier, when Clinton told Diane Kincaid, the political science professor at Arkansas, how much she reminded him of Rodham and made him miss her, the professor asked him why he did not just marry Rodham and bring her to Arkansas. "Because she's so good at what she does, she could have an amazing political career on her own," Clinton said. "If she comes to Arkansas it's going to be my state, my future. She could be president someday. She could go to any state and be elected to the Senate. If she comes to Arkansas, she'll be on my turf."

That turf, Clinton realized, could appear inhospitable to his Yankee girlfriend. His mother and younger brother made little effort to hide their distaste for her. Whenever the Frays visited Hot Springs during the campaign, Virginia would complain to them about Hillary. "Virginia loathed Hillary then," Mary Lee Fray recalled. "Anything she could find to pick on about Hillary she would pick on. Hillary did not fit her mold for Bill." But even if it was not a natural fit, Clinton seemed determined to lure her to stay in Arkansas. He encouraged his friends and political aides to make her feel welcome. "She was someone you had great expectations for and wanted to know because Bill kept talking about her," recalled Rudy Moore.

Yet at the same time that Clinton was earnestly recruiting Rodham to his state, he was still involved with the student volunteer, a relationship that had been going on for several months. The tension at campaign headquarters increased considerably when Rodham arrived as people there tried to deal with the situation. Both women seemed on edge. The Arkansas girlfriend would ask people about Hillary: what she was like, and whether Clinton was going to marry her. When she was at headquarters, someone would sneak her out the back door if Rodham was spotted pulling into the driveway. Mary Lee Fray, who liked both women, felt trapped in the middle of the triangle. She remembers times when Clinton wanted her to chaperone the Arkansas girlfriend and make sure that there were no confrontations with Hillary. "Bill would say, 'Go take her somewhere. Get lost,'" Fray recalled later. "It would put me in a funny position. He'd say, 'Go do something. Move it. Scoot it.' He'd get us out of there." If Clinton had made it clear that Rodham was his only romantic interest, Fray thought, the other woman would have disappeared. But Clinton would not say anything so direct.

Fayetteville, a university town, was the most culturally liberal enclave in Arkansas, but the mores of the wider Third Congressional District made it politically impractical for Clinton to live with a woman outside of marriage. Rodham took her own place when she arrived. She rented a three-bedroom house, an architectural showpiece replicating a Frank Lloyd Wright design, bow-shaped and glassy, full of odd-shaped rooms, with a large swimming pool in the backyard. The house belonged to Rafael Guzman, who was on temporary leave from the law school to teach in Iowa, where he was soon joined by his wife, Terry Kirkpatrick, who had served with Rodham on the impeachment inquiry staff. The place quickly looked like campaign headquarters, with Clinton signs everywhere.

To some Arkansans, Rodham seemed too aggressive at first, especially in contrast to Clinton, who was soft and ambiguous. On the opening day of school, when Rodham first walked into the criminal law classroom, Woody Bassett, who was then a first-year student, thought she "looked out of place. She dressed like a throwback to the sixties. There were not many women in the law school. It took a while to adjust to someone with a different accent who was as aggressive as she was." Some students were intimidated by Rodham's brilliance, and others, according to Bassett, "downright resented it. People were never indifferent about her. Some of the guys were not used to being taught and led by a strong woman. And there was no question she was a role model for some of the female students."

Anyone who entered her classroom expecting her to follow Clinton's pedagogical style was mistaken. Clinton was diffuse and easygoing. Rodham was precise and demanding. Clinton was amenable to a filibuster, Rodham was less willing to waste time. Clinton rarely confronted students, preferring to engage them in freewheeling conversations. Rodham would come straight at her students with difficult questions. She was more likely than Clinton to offer clear opinions on legal issues and not leave the class hanging, and she had what Bassett thought was an "unusual ability to absorb a huge amount of facts and boil them down to the bottom line." And unlike Clinton, notorious as the friendliest grader on the faculty, Rodham wrote rigorous exams and was a tough grader. Most members of the law school faculty regarded her as a better professor than Clinton, if not as animated in the lecture hall, more committed to the craft, as demonstrated by her writings in law journals about the rights of children.

Rodham was approachable but serious, Mort Gitelman thought. "She would not sit for idle chitchat. She was not a chew-the-fat type of person. She was always working on something and wanted to bring the conversation around to what she was working on. She was all business." During that first semester, along with teaching criminal law, Rodham also became the first director of the University of Arkansas Legal Clinic, in which law students took on needy clients under the supervision of licensed attorneys. Before Rodham arrived, preliminary work on the clinic had left several faculty members frustrated by resistance from the legal establishment and the paperwork demanded by the federal bureaucracy. Gitelman handed Rodham a ten-inch file that needed to be processed to get federal money for the program. He was impressed by how quickly Rodham sorted through the forms and got the money. Burdened as an outsider and a woman in what was then still a clubby male domain, she persuaded local judges and lawyers to endorse the program. She went to the county bar and negotiated approval for indigence guidelines on who could qualify for clinic assistance, in return agreeing that the clinic would take unprofitable criminal case appointments from the local courts. David Newbern, who helped Rodham with the idiosyncrasies of the legal world in Fayetteville, regarded her, above all, as "a prodigious worker."

"IF you are looking for a battleground, go outside onto the streets where I grew up. Lift your eyes to the hills of north and west Arkansas! There is a fight in this Third Congressional District which is a clear and unmistakable struggle between what we are for and what we are against. For, in the words of Harry Truman, when you strip away the 'small talk and double talk, the combination of crafty silence and resounding misrepresentation,' you find this seat in Congress occupied by one of the strongest supporters of, and apologists for, the abuse of presidential power and policies which have wrecked the economy. Today we must deliberate. Tomorrow we must take out of this hall the will to set things straight. Let us begin!"

It was at the Democratic state convention in Hot Springs on September 13 that Clinton delivered that fiery oration. He had been building a name for himself for months, and now, as the stretch run of the general election campaign began, party regulars who had considered him a long shot thought it possible that he had a chance of winning. His challenge was the hot race, the only tightly contested match in what was still a one-party state everywhere but in northwest Arkansas. Clinton packed the fall convention, bringing carloads of supporters from Fayetteville and supplementing them with a boisterous home-town contingent. Although he still privately feared that Nixon's resignation had cut short his chances, he regained some measure of hope the week before the convention when Gerald Ford pardoned Nixon. Hammerschmidt had swiftly tried to reposition himself as more of a Ford man than a Nixon man in the days after the resignation, bringing out newspaper ads that depicted him working closely with Ford during their days together in the House. But no sooner had the ads appeared than Ford's popularity sank when he pardoned his predecessor.

Clinton portrayed the pardon as the final dishonorable act of the Watergate scandal. "We have come together in the midst of one of our country's most difficult periods," he said. "After two years of turmoil, a president of the United States has resigned his office. His chosen successor, in whom Democrats and Republicans alike had at first placed such hope, has granted a 'full, free and absolute' pardon to the fallen president in advance of any charges being filed against him. This pardon has again opened the wounds of Watergate. It has undermined respect for law and order. It has prejudiced pending trials. It has tormented the families of those already in prison for the administration's political crimes. It is yet another blow to that vast body of law-abiding Americans, whose faith in equal justice under law has been shaken, then repaired, and is now shaken again."

The rest of Clinton's keynote speech was devoted to the economy, his rhetoric more strident and class-conscious than it would later become. He came across as a defender of the middle class and the working class against rapacious corporations and Republican policies. He deplored the "record deficits and recession" brought on by "six long years" of Republican control of the White House. He accused Republicans of keeping "prices high and profits high for the biggest corporations, while trying to hold down minimum wages and telling working people to tighten their belts." He spoke of a member of a road crew in Scott County, his apocryphal everyman, who told him that working people "want a hand up, not a hand out." If President Ford "wants to pardon somebody," he concluded, "he ought to pardon the administration's economic advisers."

Clinton's principal issues adviser for the fall campaign was Steve Smith, the young turk of the Arkansas legislature who had spent the summer in graduate school at Northwestern University. His return to Fayetteville came shortly before Rodham's arrival, at once lending the campaign more intellectual weight and making it more chaotic. Smith was a voracious reader who could match Rodham and Clinton's brainpower, and week by week he grabbed more of the candidate's time and interest as they developed issues together. "It was wonderful to work issues for the guy," Smith said later. "Every week I'd spend eighty hours doing research. I'd set up an issue of the week. We'd open Monday with a press conference, lay out our position and a handful of Hammerschmidt votes. I'd brief him on Sunday for the press conference on Monday. He would absorb everything I said, every detail, and draw conclusions and connections that I had missed."

The weekly news conferences began the Monday after the state convention and continued through November. At one in Van Buren, Clinton attacked the administration's agricultural trade policies, saying that wheat exports to the Soviet Union should be restricted and tighter limits should be placed on beef imports. "If we do not reverse these suicidal trends," he said, "the small, independent farmer will be forced from his land, and large multinational corporate farms will dominate Arkansas and the nation, manipulating the price of food much the same as the giant oil companies do the price of gasoline." Clinton called on Earl Butz, the Secretary of Agriculture, to "resign and return to the board of directors of Ralston-Purina."

Although Clinton was mechanically inept and had no real experience on the farm or in the factory, he now offered himself to the farmers and workers of his district as one of them. His childhood friends from Hot Springs might have snickered at this transformation. Clinton's potential as a skilled laborer was revealed to them in seventh-grade shop class. The teacher would not let students proceed to more complicated tasks until they had squared a block to his satisfaction. While most of the boys went on to craft breadboards and tables, Clinton spent the entire year trying to square his block. "Bill planed more blocks than any kid in the history of junior high," according to his classmate Ronnie Cecil. As to his aptitude on the farm, his formative experience there came at age seven when he was bruised and battered by an angry ram that had pinned him to the ground.

Now, as a candidate, he was the son of soil and toil. It was part of a strategy that had been outlined to Clinton by Jody Powell, an aide to Jimmy Carter, the former governor of Georgia who was heading the Democratic National Committee's 1974 campaign team. Powell came to Fayetteville to advise the Clinton campaign for a few days in the early fall. Clinton's aides remember that Powell looked disheveled and "more hippieish" than he would two years later when his boss was running for president. He left behind a seventeen-point memo. Point number seven read: "Find a dramatic way to identify with agricultural interests before [Hammerschmidt] can label you as some sort of 'pseudo-intellectual liberal professor' who doesn't know or care about agriculture."

At the same time that Clinton plowed the populist turf, and attacked the corporate mentality of Republicans, he relied heavily on support from the Tyson family, owners of Tyson Foods Inc. Don Tyson, the chairman, was an eccentric, hardworking, hard-playing character who would later redesign his corporate suite in the shape of the White House's Oval Office. He wore the khaki work uniform he required of all his employees, including the top executives. He had shiny doorknobs in the corporate suite made in the shape of eggs. He was also a yellow dog Democrat who had long ties to the recently defeated Fulbright and most other leading politicians in the state. His chief outside legal counsel was Jim Blair, who had been Fulbright's campaign manager and counsel to the state Democratic party and was one of Clinton's friends and advisers.

Tyson Foods was aggressively buying out competitors in the early 1970s on its way to becoming the leading poultry firm in the nation. But 1974 was a difficult year, the only one in its history when the company lost money, going back to 1936 when John Tyson loaded five hundred spring chickens into crates and trucked them up to Chicago where he sold them for a $235 profit. Don Tyson, the founder's son, placed much of the blame for the slump on the Republican administration in Washington, charging that huge grain sales to the Soviet Union had caused feed prices to rise sharply, destroying the poultry market. The Third Congressional District was home to Tyson's corporate headquarters, based in Springdale, as well as to hundreds of small farmers who raised chickens for the company. The growers were largely dependent on Tyson Foods and suffered when the company suffered. Clinton emphasized their plight, rather than the Tyson operation's annual loss, in his speeches and commercials. One of his radio spots featured an announcer who sounded like Johnny Cash, inquiring, "Pay too much for greens 'n beans? Forget what pork 'n beefsteak means? Push Earl Butz away from the trough!"

Don Tyson stayed in the shadows of the campaign, but would be called in occasionally by Blair when fund-raising problems arose. Clinton would meet Tyson and other major financial patrons in the back room of an old stone house up the road from headquarters, an unmarked restaurant that specialized in thick steaks and saltine crackers with picante sauce. Don Tyson's stepbrother, Randal Tyson, spent much of his time at Clinton headquarters during the final months. "He busted his butt," recalled Paul Fray. "Randal wanted Clinton to win that race something fierce." The Tysons also donated a campaign telephone bank which operated out of an apartment near the university.

ONE way to catch fish, according to an old Arkansas folk tale, is for people to wade into a stream and kick their feet around the bottom until the water becomes so disturbed and muddy that the fish rise to the top. The story serves as an allegory for politics, which in Arkansas is both a popular sport and a muddy one. Bill Clinton was a fish swimming in muddy water from the beginning of his political career. Even then, in his first Arkansas campaign, rumors swirled furiously around him.

One rumor, which came to be known as "The Boy in the Tree," or "The Man in the Tree," was the easiest to disprove and yet the most persistent. In the fall of 1969, President Nixon, an inveterate sports fan, had traveled to Fayetteville to attend a football game between the Arkansas Razorbacks and Texas Longhorns, two of the nation's best college teams. The lasting photographic symbol of that Saturday afternoon in Fayetteville was a picture of a protester sitting in a tree holding a sign urging Nixon to go home, which was later reprinted in the college yearbook. The young man's face was not clearly identifiable. He resembled the Bill Clinton of 1969 only in that he had long curly hair and a beard. Brenda Blagg, who covered Nixon's visit for the student newspaper, was standing under the tree that day and knew the protester, a familiar campus character who was "certainly not Bill Clinton." At the time of Nixon's visit, Clinton was against the war and no fan of Nixon's, but it was impossible for him to have been in a tree in Fayetteville. He was at Oxford, beginning his second year as a Rhodes Scholar.

Yet five years later, during the congressional campaign, the word went out that Clinton was the boy in the tree. A woman called several newspapers in the district and, without identifying herself, said, "We're trying to get a copy of that picture when Bill Clinton was sitting in the tree. Do you happen to have that picture in your files?" At political rallies, unmarked handbills were distributed showing the tree picture and no explicit mention of Clinton, simply the inference in a question: "Do You Want This to Be Your Congressman?" The rumor was accompanied by whispers that Clinton had been a draft dodger, though his letter to Colonel Holmes and other ROTC records had not surfaced, and no one made the draft-dodging charges in public. Many of Clinton's aides noticed a level of vitriol in the attacks on Clinton that exceeded even the rough norms of Arkansas politics. "This was his first race, he had no political history to speak of, yet the level of feeling for and against him was so intense," recalled Doug Wallace. "It was amazing to me. There was something in his personality and style that engendered that kind of passion on the part of people who wanted to keep him from being elected."

The boy-in-the-tree story hovered around Clinton for several years, until finally it was transformed into a joke by the journalists who covered him in later campaigns. One year, the press association in northwest Arkansas presented a satirical Gridiron show that included a skit in which Clinton was on trial as the boy in the tree and was found innocent based on "butt prints."

Rumors about Clinton's sexual behavior also began in that first campaign. As a bachelor, he was immune from charges of marital infidelity, but little else. John Baran, who had taught Clinton art in junior high school, heard rumors at his church, Grand Avenue Methodist of Hot Springs, during the final months of the congressional campaign that "Bill was a homosexual." Some of the same churchgoers spreading that story would later attack Clinton for living with a woman before he was married. Mary Lee Fray attended a Baptist church in Fayetteville where Clinton was criticized from the pulpit. She quickly learned that "some conservative preachers were crusading against him. They were constantly talking about drugs and women in the Clinton campaign." Nearly every week, Paul Fray would field a call from a labor organizer in Fort Smith who would utter the same lament. "We're catching hell down here about all you left-wing dope smokers up there at that damn yoo-nah-ver-sity, Paul. We're just catchin' hell down here!" Neil McDonald, a Clinton volunteer, was frequently confronted by hostile questioners who wanted to know about women and the campaign. "They were trying to pin Bill down on the women issue or anything else they could find. They would ask if Clinton was dating women out of the campaign. Most of us knew better than to answer that one."

Several office affairs bloomed at the College Avenue headquarters, but they seemed more a reflection of the sexually combustible nature of political campaigns than of any loosening of sexual mores among the under-thirty generation. There was a discussion once among Clinton advisers about taking the offensive and resurrecting a slogan that cropped up during Hammerschmidt's first campaign: "Send John Paul to Washington, the wife you save may be your own." That idea was proposed by Paul Fray, but vetoed by Rodham, according to Doug Wallace. "Paul wanted to play hardball, cut and slash. Hillary did not like it."

The campaign was not a haven for the drug culture, but neither was it a marijuana-free zone. Randy White, a college freshman who joined the campaign as a volunteer, was sent to work at a phone bank one night at an apartment in Fayetteville. When he entered the apartment, he saw "seven or eight people in there smoking pot." He felt "terrified that the place would be busted" while he worked through his list of calls in another room. Whenever eighteen-year-old Roger Clinton, the candidate's younger brother, came up to Fayetteville, the scent of marijuana trailed him. "It was no secret Roger was blowing smoke," recalled Neil McDonald. "It ain't too hard to tell when you go into a room that Roger had just been in, and it smells like burnt rope. He and his buddies would be in the basement stenciling signs, and actually smoking joints." McDonald thought that Clinton knew that Roger was smoking pot in 1974. "Bill . . . tried to lecture him in a big-brotherly way."

INSIDE the Clinton campaign, Addington was known as "Ronnie Paul," Wallace was "Dougie," Fray was "P.D.," and they all called Clinton "the Boy." "The Boy's on a roll today," they would say. Or, "The Boy's in a pisser of a mood."

The nickname was in part complimentary: it evoked Clinton's youth, friendliness, and achievement. But it also had a subtext that addressed the immature aspects of his personality. The Boy never wanted to go to bed. The Boy had no concept of money. Once, early in the campaign, he called Addington and announced that he had to come over to Addington's apartment to take a shower and shave because he had forgotten to pay his utility bills and his water and power had been turned off.

The Boy had a tendency to talk too much and could not always be trusted to keep campaign matters in confidence. One day he told reporters about internal poll results, prompting Doug Wallace and David Ivey, the two aides in charge of press matters, to issue a blistering memo that was labeled "To all Distrist Headquarters Staff," but was directed primarily at Clinton. "The damage done by the release of the last poll without the accompanying previous poll can only be judged after some time, but it is obvious that it has hurt," they wrote. "From now until the time Bill Clinton finishes this campaign, NO ONE will talk, or even breathe in the direction of a news reporter, without first clearing it with David Ivey or Doug Wallace. THIS ALSO MEANS THE CANDIDATE." If Clinton ignored this edict, they declared, "All hell will break loose."

The Boy was sentimental and easily touched. He was near tears one day when he received a fifty-dollar contribution from two friends from Yale Law School who had little money. "It's like the widow's mite," Clinton said, comparing the contribution to the biblical story of the widow who gave more than she could afford at the temple, the smallest denomination of coin, a mite, which prompted Jesus to say that her contribution was worth more than all the riches donated by the wealthy.

The Boy could throw a fit when he felt frustrated. His temper was an accepted part of the campaign. There were testy notes if he thought the follow-through on something was not quick enough. He would explode in a flash, then act as though it had never happened. Neil McDonald witnessed some of Clinton's explosions: "There was a minor snafu and he blew off at us for no reason. But most of us knew better than to take it personally. He was under a great deal of stress." Harry Truman Moore, a law student who often traveled with Clinton and served as his photographer, remembered that Clinton would often snap at his travel aides when they tried to pull him away from a crowd to keep him closer to his schedule. "He'd say, 'Don't ever pull me away from a crowd like that again!' Then, ten minutes later, he'd say, 'Why are we late?' We'd all get used to it, the Clinton temper."

His most memorable eruptions came in arguments with Rodham, who seemed not the least bit timid about snapping back when he erupted. "They'd have the biggest damn fights, shouting and swearing," Addington recalled. "They had two or three battle royals." One day Addington, Clinton, and Rodham were starting out on their way to an event in Eureka Springs. Clinton and Rodham were debating how to handle a campaign issue. "Bill wanted to do one thing, she wanted to do another. They started shouting at each other. I was driving. Bill was in the front seat, Hillary in the back. He was hitting the dashboard. She was hitting the seat. They were really going at it. We drove up a street near the headquarters and stopped at a light. Hillary said, 'I'm getting out!' She got out and slammed the door. And Bill said, 'Go on.' We got out on the highway and I was going fast because we were late. Bill started venting his anger on me. It was one of the most uncomfortable times I've ever spent with him. Then he took a short nap. When he woke up, everything was fine."

Rodham was a central figure during the final weeks of the campaign. She was, thought Mary Lee Fray, "fighting for her man" romantically and politically. After sending Clinton's University of Arkansas girlfriend into exile (the young woman was not seen around the campaign from October through election day), Rodham took on several aides whose style she disapproved of, especially Addington and Paul Fray. Addington, who was sent to the Fort Smith office, came to think of Rodham as a negative force. "Our organization went to shit. We lost the spirit because of her. Everybody started bickering with everybody else," he said later. In a memo to Clinton, Doug Wallace noted that though he thought Rodham's "intentions were the best," her presence was more negative than positive. "She . . . rubs people the wrong way, and boy, did she ever," Wallace wrote. "She managed to antagonize almost the entire staff. . . ."

Most of Rodham's bickering was with Paul Fray, a strong-willed political operator accustomed to playing a dominant role. It is an understatement to say that their styles clashed. "Paul was rough around the edges in how he dealt with people, real colorful and country, and that style didn't mesh too well when Hillary was around," Wallace recalled. The power struggle between Rodham and Fray reached a critical stage near the end when they got into several arguments over money. The campaign needed more funds to compete with Hammerschmidt on television and to ensure a strong get-out-the-vote effort, but Rodham advised against borrowing too much or taking it from questionable sources. In one instance, according to the accounts of Fray and several other campaign aides, Rodham took the ethical high ground, Clinton vacillated, and Fray was willing to do whatever it took to win. Fray says that he was contacted by a lawyer representing dairy interests who had $15,000 ready for the campaign that could be used in Sebastian County "to ensure that you are able to win the election." The implication was that the money was dirty coming and going: it would come from the dairy industry with expectations that if Clinton became congressman he would serve their interests, and it would go to election boxes in Fort Smith where votes could still be bought. In several parts of Arkansas in those days, voters still cast paper ballots that went into cardboard boxes. There were frequent allegations that different boxes were stuffed and that payoffs were required to prevent stuffing. "The attorney already had the money," Fray said later. "It was a question of me picking it up and delivering it. I knew there were places where we could spend a little money and it would turn out right."

At a late night meeting at headquarters, Fray discussed the deal with Clinton and Rodham. Clinton did not have much to say. Rodham flatly rejected the proposal. "She nixed it," according to Fray. "She got adamant. She said to Bill, 'No! You don't want to be a party to this!' I said, 'Look, you want to win or you want to lose?' She said, 'Well, I don't want to win this way.' If we can't earn it, we can't go [to Washington].' "

ON November 5, election night, the mood was buoyant at Clinton headquarters. Any disputes within the campaign seemed inconsequential compared with the energy and enthusiasm that Clinton had put into his candidacy, and now it was as though that energy was all that mattered. Reports from the field indicated that the race was close and that Clinton had the momentum. He had been out there traveling the back roads for eight months, while Hammerschmidt, slow to realize the seriousness of the challenge, had been back in the district only for the final three weeks. The campaign had election teams stationed in the courthouses in all twenty-one counties, calling in reports box by box. Fray and Clinton had determined the minimum number of votes they figured they needed in each rural county to overtake what they expected to be a significant Hammerschmidt edge in Fort Smith. They tallied the results on a large tracking board. Hammerschmidt's totals were on the left side of the board, Clinton's on the right. The early results were encouraging. Rodham sat at a desk working a calculator. Fray stood by the tally board analyzing the numbers as Harry Truman Moore wrote them down. Clinton worked the phone, taking and making calls to the counties. He started getting concerned when the calls came from Garland County, which included his home town of Hot Springs. They knew that Garland County was conservative, but assumed that the favorite son could at least break even there. "What the hell's going on down there?" Clinton asked. Somehow, he had lost Garland County.

By midnight, every county had reported except the largest and most conservative one, Sebastian County, home to Fort Smith. Clinton was still leading by several thousand votes. Steve Smith was thinking about finding an apartment in Georgetown. But what was happening down in Fort Smith? Clinton supporters at the Sebastian County courthouse were picking up reports of vote tampering. "Let me call the sheriff," Clinton said. "He's a friend of mine." The sheriff told Clinton he was looking into it. Steve Smith and several other aides piled into a car and drove to Fort Smith. Ron Addington met them at the courthouse, and they milled around for a while, grumbling, but determined that there was nothing they could do and drove back to Fayetteville. Fort Smith finally came in with an enormous swing in Hammerschmidt's direction. The board showed that Clinton had lost by 6,000 votes. Fray started swearing and throwing things out the window. "It was the goddamn money!" he said.

The staff talked about challenging the election results, but Clinton chose not to. He realized that he had won for losing. His race was the most talked about contest in the state. He had become the darling of the Democratic party by taking on Hammerschmidt and coming within 2 percentage points of defeating him, by far the best showing any opponent ever made against him. He had been on the same stage with Dale Bumpers and David Pryor and compared favorably to them. "We accomplished a miracle out here," Clinton told his staff. "We started with no name recognition and look what we accomplished. We scared the pants off that guy." He then sent a telegram to Hammerschmidt: "Congratulations on your victory yesterday. I hope you will consider the merit of the positive positions I took during the campaign. They grew out of the long months of discussions I had with our people. I wish you well in the next two difficult years. If ever I can be of service to you in your attempts to help the people of the Third Congressional District, please call on me."

ONE morning after the election, Clinton drove to the square in downtown Fayetteville and started shaking hands. "Thank you for your help," he said to passers-by who had voted for him. To others, he expressed thanks simply for voting, or for listening to him. He stood in the square all day, talking and shaking hands. He was cooling down after nine months of nonstop campaigning, his friends thought. No, there was more to it than that. He was warming up. The next race had already begun.

CHAPTER NINETEEN

GOVERNOR-IN-WAITING

GARY HART OF Colorado arrived in the Senate. Jerry Brown became the new governor of California. Michael Dukakis took over in Massachusetts. Paul Simon of Illinois, Paul Tsongas of Massachusetts, and Tom Harkin of Iowa were elected to the House of Representatives. All of these Democrats were set on the path of presidential ambition by the elections of 1974. They were among the winners in what came to be regarded as a transformational year in modern American politics, a year when the old order started to give way to the next generation. The most dramatic change took place in the House, where ninety-two freshmen, including seventy-five Democrats, stormed Capitol Hill. They were known as the Watergate class or the Watergate babies. With equal measures of impatience and righteousness, they undertook the work of institutional reform, changing the rules of the place, upsetting the seniority system, overthrowing old committee chairmen, demanding a share of the power.

The road of ifs usually leads nowhere, but in the case of Bill Clinton and 1974 a brief journey down the path of historical speculation seems appropriate. If four thousand people in the Third Congressional District had voted for him instead of for John Paul Hammerschmidt, Clinton would have been one of the rambunctious Watergate babies. He would have moved to Washington that winter, meaning that his stay in Arkansas, the land to which he had always said he longed to return, would have lasted a mere sixteen months. Hillary Rodham, after four months in Fayetteville, certainly would have left with him, resettling in a place and a culture where they were on more equal standing and where she could pursue her interests in politics and law on a national rather than provincial stage. While the removal of geography as an issue might have made it smoother for the partnership in the short term, it is also conceivable that life in Washington eventually would have unraveled the couple's relationship by making them less dependent on each other than they would become during their long haul in Arkansas.

Everything in Clinton's history leads to the conclusion that he would have emerged as a leader of the Watergate babies in Congress, impressing his colleagues on Capitol Hill if not always his constituents back in Arkansas. In settings where he found himself among high-powered peers, whether with the Rhodes Scholars at Oxford or, much later, with the governors of other states, Clinton rose quickly to prominence, outpacing others with his ambition, affability, and appetite for ideas and dealmaking. But where would that have taken him in Washington? To a House committee chairmanship, eventually, or more likely, given his restless electoral nature, to a bid for a Senate seat, either in 1978 or in 1980, when he would have to challenge Dale Bumpers. Bumpers and Governor Pryor, who also had senatorial ambitions, were always there ahead of Clinton, two formidable vote-getters in his own party. Had he gone to Washington in 1974, at some point he would have been unable to repress an urge to try to run over one of them; instead, from back in Arkansas, he found a way around them.

Losing the congressional election did not hurt Clinton's political status in Arkansas, and enhanced his image as an emerging star of the Democratic party. He came out of the contest with what all politicians covet—an aura of inevitability. The question was not whether he would run again, but what office he would seek. By early 1975, he was weighing two options: challenging Hammerschmidt again or running for attorney general. While resuming his teaching at the law school, he maintained his political contacts around the district and solicited advice on which election path to follow. Doug Wallace, his press secretary during the congressional campaign, wrote a memo outlining the potential dangers of another race against Hammerschmidt. The attorney general's race, on the other hand, seemed "very attractive with relatively few drawbacks," beyond its paltry annual salary. "The office of attorney general would allow you to work on consumer affairs, white collar crime, energy matters and other issues of interest," Wallace wrote. "It would also provide a proving ground for the future by giving you the experience in government that some people in 1974 said you lacked."

Long before he revealed his intentions publicly, Clinton began taking steps helpful to the waging of a statewide campaign. The Democratic State Committee, now chaired by Mack McLarty, appointed him to head its affirmative action committee, whose mission was to study the state's new presidential primary law and set guidelines for the selection of delegates for the next national convention. This convenient assignment allowed Clinton to travel the state at party expense to meet with Democratic activists.

He also obtained a part-time teaching post at the University of Arkansas-Little Rock, traveling down to Little Rock each week to teach a class on criminal justice and law enforcement in addition to his courses in Fayetteville. Many of his students in Little Rock were law enforcement personnel, a group he had also taught during his Yale Law School years when he was a part-time instructor of criminal justice at the University of New Haven. Teaching police officers strengthened the resume of a prospective attorney general, and furthered his efforts to toughen his image following his graduate school days as a long-haired war protester who had avoided military service.

HILLARY Rodham was deeply immersed in the university community by 1975. She taught trial advocacy and criminal procedure at Waterman Hall, directed the legal aid clinic, and helped run a prison project in which law students assisted inmates with post-conviction problems. At the legal clinic, she was meticulous about maintaining casework files on every person who walked in the door. Van Gearhart, one of her student assistants, worried that the recordkeeping would be too burdensome, but Rodham persuaded him that "a strong statistical base could help cement the future of the clinic," which it did. In the first year, the clinic handled three hundred clients and took fifty cases to court. For years afterward, Rodham would recall her experiences in the courthouses of northwest Arkansas with a touch of wistfulness, often retelling her favorite stories, including the time when a small-town jailer called her and said that a traveling preacher-lady was about to be committed by a judge who thought she was insane. Rodham drove to the town and in the course of interviewing the babbling preacher discovered that she had relatives in California. "People need the Lord in California, too," Rodham told the woman, who left for the West Coast after the judge was sold on the argument that a one-way plane ticket was the easiest and cheapest resolution of the case.

The prison project took Rodham and her Fayetteville associates into an unfamiliar world. Once she and another supervisor drove down to the Tucker Unit for youthful offenders near Pine Bluff. As they entered the prison farm, they noticed a building near the main unit that was identified as the dog kennel. Robert Newcomb, a lawyer stationed at the prison farm on a federal grant, recalled that when the two women lawyers got out of the car, one remarked to the other that she "didn't realize that the Arkansas prison system was so progressive that it would allow inmates to have their own dogs." It was left to Newcomb to break the news that the dogs were there not to serve as the inmates' best friends, but to track them down if they tried to escape.

In Fayetteville, Rodham often met Diane Kincaid for lunch: they would buy yogurt and walk around campus, talking about the university, their careers, feminism, and the joys and frustrations of life in their adopted small town. Kincaid, who had grown up in Washington, moved to Fayetteville a decade before Rodham and had gone through various stages— "resistance, resentment, anger, disbelief, resignation, and finally smugness about how good things were." They played tennis on weekends, scrappy singles matches, Rodham and Kincaid both diving and scraping their knees, good athletes but lacking in classic form, each with a burning desire to win, their hair a mess by the end in the summer humidity. One day, moved by what Kincaid termed "a burst of patriotism," Rodham decided to visit the local U.S. Marine Corps office to see if she could enlist. She told Kincaid that the Marines informed her she was not one of the few and the proud they were looking for: she was a woman, she was too old, and she had bad eyesight, the recruiter said, suggesting that she "oughta go try with the dogs"—the Army. If there was a political component to this odd episode, an attempt to balance Clinton's lack of service with Rodham's bold enlistment, or a test of the equal rights policies of the military, it never went any further, and the incident remained a closely held joke among friends.

Rodham's Arkansas circle widened when her two fun-loving brothers, Hughie and Tony, enrolled at the university at their sister's urging. They shared an apartment south of campus with Neil McDonald, the former campaign volunteer. Tony "liked to keep his stuff put up, semi-neat," but Hughie, who had long hair and talked earnestly about Che Guevera, was another story, according to McDonald. "As far as housekeeping, forget Hughie. He was the biggest slob in the world. He made 'The Odd Couple' seem tame." Their father, Hugh Rodham, paid for most of their expenses and came down from Park Ridge to visit during fly-fishing season.

Although they still lived apart, Rodham and Clinton spent most of their free time together, playing volleyball and charades with friends, attending Razorback basketball games, and going for steaks and chicken afterward with Coach Eddie Sutton and Don Tyson and his pals. Pressure was building on the pair to marry or separate. Should Clinton marry Rodham? He told friends that he wanted to get married and that it was Hillary or nobody: but he also realized that while their partnership was intellectually invigorating and politically complementary, their personal relationship was stormy. "All we ever do is argue," he confided to Carolyn Yeldell Staley, his high school friend. Betsey Wright, who had befriended the pair during the McGovern campaign and now worked in Washington recruiting women to run for public office, was also "aware of lots of tension between them." She had heard Clinton complain after a round of arguing with Rodham that he had tried to "run Hillary off, but she just wouldn't go."

Should Rodham marry Clinton? She studied the question from every angle, asking several women friends how they balanced their own political objectives with family responsibilities. Her questions came at a time when feminism was an urgent subject for her and the professional women with whom she associated. The equal rights amendment (ERA), which had narrowly failed in the previous session of the Arkansas legislature, was up for another vote, and a central event of the House deliberations was a Valentine's Day debate between ERA opponent Phyllis Schlafly and Diane Kincaid, who was chairwoman of the governor's commission on women and had been asked at the last minute to fill in for Sarah Weddington, the feminist lawyer from Texas. Rodham and Clinton came over to Kincaid's house and prepped her for the confrontation. They sat in the living room and rehearsed different arguments and counterarguments, when suddenly Kincaid's six-year-old daughter Kathryn called out "Mommy!" from the floor behind them. They turned around and saw the little girl holding the plastic symbol of the prefeminist era. "Here we were fighting for feminist rights and Kathryn was there with a Barbie doll!" Kincaid later recalled. The scene, she said, provoked a long, loud, infectious belly laugh from Hillary Rodham.

Among the feminists, there were differences of opinion over how best to resolve the conflicting demands of wife and sisterhood. Ann Henry, who was married to a state senator and toiled as a Democratic party activist while rearing three young children, argued with Rodham about the role that a political wife could play. Rodham thought that Henry should be more independent. "Hillary was very curious to see how women integrate family and politics. She knew politics is where she wanted to be. She had a sense of what she wanted to do. She would say, why don't you do certain things?" Henry later recalled. "And I would say that I felt certain limits as a wife. She thought she could do as much. I didn't agree with that. There's a gap between what you think you can do and what the reality is. I was not willing to push my own [career] at the risk of jeopardizing what my husband wanted to do. She didn't agree with me. I said, 'Well, that's my opinion.' " It was clear to Henry that Rodham was on her way to marriage and looking for the role she could play in a partnership where her husband would be the candidate.

Rodham told Henry that Eleanor Roosevelt was her role model. "She said, 'Look at Eleanor Roosevelt!' Well, I had just finished reading Joseph Lash on that subject, so I said, 'That's right, but Eleanor never found her voice until after that marriage was over—until she didn't care about the marriage!' "

Before the start of her second year in Fayetteville, Rodham returned to the East Coast and talked with several friends about her future. Should she

make Bill Clinton and Arkansas the center of her life? Many of her friends
worried that she was selling short her own ambitions. They saw that it was
hard for her. It was obvious to them that she was not fooling herself about
what she would be getting into with Clinton. She understood his talents
and his flaws. He might not be faithful, but together they could be faithful
to their larger mission in life and achieve things beyond their individual
reach. And there was, at the same time, an old-fashioned infatuation that
went beyond shared goals. When Rodham visited Carolyn Ellis, her Yale
Law School classmate, who was now living in New York, Ellis encouraged
her not to let Arkansas be a factor in the decision. Ellis had grown up in
Mississippi and felt a southern kinship with Clinton and Arkansas. "I was
one of the big believers," she said. "I told her to go back. I said that
Arkansas wasn't Mars. I told her that to love somebody and not marry them
because of where they were living was the height of foolishness."

When Rodham arrived back in Fayetteville, Clinton was waiting for her
with a present and a proposal. The present was a house he had bought, a
little red-brown brick cottage at 930 California Street on the southwest
side of town. The proposal was that she live there with him as his wife.
Rodham accepted. In the days before the ceremony, she showed little
interest in the details, according to Ann Henry, and "was looking more at
life to come than at the wedding itself. What happened that day she didn't
want to worry about." In fact, she and her mother, who had come down
from Illinois, spent most of their time painting the cottage and putting in
bookshelves. They were quite willing to leave most of the wedding plans
to Henry, who was giving the reception at her house. The one concession
Rodham made was to go downtown and register a Danish modern pottery
style that guests could buy as wedding presents.

The wedding took place on October 11, 1975, in the living room of the
little cottage on California Street. Victor Nixon, the Methodist minister
Clinton had met during his first foray into the Ozarks with Carl Whillock,
performed the ceremony. It was a traditional Methodist service, using the
King James Version—"I, Hillary Rodham, take thee, Bill. . . ." Rodham wore
a Victorian dress with a high collar and long sleeves that she had selected
off the rack. The couple exchanged heirloom rings in the company of a
few family members and friends. Betsy Johnson Ebeling, Hillary's close
friend from Park Ridge, got to the wedding midway through the service
after relying on Hughie Rodham's vast underestimation of how long it
would take her and her husband to drive from Chicago to Fayetteville.
Roger Clinton, now a nineteen-year-old college student, stood as his big
brother's best man. Even though Bill and Roger were growing apart in
those days, not as close as the Rodham brothers, the choice of Roger as
best man signaled Clinton's yearning for a family bond. It also reflected a

characteristic of his adult life: he was a man with hundreds of close friends but no best friend. Virginia Dwire, widowed for a third time the year before and between husbands, listened to the wedding vows with a mixture of pride and dismay. That morning at the Fayetteville Holiday Inn, as Virginia was having breakfast in the coffee shop with her friend Marge Mitchell, Bill had dropped by to say hello and give her an early warning. "Hillary's keeping her own name," he had said, a pronouncement that brought tears to Virginia's eyes. It would take time for her to accept this assertive Yankee daughter-in-law.

After the private ceremony, the wedding party adjourned to the Henry house for a reception that more obviously represented "the gregariousness of Bill," as Ann Henry later described it. Hundreds of friends from all eras of Rodham and Clinton's lives mingled on the spacious back lawn on that gentle autumn Saturday night, drinking champagne and talking about Clinton's political future. "Everybody, even at the wedding, was talking about the next campaign," Henry recalled. "Everybody knew that he was going to run."

If Rodham and Clinton felt an urge to get out of town, they had made no honeymoon preparations. It was only because Dorothy Rodham noticed a special vacation package to Acapulco that they made a getaway later that year. For a politician whose idol was John F. Kennedy, there was a poetic touch to the trip. A generation earlier, Kennedy and his bride Jacqueline Bouvier had also gone to Acapulco after their marriage. It is safe to assume that he did not have anything resembling Clinton's peculiar entourage: at the hotel it was Bill and Hillary and Hugh and Dorothy and Hughie and Tony. Clinton took along a copy of the cultural anthropologist Ernest Becker's *The Denial of Death,* a book that regards the idea of death as "the mainspring of human activity—activity designed largely to avoid the fatality of death, to overcome it by denying in some way that it is the final destiny for man." Clinton also wrote thank-you notes to wedding guests.

THE old boys were not what they used to be, according to that year's progress report by Bob Reich, secretary of the Rhodes class of 1968. Approaching their thirtieth birthdays, they seemed anxious and compromised, looking inward for fulfillment, viewing the outside world with disillusionment or confusion.

Mike Shea was now a lawyer in Honolulu, "fighting the losing battle against middle age" by running marathons, but discouraged that he "could not find a political candidate to support at any level of government." Tom Reinecke, a scientist at the Naval Research Laboratory near Washington, D.C., lamented "the dullness and blandness of the Washington scene—

especially the great Washington suburbia." Bob McCallum, a lawyer in Atlanta, had learned to ski and was "trying to figure out more ways to avoid getting older." According to Reich, who occasionally interjected his own sensibilities into the reports of others, McCallum was "concerned about losing sight of the forest for the trees as his career progresses." Rick Stearns was dabbling in presidential politics again, "doing some consulting" for Arizona congressman Morris Udall. Strobe Talbott was married to Brooke Shearer and working in the Washington bureau of *Time,* where on occasion "he chases around after President Ford, in pursuit of further proof that the Peter Principle applies even—yea especially—at the highest levels of leadership in the Free World." Reich, married to Claire Dalton, the girl he had met at a Univ College audition, was also in Washington, working for the Justice Department, where he was "still filing indefensible briefs before the Supreme Court on behalf of our government."

And of his friend from Arkansas, Reich wrote: "From the political heartland of America comes news of Bill Clinton, who is now married to Hillary Rodham and living in a comfortable suburban bungalow.... He is at this moment spending most of his time running for Attorney General of the state, and he expects to be spending most of his time a year from now being Attorney General of his state." Although Clinton's ambitions seemed clearer than most, he, too, expressed a sense of uncertainty. "He says he is concerned that, in spite of his intense political involvements of late, he does not really have a good grasp of what is happening in this country, where we are going and what we can do to make it better. So like most other people he lives and works as best he can."

CLINTON took an unpaid leave of absence from the law school for the 1976 spring semester to begin his campaign for attorney general. In fund-raising letters to out-of-state supporters, he revealed the practical politics dictating his choice: "My opponent in the last election—with an eye over his shoulder—has changed his vote on a number of critical issues, including public jobs and the oil price rollback, and, therefore, is less vulnerable than he was." He made his formal campaign announcement on March 17 in the rotunda of the state Capitol, with Hillary Rodham at his side, calling the attorney general "the principal protector of the people" and promising to expand the consumer protection office and push for stronger antitrust laws.

Although Clinton thrived on the electoral process, he wanted an easier ride this time. He had lost an election, and it was always possible that he could lose again, which would greatly damage both his ego and his nascent career. He was relieved when one potentially difficult opponent, Beryl Anthony, decided not to enter the Democratic primary, but no sooner had

Anthony declined than George Jernigan, the secretary of state, entered the race. Clinton turned to Governor Pryor, who was Jernigan's political benefactor, and pleaded with him to change Jernigan's mind, but Pryor was unwilling to play that slate-making role. On filing day there were three candidates: Clinton, Jernigan, and Deputy Attorney General Clarence Cash. That might have been two more candidates than Clinton wanted, but on the positive side, all he had to do was to win the primary and he had the job—the Republican ticket lacked a candidate for attorney general.

The primary turned out to be a mismatch. Jernigan and Cash could claim experience in state government that Clinton lacked, but they had none of his abilities as a political networker. Clinton had found a way to reach virtually every courthouse in the state, and in those areas where he was less well known, the word was spread by former law students—another advantage of teaching at a public university that took scholars from every corner of the state who tended to return home to practice law. Newspaper ads listed the scores of former law students who declared that they could ease any doubts voters had about Clinton. Jernigan later acknowledged that when he was on the road, he would retire to his motel room at an early hour, turn on the television, and order room service. It is hard to imagine Clinton following a similar routine. He was too overloaded with energy and ambition to keep to himself for long. He was alert to danger and opportunity, plotting the next move, studying the landscape, looking for allies. Political campaigns tend to imitate the rhetoric of military campaigns, with battles and skirmishes and armies and war rooms, but in Clinton's case the war metaphor runs on a deeper psychological level. The campaign became the equivalent of the war that he never fought. It was a means of pardoning his past and making himself feel worthy. His speech at the party's kickoff rally in Russellville was like something out of the Civil War era: one can hear the strains of first Whitman and then Lincoln as Clinton strove to create the aura of a veteran in a noble cause.

"This morning as I drove up Highway 7 from Hot Springs in the breathtaking beauty of our Arkansas spring," Clinton said, "I thought of all the long roads so many of us have walked together, up and down this river valley—not just through the main towns, but also to the hamlets of which so many others are dimly aware—to Houston, Casa and Adona; Havana, Briggsville and Chickalah; Coal Hill, Hartman and Lamar; Hector, Appleton and Dover and more. I know them all because they are home to me, because of you. I believe there is an unbreakable bond between us and I have tried to keep faith with it.... Now I need you once more to fight another battle. If you will do it, it will be an exhilarating reaffirmation of the work to which I have given the fullest measure of my time and strength and spirit."

Some bonds were less unbreakable than others. When Clinton appeared before the state AFL-CIO convention in Hot Springs in April, the convention hall rustled with rumors that he considered organized labor support a mixed blessing and wanted to shed his image as a tool of the trade unions. In 1974, at that same convention, Clinton had received rousing standing ovations and an endorsement that helped him get through the congressional primary, and in his general election campaign against Hammerschmidt trade union contributions accounted for 25 percent of his treasury. But now, only two years later, he lost the endorsement by rejecting labor's litmus test: he refused to sign a petition to place an amendment on the November ballot calling for repeal of the state's right-to-work law. State labor leaders considered Clinton's action a gratuitous political ploy in which he used labor to revise his public image in a southern, agrarian state that lacked a strong union tradition. It was a characterization which Doug Wallace, who once again served as Clinton's press secretary, did not dispute. "There was a sense that labor was not that critical to the attorney general's race," Wallace said later. "And we had to move away from the 1974 image."

Clinton's strategic straight-arming of labor at the 1976 convention is important to an understanding of his political evolution. First, it shows that he was adjusting to what he perceived as the temper of the time. In one labor questionnaire in which Clinton explained his refusal to support repeal of the right-to-work law, he argued that "this is a bad time because our people generally are in a conservative mood." Second, it set a precedent that Clinton would follow throughout his career: to demonstrate independence, he would rebuke traditional allies, from labor leaders who wanted union shops to schoolteachers who opposed teacher testing to African American leaders who would not repudiate a rap singer's militant remarks. There was a certain fail-safe method to Clinton's rebukes: they were directed at groups who had fallen out of public favor.

That is not to say that Clinton's political positioning was one-dimensional. If he reacted to the public sentiment in 1976, he also studied it with intensity. Sensing a prevailing mood of disillusionment, he began writing out his thoughts on yellow legal pads, and eventually put them together in a series of speeches. At the graduation ceremonies for political science majors at Arkansas State University in Jonesboro on April 27, he defended the profession of politics and noted that he had "devoted twelve years to becoming well educated, well disciplined and well motivated in politics," only to arrive on the political scene at a time when "most people believe that politicians are either corruptible, weak or ineffective." He still believed that politics could be "honorable and important work," he said, but worried that the public was losing faith and interest because of the disconnected nature of modern American culture.

In one speech at a bicentennial celebration in Ashdown, he identified television as a villain. "More and more, especially in our cities, people withdraw in their nonwork hours, to the isolation of their TV rooms, where for hours on end they can pass the time without having to feel, without having to take the initiative to be creative and to improve their lives," Clinton said. The resentment that people expressed against their government, he reasoned, was "a reflection of the bitterness they felt about themselves and their inability to change." How to change things? Clinton offered regular town meetings as one solution. "Although they would almost surely be sparsely attended at first, they can be the beginnings of a new involvement."

On primary day, May 26, Clinton avoided a runoff by amassing 55.6 percent of the vote against Jernigan and Cash. He carried all but four Arkansas counties and trounced his opponents in the Third Congressional District. He thought he might take every ballot in Newton County, one of his favorite pockets along the Buffalo River in the Ozarks, where he had talked to almost every voter, but settled for nine out of ten, vowing that next time he would win over the seventy-three people who chose Jernigan and the eighty-one who preferred Cash.

As his thirtieth birthday approached, Clinton traveled to Hope and walked the paths of Rose Hill Cemetery to the grave of William Jefferson Blythe, the father he never knew. He thought to himself, he said later, about how he had passed another milestone that his father, killed at twenty-eight, never reached. That Blythe died at such an early age haunted Clinton and made him anxious, despite all that he had accomplished. He had his first elected post locked up, he was mixing with the richest and most powerful people in Arkansas, he was the golden boy of the state Democratic party, and yet he still felt "an urgent sense to do everything" he could in life as quickly as possible. He had grown up, subconsciously, on his father's timetable and felt that in some ways he was living for both of them. If he was not obsessed with death, mortality was never too far from his mind. He was "acutely aware that you never really know how much time you have."

Clinton paused at one point on his birthday to write a note to Betsey Wright in Washington. "All is madness here," he exclaimed to his friend from the Texas McGovern campaign. Without a general election of his own to worry about, he signed up to work for the presidential campaign of fellow southerner Jimmy Carter. He indicated to Wright that he could not arouse much animosity toward Gerald Ford, but felt freer to attack the Republicans "now that the biggest prick in Congress is on the ticket"—a reference, presumably, to Ford's runningmate, Senator Bob Dole of Kansas.

At a meeting in Atlanta with Tim Kraft, Carter's national coordinator, Clinton was invited to run the Texas operation again. But it made no sense for him to work outside Arkansas in the months before he would take over as attorney general. He declined the offer and stayed home, where as Carter's state chairman he could prepare for his new job and build more contacts for his political rise. Hillary Rodham felt no similar compunction to stay on in Arkansas. After a vacation with Clinton in Spain, she took a leave from the law school and left for Indianapolis, where she served as Carter's state field director through the November election.

The effort in Arkansas could not have been more different from what Clinton had gone through for McGovern in Texas four years earlier. Whereas in Texas, Clinton was constantly on the defensive, mediating factional disputes, trying to interpret a northern liberal to a southern conservative electorate, facing a hostile rebellion from the business establishment, this time he had a candidate who was from the same southern culture and who was on intimate terms with the key financial players in the state. Georgia, like Arkansas, was a major poultry center, which led to a strong connection between Carter and Don Tyson. Tyson raised tens of thousands of dollars for Carter within the poultry industry. Even more valuable were Carter's personal ties to Jackson Stephens, head of Stephens Inc., the largest investment bond firm outside Wall Street and the most politically potent financial enterprise in the state. Stephens, a conservative who often supported Republicans on the national level, had been Carter's classmate at the Naval Academy. When Carter visited Little Rock, he stayed at Stephens's house. Stephens's son-in-law, Craig Campbell, worked side by side with Clinton on the Carter campaign. And, of course, the biggest difference of all with the McGovern campaign was that Carter won, in Clinton's state and in the nation.

LITTLE ROCK was a new world for the new attorney general and his wife, as different from Fayetteville as Fayetteville had been from New Haven and Washington. Fayetteville was informal and collegial, more progressive than the rest of the state, a town of easy friendships. Little Rock was more formal, striving to be a little Dallas, with stratified social sets, a city of country clubs and debutante balls and corporate lunches. Rodham and Clinton found a small house in the historic Hillcrest neighborhood to the west of the state Capitol and cultivated another circle of friends in government and law. The transition was more dramatic for Rodham. She went from directing a legal aid clinic at a state university to practicing law at the Rose Law Firm, the oldest and most traditional legal house in Arkansas, with an impressive roster of deep-pocket corporate clients. Law school colleagues were reluctant to lose Rodham, whom they considered a future star ("Divorce him and stay here!" her colleague Mort Gitelman had said jokingly one day), but financial and political considerations ruled out a commuter marriage. As much as Clinton and Rodham enjoyed the relaxed style of living in Fayetteville, there were names to be made in Little Rock.

There was never any doubt that the attorney general's office was nothing more than a brief stop on the road for Clinton. When raising money for the election, his supporters promoted his grander intentions. H. T. Moore, who had worked on Clinton's congressional campaign as a law student in Fayetteville and then set up a law practice in the town of Paragould in northeast Arkansas, sent out fund-raising letters for the attorney general's race with the message that it would be smart to "get on board early." It was accepted that Clinton, when he arrived in Little Rock, was the governor-in-waiting.

The attorney general's job played to his strengths. He could position himself as a populist, give speeches, travel, expound on the state code, shape broad policy decisions, and he did not have to spend much time behind a desk making difficult decisions on appointments and programs that might antagonize people. He created the position of chief of staff and gave the job to a nonlawyer, Steve Smith. Lawyers who had worked for Clinton's predecessor, Jim Guy Tucker, detected a change in the office when Clinton arrived. Although Tucker, who left for a seat in Congress, was a political animal, Clinton was more of one. He seized on one of the populist issues of the day, utility rates, and created a division of energy conservation and rate advocacy with double the previous litigation staff. He challenged the telephone companies when they raised the pay-phone rates to a quarter and often appeared at hearings to cross-examine utility officials.

Clinton and Rodham now found even more networks open to them. They made the extended guest list for dinners at the Carter White House, and Clinton was summoned to Washington occasionally for national briefings. As the state Democrat most closely associated with Carter, he was given an informal role reviewing all federal patronage appointments from Arkansas. When a vacancy arose, Carter named Rodham to the board of the Legal Services Corporation, and she quickly became its chairwoman. Clinton developed a friendship with Eddie Sutton, coach of the University of Arkansas basketball team. They would talk about the similarities of their two professions: in politics and basketball alike, you battle all the time and you get immediate results.

All in all, Clinton seemed delighted with himself in his first elected job. He had his own office with his own staff and his own private quarters. On the inside door of his private bathroom, he put up a life-sized poster of fleshily abundant Dolly Parton in a skimpy outfit. Terry Kirkpatrick, who worked in the criminal division of the attorney general's office, spotted Clinton ambling down the hallway one night when she was staying late to write a brief. "He was just walking around, looking in all the offices, like he was surveying his fiefdom. He had a big grin on his face." After encountering Kirkpatrick, Clinton strolled into the office of another assistant, Joe Purvis, who had been his friend since they attended nursery school together in Hope. "He put his feet on my desk, which means they were on top of a pile of papers," Purvis later recalled. "He offered me a stick of gum. I think I said, 'What in the hell do you want?' It was like, say what you came to say and get the hell out. Bill said, 'I said, are you having fun? If you're not having fun, it becomes just work, and it's time to move on to something else.' "

Clinton was having fun, yet thinking about moving on to something else at the same time. Rising to the position of attorney general of Arkansas would not be enough to place an asterisk next to his name in the billion pages of the book of life, the goal he had set for himself in a letter to Denise Hyland long ago. Thoughts of premature death came back to him again three days before his thirty-first birthday. On August 16, 1977, he was in Fort Smith to deliver a speech when he heard that Elvis Presley had died. Elvis was more than a slick-haired crooner in the Clinton family culture. He was a cherished icon. Clinton's mother idolized Elvis and Bill, two southern charmers with sleepy eyes and soft voices and talents beyond their backwater roots. Clinton memorized the lyrics to many of Elvis's songs as a teenager, and even during the sixties, when the King seemed out of style, there was some part of Clinton that held on to that corner of his past. Elvis's death left Clinton transfixed. He visited the home of a longtime supporter, Marilyn Speed, after his speech, and did not want to leave and miss any of the television coverage. Terry Kirkpatrick, who traveled with him that day, remembered that the end of Elvis was all her boss would talk about: "All the way home on the plane he talked about it. He talked about the passing of an era. His youth. What a wasted life. It moved him deeply."

EARLY that fall of 1977, Clinton's chief of staff, Steve Smith, placed a call to a young political consultant in New York named Richard Morris who had been soliciting new clients around the country and had some novel ideas about how polls could be used to shape rhetorical arguments in campaigns. Morris flew down to Little Rock and met with Clinton at the attorney general's office. At that meeting, according to Morris, Clinton said that he had a difficult decision to make about whether to run for governor or senator. He said he could "walk into the governor's office" if he wanted to, but that he would rather be a senator and wanted to run for the seat being vacated by John L. McClellan. Part of it had to do with length of tenure, he told Morris: governors had to run every two years while senators were safe for six. He also felt there were more challenges in Washington. But the problem was that he was not sure he could win the Senate primary. Two Democratic congressmen, Jim Guy Tucker and Ray Thornton, were already in the race, and it seemed likely that Governor Pryor would join them.

Morris agreed to do a poll for Clinton on the two races. The results showed that Clinton could win the governorship with no problem, and he "could probably win" the Senate race, though it would be an iffy proposition, Morris said. The problem was not Pryor. The poll found that Pryor was likable but not electable and would fade in a tough primary "against a young charismatic candidate." This was contrary to the conventional wisdom of the time, which held that Pryor was the strongest candidate. Clinton was impressed by Morris's conclusions. He felt the same way, he said. But he was still nervous about the Senate race. He said that he would probably run for governor, depending on what Pryor decided.

A few weeks later, Pryor invited Clinton to ride with him from the state Capitol to Hot Springs, where the governor was to deliver a speech. Clinton had been seeking a private meeting where the two men could talk about their political futures, and Pryor decided that now was the time. They sat in the back seat of the state-owned Lincoln and chatted all the way down and back, and then went on to the Governor's Mansion and talked some more. At the start of the discussion, Pryor could not tell whether Clinton wanted to run for senator or governor. He made the first move. "I told him that I was planning to run for the Senate," Pryor recalled. He said he hoped Clinton would not join the already crowded field. Clinton "opened up" to Pryor as the conversation progressed. With Bumpers and Pryor both ahead of him, he said, he feared that he might find his career stymied.

"Bill," Pryor told Clinton, seeking to reassure him, "you could run for governor and be elected and serve longer than Orval Faubus," who was in the Governor's Mansion for six two-year terms from 1955 to 1967. "You could break Faubus's record." For the rest of the conversation, Clinton asked Pryor questions about what it was like to be governor. He did not say what was really on his mind: he would settle for governor, this time, but he had no interest in breaking Faubus's record in Little Rock.

From the moment Clinton announced for governor, he began running two campaigns at once. In public, he was the candidate for governor, facing token opposition in the Democratic primary against four relative unknowns. He easily garnered support from labor and business, and was hailed as "the only truly distinguished figure" in the field by the *Arkansas Gazette,* though the editorial writers there occasionally upbraided him for being too cautious. His opponents assaulted him for using the attorney general's office "as a political tool," for "never working a day in his life," and for having an assertive wife who would not use his last name. Internal campaign news summaries frequently noted that "the Name business," as they called it, had surfaced in stories about Hillary Rodham. One candidate, Monroe Schwarzlose, an old turkey farmer, harrumphed about Rodham's law degree. "We've had enough lawyers in the Governor's Mansion," he said. "One is enough. Two would be too much." Another candidate, Frank Lady, blasted Rodham, saying there was an inherent conflict of interest between her membership in the Rose Law Firm and her position as the governor's wife.

Clinton reacted to these attacks with varying degrees of righteous anger. He exploded once at Lady, the candidate of the religious right, saying that Lady's "religious convictions tell him it is wrong to lie, but he does it anyway." Another time he offered an emotional defense of Rodham. "If people knew how old-fashioned she was in every conceivable way," he said. "She's just a hard-working, no-nonsense, no frills, intelligent girl who had done well, who doesn't see any sense to extramarital sex, who doesn't care much for drink, who's witty and sharp without being a stick in the mud. She's just great."

But in private, Clinton worried little about his primary, which his polls showed he had clinched. He busied himself with another political role as back room strategist for Pryor's race in the Senate primary. He confided to a few friends and advisers that he wanted Pryor to defeat Jim Guy Tucker, whom he viewed as his main competition as the rising star of state Democratic politics. During Morris's frequent trips to Little Rock in the spring of 1978, he later recalled, he and Clinton would spend a few minutes talking about the governor's race, then spend hours plotting how Pryor could beat Tucker. Morris noticed something extraordinary about their discussions. They talked not like consultant and client, but like two consultants. He came to regard Clinton as "a highly sophisticated colleague" in the profession.

As Morris had predicted in his early polls for Clinton, Pryor proved to be vulnerable. On the night that Clinton swept the gubernatorial primary with nearly 60 percent of the vote, Pryor barely survived the Senate primary and was forced into a runoff with Tucker. Clinton, according to Morris, was becoming "increasingly frustrated with the Pryor campaign." He complained that Pryor was "being too nice a guy and wasn't aggressive enough in the campaign." For the two-week runoff, Tucker began a media campaign based on the theme that Pryor might be a nice guy to go fishing with, but he was not an effective politician who could solve the state's and nation's pressing problems. Clinton, the back room political consultant, spent hours devising a response that would show Pryor's strength. When the firemen in Arkansas had threatened to strike, Pryor had said that he would call out the National Guard to replace them. He had acted boldly and decisively in a situation where another governor in another state had not and some fires had burned out of control. They could make an ad showing David Pryor standing tall. Clinton wrote out the ad copy and gave it to Dick Morris, who revised it and took it to Pryor, who authorized it.

Pryor felt uneasy about this outside consultant Clinton had brought into the campaign. He had rejected Morris's services earlier, and was only using him now because Clinton insisted on it. Pryor's wife, Barbara, found Morris especially disagreeable and banned him from the Governor's Mansion. She thought he was too negative, too much of an operator. Clinton had no such qualms, at least not during the election season. His theory of politics, he told Morris, was that you do what you have to do to get elected. Pryor won the runoff.

Clinton still had a general election to win. The Republicans had put up an opponent this time, unlike the attorney general's race two years earlier. But it was not an even match. Lynn Lowe, a GOP official and farmer from Texarkana, was underfinanced and unknown. So confident were Clinton and his top campaign aides, Steve Smith and Rudy Moore, that they began preparing for his first year as governor. They were determined, Moore said, to "define and set the agenda for the legislature in 1979."

WITH Bill Clinton it is often tempting, but usually misleading, to try to separate the good from the bad, to say that the part of him that is indecisive, too eager to please and prone to deception, is more revealing of the inner man than the part of him that is indefatigable, intelligent, empathetic, and self-deprecating. They co-exist. There is a similar balance to his life's progression. In his worst times, one can see the will to recover and the promise of redemption. In his best times, one can see the seeds of disaster.

The final months of 1978 reflected the second of those two conditions. He was on the edge of glory. At the early age of thirty-two, he was the governor-apparent of Arkansas. He had a determined wife and a finely tuned political machine and an army of friends. He had come further, faster in the political world than any member of his generation. And yet it was in those promising days of 1978 that Clinton perplexed his aides by hanging out in racy nightclubs surrounded by admiring women. It was then that he and Rodham signed the first papers in a land deal along the White River in the Ozark hills. It was then that Rodham entered the risky livestock commodities trading market and made a huge profit in a way that would later be questioned. And it was then that Clinton was confronted with accusations that he had dodged the draft.

Of those events, only the draft issue was played out in public at the time. The others seemed of less consequence then. Not that the draft story loomed particularly large either. It was not so much a crisis as a two-day problem, raised and dealt with and quickly forgotten—but not forever gone. In the final week of the campaign, Billy G. Geren, a retired lieutenant colonel in the Air Force, held a news conference on the steps of the state Capitol in which he accused Clinton of being a draft dodger. Geren charged that Clinton had received a draft deferment in 1969 by agreeing to join the University of Arkansas ROTC, but had then reneged on his promise and returned to Oxford University. The lieutenant colonel, who was accompanied to the press conference by a top aide to the Republican gubernatorial candidate, laid out the case. Clinton easily rebuffed the charge by offering a fuzzy response. He claimed that he had never received a draft deferment because he had canceled the agreement with the ROTC and reentered the draft pool before a deferment could be granted. When reporters asked Colonel Eugene Holmes, the former head of the ROTC program, about the incident, Holmes said that he could not remember the Clinton case. With no documents to substantiate either side, the issue disappeared.

Geren, who had served on the University of Arkansas ROTC staff from 1972 to 1976, was closer to making a strong case than Clinton or the press realized. He had heard about the letter that Clinton had written to Colonel Holmes from Oxford in which Clinton thanked the officer for saving him from the draft. But Geren could not find a copy of the letter. Ed Howard, who had been the drill sergeant on the ROTC staff and had left the service to sell real estate in Malvern, recalled that Geren called him at home late one night shortly before the press conference. "He told me they were looking into Clinton dodging the draft," Howard said. "He knew that I knew about the Clinton file and the letter. He was trying to get me to help them. He wanted me to tell the press that I knew about it."

Howard refused. He was a Clinton supporter by then and did not think the draft should be an issue in the governor's race. But the day after the press conference, when he read in the papers that Clinton denied ever receiving a draft deferment, Howard felt the same way that he had back in 1969 when he first heard about the letter to Colonel Holmes. "I was disappointed with Bill," he recalled. "And angry—again."

.   .   .

PROMISE, pain, an augury of future trouble—they were all there again on election night in 1978.

The promise was evident in Clinton's overwhelming win. He swept the state with 63 percent of the vote and became the youngest governor in the United States in four decades.

The pain came five minutes before the first evening news report on the election. Jim Ranchino, Clinton's friend and in-state pollster, who also served as an analyst for KATV in Little Rock, was exuberant that his numbers showed young Clinton scoring a resounding victory. An ebullient bear of a man, Ranchino had been slowed by what he thought was the flu that day but was eager to get on the air so that he could discuss the rise of Arkansas' bright new star. He never made it to the microphone. As he was walking up the stairs toward his seat in the studio, he was felled by a massive, fatal heart attack.

The omen of future trouble came in a congratulatory note from President Carter, who wrote to Governor-elect Clinton: "You and I will succeed in meeting the goals for our country by working closely together to serve those whom we represent."

CHAPTER TWENTY

GREAT
EXPECTATIONS

BILL CLINTON WAS ensconced in the back seat of a limousine transporting him in unaccustomed luxury through the ice-slicked streets of Little Rock. At his side was Dave Matter, an old friend from his undergraduate days at Georgetown. Matter had been the campaign manager for Clinton's first tough defeat, when he lost the student council presidency because his classmates had grown bored with his smooth patter and his ingratiating manner with the school establishment. Now, on this January night twelve years later, the two were reunited for Clinton's inauguration as the youngest governor in the United States since before World War II. As they rode from one event to the next, Clinton turned to Matter and professed surprise at what had become of his life. "Matter," he said, in his soft, hoarse voice. "Did you ever think it would come to this?" For Matter, who had been invited into the limousine in one of Clinton's characteristic share-the-moment impulses, as for scores of other friends from various chapters of Clinton's life who converged on Little Rock for his ascension to the governorship, the answer was . . . yes, of course. Yes, of course, he would be Governor Clinton or Senator Clinton some day. And yes, of course, that might only be the beginning.

This first inaugural, for the friends of Clinton and Rodham, had the aura of a generational rite. From all sections of the country they made the pilgrimage to gray, freezing Little Rock. They were there to witness the coming of age of one of their own, the first in their class to reach such prominence on the political stage. Matter and Tommy Caplan represented the Georgetown crowd. Betsey Wright, who had worked with Clinton and Rodham during the McGovern campaign in Texas, came out from Washington. Fred Kammer and Alston Johnson, who first encountered Clinton when they were pro-civil rights senators at Boys Nation, arrived from Louisiana. From the Yale Law School group came Carolyn Ellis from Mississippi and Steven Cohen and Greg Craig from Washington. Carolyn Yeldell, Clinton's high school friend, returned from Indiana to sing Verdi and Mozart arias in the Capitol rotunda. She was Carolyn Staley now, married to an art teacher, and ready to move home, believing that "this was a good time for the family to be aligned with the Clinton administration."

Along with these generational cohorts, the inaugural congregation included a colorful mix of elders. Don Tyson strutted down to the state capital to host a pre-inaugural bash at the Camelot Hotel. From Washington came Sara Ehrman, Rodham's landlady during her stay in Washington for the Watergate inquiry, who five years earlier had warned that moving to provincial Arkansas would be a grave mistake. Arriving by private jet from Norton, Virginia, were Carl McAfee and Charlie Daniels, the gung-ho lawyer and patriotic plumber who had encountered Clinton during his journey to Moscow eight years earlier when they were seeking the release of American POWs from North Vietnam. McAfee kept teasing Rodham about not changing her name. Daniels, a University of Tennessee football fanatic who owned an orange limousine that he would ride to Volunteer football games, showed up at the Diamonds and Denim ball in his bright orange tuxedo, an outfit that delighted Clinton's mother.

All of them traveled to Little Rock with the notion that the rise of Clinton and Rodham transcended that time and place. At a party the night before the swearing in, Clinton strolled up to Steven Cohen and asked, "Well, what do you think?" Cohen was an idealist, going back to his days in the antiwar movement and the McCarthy campaign, but his idealism dissolved into disillusionment when people he believed in let him down or when he thought the country was losing its way. He came to Little Rock in a dispirited mood, worn down by the controversies surrounding his job in the human rights office at the State Department and by the increasing disarray of the Carter administration. But none of that weary cynicism seemed evident in Clinton's Arkansas. "I'll tell you what I think," Cohen said to Clinton. "I feel two emotions in this room that I hadn't experienced in a long time—pride and hope."

The next day, Cohen and Greg Craig, now an attorney at the Williams & Connally law firm in Washington, stood side by side listening to Clinton's inaugural address, and were transfixed by the rhythmic cadence with which he laid out the credo of their generation. "For as long as I can remember," Clinton said, "I have believed passionately in the cause of equal opportunity, and I will do what I can to advance it. For as long as I can remember, I have deplored the arbitrary and abusive exercise of power by those in authority, and I will do what I can to prevent it. . . . For as long as I can remember, I have loved the land, air and water of Arkansas, and I will do what I can to protect them. For as long as I can remember, I have wished to ease the burdens of life for those who, through no fault of their own, are old or weak or needy, and I will try to help them." Cohen then heard his own words come back to him. "Last evening, after our Gala, a friend of mine from Washington who travels this country and speaks to many groups in many places, said that he felt in that crowd two emotions which are not found in other places today. Pride and hope. Pride and hope. With those two qualities, we can go a long way. . . ." At that moment, it seemed to Cohen and Craig that their old Yale Law friend deserved his status as a generational leader.

Craig returned to Washington "absolutely euphoric." Later he would say that he could not think of a political event that had excited him more than Clinton's first inaugural.

THE young governor arrived with an ambitious agenda. An in-house study showed that he had made fifty-three specific promises before he took office. Two promises were unmet on the first day. He was so eager to get going that he promised that he would have a budget summary book on the desk of every legislator for the opening day of the General Assembly and that he would have all his bills drafted by that day as well. Both were late. When the budget summary did appear, it was so thick that some legislators joked they would strain their backs lifting it. Clinton assumed, because of his overwhelming numerical victory in the election, that he had a mandate to transform the state. Creating new departments in energy and economic development, revamping the rural health care system, reorganizing school districts, reordering the education system—he wanted to do it all in two years. His state of the state address was so detailed that it contained a section on the length of time landlords could hold security deposits from renters. Old-line legislators looked at the legislative package with glazed eyes.

Clinton and his top assistants bubbled over with ideas that they had been collecting from progressive policy thinkers around the nation, from preschool programs to solar energy projects. It was what one adviser called "a pent-up idealistic agenda." But the young governor was also conscious of the need to be perceived as a cautious spender. Most of the programs were crammed into the first budget as demonstration projects,with little money behind them. With his new fascination for polls, Clinton asked Dick Morris to survey Arkansas voters on the dozens of ideas that he had put into the budget, and then rank them in popularity and construct an overall theme. Morris conducted the poll, but could not find a theme. "He was left with a program that was thoroughly admirable but indescribable," Morris recalled. "There was a bit of everything. Like a kid in a candy store, he wanted to do it all."

Along with his diffuse experimentation, Clinton chose one larger issue to define himself: roads. He used as his impetus a legislative report that had declared the state highway system a disaster in need of $3.3 billion worth of improvements. Better roads were essential to the economic future of the state, Clinton said. In private, he also expressed the belief that a major roads program would show that this Yale Law grad and Oxonian understood rural Arkansas. Before presenting his highway proposal, Clinton directed Morris to conduct polls on the acceptability of various taxes to fund it. His revenue specialists told him that the quickest way to raise large sums was to increase the annual car license fees. His program people told him that the largest burden of the road improvements should be placed on eighteen-wheel trucks, which were causing most of the road damage. Morris's polling showed that 53 percent of the people would support an increase in the car license fees to build better roads, while 37 percent opposed such a tax. Clinton thought the poll meant a majority would support him if he raised the fees.

The administration drafted a proposal that placed most of the tax burden on heavy trucks but also raised car license fees, basing the rate of increase on the value of each car. The plan immediately encountered intense opposition from two powerful lobbies, the trucking industry and the poultry industry, a major user of trucks, both already upset at Clinton for backing away from a campaign promise to increase the weight allowed for trucks driving in Arkansas from 73,000 pounds to 80,000 pounds, the weight allowed in several neighboring states. Several trucking firms threatened to leave Arkansas. The poultry industry, which had its operatives as far inside the legislative process as possible—its paid lobbyists were elected members of the legislature—stymied the administration bill in committee. Determined to find middle ground, Clinton signed off on a compromise that angered all sides. The major tax burden was shifted from trucks to cars and pickups, but the trucking and poultry industries remained upset that they were hit with higher taxes and hammered at Clinton for the rest of the term trying to get him to push for repeal. Meanwhile, the car license increase was altered so that it was based on weight rather than value. Owners of new, smaller, lighter, and more expensive cars would be asked to pay less to renew their licenses than poorer citizens who drove around in heavy old clunkers. This was not a politically wise concept in a rural state full of jalopies and old pickups.

ON his first official trip in office, Clinton took a chartered flight to northwest Arkansas for a series of appearances in Fort Smith, the conservative military town, where most voters regarded him skeptically. When he arrived at the terminal, he turned to his travel aide, Randy White, and asked,

"What are we doing? What's the story?" White, who had secured a job in the governor's office after serving as student manager for the Arkansas basketball team coached by Clinton's friend, Eddie Sutton, pulled out a schedule. "I know the schedule," Clinton snapped. "Where's the briefing book?" White was at a loss. There was no briefing book. Clinton's face reddened and he slammed his fist on the counter. "God damn it!" he fumed. "When we go somewhere, you've got to know who we're meeting with and what's going on and what grants the county is getting!"

As Clinton "pounded like crazy" on the counter, White thought to himself, "Oh, shit!" This was the first test of his job and he had flubbed it. Clinton wanted to know everything and White knew next to nothing. Terrified, he found a telephone and placed a call back to his boss, Rudy Moore, Jr., the aide in charge of day-to-day administration of the governor's office. Calm down, Moore told him: things would get straightened out, and in any case the mess-up was not the travel aide's responsibility. White feared that Clinton would remain mad at him all day, but as soon as they left the air terminal, the anger vanished, replaced by a compulsive urge to mingle and tell stories. "Whenever we'd pass something, he'd have a story," White recalled later. "We'd drive through a precinct and he'd say, 'Oh, I lost this box 48 to 175, and then go on to explain why he'd lost it. Then we'd pass by a store and he'd say, 'Oh, stop here' for Miss so-and-so, 'I've known her forever.' He'd go in and drink a Coke and stay. It went all day like this. Good Lord, we were off schedule. Way off." Finally, late in the day, White called back to Little Rock again. Now Moore was mad. Several questions had come up back at the office that needed Clinton's consideration, Moore said. In the future, they should never go that long without checking in. It was White's first trip, and he "caught it from both ends."

Randy White's predicament on that initial trip to Fort Smith came to symbolize much of the frustration and confusion in the governor's office during Clinton's first term. Catching it from both ends was all too common for a staff whose boss was both extremely demanding and exceedingly lax, and who could seem, at the same time, obsessively in touch and yet remote. To the outside world, it often appeared that the governor's aides during that first term were getting him in trouble and letting him down. But the staff's mistakes in large measure reflected Clinton's loose, free-ranging management style, his conflicted personality, and his urge to be all things to all people.

A few months into his tenure, Clinton gained a reputation that seemed contrary to his political nature. Legislators, lobbyists, and citizens began voicing complaints that they were having difficulty getting through to him. How could this be? How could this obsessively gregarious politician suddenly become isolated? Most attributed it to an overprotective staff. At

Clinton's urging, visitors from other parts of the state showed up at the governor's office only to be turned away by aides. Powerful state senators fumed at a letter in which Rudy Moore said that they should see him if they wanted to deal with Clinton. Labor leader J. Bill Becker groused that Clinton was "insulated by staff people." But most of these problems resulted from a classic Clinton paradox: his eagerness to please people often ended up angering them; wanting to be open, he ended up appearing closed.

"Clinton was so friendly, people would come up to him on the road and say, 'I've got a problem and I need to talk to you,' and Clinton would say, 'Well, if you'll be in Little Rock next week, come by my office'—and they would," Moore recalled. "Then he wouldn't be in or he'd have someone else scheduled or he'd tell us to handle it. So expectations would be raised and people would be disappointed." The worse the problem became, the harder it was for Clinton to appreciate that he was the principal cause of it. His solution was to beef up his scheduling staff and complain more about his overcrowded schedule. Not long after Randy White was moved to scheduling, he received a note from Clinton saying that too many people were getting through the system to see him.

"I have no time to be governor!" Clinton lamented. White responded with a two-page memo that began: "Grab this week's schedule and let's review it." Every person on the schedule, White noted, was someone with whom Clinton had agreed to meet. "Anyone who could get through and whine to him, he'd let them through," White said later. "And then he'd blame it on me."

One reason many people could not reach Clinton at the governor's office was that he was not there when he was expected to be. His tendency to straggle and talk to anyone who wanted to talk to him had reached the point by 1979 that his staff operated by what they called Clinton time. They would often lie to him about when he was due somewhere, giving him an earlier time than the actual one, hoping that might keep him on schedule, but by the end of a day he could still be an hour or two behind. Some appointments were more important not to be late for than others, but Clinton was egalitarian in that regard: he could be as late for a meeting with high-rolling corporate executives as for one with poor farmers. Once, when the state's powerful poultry barons were upset about a tax proposal, Clinton's staff arranged a summit meeting in the governor's office. The hostility that they brought with them to Little Rock only increased once they reached Room 250 and were asked to wait in the lobby until Clinton returned. He finally arrived two hours late.

After the tense meeting, Clinton raged at his scheduling staff, blaming them for the disaster. The session with the poultry executives, he grumbled, was not on his schedule. "You back off!" Rudy Moore told him. "You're wrong. You were late!"

The habit was never broken, but eventually Clinton's aides learned to accept it with gallows humor. Randy White noticed an advertisement in the newspaper that seemed especially aimed at Clinton. "Will you commit larceny today?" the ad asked. "You could be stealing from someone important to you. If you steal time, someone else suffers." Readers were urged to tear out the ad and "hand it to a thief." White gave it to Clinton, who laughed. On another occasion the governor's receptionist sent a note to Rudy Moore warning him that an uninvited and potentially dangerous visitor was in the building. "Security downstairs holding guy in their office who said he was sent here to kill the Gov.," her note read. Moore took the note and sent it on to White in scheduling with this deadpan notation: "RW—see if you can work him in."

HE was thirty-three, and his nicknames had regressed from the juvenile to the infantile. Where during his Fayetteville days he was sometimes referred to as "Wonder Boy" or "the Boy," he now occasionally answered to "Baby" —as in "Baby's getting too big for his britches," or "Maybe Baby's growing up!"—a monicker given to him by Frances Walls, a longtime Democratic activist in northeast Arkansas. Even a friendly cartoonist portrayed the child governor riding around on a tricycle or peering from the turret of a tank. "It was not easy for a boy to lead in such a conservative state," reflected Ray Smith, Jr., a Hot Springs legislator who had counseled young Clinton on politics. "To be led by a child, well, Alexander made it, but Jesus didn't."

Clinton had no chief of staff. Three executive assistants held nearly equal status. They were young, liberal, and hirsute, and became known as "the Three Beards," the leaders of the Children's Crusade. Moore, the oldest at thirty-five, took the lead in politics and legislative matters. Steve Smith, who was Moore's former seatmate in the Arkansas legislature, supervised the governor's dealings with state agencies and economic development. Smith had entered the legislature at the dawn of the seventies at the minimum age of twenty-one. Now, after pursuing a doctoral degree in communications and working for Clinton in the attorney general's office, he was a veteran of state political wars and still only twenty-nine. The third beard belonged to John Danner, thirty-one, who oversaw state-federal relations and long-term planning and took delight in thrashing about in the vast ocean of policy ideas. At his most enthusiastic, Danner, a Berkeley Law School graduate, would march into a meeting with a roll of butcher paper, unroll thirty feet, tape it to a wall, and swiftly write out ten new ideas for the Clinton administration before anyone else in the room could think of one. He and his wife, Nancy Pietrafesa, who also worked in the governor's office and went by the nickname "Peach," had met Clinton and Rodham during the Yale years and were two out-of-state friends who heeded the generational call and moved to Little Rock.

Of the triumvirate, only Rudy Moore survived the two years. Danner and Pietrafesa's stay in Arkansas was short and stressful, marked by constant friction with other aides. When a staff revolt made it obvious that Clinton had to ask them to leave, he could not bring himself to fire them personally and asked Rudy Moore to do it. Smith also left before the term was over, and, like Danner, he left in a way that revealed as much about Clinton as about himself.

As Clinton came to power, one of the high-profile public issues was the clear-cutting of forests by the giant timber companies, especially Weyerhaeuser, a Pacific Coast–based firm that had arrived in Arkansas earlier in the decade and was leveling forest tracts in the Ouachita Mountains and along the route from Little Rock to Clinton's home town of Hot Springs. Aside from the scientific debate about whether clear-cutting (in which acres of timberland were bulldozed at one time) harmed the wildlife and created pollution runoff problems, the practice enraged citizens driving along scenic highways. Clinton himself, who had grown up surrounded by a national park, was enraged. On a helicopter tour of the clear-cutting acreage near Hot Springs, he was told by a timber lobbyist that clear-cutting looked worse than it was. "Some of the wonderful things in this world don't look good at first—like the birth of a baby," the lobbyist said. "Yeah," Clinton responded, "but at least babies are only born one at a time."

The struggle around the leveling of the forests of Arkansas was part of a larger and longer one in the economic development in the South. Clinton and Smith had studied the works of C. Vann Woodward and other historians who had chronicled the complicated and sometimes tragic effects of industrialization on an agrarian society. Starting in the 1870s, after the northern timber barons had virtually wiped out the hardwood stands of the Great Lakes region, they were lured south into states like Arkansas that were so eager for what they viewed as capitalist progress that they offered cheap land, cheap labor, and little regulation. The timber companies slashed through the state with no regard for the environment, leveling soft pine forests, setting up sawmills, then abandoning the sites as soon as the resources were exhausted. By 1920, the cut-and-run tactics of the timber companies had denuded Arkansas: more than 20 million acres had been cut, leaving less than 2 million acres of virgin forest. Although Arkansas in later years boasted of prudent forest management, the new clear-cutting practices raised fears of a return to the rapacious timber baron days of old. With these concerns in mind, Clinton established a timber management task force and assigned Smith to serve as staff director.

The task force held thirteen hearings around the state in which they listened to public comments on the issue and examined the effects of clear-cutting from various scientific perspectives. To show the depth of his commitment, Clinton traveled to Nashville, a county seat deep in southwest Arkansas timber country, to chair the first public hearing. As the hearings progressed, the debate became polarized. Smith expressed outrage at the clear-cutting practices, charging that Weyerhaeuser had created the need for the task force because of its "public insensitivity and environmental disregard." In private meetings of the Arkansas Forestry Association, other timber companies chastised Weyerhaeuser for embarrassing the entire industry by clear-cutting along roadways where the practice was so obvious to passers-by. The message was: If you're going to clear-cut, at least do it where the public cannot see it so easily. But most of the industry's wrath was directed at Smith and the governor's office. John Ed Anthony, the Forestry Association president and the cousin of Democratic congressman Beryl Anthony, called the hearings "zoos" and accused Clinton of "releasing crazies" on the industry.

Anthony began a letterwriting campaign in which he charged that Clinton was no friend of the forest industry and claimed that the governor's aim was to impose state control of private lands and threaten the livelihood of forty thousand Arkansas voters who made their living in the timber and forest products business. By the end of the hearing process, Clinton was feeling intense political heat. "Every log driver, every sawmill hand, every mill worker was mad at Clinton," Anthony recalled, and sharing that anger were state legislators from the timber counties who were hearing from the large companies as well as the 240,000 land owners who held timber rights on their property. Clinton arranged a meeting in Pine Bluff with Anthony and the executive committee of the Forestry Association. Without telling Smith, he brought along a draft copy of the task force report, which was critical of the industry and argued that the governor could ban clear-cutting by executive fiat.

Clinton complained to the timber executives that he was being lied about. They were exaggerating his position, he said. He had not made any decisions on the issue and should not be held responsible for speculation in the press or by staff members on what he would do. "Every time I go south of Pine Bluff I run into a buzzsaw of criticism," he said, according to Anthony. "I don't think it's fair and I want it stopped." When he returned to Little Rock, Clinton ordered several changes, softening the criticisms of the timber industry and removing the threat of mandatory state action against clear-cutters, calling instead for voluntary changes in industry practices. It was also around that time that he appointed a new state forestry commissioner recommended by the timber lobby. Smith responded by submitting his resignation from the task force. He tried to resign from Clinton's staff altogether, realizing that his longtime friend now considered him a political liability and that he was "not going to be made a knight of the realm." Rudy Moore persuaded him to stay on for several more months, but his role and enthusiasm were greatly diminished, and Smith eventually left Little Rock to join another departed member of the governor's staff in the operation of a small bank in Madison County in the hills of northwest Arkansas.

Smith had mostly loved working for Clinton. And yet, in the end, Clinton turned from him when his political survival was endangered. "Bill Clinton pulled the rug out from under Steve Smith," said Rudy Moore. "Steve thought that he was doing exactly what Bill Clinton wanted. Be a lightning rod. He was willing to accept that role. But Bill then backed away. He felt Steve had cost him politically. That's when Steve decided to hang it up. He felt he had had enough of doing what he was supposed to do and get chewed on."

The larger lesson involved fundamentally different perceptions of how politics worked. Smith believed in the straight dialectic. "You win, you do what you can for your side, you screw the opposition. Then if the other side wins, you take what's coming." Whereas Clinton's philosophy, as Smith determined it, was "that you can reach a satisfactory compromise of polar positions that is superior to either side. I see that as more often pissing off both sides."

Clinton's conciliatory efforts in the timber controversy were of little avail. In the end, he did end up "pissing off both sides." It was a case where he seemed to have difficulty appreciating who would be in his corner when he needed them. The industry would work hard to defeat him in the next election and maintained a distrustful relationship with him in later years, even though, as Anthony later boasted, "Bill never really bothered us again."

In his formative years, Clinton was rarely around anyone who thought that getting rich was an important goal. Eldridge Cassidy, his beloved pappaw, the town iceman and grocer from Hope, was a generous soul who had little money and would just as soon give away what he had. His mother Virginia wanted only enough to free herself from the chains of an abusive marriage and to place two-dollar bets at the racetrack. Although romanticized accounts of his childhood in Hope and Hot Springs would sometimes make it seem that Bill Clinton rose from poverty, his family was middle class and comfortable by rural Arkansas standards. As a teenager he played golf at a country club and swam at the country club pool and drove his own car. He was never poor enough to be consumed by envy for the wealthy boys and girls around him. If he felt any impulse to prevail over the social elite, he saw the political realm, not the business world, as his arena.

From his high school years through his rise to the governorship, Clinton had steered clear of jobs in private industry and never held a post that paid more than $35,000 a year. He always worked but seemed to have little money. Travel aides remember how he would bum quarters from them on the road to buy soft drinks or a newspaper. Though he wanted to look sharp enough to impress women, he seldom took the trouble to buy new clothes and was known for wearing pants that were an inch too short and an inch too tight. When his brother won a magazine subscription contest in junior high, Clinton boasted only half-jokingly that at least someone in the family had practical abilities. He often told friends that he only wanted enough money in life to buy books, see the world, go to movies, and go out to eat. To be sure, he was usually the last one at the table to pick up a check. Rudy Moore often told the story of accompanying Clinton to the Democratic National Committee mini-convention in Memphis in 1978. Clinton, in his usual position at the center of a conversational huddle in a restaurant lounge, ended up getting the tab. Looking at the ninety-dollar check for a group of eight or ten, he smiled and said, "Gol, this ain't so bad!"

"Well, um," Moore felt obliged to note to his boss, "that's just the bar bill."

That is not to say that Clinton viewed money as the root of evil or disdained moneymakers. His attitude was more neutral than hostile. In fact, when he could see a direct correlation between money and political success, something that truly motivated him, he excelled at going after the cash. Whether it was sending fund-raising letters to the thousands of friends and contacts whose names found their way into his index card files, or spending an hour trying to charm a donation out of a truck company owner, or taking out a large personal loan from a friendly country banker, he had no qualms about asking for money, as long as it was for politics.

It has become an accepted description of the Clinton-Rodham partnership that Clinton was a zigzag and Rodham a straight line; he deceptive and she blunt; he confused and she clearheaded. These characterizations hold up in many areas, but not in all. When it came to money, Clinton's philosophy seemed clear and his actions tended to follow his philosophy. It was Rodham, here, whose attitudes shifted and whose actions followed a sinuous path.

Rodham's father taught her how to read the stock tables. The family lived in a suburb populated by the upwardly mobile middle class, where money was considered a measure of virtue, gained through hard work and ingenuity. Then, in college, she came to reject what she described in her Wellesley commencement address as "our prevailing, acquisitive and competitive corporate life." At Yale Law School, she turned down opportunities to clerk at high-salaried East Coast firms and again avoided that career path after receiving her law degree, choosing instead the nonprofit Children's Defense Fund, the Watergate impeachment inquiry staff, and a faculty position at the University of Arkansas Law School. As her boyfriend's and then husband's political adviser, she often warned him away from taking what she considered tainted money from lobbyists and discouraged him from incurring heavy debts. To some of Clinton's Arkansas friends, she seemed prudent if not parsimonious.

Then, when Rodham and Clinton reached Little Rock for the start of Clinton's career in government, Rodham seemed to have little difficulty embracing the acquisitive and competitive corporate life that she had once repudiated. Nothing could have taken her further into the blueblood establishment of Arkansas's capital city than her decision to join the Rose Law Firm, which traced its roots back to 1820 and claimed to be the oldest legal firm west of the Mississippi. The Rose Law Firm was the legal arm of the powerful, representing, among others, the holy trinity of Arkansas business and industry: Stephens Inc., Tyson Foods, and Wal-Mart. Her position at Rose Law provided Rodham with status and security, but she turned to other ventures in search of fast money. She became, at once, her father's daughter, a market-watching practitioner of unfettered capitalism, and her family's provider, trying to look after the financial side of life in a way that her husband would never do. In keeping with the interdependent nature of the Rodham and Clinton partnership, Rodham's early moneymaking ventures were undertaken in concert with Clinton's friends.

One of the iconic scenes from the sixties decade came in the 1967 Mike Nichols film *The Graduate* when Benjamin, the young graduate played by Dustin Hoffman, was approached by a businessman who had a word of advice for him: "Plastics." That one word in that one scene captured a generation's struggle between innocent idealism and capitalist realism. In the life of Hillary Rodham, the sequel came eleven years later, in October 1978, when Jim Blair uttered two words to her: "Cattle futures."

Blair, a Springdale lawyer who served as outside counsel to Tyson Foods, was among the most trusted friends of Clinton and Rodham from their Fayetteville days. He was a longtime Democratic party insider who had served as a behind-the-scenes adviser in Clinton's campaigns. He was romantically involved with, and soon to marry, Diane Kincaid, the political science professor at the University of Arkansas who was in Rodham's circle of professional women friends and who had known Clinton since the McGovern campaign. Governor Clinton would perform the marriage ceremony for the Blairs in September 1979 and Rodham would attend as their "best person." The foursome would vacation together for years thereafter, often at the Blairs' summer cottage on Beaver Lake. They read books together and held rambling discussions on literature, politics, and the fate of the world. As happens with many pairs of couples, Jim often sided with Hillary, practical and lawyerly, and Bill with Diane, more empathetic and political. There was, however, at least one notable occasion when the split followed gender lines. They had all read Joan Didion's *Play It As It Lays*, a novel describing the disillusionment of a woman in her thirties who has divorced her husband, turned away from her friends, and is emotionally adrift in the emptiness of the California desert. Diane and Hillary identified with the character, while Jim and Bill said they could not understand the book. "How," Clinton asked, "could a woman walk off and do that?"

Clinton and Jim Blair bonded in other ways. They had both grown up in troubled homes. Blair was abandoned by his mother and reared by his paternal grandparents in a modest apartment above an old grocery store in Fayetteville. He and Clinton both had quick and lively minds—Blair graduated from college in two years and had his law degree by age twenty-one. And both loved the art of Arkansas storytelling. They were Southern Baptists who could drop a line of scripture into any conversation or argument. A decade older and more sure of himself, Blair functioned as Clinton's smooth and confident big brother, introducing him to business figures, offering him confidential advice, helping him out of tight spots. They were both ambitious men who could become obsessed by games. Clinton was obsessed by the politics game. Blair, occasionally, by the money game.

When Blair found a way to win big at the money game by trading on the commodities market, he encouraged several friends and associates to get in on the action, including Rodham, knowing that she understood that world while Clinton did not. By the time he recruited Rodham, Blair had already been playing the cattle market for several months, using the Springdale branch of Ray E. Friedman & Company (Refco) brokerage house to buy and sell on the Chicago Mercantile Exchange. His broker there was another member of the extended Tyson network, Robert L. (Red) Bone, a beefy, red-faced good old boy, once described admiringly as "a real razorback," who had worked his way up from driving a chicken truck to being a Tyson vice president before leaving the poultry industry for the brokerage profession. Clients were plentiful in northwest Arkansas: the Tyson company alone had three corporate investment accounts going through Refco. Brokers were making between $10,000 and $100,000 a month. One young broker boasted that within a two-year period he had accumulated four Corvettes, a Ferrari, a Mercedes, and a boat.

Blair could have kept the branch office in business almost by himself. From the time he started buying and selling cattle futures in March 1978, after determining that Refco had an inside track on where the cattle market was going, he was trading enough to pay Refco an average of $50,000 a month in commissions. There is an old Arkansas saying that even a blind hog finds an acorn once in a while, but Blair was counting on anything but blind luck. He maintained a special computer program at his office that analyzed the market averages over four-day, nine-day, and eighteen-day periods. Within easy sight on his desk stood a quote machine, a stock ticker, that allowed him to watch the market all day, "tick by tick," as he once put it. He had a telephone at his side at all times, in his car, in his airplane, to ensure that he would never be out of position to make a necessary trade. At two-thirty every afternoon, he was allowed to listen in on a conference call coordinated by Refco that included cattle buyers, feedlot operators, Chicago pit traders, and Refco's Las Vegas—based president, John Dittmer. At its best, his formula of information and intuition brought in more than a half-million dollars in less than a two-week span.

Rodham followed the high-rolling Blair into the market with a thousand-dollar investment on October 11, 1978, less than a month before her husband was elected governor. She kept playing the cattle futures game for nine months, through the middle of July 1979, by which time she had parlayed that first $1,000 into an extraordinary profit of $99,537—more than the combined salaries of herself and her husband that year. It was a wild ride, one in which Rodham, from her long-distance post in Little Rock, benefited from Blair's advice, his major trading status, and his relationship with Bone and Refco in Springdale.

Playing the commodities market is not like playing the stock market. In the stock market, the most investors can lose is the amount they invest. In the cattle futures market, investors can buy and sell cattle in separate transactions and have to guess correctly whether the prices will rise or fall. If they are locked into contracts to sell at one price at a future date, they hope prices will fall so that they can then buy contracts for that number of cattle at a lower price before the sell date: selling high and buying low. If they buy cattle first, they want the market to rise so that they can sell at a higher price: buying low and selling high. Either way, if they guess right, they can make huge profits; but if they guess wrong, they can lose more than their investment, they can lose the margin between the two prices. If the market moves in the wrong direction and there is a significant potential loss in a client's position, the broker will ask the investor to cover the loss.

It is a nerve-wracking game, and one that not all of Jim Blair's close friends wanted to play or understand. Diane Kincaid, who was not yet married to Blair when the investments began, said he invested money for her and her children even though she wanted "nothing to do with" the trades. "I thought it was terrible. I hated it. I was very concerned about the stress it put on him and I thought it was an excessive preoccupation," she said later. "The things that I enjoyed about him were the conversations and the books we'd read together, and this was taking away from all that. I thought whatever the financial reward, there was a negative impact on the quality of our relationship. I was on a roller-coaster unwillingly. He would say, 'This is a brief wave and I'm going to ride it and then get out.' "

Rodham was more interested than Kincaid. She wanted to learn the game. Following Blair's advice, she played aggressively, sometimes opening and closing trades on the same day. There were times when she guessed wrong, however, and should have faced margin calls, but she never got one. She seemed to get a break even on her first day in the market, when records show that she ordered ten cattle futures contracts with her $1,000 when that normally requires a $12,000 investment. At one point in July, shortly before she quit playing, she was $60,000 in the red and had only $40,000 in her account, but was not asked to pay the margin, and the market soon turned to her favor. Some other Refco clients caught in similar positions apparently were not given such leeway. A client named Stanley Greenwood later claimed in a lawsuit that during that same period of July he was directed to put in $48,000 to cover his losses. What was special about Rodham? The reason she was allowed to keep playing when she did not have enough money in her account to maintain her trading positions was Jim Blair. He was such a good Refco customer that he protected not only himself but his friends. "They weren't going to hassle me," Blair later acknowledged. "And if I brought someone in, they weren't going to hassle them."

Rodham closed her Refco account, she would later explain, because the game was so nerve-wracking and she had become pregnant that summer. She could not withdraw cold turkey, however. She opened a new account closer to home, with Stephens Inc. in Little Rock, and let her broker make all the investment decisions. She closed that account in October. Not long thereafter, the cattle market collapsed, sending many investors and brokers into court, where they sued one another and filed for bankruptcy. Hugh Rodham's daughter was lucky and had the right friends, but she also exhibited a sixth sense about when to stay and when to go—a talent that she would exhibit many times in many ways over the ensuing years.

Her intellect and intuition could not always save Hillary Rodham, however, if the connection turned out to be less reliable than the one she had with Jim Blair. She had less good fortune that year with another investment, a partnership involving the Clintons and another couple, Jim and Susan McDougal, in which they acquired 230.4 acres of undeveloped land along the White River in the Ozarks of north-central Arkansas.

For the first year of Clinton's term, Jim McDougal was a member of Clinton's staff, the governor's liaison to banking and industrial development. At thirty-nine, he was the old hand among the youthful crusaders and the one with the longest connection to Clinton, going back to the Fulbright campaign of 1968. He could often be found with his feet propped up on his desk, gesticulating with his ever present FDR-style cigarette holder, telling a colorful story about his days with Fulbright or making a classical allusion while enhancing an otherwise prosaic bureaucratic encounter. He had a rich speaking voice and what one acquaintance called "a command of the English language better than that of an Oxford don." His young wife Susan, who had been his student when he taught political science at Ouachita Baptist University in Arkadelphia during the mid-1970s, dressed like a New York fashion model and caused quite a commotion during her frequent visits to the Capitol. "She was young and attractive and all that, but we always sort of wondered, 'What's her deal?' " recalled Randy White. "She would float in with an air about her, kind of sweeping in. It seemed like a major production when she swept through, calling attention to herself. We kind of looked at them and went, 'Hmmm.' "

In the summer of 1978, when Clinton was still attorney general but he and Rodham seemed sure bets to occupy the Governor's Mansion, McDougal had encountered them at a Little Rock restaurant and made his sales pitch on the White River land. He said later that he was in the middle of buying the property when he bumped into the Clintons, and invited them to join in the venture because he thought it would prove profitable and he always enjoyed having partners with whom he could discuss the deal's progress. Other acquaintances of McDougal said he had another motive as well: he thought having the next governor of Arkansas involved in the deal would make it easier for him to develop and sell the land.

McDougal had been an aggressive entrepreneur since the age of eight and had traveled around the mountain villages of the Ozarks with his great-uncle, selling feed and seed from the back of a truck. He had been making land deals since he was twenty-seven, and had pulled off several successful ones with friends and political associates, including Senator Fulbright, who went in with him on a deal in Conway where they bought the land for $100 an acre, improved and subdivided it, and sold it for $350 an acre. Clinton knew nothing about real estate and had no interest in it, according to McDougal. When he talked to the Clintons, McDougal said later, he dealt with Rodham. They formed a corporation, Whitewater Development

Company Inc., and took out a $20,000 loan from the Union National Bank of Little Rock for the down payment on the land and then a $182,000 loan from Citizens Bank and Trust of Flippen to buy the property. They secured the loans with the property itself, and expected to pay off the interest by subdividing the land into forty-two lots and selling them as vacation home sites.

Although Jim McDougal brought the Clintons in on the deal, his wife Susan was the most excited about the property, which the Clintons had never seen and never would bother to visit. Susan had picked it out and was convinced that the land would pay for itself as they developed it. "It was a beautiful development. The water was gorgeous up there," she said later. "It was a fabulous idea." In theory, perhaps. But the real estate market soon soured. The lots did not sell quickly. Interest rates soared from 8 to 18 percent. The McDougals, as managing partners, and to a lesser extent the Clintons, began making interest payments on the loans from their own money. For Hillary Rodham, there was no quick cash to be made on the White River.

As to the larger question of Rodham's changing attitudes toward the acquisition of wealth during that period, the argument can be made that there was a higher consistency at work: her practical sense of doing what it takes to move toward her ultimate goals. Reasons for her saddling up for Jim Blair's cattle roundup, for instance, were plentiful: Her husband would never be the sort to worry about the family's financial security; she was an intelligent feminist, who saw no reason not to compete in what was largely a man's world, and who viewed financial strength as an important means of gaining power and independence. A higher personal income would make it less risky for Clinton to borrow money for political campaigns in the future. All of these are legitimate explanations, and yet there is evidence that Rodham felt her own zigzag, the internal contradiction, and that she was not entirely comfortable with what she was doing.

Rodham and Clinton took a vacation in England the year when she was playing the market. One day they were invited to tea at the home of John and Katherine Gieve. Katherine Gieve, formerly Katherine Vereker, had been a friend of Clinton's during his Oxford days. Two other close friends from that era, Sara Maitland and Mandy Merck, also came to the tea, along with several left-wing members of a women's reading group whose slogan was "Why be a wife?" Clinton, according to Merck, seemed years younger than the heavy-lidded, bearded Rhodes Scholar she had remembered from Oxford: "much thinner, closer shaven, with chestnut hair, a shiny blue blazer—not anything like what he wore at Oxford." Rodham wore large glasses and kept rather quiet. The subject at the tea was equal pay for women. Clinton jumped right into the conversation, saying how hard it was to measure value. "How do you compare the value of a truck driver to the value of a beautician?" he asked. The women were impressed by his knowledge and sensitivity on the issue. "Who is that?" one whispered to Merck. "None other than the governor of Arkansas," she responded.

Finally the conversation moved on to Rodham. What did she think? "You know," she said, "I'm beginning to think there must be more to life than this greasy pole, this rat race." She was talking about the greasy pole of politics and the rat race over money. And she added: "I'm thinking about getting back into religion." The other women were stunned. They were utterly political creatures who had no context in which to place her remarks. "If she had said, 'I think I'm going to be a Moonie,'" Merck said later, "she could not have appalled her audience more."

CHELSEA Victoria Clinton was born on February 27, 1980, seventeen days early. Clinton had been home from a trip to Washington less than fifteen minutes when Hillary went into labor. He had studied the Lamaze method and planned to be in the delivery room, but the birth was difficult and required a Caesarian section. When a nurse finally handed his infant daughter to him, he would not let go of her. "He walked all over the area . . . holding the baby in his arms," a hospital official reported. As he looked at his daughter, he realized that he was experiencing something that his own father had never been able to do. "Well," Clinton later recalled saying to himself, "here's another milestone he didn't reach." The date was reminder enough. February 27 was the date that the family honored as the birthday of W. J. Blythe.

Not long after mother and daughter returned home from the hospital, Carolyn Yeldell Staley, Clinton's old high school friend, an opera singer who had moved back to Little Rock with her family to work on the state arts council, wrote a song about Chelsea. She sang it in the Governor's Mansion, accompanying herself on the piano. It was a sentimental ballad written from the perspective of humble parents in awe of their creation. One stanza included the lines, "We may not be worthy, but we'll try to be wise." After listening to the song, Rodham approached Staley and said rather coldly, "That's a nice song, Carolyn. But who's not worthy? You and your tape recorder?"

THE birth of Chelsea might have been the last good thing to happen to Clinton in 1980. On the American public stage, this was another year of confusion and disillusionment not unlike 1968, except this time along with tragedies and crises there were moments of incompetence and rotten luck

piling up in rapid succession. Jimmy Carter went into that final year of his
first term with the lowest ratings of any president in modern times, viewed
by the liberal wing of his own party as too moderate and tight-fisted on
domestic policy and by the larger public as weak and indecisive in foreign
affairs. When he attempted to take strong action to counter the latter
image, it seemed to compound the problem. When the Red Army invaded
Afghanistan, he imposed a grain embargo on the Soviet Union and ordered
a boycott of the Summer Olympics in Moscow, actions which angered
midwestern wheat farmers and demoralized the public. When the Iranians
would not respond to diplomatic efforts to free dozens of Americans held
hostage in Tehran, he ordered a rescue mission that aborted when a U.S.
Navy helicopter crashed in the Iranian desert, killing eight servicemen.
One unpredictable event after another left Carter and the nation reeling.
There were race riots in Miami. Mount St. Helens erupted in Washington
State. More than one hundred thousand Cuban refugees, encouraged to
leave by Fidel Castro, landed on the beaches of Florida in what was known
as the Mariel boatlift.

The state of Arkansas in 1980 was a microcosm of national unease and
disarray. Truckers were striking, Ku Klux Klansmen were on the march,
tornadoes ripped through the countryside. The economy was turning
downward, forcing state revenues below the overoptimistic estimates and
costing public school teachers the raises they expected. Although Clinton's
poll ratings remained higher than Carter's that spring, he sensed that he
was in trouble. When Frank White, a beefy, jovial savings and loan executive and former economic development official in the Pryor administration,
switched parties and announced that he would challenge Clinton as a
Republican in the fall election, Clinton told Rodham that White would
start the race with 45 percent of the vote. The young governor feared that
he had already angered at least that many people during his first year in
office.

A seconding motion came sooner than expected, in the Democratic
primary in late May, when Monroe Schwarzlose, the seventy-seven-year-
old turkey farmer, drew 31 percent of the vote. The old farmer's showing
was a stunning expression of no confidence in Clinton, since Schwarzlose
was the ultimate fringe candidate, who had carried only 1 percent in the
same primary in 1978. It was also a signal to Clinton from the timber industry, which was still raging over the clear-cutting controversy. Schwarzlose fared best in south Arkansas timber counties, where he received
behind-the-scenes encouragement from John Ed Anthony.

A few days later, on June 1, a bad situation deteriorated. Suddenly,
perhaps inevitably, the troubles of Governor Clinton and President Carter
converged in northwest Arkansas, when several hundred Cuban refugees
who had come to the United States in the Mariel boatlift rioted and broke

out of their resettlement camp at Fort Chaffee. Clinton would be given high marks for his performance under pressure in dealing with the Cuban refugee crisis, but his close friendship with Carter, which became strained in private but did not break in public, was held against him by Arkansas voters. It was also used to great advantage by Republican challenger Frank White and his handlers, who replayed footage of the Fort Chaffee riot to associate Clinton with images of disorder and bad times.

The buildup of tension at Fort Chaffee began in mid-May with the arrival of the first Cubans. Although the sprawling military base had been used as a resettlement center for Vietnamese refugees earlier in the decade with little controversy, nearby residents were alarmed this time by reports that the Cuban contingent included criminals and mental patients. Most of the eighteen thousand refugees sent to Arkansas waited patiently to get processed. But a number of rebellious young men grew more agitated day by day at their confinement. Several hundred of them broke out of the camp on May 26 and created a minor disturbance in a nearby hamlet. Clinton had urged federal officials to tighten security after that to prevent a more serious confrontation with posses of shotgun-toting citizens in towns near the fort. If the federal authorities did not secure the camp within seventy-two hours, Clinton said, he would take action to secure it himself.

Clinton took precautionary steps in that direction. He activated a few dozen National Guardsmen and authorized state police to send troops to the Fort Smith area from all eight sectors of the state. But he was surprised and embarrassed by a second round of disturbances, believing wrongly that the Carter administration by then had resolved a dispute among federal officials over control of the refugees. White House aide Eugene Eidenberg had insisted in conversations with Clinton that the post commander, Brigadier General James (Bulldog) Drummond, had been granted the authority to contain the Cubans inside their relocation camp. Drummond maintained that he had no such authority. On the morning of June 1, after staging a sit-in at the main gate, several hundred Cubans bolted past the military guards, who did nothing to stop them, and marched onto a nearby highway chanting *"Libertad! Libertad!"* They were met by a state police squad and retreated to the fort. But late that afternoon, they congregated at the main gate again, this time more than a thousand strong, and again met no resistance from the military guards as they ran out the gate and down the highway, carrying sticks and bottles. The state police had formed a protective line at the edge of the town of Barling. When the Cubans reached them, there was a brief confrontation in which sixty-seven people were injured, including several officers, but mostly Cubans, some of whom had their heads cracked open.

Clinton and James H. Jones, the adjutant general of the Arkansas National

Guard, and Jones's chief of staff, James A. Ryan, flew by helicopter from Little Rock to Fort Chaffee soon after they heard about the riot. Their first meeting was with General Drummond. Ryan had never seen the young governor in a tense situation of that sort before and thought "he asked some very intelligent questions, questions that were relevant." Jack Moseley, editor of the *Southwest Times Record* in Fort Smith, was eavesdropping outside the open door. He heard "a lot of shouting and loud voices" and Drummond saying that it was not the Army's fault because it was restricted by law from intervening. A voice that Moseley identified as Clinton's responded by saying, "Well shit, General, who left the wirecutters in the stockade if none of this was the military's fault?"

After the meeting with Drummond, Clinton activated two National Guard battalions and an infantry company and had them stationed outside the gates. He then had his staff arrange a meeting with community leaders and concerned residents, first in Barling, then in Jenny Lind. The crowds were hostile at first. At Barling, one local official jumped up on his chair and shook his fist at the governor. At Jenny Lind, Clinton hopped up on the back of a pickup truck parked under a shade tree, surrounded by angry local men carrying shotguns. Moseley, who would endorse Frank White later that year in editorials that excoriated Clinton, nonetheless came away from the Fort Chaffee incident impressed by Clinton's behavior under pressure: "I think he showed a tremendous amount of fortitude. He took charge. He accepted responsibility. He behaved in a responsible manner. He listened to what the military commander had to say and went toe to toe with the White House." Eidenberg, the White House official in charge of the refugee situation, arrived at Fort Smith in the middle of the night and was met by Clinton, who "in no uncertain terms" made clear to him that "it was his judgment that the dispute over the law enforcement authority question had made possible an event that did not have to happen."

Eidenberg agreed. At a press conference held at two-thirty that morning, he pledged that no more Cubans would be sent to Arkansas.

WITH more troops stationed outside the gates and the dispute over military authority resolved, there were no more refugee uprisings that summer. But the Fort Chaffee drama was only at intermission, soon to be resumed, and other troubles kept coming at Clinton nonstop. A sense of imminent disaster permeated the governor's office. If a telephone rang after office hours, aides would joke, "Don't answer it—they'll probably want the National Guard!" The state broiled in a heatwave that took the lives of several older citizens, led to the suffocating deaths of thousands of poultry chicks, and made life generally miserable for an already grousing populace. Even more troublesome was the car tags issue, which would not go away. Every month, one-twelfth of the car owners in the state erupted in anger as they had their license tags renewed and were required to pay fees that had increased by as much as tenfold. Although the licenses still went for relatively modest sums, the tax became an easy and obvious target of public discontent—all of it directed not at the legislature but at Clinton.

It reached the point where chief of staff Rudy Moore felt that they could not please anybody. He thought of it as a wave of hostility building, month after month. By July, Clinton realized that the wave might drown him. One day, after giving speeches in El Dorado and Texarkana, he returned to the office staggering from the negative reaction he was getting.

"Rudy, they're killing me out there!" he said to Moore. "They hate my guts!"

"What are you talking about?" Moore asked.

"The car tags," said Clinton. "A man came up to me and said, 'I'm havin' a hard enough time makin' a livin', and you're kickin' me while I'm down.' They're killing me out there, Rudy."

On August 1, Clinton came to believe that his own president was among those killing him. Word came from the White House that all Cuban refugees still being housed at resettlement camps in Wisconsin, Pennsylvania, and Florida would be transferred to a single consolidated camp at Fort Chaffee. Only two months earlier, Gene Eidenberg had visited Fort Chaffee and promised that no more Cubans would be sent there. Now, the White House officials had changed their minds. Travel aide Randy White was in the room at the Governor's Mansion when Clinton got the news and remembers that his boss pounded his desk and launched into an obscenity-laced protest that, considering the circumstances, amounted to a rather normal reaction.

"You're fucking me!" White heard Clinton shout into the phone at a White House official. "How could you do this to me? I busted my ass for Carter. You guys are gonna get me beat. I've done everything I could for you guys. This is ridiculous! Carter's too chickenshit about it to tell me directly!"

Clinton nonetheless promised to keep the story quiet over the weekend until Eidenberg could travel to Arkansas to explain the situation directly to people in the communities near Fort Chaffee. Word leaked out later that day from Senator Pryor's office. When the press asked Clinton if he could confirm Pryor's claim, he acknowledged that he had known about the White House decision. He had agreed to Eidenberg's request to keep quiet, he said, because he hoped to spend the weekend persuading administration officials to change their minds. The decision, Clinton told reporters, was the most politically damaging one Carter could make. Placing the final resettlement camp in Wisconsin, Pennsylvania, or Florida would have been smarter, he argued, because Carter had a better chance of carrying Arkansas in the fall election than any of those states. Now, he shared Pryor's assessment that Carter's chances in Arkansas were shot.

What more could Clinton do besides cuss out the White House in private and bemoan the political consequences in public? Many of his aides thought that he should "kick and fuss and holler and just tell Jimmy Carter no," in Rudy Moore's words. Clinton was not prepared to go that far. One reason was historical and emotional: he saw too many modern-day parallels to what he considered to be Arkansas' day of infamy in 1957, when Governor Faubus evoked states' rights to defy federal authorities seeking to desegregate Little Rock Central High School. If the people of Arkansas wanted a provincial demagogue, they would have to look elsewhere. There were many things Clinton would do to try to win an election, but that was not one of them.

There was, to be sure, a broader political consideration as well. As unpopular as Carter might be in Arkansas, he was still president; he was still heavily favored to prevail over challenger Edward Kennedy and win renomination at the Democratic National Convention to be held in New York less than two weeks later. Clinton had signed up as a floor whip for Carter at the convention. He had been chosen to give a prime-time convention speech as the spokesman for the Democratic governors, after being among those considered for an even more coveted assignment as the keynote speaker. He had strong connections to the chairman of the Democratic National Committee, John C. White, the former Texas agriculture commissioner who had been one of Clinton's patrons since the 1972 McGovern campaign. He was still enjoying insider status as Carter's man in Arkansas, sought out for patronage decisions, consulted on domestic programs, invited to briefings on foreign affairs. A too-public break with Carter now might jeopardize what remained of their special relationship.

That weekend Clinton traveled to Denver for the annual meeting of the National Governors Association, where most of the talk among the twenty-four Democratic governors in attendance was about maneuvering between Carter and Kennedy on convention rules and the party platform. Suppressing his sense of betrayal, Clinton worked to shore up support for the president among the other governors. On the afternoon of August 4, he talked on the telephone with Carter, who was at the White House. Gene Eidenberg, who was also at the governors' conference, monitored the conversation. Clinton tried but failed to talk the president out of the Fort Chaffee decision, instead only gaining a promise that the state would play a central role in the development of a new security policy at the refugee camp. Although most people viewed the decision through a political lens,

Carter insisted that politics had nothing to do with it. Fort Chaffee was chosen on its merits, as a warm-weather site that had the most suitable facilities. At a meeting at Fort Chaffee the next day, Eidenberg officially announced the consolidation plan and tried to explain that his earlier pledge not to send any more Cubans to Arkansas was rendered "inoperative" by circumstances which could not have been foreseen. "I understand," Eidenberg said, "why that statement made then and the decision made now, being announced now, is being viewed, let's be frank with each other, as a lie, as a breaking of my word, and worse, a breaking of the word of the President of the United States."

CLINTON and Rodham had friends on both sides of the Carter and Kennedy fight. Some called it a struggle for the soul of the Democratic party, but it was fought as much out of weariness and confusion as out of passion. Kennedy supporters thought Carter was foundering because he had turned away from fundamental liberal doctrine and had gotten lost in compromise and vacillation. Carterites believed that Kennedy was waging a futile symbolic struggle for a governing philosophy from which the American public had long since turned away.

Although Rodham was considered the more liberal member of the partnership, she had no trouble choosing sides in this dispute. On a trip to San Francisco, she stayed at the home of Fred Altshuler, her friend from the House impeachment inquiry staff, who held a dinner party in her honor. The Kennedy versus Carter battle dominated the conversation. Altshuler was highly critical of Carter and made an impassioned case for Kennedy. Rodham derided him, defending, it seemed, not only the president but her husband by inference. "She said she was talking about practical politics and I was talking about impractical politics," Altshuler recalled. "She was saying, 'You have to look at who can get elected and what he can accomplish.' She was definitely in a minority. There were not any other Carter supporters at the dinner. But she held her position."

Clinton's friends in the Kennedy camp had no better luck. Carl Wagner, a Kennedy aide who had worked with Clinton at Project Pursestrings and served as George McGovern's coordinator in Michigan when Clinton was in Texas, talked with Clinton often that summer. He found Clinton's support of Carter unshakable, even after the Cuban refugee fiasco. Wagner understood. All his friends were seeing their way through that race on their own terms. As a southern governor seeking reelection, an association with Teddy Kennedy would have done Clinton no good.

Clinton was now more than a decade removed from his Oxford days as an antiwar protester, eight years beyond the McGovern struggle, six years past the Watergate scandal. It all seemed so long ago. Mandy Merck, the radical lesbian who had befriended Clinton at Oxford, realized what a different world he was now moving in when she looked him up at the Democratic National Convention in New York. Merck was covering the convention for *Time Out,* a counterculture magazine in London. She had no credentials, only a note on Clinton's official stationery inviting her to a reception for the Arkansas delegation. All of the stereotypes that Merck had carried about Clinton's Arkansas, impressions that he had fostered with his stories of old farmers and huge watermelons, were smashed when she walked into the reception room. Here was a congregation of yuppies: lots of dark suits, a smattering of jewel-studded denim jeans, the aura of money and power and sex in the air. Clinton looked like a well-groomed young banker. He greeted her warmly, and started to introduce her around the room. In his thickest Arkansas accent, his eyebrows raised in his classic can-you-believe-this? style, he would say, "I want you to meet a real Marxist-feminist from London, England."

Two days later, Merck met Clinton in his hotel room for an interview. She told him she was surprised to learn that he was working as a floor whip for Carter opposing a platform plank on federally funded abortions. If women were seeking abortions as a matter of choice rather than health, Clinton told her, then he thought they should pay rather than the taxpayers. Merck was tempted to argue with him, but decided, "What's the point? I'm not going to change his mind." Clinton changed the subject to his convention speech. He hoped it would be in prime time.

Hours before delivering the speech, Clinton received a telegram from Carolyn Yeldell Staley. "Energize us," she wrote. "Renew our flickering faith that leadership does care, and that government can respond. America waits." Whether Clinton energized his audience that night is open to debate. But it is fair to say that his speech, which he wrote himself, was the shortest, clearest address that he would ever give at a Democratic convention—a cogent analysis of the troubled, transitional period that the Democratic party was enduring.

Simply putting together the old elements of the Democratic coalition and repudiating Ronald Reagan was not enough anymore, Clinton said. The Democrats had to start looking for "more creative and realistic" solutions to the nation's problems. "We were brought up to believe, uncritically, without thinking about it, that our system broke down in the Great Depression, was reconstructed by Franklin Roosevelt through the New Deal and World War II, and would never break again. And that all we had to do was try to reach out and extend the benefits of America to those who had been dispossessed: minorities and women, the elderly, the handicapped and children in need. But the hard truth is that for ten long years through Democratic and Republican administrations alike, this economic system has been breaking down. We have seen high inflation, high unemployment, large government deficits, the loss of our competitive edge. In response to these developments, a dangerous and growing number of people are simply opting out of our system. Another dangerous and growing number are opting for special interest and single interest group politics, which threatens to take every last drop of blood out of our political system."

GOVERNOR Clinton was a creature of habit. When someone went in to brief him on a subject or upcoming event, his habit was to keep doing some other activity, either reading or writing, at the same time that he was being briefed. Every half-minute or so, without looking at the aide, he would blurt out, "What else"—not as a question but as a sign that he had catalogued the information and it was time to move on. They were two of Clinton's most frequently uttered words: What else. What else. What else. He was always working the telephone in search of inside information: much like his friend Jim Blair, who sought constant reports on cattle futures, only Clinton wanted the latest reading on Clinton political futures, up or down. He would end many conversations with another of his favorite phrases: "Keep your ear to the ground." He was a young man of oversized appetites. Any aide who spent time with him could tell stories of his inhaling apples in a few massive bites, swallowing them core and all. Hot dogs went down so fast that they barely touched his teeth. The mansion cook could not bake chocolate chip cookies fast enough. Plates of enchiladas and nachos disappeared in seconds. What else. What else. What else.

He was competitive, always looking for a challenge. He put a pinball machine in the game room in the basement of the red brick Governor's Mansion. One day seven-year-old Matt Moore, Rudy's son, stood on a box to reach the levers and rang up a score of 800,000 points, lighting up the whole machine. The governor could not believe it. A child had broken his record. When everyone had left for the night, Clinton stayed up, Billy the pinball wizard, shooting, pounding, leaning, tilting, until two in the morning, determined to reclaim the record. What else. What else. What else.

For all of the frustrations that came with being around Bill Clinton, most of the people who fell into his orbit found it exhilarating. Life around him, they said, seemed more vital, closer to the edge, less routine, more physically and intellectually challenging. But in the final months of the 1980 election, Clinton's "what else" personality took a dangerous turn. It started to seem less a product of boundless energy and more a reflection of self-absorption. To Moore, he seemed distracted, unable to focus as he should, unwilling to make clear decisions. People would approach travel aide Randy White and ask what was the matter with the governor: "They'd tell me when they would meet him or shake his hand, it seemed that he was looking at the next person in the room, the next person to talk to. I had a lot of friends comment that he really wasn't listening to them." Moore thought it might be a midlife crisis, a private conflict between Clinton and Rodham, something involving Clinton and the other women who hovered nearby wherever he went.

Clinton's behavior was a symptom of something larger. He was fighting his own emotions related to ambition and expectations. For most of his life, people had been talking about how he would be president someday. Those great expectations had both carried him along and circumscribed his path. He often seemed to be doing things because they were what someone who might be president should do. Or, occasionally, in rebellion, because they were precisely what a future president should not do. In either case, it was reactive. And when the public started to turn against him, it left him at a loss.

His reelection campaign organization provided little help. It was directed by well-meaning but inexperienced newfound friends from the Little Rock country club and business set who had little sense of how to react in an unexpectedly tense situation. When Frank White's campaign team began running television commercials depicting the Cuban refugee riot at Fort Chaffee, Clinton's lead dropped 10 percentage points in one week. There was no response. Clinton could not believe that people would blame him for it. When he tried to turn the Fort Chaffee aftermath to his advantage by traveling up to Fort Smith and personally handing out federal reimbursement checks, he was blasted for partisan pandering by editor Jack Moseley in a front-page editorial in the *Southwest Times Record.* The publisher of the *Times Record,* who owned several newspapers in Arkansas, ordered Moseley's editorial reprinted on the front page of all of them, including the newspaper in Hot Springs, Clinton's home town, which so enraged Virginia Dwire that she stormed down to the office of the *Hot Springs Sentinel-Record* and canceled her subscription.

Hillary Rodham, who again had become an issue because of her use of a different last name, was enraged, too, and tried in the final weeks to assert control over the campaign. She began reworking her husband's schedule day by day. With eight days left, she placed an emergency long-distance call in search of Dick Morris. The New York pollster had been deposed from Clinton's inner circle before the campaign, replaced by Peter Hart, a nationally regarded Democratic pollster. The marks against Morris were varied. Some of Clinton's aides distrusted him as a mercenary who represented Republicans as well as Democrats. Others thought of him as an evil force willing to do anything to win a campaign. Clinton himself had contradictory feelings about Morris. Before the 1978 election, when they were plotting Pryor's race together, they were brothers. Once Clinton was in office, Morris felt a distance in their relationship. It was, he said later, as though Clinton "had gone from being a practical hard-nosed political operative to being a Boy Scout." Morris started to feel that Clinton thought of him as "something dirty, that he didn't want to touch without gloves."

When it came time to fire Morris, Clinton backed away from doing it face to face. At their final meeting, the governor complained that Morris's polls did not seem as thorough as Peter Hart's. He also, according to Morris, declared at that meeting: "You are an assault to my vanity. Politics is what I do best and you do it as well as I do." Morris later concluded that Clinton was setting him up to be fired. Two weeks afterward, an aide in the governor's office called and said his services were no longer needed.

Until now, when the campaign was disintegrating with eight days to go. Now, Hillary Rodham made the practical decision that they needed Morris back. She called his house in New York City. Morris's wife, Eileen McGann, answered the phone. "We're losing. Frank White's gaining. He's hitting us with negatives. They're working. We need Dick," Rodham said. "He's got to come to Arkansas right away."

Morris was not home, McGann said, and in any case, Clinton had fired him and he had other candidates to work for now. Rodham tracked him down in Florida, where he was advising the Republican Senate candidate, Paula Hawkins. She persuaded him to come to Arkansas for the final days of the campaign. Morris took a final poll that showed Clinton under 50 percent, which for an incumbent he took to be fatal. They put up a final negative ad against White, but with little hope that it could make a difference. Nothing could go right. On Saturday, November 1, Clinton attended a Razorback football game at Little Rock's War Memorial Stadium. Arkansas was playing Rice, the perennial doormat of the Southwest Conference. Rice won 17–16. "This," Clinton said, "is the last straw." In private, he started attacking himself. "God, I'm an idiot!" he said. "I should have seen it coming. How could I be so dumb!" Morris noticed a clinical detachment in Clinton's lament. It seemed to him that Clinton "was more hurt that he had screwed up as a politician than that he had screwed up as a governor."

Clinton ended the campaign with a fund-raiser in El Dorado at the home of Richard Mason, an environmental activist who owned an energy company. The crowd was large and enthusiastic, which temporarily lifted Clinton's spirits. But while the guests mingled, he spent much of the night in the kitchen, working the telephone, getting reports from his county coordinators around the state. The reports were not encouraging. There were not enough volunteers for the get-out-the-vote effort on Tuesday.

After the event, Clinton retreated to Mason's guest house down the path from the main residence. His light stayed on most of the night. The next morning, after Clinton had gone, Mason went to the guest house to clean up. He found a deck of cards that Clinton had left behind. The governor had been playing solitaire; he had lost the last game. Mason noticed that the playing cards were adorned with pictures of the presidents of the United States.

CHAPTER TWENTY-ONE

THE ONLY
TRACK

"Someone once said you don't understand politics until you've been defeated—then all the mysteries become apparent."
—JOHN F. KENNEDY

CLINTON AND RODHAM were still at the Governor's Mansion when the early returns started coming in on election night. They had an open line to Rudy Moore in the campaign headquarters war room on the second floor of an old Victorian house near the Arkansas Capitol. As soon as Moore received the first results from Texarkana, he passed them along to Clinton, who immediately grasped their meaning. He could analyze the voting boxes better than anyone in the campaign. He knew the precise totals that he had received in every county in the state in the past two elections. Now he was carrying Texarkana, but with numbers far below what he needed. At the same hour that his supporters at the Camelot Hotel were shouting with joy at a television network's premature declaration that he would win, Clinton was swearing into the telephone, raging at his fate. It was over. He had lost.

His first wave of anger passed quickly, and by the time he and Rodham reached campaign headquarters he appeared calm and analytical, the political scientist again picking apart the data of defeat. Rodham remained more emotional. One friend noticed that she was trembling slightly, struggling to keep her composure, as she walked down the hallway with her husband and entered a private room to take a condolence call from Ted Kennedy.

Clinton had lost before, but none of his previous defeats compared with this one. This was catastrophic. Maybe the Oxonian curse had found another victim. At thirty-four, he fit the ironic description of the quintessential Rhodes Scholar: someone with a great future behind him. He had attained the achievement of being the youngest defeated governor in

American history and only the third Arkansas governor in the twentieth century to be denied a second two-year term. His reaction, characteristically, was of two parts. Here he was whining, feeling sorry for himself. There he was resolved, plotting a comeback course.

The petulant side of Clinton's personality sought to place blame on people and factors beyond his control. The press was his first target. He phoned Bill Simmons, the Associated Press bureau chief in Little Rock, a journalist known for fair-mindedness, and screamed about how Simmons had conspired to get him defeated. Simmons was puzzled by the attack and thought the governor seemed out of control. That Clinton deigned to talk to him was unusual: he gave most of the statehouse press corps the silent treatment for several weeks, brushing them off at public appearances with a wave of the hand. He was more accommodating to national journalists, although when David Broder of *The Washington Post* visited Little Rock shortly after the election, Clinton chided him, only half-jokingly, for mentioning the young governor in a *Parade* magazine account as someone who might someday be president. Clinton later carried a similar complaint to a meeting of the Society for Professional Journalists in Little Rock, where he broke his post-defeat silence by claiming that he had been unfairly portrayed as an overambitious young man interested in the governor's job only as a steppingstone.

Clinton also took aim at Jimmy Carter, who had lost to Ronald Reagan. "The guy screwed me and never tried to make amends," he told Rick Stearns, his political confidant from the Oxford days, in a late night telephone conversation. During an informal meeting with David Broder over a cup of coffee at the Governor's Mansion, Clinton seemed consumed by bitterness toward the president. He said that he had warned Carter administration officials that their handling of the Cuban refugee crisis at Fort Chaffee would be a political disaster for everyone, but that the White House would not listen. When Carter belatedly expressed regret that Fort Chaffee might have played a role in Clinton's defeat, Clinton responded with a touch of sarcasm that did not humor the earnest president: he told the press that he was "coming to Washington with a few refugees" for Carter to sponsor.

In the interregnum before the end of his term, Clinton traveled to Washington frequently and spent less time than usual in the governor's office. When he was in Arkansas, he seemed sometimes to be overtaken by self-pity. One day he invited several aides to lunch at the Tracks Inn at the old railroad station down the hill from the Capitol. As they sat around the table after lunch, Clinton launched into a melodramatic soliloquy on what he should do next. Should he practice law in Little Rock? Should he compete for the chairmanship of the Democratic National Committee, which would entail a move to Washington and a six-figure salary? Should he take another high-visibility public interest post being dangled in front of him by a progressive alternative to the religious right, People for the American Way, which was looking for a new chairman, preferably a Southern Baptist?

This was not his most sympathetic audience. No one else at the table had any plans or job offers because they had not expected to be out of work so soon. "You sonofabitch!" said Randy White. "You've got every offer. You can do all these things. What are we gonna do? What am I gonna do? You've got everything in the world!" After they returned to the office, a chastened Clinton spent the remainder of the afternoon strolling from desk to desk, asking his staff members what he could do for them and how he could help them find new jobs.

Clinton's own job offers included more than those he had mentioned to his staff at lunch. One day he took a call from Governor Jerry Brown of California, who suggested that Clinton and Hillary should move to the West Coast and reestablish a political base there, in a state more attuned to their progressive politics. To help Clinton get started, Brown offered him a job as his chief of staff in Sacramento. Clinton mentioned the proposal to Mickey Kantor, a longtime Brown friend and Los Angeles lawyer who worked with Rodham on the board of the Legal Services Corporation. "I indicated to him for a lot of reasons that might not be the most productive thing you could do," Kantor later recalled. At the same time, Kantor was also serving a dual role in the maneuvering for the Democratic National Committee (DNC) chairmanship. As the law partner of Charles Manatt, he was leading the campaign to get Manatt the job; and as a friend of Bill Clinton and Hillary Rodham, he was advising Clinton that it would be the wrong move for him. Kantor was awed by what he saw as Clinton's political potential: after their first meeting a few years earlier, he had gone back to California and told his friends that he had just met a young man who would be president someday. But running the DNC, Kantor told Clinton now, would not help him reach that ultimate goal. The national party was not held in high repute, especially in the South. Anyone who wanted to run again in Arkansas would have difficulty surviving the association with the party.

There was, in Clinton's case, often a fine line between self-absorption and humility. At any hour of day or night he would flip through his bulging file of index cards, dialing friends from around the country for long talks and confessionals. He had blown it, he would say. He had his career exactly where he wanted it, and he had blown it. In grocery stores, he cornered friends and asked what he had done wrong. He took solace wherever he could find it. One day he invited a group of Pentecostal ministers in to pray with him. He called himself "about as popular as the plague."

During a trip to Fayetteville, Clinton made a guest appearance at Diane Blair's class on politics and literature. He analyzed some of the more complex and compelling political characters in literature, including Willie Stark, the corrupt, populist southern governor in Robert Penn Warren's *All the King's Men,* and Pietro Spina, the disillusioned hero of Ignazio Silone's anti-Fascist novel *Bread and Wine.* He also discussed several biographies that had helped shape his perspective, including ones of Lincoln, Hitler, and Churchill. Political leaders, he said, were usually a combination of darkness and light. The darkness of insecurity, depression, family disorder. In great leaders, the light overcame the darkness. Near the end of class, one student asked why, given all the choices open to him, Clinton had committed himself to the political life. His response revealed that his urge was so deep and strong that he never saw it as a choice. He framed his answer in the language of his mother, a woman who loved nothing better than to watch the races of her thoroughbreds: the ponies at Oaklawn and her son Bill the candidate.

Why politics? Clinton was asked.

"It's the only track I ever wanted to run on," he replied.

THE only track. . . .

When Billie Carr, the tough old Godmother of Texas liberals who had trained Clinton in the ways of Lone Star politics in 1972, heard that he had lost, she thought it was "the end of his dream." Then he called her one night and launched into one of his patented, breathless assessments of what went wrong.

"What now?" Carr asked when he was through.

"Well, Billie," he said. "I'm gonna start working for the next time." . . .

Woody Bassett, a young Fayetteville lawyer who had taken classes from Clinton and Rodham when they taught at Arkansas, was heading toward his seat at Razorback Stadium on a bitterly cold Saturday afternoon a few weeks after the election. Through the din of the college football crowd, Bassett heard someone shouting his name: "Woody! Hey, Woody! Bassett!" He turned around. There was Bill Clinton, running toward him. It was the first time he had seen Clinton since his defeat.

"Governor," he said, "I'm awfully disappointed that you lost."

"Tell you what," Clinton said, pointing his oversized index finger at Bassett's chest. "I'm gonna run for governor again. I'm gonna get that job back. I want you to help me." . . .

Clinton called Rudy Moore out to the mansion. He and his wife had been brainstorming. "Here's an idea, let's talk about it," Hillary Rodham said, as Clinton and Moore shot a casual game of pool. The idea was to call a special session of the legislature to repeal the unpopular increase in car license fees which had played a role in his defeat. Frank White would repeal the fee increases as soon as he got in office, Clinton said. "If it's gonna happen anyway, why should that guy get the credit?" Moore argued against the special session, saying it was too late to placate the general public and that all this would do was rile the highway lobby, which was already planning how to spend the money to build more roads. Moore won the argument, but he and Randy White, who was also at the mansion, came away with one overriding thought: Clinton was already running for election.

The only track . . .

THE comeback began with two telephone calls. Rodham called Dick Morris again and said he had to return to Little Rock immediately to begin working on the next campaign. And Clinton called Betsey Wright. His political life was a mess, he told her. His staff was demoralized and despondent. Some of them were mad at him. He felt, to some degree, that he had let them down, and vice versa. Hillary had tried to make it clear to the staff that there was a lot of "cleaning up" to do before they turned things over to Frank White. She had assumed the role of bad cop to get that word across, but it had only ended in a harsh exchange with Rudy Moore. "The problem here is that these people have to look for other jobs," Moore had explained, to which Hillary had replied, "Well, that may be true, but we've got to get this goddamn work done!" But Clinton did not feel comfortable turning to his staff for much help, which he needed immediately.

He told Wright that he needed an outsider to come down to Little Rock to gather all of his records and sort through the substance and the remains of his career. He needed a trainer to get him back on the track. Wright, who was between jobs after having spent most of the seventies as an organizer in the women's political movement in Washington, was intrigued. She had known Clinton and Rodham since the McGovern campaign, and she felt both an intuitive understanding of him and an impulse to help him. She was, in a sense, almost part of the family. Within days of taking the call, Wright was on the job. She slept in the guest house at the mansion at first, until Tom Williamson, Clinton's Oxford friend, arrived for a buck-up visit, and they moved her to the basement, where she slept amid the sea of files. She worked day and night and on weekends, assisted by Gloria Cabe, the Clinton campaign worker and former Little Rock representative, who had also been defeated that year. On Thanksgiving Day, Clinton and Rodham took baby Chelsea with them down to Virginia's house in Hot Springs, leaving Wright behind. They forgot to bring her back any leftovers.

Some of the raw political data Wright and Cabe sorted through had been computerized over the years, but most of the essential information about his political network of supporters remained on loose slips of paper or on three-by-five-inch index cards, now totaling more than ten thousand, that had been maintained by Clinton and his aides over the years, and were stored in shoe boxes and old wooden library card catalogue files. If Clinton was to rebuild his political career, these cards were the bricks with which he would do it. Each card recorded a piece of his history and reflected his relentless campaign style. On the top right corner was the county where the subject of the card lived, or, if the name was from out of state, the era in which that person came into Clinton's life: Georgetown, Oxford, Yale, McGovern campaign. Running down the left-hand side of the card were dates, starting with the first time Clinton had met the person and every important contact they had had since. In the middle were names, telephone numbers, addresses, sometimes contribution amounts. Another row of dates noted when that person had received a letter from Clinton or his aides known as a GTMY: for Glad to Meet You.

THE youngest former governor in American history left the mansion one morning in January 1981 with his wife and daughter and moved to Midland Avenue on the near west side, to a yellow frame house tucked under the trees, with a wraparound porch and a carport. They lined the walls with built-in bookcases. In an unlikely binge of consumerism, Clinton went on a shopping spree, buying kitschy gingerbread pieces and garish knick-knacks and gargantuan German furniture. Hillary would come home from work and sigh, "Oh, Bill's been shopping again!" They hired a nurse from the former mansion staff to take care of Chelsea. Clinton went off to work every day at the law firm of Wright, Lindsey & Jennings in the Worthen Bank Building, where he held an office and the title "Of Counsel."

He pretended that he was enjoying this new private life, but his friends and associates could see that he hated it. He had to worry about things that had not concerned him before, from laundry to baby-sitters. He looked pathetic and out of place in the law office, thought Dick Morris, who often visited him there on political missions. "Everything about it smacked of penance and defeat," Morris recalled. "Everything about it was 'This is what I'm doing because I screwed up.' The image that stays in my mind is of this tall guy, folded into a chair, stuffed underneath a small desk in a small room with the walls crowding him closely, and having to go out and search for someone in the steno pool to do his work, and just being incredibly oversized for the environment in which he was cast. He would very often be soulful: 'Gee, do you think I can come back? Do you think I've had it?' He would talk about the great people who got voted out of office. He was like a patient afflicted with cancer wondering if he had any chance of survival."

Just as Clinton had to find his way through the psychological debris of defeat, so, too, did Rodham. She had not expected to be the wife of a former politician so soon. For Arkansans to reject her was one thing; but for them to reject Clinton, whom she had regarded as the state's favorite son, seemed unthinkable. In a letter to Don Jones, her former Methodist youth minister who was now teaching theology in New Jersey, she tried to sort out what had happened. "I've been thinking a lot about the irratio-nality of politics and why people become so irrational," she wrote. "I remember once talking to you when I was in high school about a relative of mine who every now and then became caught up in an irrational mood, and how you put it in such simple terms and said, 'Have you ever seen anyone lose their temper? And how people can lose control of their good sense in moments of passion?' And you helped me in understanding."

Nowhere in the letter did Rodham mention what had happened in the election. Years later, rereading that letter, Jones pieced together what was going through her mind. In bringing back his old advice, she had reached a classically Rodhamesque conclusion. She considered herself rational and her logic told her that her husband should have been reelected. Therefore his rejection was an act of irrationality inflamed by passion.

Rodham offered a more political analysis of her husband's defeat at a conference in late February at the University of Arkansas-Little Rock. Her performance there was characterized by the *Arkansas Gazette* as "semi-gracious" but "totally spunky and eloquent." The losing campaign's first problem, she asserted, was that too many Clinton supporters thought it would be an easy election and were not as energized as they should have been. Furthermore, she said, "a political campaign has come down to a thirty-second war on television"—and the Clinton organization lost that war badly to Frank White. Their television commercials were ineffective, she said, and they reacted too slowly to White's negative attack in which he used grainy black and white film of the Cuban refugees rioting at Fort Chaffee to portray Clinton as an ineffective leader. When she first saw the Cuban refugee ad, Rodham thought, "I can't believe anyone will believe this." She considered it racist, noting that all the rioters in the film were black. Only too late, she said, did they realize that "it was not fair or accurate, but it was very effective."

Many of her friends from outside Arkansas were concerned about Rod-ham's well-being in the aftermath of the election. Did she feel stuck in that remote place with an embittered husband whose ambitions had been stymied? Fred Altshuler decided to check up on her. "I knew what she had gone through just to go to Arkansas in the first place," Altshuler recalled.

"I wanted to see how she was doing." He ventured out to Little Rock from San Francisco and slept on their couch at the Midland Avenue house. After hanging out for a few days, he decided that he had been too apprehensive about his friend's trauma. He visited Hillary and Bill at their law offices. She seemed engrossed in her work and Clinton bored by his. Altshuler talked about referring some cases to Clinton, "but he seemed much more interested in politics." They held a large dinner party at their house and Betsey Wright was there along with several professors—Arkansas people all talking Arkansas politics for hours on end. Hillary was right in the middle of the conversation.

She seemed perfectly at home there, Altshuler decided, more comfortable than when she had visited him in San Francisco and defended Jimmy Carter at a dinner party full of liberals. Hillary, Altshuler concluded, "was as much into the Arkansas kind of situation as Bill, which was the thing I had been curious about. I didn't know how she would react, having lost. She seemed to be doing fine."

As the weary winter dissolved into spring, Rodham spent some of her spare time planting a flowerbed in her yard and asked for advice on colors of lawn furniture. Clinton once called a friend and proudly boasted that he had just finished cleaning the kitchen: "It's spick and span," he said. But these were only random scenes of domestic bliss. The Clinton and Rodham relationship was rarely without tension, and in the months after the defeat the tension had heightened. Clinton seemed the more unhappy and distracted. One Saturday morning a friend stopped by the house and found him in the den, playing on the floor with Chelsea. Rodham was in the kitchen. As he smiled and laughed with his one-year-old daughter, Clinton sang softly in the lilt of a gentle lullaby, but loud enough for his guest to hear: "I want a div-or-or-or-orce. I want a div-or-or-or-orce."

NEVER fond of the deskbound life, Clinton spent several months in 1981 traveling the state, running as long and as hard as a noncandidate could run. Randy White, who had not found other employment, often served as his driver and travel aide. They would take White's Thunderbird, and scrounge around for gasoline money and a quarter to buy the *Gazette*. Betsey Wright, from her post outside Clinton's law office door, was running the show, setting up appointments at the same time that she was overseeing the transfer of his index cards onto a new computer system, bringing his political operation into the high-tech era. High school graduations, community meetings on toxic waste dumps—Clinton would go anywhere and talk to anyone who would listen to him. When asked pointblank, "Are you running for governor again?" he would demur, saying he was still weighing his options. Then, back in the car with White, he chortled, "Man, this thing is taking off. Talk up the rematch! Talk up the rematch!"

The traveling show of 1981 provided another chapter for Clinton's Close Calls in Cars. He and Randy White were in Fayetteville one morning for a commencement ceremony. As usual, Clinton chatted at length after the program, so that by the time he and White got back in the T-bird they were late for the next appointment, a graduation speech at the small town of Fifty-Six in north-central Arkansas. White's best-case scenario was that they could make it fifty minutes late. "Let's do it!" Clinton said. They took off, laughing and telling stories. Beer cans from a six-pack White had emptied the night before were rattling around on the floor of the car. The speedometer soon reached one hundred. Clinton was into a nap. White looked out the side and noticed that he had whooshed past a parked state trooper. He hit Clinton on the leg and said, "Uh, guess what, I just passed a state trooper!"

By the time the trooper caught up to them, Clinton and White were standing casually outside their car, parked on the shoulder of the road. "The trooper got that 'Oh, shit' expression on his face when he saw who it was," White later recalled. Clinton coolly gave him instructions. "We're trying to get to Fifty-Six and we need you to radio ahead and let them know we'll be late." Then they jumped back in the car and took off. Perhaps the trooper had forgotten that Clinton was no longer governor. In any case, not only did he spare them a ticket, but he radioed ahead as ordered. By the time the Thunderbird reached the school at Fifty-Six, the whole town was waiting. A special parking place had been set aside right in front. White's engine was smoking. Clinton was pumped by the journey and the crowd. He jumped out of the car—and a few beer cans fell out with him and rolled and clanged down the hill. They loved him in Fifty-Six.

Now that Clinton needed friends wherever he could find them, his on-and-off relationship with labor was on again. He visited with Bill Becker and other state labor leaders several times, expressing regret that he had not worked more closely with them in the past. The AFL-CIO summer convention in Hot Springs received his denunciation of Frank White's anti-labor record with shouts and several standing ovations, and Becker followed his speech by saying, "I suspect that that good-bye is only temporary." The labor movement contributed money to the fund that paid Betsey Wright's salary and his exploratory campaign work. The Democratic National Committee also helped him stay active by giving him a part-time mission as the head of the state and local elections effort, a job that could pay for some of his travel until he officially began his own state election campaign.

In his travels for the DNC, Clinton brought with him the lessons learned from his loss. The main tactical lesson, he thought, concerned how to respond to negative advertising. Since his first campaign on behalf of Judge Frank Holt in the 1966 gubernatorial primary, Clinton had remembered Holt's assertion that the public expected more of its candidates than to respond in kind to mudslinging from the other side. After what Frank White did to him with the Cuban refugee ads, Clinton finally became convinced that Judge Holt's credo was noble but naive and ultimately fatal. At a DNC election workshop in Des Moines, Iowa, Clinton delineated his new policy. "When someone is beating you over the head with a hammer, don't sit there and take it," he said. "Take out a meat cleaver and cut off their hand."

Doug Wallace was in the luncheon audience that day when Clinton let loose. In the years that he had worked with Clinton, first as his press secretary in the 1974 congressional race and later as executive director of the Arkansas Democratic party, Wallace had heard many colorful comments from his friend, but none quite so ferocious and bloody as that. Yes, Clinton was eager to please; yes, he was known as a conciliator; no, he had no combat experience; no, he had never shown much skill with tools or cutlery; no, he was not the brutish sort; yes, he often seemed conflict averse—and yet he had a peculiar attraction to violent figures of speech. "Take out a meat cleaver and cut off their hand," Bill Clinton had said.

One evening later that year, when Clinton took his traveling show up to Bentonville in northwest Arkansas, Rudy Moore felt as though it was his hand and those of other former assistants that Clinton's meat cleaver was cutting off. Moore had gone to a reception for Clinton at a private home. During a question and answer period, a local banker got up and started criticizing Steve Smith and other members of Clinton's first-term staff. It did not surprise Moore that Clinton chose not to defend Smith. But Moore was disappointed to hear Clinton give a long answer about the mistakes of his first term in which it seemed that he placed most of the blame on the staff. Moore left the reception feeling that "the rug had been pulled out from under" him. He had done nothing but work hard and be loyal, he thought to himself. He had given up his life in Springdale for a few years to devote himself to Clinton, and now "all of a sudden I'm getting the feeling that for his own well-being the staff becomes expendable at this point."

Moore later wrote Clinton a letter questioning whether he had sacrificed his old staff to the political gods in his bid for redemption. In his reply, Clinton argued, "Whatever you may think, I consistently defended you and your role on my staff in private meetings all over the state. . . . I always acknowledged that we had some serious staff problems but I tried to take full responsibility for them."

He had been misinterpreted, Clinton claimed.

Late that summer, national political columnists Jack Germond and Jules Witcover wrote in their column that Clinton had hired Betsey Wright to help him lay the groundwork for his 1982 campaign for governor. Wrong, Clinton responded, when local reporters asked him about the column. His actions were being misinterpreted. Germond and Witcover had "made too many assumptions." Although Wright was working for him at a desk outside his law office, "her job was not politically related." She was just helping him establish a computer filing system for his gubernatorial papers. "There is no campaign," he said.

FOR a few days each month, Dick Morris had been commuting to Little Rock from New York to help plot Clinton's comeback. It did not start out as a pleasant task. He felt some competition with Betsey Wright, who was there doing the same thing. On first sight, they hated each other. Wright viewed Morris as a slick, negative eastern sharpie who was "trying to take this moral man and corrupt him in the evil ways of politics." Morris viewed Wright as a "rigid left-wing idealogue who was so obsessively opposed to modern political campaigning that she would lead him back into the Stone Age politically." Each saw the other as a mortal threat. But the animosity dissipated, until finally Wright and Morris found themselves agreeing on almost every political move. They became allies in the resurrection of Bill Clinton. Wright would compliment Morris by calling him "one of the smartest little sons of bitches" she had ever met. "Mean. But God was he good."

Early in the fall of 1981, Morris polled Arkansas voters to gauge their feelings about Clinton. He feared that the public regarded Clinton as an alien figure, trained at Yale and Oxford, who had patronized them and had no sense of their state, and that they would feel no remorse about having got rid of him. But the poll results showed that the voters had a paternal attitude toward Clinton. Frank White had not won the election so much as Clinton had lost it. Morris and Wright began to construct a family parable out of the poll results. The citizens of Arkansas viewed Clinton as a prodigal son who had grown too big for his britches, who had thought that he knew everything and had tried to tell the other family members what was best for them rather than listening to their suggestions. They had voted against him to teach him a lesson, to give him a public spanking, but they had not necessarily intended for him to lose. The parable allowed for forgiveness. It meant, Wright concluded, that "a comeback was doable."

But first Clinton had to apologize. Morris conceived the notion of a public mea culpa, a television advertisement in which Clinton announced his comeback bid by saying he was sorry. In discussing it with Wright,

Clinton, and Rodham, Morris, who was Jewish, put it in terms of the theological metaphor of Christian forgiveness. "You have to recognize your sins, confess to them, and promise to sin no more and then sin no more," Morris said. "And in the act of contrition, you have to be humble. You can't be self-justified. You have to say, 'I'm very sorry, ashamed, I know I did wrong and I'll never do it again.' " Rodham and Wright immediately took to the idea. Clinton had somewhat of a hard time fully accepting it. He felt humbled, certainly, and stupid for losing to Frank White, but the part he could not get past was being restrained from trying to explain and justify what he had done. On one level, he would say, "I screwed up." But on another level he would ask, "Which of the things that I did would I do differently? Would I not fulfill my campaign promise to build better roads?" He could justify every specific action he had taken.

It was bigger than specifics, Morris insisted. It was his attitude, his approach to governing. The voters thought he was patronizing. He had to learn how to sail into the wind, Morris said. "You don't abandon where you want to go, but you have to tack to get there. You have to one minute go right for the objective, and then at some point when you find the boat is about to tip over, you steer in another direction until the boat regains stability, then once more head toward the objective. You approach it in a series of triangular moves, instead of head-on." The objective here was to get back in office. The triangular move was to apologize in a paid public television advertisement.

Clinton agreed to go ahead with the mea culpa, but continued to argue with Morris about the wording. The language was too apologetic, he complained.

"Well," Morris responded, according to his later recollection, "you can't say, 'So I robbed the store but I needed the money badly because my sister is starving.' That's a very nice justification for robbing the store, but it implies that you don't think it was all wrong to rob the store."

"But I don't!" Clinton said.

"But you do!" Morris said.

At one point, the two men spent several hours arguing over whether the word "apology" should be in the ad. They finally agreed to the language for two spots, one a general apology for mistakes including the car tags increase, and another addressing his decision during the final days of his term to pardon scores of violent criminals whose release had been recommended by the state parole board. They went to New York, to the West 57th Street studios of media consultant Tony Schwartz, for the filming. Before the cameras went on, Clinton revealed to Morris that he had fiddled with the words one last time. Morris was in shock. "I'm not gonna tell you what I did—I just want you to see it," Clinton said.

In the end, Clinton managed to say he that he was sorry without saying he was sorry. He did it by using down-home Arkansas language. Morris was elated by the change. When he was growing up, Clinton said, his daddy never had to whip him twice for the same thing. If the voters gave him another chance, he said, he would never make the same mistakes again. He had learned that he could not lead without listening.

The ads began running on three Little Rock television stations on February 8, 1982. Clinton's face filled the screen, barely leaving room for his name and the tag line identifying the commercial as paid for by the Clinton for Governor Committee. What the public saw was that Clinton was chastened. Political observers in Little Rock had never seen anything like it—someone announcing for governor via a thirty-second commercial, and doing so with an apology. But the strategy was apparent: By admitting his mistakes and seeking absolution before the first tough question of the race could be asked, Clinton was able to say that criticisms of his previous actions were irrelevant.

ANOTHER problem needed fixing as the comeback campaign began, this one involving Hillary Rodham and her name. Since his first race for governor in 1978, Clinton's opponents had tried to make something out of that. It was very un-Arkansan, they would imply, marking Rodham as an outsider who stubbornly resisted the traditional mores of her adopted state. This sentiment was shared by many of Clinton's friends, including his own mother. During the 1980 campaign, one powerful member of the Arkansas House offered the opinion to Representative Ray Smith, Jr., of Hot Springs that "Hillary's gonna have to change her name, and shave her legs." Rodham had ignored the issue in the past, but now, as she saw her and her husband's political ambitions on the line, she reconsidered.

Her change, in typical Rodham fashion, was more intellectual than emotional. When Carolyn Staley dropped by the Midland Avenue house the morning after a party in Little Rock, Rodham asked her a question that Staley had never heard from her before: "What were people wearing?" It was clear to Staley that Rodham was "making the transformation from studied feminist. She started to key in on the fact that the name was political, that what she wore was political." Years later, when asked about the name change, Clinton recalled a conversation he had with his wife in which she approached him and said, "We've got to talk about this name deal." As Clinton remembered it, Rodham told him that she did not want him to lose the election because of her last name. Clinton said he protested. Then, by his account, she placed the decision in the most pragmatic political terms: "We shouldn't run the risk. What if it's one percent of the vote? What if it's two percent?"

If Clinton protested, it was not very strenuously. In conversations when his wife was not around, he often joked about their different names in a way that made it clear he thought it would be easier if she became Hillary Clinton. Once, while eating Mexican food with some old friends from the McGovern campaign during a visit to Austin, Clinton noted that he and his wife disagreed on an issue and then added, "Hell, I can't even get her to use my last name!"

All that changed on February 27, 1982, the day of Clinton's formal announcement, when Hillary referred to herself as "Mrs. Bill Clinton." Was it really a change, and was it something that she wanted to do? Her answers that day left room for confusion. "I don't have to change my name," she said. "I've been Mrs. Bill Clinton. I kept the professional name Hillary Rodham in my law practice, but now I'm going to be taking a leave of absence from the law firm to campaign full-time for Bill and I'll be Mrs. Bill Clinton. I suspect people will be getting tired of hearing from Mrs. Bill Clinton." But when asked whether she had legally changed her name and was now registered to vote as Hillary Clinton, she said, "No." The press accounts of that exchange made it clear that she still had some convincing to do.

The *Times-News* of McGehee put it this way: " 'No,' came the ice cold answer from Arkansas' former first lady."

THE public reaction to Clinton's mea culpa ad was swift and sure. People hated it. In a three-way race in the Democratic primary for governor against Jim Guy Tucker and Joe Purcell, Clinton fell from the top spot, from holding about 43 percent of the vote, down to the mid-20s. Voters who said they held a favorable view of Clinton dropped. The number who held an unfavorable view doubled. Tucker, the politician he had conspired to defeat in the 1978 Senate race against David Pryor, was now ahead of him. And all because of a self-inflicted wound. Morris's polls showed that the mea culpa caused the precipitous decline in Clinton's ratings, reminding voters of the reasons they turned away from him in the first place. The consultant flew out to Arkansas to deliver the grim news, and met Clinton and Rodham in a small town where Clinton was giving a speech. He tried to put the best spin on the poll results. The apology was like a smallpox vaccination, he said. You get a little sick, but then you are immune. He said it, Morris recalled later, with "great bravado and self-confidence." But he did not mean it. He thought he had destroyed his client.

The immunization theory was quickly tested. It was a bitter, unenlightening primary, with most of the enmity flowing between Tucker and Clinton, who were both in desperate, anything-goes moods, fighting for political survival. They attacked each other daily, each trying to prove that he was tougher and more conservative. Tucker attacked Clinton for commuting or cutting the sentences of thirty-eight convicted murderers during the final weeks of his first term. Clinton attacked Tucker's poor attendance record in Congress and portrayed Tucker as a tool of labor and the special interests and as a bleeding heart on welfare issues. He criticized Tucker for supporting liberal food stamp standards. It was left to the *Arkansas Gazette* to point out that Tucker had merely voted against an amendment that would have eliminated food stamps for striking workers. In an editorial entitled "Bill Clinton on the Low Road," the *Gazette* concluded of his food stamp attack: "It is an uncharacteristic place for Bill Clinton to take his stand, and in the sanctity of his own thoughts he must be ashamed."

Shame was not foremost on Clinton's mind that year. His main concern was to stay alive. The intensity of his mood was revealed in April when he got into a dispute with the Arkansas Education Association (AEA). At a meeting with a screening committee for the teachers' union, Clinton was asked what kind of relationship he would maintain with the AEA if they did not endorse him. According to Larry Russell, a teacher at Lake Hamilton High who was chairman of the committee, Clinton "said he would tear our heads off and beat our brains out if we endorsed another candidate." Russell and Lyle French, the president of the union, took Clinton's statement to mean that he might hold a grudge against them.

"Nothing could be further from the truth and I resent this!" Clinton bellowed during a rally in Hot Springs a few days later. In Clinton's version of the event, when the screening committee asked him how he would respond if he failed to get their endorsement, "I told them this is a political race and they would be trying to end my political career and that I would beat their brains out." But, Clinton said, he left no implication that he would hold it against them. The teachers endorsed Tucker.

But Clinton's negative approach was working. The next round of internal polls found that all of Clinton's negative attacks on Tucker scored, driving his poll ratings down fifteen points, while none of Tucker's attacks hurt Clinton. It seemed that Clinton had indeed been immunized. "The polls showed a tremendous backlash of sympathy for Clinton because he had already apologized," Morris recalled. "People said, 'What's Tucker dumping on him for? He already apologized. It's a rare man who can admit his mistakes.' The immunity was so palpably there that it was a tremendously useful thing to have gone through." Clinton and Rodham filed it away in their briefcase of effective political tactics, to be pulled out now and again when Clinton got caught in uncomfortable situations. The calculated act of contrition: when in trouble, go directly to the people and confess on your own terms.

As often happens when two candidates bury each other in mud during a three-way primary, the voters became interested in the third candidate. Joe Purcell, a soft-spoken former lieutenant governor, made it into a runoff with Clinton, while Tucker was eliminated. Clinton and his strategists would have preferred to have faced Tucker again. "Tucker had a record we could run against," Betsey Wright said later. "Joe Purcell was a lovable old slipper. We didn't know what to do with him." Purcell was in the Judge Holt mold, a dignified man who refused to make personal attacks against his opponents. Clinton could not claim that someone was going at him with a hammer, but he was forced to use the meat cleaver anyway. Morris's first poll during the two-week runoff showed Purcell ahead, with most of the Tucker vote going to him. They put up one negative ad and spread the word that Republicans were interfering in the runoff on Purcell's behalf. Luckily for Clinton, runoffs, with traditionally low voter turnouts, depend largely on campaign organizations, and Purcell did not have one. The results on June 8 gave Clinton 54 percent of the vote. "We want Frank! We want Frank!" Clinton's supporters shouted that night. They got Frank. The rematch with Governor White was at hand.

THE general election of 1982 was almost completely devoid of the internal bickering of many other Clinton campaigns. It combined the optimism and freshness of his 1974 congressional campaign with the technical skill of his later efforts. With Hillary, Betsey Wright, and Dick Morris at the head of the campaign organization, there were enough decisive people to offset Clinton's indecisiveness, which was less noticeable than usual anyway because of the urgency of his cause. He had a clear mission: redemption. "Hell, he knew what was at stake," Woody Bassett, who organized Washington County for him, later recalled. "He knew that if he lost, it was the end for him in elected politics."

His supporters had various missions of their own. Some hated Frank White. Some thought Clinton deserved another chance and felt guilty that they had not worked harder for him in 1980. Some were embarrassed that the state had regained a backwater image with the enactment of fundamentalist legislation requiring public schools to teach creationism along with evolution. Young black professionals who moved back to the state at the start of the 1980s saw Clinton as the conduit for their rise. The vibrancy of a political campaign can be measured by the ratio of volunteers to paid staffers. In 1980, Clinton struggled to find volunteers. This time, the headquarters overflowed with volunteers and there were only a handful of paid staff members. Betsey Wright called it a crusade—her first, and her best—in Arkansas. If the volunteers were the soul of the campaign, the computer system was its brain. The dedicated computer room in the campaign headquarters near the Capitol ran around the clock, churning out Glad-to-Meet-You letters, fund-raising solicitations, special letters for black supporters, for first-time supporters, for teachers, for the elderly. Letters to friends of Bill went out in an endless stream. No other politician in Arkansas had anything comparable. The computer became the mechanical extension of Clinton's tireless personality. What else. What else. What else.

The airwaves were glutted with negative advertising from both sides, but White's ads made little difference. With every exchange of the hammer versus the meat cleaver, Clinton's numbers rose. "It got to be almost a joke," Morris recalled. "We felt like we were behind bulletproof glass watching somebody aim at us and pull the trigger and watch the bullets splatter harmlessly." He started to call Clinton "Achilles without the heel."

Clinton narrowed his message. He talked constantly about jobs and utility rates. He had needed a villain against which he could assume a populist pose, and a calculated decision was made to cast the utility companies in that role. Other villains were considered, according to Morris, including the trucking-poultry lobby, but Clinton did not want to refight a lost battle of the first term and in fact had promised to support the industry's bid for an increase in truck weights to 80,000 pounds. Utility companies were better villains in the sense that they were less feisty and threatening. He promised that in a second term he would work to make the Public Service Commission, which controlled utility rates, an elected body accountable to the people. He brought in old-line, middle-of-the-road Democrats to help him raise money, including W. Maurice Smith, a wealthy farmer and banker from Birdeye, and George Kell, a former third baseman for the Detroit Tigers. He raised and spent more money than any candidate in Arkansas history. He spent most of his Sundays in black churches, and recruited three black organizers to help him with the black vote: Rodney Slater, Carol Willis, and Bob Nash, all of whom would become part of his team for the next decade.

Willis, a former law student of Clinton's in Fayetteville, had developed a militant reputation in the impoverished Delta region of southeast Arkansas. He called Clinton one day and said, "They're about ready to run me out of McGehee, Bill, I need work." To which Clinton responded, "Well, shit, I ain't got no jobs unless I get elected. Come on and help." Willis, Slater, and Nash split up the state, Willis taking the Delta, Slater the Little Rock area, and Nash the southwest. They called themselves the three amigos: Willis the radical, Slater the moderate, and Nash the technocrat. "And we humped," Willis recalled later. "We worked twenty-four hours a day, Saturday and Sunday. If there was an event involved black people, we were there. And we would get Clinton there." No one in Arkansas political annals locked up the black vote the way Clinton did in 1982.

On election night, everything was different from the way it had been in

1980. Rodham and Clinton and Betsey Wright were superstitious. They stayed away from the Camelot Hotel. They set up a stage on the street outside the headquarters on Central Avenue. Clinton watched the results in a back room with Hillary and his mother and brother Roger, who was wearing an open-necked Mexican shirt and gold chains. Wright ran the tally board. She tried to stay cool, but could barely contain her excitement. Every few minutes, she emerged from the room and shouted out new numbers. "Craighead County by fifty-four percent. Complete!" she barked, denoting another county that Clinton had lost two years earlier but carried this time. Clinton had won. He pumped his clenched left fist high into the air and rushed out the front door of the headquarters, out into the street, where his army of supporters, intoxicated by victory, chanted his name as he disappeared in the delirious sea of outstretched hands.

CHAPTER TWENTY-TWO

THE
PERMANENT
CAMPAIGN

Two MONTHS LATER, on the afternoon of January 11, 1983, the faithful and curious waited single-file in a queue that circled from the second floor of the Arkansas Capitol down to the rotunda and out the steps into the warm winter wind. It was the largest crowd that had ever gathered for an inauguration in Little Rock, there to celebrate the return of the favorite son. Bill Clinton stood in the receiving line inside the governor's conference room, surrounded by portraits of his predecessors, one of whom was himself. Already that day he had belted out redemptive hymns with his Immanuel Baptist Church choir. He had swept back to the Capitol for the swearing-in ceremony in the House, the click of his heels echoing in the marble halls as he moved through his old haunt. He had delivered his inaugural address on the Capitol steps and felt the applause wash over him. Now the welcome-back handshakes and bearhugs made the restoration complete. He was blessing and being blessed in the sacred rite of Arkansas politics.

Clinton was back in power; but he was not picking up where he had left off a few years earlier. Everything was different this second time around. The youth crusade atmosphere of the first term was long gone. His staff was almost entirely recast in a more reassuring image, with a grandmotherly receptionist and a good ole boy executive assistant, old enough to be his father, and another senior aide whose duties included praying with fundamentalist preachers when they visited the governor's office. "He realized that he needed some older folks on his staff," recalled Paul Root, who had been Clinton's high school world history teacher and was recruited at age fifty to work in the governor's office on education and church issues, which often intersect in the Bible Belt. "He said the first term he had some of the brightest people he knew, but they were all policy people, and if a right-wing preacher came in, he didn't have anyone to pray with him." The emphasis this time was on how aides got along with the public, state agencies, and the legislature. To sharpen his focus and open up the decision-making process, Clinton began chairing staff meetings every morning at seven while the legislature was in session during the first few months of the year. They were freewheeling, open-door discussions at which interested legislators were welcome to get some coffee and take a seat.

The state's mood had also changed. In place of the pride-and-hope theme of his first inaugural, Clinton now spoke of a battle "with an old and familiar enemy: hard times." Arkansas was in the midst of a recession, with three bad years on the farms and double-digit unemployment in the towns. He attributed the recession in part to the Republican policies of the Reagan administration in Washington, and in part to a larger state and national lethargy in adapting to a changing world economy through a renewed focus on education, information services, and worker retraining, themes that his Rhodes Scholar friend Bob Reich was expounding in his book *The Next American Frontier.* But the central parable of Clinton's inaugural speech came not from his generational experience but from Depression-era family folklore: the story of when Pappaw Cassidy fell to his knees and cried because he could not afford to buy young Virginia a two-dollar Easter dress.

If the public image Clinton conveyed was one of earnest determination, in private he feared that the state's condition, and his political situation, were more precarious than he had let on. In this moment of vindication, he was nagged by a sense of impending disaster. The bad news had started on the morning after the election, when Frank White's chief of staff had called Betsey Wright, who would be Clinton's staff director, and revealed that there was a $30 million shortfall in state revenues. Much of the transition had been consumed with targeting budget cuts. And there were other worries. In his comeback campaign, Clinton had pounded away at utility companies, portraying them as greedy villains and himself the returning champion who would give consumers a break on spiraling rates. The populist theme had helped him get elected, but now he had to deal with the raised expectations. He did not yet control the Public Service Commission, which set rates. Legislators and editorialists were lined up against his pledge to require that the utility commissioners be elected rather than appointed. A federal ruling on the state's financial obligations to a regional nuclear power consortium might force rates higher. In the end, he worried, he might appear no better on the issue than White.

An even more difficult predicament loomed. The Arkansas Supreme Court was considering a lower court ruling that had declared the state's system of financing public education unconstitutional because it denied equal opportunities to students in poor districts. A final decision, almost certain to uphold the lower court ruling, was expected sometime during the new two-year term. Clinton's options looked unappealing. He could try to take money from rich districts and give it to poor ones, which would invite class warfare and be of minimal value since education was severely underfinanced in the entire state. Arkansas was at the bottom nationally in student spending and teacher salaries. He could make a concerted push for consolidation among the state's rural school districts, an effort that might reopen the old desegregation wounds and was sure to hurt him politically in areas that would lose their high school sports teams and school identities. Or he could raise taxes for education, the most likely alternative, yet a disturbing prospect for a governor who could not forget that he had lost his job attempting to get more money for better roads.

But among the things that had changed since his first term was Clinton's strategic approach. His political personality was largely unchanged: he was still restless, eclectic, intellectually hungry, eager to please. But this time he had a survival plan: the permanent campaign.

SINCE his period of exile, Clinton had been spending endless hours talking with Dick Morris about political theory and strategy. Morris was a nonstop plotter, constantly spinning out strategies and scenarios, calling his favorite clients late at night or flying in for intense, secretive head-to-head consultations in which he often left them mesmerized and reassured. He was competitive and contentious, always asking for his next check, and tended to drive other staffers crazy. To the extent that his flexible ideology was apparent, he was moderate and moving rightward. Of the politicians of both parties who dealt with him, none listened with more rapt fascination or engaged him in more debate than Clinton. Morris also established a special bond with Hillary, who shared his dark, untrusting perspective on politics.

Clinton's problem, Morris told him, was that in the past he had bisected means and ends with "an almost Catholic splitting of virtue and sin." Candidate Clinton would do whatever it took to get elected, but Governor Clinton would "go about serving without any significant thought to the political connotations, with almost a shunning of that which would be politically useful." Means and ends, pragmatism and idealism, had to be "completely interwoven," Morris advised. "When you lead in an idealistic direction, the most important thing to do is to be highly pragmatic about it. And when necessity forces upon you a problem of great pragmatism, you need to use idealism to find your way out of the thicket." This axiom became one of the three basic tenets of Clinton's permanent campaign.

A second arose from the benchmark poll Morris had conducted in 1981 in which the intensity of disillusionment with Clinton was measured to see whether a comeback was possible. The survey had found a widespread perception among voters that Clinton had probably done some good things in his first term but they could not remember any specific accomplishments. All they could recite were actions he had taken which they disliked. Morris, Clinton, Hillary, and Betsey Wright, the quartet that comprised the inner circle, decided that they would never again rely on the "free media" —newspaper, radio, and television reporters—to define Clinton and his programs. Interweaving means and ends, they would use paid media, commercials and grass-roots mailings, whenever they wanted to get their message to the public, even during a midterm legislative session. Individual journalists might be courted, especially the peskiest ones, such as *Arkansas Democrat* managing editor John Robert Starr, who would nip at the governor in his daily column unless he was made to feel like an insider. (Starr remembered Clinton calling him the day he got back to the governor's office and saying, "Okay, what do you want?") But for the most part, the press was not part of the plan. "His entire strategy in governing the state," Morris recalled, "was based on flanking the press through the paid media."

The third aspect of Clinton's permanent campaign involved the use of voter surveys in similarly perpetual fashion, taking poll results to shape the substance and rhetoric of policy debates. The goal was to discover more than whether voters supported or opposed an initiative. Word by word, line by line, phrase by phrase, paragraph by paragraph, rhetorical options would be tested to see which ones were most effective in moving the public a certain direction. It was polling as a form of copy writing, as a way for Clinton to organize his thoughts. Although Morris conducted the polls, each of the four played a role in the process. Hillary Clinton was usually the one to articulate the larger problem. Wright was there to lay out the facts. Clinton and Morris would play endlessly with the words and arguments. Clinton became so hooked on the process that his rhythms could be charted by it. When polls were out in the field, he seemed passive and noncommittal. Wright and Morris discovered that Clinton was never happier than when he got the results.

Morris would read an answer, and Clinton would shout, "You know, I feel it! I feel it! I'm out there and that's just what I feel! That's absolutely right!" Then he would practice the rhetorical argument again, elaborating, rehearsing, seemingly overcome by joy as things that had been unclear became clear to him and he sang from a political score that he and the voters had jointly composed.

All of these elements of his permanent campaign were put to the test during Clinton's first year back on the job. It was a difficult stretch that started slowly and ended in controversy, yet it was also the year of Clinton's greatest legislative triumph. On the surface it seemed at first that he had no better grasp of how to operate than he had displayed during his first term. His means and ends were snarled. The state press corps found his agenda unenterprising. The only apparent resolve he exhibited was on utility issues, which were going nowhere. One February day, Clinton spent ninety minutes beseeching the House Insurance and Commerce Committee to endorse his bill that would require the election of Public Service Commissioners. He brought in an expert witness from North Dakota to testify with him. When their presentations ended, not a single member of the committee made a motion to endorse the bill. A local columnist described it as "one of the most embarrassing defeats any governor has suffered."

It was being said that Clinton was indecisive, reluctant to move on issues ranging from school consolidation to taxes. His maneuverings in the renewed battle between the highway lobby and the trucking-poultry lobby did nothing to enhance that image. First Clinton endorsed the highway commission's bill to impose a weight-distance tax to cover additional damage incurred by trucks weighing up to 80,000 pounds that were soon to roll down state highways. When that bill got through the Senate, leaders of the lobby, organized as the Forward Arkansas Committee, expressed outrage, saying they thought Clinton had told them that he opposed the measure because it raised more money than was needed. A few days later, the trucking forces pushed their less costly alternative through the House, this time with Clinton's endorsement and the help of his legislative aides. The state highway director was now shocked, calling the governor a "double-crosser." Clinton eventually took a third position, saying that he supported both bills and that whichever one passed was fine with him. In an end-of-session interview with the *Arkansas Gazette,* published under the front-page headline, "Wasn't Weak, Vacillating, Clinton Says of His Stands," he argued, without irony, that it was unfair to say that he tried to please everybody because "in reality the effect probably was that I ended up displeasing both sides."

Although these apparent blunders might not have been deliberate ploys, they did fall into a larger strategy. Clinton and his inner circle had already chosen education reform, not utility reform or highway improvements, as the central issue of his governorship, the one for which they planned to put to full use the tactics of the permanent campaign. Clinton was eager to become known as the education governor. For all his romance about the regular folks of Arkansas, he was frustrated by the state's inferiority complex, a sense that "God meant for us to be last, that God meant for us to be poor." Basic education was the "key to our economic revival and our perennial quest for prosperity." But the Supreme Court had not yet ruled on the school-funding case. Morris had just begun testing the tax possibilities and the rhetoric that would shape the public debate. Hillary Clinton was preparing to serve her husband as chairman of the Education Standards Committee that would design the substance of reform. The serious work awaited a special legislative session.

Before that, during the regular legislative session, Clinton's essential objective had been to buy time. His goal with truck weights was to try to avoid being viewed as the central force responsible for a new tax, whichever way the tax went. He managed to do that, at the calculated expense of angering both sides and appearing equivocal. On utility reform, his aim had been to push hard in public so that he would not appear to be backing away from a campaign promise, while essentially conceding the issue in private. "He knew he couldn't succeed, but he had to show that he had tried and failed," Morris recalled. "He had to keep up the rhetoric." This strategy also had mixed results. While it enhanced Clinton's pro-consumer image, it infuriated some utility reform advocates who concluded that he had been grandstanding. One of his longtime energy advisers, Scott Trotter, finally turned on him, issuing a seven-page critique in which he said, "Clinton's actions on utilities during the current term have been phony and inconsequential. What is worse, this is not a mistake but a politically calculated policy." Trotter bitterly cited a meeting in early summer at which he said Clinton told him that he no longer needed the utility issue because he was now focused on education reform.

FEW people in Arkansas were surprised when the state Supreme Court ruling came out in the final week in May declaring public education financing unconstitutionally inequitable. Here was a state with 367 school districts, more than twice as many districts as neighboring states, some so remote and poor and with such meager property tax bases that they could barely pay teachers a living wage or supply basic educational services. In some schools in southwest Arkansas, not far from Clinton's birthplace in Hope, teachers were making less than $10,000 a year and qualified for food stamps, with their own children in federally subsidized free lunch programs. The need for more money to spread around to those districts was obvious. But it was also Clinton's great practical dilemma. Even though Arkansas ranked next to last in the nation in the tax burden imposed on state residents, above only Alabama, there was a prevalent notion among Arkansans that they were poor and overburdened already. As the car tag revolt of 1980 had made clear to Clinton, any tax hike could be rejected as an unwarranted imposition, especially during economic hard times.

How to raise taxes? How to solve this practical dilemma? Rule number one of the permanent campaign: Turn to idealism. The first decision of Clinton and the inner circle was to move the focus away from the tax by making it an idealistic crusade. Rather than merely raising enough money to satisfy the court mandate, they would seek twice as much, and build an entire program around it. There was a national context to this approach: the National Commission on Excellence in Education had just issued a landmark report citing a "rising tide of mediocrity" in the nation's schools and detailing a long list of needed reforms. Some southern states had already launched education reform efforts, most notably Mississippi, whose threadbare schools usually ranked fiftieth, below Arkansas' forty-ninth, in comparative studies of the states. The traditional sarcastic cry in Arkansas, "Thank God for Mississippi!", might no longer apply.

Hillary Rodham, now going by Hillary Clinton or Mrs. Clinton, took a leave of absence from Rose Law Firm to spend the summer and early fall chairing the Education Standards Committee. It was not the first time she had worked for her husband (in the first term she had chaired a committee on rural health care), but it was her widest public exposure, reflecting her idealistic and pragmatic sides: her profound interest in children and education issues and, even more, the extraordinary commitment she had begun making to advance Clinton's cause since the 1980 defeat. In selecting her for the committee, Clinton had said, "This guarantees that I will have a person who is closer to me than anyone else overseeing a project that is more important to me than anything else." From then on, increasingly, he would turn to her for critical tasks that he needed done or was not good at himself.

The Education Standards Committee held seventy-five meetings, in which it took public testimony at the same time that it prepared the public for a largely predesigned set of reforms, from mandatory kindergarten to smaller class sizes in elementary school to competence tests for students in third, sixth, and eighth grades to minimum standards and scorecards for every school. The inadequacies the committee members found in many Arkansas school districts were stunning: no physics classes in 148 high schools, no advanced math in 135, no foreign languages in 180, and no music in 204 schools. At every session, parents would hover around Hillary Clinton after the meetings and tell stories about their troubled schools. Gradually, over the course of the hearing process, it seemed that Hillary, after living in Arkansas for nearly a decade, was finally being accepted as a member of the family, viewed less as a professional outsider and more as an intelligent public servant. When she appeared before an interim committee of the legislature to outline the reforms that her panel was considering, Representative Lloyd George said into his microphone, "I think we've elected the wrong Clinton!"

While Hillary concentrated on substance, Clinton and Morris experi-

mented with tax strategies, testing a variety of options in polls which they
wrote and rewrote together. Clinton finally decided to try to raise most of
the money by increasing the sales tax 1 percent. It was the least progressive form of taxation, unpopular with organized labor and advocates for
the poor, but it was also the surest way to get the money. It required only
majority approval in the legislature, whereas most other tax hikes would
require three-quarters approval. Some of Clinton's allies thought it was
time to reform the sales tax by eliminating food from items that could be
taxed or expanding it to include a variety of exempted services. But Morris,
strongly supported by Hillary, argued that it would be counterproductive
to make the tax that interesting because it would then become the issue,
"rather than the good things it would achieve."

As the final education package was prepared for the special session
which was to begin in early October, an idea that had not been part of the
committee's recommendations took on a central role: competence tests
for public school teachers. It was a concept that Hillary had considered
privately, especially after coming home from hearings where she heard
horror stories about some teachers. In their strategy sessions, the Clintons
would recall the teacher who taught his class about "World War Eleven"
—apparently mistaking the Roman numerals of World War II. But the
overriding reasons for adding the teacher tests to the program were political. Frank White, the former governor, who represented the conservative
business establishment, announced in a speech a few weeks before the
special session that he would support the tax increase and pay raises for
teachers only if they were accompanied by teacher tests.

Morris offered two other reasons to include teacher tests in the package
in tandem with teacher salary increases. In surveys he had conducted
going back to 1978, one of Clinton's highest negatives was that people
thought he was the tool of special interests, which to many Arkansas voters
meant not powerful business forces but liberal groups such as the Teachers
Association, labor unions, and blacks. Public employee unionism was unpopular in the state. When Morris polled on the teacher tests, he found
that the support for it was overwhelming, exceeding 75 percent. "It distills
the quality of helping children from the soup of helping children and
helping the teachers' union," Morris told Clinton. "It boils off what people
didn't like, which was caving in to the teachers who want more money,
and shows the purity of your motivation of helping children, because you
are offending the special interest that would be most gratified by what you
are doing." It was also, Morris noted, a decisive break from the Democratic
left.

On the day before Clinton appeared on statewide television to unveil
his proposal, Betsey Wright invited Kai Erickson, executive director of the

Arkansas Education Association (AEA), to her office in the Capitol and told him what was in the package, including the teacher tests. Erickson was stunned. He told her that the teachers had worked with Clinton and Hillary throughout the hearing process and had never been informed that the competence tests were on the table. He asked whether it was something that could be discussed and negotiated. Wright said no.

RULE number two of the permanent campaign: Never rely on the press, the free media, to get your message across. The education campaign started before the special session began, and it was almost indistinguishable from an election campaign. Clinton formed a finance committee, Arkansas Partners in Education, that raised and spent $130,000 for radio and television commercials promoting the reform package. Another support group, the Blue Ribbon Education Committee, distributed satin blue ribbons and 250,000 brochures explaining the program along with postcards that could be mailed to legislators by citizens supporting the reform effort. Most of the money was raised from financial institutions and corporations in a four-day solicitation blitz orchestrated by Clinton and his executive secretary, W. Maurice Smith, the rural financier and farmer, who also began making personal loans to Clinton from his own bank to sustain the permanent campaign.

On Tuesday, October 4, in an address opening the special session, ten months into his term, Clinton declared that the legislature was presented with a "magic moment" to change Arkansas history. It was an emotional speech, infusing his personal struggles with his hopes for his state. "In the life of our state, as in the life of a person, there are times of growth and decline, times of joy and sadness, times of triumph and tragedy, and times of ordinary getting along," Clinton said. "Much of what life brings is a matter of circumstance beyond our control. Yet always our will makes some difference, and sometimes our will can make all the difference. We are here tonight in such a time." He cited one of his favorite quotes from Oliver Wendell Holmes: " 'I think that, as life is action and passion, it is required of a man that he should share the passion and action of his time at peril of being judged not to have lived.' " He read from Robert Frost: " 'Two roads diverged in a wood, and I—/I took the one less traveled by,/ And that has made all the difference.' " And, mindful of Morris's polls indicating that the public was overwhelmingly behind teacher tests, he called mandatory tests a "small price to pay for the biggest tax increase for education in the history of the state and to restore the teaching profession to the position of public esteem that I think it deserves."

What had been a last-minute, throw-in idea now became the symbolic center of the reform package. The Teachers Association accused the Clintons of labeling their entire profession incompetent. One of the major fears of the AEA leadership was that a standardized teacher test, like many standardized tests, would prove to be culturally biased against some black teachers, but they were reluctant to make that case in public, fearing a backlash among redneck legislators. Carol Willis and other black aides on Clinton's staff also thought that the tests would have racial implications: they drafted their own satiric version of a test with a cultural bias toward the inner city, with such items as "Q. When is Mother's Day? A. The day the welfare checks arrive." Clinton expressed chagrin at the AEA's charges that he and Hillary were smearing the teaching profession. But in private, according to Morris, he appreciated the political benefits of picking a fight.

With the poll numbers behind him, Clinton struck an unyielding position. If the legislature killed the testing plan, he said, he would drop the entire package. Angry teachers roamed the halls of the Capitol and packed the Senate gallery for the crucial vote, which was close enough to go either way. Clinton did much of the last-minute lobbying himself, calling senators out of the chamber and displaying the full range of his abilities to plead, cajole, and persuade. He cornered Vada Sheid, the former treasurer of Baxter County who had been his friend and ally since the day in the spring of 1974 when he had stopped at her furniture store in Mountain Home to ask for her support in the congressional race against John Paul Hammerschmidt and she had sewed a loose button on his shirt. Sheid wanted to vote with Clinton, but the teachers in her district were putting pressure on her to go against the tests. "Bill Clinton comes to the Senate and he calls me out and he says, 'Vada, you're not thinkin' clear, you've forgotten your grandchildren have always had priority with you,' " Sheid recalled. "He said, 'You're afraid, Vada. But I have to have one more vote to pass this thing.' "

Clinton "had tears in his eyes," according to Sheid. "He had to have that one vote. He was dead meat. He was emotional about it." She told him that she was nervous about reelection. "This will defeat me," she said.

"No it won't," Clinton promised. "It will help you."

Sheid voted for the tests. The teachers campaigned door to door in her district against her. She lost the next election, but did not hold it against Clinton, who rewarded her act of loyalty by appointing her to the state police commission.

In the legislative endgame, Clinton also had a problem with the tax aspects of the package, and he resorted to a different sort of gamesmanship to prevail. Among the issues still in dispute were his insistence that the sales tax hike include an emergency clause making its effect immediate, and an amendment pushed by labor and public action groups giving an annual rebate to low-income families for the sales tax on food. At a meeting in the governor's office, Clinton struck a deal with J. Bill Becker of the AFL-CIO and citizen activist Brownie Ledbetter, two vocal advocates of the food tax rebate. If they would lobby for his emergency clause in the House, he would support their amendment. The deal was witnessed by two legislators, one of whom interrupted Clinton and repeated the terms to make sure the governor understood what he was saying. Clinton said yes.

The House then passed the tax measure with the rebate amendment, but the emergency clause failed by a narrow margin. The rebate lobbyists, satisfied that Clinton was upholding his end of the deal, joined forces again with the governor's aides the next day and pushed through the emergency clause. The following day, however, when leaders of the Senate said they had troubles with the rebate amendment, Clinton started backing away from it. By the time the Senate had passed the bill without the rebate and sent it back to the House for final action, the governor and his lobbyists were actively working against it. Clinton said that the deal was only temporary, and that he had to turn away from it in the interest of getting the reform package enacted. Whatever savings low-income residents might gain from the food tax rebate, he said, were of transitory and minimal value compared with the permanent benefits of better educational opportunities.

Becker was enraged. He complained that Clinton had turned away from the rebate amendment too hastily. The vote in the Senate would have been close, he agreed, but with a full-scale lobbying effort by the governor it might have passed. When he was lobbying the House for the emergency clause as part of the deal, Becker said, several representatives had warned him, "Clinton's lying to you! He's lying to you! He's not going to do it!" Becker had not believed them then, but now he decided that they had been right. He had been a presence in Arkansas politics since the days of Orval Faubus, Becker said, but never before had he felt so deceived by a governor. He called Clinton's maneuver "inexcusable" and one that he would not soon forget.

Becker held his grudge, and so, for a long time, did the teachers. The AEA spent most of the next three years and two elections trying to defeat Clinton and repeal the competence tests. But as influential as it could be in isolated legislative races, such as Vada Sheid's, it was rendered powerless against Clinton. The more it took him on, the more his popularity grew statewide. The substantive results of the education reform package were uneven. Over four years, all of the school districts eventually complied with the new standards on class size and course offerings. Advanced math, science, and foreign languages eventually became available in every district. The number of graduating seniors who moved on to college increased from 38 percent to 50 percent. Teacher salaries went up, but still remained near the bottom nationally, as did student test scores. Statistics from the U.S. Department of Education indicated that scores for Arkansas high school seniors taking the American College Test declined in the four years after the reforms were enacted.

Still, Bill Clinton now had a cause, a story, a political identity. From the passage of the reform package in November 1983, in every poll, the people of Arkansas could cite something they liked about him as governor: he was the one who had improved the schools and forced the teachers to prove their competence. He was the education governor.

JOGGING was the craze in Little Rock during that era, and Clinton took up jogging. One day he ran in a four-mile race on a course that weaved its way past the Victorian homes in the historic Quapaw District, around the Arkansas Governor's Mansion, and back down to the Capitol. Jim Blair, his lawyer friend from Fayetteville, was in town and ran the race at the governor's side. As they jogged by the mansion, Clinton decided to take a break. He walked for a few minutes, catching his breath and playing with his dog Zeke. Then he started up again, lumbering down the street to catch Blair. "Let's finish strong!" Clinton huffed as they crossed the highway and neared the Capitol, and suddenly he sprinted past his friend to reach the finish line first. It was a fitting performance for Clinton's second act as governor. Now he was the long-distance runner, plodding along mile after mile for his state. To stifle the inevitable talk that he was looking for a faster track, he said that he hoped and intended to serve as governor for another six to eight years. He was in it for the long haul, the marathon man.

Clinton's Arkansas experience became a testing ground for strategies and policies that might be applied on the national level. Since the morning after he and Jimmy Carter had been defeated in 1980, Clinton had focused on what it "would take to re-create a new majority for change in America," which is to say what it would take for an activist Democrat to make it to the White House. He felt that his party had become stuck in "no-win situations" and become known as "the party of blame." It got in trouble, he said, when "the need for change conflicted with people's most deeply ingrained habits or most cherished values. If you want to be for change, you have to render that change in ways that people can understand and relate to."

That did not mean, he said, resorting to the familiar nostrums of the New Deal coalition. Clinton had long since turned away from what he viewed as the politics of nostalgia. Going back even a decade before his defeat to Frank White, back to the Duffey Senate campaign in Connecticut in 1970, he had been searching for new formulas for Democratic success.

By the time his party gathered in August in San Francisco for the 1984 Democratic National Convention, he believed that the great divide that needed to be narrowed was not so much between liberals and conservatives as romantics and realists. Although he had remained neutral in the presidential primary battle that year between former Vice President Walter Mondale and Senator Gary Hart of Colorado, and although he eventually cast his convention vote for Mondale, his intellectual sympathies rested with Hart, his onetime boss in the McGovern campaign, who was basing his challenge on generational change. During an informal gathering at the convention, Clinton asked one of his colleagues, Governor Richard Lamm of Colorado, what he thought of the keynote address by Governor Mario Cuomo of New York, a rhetorical masterpiece that had stirred the crowd with its rich evocation of the core Democratic principles of empathy and equality. Lamm said he was impressed and moved, to which Clinton responded, "Come on, what did it really say about the issues we're trying to raise?"

In Clinton's own speech to the convention that week, he cited Harry Truman to talk about the future of the party. "Harry Truman would tell us to forget about 1948 and stand for what America needs in 1984," Clinton said. "That's the way to attract the millions of Americans who feel locked out and won't vote because they think we're irrelevant. That's the way to attract millions more, mostly young and well-educated, who intend to vote against us because they think we have no program for the future. Harry Truman would say: America has a productivity problem. What are we going to do about it? America is getting its brains beaten out in international economic competition. What are we going to do about it? America has millions of people who want to work but whose jobs have been lost because of competition from low wages abroad or the necessity to automate at home. What are we going to do about it? America is mortgaging its future with high deficits, driving interest rates too high, making our dollar too expensive and our trade deficit enormous. What are we going to do about it? . . . America is pricing itself out of affordable health care. What are we going to do about it? America needs an invigorated education system based on high standards and real accountability, as well as more money. What are we going to do about it?"

In the aftermath of Mondale's defeat, Clinton began to place his programs into a broader philosophy of opportunity and responsibility, which he saw as a theme that could lead to change without alienating the middle class. His education reforms in Arkansas set the model: the opportunity was for teachers to get more pay and more flexibility, the opportunity was for students to get more course offerings and smaller class sizes, and the responsibility was for both teachers and students to document their skills through standardized competence tests. During the mid-1980s, as he took an increasingly active role in the National Governors Association, he pushed that theme and expanded its scope to include other issues such as welfare, where workfare-style proposals Clinton helped design and push offered opportunity for work, education, and child care, but linked them to the responsibility of welfare recipients to work their way off the rolls and find jobs. In Arkansas, he offered major industries the opportunity to expand through major tax breaks, with the responsibility of staying in the state and expanding their workforces. He was merging ends and means, strategy and philosophy. And as he followed that course, his critics argued that his efforts to develop win-win situations made him so malleable that his word was unreliable. Of his opportunity-responsibility theme, some complained that more of the responsibility seemed to be placed on the less powerful and more of the opportunity seemed to be going to those who already had ample clout and, not incidentally, the wealth that Clinton needed to fund his political rise.

The essential question of his permanent campaign became whether his will to survive would overwhelm his convictions.

CHAPTER TWENTY-THREE

RELATIONSHIPS

FOR MORE THAN a decade, since his return home from his long odyssey through Georgetown, Oxford, and Yale, Clinton had been preoccupied with the task of becoming. Only rarely was he jolted into periods of introspection during which he would consider why he was what he was. It had happened when his daughter was born, and again when he was defeated for governor. Now that question engulfed him once again. This time it began when a young man named Rodney Myers approached Arkansas State Police narcotics investigator Robert Gibbs and Hot Springs detective Travis Bunn in the spring of 1984 and told them that Roger Cassidy Clinton, the governor's younger brother, was a cocaine dealer. The investigators heard Myers's story, which meshed with other information they had been gathering during a state-federal narcotics probe of cocaine use in Arkansas. They took him to see Sergeant Larry Gleghorn, Gibbs's supervisor at the criminal division, who set in motion a sting operation in which they would wire Myers with a hidden tape recorder and place a video camera in his apartment to record Roger Clinton selling cocaine.

The awkwardness in having the Arkansas State Police investigate the brother of the Arkansas governor was compounded by the fact that both Gibbs and Gleghorn knew the Clintons personally. Before transferring to the criminal division, they had been assigned to the state police security detail at the executive mansion, serving as bodyguards, chauffeurs, and at times valets for the governor and his family. Gleghorn had been friendly with the extended Clinton clan, including Roger and his mother Virginia, who was now married to her fourth husband, Richard Kelley, a food broker. During Gleghorn's two-year stint at the mansion, Roger had been a frequent visitor and an occasional problem. The governor's younger brother was a good-times fellow, gold-chained and open-collared, and though he detested the memory of his father and namesake, who died when he was eleven, he seemed to have taken on a measure of the old man's personality: the gregarious and unreliable "dude," surviving on guile and charm. He had partied and performed with his rock band at after-hours

clubs in Little Rock that stayed open until dawn. More than once, according to Gleghorn, Governor Clinton had asked a member of the security
detail "to kind of go and keep an eye on that situation." Now the eye was
a surveillance camera.

One day soon after the investigation began, a state police official alerted
Clinton's law enforcement aide, who told chief of staff Betsey Wright.
Wright called the Rose Law Firm in search of Hillary, who had rejoined the
firm after her service on the education task force, and found her eating
lunch with friends at a restaurant on Kavanaugh Street. Wright and Hillary
drove to the mansion and told the governor. According to Clinton's later
recollections, he was also informed of the investigation separately by State
Police Colonel Tommy Goodwin. It was not, in any case, the most closely
held secret. Nor was it normal procedure to advise the brother of a drug
suspect that a sting operation was under way. Although Clinton had no
authority over the matter, he wrote a note to Colonel Goodwin stating
that he would not interfere in the investigation and that he expected it to
be handled in routine fashion.

Clinton's private reaction to the news was a mixture of guilt and dread.
When he and Roger had lived in the same home on Scully Street, and even
during the early years at Georgetown, he had included his little brother in
many of his activities and had written and talked about him with parental
love and concern. But then he "got so wrapped up in" his career, Clinton
said later, that he paid less attention to his brother. Did the news that
Roger was a cocaine dealer take him by surprise? Clinton said later that it
did, and that he felt guilty about not being more involved during those
years as Roger dropped out of college three times and bounced around
with rock bands. But the fact that, even before the drug investigation
began, Clinton occasionally had asked members of his security detail to
watch out for Roger indicates that he had some suspicions. The heads-up
from the state police, according to Betsey Wright, was "not the first time
the possibility of his brother using cocaine had ever crossed his mind, yet
it took him by surprise. Suspecting is not mutually exclusive from being
taken by surprise. You hope against hope."

Part of Clinton's dread came from the realization that he had to keep
quiet about what he had learned. The painful prospect of allowing his
brother to be stung, arrested, and sentenced to prison was balanced against
the politically damaging repercussions of interfering in an official investigation. The surveillance dragged on for weeks. With Officer Gibbs hiding
under a blanket in the back seat of the car, informant Myers drove out to
Roger's apartment and emerged with cocaine and a secret tape-recording
of the transaction. Four more deals were made and recorded, as investigators gathered evidence on Roger and a cocaine scene that involved a

Colombian national supplier operating between Arkansas and New York and a circle of cocaine users in Hot Springs and Little Rock that included wealthy young lawyers and bond brokers. Roger was heard boasting about how untouchable he was, how nobody would mess with the brother of the governor.

During that period, Clinton talked to both Roger and his mother several times without mentioning the investigation. Alone with Hillary or Betsey Wright, he would ask, "Do you think they are ever going to finish this?" Finally, the investigators confronted Roger and told him they were charging him with distribution of cocaine. According to Gibbs, Roger tried to deny that he had done anything wrong until he was made aware of the recordings and videotapes. Bill Clinton's sadness at the fall of his brother was tempered by relief that the period of uncertainty was over. He held a press conference in Little Rock that afternoon and then drove down to Hot Springs for a family meeting with his mother and Roger. It was an emotional scene, as later described by Virginia, who said that Roger had arrived in tears, threatening to kill himself because of the embarrassment and pain he was bringing to his devoted mother and famous brother. "I caused it! I can end it!" he sobbed. The suicide talk enraged Bill, who shouted, "How dare you think that way!", leaped up from his chair, and started shaking Roger furiously.

For Clinton, a period of intense introspection began soon after his brother's arrest, when Roger entered therapy for his drug addiction. The counselor, Karen Ballard, requested that Bill and Virginia join the sessions. For the first time, the mother and two sons talked openly about alcoholism and the effects it had had on their family. It came out that Virginia had developed a tendency to avoid unpleasant truths and block out difficult parts of her life. Just as she had once been reluctant to acknowledge that her angry and skeptical mother might have been right about the failings of Roger the husband, it was hard for her to accept now that Roger the son had a chemical addiction of his own. Virginia had faced so many obstacles in her life that she had taught herself to create her own version of reality and function within it, allowing her to maintain her optimism and to persevere. Bill discovered that he had the same characteristics, including the denial mechanism, he told friends. It had always been easier for him to discuss the premature death of his biological father, and how that pushed him to achieve at an early age, than to consider how he was shaped by his stepfather's alcoholism, which he had never mentioned to most of his closest friends. In the sessions with his brother and mother, Clinton said later, "We learned a lot about how you do a lot of damage to yourself if you're living with an alcoholic and you just sort of deny that behavior and deflect it all. You pay a big price for that."

For several weeks, Clinton delved into the literature of alcoholism and co-dependence, the emerging fashionable theory, which placed addiction in the realm of family relationships. According to Betsey Wright, Clinton often came back to the office talking about the latest book he had read and relating it to his own experience. It was the first time she had heard him talk about alcoholism in his home, and how it had made him so averse to conflict. "He did a lot of introspection that I had never seen him do like that before," Wright recalled. "He got a much better understanding of why he did things the way he did. It was in the context of learning about how that comes out of an alcoholic home. Most notable was why he was always trying to please people. He was fascinated by it, and it rang so true that it was kind of like he was being introduced to something that he wished he had known a long time ago." This did not mean that Clinton changed his behavior, Wright thought, but simply that he could "see what he was doing far better."

In a discussion with Carolyn Yeldell Staley, Clinton indicated that he was struggling with his self-awareness. "I think we're all addicted to something," Clinton told her, according to Staley's recollections. "Some people are addicted to drugs. Some to power. Some to food. Some to sex. We're all addicted to something." It seemed to Staley that Clinton was "coming to grips with the fact that he had places of real weakness. He was trying to sort all of that out in his life."

Clinton, Virginia, and Hillary Clinton all sat in the federal courtroom on the day in January 1985 when Roger was sentenced to a two-year prison term at the federal correctional institution in Fort Worth, Texas. As part of his plea, Roger agreed to testify, with immunity, for the government in several other cocaine cases. One resulted in the conviction of his childhood friend, Sam Anderson, Jr., a limousine-riding Hot Springs attorney. Another led to a six-month prison term for investment banker Dan R. Lasater, a flashy young financier, racehorse owner, and recreational cocaine user who set out lines of the white powder at his lavish parties.

The connections between Lasater and the Clintons throughout the decade raised questions about the propriety of the relationship. Roger, who had been one of Lasater's cocaine suppliers, had worked briefly for him at one of his horse farms and as his driver, and had borrowed $8,000 from him to pay off a drug debt. At the same time, Lasater was a major contributor to Clinton's permanent campaign, donating money to his gubernatorial races and holding fund-raisers. His brokerage house, meanwhile, received $1.6 million in fees for its role in handling tax-exempt bonds for the state. Clinton personally lobbied the legislature in 1985 to give Lasater's firm a contract to sell bonds for a state police radio system. The governor and his wife occasionally flew on Lasater's corporate jet. When Lasater was promoting a special vacation package at Angel Fire, his 22,000-acre ski resort in New Mexico, he used Governor Clinton's name in his mailings, although Clinton did not make the trip. Patsy Thomasson, the executive vice president of Lasater Inc., was a Democratic party activist who had been appointed to the state highway commission by Clinton, her long-time friend. After serving time in prison, Lasater was later pardoned by Clinton.

The prosecution of Roger Clinton did have some positive side effects. Asa Hutchinson, then the Republican federal prosecutor in Little Rock, believed that Roger's conviction and his later testimony in other cases helped stem an emerging cocaine party scene in central Arkansas. "Here the brother of the governor was saying, 'Hey, nobody touches me, look who I am!' And people had come to think it was all right," Hutchinson recalled. "The case was important in showing people they couldn't do that." It was also important, Bill Clinton came to believe, in saving his brother's life.

"WE'RE closer than any brothers you've ever known," Roger Clinton was heard saying about his relationship with his brother the governor during one of the secretly tape-recorded conversations with Rodney Myers. "See, I didn't have a father growing up and he was like a father to me growing up, all my life, so that's why we've always been so close. There isn't anything in the world he wouldn't do for me."

Minutes before he described that brotherly bond, twenty-eight-year-old Roger had inhaled cocaine through his nose. He and Myers were in the middle of a rambling discussion during which they rated the quality of their cocaine (*Myers:* "Boy, this is some good coke!" *Clinton:* "It's decent. It's decent") . . . and discussed the high-rolling lives of wealthy lawyer friends who rode in white limousines and partied in hot tubs . . . and told tall tales about busting heads in a Fayetteville brawl . . . and fantasized about how they were going to make so much money in condominium deals that they could have generous clothing allowances and new cars (*Clinton:* "What I've been saving up for is a Porsche." *Myers:* "What kind?" *Clinton:* "Just any kind. Just any kind." *Myers:* "Right. You want a Porsche?" *Clinton:* "I want a Porsche so bad I can spit") . . . and agreed that Roger's name would help them put the deals together (*Myers:* "If I had you on my side, I could make a hell of a lot of money, you know, with your last name." *Clinton:* "Oh, listen, I realize exactly what you're saying." *Myers:* "You got good bullshit. You got your bullshit but your last name would also make, you know, you could make a hell of a lot." *Clinton:* "Good at bullshitting and public relations. I can sell a product.").

Roger Clinton would call Bill "Big Brother" when talking about him to other people. Not "my big brother," just "Big Brother," with the double meaning explicit. They were of different generations, though separated only by ten years, each with soft blue eyes and big hands, raised by the same woman with the same unconditional love. When her boy Bill had left for good from Scully Street, Virginia had taken down his plaques and awards and rearranged the house to make it more accommodating as a rehearsal space for Roger's first rock band, The Hundred Millimeter Banana, which he formed at age ten. She wanted him to become the next Elvis as much as she wanted Bill to become the next JFK. When he started to get club dates with another band, Dealer's Choice, she went to see him perform, even at a topless lounge named the Black Orchid, and listened to him sing with the same pride with which she listened to her son the politician talk. She got a list of Roger's club dates and studied it with the same pleasure that she perused Bill's weekly schedule, sent to her by the governor's office. She loved her sons with equal intensity, she told her friends. But one son had the will and one son did not.

How could two brothers be so different: the governor and the coke dealer, the Rhodes Scholar and the college dropout, one who tried to read three hundred books in three months and another who at his most addicted snorted cocaine sixteen times a day, one who could spend hours explaining economic theories and another whose economic interests centered on getting a new Porsche? In the case of the Clinton brothers, the contrasts become more understandable when considered within the context of their family history and environment. They grew up in a town of contrast and hypocrisy, in a family of duality and conflict. Bill and Roger were not so much opposites as two sides of the same coin. Each essentially grew up without a father. Bill was constantly searching for older male role models: his pappaw Eldridge Cassidy, Virgil Spurlin at school, his grandmother's brother Buddy Grisham, his friend Jim Blair, his adviser Maurice Smith, his minister W. O. Vaught. Bill was the closest thing to a role model Roger could find.

By their chosen careers, Bill the politician and Roger the rock musician revealed a common desire to perform and to gain approval from large audiences. Virginia often said that her boys resembled her in that respect. Like her son Roger, she loved to jump on stage and sing along with the band; and like her son Bill, she would walk into a room and try to win over every person there. Another common denominator for the politician and the rock musician is sex. Performers in both realms are often surrounded by groupies, their sexual charisma enhanced by power and unrestrained ego. The desire to perform, the need for approval, and the supply of idolaters can be a habit-forming triangle.

There was little history of sexual restraint in Bill and Roger's family culture, no puritanical sense that sexual propriety was the barometer of goodness and morality. Suspicion, gossip, and mystery were always part of the sexual mix. Edith Cassidy constantly accused her husband Eldridge Cassidy of cheating on her, while at the same time she developed a reputation for engaging in affairs with certain doctors in Hope. William Jefferson Blythe may have had five or more wives in his short life, wooing and discarding women with dispatch. Virginia married Roger Clinton even though she knew he was a philanderer. During their tumultuous marriage, Roger was often overcome by jealousy after catching Virginia flirting at nightclubs or hearing the gossip that she had been seen around town with other men. Bill Clinton came out of that environment, and took from it the competing impulses of a youth who had walked to church alone in a city of earthly pleasures. He was, at once, the good boy, the Family Hero, and the inveterate flatterer and flirt, constantly searching for more girls—and later, women—who would be charmed by him and feed his ego.

His marriage to Hillary Rodham in 1975 seemed to have little inhibiting effect on him. During the 1978 gubernatorial race, campaign manager Rudy Moore had to fire a travel aide who boasted publicly about the nightclubs he had visited with the candidate. Provocative women seemed to find their way to the governor's office, "hangers-on who could get you in trouble," as Moore described them. Clinton's judgment at times was not as good as it should have been, Moore thought, though he believed that "appearances were more than what was going on." Clinton's travel aide during his first term, Randy White, said that the governor enjoyed nothing more than to go on the road, especially to Fayetteville, where he would frequent a club in the bottom of the old post office, and dance and hang out "until they threw us out." Wherever they went, White said, Clinton's table attracted a crowd of pretty women drawn to the powerful young governor, who enjoyed the attention. "He loved the road," White said. "He loved it."

In more than two years at Clinton's side, White said later, he saw no evidence that the governor was having extramarital affairs and was not asked by Clinton to conceal his activities. In contrast, several state troopers who worked on the governor's personal security staff after his return to power in 1983 claimed that Clinton was promiscuous and that he frequently used them to solicit sexual partners. Trooper L. D. Brown, who was on the security staff from 1983 to 1985, alleged that he was asked to try to solicit more than one hundred women for Clinton during those two years. On the matter of how many, if any, of those women acceded to Clinton's desires, Brown was unclear. He called himself "the go-between, the buffer" for a politician with a voracious sexual appetite.

• • •

HILLARY Rodham Clinton and Carolyn Yeldell Staley were on the back lawn of the Governor's Mansion one summer day, sticking croquet hoops into the grass and talking about their husbands. Carolyn had married a soft-spoken photographer and art teacher named Jerry Staley, who remained in the background, content in his role as the dependable husband and father of two daughters and a son, willing to let his wife be the star of the family as the aspiring singer and longtime friend of the governor of Arkansas. Hillary said she could never marry someone as quiet as Jerry. She liked to spar, she said. She liked to "get into it." She had to have an equal. Then, pondering the ups and downs of her life with Bill Clinton, she said, "I wonder how history is going to note our marriage."

The long haul, the view toward the future and history, was evident in the Clinton and Rodham partnership from its formation. For Clinton, perpetually infatuated with a shining new idea or a fresh face, Hillary was the rare constant, her intellect, resilience, and ambition always there, equal to his. When he had thought about marrying her, it was not so much the sight of the young woman that overwhelmed him as an image of an older version: Hillary, he told friends, was the one woman with whom he could imagine growing old and not getting bored. Her feelings about him seemed more immediate and passionate; she adored him, one friend said, with "a romantic, fifteen-year-old, poetic, teenage love." By the mid-1980s, those early dynamics were still apparent, although there had been several adjustments in the partnership, most of them made by Hillary. Year by year, in their joint political enterprise, she had taken on more tasks—some that her husband had asked her to do, some that she felt obliged to perform because it was clear to her that he did not want to do them or was not good at them. After ten years of marriage, those tasks were starting to define her.

One of Hillary's missions was to protect her husband by being his gate-keeper. During her early years in Arkansas, she often deferred to Clinton's judgments about people; but that had changed forever after his defeat in 1980, when she thought that he had been ill served by poor advice and by his own amiability and that she needed to take a more direct role in his career. After their return to the Governor's Mansion, she would tell friends that she understood him better than anyone, better than his sycophants or critics, and that it was her responsibility to allow him to be his true self. One way to do that was to prevent other people from imposing on him if they seemed against his best interests. She said that she wanted him to be free to use his own mind, which she considered creative and even vision-ary. Although she was naturally skeptical and direct, even hard-edged in her dealings, Hillary's role as her husband's protector exaggerated those character traits. Her concerns were largely political, though at times there seemed to be a sexual component to her protectiveness. A male friend of Clinton's noticed that Hillary was classifying the people around Bill as either "one of the goods or one of the bads. If you were bad, you had to be kept away from Bill, because if he was with the bad guys he would relax and enjoy himself and make comments about attractive women waving at him in the crowd."

In her effort to protect Clinton, Hillary was assisted by two women whom she did not consider threats: press secretary Joan Roberts, who insisted on being in attendance whenever Clinton or another member of the staff spoke to the press; and chief of staff Betsey Wright, whose relationship with Clinton resembled that of a bossy big sister. Wright was constantly checking on his whereabouts, sending out scouts to see what he was doing and what his enemies were saying about him, thinking up explanations to put his actions in the best possible light, and trying to keep him away from people she thought wanted to exploit him. These three strong women around Clinton became known in Little Rock as "the Valkyries," named for the wise and immortal maidens of Old Norse mythology who selected the heroic warriors fit to die in battle and be escorted to Valhalla.

Clinton both encouraged the defensive cordon put up around him and bristled at the way it inhibited him. "I won't have it! I won't have it!" he once shouted at Wright when she insisted that a state policeman escort him on his morning jogs. The almost sibling nature of Wright's relationship with Clinton at times stretched the boundaries of boss and chief of staff. His habits began to grate on her, and hers on him. Once when he was noisily chomping on an ice cube, his mouth impolitely open, and reached into his cup to get another cube, Wright swatted it out of his hand, which caused him to slap her, reflexively, like a brother hitting his sister. It was only a tap, and it was the only time he struck her, but it was by no means their only fight. She was the aide on whom he vented his frustrations. He staged so many temper tantrums in front of her that he would send her earplugs as an expression of apology. His quarrels with Hillary were even louder and more frequent. But as Hillary told Carolyn Staley that day when they were setting up for croquet on the back lawn, she liked to spar. Mansion workers confided to frequent guests that there were times when they would have loved to disappear while the Clintons screamed at each other.

Another continuing task for Hillary was that of moneymaker. It had been apparent since the beginning of their partnership that Clinton cared little about money outside the political campaign context, and that she would carry the financial burden for the family. But as they entered the prime wage-earning years of middle age, the arrangement became lopsided. Clinton's part of the deal was to be governor and make a national name for himself while bringing home $35,000 a year in salary. Hillary felt the need to build the family savings account at the same time that she was taking on more political assignments that consumed hours she could have been billing law clients. Her dealings in the cattle futures commodities market with Jim Blair in the late 1970s marked the first of several forays into the financial world.

Roy Drew, then a stock broker at E. F. Hutton in Little Rock, had received a call from Hillary in the spring of 1983, just as she was getting into her work on the Education Standards Committee. She told Drew that she and two of her partners at Rose Law, Vince Foster, Jr., and Webster Hubbell, had $15,000 each that they wanted him to invest. They called their account Midlife Investors. Foster and Hubbell were placid partners while Hillary was constantly checking in with Drew. "I recommended Diamond Shamrock and a movie deal and Firestone," Drew recalled. "And Hillary would call and say, 'What's Firestone doing?' and I'd say, 'Well, it's up an eighth today,' and she'd say, 'Why isn't it doing anything?' She was used to the fast action of cattle futures. The next day she'd call and say, 'Where's Firestone?' and I'd say, 'Down a half,' and she'd say, 'Oh, no, what's the matter?' She'd call three or four times a week."

Some people sensed a growing resentment in Hillary that she had to take on so many private duties in the partnership while at the same time she was being asked, unfairly, she thought, to sacrifice material things. In 1985, Hillary told consultant Dick Morris that she wanted to build a swimming pool on the mansion grounds. She said among other things it would be great for Chelsea. "I said, 'How could you even think of that? You'll get killed for that!'" Morris recalled. "And she said, 'Well, it's really not for us, the mansion is for all future governors of the state and they'll all be able to use it.' And I said, 'You'll never be able to sell that argument. The next time you fly over Little Rock, look down and count the number of swimming pools you see.' She said, 'Well, a lot of people have swimming pools.' I got really sarcastic with her and said, 'On the next poll, do you want me to ask whether people have swimming pools?' She was really mad. Very angry. She said, 'Why can't we lead the lives of normal people?' I saw in that flash the resentment from a lot of those issues, the sacrifices they were making staying in public life." Clinton, for his part, lamented to friends that he held a job with little income, one where it was politically impractical to seek a raise. He said he felt bad that he was not living up to his responsibility to support the family. But politics was still his only track.

Another role that Hillary assumed was related to the first two—protector and financial guarantor. She was her husband's public relations troubleshooter and legal problem solver. She provided a full range of formal and informal services. As the public relations consultant, she would devote hours to courting John Robert Starr, the managing editor of the *Arkansas Democrat,* in an occasionally effective effort to persuade him to go easier on her husband. As the lawyer, she would quietly represent Clinton's interests, working to resolve some of the most politically sensitive issues in Arkansas, including the resolution of the long-running desegregation case in the Little Rock school district and the state's financial dispute over its disengagement from the costly Grand Gulf nuclear power plant near Port Gibson, Mississippi.

The Grand Gulf case provoked questions, even from Clinton allies, about potential conflicts of interest involving the governor's wife's law firm and state issues. Dick Morris said that when he told his wife Eileen McGann, who was also a lawyer, that Rose Law was representing the Public Service Commission in the Grand Gulf matter, McGann thought it looked like a conflict and said of Hillary, "She's got to be out of her mind!" On his next visit to Little Rock, according to Morris, he raised the issue with Clinton, who said that he needed Hillary and the Rose firm on the case because "anybody else would mangle it." Morris said that Hillary reacted angrily when he asked her about it, reminding him that Rose was a respected firm which had been doing business with the state long before she came along. Her solution was to dissociate herself from fees Rose Law received in the case.

During the 1986 gubernatorial race, in which Clinton prevailed over Frank White in a bitter rematch, White raised the conflict of interest question regarding Hillary and Grand Gulf. In response, Rose Law issued a statement saying that fees from the case "were segregated from other income and were distributed to members of the firm other than Mrs. Clinton so that she in fact received no direct or indirect benefit from the fees." The question was framed in financial terms, disregarding the larger notion of Hillary Clinton as the private lawyer watching out for her husband's political interests. The Clinton team's political response to White was to belittle him for picking on the governor's wife. They printed bumper stickers and put up billboards with the message: "Frank White for First Lady." It was another tactic, like the mea culpa commercial of 1982, that worked so well that the Clintons stored it away for future use.

There were other potential conflicts involving Hillary's work as a Rose lawyer and institutions with political or personal connections to her and her husband the governor. In one case, Dan Lasater, the bond broker and major Clinton campaign contributor who had gone to jail on a drug conviction, was sued for fraud in the collapse of a savings and loan in

Illinois. Hillary, representing the Federal Deposit Insurance Corporation, helped arrange an out-of-court settlement for less than one-tenth of what the government orginally sought. In another, she helped represent Jim McDougal when the thrift he owned, Madison Guaranty Savings and Loan, sought permission from the state securities commissioner to raise money by issuing preferred stock in an effort to maintain the minimum capital requirements and avert insolvency. The Madison case underscored the professional, personal, and political triangle of interests in the Clintons' lives during that era.

At one point of the triangle was Hillary's corner office on the third floor of the red brick Rose Law building, a handsomely converted downtown YWCA with hardwood floors and an indoor swimming pool. It was from that office that she signed a letter to the securities commissioner on behalf of McDougal and received a "Dear Hillary" letter in reply. It would later be a question of dispute as to how Hillary became McDougal's lawyer in that matter. According to her account, she was merely helping a young Rose associate who did most of the work. According to McDougal and his wife Susan, Hillary actively solicited the savings and loan's business, showing up at Madison's Art Deco–style Little Rock branch office one day and saying she needed new clients and would like the thrift to put her and Rose on retainer. "Hillary came in and was telling us about the problem; the problem was finances and she was not bringing enough in to her law firm," Susan McDougal later said. "I remember Jim laughing and saying, 'Well, one lawyer's as good as another, we might as well help Hillary.' "

At the second point of the triangle was the Georgian-style Governor's Mansion several blocks south of downtown where Bill and Hillary Clinton kept their personal papers related to their private financial relationship with the McDougals in Whitewater Development Company. The land development enterprise along the White River had never made the money McDougal had promised it would, and now, by the mid-1980s, it apparently had cost the Clintons tens of thousands of dollars in interest payments on the original loans they had taken with the McDougals to buy the property. McDougal was feeling regret that he had lured the Clintons into the deal. It was, he said, "the dumbest thing I had ever done in my life, from start to finish."

The final point in the triangle was the governor's office on the second floor of the Capitol. It was from that office that Clinton, as governor, appointed the securities commissioner who regulated McDougal's savings and loan. And it was also from that office that Clinton, the politician, operated his permanent campaign, which included the expensive concept of using paid media to advance his legislative and political agenda. McDougal had a connection to that as well. In January 1985, he replenished the coffers of the permanent campaign by holding a fund-raiser at his Madison branch office in Little Rock, helping to pay off Clinton's political debts, including unsecured personal loans from the Bank of Cherry Valley, which was owned by Clinton's aide and fatherly adviser, Maurice Smith. Clinton and Betsey Wright attended the McDougal fund-raiser for "about twenty-five minutes," Wright recalled. Wright viewed the event as an effort by McDougal to "heal a breach with Bill" that had formed since the disappointment of the Whitewater deal. McDougal later said it was Maurice Smith who asked him to stage the event, and that he and Smith, both nondrinkers, had sat up in his office on the second floor while Clinton made the rounds down below. Wright collected the contributions from McDougal and deposited the checks in Clinton's campaign account that night.

Hillary Rodham Clinton, who touched all three corners of the triangle, saw no conflict in her actions. As a lawyer, she said that she was acting professionally, dissociating herself from fees gathered by Rose in its dealings with the state, giving her best advice to clients, whether they were the FDIC or Madison Guaranty. As a wife and mother, she was trying to bring her family financial security. As a political adviser and pro bono public servant, she was devoting her time and intellect to the betterment of the state. Her motives always seemed practical—she was looking for solutions—but there was also a sanctimonious aspect to it that tended to blind her and her husband to the appearances of what they were doing. Clinton considered her the ethical pillar of their partnership. If she handled a matter for him, he assumed that it would be done extraordinarily well; hence his decision to pick her to lead the Education Standards Committee, because she was "the person closer to me than anyone else," and his statement to Morris that "anyone else would mangle" the Grand Gulf dilemma. He thought she would keep him out of trouble.

Hillary dismissed those who questioned her actions as quibblers who did not appreciate that what she was doing was for the greater good. She framed her actions in moral terms. Beyond all the particulars, in the grand scheme of right and wrong, she felt with almost religious conviction that she was on the side of right. Don Jones, the Drew University theology professor who had been her religious mentor during her youth in Park Ridge, and who admired her greatly, got into an argument with her during a visit to Little Rock. They were discussing the works of the theologian Reinhold Niebuhr, and soon enough Jones found himself disputing Hillary's contention that some causes were closer to the will of God than others. "I said, 'I don't think you can equate any cause, however good, to the will of God,'" Jones recalled. "I began a discourse on the dangers of idolatry and quoted from Lincoln's second inaugural address—the North thinks God is

on its side, the South thinks God is on its side, but the Almighty has his
own purposes."

RELIGION played an increasingly important role in the lives of the Clintons
through the eighties, the most demanding decade of their partnership.
They came out of vastly different religious cultures and attended separate
churches on Sunday, yet Hillary, the United Methodist, and Bill, the Southern Baptist, both found that faith eased the burden of their high-profile
lives, sometimes offering solace and escape from the contentious world of
politics, at other times providing theological support for their political
choices. Their religious evolutions were similar, reflecting a generational
trend: churchgoing was an essential part of their early adolescent years,
less apparent during their late teens and twenties, and more vital again
as they moved through their thirties into mature parenthood and middle
age. The intensity of their faith seemed to increase in proportion to their
growing ambitions and responsibilities in careers where the rewards of
adulation and accomplishment were counterbalanced by the strains of
compromise and criticism.

Hillary Clinton seemed to fit her religion and her church so well that
one of her ministers called her "a model of Methodism." She was, in fact,
the human model and inspiration for her husband's emerging political
theme of opportunity and responsibility, which she traced back to the
founder of Methodism, John Wesley, an eighteenth-century Anglican priest
who mixed social reform with evangelical piety. "As a member of the
British Parliament, he spoke out for the poor at a time when their lives
were being transformed by far-reaching industrial and economic changes,"
she said in a speech explaining why she was a Methodist. "He spent the
rest of his life evangelizing among the same people he had spoken up
for in Parliament. He preached a gospel of social justice, demanding as
determinedly as ever that society do right by all its people. But he also
preached a gospel of personal responsibility, asking every man and woman
to take responsibility for their own lives . . . and cultivate the habits that
would make them productive."

Hillary's church in downtown Little Rock, First United Methodist, was
dominated by productive, achievement-oriented professionals with an interest in modest social reform. It seemed to have a special attraction for
lawyers: there were seventy-six in the membership, including many of the
leading legal lights in the city. The local bar association held its meetings
at the church every month. From its earliest days, United Methodist had
played a benevolent function in the community. It sponsored a home for
unwed mothers at the turn of the century, and later opened a major child

development center and launched the first telephone crisis hotline service in Little Rock. Hillary donated funds for the child care center, served on the administrative board of the church, performed free legal work for the Methodist Church in Arkansas, and traveled the state giving speeches on the personal meaning of Methodism.

In those speeches, she would talk about John Wesley and Methodist history, about her church youth group experiences in Park Ridge, about the balance between personal and social behavior, and finally about her personal relationship with God. Somewhere in her speech she would recite her favorite exhortation from Wesley: "Do all the good you can, by all the means you can, in all the ways you can, in all the places you can, at all the times you can, to all the people you can, as long as ever you can." Yet at the core of her belief, thought one of her ministers at United Methodist, Reverend Ed Matthews, was a personal need as strong or stronger than the social commitment. "One of her favorite thoughts," Matthews later reflected, "was that the goal of life is to restore what has been lost, to find oneness with God, and until we find this we are lonely."

It could be said that Bill Clinton also turned to religion in search of something that had been lost: a father.

His church was Immanuel Baptist, an imposing, rectangular shrine of gold and tan that occupied two full city blocks, standing alone on a hill at Tenth and Bishop, looming above the Capitol and the workday world of Little Rock. It was the largest church in Arkansas, with more than four thousand members and a statewide television audience for the live broadcast of the eleven o'clock Sunday services. The differences in the Clintons' churches were as obvious as Hillary's midwestern reserve and Bill's unabashed southern manner. Hillary, as Reverend Matthews once said, was "not going to tote her Bible to church; she wasn't going to flaunt it. Baptists like Bill carried their Bibles to church." Clinton's Bible was old and dog-eared, an expression of his desire to master this course of study as he would any other. He was a second tenor in the church choir, and though he never had time for choir practice, on Sundays he "would get up there and act as though he had rehearsed the whole thing," recalled Mary Frances Vaught, the wife of the minister. "He would sing as big as anything."

Clinton did not go to church for social activism, nor did he go for fire and brimstone judgment and guilt-ridden repentance; he went, largely, to search for the better part of himself in a place where he could be accepted at face value. Dr. Worley Oscar Vaught, the leader of Immanuel Baptist, provided that atmosphere. They seemed an unlikely pair: Clinton the tall, bushy-haired, effusive, ambitious, freewheeling and liberal-leaning young politician, and Vaught the short, bald, bespectacled, stern-voiced, conservative religious scholar, who had been preaching since the year before

Clinton was born. But Vaught was, like Clinton, at once a storyteller and an intellectual, translating the Old and the New Testaments from Hebrew and Greek and giving his worshipers detailed syntactical and semantic explications of the text. He was methodical and patient, taking more than a year to get through Genesis and devoting two or three years to Romans and Matthew. He would start every service by leading his congregation in reciting Hebrews 4:12: "The word of God is alive and powerful, sharper than any two-edged sword, to the dividing asunder of the soul and spirit, and of the joints and marrow, and is a discerner of the thoughts and interests of the heart." Later, somewhere in each sermon, he would pause and in his surprisingly strong and authoritative voice, inquire, "Are you listening?"

Clinton was always listening to Vaught, during the sermons and in their frequent conversations. As someone who tended to think in metaphors, Clinton related the Bible to his role as governor. Each morning when he reached his office in the Capitol, there would be a quote from scripture on his desk, placed there by his personal secretary, Lynda Dixon, who also worshiped at Immanuel Baptist. He and Dixon would talk about the passage for a minute before getting to work. During the course of the day, according to Betsey Wright, Clinton would include Vaught in his round of calls, and later, "in the course of a conversation, he would say, 'Well, Dr. Vaught told me such-and-such.' " Although Vaught did not presume to tell Clinton what to do, he had a profound effect on the governor's thinking on several important social issues, most notably the death penalty and abortion.

On capital punishment, Vaught took the initiative when it became apparent that Clinton would soon have to start setting dates for executions and make his first life-or-death calls concerning death-row inmates. Since his race for attorney general in 1976, Clinton had stated publicly that he supported the death penalty, but Vaught sensed that Clinton was still struggling with the issue a decade later and that he was deeply ambivalent. He called Clinton one day and said he would like to talk to the governor about it. Clinton invited him to the mansion for breakfast. He had "gone over it a thousand times," Clinton told Vaught, and was now asking himself the question about capital punishment, "Not is this the right thing to do, but is it always the wrong thing to do." Vaught told Clinton that in the original translations of the Ten Commandments, capital punishment was not prohibited. In ancient Hebrew and Greek, he said, the phrase was "thou shalt not murder," not "thou shalt not kill"—which he said meant it was not the same thing as the laws of the land applying capital punishment. Clinton said he appreciated that interpretation because he had "instinctively thought you could make arguments for and against capital punishment, but didn't think it was a violation of Christian faith." You can make your own judgment about whether you think it's right or wrong, Vaught told him, "but you must never worry about whether it's forbidden by the Bible, because it isn't."

On the abortion issue, it was Clinton who solicited Vaught's advice. He had ambivalent feelings about it personally, though he agreed with the pro-choice argument intellectually and was surrounded by strong pro-choice women, including Hillary and Betsey Wright. Yet he was struggling with the notion of the definition of a human life, and he wondered whether Vaught could provide some insight from his readings of the Old and New Testaments. Vaught, who was not among the active anti-abortion clergy in Little Rock, said he shared some of Clinton's ambivalence. He told the governor that he was almost always opposed to abortion, but had seen "some extremely difficult cases" in his life as a pastor and did not believe that the Bible forbade it in all circumstances. In the original Hebrew, Vaught said, the meaning of life and birth and personhood came from words which literally meant "to breathe life into." From that he concluded that the literal meaning of life in the Bible would be that it began at birth, with the first intake of breath. That did not mean that abortion was right, he told Clinton, but he did not think one could say it was murder. In all of his discussions about abortion thereafter, Clinton relied on his minister's interpretation to bolster his pro-choice position.

Some of Clinton's progressive friends were shocked by his relationship with Vaught, who was considered a symbol of Little Rock's old guard. They worried that the minister's influence was making Clinton more conservative, or alternatively that the governor was using the minister. In fact, Clinton and Vaught shared a common condition. Vaught was a transitional figure in the long-running fight between fundamentalists and moderates within the Southern Baptist Church. He used the devices of the fundamentalists, the reliance on scripture, but he supported the intellectual curiosity and openness of the moderates. Clinton considered himself a transitional figure between political liberals and conservatives. He was using the political equivalent of biblical language in an effort to bring about change. Vaught delighted in this aspect of Clinton, and thought it eventually would take him where he wanted to go.

At a small dinner for the Vaughts' fiftieth wedding anniversary at a restaurant atop the Union Bank Building overlooking the broad expanse of Little Rock, the elderly preacher turned to his young disciple and said, "Bill, one of these days I want to sleep in the Lincoln Bedroom."

CHAPTER TWENTY-FOUR

SAYING THE WORDS

EIGHTEEN YEARS AFTER the Rhodes Scholars of the class of 1968 sailed across the Atlantic aboard the S.S. *United States* on their way to the ancient colleges of Oxford, where they were trained as "the best men for the world's fight," the old boys were reaching forty. Of their class of thirty-two scholars, all were still alive except Frank Aller, the draft resister who committed suicide. Doctor, lawyer, scientist, professor, journalist, investor, art curator, military officer—most of them had reached some level of achievement in their professions. Bob Reich was teaching politics and economics at the Kennedy School of Government at Harvard, and Strobe Talbott was Washington bureau chief of *Time* magazine. Both had gained acclaim as authors, Reich writing about industrial policy and world trade, Talbott about nuclear arms control. But only one class member seemed intent on engaging in the world's fight in the largest sense of Cecil Rhodes's imperative. In his annual class letter in the *American Oxonian,* secretary Reich finally broached a subject in 1986 that he and many of his classmates had contemplated since their days together in England: Bill Clinton running for president.

"The latest polls in Arkansas show that the governor has a seventy-two percent approval rating, which places him in the same category as McDonald's hamburgers and Dan Rather, ahead of Ronald Reagan and the new Coca-Cola," Reich wrote. "Rumor has it that Bill will be the Democratic candidate for president in 1988. I just made up that rumor, but by the time you read this, the rumor will have spread to the ends of the nation."

The expectation was always there. It had started long before there was any sense to it, back when Clinton's mother boasted that a second-grade teacher had told her that her boy could be president. Or perhaps it went back generations further, back to his poor southern forebears who con-

nected themselves, if only in name, to things presidential: back to Thomas
Jefferson Blythe, a Confederate private from Tippah County, Mississippi,
who once bet a saddle on the outcome of a sheriff's race; and to Andrew
Jackson Blythe of Tennessee; and to George Washington Cassidy of Red
Level, Alabama. Wherever it came from, it was always there, not a matter
of predestination but of expectation and will, and it had built up year by
year, decade by decade.

ON August 26, 1986, one week after he turned forty, Clinton ascended to
the chairmanship of the National Governors Association (NGA) at the
group's summer meeting in Hilton Head, South Carolina. In his acceptance
speech that night, he satirized his passage into middle age, wondering
whether this would be a "milestone or millstone" year for "the first of the
over-the-hill baby boomers." He also stirred the audience with a campaign-
style oration in which he said his priority as chairman would be to help
create more jobs. "Let me be clear," he said. "We do not need further
studies. We have a wealth of excellent material outlining the dimensions
of the problem. What I want are action plans and programs."

The chairmanship of the NGA was part of Clinton's own action plan. It
allowed him to develop issues that he cared about, that he thought were
essential to the revival of the Democratic party, especially jobs creation,
education reform, and an overhaul of the welfare system, while at the same
time providing him a forum to expand his reputation. He felt relaxed and
at home with this collegial group of state executive peers. Here was a place
where he could fit in and yet easily stand out. Harry Hughes, the governor
of Maryland, recalled that his lasting image of Clinton at NGA conventions
was of him "always standing, never sitting." Hughes contrasted Clinton's
style at the meetings with those of two other ambitious governors, Michael
Dukakis of Massachusetts and Mario Cuomo of New York. Dukakis was
usually seated, Hughes said, plugging his way through plenary sessions,
talking earnestly, while Cuomo rarely bothered to show up at all, and when
he did, tended to remain apart from the gang. Clinton was always in the
middle of the action, working the room, leaning against a wall perhaps,
surrounded by governors and staff members, telling a joke or leading an
informal discussion about the latest book by urban historian Jane Jacobs
or sociologist William J. Wilson or his friend Bob Reich.

Along with the camaraderie, the Governors Association gave Clinton
opportunities to travel outside Arkansas and deliver speeches. He took on
another post earlier that year that offered him additional national visibility,
as chairman of the Education Commission of the States, a Denver-based
nonprofit commission that provided research on education issues to state

officials. Little Rock state representative Gloria Cabe, whose loyalty to Clinton went back to the bleak days after his 1980 defeat, served as his educational liaison to both national groups. "Nobody ever told me to behave in this manner, so it was largely my attitude, but through all the work I did for him in national organizations, it was with the notion that he was going to run for president," Cabe recalled. There was no reason for Clinton to make his national ambitions too explicit at first, especially not until after his reelection that November in his noisy but not particularly close rematch with Frank White. After the election, as he began his fourth term as governor, it became increasingly obvious to his staff, as well as to Arkansas legislators and journalists, that his attention was elsewhere.

EARLY on the evening of March 20, 1987, the office of Senator Dale Bumpers of Arkansas issued a brief statement announcing that he would not be a candidate for president in 1988. The announcement came as a surprise to some in the political world. Since the beginning of the year, Bumpers had been traveling the country, meeting with prominent Democratic party financiers and operatives, seeming to prepare the groundwork for a presidential campaign. Only the week before, New York Governor Mario Cuomo, who had already issued the first of many statements of noncandidacy for himself, predicted that Bumpers would make the race. But this was not the first time that Bumpers had edged toward the national spotlight and then receded from it. He had first been urged to run for president in 1976, shortly after he left the governor's office for the Senate. He had considered it again in 1984. Now, at sixty-one, he was taking himself out of consideration for the last time. Running for president, he said in his statement, "means a total disruption of the closeness my family has cherished. If victorious, much of that closeness is necessarily lost forever. So I'll turn to other challenges."

The quiet announcement from the office of Senator Bumpers in Washington reverberated loudly in the office of Governor Clinton in Little Rock. Whatever Bumpers did or did not do was always of great interest to Clinton. Their relationship had gone through brief periods of hostility and longer periods of reconciliation and alliance, but it had always been marked by a certain amount of tension. They were separated by twenty years, yet often got in each other's way. Only a year earlier, Clinton had talked to friends about challenging Bumpers for the Senate seat, but was dissuaded by Hillary, who thought he would be unhappy in the Senate, and by polls that showed Bumpers would beat Clinton in a primary. Now, with Bumpers out of the presidential derby, Clinton seriously considered making the race. Alone in his office or in the kitchen of the mansion, he worked the telephone day and night talking to friends about the pros and cons. Legislators noted that he seemed distracted, disinterested in state affairs. He was losing the major tax initiatives that year which he had hoped would pay for the final parts of his education reform effort.

Clinton and Betsey Wright dispatched scouts to Iowa, New Hampshire, and several Super Tuesday primary states to gauge how a Clinton candidacy might be received. Gloria Cabe ventured up to New Hampshire and spent three days in a Holiday Inn calling campaign activists from a list Clinton had compiled. She was preparing the way for Clinton's first campaign-style swing through the state, which went so well that he returned home "flying like a kite," convinced that he could finish second there and then win the southern primaries. Fund-raising letters were sent to the extensive network of out-of-state friends Clinton had accumulated over the years. Charlie Daniels, the old plumber from Virginia who had met Clinton in Moscow, mailed back the first contribution. He and his wife Ethel received a note from Clinton: "Your willingness to help us defray costs while we are testing the waters is a very special vote of confidence and I'm very grateful. You've been wonderful friends—Thanks for everything—Things are going well—Bill." In Arkansas, Clinton began working on seed money commitments for the $1.5 to $2 million he had been told he would need to raise within his home state to make a creditable race. Betsey Wright thought about taking a leave from the governor's staff to concentrate on the presidential effort.

In the early morning of May 7, another Democrat was scratched from the field. This time it was Gary Hart who was forced to withdraw in the face of questions, allegations, and documented evidence regarding his extramarital sex life, which Hart had helped turn into an issue by denying that he was a philanderer and challenging reporters to tail him if they doubted his word. It was an unfortunate challenge which the *Miami Herald* took up, leading to an article in that newspaper and subsequent pictures in a tabloid detailing Hart's dalliance with a model named Donna Rice. Hart's sudden fall increased the pressure on Clinton from both ends. From one end came more longtime political pros from the McGovern era who had been allied with Hart but were now looking to Clinton as an alternative. And from the other end came the question: Did Bill Clinton have a Gary Hart problem?

As journalists and party activists in Washington asked the question among themselves, and in so doing advanced Clinton's reputation as a womanizer, Clinton and his friends and advisers struggled with how to deal with it. Bob Armstrong, the former Texas Land Commissioner who had developed an easygoing, big-brotherly friendship with Clinton since they worked together in the McGovern campaign, had several telephone conversations with Clinton in the aftermath of the Hart implosion. One of the issues Clinton brought up, according to Armstrong, was whether there was "a statute of limitations on infidelity—whether you get any credit for getting it back together." Armstrong told Clinton that he thought not. Clinton and Betsey Wright also had several private debates over the lessons of the Hart episode. Clinton "wanted to believe and advocated that it was irrelevant to whether the guy could be a good president," Wright recalled. She argued that it had a significant bearing in Hart's case "because it raised questions about his stability." Any previous affairs might have been irrelevant, she said, but "to have one while he was running was foolhardy."

Clinton agreed. Hart, he said, was foolish to flaunt it.

Dick Morris, still a Clinton pollster and consultant though his other clients by then were almost exclusively Republicans, was also brought into the discussions. Clinton questioned Morris at length about how he thought the public would react to the infidelity issue and whether it would be held against him. They gingerly explored different ways to address the topic or sidestep it. Morris sensed that Clinton had "a tremendous terror of the race because of the personal scandals that were visited upon candidates who ran. His experience watching candidates be destroyed by those scandals or impaired by them chilled him, and led him to a feeling that this was a terribly inhospitable environment upon which to tread." The sex issue, Morris said, "loomed large in his consideration. It loomed very large."

But the momentum kept building for Clinton to run. He traveled to Washington for a foreign policy briefing set up by Steve Cohen, the friend of his and Hillary's from Yale Law who had attended the first gubernatorial inaugural in Little Rock eight years earlier, where he had told Clinton about how taken he was by the "pride and hope" he felt there. Sandy Berger and John Holum, two veterans of the McGovern and Hart campaigns, helped Cohen with the briefing. Back in Little Rock, Wright and her assistants prepared for a possible announcement. Their first choice was the House chamber inside the Capitol, but state law prohibited its use for political events of that sort, so they rented a ballroom at the Excelsior Hotel for July 15.

Rumors about Clinton's extramarital sex life began making the rounds in Little Rock. A few days before the announcement, Wright met with Clinton at her home on Hill Street. The time had come, she felt, for Clinton to get past what she considered his self-denial tendencies and face the issue squarely. For years, she told friends later, she had been covering up for him. She was convinced that some state troopers were soliciting women for him, and he for them, she said. Sometimes when Clinton was on the road, Wright would call his room in the middle of the night and no one would answer. She hated that part of him, but felt that the other sides of him overshadowed his personal weaknesses.

"Okay," she said to him as they sat in her living room. Then she started listing the names of women he had allegedly had affairs with and the places where they were said to have occurred. "Now," she concluded, "I want you to tell me the truth about every one." She went over the list twice with Clinton, according to her later account, the second time trying to determine whether any of the women might tell their stories to the press. At the end of the process, she suggested that he should not get into the race. He owed it to Hillary and Chelsea not to.

The next day, Wright drove to the airport and picked up Carl Wagner, the first of a group of Clinton friends who had planned to gather in Little Rock for the presidential announcement. Wagner was a generational co-hort who had met Clinton during the Project Pursestrings antiwar effort in the summer of 1970. They had gone through the McGovern campaign together, Wagner running Michigan while Clinton ran Texas, and had kept in touch ever since. Wagner, like Clinton, loved to talk on the phone. Clinton had asked him to come down to Little Rock a day early to help "think this thing through." On the way back from the airport, Wright did not tell Wagner about her encounter with Clinton the day before. She did offer her opinion that her boss seemed "too conflicted" and "might not be ready."

Wagner met with Clinton and Hillary at the Governor's Mansion that night. They sat around the table in the kitchen and talked for several hours. It was, Wagner recalled, an intense, blunt conversation in which he and Hillary assessed the practicality of Clinton making the presidential race, element by element. Could Clinton raise $20 million? Did he have the time he needed? They analyzed the strengths and weaknesses of the other candidates, especially the probable Republican nominee, Vice President George Bush. Wagner thought that the economy would be strong enough to make Bush difficult to beat. Clinton was surprised by that argument and launched into a long discussion of economic policy. Wagner noticed that Clinton was more comfortable talking about policy, depersonalizing the discussion. He wondered whether Clinton was prepared for the conse-quences if he became a candidate. At the end of the evening, as Clinton and Hillary moved toward the stairs leading from the kitchen up to their second-floor bedroom, Clinton turned to Wagner, who was still seated at the table, and asked, "So what's the bottom line?"

"I tell you what," Wagner responded. "When you reach the top of the steps, walk into your daughter's bedroom, look at her, and understand that if you do this, your relationship with her will never be the same. I'm not sure if it will be worse or better, but it will never be the same."

After Clinton disappeared up the steps, Wagner went to the phone and called Steve Cohen, who planned to be at the announcement. "Jesus Christ," Cohen remembered Wagner telling him, "this guy doesn't know

whether he wants to run!" Cohen called Sandy Berger, who also had airplane reservations for Little Rock. There was a chance Clinton might not
run, Cohen said. They decided to go anyway.

By early afternoon the next day, a dozen Clinton friends from around
the country had congregated at the Governor's Mansion for an announce-
ment-eve luncheon. Most waited in the living room as Clinton sat on the
porch steps leading out to the back lawn, engaged in a final conversation
with Wagner and Mickey Kantor, the California lawyer and Democratic
activist who had been part of Clinton's network since the Carter era. If
Clinton had privately made up his mind after the encounter with Betsey
Wright, if he had reached a decision after the discussion with Wagner in
the kitchen the night before, he still felt a need to weigh the options to the
last possible moment. Kantor took the lead as they talked about the level
of commitment that a national campaign required. As they talked, Chelsea,
then seven years old, approached her father and asked him about a family
vacation planned for later that summer. As Kantor remembered the scene,
Clinton told his daughter that he might not be able to go because he might
be running for president. "Well," Kantor recalled Chelsea responding,
"then Mom and I will go without you."

Chelsea always had a powerful effect on Clinton. He carried pictures of
her around in his wallet and showed them to friends whenever he was on
the road. He could get misty-eyed talking about her. They held hands
whenever they were together. When he was in town, he tried to drive her
to school every morning. Earlier that year, on a Sunday morning at the
start of the legislative session, his aide and former high school teacher,
Paul Root, and Root's wife Mary, who was also a teacher, accompanied
Clinton and Chelsea to a prayer breakfast at the First Baptist Church in
Benton. When father and daughter came out of the mansion and got into
the car, Root recalled, Clinton said that he might not talk to them much
on the ride down to Benton because he did not get that much time with
Chelsea and their favorite thing to do together was read books. Chelsea
opened her church book and found her favorite story. Father and daughter
read it aloud together. They did the same thing on the way home from
Benton. As they neared the mansion, Clinton turned to Mary Root and
asked, "Is that okay? The way I was reading to her?"

The subtext of Clinton's relationship with his daughter was his own
unfortunate history with fathers. He did not want to be considered a ne-
glectful father himself, yet his political obsession gave him little time with
Chelsea. He would try to soften the guilt by joking about it, often telling
the story of how, when Chelsea was asked to describe what her father did,
she said, "He gives speeches, drinks coffee, and talks on the telephone." It
was as true as it was amusing. Now, when Kantor saw the look on Clinton's

face after Chelsea matter-of-factly scratched her father from the family vacation plans, he was sure that Clinton would not run for president that year. "It was the turning point of the conversation," he said later.

Clinton faced the gathering of friends in the dining room and apologized for luring them all down to Little Rock for no reason. No problem, they said, one after another, some fighting to keep their composure. The struggle between family and ambition was something all of them had dealt with in various ways. John Holum helped Clinton draft a statement. Clinton did not want the news to slip out haphazardly. He had friends around the country who were expecting him to run, and he wanted them to learn about his decision at the same time. Betsey Wright and Gloria Cabe and several other aides and friends worked the telephones, setting up the calls for him and alerting the national press that there was no need to make the trip to Arkansas. Wait for another day, he said to many of those he called, "because it's coming." One of those who heard from Clinton was Billie Carr in Houston. It was a sentimental conversation during which Clinton talked about the importance of "putting his house in order." Carr said she understood. "All of us in politics feel bad about neglecting our families," she said later. "We feel bad about it—but not too bad."

Clinton's statement was issued late in the day. "I need some family time: I need some personal time," he said. "Politicians are people too. I think sometimes we forget it, but they really are. The only thing I or any other candidate has to offer in running for president is what's inside. That's what sets people on fire and gets their confidence and their votes, whether they live in Wisconsin or Montana or New York. That part of my life needs renewal. The other, even more important reason for my decision is the certain impact that this campaign would have had on our daughter. The only way I could have won, getting in this late, after others had been working up to two years, would be to go on the road full time from now until the end, and to have Hillary do the same thing.... I've seen a lot of kids grow up under these pressures and a long, long time ago I made a promise to myself that if I was ever lucky enough to have a child, she would never grow up wondering who her father was."

That night, a group of Clinton's high school friends gathered at Carolyn Staley's house near the mansion in Little Rock. Clinton, his staff had said, would be too busy to attend, but he came over anyway. The friends had suspected that he would find his way there: Bill usually sought them out when he needed to ease the pressure and emotion of his public life. Just looking at David Leopoulos could make him feel better. "So," Leopoulos said at one point that night, "this reminds me of the Fuhgawe Indians." Clinton was the only one in the room who knew what Leopoulos was talking about. They both started laughing. It was their oldest, corniest joke, one they used to tell as they sat atop the mountain above Hot Springs. It was about the Indians who had no name until they got lost in the mountains and one of them asked, "Where the fuhgawe?"

ON a Sunday morning in early February of 1988, Clinton was asked to talk to a class of single adults at Immanuel Baptist Church. Most members of the group were professionals in their twenties and thirties. The theme he chose was "the conflict between the idea of progress and the certainty of death." Sometimes, he said, it is hard "to keep going when you know that the sand's running out of the hourglass. Yet you still have a moral obligation to try to make tomorrow better than today." A few days later, in a speech at the University of Arkansas at Little Rock, Clinton recalled his Sunday School sermon and said that in his own life he had two hourglasses going at once, one his mortality as a person and the other his mortality as a politician. Knowing about the first made him feel more urgency about the second and all that he still hoped to accomplish. "I think about it," he said, "as the time ebbs away."

ATLANTA, Georgia: July 20, 1988. This was the third consecutive convention at which Clinton had made the coveted list of speakers. In 1980, he had been selected to present the issues affecting the nation's governors. In 1984, his assignment was to deliver a tribute to Harry Truman. This 1988 Democratic National Convention might have been the time he talked about himself. But another governor, Michael Dukakis of Massachusetts, had top billing, and another governor, Ann Richards of Texas, became a star as the keynote speaker. Jesse Jackson had already stirred the convention hall with an emotional speech. Clinton would give the nominating speech for Dukakis. By tradition, several speakers nominated a presidential candidate. Clinton would do it alone, in prime time, before all the audiences he wanted to reach. It could be the first speech of his future campaign.

Clinton had stayed up all night revising his speech, going through nine full drafts. Ordinarily he spoke extemporaneously, working off notes, but this speech had to be a finished document, to be read and approved by Dukakis and his aides. Hillary had never seen him work so hard on a speech, she told friends. He would tackle a section, go over it with his advisers, and then scrap it and redo it, again and again, adding more themes, inserting paragraphs. His secretary got so worn out typing and retyping drafts overnight that she ended up needing medical treatment for exhaustion. By midmorning, when the manuscript was essentially finished, Clinton was concerned that it was too long, yet Dukakis aides called three more times with suggested additions. Clinton had been allotted twenty minutes, including pauses for applause and demonstrations, and it was timed with no interruptions at sixteen minutes. His advisers had other concerns. Betsey Wright, Gloria Cabe, and Bruce Lindsey, the Little Rock lawyer who was becoming Clinton's most trusted traveling aide, had all listened to him give countless rousing speeches that brought his audiences to standing ovations. They knew that it would be hard to turn an introduction into a scintillating oration. But this text, Cabe thought, had been redone so many times by Clinton and had so many inserts from the Dukakis camp that it had become plain vanilla. After reading it with Lindsey and Wright, she turned to them and said, "All the Bill Clinton's been taken out of it."

After the dress rehearsal at the convention hall in late afternoon, Clinton and Hillary paid a visit to the Dukakises at their hotel room. The speech, Dukakis said, was exactly what he wanted. He loved it. "No matter what happens," Clinton later recalled Dukakis telling him, "give the speech."

Clinton went to the microphone confidently that night, to the theme of *Chariots of Fire* playing on the sound system. "I'm honored to be here tonight to nominate my friend Michael Dukakis for President of the United States," he began. That was the rhetorical high point. It went downhill from there. Clinton and his aides had hoped that the house lights would be dimmed and the crowd silenced for a thoughtful presentation. But the lights stayed on, and Dukakis delegates, who had remained relatively subdued for two days while Jackson delegates dominated the scene, were now being whipped up by cheerleaders on the convention floor. Inside the convention hall, Clinton's words were an inaudible drone. It was no better on television.

Betsey Wright stood at the back of the podium, overtaken by a "completely helpless feeling." She tried to have the lights lowered. No one would do it. Hillary was posted nearby, furious about the lights and the sight of Dukakis floor whips instructing delegates to cheer every time Clinton mentioned his name. Gloria Cabe was seated with the Arkansas delegation, "pissed off" that she could not hear the speech above the orchestrated commotion. Harry Truman Moore was also on the floor, with his camera out, recording the scene for the *Paragould Daily Press*. Caught between two clumps of Dukakis and Jackson delegates engaged in a shouting match, turning his lens first up at his longtime friend who seemed to be dying on stage, then back at the painful faces of his colleagues in the Arkansas delegation, Moore felt he was witnessing "one of the most miserable political experiences" he had ever been through. As the speech dragged on, past sixteen minutes, past twenty minutes, it got even worse.

ABC cut away at the twenty-one-minute mark and began showing a film. On NBC, Tom Brokaw uttered forlornly, "We have to be here, too," and then gave up on the speech. CBS showed a red light flashing on the podium, a signal for Clinton to shut up, then found a delegate in the audience giving Clinton the cut sign with the hand slash across the throat. People could be heard shouting: "Get the hook! Get the hook!"

A few minutes into his speech, Clinton had seen that he had lost the audience. He considered abandoning the text and firing up the crowd with a few campaign-style exhortations and getting off the stage. But as he later explained, or rationalized, he kept his word to Dukakis to read the entire speech. After thirty-two excruciating minutes, when he uttered "In closing"—one of the few ad-libbed phrases in his speech—the hall erupted in mocking applause. Clinton and his entourage knew it was a lost opportunity, but they did not realize how disastrous until Bruce Lindsey called Cabe's husband in Little Rock and asked what it had looked like on television. "God, Lindsey, Bill was awful!" Robert Cabe said. Clinton, Hillary, and Betsey Wright decided on a swift counterattack. They would spread the word on the problems in the hall as Clinton was giving his speech, without saying anything negative about Dukakis. Clinton, meanwhile, worked the hospitality suites and parties around town, talking to activists and journalists and anyone who would hear him out. The strategy recalled the days after his loss to Frank White in 1980, when he talked obsessively about what had happened to him and what he had done wrong, confronting friends and strangers in supermarkets and bookstores and anywhere he could find them.

The morning after was unforgiving. Deborah Norville on NBC's *Today* asked Tom Pettit how Clinton could have been described as "someone to watch" on the national scene. "Now we know better," deadpanned Pettit. Frank Greer, a media consultant who admired Clinton and wanted to work for him on a political campaign, was quoted repeating a line he said he had heard after the speech: " 'It was either the longest nominating speech or the shortest presidential campaign speech in history.' " Television columnist Tom Shales of *The Washington Post* described it under the headline "The Numb and the Restless." While Jesse Jackson had electrified the crowd the night before, Shales wrote, Clinton had calcified it. Johnny Carson's writers delighted in the material Clinton had provided them for *The Tonight Show.* Carson would begin his next monologue by saying, "In closing . . ." Then he would note that the Surgeon General had just approved Governor Bill Clinton as an over-the-counter sleep aid, and that Clinton's speech went over "about as big as the Velcro condom," and that when it came to drama, Clinton was "right up there with PBS pledge breaks."

The Clintons tried to defuse the situation with humor. "It was the worst hour of my life—no, make that hour and a half," Clinton told the *Boston Globe.* "Last night was just weird," Hillary told a forlorn caucus of Arkansas delegates who gathered the next morning at the Embassy Suites for a postmortem. She quoted her husband as telling her, " 'Well, that's the last time I'll nominate anybody for anything!' " She hoped that the speech would soon be forgotten. "Political history remakes itself every twenty-four hours. Every day is an opportunity to make a new speech." Still, she was fighting for her husband and the future of their political partnership, and she could not entirely control her competitive bent. "If the criticism is that Bill talked too long and was ponderous," she said, "hey, that's criticism of all the Bill Bradleys and all the Mike Dukakises of the world." She was still simmering on the plane ride back to Little Rock Friday morning, according to Gloria Cabe, who sat next to her. "We felt like we had made some small steps toward recovery but were still flabbergasted by the enormity of the event," Cabe recalled. "And of all things, for people to think he was a bad speaker! You could say a lot of things about him, but that was just not accurate."

Betsey Wright had flown back a day earlier, before the convention was over, and she called a staff meeting. Several members of Clinton's staff had watched the speech at the Oyster Bar restaurant in Little Rock and were confused and demoralized when they gathered to hear Wright's account. Wright intended to give a calm assessment of what had happened. But not long after she began her explanation, she started sobbing.

IF Clinton intended to finish his political career as the governor of Arkansas, the recovery from the speech could have ended with the adjournment of the convention. But the permanent campaign was a national endeavor now. The vast network of friends that he and Hillary had constructed across the country was seeking reassurance. Judy Trabulsi in Austin, his friend from the McGovern days, was flooded with calls from acquaintances eager to tease her. "So this is the guy you say is going to be president? What a joke!" There was more face-saving work to be done. Clinton needed to transform the disaster into an opportunity by doing something creative and dramatic. Friends in Hollywood, producers Linda Bloodworth Thomason and Harry Thomason, an Arkansas native whose brother Danny was the Clintons' optometrist, conceived the answer. They arranged for him to appear on *The Tonight Show,* where he nervously played "Summertime" on his saxophone and made self-effacing jokes that inspired Johnny Carson to laugh with him, not at him. More Americans watched that show than had listened to his convention speech.

That summer and fall of 1988 marked the first even-numbered year since 1974 that Clinton was not engaged in his own political race. Including primaries, runoffs, and general elections, he had been involved in fifteen elections in fourteen years—more elections, he stated with probable justification, than any other politician in America during that stretch. But state election laws had been changed before the 1986 elections to make the gubernatorial term four years instead of two. Now Clinton was without a race, and he was restless, bored, and increasingly distraught about the Dukakis campaign. Gloria Cabe said there were times when she thought he wanted to enlist as Dukakis's campaign manager. George Bush's campaign team, led by Lee Atwater, was beating Dukakis over the head with a hammer, making him appear soft on crime by exploiting a case where a Massachusetts felon named Willie Horton had killed again after being released on parole. Clinton knew what he would do in that situation. To continue the metaphor which had been his creed since Frank White had pounded him with negative ads in 1980, he would get out a meat cleaver and cut off Bush's hands. Dukakis did not respond adequately. Once during that fall, as he was driving from the airport in Fayetteville to give a speech at the University of Arkansas campus, Clinton raged about Dukakis to Woody Bassett. "He was upset that Dukakis had not fought back on Willie Horton," Bassett later recalled. "He said that he had written a response ad for them, but they had never used it."

Not long after Dukakis lost, Bob Reich, in his annual letter in the *American Oxonian,* put into Rhodes classmate Strobe Talbott's mouth the words that both he and Talbott were thinking. "America," he wrote, "will survive the next four years the same way it survived the last 20 since we set sail for England: waiting for Clinton to become president."

Clinton was already making plans. Two days after Christmas, nearly a month before Bush would be inaugurated, Clinton met with John Pouland, a Dallas lawyer who had been the southern coordinator for Gary Hart's presidential campaign. Pouland had flown up to Little Rock with Randy White, who now worked as an assistant to Pouland's law partner, Congressman John Bryant. They arrived at the Governor's Mansion just as Clinton was returning from a jog and adjourned to the study, where they sipped coffee and talked presidential politics for two hours. Clinton was full of questions. Should he run for governor again in 1990 if he wanted to run for president two years later, when he would be in the middle of his term? How much money did he have to raise in Arkansas? Could he be the regional candidate? What about another young southern moderate—Tennessee Senator Al Gore? White left the meeting thinking that Clinton could hardly wait for 1992.

· · ·

GETTING from here to there would not be easy. Throughout his political career, Clinton often demonstrated a keen ability to foresee obstacles that he might encounter, though he could not always find the surest way around them. Now he seemed anxious about how he would get through the next few years. As his permanent campaign took on a national focus, it lost energy in Arkansas. And he still had to survive in Arkansas. When he went before the General Assembly on January 9, 1989, for his state of the state address, he spoke as the first Arkansas governor in more than a century to open a regular legislative session without just having been inaugurated. More than two years had passed since his last election, and that gap, he told his aides, could prove troublesome. His last major effort to raise the sales tax to fund education programs, in 1987, had been defeated after a heavy lobbying effort against it by the state's business interests, who opposed the expansion of the tax to cover professional services that had been exempted. This time he had worked with the corporate powers to devise an education agenda and a tax plan that they could support, but the public mood seemed determinedly antitax. George Bush had just won the presidential election lip-reading his promise of no new taxes. Without a fresh mandate from the voters, Clinton feared, it would be hard for him to move a recalcitrant legislature.

During the six years of his second act as governor, state aid to education in Arkansas had increased by a greater percentage than in all but six other states. Yet local support of the schools through property taxes had trailed the national average, meaning that Arkansas still lingered in its traditional spot near the bottom in overall education spending. Clinton had built his career on the education issue. He felt there was more to be done. Before the session, during the time when in earlier years he would have been campaigning for reelection, he spent seven months with his staff and a statewide task force preparing a new agenda for expanded preschool, vocational, and higher education programs. But he realized that getting the taxes to pay for it would be harder than ever. "The Great Communicator in Washington, who's told us that all taxes are evil, has made it hard for us to do what we need to do here," Clinton said in his state of the state address. "I have two answers to that: First of all, President Reagan said in 1983 that education was the business of the states and if funding had to be increased, the states should raise the taxes to do it. . . . And secondly, unlike our friends in Washington, we cannot write a check on an account that is not funded. We either raise and spend or we don't spend."

That final phrase, taken out of context, would be used against Clinton later, but at the time it was accurate. The 1989 legislature declined to raise taxes; Clinton had no new money to spend on education. His early premonition of trouble had been fulfilled—and more trouble was on the way.

· · ·

Betsey Wright had been at Clinton's side for nearly a decade, since his loss to Frank White. Nothing that concerned Bill Clinton was too trivial for Major Betsey, as some staff members called her. During his exile, she had sat in his basement and organized his political files, then had followed him to the law firm and took a desk outside his door, in the bullpen with the secretaries. After his restoration, she had followed him back to the Capitol and become his top aide. She was a chronic chain-smoking overworker, deep-voiced, literate, who reported before dawn and stayed late into the night. Now she was exhausted. Her face, said one friend, seemed frozen in a gaunt expression of pain. Year by year, she had become more of a target of criticism from some good ole boys in the Arkansas legislature, who found her too protective and abrasive. Her relationship with Clinton had grown increasingly tumultuous. They yelled and cursed each other like sailors, but now Wright was becoming more emotional. Policy, personality, private life—everything was getting mixed up into one unsettling stew.

After years of legal deliberations, the first death penalty decisions were approaching in Arkansas. Wright opposed capital punishment but knew that Clinton supported it. They had argued over the death penalty since she had gone to work for him. She wanted to believe, she said later, that his position was based on conviction, not political pragmatism. On the night that mass murderer Ronald Simmons of Russellville was to have been executed, she persuaded Clinton to cancel an appearance at a social function, which she thought would look inappropriate. At the last hour, the court granted a stay of execution. Wright called the governor to tell him, but could not find him at the mansion. She discovered that he was out having dinner with actress Mary Steenburgen, a longtime friend of the Clintons who had grown up in Arkansas.

He was into self-denial again, she told her friends. She concluded that he was going through a severe midlife crisis. She said that he was having a serious affair with another woman, and was not even being discreet about it. Everyone knew, she said. She knew, the troopers knew, Hillary knew. There were great screaming matches at the mansion. Once a counselor was called out to mediate. Clinton was broaching the subject of divorce in conversations with some of his colleagues, governors from other states who had survived the collapse of their marriages. But he told his friends in Arkansas that he wanted to save his marriage. And Hillary wanted to save it, too. She told Wright that she was unwilling to abandon the partnership. She had invested too much in Bill Clinton and was determined to see it through. Wright felt that she had to get away. She was irritable beyond any measure that even she could justify. She was so mad at Clinton that she told him she felt like boiling a pot of water and pouring it over his head. She was, as she would discover later, suffering from a deep clinical depression. Late in the summer of 1989, she told Clinton that she was burned out. She asked for and got a leave of absence.

In the midst of this personal turmoil, Clinton was losing another father. His minister, W. O. Vaught, was in the final stages of bone cancer. Nearly every week Clinton stopped by Vaught's house to check on him. Once he brought along the evangelist Billy Graham. They stood at Vaught's bedside and Graham said a prayer. A few days before Christmas, Clinton was among a group of friends who came over to put up the Vaughts' Christmas tree. When the ailing minister said that he wanted to see it, Clinton picked up the tree and carried it into his room. On Christmas Day, 1989, the old Baptist preacher died. Clinton served as a pallbearer at the funeral, leading the procession down the front steps of Immanuel Baptist Church on the way to Roselawn Memorial Park. At the graveyard, Vaught's son, Carl Vaught, gave a final speech about his father and the irony of his not being there at this time when everyone needed him. His father, he said, "was doubly aware of how important it was to be present at crucial times." At that moment, he looked across the grave and caught the watery eyes of Bill Clinton. A few days later, he wrote Clinton a note recalling that moment at the graveyard and saying that he knew Clinton was thinking about some of those special occasions. Clinton wrote back and said he was surprised that Vaught could read his face so clearly.

There is a temptation to dismiss the pious Clinton as somewhat of a poseur, seeking to cover up less righteous aspects of his life. But he was always a man of contrasts and contradictions. Within hours in one day, he could eat pork ribs and listen to the Delta Blues music at Sim's Bar-B-Que in the lowlands of Little Rock's predominantly black south side; then drive up to the Heights for a round of golf at the Country Club of Little Rock, an elite hideaway with manicured fairways and no black members; then, on the way home, he might pop in his favorite tape of white Pentecostal gospel music from the Alexandria Sanctuary Chorale. Clinton could go from a meeting with deer hunters in Scott County, furious because the state Game and Fish Commission would not let them run their dogs in December, to an education summit in Charlottesville staying up all night crafting an agenda of education goals for the fifty governors and the Bush administration, to a West Coast fund-raising dinner at Norman Lear's house where he mixed with the Hollywood glitterati. If Clinton had the ability to move easily through so many different worlds, he could also appear a chameleon, forced to balance one world off against another. Capable as he was of great bursts of energy and concentration, no single world could keep him content for long.

• • •

THE year 1990 presented Clinton with one of the toughest political decisions of his career. He had been governor for ten of the last twelve years.
What more could he do? he asked his advisers. He seemed tired of the job
and feared that the people of Arkansas had grown weary of him. Those
were strong reasons not to seek a fifth term. His concern about losing a
forum could be alleviated somewhat by another national leadership position that he was assuming, as chairman of the Democratic Leadership
Council, a faction of moderates, many of them from the South, who sought
to reorient the party toward the white middle class. There were also
persuasive reasons to remain in the governor's office. If he left and started
running for president as a former governor, he would be depriving himself
of status and a financial power base, especially if President Bush appeared
unbeatable in 1992 and Clinton ended up postponing his national run until
1996. He was getting strong advice from former governors, including Jim
Hunt of North Carolina and Richard Riley of South Carolina, not to give up
the job until he had to: they missed it, they said, and he would, too.

Clinton's state of mind further complicated the decision. Although he
was developing new themes on the national level, back home, in his role
as governor, he seemed to be "dithering and depressed," in the view of
Dick Morris, who had helped construct the permanent campaign that had
carried him through the eighties. Clinton's dilemma, as Morris viewed it,
was that he was temporarily without a crusade, such as education reform
or economic development, and that he was incapable of being a caretaker
chief executive. He had to be engaged in "some important, valiant fight for
the good of the world to lend coherence and structure to his life, and
when he didn't have those fights he would turn on himself, he would eat
away at himself, he would become depressed, paranoid, surly and, one
suspects, escapist." Clinton was an activist, Morris concluded, "because it
was the only way he could maintain any reasonable degree of psychological coherence."

Clinton's decision-making process in 1990 followed the same wavering
pattern as his deliberations about running for president in 1987. During
the first two weeks of February, there were fresh rumors every day. One
of the most popular, promoted by several of her friends in the Little Rock
legal community, was that Hillary would run instead. She seemed as unclear as anyone else about her husband's plans, even after he had scheduled
a press conference at which he was to announce his decison. On the day
before the event, according to Gloria Cabe, Hillary called her and asked
whether she had any inside information on what Clinton had decided.
Betsey Wright, who was still on leave from her post as chief of staff, talked

to him the morning of the announcement and was convinced that up to thirty minutes beforehand he intended to relinquish the governorship. Cabe was among those who thought he had decided not to run but changed his mind when he entered the room and began to speak. David Leopoulos, Clinton's high school friend, later recalled that "you could have knocked Hillary over with a feather" when Clinton declared that he was seeking another term. "She did not expect it. None of us did."

THE notion that Bill Clinton began his political career as a radical and moved inexorably rightward over the decades is misleading. He was a cautious defender of the establishment during his student politics days at Georgetown. In his Oxford and Yale years, he was in the moderate wing of the antiwar movement. From the beginning of his ascent in Arkansas, he would attack organized labor and court corporate interests when it served his political purposes. He had supported the death penalty since his 1976 race for attorney general. As early as his 1980 speech at the Democratic National Convention in New York, he was turning away from traditional liberal Democratic rhetoric. The sphere in which his movement from left to right seemed most apparent was foreign policy. There is a considerable ideological gap between his antiwar letter to Colonel Holmes, in which he disparaged the military, and his decision in the late 1980s to let the Arkansas National Guard participate in controversial training missions in Central America, at a time when some other governors, who opposed the Reagan administration policies there, refused to let their troops go. But in the full context of his political life, his letter to Colonel Holmes was the aberration, his decision on the National Guard the norm.

On race relations, Clinton used his power as governor to accomplish many of the integrationist goals he had carried since his youth in Hot Springs. He appointed more blacks to state boards and commissions than had all previous Arkansas governors combined. He appointed the first black lawyer to the state Supreme Court, instilled a black woman as the state health chief, and surrounded himself with African Americans in key financial posts, including director of the Department of Finance and Administration. He and Hillary sent Chelsea to a public school in Little Rock that was 60 percent black. But as a politician seeking to survive in a state dominated by conservative white voters—the black population in Arkansas was about 15 percent, the lowest percentage in the South—Clinton was not always able or willing to advance the causes of black activists. Arkansas was one of only two states without a state civil rights law, and he could not persuade the legislature to fund a human rights commission. In 1989, as one of three members of the state Board of Apportionment, Clinton disappointed many of his black supporters by voting to appeal a federal court ruling that substantially increased the number of majority-black legislative districts. He said that he voted for the appeal, which eventually was dismissed, for technical reasons: the apportionment board needed guidance from the high court on its role in redistricting because the 1990 census was approaching.

Clinton's policy choices throughout the 1980s reflect an activist nature more than shifting ideology. In his effort to reform the education system, he turned to the regressive sales tax as the surest way to get the money. In seeking to lower the state's unemployment rate, which hovered above 12 percent when he returned to office in 1983 but had dropped to under 7 percent by the end of the decade, he often backed away from strict environmental enforcement and gave major corporations large tax breaks to stay in Arkansas and expand their operations. Tyson Foods received $7.8 million in tax breaks from 1988 to 1990 at a time when the world's largest poultry firm had a budget twice as large as the state's. After occasional battles over taxes, lobbying laws, and municipal bond practices, Clinton and the Arkansas business establishment had reached a level of mutual accommodation. He was accepting free rides in corporate jets (Tyson had flown him on nine trips) and soliciting large contributions from corporate leaders for the public relations arm of his permanent campaign. If he was not exactly one of the money boys, he was accepted to the point where Little Rock bankers called him "Pards," the abbreviated form of "Partner" in the southwestern subculture of oil and finance. Hillary, in her pursuit of financial security, had joined the boards of several corporations, including two of the largest in Arkansas, Wal-Mart and TCBY, the yogurt enterprise.

By the time Clinton began his campaign for a fifth term, which would make him the longest-tenured governor in Arkansas history, he was such a large, familiar figure in the state that he faced the ultimate political paradox. His self-image had always been one of action and change, yet now, inevitably, he had come to represent permanence and stability. He was approaching a potential fatal point where polls showed that he was more popular than electable: more people gave him a high approval rating than wanted to vote for him. His opponent in the Democratic primary, a liberal policy analyst named Tom McRae, played on this mood with an anti-Clinton ad that showed a line of clocks stretching into infinity. Clinton's campaign was burdened with a sense that he was stretching his time in office. Many of his longtime county chairs were exhausted from the permanent campaign and unprepared for another grueling round. Gloria Cabe, who had taken over as campaign manager for Betsey Wright, had to recruit an almost entirely new network of workers. Wright felt that Cabe had betrayed her by taking the job. Dick Morris, an ally of Wright's, would not deal with Cabe and kept pestering Clinton to rehire Wright. Cabe wanted nothing to do with Morris and was furious that Clinton and Hillary still dealt with a political operative whose other clients were Republicans.

One day at the Governor's Mansion, after a meeting of Clinton, Hillary, Cabe, and Morris, the relationship between the governor and his consultant exploded. Clinton was on edge, worried that he had made a mistake by entering the race. Morris was hounding Clinton about his treatment of Betsey Wright. They got into a shouting match near the side porch, with Morris, nearly a foot shorter than the governor, screaming up into his face. As Hillary and Cabe stood by, Clinton suddenly lost control, according to Cabe, and slugged Morris, sending him reeling. "Clinton apologized," Cabe later recalled. "But he was still pissed." Morris did not resign. He stayed on for the rest of the campaign, though every now and then, according to Cabe, he would mutter, "I can't believe Clinton hit me!"

The most memorable moment in the primary came when Tom McRae held a press conference at the Capitol and Hillary started heckling him from the back of the crowd. "Get off it, Tom!" she shouted, as McRae criticized Clinton's record. It had the feel of a spontaneous encounter, the proud wife defending her man. In fact, it had been scripted. At a strategy meeting the day before, the Clinton team had decided that McRae needed to be confronted. "We have to take this guy on!" Hillary had said, and then she went out and did it. What effect it had is a matter of dispute. McRae later claimed that he won the rural women's vote because of it. But Clinton won the primary.

In the general election, Clinton faced Republican Sheffield Nelson, a former Democrat who ran Arkansas-Louisiana Gas Company, the state's largest gas utility. During Clinton's first term, he and Nelson had been allies. "If Sheffield Nelson called the office, he was talking to Bill Clinton," former aide Randy White recalled of those early days. "If Nelson wanted Bill Clinton in his office, he would be there." They had several mutual friends, including Clinton's childhood pal, Mack McLarty, who would succeed Nelson at Arkla, but over the years Clinton and Nelson grew to hate each other. They both came out of small-town Arkansas, Nelson with an even more deprived background than Clinton. They were competitive, ambitious, complicated men who enjoyed nothing more than gathering rumors and private reports on the other's actions and then spreading the word around town. There was enough material on both sides to keep the gossip flowing. It was a private war conducted at a level beneath the public campaign.

Clinton had reinforced his general election team with outsiders, including Frank Greer, a Washington-based media consultant, and pollster Stanley

Greenberg, an expert on the use of focus groups. Greer had long considered Clinton presidential material and viewed the gubernatorial race as a warmup for 1992. In recruiting Greer, in fact, Clinton had said, "You always wanted me to run for president. But let me tell you, if I lose this race for governor, I'll never get elected dog catcher." Not long after Greer signed on, Clinton attended a debate at which he was asked whether if he won the election he would serve out his full term as governor. "You bet," he said impulsively.

Cabe called Greer from the debate. "You're not going to like this," she said. "Clinton just took himself out of the '92 race."

Greer was shocked. "We had talked a lot about running for president," he recalled. "I died a thousand deaths. I thought perhaps it wasn't going to happen. I was bound and determined to tell him to run in 1992."

Clinton remained comfortably ahead during the final month of the campaign. In response to the findings of Greenberg's focus groups, he had repositioned himself as the agent of change, with a new agenda for his next term that concentrated on middle-class concerns. The strategy was effective, but every day in October it seemed that the contest got nastier. Calls were streaming into the campaign office about Clinton's extramarital sex life. On October 19, Larry Nichols, a former employee of the Arkansas Development Finance Agency, held a press conference announcing that he was filing a lawsuit against Clinton in which he contended that the governor had used a slush fund to entertain at least five women with whom he had affairs. Nichols offered no proof, and the Arkansas press declined to write about the suit or the press conference. Nichols was a familiar character to the local press. He had been fired from the state agency in 1988 after it was discovered that he had made 142 long-distance telephone calls at taxpayer expense to leaders of the Nicaraguan contra movement. Although Nelson maintained that he had no connection to the Nichols lawsuit and the allegations about Clinton's sex life, workers at his campaign headquarters spread the story to anyone who called.

According to Nelson's campaign manager, Paula Unruh, they had taped a commercial attacking Clinton's personal character but decided not to run it. Instead, during the final days of the campaign, they ran another negative ad portraying Clinton as a big-tax liberal. What has Clinton done and what will he do if he is reelected? the spot asked. The answer, "Raise and spend, raise and spend," was delivered in Clinton's voice, taken out of context from his 1989 state of the state address.

At eleven o'clock on Saturday night of the final weekend before the election, Dick Morris was at a tavern in Westchester County, New York, and about to leave for his home in Connecticut when he decided to call the firm in Atlanta that was doing the tracking polls for Clinton. With

Clinton apparently ahead by 15 percentage points, Morris did not consider the final tracking poll a matter of urgency, and acknowledged later that he had it done "just to make it look good as much as anything else." But when he reached the people in Atlanta, they told him that Clinton had fallen 10 points in three days and was now down to 46 percent. According to Morris, the open-ended question on the poll that asked people what they liked least about Clinton showed that Nelson's tax ads were having a profound effect. It was well past midnight when he called Clinton at the mansion and gave him the numbers. "I knew it! I knew I was getting killed by that ad!" Morris recalled Clinton saying. "I can feel it!"

From that point, Morris said, Clinton reacted "as clearheaded as a quarterback under a rush." They wrote a response ad overnight and produced it early the following morning. The response noted that Nelson had misappropriated Clinton's state of the state message by lifting the words "raise and spend" from a paragraph that in fact was a criticism of the Reagan administration. To pay for the ads, Clinton took out another personal loan from one of the banks that helped him fund the permanent campaign, the Bank of Perry County, which was owned by Herbie Branscum, a longtime Clinton ally and former chairman of the state Democratic party. Television station managers around the state were called and persuaded to take the response ads immediately and run them Sunday and Monday. Gloria Cabe recruited her teenage daughter to serve as the delivery woman. She and a pilot flew around the state in a thunderstorm to get the tapes to the stations. Another team of volunteer drivers carried the audio responses to dozens of radio stations.

Clinton defeated Nelson handily that Tuesday, so easily, in fact, that Cabe wondered whether Morris's final poll could have been accurate. When Morris called her and asked for his payment for the poll, she said she would not give it to him until he provided her with the detailed results. She never got the results, she said later, and she never wrote Morris the check.

ONE day in December, in the month after the election, Clinton called Gennifer Flowers, one of the women who had been named in the Nichols lawsuit. Clinton did not know that Flowers was tape-recording their conversation. They talked about the lawsuit and Sheffield Nelson. "I stuck it up their ass," Clinton said. "Nelson called afterwards, you know." He said that Nelson had claimed that he had nothing to do with the infidelity allegations. "I know he lied. I just wanted to make his asshole pucker," Clinton said to Flowers. "But I covered you. . . ."

When AP reporter Bill Simmons had first called him and read him the list, Clinton told Flowers, his response was, "God . . . I kinda hate to deny that!" He had good taste, Clinton told her. Then he added: "I told you a couple of years ago, one time when I came to see you, that I had retired. And I'm now glad I have because they scoured the waterfront."

As Ed Howard was moving through the crowd at Oaklawn race track in Hot Springs on Derby Day, April 20, 1991, he saw Governor Clinton approaching from the other direction. Howard was a real estate agent in Malvern. He was a Clinton supporter. He had known Clinton since the summer of 1969, when he served as a drill instructor for the ROTC unit at the University of Arkansas in Fayetteville. He was there when Clinton had signed up for the reserve program as a means of avoiding the draft, and he had been there when Clinton's letter to Colonel Holmes arrived from Oxford. Nearly ten years later, when Clinton was in his first campaign for governor, Howard had received a call from a Republican political operative who wanted him to go public with his knowledge of Clinton's actions to avert the draft. Howard had declined. Now another decade had passed, Clinton seemed to be on the verge of running for president, and the questions were coming again. Howard was being pursued by a reporter for the *Arkansas Gazette* who had heard from an ex-student in Fayetteville about the possible existence of a controversial letter from young Bill Clinton concerning the draft. The reporter had called Howard several times. It was the first thing that crossed Howard's mind when he saw Clinton at Derby Day. Maybe, he thought, he should tell the governor.

They shook hands and chatted a minute, and then Howard said that a reporter was on the trail of the letter and the draft.

"Oh, don't worry about that," said Clinton. "I've put that one to bed."

"Okay," said Howard.

There was a pause, and then Clinton asked, "What did you tell 'em?"

"Nothing," said Howard.

"Good," Clinton said.

LESS than three weeks later, on the morning of May 6 at a convention hall in Cleveland, Ohio, Clinton walked to the podium to give the keynote address at the national meeting of the Democratic Leadership Council (DLC). The session had generated controversy even before it began, with the decision to exclude Jesse Jackson from the list of speakers. Clinton, as the president of the DLC, had taken the brunt of Jackson's wrath, along with a few sharp criticisms from Ron Brown, chairman of the Democratic National Committee. As Clinton prepared to speak, he took out a single piece of paper that had twenty words scratched on it. From those one-word cues he delivered what many in the audience regarded as the finest political speech of the year. "We're here to save the United States of America," he declared, not just the Democratic party. "Our burden is to give the people a new choice rooted in old values. A new choice that is simple, that offers opportunity, demands responsibility, gives citizens more say, provides them responsive government, all because we recognize that we are community. We're all in this together, and we're going up or down together." The buzz in Washington among journalists and political opinion makers was that the Cleveland speech had established Clinton as a serious national figure, one who seemed to have a clear idea of what he wanted to do as president.

Two days later, back in Little Rock, Clinton made an appearance at the Governor's Quality Conference in a ballroom at the Excelsior Hotel. Paula Corbin Jones, then a twenty-four-year-old secretary for the Arkansas Industrial Development Commission, which was sponsoring the conference, was working at the reception desk outside the ballroom. According to an account she would give three years later, which Clinton denies, the governor stared at her as he stood nearby, and then later dispatched one of his state troopers to solicit her. Handing her a piece of paper with a room number on it, the trooper, according to her account, said that Clinton wanted to meet her in his room. She said that she went out of curiosity. Inside the room, she said, Clinton kissed her on the neck, placed a hand on her thigh, said that he liked the curves of her body and the flow of her hair, turned "beet red," and asked her to perform a sex act. She refused, she said, and quickly left.

IN June and July, Clinton talked to scores of friends about whether he should run for president. He could present a convincing case either way, as he always could. One of his arguments on the negative side had echoes of 1987. He would say that he was not sure that Chelsea was ready. There was a new problem as well: his promise to the voters of Arkansas that he would serve out his term as governor. Hillary seemed not merely ready this time, but eager, as were most of their friends. On August 14, Hillary Clinton went up to Bentonville for a meeting of the Wal-Mart environmental board, which she chaired. Texas Land Commissioner Garry Mauro, and Roy Spence, head of an Austin advertising firm, were also there. They had known Clinton and Rodham since the McGovern campaign in Texas in 1972. Now Mauro was on the Wal-Mart environmental board with Hillary, and Spence had the company's advertising account. After the meeting, Hillary turned to Spence, who had rented a car, and said, "Let's drive around." Spence drove aimlessly. Mauro sat in the back and Hillary in front. "We're thinking about doing it," Hillary said. "We're thinking about going forward with this great adventure. What do you all think?"

"This is what we've been waiting for, for a long time," Spence said.

Hillary said there were some problems and she needed their advice. "Bill made a contract with the people of Arkansas to not run and he's really worried about it," she said.

Spence said it was important to "lance that boil."

How? asked Hillary.

"Your enemies will hold it against you, but your friends don't have to," Spence said. "They'll want you to run. Get in the car and drive around Arkansas and seek the counsel of the family members."

They drove around for another half-hour, and then Spence circled back to the Wal-Mart parking lot and turned off the engine. "You know, Roy, they'll say a lot of things about our marriage," Hillary said.

"Yeah."

"What should we do about that?"

"Admit it. Early."

A few days later, Clinton drove around Arkansas in what was called "The Secret Tour." In town after town, he told supporters that he felt troubled about breaking his pledge to serve out his term. Everywhere he went, people told him to run. He was participating in a well-scripted skit. Not long after he finished, he announced the formation of an exploratory committee, the first formal step on the way toward an announcement. The next three steps were taken in sequence when the Clintons visited Washington in mid-September. First, in a day-long session chaired by Mickey Kantor in a meeting room at the Washington Court Hotel, they met with about twenty political friends and allies and plotted the strategy and mechanics of a campaign: what issues to emphasize, how to put together a staff and raise money. Kantor gingerly broached the subject of how Clinton intended to deal with questions about infidelity.

That subject got a more thorough vetting later at a meeting in Frank Greer's office attended by a smaller group that included the Clintons, Bruce Lindsey, Greer, and Stan Greenberg. In dealing with reporters and political operatives all summer, Greer had come to realize that Clinton had "an incredible reputation around town" for philandering. The next morning, Clinton was scheduled to meet the elite of Washington's political press corps at a traditional function known as the Sperling Breakfast, founded by Godfrey Sperling, Jr., of the *Christian Science Monitor.* What should he do, if anything, to assure this crowd that his personal life was under control, that he would not implode like Gary Hart? The mention of the subject irked Clinton. The rules had changed since Hart, he said. Now there was so much hypocrisy involved. If you just go out and divorce your wife, you never have to deal with this. But if you work at your problems, if you make a commitment, then you do. So people are rewarded in politics if they divorce their wives. That was the genesis of the answer they decided Clinton should give at the Sperling Breakfast. He would say that he had had some problems, but that he and Hillary worked things through and they were committed to their marriage.

Clinton and Hillary left for dinner. When Clinton came back a few hours later, he told Greer, "Hell, I just had dinner with Vernon Jordan and Jordan said, 'Screw 'em! Don't tell 'em anything!' "

That probably would not work, Clinton was told.

The next morning, before the breakfast, Greer encouraged several reporters to ask a question about Clinton's sex life. No one seemed eager to do it. Finally, as the session was nearing an end, the question came up. Clinton replied that it was the sort of trivia that people obsessed about while Rome was in decline. But on this occasion, with Hillary at his side, he added: "Like nearly anybody who has been together for twenty years, our relationship has not been perfect or free from difficulties, but we feel good about where we are and we believe in our obligation to each other, and we intend to be together thirty or forty years from now, whether I run for president or not."

IN the early morning of October 3, Clinton, in his jogging shorts and shoes, headed down the mansion driveway and out the gate, heading north through his neighborhood of Victorian homes and across the bridge over I-630 into the quiet downtown. The streets counted down as he ran, past Tenth and Ninth and Eighth and Seventh and Sixth and Fifth and Fourth and Third and Second, until he arrived at East Markham Street, one block from the Arkansas River. He loped past the Old State House. In a few short hours, at noon, he would stand there, on a platform framed by twelve American flags and four grand white columns, and say the words he could not bring himself to say four years earlier, words that he had wanted to say for so long.

He had been up until at least two-thirty the night before, sitting at his oversized chair in the breakfast nook next to the kitchen, making telephone calls, nibbling on a banana with peanut butter spread on it, working through the final drafts of his speech with a team of writers: Bruce Reed from the DLC, pollster Greenberg, consultant Greer, and the author Tommy Caplan, his friend from Georgetown. Now the speech was typed and printed, and Greer had already slipped embargoed copies to the wire services, hoping that he could thereby prevent Clinton from making too many of his last-minute revisions. Greer and Reed were waiting for him when he returned from his jog. It looked beautiful down there at the Old State House, he told them. With Clinton still sweating in his running clothes, Greer positioned him in front of a portable bar, which they pretended was a podium, and had him rehearse the speech. His allergies were flaring and they worried about his voice. The speech seemed too long; they cut several lines. The last thing Clinton wanted was to remind anyone that he was the guy whose most famous speech prompted members of the audience to chant: "Get the hook!"

At eleven-thirty, everyone was ready to go except Clinton. He was in his room, rummaging through his closet, searching for a tie that looked presidential. He settled on one that was dark blue with diagonal stripes.

It was a glorious high autumn day, clear and golden. The crowd gathering in front of the Old State House was in a festive mood. There were a few thousand people there, legislators, state workers, curious onlookers, staff members, friends. As Diane Blair approached the black iron gate leading onto the lawn, she stopped for a moment. There on the sidewalk in front of her stood Orval Faubus, symbol of the Old South, an ancient and lonely man, reduced to a sideshow, hawking one of his books. A television crew swept past, oblivious of the old governor's presence. History rises, Blair thought, and history rejects.

Clinton gave a speech that lasted thirty-two minutes, the precise length of his ill-fated address in Atlanta. Few complained. No red lights flashed. He mentioned the middle class twelve times. He recalled the lasting message of his favorite professor at Georgetown, Carroll Quigley, who said that America was the greatest country in history because it was rooted in the belief that the future would be better than the present. He talked about how his grandparents had taken care of him while his mother was away at nursing school. He said that southerners had been divided by race for too long. Twice he evoked John F. Kennedy. He delivered his New Democrat riffs on opportunity and responsibility and how he favored change that was neither liberal nor conservative but both and different. But there was one line in the speech that had been the easiest to write and that he now proclaimed with the most energy and emotion. It was the first line of the twenty-third paragraph. It went: "That is why today I am declaring my candidacy for President of the United States."

His mother was there to hear him say those words. She had been waiting to hear them since he was a boy. She was the one who had taught him how to block things out and keep going through tough times. She gave him his perseverance and his optimism. Now she was determined to play out one final act of will. Four months earlier, her doctor had told her that her breast cancer had spread and that she was dying. She had not told her son. She hoped not to tell him until he was president of the United States.

Carolyn Staley and David Leopoulos were nearby, amid a group of special guests in a front-row section cordoned off with a golden rope. The two friends from Hot Springs were overwhelmed when Clinton finished speaking and stood on the podium with Hillary and Chelsea. They were so close to him that they could reach out and touch his feet, yet they felt oddly further from him than ever before. All three Clintons had tears in their eyes and Leopoulos thought they looked "scared to death," as though they had stepped past a point of no return.

Tommy Caplan, Clinton's Georgetown roommate, lingered off to the side, thinking back to their senior year in college, before Robert Kennedy was killed, when he and his friend both believed it was possible for a politician to heal a country.

Bob Reich had flown down to Little Rock that morning, unexpected, and stood under the shade of a column as he listened. When he noticed the tear in Chelsea's eye, he became overtaken by emotion himself and thought, "I just hope to God they know what they're getting into." At that moment, he would say later, he had a vision that he was witnessing a momentous occasion "in an extreme and classic sense of momentous." His vision was that his old Rhodes pal at Univ College would be elected president. He left for the airport soon after the speech, without even letting Clinton know that he had been there, and flew back to Cambridge, where, once again using Strobe Talbott as his foil, he would write in the annual class letter: "Bill Clinton's candidacy makes Strobe Talbott feel old. However, the prospect that all of us will flock to Washington when Bill wins makes him feel good."

Carl Wagner, who had spent several hours talking to Clinton and Hillary on the eve of his decision not to run four years earlier, had a sensation similar to Reich's. He thought back two decades to the summer of 1970 when he and Clinton walked up to Capitol Hill to try to persuade congressmen to cut off funds for the Vietnam War. Here, finally, is the day, Wagner thought. Here is the day for their generation.

Diane Blair looked up at Hillary, with her rich red suit and brilliant red lipstick, her face made up and her hair coiffeured, and remembered their days as young professors in Fayetteville. She grinned to herself, Blair recalled, as she thought back to the era when Hillary "had looked so much less glamorous." Then she felt a chill. It is different, she thought. Nothing will ever be the same.

Betsey Wright could not bring herself to drive over to the Old State House. After devoting a decade of her life to Clinton's political advancement, she was feeling demoralized about him again. With Clinton's help and encouragement, she had reentered the political world in late 1990 and become the head of the state Democratic party. But one month before Clinton's announcement, their reconciliation had collapsed in a bitter misunderstanding over money: she had been trying to raise it for the state party and felt that he had directly competed with her by soliciting funds for the DLC. The dispute had prompted her to quit as director of the state party. While Clinton was announcing for president, thanking his friends for "filling my life full of blessings beyond anything I ever deserved," Wright was back at her house on Hill Street, alone.

Cliff Jackson was also at home in Little Rock, sitting at his desk, his television tuned to the speech. Jackson, who had first met Clinton when they played basketball together at Oxford, had been following his fellow Arkansan's political rise with dismay and a sense of inevitability. He had distrusted Clinton since the summer of 1969, when he thought that Clinton had manipulated him in an effort to avert the military draft. He had been mostly silent about it for decades, but no more. He and several conservative associates had just formed an anti-Clinton group called the Alliance for Rebirth of an Independent America. They were raising money to fund newspaper and radio commercials attacking Clinton's record. The first one ran in the *Arkansas Democrat* on this morning of the announcement. Now Jackson, a lawyer, was spending his lunch hour alone in his den, watching his long-ago rival declare that he was a candidate for president. "I've always known that we would come to this time and place," Jackson said to himself. "I've always known."

When the cheering stopped, Clinton and his family entered the Old State House for a small reception. Chelsea took a place in line, and when she reached the front she shook her father's hand and said, "Congratulations, that was a fine speech, Governor." Clinton spent several hours that afternoon shaking hands at a larger reception at the Excelsior. There were more receptions that night back at the mansion. By eleven, Hillary was tired and ready for bed. Clinton stayed up with a small band of friends who had gathered around Carolyn Staley at the piano. They sang a medley of Motown songs, followed by "Abraham, Martin and John," the anthem to political martyrs. Clinton sat beside Carolyn on the bench and sang every verse. He knew all the words.

Soon the room fell quiet as Carolyn played the opening chords to her friend's favorite hymn. It was approaching midnight on the first day of his campaign for president and William Jefferson Clinton was in full voice. "A-a-ma-zing grace!" he sang. "How sweet the sound. That saved a-a wretch like me. I-I once was lost, but now am found. Was blind, but now I see."

NOTES

Prologue: Washington, D.C., 1963

11   The boys rode down: Ints. Larry Taunton, March 12, 1993; Daniel O'Connor, April 6, 1993; and Jack Mercier, April 6, 1993.
12   They made no secret: Int. Richard Stratton, April 5, 1993.
12   O'Connor knew: Int. Daniel J. O'Connor, April 6, 1993.
14   In his speeches: Int. Thomas McLarty, April 19, 1993.
15   "It's the biggest thrill": *Hot Springs Sentinel-Record,* June 1963.
15   Amid the excitement: Int. Larry Taunton, March 12, 1993.
15   She loved to tell: Int. Virginia Kelley, Jan. 13, 1992.
15   The eighteenth annual: Boys Nation program, July 19–26, 1963, The American Legion.
15   The official politicking: *Senior Scholastic,* Sept. 23, 1963.
16   The looming danger: *The Washington Post* (cited hereafter as *WP*), July 24, 1963.
16   where the local Lions: Int. Ron Cecil, Jan. 3, 1994.
16   His mother would: Int. Virginia Kelley, Jan. 13, 1992.
16   Most of the boys: Int. O. L. Johnson, March 10, 1993.
16   With both parties: *Senior Scholastic,* Sept. 23, 1963.
17   The Arkansas luncheon quartet: Int. Larry Taunton, March 12, 1993.
17   "the cat's meow": Int. Bill Clinton, Aug. 6, 1992.
17   Clinton wanted to be vice president: Int. John E. Mills, March 11, 1993.
18   Fred Kammer squirmed: Int. Fred Kammer, Feb. 26, 1993.
18   A year later: Int. Richard Stratton, April 5, 1993.
18   It got quiet: Ints. Richard Stratton, April 5, 1993, and Larry Taunton, March 12, 1993.
19   At quarter to ten: Transcript and tape of President Kennedy's speech to Boys Nation, July 24, 1963, JFK Library.
20   After an early lunch: Int. O. L. Johnson, March 10, 1993.
20   The next morning: Ints. Larry Taunton, March 12, 1993, and Jack Mercier, April 6, 1993.

One: Hope and Chance

21   Details of William J. Blythe III's birth from Edith Cassidy's records, in possession of her niece, Myra Irvin, and from *Hope Star,* Aug. 20, 1946.
22   one of Hope's dazzling characters: Ints. Myra Irvin, Feb. 9, 1993; Falba Lively, Feb. 8, 1993; Jack and Jimmy Hendrix, Feb. 10, 1993; and Virginia Kelley, Jan. 13, 1992, and July 12, 1993.
22   He came off the farm: Ints. Mary Nell Turner, Feb. 9, 1993; Dale Drake, Aug. 3, 1994; Jack and Jimmy Hendrix, Feb. 10, 1993; and Virginia Kelley, Jan. 13, 1992, and July 12, 1993.
23   Virginia worked: *Hope Star,* Hope High School tabloid edition, May 28, 1941.
24   "There was a sense": Int. Jack Hendrix, Feb. 10, 1993.

24 Virginia got away: Int. Virginia Kelley, Jan. 13, 1992.

24 in his military records: Obtained in FOIA request from National Personnel Records Center, Military Personnel Records, St. Louis. Also, W. J. Blythe military discharge records on file at Hempstead County Courthouse, Hope, Arkansas.

24 Blythe was "a handsome man": Int. Virginia Kelley, Jan. 13, 1992.

25 She flirted through eye contact: Virginia Kelley, *Leading with My Heart* (cited hereafter as *Leading*), pp. 40–42.

25 There is a contradiction: W. J. Blythe Army discharge papers filed at Hempstead County Courthouse, Dec. 13, 1945, and Military Personnel Records in St. Louis.

25 Anyone doubting: *Leading,* p. 45.

25 She knew that he had: Ints. Virginia Kelley, Jan. 13, 1992, and July 12, 1993.

26 She did not know about the December ...: Blythe's marital past is documented in courthouse records in Medill, Oklahoma; Oklahoma City; Dallas and Austin, Texas; and Ardmore, Oklahoma. Bill Clinton and Virginia Kelley were first told about Blythe's history during the 1992 presidential campaign, after Clinton's campaign office received inquiries from possible relatives. They said nothing publicly until an article by Gene Weingarten in *The Washington Post* dated June 20, 1993, revealed the possibility that Henry Leon Ritzenthaler was fathered by W. J. Blythe.

26 sailing away on a troopship: Blythe's wartime experiences are based on historical records of the 125th Ordnance Base Auto Maintenance Battalion, stored at the National Archives.

27 *Hometown News:* Anderson's letters were later compiled by Hope historian Mary Nell Turner and reprinted by the Hempstead County Historical Society journal in 1991.

27 no plans to stay: *Leading,* pp. 54–55, has Virginia Kelley's version. Military records, with dates that conflict with Kelley's, are taken from Blythe discharge papers filed at Hempstead County Courthouse on Dec. 13, 1945, and from Military Personnel Records in St. Louis.

28 little time to get to know: Int. Virginia Kelley, Jan. 13, 1992, and *Leading,* pp. 56–59.

28 May 17 was a Friday: Descriptions of Blythe's trip home and his fatal automobile accident come from interviews with Virginia Kelley, Jan. 13, 1992; Buddy Grisham, Feb. 11, 1993; and Elmer Greenlee, Jan. 14, 1992, and July 20, 1993. Also articles in *Hope Star,* May 18, 1946; *Sikeston Standard,* May 20, 1946; and *WP,* June 20, 1993.

29 day that Billy Blythe was born: *Arkansas Gazette,* Aug. 20, 1946.

29 the race issue still defined Hope: Ints. Mary Nell Turner, Feb. 9, 1993; Al Graves, Sr., Feb. 9, 1993; George Wright, Feb. 11, 1993; and Dale Drake, Aug. 3, 1994.

30 His days as the iceman: Ints. Virginia Kelley, July 12, 1993; Margaret Polk, Feb. 22, 1993; and Dale Drake, Aug. 3, 1994. *Leading,* pp. 74–75.

30 Edith kept him occupied: Ints. Virginia Kelley, Jan. 13, 1992, and Myra Irvin, Feb. 9, 1993. *Leading,* p. 74.

31 Clinton had a wife and two stepsons: From records of Ina Mae Clinton's divorce from Roger Clinton, filed at Garland County Courthouse in Hot Springs, Aug. 17, 1948.

31 that he was a philanderer: *Leading,* p. 85.

31 "I'm fixin' to marry": Int. Buddy Grisham, Feb. 11, 1993.

32 Billy would "light up": Int. Donna Taylor Wingfield, Feb. 10, 1993.

32 He called Roger Clinton "Daddy": The fact that Roger Clinton did not legally adopt Bill Clinton is established in the papers Bill filed on June 12, 1962, at the Garland County Courthouse to change his name from William Jefferson Blythe to William Jefferson Clinton.

32 he hauled out a gun: Ints. Virginia Kelley, Jan. 13, 1992; Margaret Polk, Feb. 22, 1993; Dale Drake, Aug. 3, 1994; and Donna Taylor Wingfield, Feb. 10, 1993.

33 Virginia hated the farm: Int. Virginia Kelley, Jan. 13, 1992. *Leading,* pp. 93–94.

33 it belonged to big brother Raymond: Raymond Clinton's ownership of the Park Avenue house is documented in divorce papers Virginia Clinton filed against Roger Clinton on May 15, 1962. Roger's financial troubles are detailed in *Leading,* p. 90.

34 The Clintons had arrived: From oral history of Raymond Clinton conducted by Dorothy Wise, Oct. 24, 1980, as part of the Leo P. McLaughlin project.

34 He spent much of his time drinking: *Leading,* pp. 110–12. Ints. Virginia Kelley, Jan. 13, 1992, and Judy Ellsworth, April 24, 1994.

35 Billy tried to carve out: Int. Bill Clinton, May 14, 1992.

36 Every boy in the school: Int. Ron Cecil, Jan. 3, 1994.

Two: In All His Glory

37 To open the side door: Ints. Carolyn Yeldell Staley, Jan. 14, 1992, and June 8, 1993.

37 an olfactory sensation: Int. David Leopoulos, June 9, 1993.

38 After secretly saving money: *Leading,* p. 119.

39 In seeking to end the marriage: The account of events leading to their divorce is taken from divorce records and affidavits filed at Garland County Courthouse, May 15, 1962. Also Ints. Virginia Kelley, Jan. 13, 1992, and June 12, 1993, and Bill Clinton, Jan. 20, 1992.

40 "Mother," he said: Int. Virginia Kelley, Jan. 13, 1992.

40 The only Roger Clinton: Records filed at Garland County Courthouse, June 12, 1962. Also Int. Bill Clinton, Jan. 20, 1992.

41 But it was not his castle: Ints. Carolyn Yeldell Staley, Jan. 14, 1992, and June 8, 1993; Virginia Kelley, Jan. 13, 1992; and David Leopoulos, June 9, 1993.

41 He had planned to run: Ints. Phil Jamison, Feb. 21 and April 2, 1993.

42 He ran for it: Ints. Carolyn Yeldell Staley, Jan. 14, 1992, June 8, 1993, and July 12, 1993.

42 Mrs. Mackey turned down some requests: Ints. Virginia Kelley, Jan. 13, 1992, and David Leopoulos, June 9, 1993.

42 When Root assigned: Int. Paul Root, July 13, 1993.

42 During his sophomore year: Int. Phil Jamison, April 2, 1993.

43 cadre of teachers: Ints. Elizabeth Buck, July 29, 1993; Ron Cecil, Jan. 3, 1994; Phil Jamison, Feb. 21, 1993; and Carolyn Yeldell Staley, June 8, 1993.

44 His speech to the Civitan Club: *Hot Springs Sentinel-Record,* Dec. 6, 1963.

44 Band teacher Virgil Spurlin: Ints. Virgil Spurlin, July 14, 1993; John Hilliard, July 12, 1993; and David Leopoulos, June 9, 1993.

45 "the opportunity to create something": *Arkansas Democrat,* Sept. 27, 1977.

45 He toted his saxophone: Int. Carolyn Yeldell Staley, June 8, 1993.

45 Virgil Spurlin saw in young Clinton: Int. Virgil Spurlin, July 14, 1993.

46 more like fraternity brothers: Ints. Carolyn Staley, July 12, 1993, and John Hilliard, July 12, 1993.

47 He never wanted to be alone: Int. David Leopoulos, June 9, 1993.

47 Graduation for the Hot Springs: The account of commencement events is drawn from *Hot Springs High Torchlight,* May 29, 1964. Also ints. with David Leopoulos, June 9, 1993; Carolyn Yeldell Staley, June 8, 1993; Phil Jamison, Feb. 21, 1993; Virgil Spurlin, July 13, 1993; and Edith Irons, Jan. 14, 1992.

48 He had the last word: Copy of Clinton's speech and Virginia's letter about it saved by Edith Cassidy, in possession of her niece, Myra Irvin.

Three: The Road Ahead

50 "Remember, at Georgetown": *The Courier* (October 1964), p. 22.

50 there were women around: Demographics from Georgetown University Registrar provided by Georgetown University archivist Jon K. Reynolds.

51 the freshman dean mused: Int. Virginia Kelley, Jan. 13, 1992.

51 Clinton's roommate reached: Ints. Tom Campbell, Jan. 22 and Feb. 3, 1993.

52 There was inevitable posturing: Ints. Tom Campbell, Jan. 22, 1993; John Dagnon, Feb. 26, 1993; and Tom Caplan, Feb. 27–28, 1993.

52 While another southern freshman: Int. Kit Ashby, Jan. 20, 1993.

52 "Dear Mammaw": Postcard to Edith Cassidy, Sept. 21, 1964.

52 He and roommate Campbell: Ints. Tom Campbell, Jan. 22 and Feb. 3, 1993.

53 Clinton returned to the dorm: Int. Tom Campbell, Jan. 22, 1993.

53 "One thing I really want": Letter to Edith Cassidy, Oct. 9, 1964.

53 Tommy Caplan had met Kennedy: Int. Tom Caplan, Feb. 27, 1993.

55 His candidacy was nonideological: The account of Clinton's campaign for freshman president is based on interviews with Kit Ashby, Jan. 20, 1993; Judith Bacher, Feb. 3, 1993; Tom Campbell, Jan. 22, 1993; Tom Caplan, Feb. 27, 1993; John Dagnon, Feb. 26, 1993, David Kammer, Feb. 6, 1993; Paul Maloy, March 2, 1993; and David Matter, Feb. 5, 1993. Also *The Hoya,* Oct. 25 and Nov. 6, 1964, and *The Courier* (December 1964).

56 "I know I'm late": Letter to Edith Cassidy, Nov. 7, 1964.

56 Robert Irving, the English professor: Int. Tom Caplan, Feb. 27, 1993.

57 under Father Joseph S. Sebes: Ints. Bill Clinton, May 14, 1992; Tom Caplan, Feb. 27, 1993; Joe Baczko, Feb. 8, 1993; and Father James Walsh, S.J., Jan. 25, 1993.

57 Hentz championed the philosophy: Int. Otto Hentz, Jan. 25, 1993.

58 "I think you should": This conversation was recalled similarly by Hentz, Jan. 25, 1993, and Bill Clinton, May 14, 1992.

58 "Half the people at Georgetown": Clinton gubernatorial inaugural speech in Little Rock, Jan. 13, 1987.

58 his course was mandatory: Description of Carroll Quigley based on interviews with Kit Ashby, Jan. 20, 1993; Tom Campbell, Jan. 22, 1993; Tom Caplan, Feb. 27, 1993; Phil Verveer, Feb. 2, 1993; Jim Moore, Jan. 21, 1993; Jon R. Reynolds, Jan. 22, 1993, and David Matter, Feb. 5, 1993. Also Quigley documents at Lauinger Library Archives, Georgetown University.

60 From the nursing home: Int. Myra Irvin, Feb. 1993. Irvin saved Edith Cassidy's possessions, including address book, envelopes, and letters from her grandson. Letters from Bill Clinton, Oct. 9, Nov. 8, and Nov. 25, 1964.

60 He went to a dance: Int. Phil Jamison, Feb. 21, 1993.

61 "Everybody else has moods": Int. Jim Moore, Feb. 1, 1993.

61 Among his fellow student politicians: The account of Clinton in student government is taken from interviews with Phil Verveer, Feb. 2, 1993; David Kammer, Feb. 6, 1993; and Paul Maloy, March 2, 1993.

63 A letter to the editor: *The Hoya,* Feb. 18, 1965.

64 still supportive of the president: Int. Tom Campbell, Jan. 22, 1993.

64 Denise Hyland left: The account of Clinton's friendship with Denise Hyland is drawn from interviews with Denise Hyland, March 4, May 14, and July 12, 1993.

65 "I met some awfully cute kids": Letter to Denise Hyland, June 1965.

65 "My grandfather is dying": Letter to Denise Hyland, June 10, 1965.

66 After the funeral: Letter to Denise Hyland, June 18, 1965.

66 "I remember the blackness": Int. Tom Campbell, Feb. 3, 1993.

67 Carolyn Yeldell was home: Int. Carolyn Yeldell Staley, June 8, 1993.

67 "What feedback are you getting": Letter to Denise Hyland, Aug. 11, 1965.

67 "Just searching": Letter to Denise Hyland, Aug. 11, 1965.

68 "This one tall proud Texas boy": Int. Denise Hyland, March 4, 1993.

Four: He Was on Fire

69 For the start: Int. Kit Ashby, Jan. 20, 1993.

70 "Bill, you've got your nose": Int. Tom Campbell, Feb. 3, 1993.

70 A medical student had once: Int. Kit Ashby, Jan. 20, 1993.

70 the most exacting course: The account of Walter I. Giles is drawn from interviews with Kit Ashby, Jan. 20, 1993; Tom Caplan, Feb. 27, 1993; John Dagnon, Feb. 26, 1993; John Spotila, Jan. 12, 1994; Phil Verveer, Feb. 2, 1993; and David Kammer, Feb. 6, 1993.

72 He was, in the football realm: Ints. Phil Jamison, April 2, 1993, and Denise Hyland, March 4, 1993.

72 When his grandmother mailed: Postcard to Edith Cassidy, Feb. 2, 1966.

73   "A small price to pay": Int. Denise Hyland, May 14, 1993.
73   "All males harbor fears": *The Courier* (April 1966), p. 7.
73   Alpha Phi Omega: Ints. Tom Campbell, Jan. 22, 1993, and Donald Pattee, Jan. 22, 1993.
74   They flew out to Little Rock: Int. Tom Caplan, Feb. 27, 1993.
74   he decided not to run: Int. David Matter, Feb. 5, 1993.
75   Lyda Holt was seated: Int. Lyda Holt, June 8, 1993.
75   Clinton had relied on: Int. Jack Holt, Jr., June 4, 1993.
75   Holt was immediately put on the defensive: Undated *Arkansas Gazette* articles in Lyda Holt scrapbook.
76   He surrounded himself with young people: Descriptions of the Holt Generation from interviews with Lyda Holt, June 8, 1993; Paul Fray, April 25, 1994; David Glover, June 4, 1993; Richard King, June 5, 1993; and Jack Holt, Jr., June 4, 1993.
76   "and warming the bench, me": Letter to Denise Hyland, June 29, 1966.
77   They were quite a quartet: Int. Lyda Holt, June 8, 1993.
77   "I never took orders": Letter to Denise Hyland, July 8, 1966.
77   His letters to Denise: Int. Denise Hyland, May 14, 1993.
77   As the fire engines: Int. Lyda Holt, June 8, 1993.
77   "I hope you saw me": Letter to Edith Cassidy, July 1, 1966.
78   Clinton made a special plea: Int. Lyda Holt, June 8, 1993.
78   "Last night I spoke for": Letter to Denise Hyland, July 8, 1966.
78   The day after the speech: Int. Lyda Holt, June 8, 1993.
79   "a good reminder": Letter to Denise Hyland, Aug. 8, 1966.
79   It was a scorching day: Int. David Pryor, June 29, 1993.
79   "I think the heat": Letter to Denise Hyland, July 14, 1966.
79   "Boy, you meet all kinds": Letter to Denise Hyland, July 14.
80   "The Holts travel": *Memphis Commercial-Appeal,* July 12, 1966.
80   In his letters: Int. Denise Hyland, May 14, 1993.
81   "Denise, he's never lost": Letter to Denise Hyland, June 29, 1966.
81   "All I can do is pray": Letter to Denise Hyland, Aug. 8, 1966.
81   "He stayed sweet and nice": Int. Lyda Holt, June 8, 1993.
81   He told Jack Holt, Jr.: Int. Jack Holt, Jr., June 4, 1993.
82   Lee Williams was always looking: Int. Lee Williams, May 12, 1993.
82   Virginia Clinton wrote Denise: Int. Denise Hyland, May 14, 1993.
82   "one of my happiest birthdays": Letter to Denise Hyland, Aug. 19, 1966.

Five: The Back Room Boys

83   "I am well settled": Letter to Edith Cassidy, Sept. 26, 1966.
84   They sorted the mail: Description of the back room boys comes from interviews with Lee Williams, May 12, 1993; Norvill Jones, May 12, 1993; Bertie Bowman, May 26, 1993; Charles Parks, June 4, 1993; Phil Dozier, June 22, 1993; and Buddy Kendrick, May 29, 1993.
84   "People dumped on our state": Clinton tribute to Senator J. William Fulbright, Washington, D.C., May 5, 1993.
85   Soon the fissure: The description of Fulbright's relationship with Johnson is drawn largely from Haynes Johnson and Bernard M. Gwertzman, *Fulbright: The Dissenter;* Lee Riley Powell, *J. William Fulbright and America's Lost Crusade;* J. William Fulbright, *The Arrogance of Power;* and J. William Fulbright, *The Price of Empire.*
85   "for the war": Int. Bill Clinton, August 6, 1992.
85   It was difficult to work: Ints. Norvill Jones, May 12, 1993, and Lee Williams, May 12, 1993.
86   Clinton and Dozier: Int. Phil Dozier, June 22, 1993.
87   If Campbell carried: Int. Tom Campbell, Feb. 3, 1993.
87   One Saturday morning: Int. Lyda Holt, June 8, 1993, and letter to Edith Cassidy, Oct. 11, 1966.
87   "Last week Frank Holt": Letter to Edith Cassidy, Feb. 6, 1967.

87   They headed back to school: Ints. Denise Hyland May 14, 1993, and Tom Campbell,
      Feb. 3, 1993.
88   "My grades for the first semester": Letter to Edith Cassidy, Feb. 6, 1967.
88   Matter realized: Int. David Matter, Feb. 5, 1993.
88   His obsession was so great: Int. Terry Modglin, Feb. 18, 1993.
89   "A Realistic Approach": Copy of Clinton platform saved by Denise Hyland.
89   "He wanted to co-opt the management": Int. Jim Moore, Feb. 2, 1993.
89   "Bill never wanted to say": Int. Kit Ashby, Jan. 20, 1993.
90   He struck an alliance: Int. Terry Modglin, Feb. 18, 1993.
90   Clinton's allies worked tirelessly: Ints. Denise Hyland, March 4, 1993, and Kit Ashby,
      Jan. 20, 1993.
90   "The Spirit of '67": *The Hoya,* March 16, 1967.
90   The second episode: Ints. David Matter, Feb. 5, 1967, and John Dagnon, Feb. 26, 1993.
90   The election was on a Friday: The account of this election night is based on interviews
      with Tom Campbell, Feb. 3, 1993; Kit Ashby, Jan. 20, 1993; Terry Modglin, Feb. 18,
      1993; David Matter, Feb. 5, 1993; Denise Hyland, March 4, 1993; and Lyda Holt, June
      8, 1993. Also *The Hoya,* March 13–16, 1967.
92   "Roger, your neck": Ints. Virginia Kelley, Jan. 13, 1992, July 12, 1993.
92   Bill visited Roger Clinton: Int. Denise Hyland, May 14, 1993.
92   Lyda Holt visited: Int. Lyda Holt, June 8, 1993.
92   "I know I have never": *Leading,* p. 165.
92   "Daddy has been so sick": Letter to Denise Hyland, 1967.
93   he and Tommy Caplan: Int. Tom Caplan, Oct. 3, 1994. Letter to Denise Hyland, June
      1967.
93   The binge left Clinton wallowing: Letter to Denise Hyland, June 1967.
93   It was a summer of uncertainty: Letter to Denise Hyland, July 29, 1967.
94   Clinton was assigned a rather odd diversion: Int. Sharon Ann Evans, June 9, 1993.
      Letter to Denise Hyland, August 31, 1967.
95   He stayed that summer: Int. Jim Moore, Feb. 2, 1993.
95   Duke Watts was about to leave: Int. Duke Watts, May 6, 1993.

Six: All Hell Broke Loose

96   The five young men: Int. Tom Caplan, Feb. 27, 1993.
96   Allen Ginsberg: *The Hoya,* Feb. 29, 1968.
96   It was an elegant affair: Ints. Tom Caplan, Feb. 27, 1993; Kit Ashby, Jan. 20, 1993; and
      Jim Moore, Feb. 2, 1993.
97   Robert Lowell's "October and November": Robert Lowell, *Notebook 1967–68,* p. 27.
97   Clinton shared the conviction: Ints. Bill Clinton, Aug. 6, 1992, and Lee Williams, May
      12, 1993.
97   "To criticize one's country": Fulbright, J. William, *Arrogance.*
98   "Sometimes he'd bring a friend": Int. David Pryor, June 29, 1993.
98   His closest friend at work: Int. Bertie Bowman, May 26, 1993.
98   His friends would plan: Int. Tom Campbell, Feb. 3, 1993.
99   Clinton not only informed Lowe: Int. Rudiger Lowe, April 8, 1993.
99   Every morning that November: Int. Virginia Kelley, Jan. 13, 1992.
100   "somewhere deep down inside": Ints. Bill Clinton, Jan. 20, 1992, and Virginia Kelley,
      Jan. 13, 1992, July 12, 1993.
100   Roger looked pitiful: The account of Roger Clinton's death is drawn from interviews
      with Mary Jo Nelson, June 9, 1993; Virginia Kelley, Jan. 13, 1992, and July 12, 1993.
      Also *Leading,* pp. 169–70.
100   The notion that Bill Clinton: Int. Tom Campbell, Feb. 2, 1993.
101   George Butte in the Southwest: Ints George Butte, Feb. 24, 1993, and Robert Reich,
      April 15, 1993.
101   The interview process: Ints. Darryl Gless, March 10, 1993; Strobe Talbott, April 19,

1993; Mike Shea, April 6, 1993; Keith Marshall, Feb. 2, 1993; and Daniel Singer, March 5, 1993.

102   Good fortune came to Bill Clinton: Ints. Tom Ward, June 18, 1993, and Kit Ashby, Jan. 20, 1993.

103   At the South regional: Ints. Keith Marshall, Feb. 2, 1993; Walter Pratt, April 28, 1993, and Paul Parish, Oct. 23, 1993.

103   Some young men: Ints. Walter Pratt, April 28, 1993; Robert Reich, April 15, 1993; and William Fletcher, Nov. 23, 1993.

104   Sobbing, he spoke lovingly: Int. Keith Marshall, Feb. 2, 1993.

104   He finally called: Int. Virginia Kelley, Jan. 13, 1992.

104   The house on Potomac: Ints. Tom Caplan, Feb. 27, 1993, and Kit Ashby, Jan. 20, 1993.

104   Supper at the kitchen table: Int. Jim Moore, Feb. 2, 1993.

105   He chided Tom Campbell: Ints. Tom Campbell, Feb. 3, 1993; Kit Ashby, Jan. 20, 1993; and Jim Moore, Feb. 2, 1993.

105   On the war in Vietnam: Ints. Jim Moore, Oct. 20, 1992, and Kit Ashby, Jan. 20, 1993.

106   Two weeks after Tet: *WP,* Feb. 17, 1968, p. 1.

106   now it came up constantly: Ints. Tom Campbell, Feb. 3, 1993; Kit Ashby, Jan. 20, 1993; Tom Caplan, Feb. 27, 1993; and Jim Moore, Feb. 2, 1993.

107   He often spoke of a high school friend: Int. Tom Campbell, Feb. 3, 1993.

107   In a paper he had written: Clinton describes the paper in a letter to Colonel Holmes, Dec. 3, 1969.

107   On the first day of March: Ints. Tom Campbell, Jan. 22, 1993, and Jim Moore, Feb. 2, 1993.

108   Within two weeks: *Facts on File,* March 14–20, 1968.

108   "a sort of never-never-land": Int. Tom Campbell, Feb. 3, 1993.

108   One Sunday morning: Ints. Carolyn Yeldell Staley, Jan. 14, 1992, and June 8, 1993.

109   A few days later: Int. Phil Jamison, Feb. 21, 1993.

110   Early on morning of June 5: *WP,* June 6, 1968.

110   Another senior, who had just: Int. John Dagnon, Feb. 26, 1993.

110   Tommy Caplan learned the news: Int. Tom Caplan, Feb. 27, 1993.

111   The following day: The account of the 1968 Georgetown graduation is drawn from interviews with Kit Ashby, Jan. 20, 1993; Tom Campbell, Jan. 22, 1993; Tom Caplan, Feb. 27, 1993; Dave Kammer, Feb. 6, 1993; David Matter, Feb. 5, 1993; and Jim Moore, Feb. 2, 1993.

111   But one member of the class: Int. Jim Moore, Feb. 2, 1993.

112   Clinton and Moore used Little Rock: Int. Jim Moore, Feb. 2, 1993.

114   Clinton went to work full time: Ints. Lee Williams, May 14, 1993, and Jim McDougal, April 23, 1993.

115   "Lately I have returned": Letter to Denise Hyland, August 1968.

115   The Frays had known Clinton: Ints. Paul and Mary Lee Fray, April 25, 1993.

116   Late in the summer: Ints. Tom Campbell, Feb. 3, 1993, and Sharon Ann Evans, July 13, 1993.

116   Clinton was a cool customer: Ints. Carolyn Yeldell Staley, July 12, 1993, and Sharon Ann Evans, July 13, 1993.

117   "From then on Sharon": Int. Carolyn Yeldell Staley, July 12, 1993.

117   "The woman I marry": *Ibid.*

117   When they reached Hot Springs: Int. Phil Jamison, Feb. 21, 1993.

118   Raymond Clinton took it upon himself: Int. Henry Britt, July 14, 1993. *Los Angeles Times* reporter William C. Rempel was the first to present an account of Raymond Clinton's efforts, Sept. 2, 1992.

118   He belonged to the local chapter: Int. Henry Britt, July 14, 1993.

118   They were unlikely associates: Ints. Henry Britt, July 14, 1993, and Ray Smith, Jr., April 25, 1994.

119   Raymond paid a visit: Int. Henry Britt, July 14, 1993.

119   The first relief. Int. Henry Britt, July 14, 1993. *L.A. Times,* Sept. 2, 1992.

119 Britt called draft board: *Ibid.*
120 The draft board in Alameda: Int. Tom Williamson, April 15, 1993.
120 they strung a banner: Int. Darryl Gless, March 10, 1993.
120 Dartmouth scholar John Isaacson: Int. John Isaacson, March 5, 1993.
120 University of Iowa scholar: Int. Mike Shea, April 6, 1993.
120 Paul Parish's mother: Int. Paul Parish, Oct. 23–25, 1993.
120 He cut a deal: Int. Willie Fletcher, Nov. 23, 1993.
120 Vanderbilt's Walter Pratt: Int. Walter Pratt, April 28, 1993.
120 Clinton was less certain: Int. Denise Hyland, May 14, 1993. Letter to Denise Hyland, September 1968.

Seven: The Great Escape

122 He arrived wearing a gray suit: Int. Denise Hyland, May 14, 1993.
122 She was known as "The Big U": Kludas, Arnold, *Great Passenger Ships,* p. 52; *S.S. United States,* p. 15.
123 "Anybody know what this song?": Ints. Keith Marshall, Feb. 2, 1992, and Paul Parish, Oct. 23, 1993.
123 "felt like an outsider": Int. George Butte, Feb. 24, 1993.
123 "something of the provincial": Int. Darryl Gless, March 10, 1993.
123 "overwhelmed by the intellectual": Int. Robert Reich, April 15, 1993.
124 "At that age": Int. John Isaacson, March 5, 1993.
124 Clinton was different: Ints. George Butte, Feb. 24, 1993; Darryl Gless, March 10, 1993; Strobe Talbott, April 19, 1993; Rick Stearns, March 4, 1993; and Doug Eakeley, Dec. 19, 1993.
124 The first day at sea: Int. George Butte, Feb. 24, 1993.
124 "What a relief!" Int. Robert Reich, April 15, 1993.
124 stunted by Fairbanks Disease: Int. Robert Reich, Sept. 16, 1994.
124 "you put his size aside": Int. Tom Williamson, April 15, 1993.
124 "He was a cartoonist": Int. John Isaacson, March 5, 1993.
125 They were quite a pair: Ints. John Isaacson, March 5, 1993, and Robert Reich, April 15, 1993.
125 *Time* magazine cover story: *Time,* June 7, 1968.
125 By the second morning: Ints. Robert Reich, April 15, 1993; George Butte, Feb. 24, 1993; Daniel Singer, March 5, 1993; and Darryl Gless, March 10, 1993. Also, *American Oxonian* (October 1978).
126 "It's wrong for me to be scared": Clinton radio interview by Christopher Matthews, May 29, 1993, simulcast on KCBS Newsradio, San Francisco.
126 "A lot of us": Int. Doug Eakeley, Dec. 19, 1993.
126 "all the boys were scared:" Int. Hannah Achtenberg, June 1, 1993.
127 Talbott was the cautious: Int. Strobe Talbott, June 2, 1993. Also Talbott Class Day Speech, Yale University, 1987, reprinted in *Yale Alumni Magazine* (Summer 1987).
127 "Reich saw nothing but forests": Int. John Isaacson, March 5, 1993.
127 He and his best friend: Int. Derek Shearer, Jan. 5, 1994.
127 "Many of us simply": Strobe Talbott Class Day Speech, June 1968.
128 "The whole scene was bizarre": Int. John Isaacson, March 5, 1993.
129 "raw political talent": Ints. Robert Reich, April 15, 1993, and Strobe Talbott, June 2, 1993.
129 "Look at him!": Int. Darryl Gless, March 10, 1993.
129 Singer lost the caravan: Int. Daniel Singer, March 5, 1993.
129 Four of them: Ints. Robert Reich, April 15, 1993, and Doug Eakeley, Dec. 19, 1993.
130 "They told me": Ints. Robert Reich, April 15, 1993, and John Isaacson, March 5, 1993.

Eight: The Dreaming Spires

131   He had a sitting room: Int. Doug Eakeley, Dec. 19, 1993.
132   Every morning during his first week: Ints. Robert Reich, April 15, 1993; Doug Eakeley, December 1993; and Rick Stearns, March 4, 1993.
132   "Sore and exhilarated": Bill Clinton interview by John Pagan, Merton College Postmaster, 1992.
132   "We were suddenly within ruins!": Int. Robert Reich, April 15, 1993.
132   It turned out that this boast: John R. Thackrah, *The University and Colleges at Oxford,* pp. 67–69.
132   "I am happy if lonely": Letter to Denise Hyland, Oct. 14, 1968.
133   America seemed very far away: Ints. Robert Reich, April 15, 1993, and John Isaacson, March 5, 1993. Also Aldon D. Bell, *London Impressions,* and *The American Oxonian* (1968).
133   "the wind that blows": From Peter Snow, *Oxford Observed,* p. 10.
133   "our cities were burning": Int. Tom Williamson, May 26, 1993.
133   "always the character": Int. Doug Paschal, March 3, 1994.
133   The cultural gap: Ints. George Butte, Feb. 24, 1993; Tom Williamson, May 26, 1993; and John Isaacson, March 5, 1993.
134   "People were starting:" Int. Nick Browne, April 16, 1993.
134   "We knew about the barricades": Int. Wilf Stevenson, March 29, 1993.
134   The protests at Oxford: Martin Amis, *My Oxford,* p. 206; Report of the Committee on Relations with Junior Members, Appendix A: Student Radicalism in Oxford, May 1969.
134   The most ferocious Oxford Union: *Cherwell,* Oct. 30, 1968.
135   "They assumed that because": Int. Darryl Gless, March 10, 1993.
135   Clinton's reaction was similar: Int. Martin Walker, Feb. 19, 1993.
135   "Got results at Rhodes House": Telegram to J. William Fulbright, Nov. 6, 1968. Note from Fulbright to Clinton, Dec. 3, 1968. From J. William Fulbright Papers, Special Collections Division, University of Arkansas Libraries.
136   British students at Oxford: *Cherwell,* Oct. 23, Oct. 30, 1968.
136   "It was easy for us": Int. Martin Walker, Feb. 19, 1993.
136   Later in his life: In the 1992 interview with John Pagan, an American who had studied at Merton College, Clinton said: "I started off studying PPE. . . ." Merton College Postmaster, 1992.
136   He began in what was called B. Litt.: Clinton's records at Oxford as described by his former tutor, Zbigniew Pelczynski.
137   He also changed supervisors: Int. Zbigniew Pelczynski, March 23, 1993.
138   First was the Totalitarian school: "Political Pluralism in the USSR" by William J. Clinton.
139   Oxford, he later wrote: Amis, *My Oxford,* p. 203.
139   Clinton lingering: Int. Doug Eakeley, Dec. 19, 1993.
140   The informal club: Int. George Cawkwell, March 24, 1993.
140   The floating seminar: Int. Maurice Shock, March 24, 1993.
140   "quite fanatically political": Int. Doug Paschal, March 3, 1994.
140   He intimidated everyone: Ints. Wilf Stevenson, March 29, 1993; Nick Browne, April 16, 1993; and John Isaacson, March 5, 1993.
141   Clinton "wasn't very good": Int. Chris McCooey, April 2, 1993.
142   He was partial to the shandy: Int. Strobe Talbott, June 2, 1993.
142   Rick Stearns had soft spot: Int. Rick Stearns, March 4, 1993.
142   " 'Oh, no thank you' ": Int. James Shellar, Feb. 26, 1994.
142   He was an actor: Int. Robert Reich, April 15, 1993.
142   "Small and twinkly": Int. John Albery, March 25, 1993.
142   Reich and Clinton were viewed: Ints. Chris McCooey, April 2, 1993, and Wilf Stevenson, March 29, 1993.
143   They hitchhiked everywhere: Int. Mike Shea, April 6, 1993.

143   At Clinton's suggestion: Int. Tom Williamson, April 15, 1993.
143   Clinton talked to him: Int. Darryl Gless, March 10, 1993.
144   Clinton had a fascination: Ints. Paul Parish, Oct. 23, 1993, and John Isaacson, March 5, 1993.
144   Clinton pondered that question: Letter to Denise Hyland, Dec. 13, 1968.
145   it had been damp and cold: Ints. Wilf Stevenson, March 29, 1993; Darryl Gless, March 10, 1993; and Daniel Singer, March 5, 1993.
145   Strobe Talbott ventured the other way: Int. Strobe Talbott, June 2, 1993.
146   Clinton made the longest journey: Ints. Hannah Achtenberg, June 1, 1993, and Virginia Kelley, July 12, 1993.
146   Dwire, in fact: Ints. Inez Cline, Sept. 15, 1992, and Virginia Kelley, July 12, 1993. Also *Leading*, p. 178.
146   "The surprise came off": Letter to Denise Hyland, Jan. 1, 1969.
146   "I had no earthly idea": Int. Virginia Kelley, July 12, 1993.
147   "Bill, you are still really interested": Int. Carolyn Yaldell Staley, July 12, 1993.
147   "Thank you for having me": Letter to Winthrop Rockefeller, Jan. 8, 1969. Winthrop Rockefeller Archives, University of Arkansas-Little Rock Library.
147   Few of the boys: Ints. David Leopoulos, June 9, 1993; Ron Cecil, Jan. 3, 1994; Herman Thomas, May 3, 1993; A. B. Jeffries, May 3, 1993; and Duke Watts, May 6, 1993.

Nine: Feeling the Draft

149   "Looks like I will finish": Letter to Denise Hyland, Jan. 1, 1969.
149   On January 13: Letter to Denise Hyland, Jan. 27, 1969.
150   For Frank Aller: Ints. Hannah Achtenberg, June 1, 1993; Strobe Talbott, June 2, 1993; and Brooke Shearer, July 1, 1993.
150   "I believe there are times": Quoted in *NYT Magazine*, Nov. 22, 1992, by Alessandra Stanley.
150   "When I decided to refuse": Letter to Brooke Shearer, Nov. 3, 1970.
150   His friends held a party: Ints. Willie Fletcher, Nov. 23, 1993; Paul Parish, Oct. 23, 1993; Hannah Achtenberg, June 1, 1993; and John Isaacson, March 5, 1993.
151   "I remember it was drizzling": *American Oxonian* (October 1978).
151   "We all knew how": Int. Daniel Singer, March 5, 1993.
151   "there was very much the feeling": Int. Sara Maitland, May 11, 1993.
151   "All of us": Int. Willie Fletcher, Nov. 23, 1993.
152   he "failed to fail": Int. Paul Parish, Oct. 23, 1993.
152   Butte even got permission: Int. George Butte, Feb. 24, 1993.
152   But every local board: Ints. Paul Parish, Oct. 23, 1993, and Sara Maitland, May 11, 1993.
152   Late at night: Int. Paul Parish, Oct. 25, 1993.
153   at Oxford she began rebelling. Int. Sara Maitland, May 11, 1993.
153   "by how well they all spoke": Bill Clinton interview by John Pagan, Merton College Postmaster, 1992.
153   "It was a very good way": Int. Sara Maitland, May 11, 1993.
153   They often discussed books: Ints. Strobe Talbott, June 2, 1993; Sara Maitland, May 11, 1993; and Paul Parish, Oct. 23, 1993.
153   "a very enthusiastic dancer": Int. Sara Maitland, May 11, 1993.
154   Cannabis was "incredibly easy": *Cherwell*, Jan. 29, 1969.
154   "We would scramble it": Int. Martin Walker, Feb. 19, 1993.
154   blacked out on the way: Int. Paul Parish, Sept. 6, 1994.
154   "We spent enormous amounts of time": Int. Sara Maitland, May 11, 1993. (Clinton's marijuana use at Oxford became an issue during the 1992 presidential campaign largely because of the way he acknowledged it after previously refusing to answer questions about drug use or answering in technically correct but elusive ways. On March 29, 1992, in a debate at WCBS-TV in New York, Clinton said: "I've never broken any state laws and when I was in England I experimented with marijuana a time or

two and I didn't like it. And I didn't inhale and I didn't try it again." Typical of his answers before that was one he gave to Fox television on March 2, 1992: "I said I've never violated the drug laws of our country, and I haven't.")

154 "He was technically correct": Int. Martin Walker, Feb. 19, 1993.
154 "this delightful, cheery": Int. Charlene Prickett, June 24, 1993.
155 Jackson knew Clinton: Int. Cliff Jackson, June 7, 1993.
155 "I was toddling to the train station": Int. Charlene Prickett, June 24, 1993.
155 All three British women: Int. Charlene Prickett, June 24, 1993.
155 Waugh was in a singular position: Int. Jim Waugh, June 25, 1993.
155 Jackson had sailed: Int. Cliff Jackson, June 7, 1993.
156 "I am an ambitious person": Letter to Leslie Campbell, May 8, 1969.
156 Those were the questions: Int. Cliff Jackson, June 7, 1993.
156 When Jackson got back to Oxford: Int. Cliff Jackson, June 7, 1993.
156 "Cliff had a personality": Int. Jim Waugh, June 25, 1993.
157 Waugh spent many evenings: Int. Jim Waugh, June 25, 1993.
157 "I was scared and anxious": Int. Cliff Jackson, June 7, 1993, Nov. 1, 1993.
158 "over a hundred politically inspired": Gitlin, *The Sixties,* p. 342.
158 "I was naive": Int. Darryl Gless, March 10, 1993.
159 Clinton would open: Int. Strobe Talbott, April 19, 1993.
159 "an end in itself": Ronald Steel, *Pax Americana,* p. 13.
159 "What we need": *Ibid.,* p. 353.
159 Another scholar at Oxford: Int. Rick Stearns, March 4, 1993.
160 When the middle term at Oxford ended: Ints. Rick Stearns, March 4, 1993, and Rudiger Lowe, April 23, 1993.
160 "Have been in Bavaria": Postcard to Denise Hyland, March 27, 1969.
160 He had been speed-skating: Int. Rick Stearns, March 4, 1993.
161 Then the tempestuous relationship: Int. Rick Stearns, March 4, 1993. (Markesun declined interview requests.)
161 Clinton headed north: Int. Rudiger Lowe, April 23, 1993.
161 She landed at Heathrow: Int. Sharon Ann Evans, July 13, 1993.
161 They spent the first five days: *Ibid.* Also, Clinton calendar of ten-day Evans trip.
162 "Times are getting tough": Letter to Denise Hyland, April 7, 1969.
162 "My friends just don't understand": Int. Sharon Ann Evans, July 13, 1993.
163 "I heard about Bert just yesterday": Letter to A. B. Jeffries, April 10, 1969.
163 Bert had lived a different life: Int. A. B. Jeffries, May 3, 1993.
163 At just after ten: U.S. Marine Corps Western Union Telegram, received by A. B. Jeffries March 24, 1969. Also letter to Mr. and Mrs. A. B. Jeffries from USMC Lt. D. T. Stevens.
163 "The thing about Vietnam": Int. Duke Watts, May 6, 1993.
164 The tutor Clinton thought so much of: Int. Zbigniew Pelczynski, March 23, 1993.
164 One week his reading list: Int. Denise Hyland, July 12, 1993.
164 They had toured Manhattan: Willie Morris, *New York Days,* pp. 137–38.
164 he had asked five people: Int. Paul Parish, Oct. 23, 1993.
164 Sir Edgar took delight: Int. Edgar Williams, March 23, 1993.
164 "The Rhodent": Ints. Mike Shea, April 6, 1993; Willie Fletcher, Nov. 23, 1993, and Paul Parish, Oct. 23, 1993.
165 "explaining what it was": Int. Edgar Williams, March 23, 1993.
165 Clinton spent days: Ints. Paul Parish, Oct. 25, 1993, Sept. 5, 1994.
165 It was a glorious spring: Ints. Sara Maitland, May 11, 1993, and Paul Parish, Oct. 23, 1993.
165 Clinton would fail to mention: In the early days of his presidential campaign, Clinton omitted mention of the draft notice in interviews with several journalists writing about candidates and the Vietnam War. They included David Kern, *Arkansas Democrat,* Oct. 28, 1991, and Dan Balz, *WP,* Dec. 16, 1991. The first story raising serious questions about Clinton's version of events was by Jeff Birnbaum of the *Wall Street Journal,* Feb. 6, 1992.
165 He called his mother and stepfather: Int. Betsey Wright, Nov. 4, 1993. (In the 1992

presidential campaign, Betsey Wright, at Clinton's request, examined his private documents related to his draft situation. Wright said her examination revealed that Clinton called his stepfather, Jeff Dwire, who was in contact with the draft board secretary, Opal Ellis.)

165 A study by the Scientific Manpower Commission: *New York Times* (cited hereafter as *NYT*), May 20, 1969, p. 6.
166 "You may have heard": Letter to Denise Hyland, Spring 1969.
166 "I really hate": Cliff Jackson letter to mother, May 7, 1969.
166 Paul Parish carried one image: Int. Paul Parish, Oct. 23, 1993.

Ten: The Torment

167 a leatherbound diary: Int. Denise Hyland, March 4, 1993.
167 "The diary you gave me": Letter to Denise Hyland, May 1969.
167 "I do hope you are finding": Int. Denise Hyland, July 12, 1993.
168 "Maintaining viability": Int. Sara Maitland, May 11, 1993.
168 "completely inconsistent": Int. Strobe Talbott, April 19, 1993.
168 "Clinton and Talbott wanted to solve": Int. Daniel Singer, March 5, 1993.
168 In telephone conversations: Ints. Betsey Wright, Nov. 4, 1993; John Spotila, Jan. 12, 1994; and Paul Fray, April 25, 1994.
168 As Jackson later recollected: Int. Cliff Jackson, June 7, 1993.
168 "I got a letter from Bill Clinton": Cliff Jackson letter, May 27, 1969.
169 "I was ambivalent": Int. Cliff Jackson, June 7, 1993.
169 "thought he was going": Quoted by Associated Press, February 1992.
169 Clinton's friends bade farewell: Ints. Doug Eakeley, Dec. 19, 1993; Darryl Gless, March 10, 1993; Rudiger Lowe, April 8, 1993; and Sara Maitland, May 11, 1993.
170 When Clinton arrived in America: Int. Denise Hyland, July 12, 1993.
170 "All the light is out": Letter to Denise Hyland, July 2, 1969.
170 On his way to Arkansas: Int. Rick Stearns, Dec. 12, 1993.
170 "They came to us in droves": Int. Lee Williams, May 12, 1993.
171 The scene awaiting Clinton: Int. Sharon Ann Evans, July 13, 1993.
171 "Bill and Jeff": Int. Virginia Kelley, July 12, 1993.
172 " 'I could do this' ": Int. Paul Parish, Oct. 25, 1993.
172 "I am home now": Letter to Denise Hyland, July 8, 1969.
172 "I was just under the maximum size": Clinton interview with Dan Balz, Dec. 16, 1991.
172 On July 10: Int. Cliff Jackson, June 7, 1993. Also, Jackson letter, July 11, 1969.
173 Jackson asked his boss: Int. Cliff Jackson, June 7, 1993. Also *Arkansas Democrat,* Sept. 17, 1992, p. 13.
173 "We were used to guys:" Int. Ed Howard, July 19, 1993.
173 His papers indicate: J. William Fulbright Papers, Special Collections Division, University of Arkansas Libraries.
174 He met with Colonel Holmes: Holmes statement, Sept. 17, 1992.
174 "On the 17th": Letter to Denise Hyland, July 20, 1969.
175 Now that he was protected. AP account of letter to Tamara Kennerley, Aug. 15, 1969.
175 Clinton drove to Houston: Ints. Kit Ashby, Jan. 20, 1993, and Tom Campbell, Feb. 3, 1993.
175 Strobe Talbott traveled to Arkansas: Int. Strobe Talbott, June 2, 1993.
176 His "gimpy knee": *Time,* April 6, 1992.
176 And so it was: Ints. Boisfeuillet Jones and Robert Reich, Sept. 16, 1994; John Isaacson, March 5, 1993; and Doug Eakeley, Dec. 19, 1993. Statistics from *Vietnam Draft Almanac.*
177 The extent to which: DOD-Gorham study on ROTC, Senate Judiciary Committee, Fall 1969.
177 Mike Shea spent his first year: Int. Mike Shea, April 6, 1993.
178 "in direct proportion": Int. Tom Ward, June 18, 1993.

178 In mid-August: Int. Rick Stearns, Dec. 12, 1993.
178 He was on the outer edge: Int. David Mixner, Jan. 31, 1994.
179 "therapy for a sick man": Letter to Rick Stearns, Aug. 20, 1969.
179 "Bill was a lot more revealing": Int. Rick Stearns, Dec. 12, 1993.
179 "I am home now": Letter to Rick Stearns, Aug. 20, 1969.
179 Stearns called Clinton: Int. Rick Stearns, Dec. 12, 1969.
179 "My mind is every day": Letter to Rick Stearns, Sept. 9, 1969.
180 Clinton stayed up all night: Recounted in Clinton letter to Colonel Holmes, Dec. 3, 1969.
180 "a month or two": Holmes statement, Sept. 17, 1992.
180 "I know I promised": Clinton letter to Colonel Holmes, Dec. 3, 1969.
180 "A lot of people": Int. Ed Howard, July 19, 1993.
181 Cliff Jackson was among: Int. Cliff Jackson, June 7, 1993. Also, Jackson letters, Aug. 27, and Sept. 14, 1969.
181 a scrappy little fellow: Ints. Jim French, April 14, 1993, and Bill High, April 24, 1994.
181 "Mike was in a fraternity": Int. Herman Thomas, May 3, 1993.
181 His platoon loved Mike Thomas: Int. Greg Schlieve, May 3, 1993.
182 In Saigon that morning: *WP* and *NYT,* Sept. 15, 1969, both p. 1.
182 Lieutenant Thomas put on his pack: Ints. Herman Thomas, May 3, 1993, and Greg Schlieve, May 3, 1993, drawn from unit history records.
182 The Army posthumously: Letter to Herman Thomas from Maj. Gen. E. B. Roberts, Department of the Army, Nov. 24, 1969.
182 took other casualties as well: Ints. Herman Thomas, May 3, 1969, and Greg Schlieve, May 3, 1969.
183 Clinton and Stearns were there: Int. Rick Stearns, March 4, 1993.
183 "The Executive Committee": Int. Taylor Branch, Feb. 28, 1993.
184 Mixner confided to Clinton: Int. David Mixner, Jan. 31, 1994.

Eleven: The Lucky Number

185 Rick Stearns rented a spacious: Ints. Rick Stearns, March 4 and Dec. 12, 1993.
185 When the *American Oxonian: American Oxonian* (Fall 1969).
185 "I was under the impression": Int. Żbigniew Pelczyński, March 23, 1993.
186 a full-blown antiwar organizer: Ints. David Mixner, Jan. 31, 1994, and Randall Scott, June 30, 1993.
186 "My friend said": Int. Steve Engstrom, May 14, 1993.
187 A Gallup Poll: *WP,* Oct. 5, 1969, p. 21.
187 a broad range of support: *WP,* Oct. 4, p. 1; Oct. 8, p. 3; Oct. 10, p. 1.
187 "And I can express": Randall Scott letter, Oct. 19, 1969.
187 "Mr. Newman Supports Students": *The Guardian,* Oct. 16, 1969, p. 3.
187 "soulmates in opposition": Int. Tom Williamson, May 26, 1993.
188 On the eve of the demonstration: Ints. Taylor Branch, Feb. 28, 1993, and Steve Cohen, May 11, 1993. Ayers confrontation reported in *WP,* Nov. 18, 1969, p. 1: "Weathermen Accused of Shakedown," by Aaron Latham.
188 The day of the Mobe: *WP,* Nov. 16, p. 1.
188 In London that day: Ints. Rick Stearns, Dec. 12, 1993; Tom Williamson, May 26, 1993; and Father Richard McSorley, Nov. 17, 1993.
189 "After my prayer": McSorley, *Peace Eyes,* p. 22.
189 After the service: Ints. Richard McSorley, Nov. 17, 1993, and Richard Stearns, Dec. 12, 1993.
189 among the Rhodes Scholars who came: Ints. Willie Fletcher, and J. Michael Kirchberg, Nov. 23, 1993. Also, *The Guardian,* Oct. 16, 1969. (Michael Boskin, interviewed Dec. 18, 1993, said that although the *Guardian* article identified him among a group of American students trying to close the American Embassy, he was not an antiwar protester. He explained: "My sole recollection of it was there were a lot of Americans

arguing different points of view. The London police asked us not to flow into the streets so much from where the discussion was. I and a number of other people started shepherding people back onto the sidewalk. A reporter came up and asked me what was going on. I tried to explain the debate.")

190 His draft records: Draft records, Garland County Draft Board.

190 His answer was largely accepted: "Ex-officer Accuses Clinton; It's Baseless, Official Says," *Arkansas Gazette,* Oct. 28, 1978.

191 the only letter Clinton wrote Holmes: Clinton letter to Colonel Holmes, Dec. 3, 1969.

191 "I expected to be called": Bill Clinton interview with Dan Balz, Dec. 16, 1991.

192 The best estimate of when: Int. Randall Scott, June 30, 1993.

193 "I didn't see, in the end": Letter to Colonel Holmes, Dec. 3, 1969.

193 This became possible because: *NYT,* Oct. 2, 1969: "Nixon Eases Rule on Draft."

193 In the weeks before: Sept. 14 front-page stories in *NYT, WP,* and *Arkansas Gazette* cited sources saying the draft would be cut. The *NYT* article began: "The Nixon Administration is considering a series of major reforms in the military draft intended to defuse domestic political opposition to the war in Vietnam."

194 "I didn't know anything about any lottery": Bill Clinton interview with Dan Balz, Dec. 16, 1991. (The lottery was headline news during that period. Lead headline in *WP,* Sept. 20, 1969: "Nixon Trims Draft, Presses for Lottery.")

194 they both loved Dylan Thomas: Ints. Rick Stearns, March 4 and Dec. 12, 1993.

195 "that you and I are queer": Letter to Rick Stearns, Nov. 19, 1969.

196 "He basically said that": Ints. Rick Stearns, March 4 and Dec. 12, 1993.

196 He had been invited: Int. Strobe Talbott, June 2, 1993.

196 "particularly shambolic": Int. Sara Maitland, May 11, 1993.

196 "graduate student bohemian": Int. Strobe Talbott, June 2, 1993.

197 She and Talbott rode bicycles: Int. Brooke Shearer, July 1, 1993.

197 "Frank and Bill shared": *Time,* April 6, 1992.

197 "I may never pick up a parchment": Letter to Denise Hyland, Nov. 27, 1969.

198 The first draft lottery: The account of the lottery is drawn from *WP,* Dec. 1–2, 1969; *Boston Globe,* Dec. 2, 1969; and *Vietnam War Almanac,* 1988.

198 "It was just a fluke": Bill Clinton interview with Dan Balz, Dec. 16, 1991.

199 "I am sorry to be so long": Letter to Colonel Holmes, Dec. 3, 1969. The letter resurfaced twenty-three years later when ABC News obtained a copy while Clinton was campaigning in the 1992 New Hampshire presidential primary. ABC producer Mark Halperin, working with correspondent James Wooten, showed the letter to Clinton aides at the Nashua, New Hampshire, airport on Feb. 10 and requested an interview with the candidate. After reading the letter, consultant James Carville said, "This letter exonerates us. We want to publish this god damn thing in the [Manchester] *Union-Leader* tomorrow!"

204 "The letter was the talk": Int. Ed Howard, July 19, 1993.

204 A dissident file was kept: *Ibid.*

204 Holmes's reactions fluctuated: *Arkansas Gazette,* Oct. 28, 1978; *Arkansas Democrat,* Oct. 29, 1991; *Wall Street Journal,* Feb. 6, 1992; and Holmes statement, Sept. 16, 1992.

205 "full of rhetoric": Int. David Tell, Dec. 13, 1993.

205 "At no time": Holmes statement, Sept. 16, 1992.

205 not above enrolling law students: Int. Ed Howard, July 19, 1993.

Twelve: The Grand Tour

206 "a modern version of the old": Int. Edgar Williams, March 23, 1993.

206 Not a nobleman's holiday: Ints. Richard McSorley, Nov. 17, 1993; Richard Shullaw, Feb. 2, 1993; Charlie Daniels, June 29, 1993; Rudiger Lowe, April 23, 1993; and Jirina Kopoldova, June 1993.

206 As he was ambling down: Int. Richard McSorley, Nov. 17, 1993.

207 It was from McSorley's account: In early October 1992, in the final month of the presidential campaign, a group of Republican congressmen led by Robert K. Dornan of California gave nightly "special order" speeches on the House floor, televised by C-Span, which questioned Clinton's Moscow trip. Dornan said that Clinton rode a "peace train" and, though he had no evidence, suggested Soviet agents were involved in arranging the trip. This sinister scenario caught the attention of George Bush, who asked his negative research team to investigate. David Tell, the head of Bush's research team, said he interviewed Dornan and listened to his "free associative lecture on the Peace Train," but found that it was riddled with suppositions and "factual inconsistencies."

208 James Durham was another: Int. James Durham, July 1, 1993.

208 Over the years: *Ibid.*

209 Again he had no schedule: Int. Richard Shullaw, Feb. 2, 1993.

209 "I have found the world's winter": Postcard to Denise Hyland, Dec. 24, 1993.

209 "Pelle did not care for Bill": Int. Richard Shullaw, Feb. 2, 1993.

209 One was H. Ross Perot: *NYT,* Jan. 1, 1970, "Soviet Denies Perot a Visa to Send Gifts."

210 "Upon entering Russia": Daily Journal of Charlie Daniels.

210 Their view of the Soviet Union: Int. Strobe Talbott, June 2, 1993.

211 He had one friend: Int. Tom Williamson, May 26, 1993.

211 Daniels was in Moscow: The account of Daniels's trip to Moscow with Henry Fors and Carl McAfee is drawn from interview with Charlie Daniels, June 29, 1993. Also Daniels's daily journal of the trip.

212 "You wonder why Bill": Int. Charlie Daniels, June 29, 1993.

213 Senator Eugene McCarthy arrived: *NYT,* Jan. 7, 1970.

213 "That figures!": Daniels's daily journal.

213 "We were all very moved": Int. John Albery, March 25, 1993.

213 "My friend Bill Clinton": Jan Kopold letter to his parents, December 1969.

214 Clinton stayed with the Kopolds: The account of Clinton's stay in Prague is based on interviews with Jirina Kopoldova and Bedrich Kopold, May 1993, and letters from Jan Kopold and Bill Clinton to the Kopold family. Also on the description of the apartment complex in *Strana* magazine, pp. 46–48.

215 "I still have a picture": Int. Rudiger Lowe, April 23, 1993.

215 The first telephone call: Int. Charlie Daniels, June 29, 1993.

215 "I would like to take": Letter from Virginia Dwire, Jan. 22, 1970.

216 with his baggy tweed jackets: Ints. Strobe Talbott, June 2, 1993; Brooke Shearer, July 1, 1993; and Sara Maitland, May 11, 1993.

216 Frank Aller counterbalanced: Ints. Strobe Talbott, June 2, 1993; J. Michael Kirchberg, Nov. 23, 1993; and Willie Fletcher, Nov. 23, 1993.

216 "looked like a lumberjack": Int. Brooke Shearer, July 1, 1993.

217 "old and heavy-lidded": Int. Mandy Merck, May 14, 1993.

217 "Frank was describing the effect": Int. Sara Maitland, May 11, 1993.

217 "As you know": Int. Tom Campbell, Feb. 3, 1993.

218 "Senator Clinton will see you": Int. Mandy Merck, May 14, 1993.

218 "Politics gives guys so much power": *Ibid.*

218 "Five of us were in the game": *Ibid.*

218 The highlight of her lecture: Ints. Sara Maitland, May 11, 1993; Mandy Merck, May 14, 1993; and Rick Stearns, Dec. 12, 1993.

219 "I thought I was going": Int. Mandy Merck, May 14, 1993.

219 Mixner was gay: Int. David Mixner, Jan. 31, 1994.

220 The breakup of the relationship: Ints. Paul Parish, Oct. 23, 1993, and Sara Maitland, May 11, 1993.

220 When the Hilary term ended: Int. Rick Stearns, March 4, 1993, Dec. 12, 1993.

220 Waiting to see them: The account of Clinton's trip to Spain is based on interviews with Lyda Holt, June 8, 1993; Rick Stearns, March 4, 1993; Peggy Freeman, June 4, 1993; and Jack Holt, Jr., June 4, 1993.

222 Leopoulos was always hungering: Int. David Leopoulos, June 9, 1993.
222 He attended special cram courses: Ints. Maurice Shock, March 24, 1993, and Alan Ryan, Dec. 14, 1993.
223 "I didn't take any kind": Int. Maurice Shock, March 24, 1993.
223 "If you were an American": Int. Edgar Williams, March 23, 1993.
223 In the end: Ints. Strobe Talbott, June 2, 1993; Doug Eakeley, Dec. 19, 1993; and Paul Parish, Oct. 23, 1993.
224 he drove to Springfield: Ints. Amy and Kit Ashby, June 19, 1993.

Thirteen: Law and Politics at Yale

226 One of the candidates: Ints. Joseph Duffey, Feb. 7, 1994, and Anne Wexler, May 11, 1993.
227 They had worked together: Ints. Tony Podesta, May 5 and May 10, 1993, and Carl Wagner, June 28, 1993.
227 "he had a baby face": Int. Virginia Kelley, Jan. 13, 1992.
227 Many from the Pursestrings contingent: Int. Tony Podesta, May 5, 1993.
228 "Bill Clinton was an unusual choice": *Ibid.*
229 "Oh, my God!": Int. Mickey Donenfeld, May 13, 1993.
229 "one of the few Yalies": Int. Irv Stolberg, May 12, 1993.
229 "I was told the new guy": Int. Chuca Meyer, May 12, 1993.
229 "He'd come over": Int. Mickey Donenfeld, May 13, 1993.
230 Wexler realized: Int. Anne Wexler, May 11, 1993.
230 "We had a lot of students": Int. Joseph Duffey, Feb. 7, 1994.
231 with his adaptability: Int. Anne Wexler, May 11, 1993.
231 "could never bridge the gap": Int. John Spotila, Jan. 12, 1994.
231 The irony here: Int. Joseph Duffey, Feb. 7, 1994. Also Eric Rennie, *From a Campaign Album,* 1973.
231 "but we couldn't get": Int. Larry Kudlow, May 13, 1993.
231 When one critic: Rennie, *From a Campaign album.*
232 The Duffey crew worked hard: Ints. Joseph Duffey, Feb. 7, 1994; Anne Wexler, May 11, 1993; Judi Gold, June 23, 1993; and Tony Podesta, May 10, 1993.
232 "It is always tempting": Rennie, *From a Campaign Album.*
233 Once during the campaign: Int. Anne Wexler, May 11, 1993.
233 "Hi, I'm Bill Clinton": Int. Nancy Bekavac, June 29, 1993.
233 "as nonchalant about it": Int. Bill Coleman, May 29, 1993.
234 "He was very quick": Int. Don Pogue, June 2, 1993.
234 entered Yale Law in 1968: Int. Steve Cohen, Feb. 3, 1994.
234 "In exams the concern": Int. Robert Borosage, Jan. 10, 1994.
234 "He never went to class": Int. James Blair, July 15, 1993.
234 He was "flabbergasted": Int. Don Pogue, June 2, 1993.
236 It is hardly surprising: *Ibid.*
237 In the law school corridor: Int. Robert Borosage, Jan. 10, 1994.
237 Bands of students: Int. Don Pogue, June 2, 1993.
237 Clinton moved easily: Int. Bill Coleman, May 29, 1993.
238 "Oh, you poor bastard": Int. Nancy Bekavac, June 29, 1993.
239 "Politics . . . was a natural part": Int. Bill Coleman, May 29, 1993.
239 "If you scratched the surface": Int. David Schulte, Jan. 27, 1994.
239 "About the White House": Letter to Cliff Jackson, Nov. 17, 1971.
240 Clinton thrived on what politics: Int. Nancy Bekavac, June 29, 1993.
240 His living quarters: The account of the Fort Trumbull beach house is based on interviews with Doug Eakeley, Dec. 19, 1993; Bill Coleman, May 29, 1993; Don Pogue, June 2, 1993; Nancy Bekavac, June 29, 1993; and Robert Reich, April 15, 1993.
242 "New Haven is the vile crotch": *American Oxonian* (Spring 1971). Also int. Robert Reich, Sept. 16, 1994.

242 "Robert Reich is now less confident": *Time,* May 17, 1971, "Class of 1968 Revisited."
243 The Rhodes Scholars had scattered: *American Oxonian* (Spring 1971).
243 Aller went to Spain: Ints. Strobe Talbott, June 2, 1993, and Brooke Shearer, July 1, 1993. Also letter to Brooke Shearer, Nov. 3, 1971, and a richly textured article on Aller's final troubled years in *NYT Magazine,* Nov. 22, 1992, by Alessandra Stanley.
244 Clinton went out to California: Ints. Brooke Shearer, July 1, 1993, and Derek Shearer, Jan. 5, 1994.

Fourteen: Rodham and Clinton

246 "Bill, this is Hillary": Int. Robert Reich, Sept. 16, 1994.
246 Struggling to hold Clinton's: Int. Jeff Glekel, Sept. 21, 1994.
247 On their first outing: *ARTnews* (September 1994), p. 141.
247 It took a little time: Int. Don Pogue, June 2, 1993.
247 "He cared deeply": Int. Hillary Clinton, Jan. 16, 1992. (Hillary Clinton declined interview requests for this book, but was interviewed by the author during the 1992 presidential campaign.)
247 "They were funny together": Int. Don Pogue, June 2, 1993.
247 "Come off it, Bill!": Int. Doug Eakeley, Dec. 19, 1993.
248 Emerson kept private numerical grades: *The Nation,* Nov. 2, 1992, Andrew L. Shapiro.
248 "Clinton had the charm": Int. Steve Cohen, Feb. 3, 1994.
248 "The story of what": Int. Carolyn Ellis, Jan. 28, 1994.
248 "mainstream, conscientious": Int. Greg Craig, Jan. 27, 1994.
248 She kept her hair long: Int. Carolyn Ellis, Jan. 28, 1994.
249 Rodham served as a commentator: Ints. James Blumstein, June 22, 1993, and Jack Petranker, Feb. 7, 1994. ("Jamestown 70" inspired an article in *Playboy,* April 1972, headlined "Taking Over Vermont—get 225,000 counterculturalists to settle in the green mountain state and exercise their franchise—and you've begun a unique social experiment.")
249 "You couldn't get away with that": Int. Rick Ricketts, June 22, 1993.
249 Dorothy Rodham often told: *A First Lady,* p. 35.
250 when one marriage disintegrated: Int. Rick Ricketts, June 22, 1993.
251 "conservative but not paranoid": Int. Hillary Clinton, Jan. 16, 1992.
251 "a much more intellectual view": Int. Sherry Heiden, March 16, 1993.
251 "We'd get our *Weekly Reader*": Int. Rick Ricketts, June 22, 1993.
251 He considered himself a liberal realist: The account of Don Jones is based on interviews with Don Jones, April 14, 1993 and May 17, 1993, and with Rick Ricketts, June 22, 1993, and Sherry Heiden, March 16, 1993.
253 The most overt case for Hillary: R. E. Levin, *Inside Story,* p. 15; Rodham, *A First Lady,* p. 42. Also *NYT,* Feb. 18, 1994, Maureen Dowd.
254 "let's-keep-it-clean": Letter to Don Jones, May 17, 1964.
254 Hugh Rodham did not spoil: Ints. Hillary Clinton, Jan. 16, 1992, and Rick Ricketts, June 22, 1993. Also *WP,* Jan. 11, 1993: "The Education of Hillary Clinton," Martha Sherrill.
254 Hillary kept up a running: Int. Rick Ricketts, June 22, 1993.
255 "a clean slate": Int. Geoffrey Shields, Feb. 23, 1994.
255 "See how liberal I'm becoming": Letter to Don Jones.
256 "We saw everything": Int. Betsy Johnson Ebeling, Sept. 27, 1994.
256 "try out different personalities": Letter to Don Jones. Int. Don Jones, May 17, 1993.
256 "personally pretty conservative": Int. Geoffrey Shields, Feb. 23, 1994.
257 "You can't accomplish anything": *Ibid.*
257 "started out thinking": Int. Alan Schechter, Sept. 8, 1994.
257 "someone can be a Burkean realist": Int. Don Jones, May 17, 1993.
257 reluctantly acquiesced: *A First Lady,* p. 79.
257 Adams described her: Transcript of Adams's introduction, Wellesley College files.

258 "I find myself in a familiar position": Transcript of "Remarks of Hillary D. Rodham, President of the Wellesley College Government Association and member of the Class of 1969, on the occasion of Wellesley's 91st Commencement, May 31, 1969."
259 "She said it had been hard": Int. Geoffrey Shields, Feb. 23, 1994.
259 21 Edgewood Avenue: Ints. Greg Craig, Jan. 27, 1994, and Carolyn Ellis, Jan. 28, 1994.
259 "I am trying to at least": Letter to Denise Hyland, Fall 1971.
259 eating breakfast at the Blue Bell: *NYT Magazine,* Nov. 22, 1992.
259 The call was from Brooke Shearer: Ints. Brooke Shearer, July 1, 1993, and Strobe Talbott, June 2, 1993.
260 They all had their own perspectives: Ints. Rick Stearns, March 4, 1993; John Isaacson, March 5, 1993; Brooke Shearer, July 1, 1993; Mike Shea, April 6, 1993; and Willie Fletcher, Nov. 23, 1993.
261 "His politics are probably closer": Letter to Cliff Jackson, Nov. 17, 1971.
262 "As to the 'disturbing undercurrents' ": Letter to Cliff Jackson, December 1971.
262 "the pluralist model": Int. Greg Craig, Jan. 27, 1994.
263 there was a Prize Trial: The account of Rodham and Clinton's performance at the Prize Trial is based on interviews with Robert and Sarah Alsdorf, April 7, 1993; Mike Conway, April 1, 1993; Elliot Brown, April 1, 1993; Mark Klugheit, April 1, 1993; and Nancy Bekavac, June 29, 1993.

Fifteen: Texas Days

265 "You said you were sending": Ints. Billie Carr, Dec. 15, 1992, Feb. 16, 1994.
265 which was how Hart wanted it: Int. Gary Hart, March 1993.
265 Despite the admonition: Ints. Robert Hauge, Dec. 8, 1992; Sissy Farenthold, February 24, 1993; and Billie Carr, Feb. 16, 1994.
266 At a reunion of Duffey workers: Ints. Anne Wexler, May 11, 1993, and Tony Podesta, May 10, 1993.
266 Stearns had sent Clinton: Ints. Rick Stearns, March 4, 1993; Steve Smith, July 15, 1993; Don O'Brien, Dec. 16, 1992; and Gary Hart, March 1993.
266 Taylor Branch brought his own share: Ints. Taylor Branch, Jan. 11, 1992, Feb. 28, 1993, and Feb. 14, 1994.
268 The McGovern headquarters: Ints. Joyce Sampson, Jan. 10, 1993; Lisa Hazel, Jan. 8, 1993; and Nancy Williams, Jan. 7, 1993.
268 from a hippie commune: Int. Mark Blumenthal, Jan. 9, 1993.
269 Branch took finances: Int. Taylor Branch, Feb. 28, 1993.
269 The Texans viewed the newcomers: Ints. Mark Blumenthal, Jan. 9, 1993; Lisa Rogers, Jan. 9, 1993; Carrin Patman, Jan. 5, 1993; and Anne McAfee, Dec. 19, 1992.
269 "good cop—bad cop routine": Int. Billie Carr, Dec. 15, 1992.
269 "Who's Linda Ronstadt": Int. Taylor Branch, Feb. 28, 1993.
270 One of his first acts: McGovern archive at Seeley G. Mudd Manuscripts Center at Princeton University. In his return telegram, LBJ wrote: "Have just returned home from hospital. Thank you for your wire and your concern. Will be delighted to see you and senator Eagleton at any time convenient to you."
270 Clinton and Branch helped the national staff: Ints. Rick Stearns, March 4, 1993, and Taylor Branch, Feb. 28, 1993.
270 sometimes with disdain: The LBJ Library file on McGovern campaign shows Johnson's annotations to a McGovern fund-raising letter. One sentence in the letter begins: "In having stubbornly pursued an unpopular, unjust war in Vietnam for nearly ten years...." Johnson scrawled the words "yes" over "unpopular" and "no" over "unjust."
271 greatly disappointed Clinton and Branch: Int. Taylor Branch, Feb. 27, 1993.
271 "a great man": *Arkansas Democrat,* Sept. 27, 1977.
271 One week before the meeting: LBJ Library. Statement was released Aug. 16, 1972. One paragraph in the statement read: "It is no secret that Senator McGovern and I have

widely differing opinions on many matters, especially foreign policy. Impelled by his conscience, Senator McGovern has not refrained from criticizing policies of mine with which he has disagreed. Neither shall I refrain from stating my disagreements with any positions of his if and when I believe, in my own conscience, that the public interest, as I see it, demands such action."

271 The day after the announcement: Memo to LBJ from aide Joan Kennedy, LBJ Library.
271 The boisterous crowd: *Austin American-Statesman,* Aug. 22, 1972: "McGovern Cheered by Huge Crowd," p. 1.
272 McGovern was startled: The account of the meeting with LBJ is drawn from an interview with George McGovern, March 10, 1994.
273 "a donnybrook of a family feud": *Dallas Times Herald,* Aug. 27, 1972, Ernest Stromberger.
273 to express their "ill feeling": *Austin American-Statesman,* Aug. 23, 1972.
273 It is clear from a series of letters: Letters from McGovern to Barrientos and Bullock are part of the McGovern Archive at Seeley G. Mudd Manuscripts Center, Princeton University.
274 "Bullshit—we're Democrats": Int. Bob Armstrong, Jan. 6, 1992.
274 "a damn good IRS audit": Int. John C. White, March 10, 1994.
274 "I cannot see a win here": *Ibid.*
274 "you had to be an optimist": Int. Gary Hart, Dec. 17, 1992.
274 "He had this bootleg cellar": Int. Taylor Branch, Feb. 28, 1993.
275 "politics as "an art form": Int. John C. White, March 10, 1993.
275 "They were right out front": *Ibid.*
275 "I'm taking some sick leave": Int. Bob Armstrong, Jan. 6, 1992.
275 He shared Clinton's political obsession: Int. Garry Mauro, Dec. 16, 1992.
275 Wright lived two blocks: Int. Betsey Wright, Feb. 15, 1993.
276 "our moral pulse": Int. Lisa Rogers, Jan. 9, 1993.
276 Many of the women: Ints. Betsey Wright, Feb. 15, 1993; Lisa Hazel, Jan. 8, 1993; Lisa Rogers, Jan. 9, 1993; and Ruth Fischer, Jan. 10, 1993.
276 There "was dope around": Int. Lisa Rogers, Jan. 9, 1993.
276 "Stories of who slept": Int. Bebe Champ, Jan. 10, 1993.
276 "women were very attracted": Int. John C. White, March 10, 1994.
276 "Where's Hillary?": Int. Ruth Fischer, Jan. 10, 1993.
276 "in awe of young women": Int. Joyce Sampson, Jan. 10, 1993.
277 aloof but intelligent: Int. Mark Blumenthal, Jan. 9, 1993.
277 "not particularly warm": Int. Bebe Champ, Jan. 10, 1993.
277 "like a little sister": Int. Ruth Fischer, Jan. 10, 1993.
277 Taylor Branch welcomed Rodham's: Int. Taylor Branch, Feb. 28, 1993.
277 The two women would sit: Int. Betsey Wright, Feb. 15, 1993.
277 It was not at all certain: Ints. Ruth Fischer, Jan. 10, 1993, and Roy Spence, Feb. 8, 1993.
277 The public lack of interest: Int. Taylor Branch, Feb. 28, 1993.
278 When the Texas staff: The account of the McGovern campaign debate over the Connally fund-raiser and rice-and-beans rally is based on interviews with Taylor Branch, Feb. 28, 1993; Tony Podesta, May 10, 1993; Gary Hart, March 1993; John C. White, March 10, 1994; and Bob Armstrong, Jan. 6, 1993.
279 A few miles away: Ann Crawford and Jack Keever, *Portrait in Power,* p. 362. Also *Austin American-Statesman,* Sept. 23, 1972.
279 "When he arrived": Int. Bebe Champ, Jan. 10, 1993.
280 "Billie Carr—Bitch": Int. Billie Carr, Dec. 15, 1992.
280 "Bill liked going out": *Ibid.*
280 "I'm gonna tell you something": *Ibid.*
281 "an endless fight": Int. Taylor Branch, Feb. 28, 1993.
281 "They were furious": The account of the dispute with Barbara Jordan is based on interviews with Taylor Branch, Feb. 28, 1993, and Feb. 14, 1994, and Tony Podesta,

May 10, 1993. Barbara Jordan declined to be interviewed and said, through her secretary, that she had no recollection of the incident.
281 "He liked what we were doing": Ints. Taylor Branch, Feb. 28, 1993, Jan. 11, 1992.
282 In Shriver's last visit: Int. Roy Spence, Feb. 8, 1993.
282 Branch and Clinton walked: *Ibid.* Also int. Taylor Branch, Feb. 28, 1993.
282 "We had this huge cadre": Int. Tony Podesta, May 10, 1993.
283 "It was unbelievable": Int. Roy Spence, Feb. 8, 1993.
283 Judy Trabulsi, camped out: Int. Judy Trabulsi, Feb. 2, 1993.
283 The lights were off: Int. Bebe Champ, Jan. 10, 1993.
283 A few days after the election: The account of the party at Armstrong's ranch is based on interviews with Bebe Champ, Jan. 10, 1993; Bob Armstrong, Jan. 6, 1993; Mark Blumenthal, Jan. 9, 1993; and Lisa Rogers, Jan. 9, 1993.
283 "You need to go hunting": Int. Taylor Branch, Feb. 28, 1993.
284 Wright headed up to Washington: Int. Betsey Wright, Feb. 15, 1993.
284 a six-year-old guru: Int. Mark Blumenthal, Jan 9, 1993.
284 "Aren't you worried": Int. Bebe Champ, Jan. 10, 1993.
284 "Coming down to Texas": Int. Pat Robards, Dec. 19, 1992.
284 "When he was traveling": Int. Mark Blumenthal, Jan. 9, 1993.
284 "He learned from that race": Int. Roy Spence, Feb. 8, 1993.
285 "He seemed to take away": Int. George McGovern, March 10, 1993.
285 "I wonder what's going on": Letter to Creekmore Fath, Nov. 25, 1972.
285 He sat in the living room: Int. Nancy Bekavac, May 29, 1993.
285 according to a summary: Int. Dean Wylie Davis, University of Arkansas Law School, March 31, 1994.
286 Bill Coleman felt "a sense of hope": Int. Bill Coleman, May 29, 1993.
286 "Let me know when you're running": Int. Robert Alsdorf, April 7, 1993.

Sixteen: Home Again

287 "a pure accident": Charles Flynn Allen, *Governor William Jefferson Clinton,* p. 50: "He had no plans to make a career of teaching, but found himself applying for a faculty position at the University of Arkansas at Fayetteville when he returned to Arkansas from Yale. Clinton said his teaching there was 'a pure accident.' . . . Clinton was driving home from New Haven, Connecticut, to Hot Springs when he stopped along the interstate in Little Rock and called the university. He spoke to Wylie Davis. . . . He was granted an interview and soon found himself a member of the U of A School of Law faculty." See also Levin, *Bill Clinton: The Inside Story,* p. 97.
288 "amusingly inaccurate": Int. Wylie Davis, March 31, 1994. Also *Arkansas Law Record* (Fall 1993).
288 He recruited a political friend: Int. Steve Smith, July 15, 1993.
288 "the entire process was": Int. Wylie Davis, March 31, 1994.
288 a curious first impression: Int. David Newbern, April 6, 1994.
288 "He charmed us all": Int. Wylie Davis, March 31, 1994. Also *Arkansas Law Record* (Fall 1993).
289 "It was very clear": Int. Mort Gitelman, June 21, 1993.
289 Clinton was offered the job: Int. Wylie Davis, March 31, 1994.
289 rented a contemporary stone: Ints. Rudy Moore, June 10, 1993; Steve Smith, July 15, 1993; and Doug Wallace, April 14, 1994.
289 On August 23: Int. Ann Henry, July 16, 1993.
290 He filed an amicus brief: Int. Steve Smith, July 15, 1993.
290 "Clinton came up": Int. Brenda Blagg, July 29, 1993.
290 Clinton called Moore: Int. Rudy Moore, June 10, 1993.
291 Whillock had previously served: Int. Carl Whillock, July 19, 1993.
291 It was not unusual: Ints. Wylie Davis, March 31, 1994, and Mort Gitelman, June 21, 1993.

291 "We had long discussions": Int. Moril Harriman, July 15, 1993.
292 "shooting the breeze": Int. Woody Bassett, June 21, 1993.
292 "There was some grumbling": Int. Rafael Guzman, April 4, 1994. Also *Arkansas Law Journal* (Fall 1993).
292 Once he accidentally: Int. Wylie Davis, March 31, 1994.
293 "wasn't terribly kind to Bill": Int. Mort Gitelman, June 21, 1993.
293 In the constitutional law: Ints. Woody Bassett, June 21, 1993, and Jesse Kearney, June 2, 1992.
293 part of the first wave: Ints. L. T. Simes, July 9, 1993, and Carol Willis, June 30, 1993.
294 perpetuating the myth: Allen, *Governor William Jefferson Clinton,* p. 53: "About his decision to run after only three months of teaching, Clinton said, 'The only reason I ran for Congress is they couldn't get anybody else to do it. I asked Diane Blair and her then husband Hugh Kincaid and Rudy Moore . . . and two or three other people. . . . I didn't intend to get into politics that early.' "
294 "He felt he had to go bigger": Int. Rudy Moore, June 10, 1993.
295 "What if you don't win?": Int. Thomas McLarty, April 19, 1993.
295 In early December: Int. Paul Fray, April 25, 1994.
296 "I've been thinking about running": Ints. Carl Whillock, July 19, 1993, and Margaret Whillock, July 28, 1993.
296 "I don't see how": Int. James Blair, June 10, 1993.
296 "a wonderful man": Int. Thomas McLarty, April 19, 1993.
296 "looked like a congressman": Int. Diane Kincaid Blair, June 10, 1993.
297 The political folk wisdom: Int. James Blair, June 10, 1993.
297 " 'Is that a good idea?' ": Int. David Pryor, June 29, 1993.
297 "Why don't you come over": Int. Ron Addington, March 29, 1994.
298 The journey ended in embarrassment: *Ibid.*
298 Addington was in Little Rock: *Ibid.*
298 They agreed to meet: Ints. Doug Wallace, April 14, 1994, and Ron Addington, March 29, 1994.
299 At eight o'clock on Monday morning: The account of the Clinton announcement is based on Doug Wallace papers from the 1974 congressional campaign, archived at University of Arkansas-Little Rock Library (UALR).
299 "All smiles": Int. Ron Addington, March 29, 1993.
299 "Billie, I'm on my way!": Int. Billie Carr, Dec. 15, 1992.
300 he responded by contributing: Federal Election Commission reports, *Clinton for Congress,* 1974.
300 "Dear Charlie,": Letter to Charlie Daniels, Jan. 7, 1974.
300 The return rate: FEC reports, *Clinton for Congress,* 1974.
301 They left at dawn: Int. Carl Whillock, July 19, 1993.
301 At the Berryville courthouse: Int. Eileen Harvey, July 30, 1993.
302 "We sat around": Ints. Carl Whillock, July 19, 1993, and Victor Nixon, Aug. 2, 1994.
302 The cattle farmer contributed: FEC reports, *Clinton for Congress,* 1974.
302 "One candidate has already": *Harrison Daily Times,* March 6, 1974.
302 "These two men walk in": Int. Vada Sheid, July 28, 1993.
303 "You do that": Int. Carl Whillock, July 19, 1993.
304 "You really missed it!": Int. Margaret Whillock, July 28, 1993.
304 "It's a little extreme": Associated Press article in *Hope Star* and *Arkansas Gazette,* April 11, 1974. Notations from Mack McLarty on copy sent to campaign and archived in Doug Wallace papers at UALR.
304 Schneider's friends gathered: Ints. James Blair, June 10, 1993; Ron Addington, March 31, 1994; and David Pryor, June 29, 1993.
305 "You and Bill get your butts": Int. Ron Addington, March 31, 1994.
305 They left on the morning: *Ibid.*
306 "God damn it!": *Ibid.*

Seventeen: And Not to Yield

307　More than twelve hours a day: Ints. Michael Conway, June 18, 1993, and Tom Bell, July 28, 1993.
307　She did not have her own: Int. Sara Ehrman, Jan. 31, 1993.
307　She and Doar had met: Int. Michael Conway, June 18, 1993.
308　He had barely settled: *Ibid.*
308　Their windows looked out on: Int. Tom Bell, July 28, 1993.
308　Rodham's section analyzed: Int. Terry Kirkpatrick, April 5, 1994.
308　Their report concluded: Report of impeachment inquiry staff, Feb. 21, 1974.
309　Doar was a seemingly: Ints. Fred Altshuler, June 24, 1993; Robert Sack, June 22, 1993; Michael Conway, April 1, 1993; and Robin Johansen, June 23, 1993.
309　Cates and Doar respected: Int. Richard Cates, July 13, 1993.
310　"He is looking for detail": Int. Tom Bell, July 28, 1993.
310　"On occasion he would call her": *Ibid.*
310　The way she would later: Radcliffe, *A First Lady,* p. 124; Warner, *Hillary Clinton,* p. 74.
310　Donaldson has no such memory: Int. Sam Donaldson, March 4, 1994.
310　"There were some tensions": Int. Tom Bell, July 28, 1993.
311　"she wasn't as ideologically pure": *Ibid.*
311　"We're lawyers, not historians": Ints. Fred Altshuler, June 24, 1993, and Michael Conway, June 18, 1993.
311　"a small but nasty": Ints. Robert Sack, June 22, 1993, and Fred Altshuler, June 24, 1993.
311　Doar was obsessive: Ints. Sandy Boone, July 8, 1993; Jeff Branchero, July 7, 1993; and Tom Bell, July 28, 1993.
312　At one point the women: Ints. Terry Kirkpatrick, April 5, 1993, and Robin Johansen, June 23, 1993.
312　"I remember that": Int. Jeff Branchero, July 7, 1993.
313　"I'm following Phil's example": Int. Phil Verveer, Feb. 2, 1993.
313　"She was absolutely, totally": Int. Terry Kirkpatrick, April 5, 1994.
313　"This is the honest-to-God": Int. Tom Bell, July 28, 1993.
313　"a little crazy": *WP,* July 1, 1993: "The Man Behind the President," Ruth Marcus.
314　They spent one week: Int. Bob Sack, June 22, 1993.
314　"It was Nixon taping himself": *New York Review of Books,* Oct. 22, 1992: "A Doll's House?", Garry Wills.
315　They developed case histories: Int. Fred Altshuler, June 24, 1993.
315　The room was somber: Ints. Michael Conway, June 18, 1993, and Robert Sack, June 22, 1993.
315　She stood in the back: Int. Terry Kirkpatrick, April 5, 1994.
316　she was "at sea": Int. Taylor Branch, Feb. 28, 1993.
316　"You have to be three hundred percent": Int. Terry Kirkpatrick, April 5, 1994.
316　She went to dinner: Int. Fred Altshuler, June 24, 1993.
316　She and Clinton had even worried: Int. Paul Fray, May 3, 1994.
317　"I mentioned to her": Int. Wylie Davis, March 31, 1994.
317　"Hillary came in dressed": Int. Mort Gitelman, June 21, 1993.
317　Ehrman was horrified: Int. Sara Ehrman, Jan. 31, 1993.
318　She persuaded Alan Stone: Int. Alan Stone, March 7, 1994.
318　Stone would remember: *Ibid.*
318　"Kind of frantic": *Ibid.*

Eighteen: Running with the Boy

319　One morning during the spring: Ints. Ron Addington, March 31, 1994, and April 23, 1994; Doug Wallace, April 21, 1994.

319   In the early stages: Int. Ron Addington, April 23, 1994.
319   "Well, how long": *Ibid.*
320   "why he was down there": Int. Doug Wallace, April 21, 1994.
320   But there were stacks of: Ints. Ron Addington, April 23, 1994; Doug Wallace, April 21, 1994; and Neil McDonald, May 4, 1994.
320   "the staff tried to ignore it": Int. Doug Wallace, April 21, 1994.
320   "Hillary had put the hammer": Ints. Paul Fray, April 25, May 3, and May 23, 1994.
321   "about broke down and cried": *Ibid.*
321   He began with 12 percent: Ints. Ron Addington, April 23, 1994, and Doug Wallace, April 21, 1994.
321   "Bill's knowledge and facility": Int. J. Bill Becker, Jan. 7, 1992.
321   "more interested in finishing": Int. Jim Daugherty, April 6, 1994.
321   At the "Y" City Café: Int. Diane Kincaid Blair, June 10, 1993.
321   On the road between stops: Ints. Ron Addington, April 23, 1994, and Harry Truman Moore, June 15, 1994.
322   "Do we really have to go?": Int. Morriss Henry, July 16, 1993.
322   Fulbright had raised and spent: Ints. James Blair, June 10, 1993, and Lee Williams, May 12, 1993.
322   Clinton intended to assist: Int. James Blair, June 10, 1993.
323   The theme of the reunion: Int. Phil Jamison, May 13, 1994.
323   "the most prominent graduate": *Hot Springs Sentinel-Record,* July 11, 1974.
323   "Lots of them": *Ibid.*
324   Jamison was cornered: Int. Phil Jamison, May 13, 1994.
324   The documentary record: Int. Ed Howard, July 19, 1993.
324   "He told me what he said": Int. Paul Fray, April 25, 1994.
324   He called the unit commander: Int. Ed Howard, July 19, 1993.
325   According to Fray: Ints. Paul Fray, April 25 and May 23, 1994.
325   He did not know: Int. Ed Howard, July 19, 1993.
325   The Lees were old friends: Ints. Mike Lee, May 13, 1994, and Suzanne Lee, May 25, 1994.
325   "went into a stall": Int. Doug Wallace, April 21, 1994.
326   Clinton's mother came home: *Leading,* p. 205.
326   Everyone at campaign headquarters: Ints. Doug Wallace, April 14, 1994, and Paul Fray, April 25, 1994.
326   When Clinton told Diane Kincaid: Int. Diane Kincaid Blair, June 10, 1993.
326   "Virginia loathed Hillary then": Ints. Mary Lee Fray, April 25 and May 3, 1994.
327   "She was someone you had": Int. Rudy Moore, June 10, 1993.
327   he was still involved: Ints. Doug Wallace, April 21, 1993; Paul Fray, April 25, 1993; and Mary Lee Fray, April 25, 1993.
327   " 'Go take her somewhere' ": Ints. Mary Lee Fray, April 25 and May 3, 1993.
327   Rodham took her own place: Ints. Rafael Guzman, April 4, 1994, and Terry Kirkpatrick, April 5, 1994.
327   To some Arkansans: Int. Woody Bassett, June 21, 1993. Also *Arkansas Law Journal* (Fall 1993).
328   "unusual ability to absorb": Int. Woody Bassett, June 21, 1993.
328   Most members of the law school: Ints. Wylie Davis, March 31, 1994; Mort Gitelman, June 21, 1993; and Rafael Guzman, April 4, 1994.
328   "She would not sit for idle": Int. Mort Gitelman, June 21, 1993.
328   "a prodigious worker": Int. David Newbern, April 6, 1994.
328   "If you are looking for a battleground": Copy of Clinton speech, Sept. 13, 1974, in Doug Wallace Papers, UALR.
329   Clinton packed the fall convention: Ints. Paul Fray, April 25, 1994; Doug Wallace, April 14, 1994; and Steve Smith, July 15, 1993.
329   "We have come together": Clinton speech, Sept. 13, 1974.
330   "It was wonderful to work": Int. Steve Smith, July 15, 1993.

330 "If we do not reverse": Sept. 23, 1974. From Doug Wallace Papers, UALR.

330 "Bill planed more blocks": Int. Ron Cecil, Jan. 3, 1994.

330 Powell came to Fayetteville: Ints. Steve Smith, July 15, 1993; Jody Powell, Sept. 8, 1994; and Doug Wallace, April 21, 1994.

331 "Find a dramatic way": Notes of Powell meeting, Sept. 5, 1974, Doug Wallace Papers, UALR.

331 He wore the khaki work uniform: *WP,* March 22, 1992: "In Arkansas, the Game Is Chicken," David Maraniss and Michael Weisskopf.

331 But 1974 was a difficult year: Schwartz, *From Farm to Market,* p. 23.

331 Don Tyson stayed in the shadows: Ints. Paul Fray, April 25, 1974, and Doug Wallace, April 21, 1974.

332 "certainly not Bill Clinton": Int. Brenda Blagg, July 29, 1993.

332 "We're trying to get a copy": Ints. Steve Smith, July 15, 1993; Neil McDonald, May 4, 1994; and Ron Addington, April 23, 1994.

332 "This was his first race": Int. Doug Wallace, April 21, 1994.

333 "butt prints": Int. Brenda Blagg, July 29, 1993.

333 heard rumors at his church: Int. John Baran, April 25, 1994.

333 "some conservative preachers": Ints. Mary Lee Fray, April 25 and May 3, 1994.

333 "They were trying to pin Bill": Int. Neil McDonald, May 4, 1994.

333 "Paul wanted to play hardball": Int. Doug Wallace, April 21, 1994.

333 When he entered the apartment: Int. Randy White, April 11, 1994.

334 "Bill . . . tried to lecture him": Int. Neil McDonald, May 4, 1994.

334 forgotten to pay his utility bills: Ints. Ron Addington, March 31 and April 23, 1994.

334 "The damage done": Undated campaign memo, Doug Wallace Papers, UALR.

334 "It's like the widow's mite": Int. David Matthews, May 24, 1994.

335 His temper was an accepted part: Ints. Ron Addington, March 29, 1994; Doug Wallace, April 21, 1994; B. A. Rudolph and Neil McDonald, May 4, 1994.

335 "He'd say, 'Don't ever' ": Int. Harry Truman Moore, June 15, 1994.

335 "They'd have the biggest damn fights": Int. Ron Addington, April 23, 1994.

335 "Our organization went to shit": *Ibid.*

335 "She . . . rubs people the wrong way": Undated Wallace memo, Doug Wallace Papers, UALR.

336 "Paul was rough around": Ints. Doug Wallace, April 21 and May 11, 1994.

336 Rodham took the ethical high ground: Ints. Paul Fray, April 25 and May 23, 1994; Doug Wallace, May 11, 1994; and Neil McDonald, May 4, 1994.

336 "The attorney already had": Ints. Paul Fray, April 25 and May 23, 1994.

336 "She got adamant": *Ibid.*

336 the mood was buoyant: The account of this election night is drawn from interviews with Harry Truman Moore, June 15, 1994; Paul Fray, April 25, 1994; Mary Lee Fray, April 25, 1994; Steve Smith, July 14, 1993; B. A. Rudolph and Doug Wallace, April 21, 1993; and Neil McDonald, May 4, 1994.

337 He then sent a telegram: Copy of telegram in Doug Wallace Papers, UALR.

338 Clinton drove to the square: Ints. Paul Fray, April 25, 1994; Mary Lee Fray, April 25, 1994; and Doug Wallace, April 21, 1994.

Nineteen: Governor-in-Waiting

340 "The office of attorney general": Wallace memo on 1976 elections, Doug Wallace Papers, UALR.

340 This convenient assignment: Clinton News Release No. 6, April 13, 1976, Doug Wallace Papers, UALR: "Clinton has traveled extensively throughout the state speaking to groups about the Arkansas presidential primary law and the Democratic Party rules concerning delegate selection."

341 At the legal clinic: *Arkansas Law Journal* (Fall 1993).

341 "People need the Lord": *New York Review of Books,* Oct. 22, 1992: "A Doll's House." Also, conversation with author, Aug. 6, 1992.

341   It was left to Newcomb: Int. Robert Newcomb, May 7, 1994.
342   they would buy yogurt: Int. Diane Kincaid Blair, Aug. 19, 1994.
342   "a burst of patriotism": *Ibid.*
342   They shared an apartment: Int. Neil McDonald, May 4, 1994.
342   Rodham and Clinton: Ints. Diane Kincaid Blair, June 10, 1993; James Blair, June 10, 1983; and Ann Henry, July 16, 1993.
342   "All we ever do": Int. Carolyn Yeldell Staley, June 8, 1993.
342   She had heard Clinton complain: Int. Betsey Wright, Feb. 15, 1993.
342   Rodham and Clinton came over: Int. Diane Kincaid Blair, Aug. 19, 1994.
343   "Hillary was very curious": Int. Ann Henry, July 16, 1993.
343   " 'Look at Eleanor Roosevelt!' ": *Ibid.*
344   Ellis encouraged her: Int. Carolyn Ellis, Jan. 28, 1994.
344   When Rodham arrived back: Radcliffe, *A First Lady,* p. 147.
344   "was looking more at life": Int. Ann Henry, July 16, 1993.
344   The one concession: Int. Bettie Lu Lancaster, July 27, 1994.
344   It was a traditional: Int. Victor Nixon, Aug. 2, 1994.
344   Hughie Rodham's vast underestimation: Int. Betsy Johnson Ebeling, Sept. 27, 1994.
345   That morning at the Fayetteville: *Leading,* p. 219.
345   "the gregariousness of Bill": Int. Ann Henry, July 27, 1994.
345   Clinton took along a copy: Int. Bill Clinton, January 20, 1992.
345   Clinton also wrote thank-you: Int. Bettie Lu Lancaster, July 27, 1994.
345   The old boys: Rhodes class letter, *American Oxonian* (1975), Bob Reich, secretary.
346   Clinton took an unpaid leave: University of Arkansas Law School records.
346   "My opponent in the last election": Copy of letter to Patricia M. Garlid, Denver, April 28, 1976, Doug Wallace Papers, UALR.
346   He made his formal campaign announcement: Int. Doug Wallace, April 21, 1994. Copy of press announcement, March 17, 1976, Doug Wallace Papers, UALR.
346   He was relieved when: Int. Doug Wallace, April 21, 1993.
347   Clinton turned to Governor Pryor: Int. David Pryor, June 29, 1993. Also, Jernigan, *As They Know Him,* p. 75.
347   Newspaper ads listed: Materials used in ads in Doug Wallace Papers, UALR.
347   Jernigan later acknowledged: *As They Know Him,* p. 74.
347   "This morning as I drove up": Speech transcript, April 10, 1976, Doug Wallace Papers, UALR.
348   State labor leaders: Int. J. Bill Becker, Jan. 7, 1992. Also, *Arkansas Democrat,* April 18, 1976, p. 1: "Clinton won't get labor's backing this time around."
348   "And we had to move away": Int. Doug Wallace, April 21, 1994.
348   In one labor questionnaire: Response to *Arkansas Advocate* questionnaire, Doug Wallace Papers, UALR. When he appeared before the AFL-CIO, Clinton said: "I know what is uppermost in your minds is the conflict between your efforts to amend the right-to-work law and my statements about it. From our past experience together, you know I am not inclined to dodge an issue and I did not dodge that one."
348   At the graduation ceremonies: 1976 campaign document, April 27, 1976, Doug Wallace Papers, UALR.
349   "More and more": Keynote speech at Little River Bi-Centennial Celebration, May 2, 1976, Doug Wallace Papers, UALR.
349   He thought he might take every ballot: Int. Doug Wallace, April 21, 1994.
349   As his thirtieth birthday approached: Int. Bill Clinton, January 20, 1992.
349   If he was not obsessed: *Ibid.*
349   "All is madness here": Letter to Betsey Wright, no date.
350   When Carter visited Little Rock: Copy of list of Arkansans Carter was to write thank-you letters to after visit, Doug Wallace Papers, UALR.
351   "Divorce him and stay here!": Int. Mort Gitelman, June 21, 1993.
351   "get on board early": "Greene County Citizens for Clinton committee mailing. H. T. Moore.

351 The attorney general's job: Ints. David Newcomb, May 7, 1994; Terry Kirkpatrick, April 5, 1994; and Steve Smith, July 15, 1993.
352 fleshily abundant Dolly Parton: Ints. Richard Morris, July 27, 1994, and Joe Purvis, September 1994.
352 "He was just walking around": Ints. Terry Kirkpatrick, April 5, 1994, and Joe Purvis, September 1994.
352 Elvis's death left Clinton: *Ibid.*
352 Morris flew down: Int. Richard Morris, July 27, 1994.
353 Morris agreed to do a poll: *Ibid.*
353 A few weeks later: Int. David Pryor, June 29, 1993.
353 "you could run for governor": *Ibid.*
354 "the only truly distinguished": *Arkansas Gazette,* May 10, 1978.
354 Internal campaign news: 1978 campaign daily news summaries, Doug Wallace Papers, UALR.
354 "If people knew how old-fashioned": Nelson, *Hillary Factor,* p. 209.
354 plotting how Pryor could beat Tucker: Int. Richard Morris, July 27, 1994.
355 Clinton, the back room political consultant: *Ibid.*
355 Pryor's wife, Barbara: *Ibid.*
355 They were determined: Int. Rudy Moore, June 10, 1993.
356 Geren charged that Clinton: *Arkansas Gazette,* Oct. 28, 1978.
356 Clinton easily rebuffed the charge: *Ibid.*
356 Geren called him at home: Int. Ed Howard, July 19, 1993.
356 "I was disappointed with Bill": *Ibid.*
357 The pain came: Int. Veta Ranchino, April 23, 1994.
357 The omen of future trouble: Carter note to Clinton, Doug Wallace Papers, UALR.

Twenty: Great Expectations

358 At his side was Dave Matter: Int. David Matter, Feb. 5, 1993.
359 "this was a good time": Int. Carolyn Yeldell Staley, June 8, 1993.
359 Arriving by private jet: Int. Charlie Daniels, Jan. 27, 1994.
359 "Well, what do you think?": Int. Steve Cohen, Feb. 3, 1994.
359 "For as long as I can": Text of Governor Clinton's Inaugural Address, Jan. 9, 1979.
360 Craig returned to Washington: Int. Greg Craig, Jan. 27, 1994.
360 Two promises were unmet: Int. Rudy Moore, June 10, 1993.
360 Clinton asked Dick Morris: Int. Richard Morris, July 27, 1994.
361 Clinton directed Morris: *Ibid.*
361 The administration drafted: Ints. Rudy Moore, June 10, 1993, and James McDougal, April 22, 1994.
361 the poultry industry: *WP,* March 22, 1992, David Maraniss and Michael Weisskopf. "The chicken connection is symbolized by the fact that a legislator, Sen. Joe Yates, is on the payroll of the poultry federation as director of industrial relations. Six lawmakers last year were guests of the federation for an all-expenses-paid golf outing out of state, state ethics records show, and four more were hosted by Don Tyson at a marlin-fishing vacation in Mexico."
361 When he arrived at the terminal: Int. Randy White, April 11, 1994.
362 As Clinton "pounded like crazy": *Ibid.*
362 "Whenever we'd pass": *Ibid.*
363 Labor leader J. Bill Becker groused: Int. J. Bill Becker, Jan. 7, 1992.
363 "Clinton was so friendly": Int. Rudy Moore, June 10, 1993.
363 "I have no time to be governor!": Int. Randy White, April 11, 1994.
363 Clinton's staff arranged a summit: Int. Rudy Moore, July 16, 1993.
364 "Will you commit larceny today?": Int. Randy White, April 11, 1994.
364 "RW—see if you can work him in": Rudy Moore note in White's files.
364 he now occasionally answered to "Baby": Int. Harry Truman Moore, June 15, 1994.

364   "It was not easy for a boy": Int. Ray Smith, Jr., April 25, 1994.
364   Three executive assistants: Ints. Rudy Moore, June 10 and July 15, 1993; Steve Smith, July 15, 1993.
365   As Clinton came to power: The account of the clear-cutting debate is drawn largely from a *WP* article, May 26, 1992: "Clinton's Hard Lesson In Pragmatism," Michael Weisskopf and David Maraniss.
365   On a helicopter tour: Int. Steve Smith, July 14, 1993
366   The task force held thirteen hearings: *Ibid.*
366   In private meetings: Int. John Ed Anthony, April 1992.
366   "Every log driver": *Ibid.*
366   "Every time I go south": *Ibid.* Also int. Steve Smith, July 14, 1993.
367   It was also around that time: Int. Steve Smith, July 15, 1993.
367   Smith had mostly loved working: *Ibid.*
367   "Bill never really bothered us": Int. John Ed Anthony, April 1992.
368   he played golf at a country club: Int. Duke Watts, May 6, 1993. (Although Clinton later developed a penchant for mulligans when his tee shots strayed, as a teenager, according to Watts, he was more honest than many of his friends. Watts said that in tournaments most of the boys would try to get in flights below their true abilities, whereas Clinton would always play in a more difficult flight. His golf talents outshone his abilities in the country club pool. Pat Parker, a lifeguard at Belevedere Country Club, once had to save a struggling Clinton who had knocked himself out doing a bellyflop off the high dive.)
368   Rudy Moore often told the story: Int. Rudy Moore, June 10, 1993.
369   Rodham's father taught her how: Hillary Clinton White House press conference, April 22, 1994.
369   "our prevailing, acquisitive": Transcript, Hillary Rodham Commencement Address, May 31, 1969. From Wellesley College archives.
369   Blair, a Springdale lawyer: Int. Jim Blair, Sept. 6, 1994.
370   They had all read Joan Didion's: Int. Diane Blair, June 10, 1993.
370   Blair was abandoned: Int. Jim Blair, Sept. 6, 1994.
370   By the time he recruited Rodham: *Ibid.*
370   Clients were plentiful: *WP,* April 10, 1994, Sharon LaFraniere and Charles R. Babcock; *Wall Street Journal,* April 1, 1994, Jeffrey Taylor and Bruce Ingersoll.
371   Blair could have kept: Int. Jim Blair, Sept. 6, 1994.
371   Playing the commodities market: Perhaps the clearest essay on the subject was James K. Glassman's "Hillary's Cows," *The New Republic,* May 16, 1994.
372   "I thought it was terrible": Int. Diane Blair, Aug. 19, 1994.
372   She seemed to get a break: *WP,* May 27, 1994: "Hillary Clinton Futures Trades Detailed," Charles R. Babcock.
372   "They weren't going to hassle me": Int. Jim Blair, Sept. 6, 1994.
373   She had less good fortune that year: The first national article detailing the Whitewater land deal was by *New York Times* investigative reporter Jeff Gerth, March 8, 1992. There had been less detailed articles in Little Rock newspapers earlier. Clinton critic Roy Drew, a stock market consultant, would later claim that he pointed Gerth in the direction of McDougal. Another Clinton antagonist, Sheffield Nelson, also pushed the story to national reporters during the early stages of the presidential campaign.
373   He could often be found: Ints. Steve Smith, April 26, 1994; Rudy Moore, April 27, 1994; and Randy White, April 11, 1994.
373   McDougal had encountered them: Int. Jim McDougal, April 22, 1994.
373   He had been making land deals: *Ibid.*
374   "It was a beautiful development": Int. Susan McDougal, March 10, 1992.
374   One day they were invited to tea: Int. Mandy Merck, May 14, 1993.
375   "I'm beginning to think": *Ibid.*
375   "He walked all over": *Arkansas Gazette,* Feb. 29, 1980: "Girl Born to Clinton and Wife."

375   "That's a nice song": Int. Carolyn Yeldell Staley, July 12, 1993.
376   Clinton told Rodham that White: Int. Bill Clinton, Jan. 20, 1992.
376   a bad situation deteriorated: The account of Clinton's handling of the Fort Chaffee
      crisis is drawn largely from *WP,* Oct. 22, 1992: "Cuban Refugee Uprising Offers View
      of Clinton's Reaction to Crisis," David Maraniss. Also from documents at the Carter
      Library, and interviews with Rudy Moore, June 10, 1993; Ron Addington, April 5,
      1994; and Jody Powell, Sept. 8, 1994.
378   Eidenberg, the White House official: Int. Eugene Eidenberg, October 1992.
378   "Don't answer it": Int. Randy White, April 11, 1994.
379   "Rudy, they're killing me": Int. Rudy Moore, June 10, 1993.
379   White was in the room: Int. Randy White, April 11, 1994.
379   Clinton nonetheless promised: Transcript of Clinton conversations with White House
      aide Gene Eidenberg, Carter Library, Atlanta, Georgia.
380   "kick and fuss and holler": Int. Rudy Moore, June 10, 1993.
380   On the afternoon of August 4: Int. Eugene Eidenberg, October 1992. Also Carter
      Library documents on conversation with Jimmy Carter.
381   "I understand": Transcript of Eidenberg statement at Fort Chaffee, Carter Library.
381   Rodham derided him: Int. Fred Altshuler, June 24, 1993.
381   Wagner understood: Int. Carl Wagner, June 28, 1993.
382   Merck was covering the convention: Int. Mandy Merck, May 14, 1993.
382   Clinton changed the subject: *Ibid.*
382   "Energize us": Int. Carolyn Yeldell Staley, June 8, 1993.
382   Simply putting together: Transcript, Address by Bill Clinton, Democratic National
      Convention, 1980. From governor's archives.
383   "What else": Int. Randy White, April 11, 1994.
383   A child had broken his record: Int. Rudy Moore, July 16.
383   To Moore, he seemed distracted: Ints. Rudy Moore, June 10, 1993, and Randy White,
      April 11, 1994.
384   Clinton could not believe: *Ibid.*
384   which so enraged Virginia Dwire: Int. Melinda Gassaway, *Sentinel-Record* editor, April
      25, 1994.
384   The marks against Morris: Int. Rudy Moore, Aug. 18, 1994.
385   "had gone from being": Int. Dick Morris, Aug. 1, 1994.
385   "We need Dick": *Ibid.*
385   "the last straw": Int. Randy White, April 11, 1994.
385   "God, I'm an idiot!": Int. Dick Morris, Aug. 1, 1994.
386   He found a deck of cards: Int. Richard Mason, June 30, 1994.

Twenty-One: The Only Track

387   They had an open line: Int. Rudy Moore, June 10, 1993.
387   she was trembling slightly: Int. Gloria Cabe, Sept. 13, 1994.
388   He phoned Bill Simmons: Int. Bill Simmons, Jan. 12, 1992.
388   although when David Broder: Int. David Broder, July 2, 1993.
388   "The guy screwed me": Int. Rick Stearns, March 4, 1993.
388   One day he invited several aides: Int. Randy White, April 11, 1994.
389   Brown offered him a job: Int. Mickey Kantor, Sept. 14, 1994.
390   During a trip to Fayetteville: Int. Diane Blair, June 10, 1993.
390   "It's the only track": *Ibid.*
390   Then he called her one night: Int. Billie Carr, Dec. 15, 1992.
390   "Woody! Hey, Woody!": Int. Woody Bassett, June 21, 1993.
390   "Here's an idea": Ints. Rudy Moore, July 16, 1993, and Randy White, April 11, 1994.
391   Rodham called Dick Morris: Int. Dick Morris, Aug. 1, 1994.
391   And Clinton called Betsey Wright: Int. Betsey Wright, June 27, 1993.
391   She had assumed the role of bad cop: Int. Rudy Moore, July 16, 1993.

391 He told Wright that he needed: Int. Betsey Wright, June 27, 1993.
391 Within days of taking the call: Ints. Betsey Wright, June 27, 1993, and Gloria Cabe,
     Sept. 13, 1994.
392 The youngest former governor: Ints. Carolyn Yeldell Staley, July 12, 1993; Betsey
     Wright, June 27, 1993: and Gloria Cabe, Sept. 13, 1994.
392 He looked pathetic: Int. Dick Morris, Aug. 1, 1994.
393 "I've been thinking a lot": Letter to Don Jones, 1981.
393 Rodham offered a more political: *Arkansas Gazette,* Feb. 22, 1981.
393 "I knew what she had gone": Int. Fred Altshuler, June 24, 1993.
395 The traveling show of 1981: Int. Randy White, April 11, 1994.
395 The AFL-CIO summer convention: *Arkansas Gazette,* June 18, 1981, John Brummett,
     p. 1.
396 "When someone is beating you": Int. Doug Wallace, April 21, 1994.
396 "The rug had been pulled out": Int. Rudy Moore, June 10, 1993. Also, Bill Clinton
     letter to Rudy Moore, no date.
397 Jack Germond and Jules Witcover: *Arkansas Gazette,* July 10, 1981: "Columnists Are
     Wrong, Clinton Says."
397 It did not start out as a pleasant: Ints. Dick Morris, Aug. 1, 1994, and Betsey Wright,
     Aug. 25, 1994.
397 Morris and Wright began to construct: *Ibid.*
398 "You have to recognize your sins": Int. Dick Morris, Aug. 1, 1994.
399 The ads began running: *Arkansas Gazette,* Feb. 9, 1981: "Clinton Makes It Official,
     Uses Taped Television Ad," p. 1.
399 "Hillary's gonna have to": Int. Ray Smith, April 25, 1994.
399 "What were people wearing?": Int. Carolyn Yeldell Staley, June 8, 1993.
399 Clinton recalled a conversation: "Hillary the Pol," *The New Yorker,* May 30, 1994,
     Connie Bruck.
400 All that changed: *Arkansas Gazette,* Feb. 28, 1981: "Rodham Takes Leave to Join
     Campaign as 'Mrs. Bill Clinton.' "
400 " 'No,' came the ice cold answer": *Times-News* editorial reprinted in *Arkansas Ga-
     zette,* March 7, 1982.
400 People hated it: Int. Dick Morris, Aug. 1, 1994.
401 "Bill Clinton on the Low Road": *Arkansas Gazette,* April 28, 1982.
401 "said he would tear our heads off": *Arkansas Gazette,* May 16, 1982.
401 "The polls showed a tremendous": Int. Dick Morris, Aug. 1, 1994.
402 "Tucker had a record": Int. Betsey Wright, June 27, 1993.
402 "Hell, he knew what was at stake": Int. Woody Bassett, June 21, 1993.
402 Young black professionals: Ints. Carol Willis, June 30, 1993, and Rodney Slater, Aug.
     7, 1992.
403 "We felt like we were behind": Int. Dick Morris, Aug. 1, 1994.
403 "They're about ready": Int. Carol Willis, June 30, 1993.
404 They set up a stage: Ints. Betsey Wright, June 27, 1993, and Gloria Cabe, Sept. 13,
     1994.

Twenty-two: The Permanent Campaign

405 Already that day: *Arkansas Gazette,* Jan. 12, 1983: "Inaugurated Before Huge Crowd,"
     p. 1; "Religious Service Starts Inaugural," p. 18. Also, int. Betsey Wright, Aug. 25, 1994.
405 "He realized that he needed": Int. Paul Root, July 13, 1993.
406 They were freewheeling: Int. Gloria Cabe, Sept. 13, 1994.
406 The bad news had started: Int. Betsey Wright, Aug. 25, 1994.
406 In the end, he worried: Int. Dick Morris, Aug. 4, 1994.
407 "an almost Catholic splitting": *Ibid.*
408 Clinton had called Starr: Int. John Robert Starr, Jan. 12, 1992.
408 "His entire strategy in governing": Int. Dick Morris, Aug. 4, 1994.

408 Although Morris conducted the polls: Ints. Betsey Wright, Aug. 25, 1994, and Dick Morris, Aug. 4, 1994.

409 "one of the most embarrassing defeats": *Arkansas Gazette,* Feb. 20, 1983: "Clinton Wants Others to Lead," Ernest Dumas.

409 The state highway director was now shocked: *Arkansas Gazette,* March 3, 1983: "Called Double-crosser by Henry Gray."

409 "Wasn't Weak, Vacillating": *Arkansas Gazette,* March 25, 1983.

409 Clinton was eager to become known: Ints. Betsey Wright, Aug. 25, 1994, and Dick Morris, Aug. 4, 1994.

410 "He knew he couldn't succeed": *Ibid.*

410 Trotter bitterly cited: *Arkansas Gazette,* Aug. 16, 1983.

410 In some schools: Int. Paul Root, July 13, 1993, and Root documents as governor's education aide.

411 There was a national context: *Arkansas Gazette,* April 23, 1983: "National Report Blueprint for Arkansas."

411 "This guarantees that I will have": *Arkansas Gazette,* April 23, 1983.

411 The inadequacies the committee members found: From report of Education Standards Committee, 1983. Also documents of Paul Root, education aide.

411 "I think we've elected the wrong Clinton!": *Arkansas Gazette,* July 29, 1983.

411 Clinton and Morris experimented: Int. Dick Morris, Aug. 4, 1994.

412 It was a concept: Ints. Gloria Cabe, Sept. 13, 1994, and Dick Morris, Aug. 4, 1994. (Gloria Cabe's daughter had a teacher who marked wrong student test answers that gave a precise number to the question of how old the United States was rather than parroting the imprecise answer in their textbook, "about 200 years.")

412 Frank White, the former governor: *Arkansas Gazette,* Sept. 8, 1983. Also int. Dick Morris, Aug. 4, 1994.

412 When Morris polled on the teacher tests: Ints. Dick Morris, Aug. 1 and 4, 1994.

412 On the day before: Int. Betsey Wright, Aug. 25, 1994.

413 Clinton formed a finance committee: *Arkansas Gazette,* Sept. 29, 1993.

413 "In the life of our state": Transcript, Governor Bill Clinton Address to Joint Session, Oct. 4, 1983.

414 Carol Willis and other black: Int. Carol Willis, June 30, 1993.

414 He cornered Vada Sheid: Int. Vada Sheid, July 28, 1993.

415 At a meeting in the governor's office: Int. J. Bill Becker, Jan. 7, 1992. Also *Arkansas Gazette,* Nov. 9, 1983, John Brummett.

415 "Clinton's lying to you!": Int. J. Bill Becker, Jan. 7, 1992.

415 The substantive results: From Paul Root documents on Arkansas education. Also numerous *Arkansas Gazette* articles 1986–87.

416 Jogging was the craze: Int. Jim Blair, June 10, 1993.

416 Clinton had focused: Int. Bill Clinton, Jan. 20, 1992.

417 Clinton asked one of his colleagues: *Arkansas Gazette,* Aug. 12, 1984, based on *New York* magazine article by Richard Reeves.

417 "Harry Truman would tell us": Transcript, Speech honoring Harry Truman by Governor Bill Clinton, Democratic National Convention, July 16, 1984.

Twenty-three: Relationships

419 This time it began: Ints. Robert Gibbs, Aug. 11, 1994, and Larry Gleghorn, Aug. 11, 1994.

419 both Gibbs and Gleghorn knew the Clintons: *Ibid.*

419 though he detested the memory: Int. Virginia Kelley, Jan. 13, 1992. Also *WP,* Jan. 24, 1993: "Oh, Brother," Laura Blumenfeld.

420 One day soon after: Ints. Betsey Wright, Aug. 25, 1994; Hillary Clinton, Jan. 16, 1992; and Bill Clinton, Jan. 20, 1992.

420 he wrote a note: Int. Betsey Wright, Aug. 25, 1994.

420 "got so wrapped up in": Int. Bill Clinton, Jan. 20, 1992.

420   Clinton occasionally had asked: Int. Larry Gleghorn, Aug. 11, 1994.
420   "not the first time": Int. Betsey Wright, Aug. 25, 1994.
420   With Officer Gibbs hiding: Int. Robert Gibbs, Aug. 11, 1994.
420   Four more deals: *Ibid.*
421   Clinton talked to both Roger and his mother: Int. Virginia Kelley, Jan. 13, 1992. Also transcript, Roger Clinton conversations with informant Rodney Myers, obtained in FOIA request. Case File 50-033-84. U.S. District Court, Little Rock.
421   "Do you think they are ever": Int. Betsey Wright, Aug. 25, 1994.
421   It was an emotional scene: *Leading,* pp. 250–51.
421   a period of intense introspection began: Ints. Virginia Kelley, Jan. 13, 1992, and Bill Clinton, Jan. 20, 1992. Also *Leading,* p. 252.
422   "He did a lot of introspection": Int. Betsey Wright, Aug. 25, 1994.
422   "I think we're all addicted to something": Ints. Carolyn Yeldell Staley, June 8 and July 12, 1993.
422   Roger agreed to testify: Int. Larry Gleghorn, Aug. 11, 1994.
422   The connections: *Arkansas Gazette,* Oct. 25, 1986. Also *Newsweek,* Jan. 24, 1994: "The Fall of a Bond Daddy."
423   "Here the brother of the governor": Int. Asa Hutchinson, Aug. 2, 1994.
423   "We're closer than any brothers": Transcript, Roger Clinton conversations with informant Rodney Myers, obtained in FOIA request. Case File 50-033-84.
423   Minutes before: *Ibid.*
424   Virginia had taken down: Int. Virginia Kelley, Jan. 13, 1992.
425   Edith Cassidy constantly accused: *Leading,* p. 23.
425   she developed a reputation: Int. Myra Irvin, Feb. 9, 1993.
425   During the 1978 gubernatorial campaign: Int. Rudy Moore, June 10, 1993.
425   Clinton's table attracted a crowd: Int. Randy White, April 11, 1994.
425   Trooper L. D. Brown: *WP,* April 11, 1994, p. 6, Michael Isikoff, following an article in *American Spectator* by Daniel Wattenberg.
426   Hillary said she could never: Int. Carolyn Yeldell Staley, June 8 and July 12, 1993.
426   "I wonder how history": *Ibid.*
427   a bossy big sister: Ints. Betsey Wright, Feb. 15 and June 28, 1993; Aug. 25, 1994.
427   "I won't have it!": Int. Betsey Wright, Aug. 25, 1994.
427   Wright swatted it: Int. Betsey Wright, Feb. 15, 1993.
428   Hillary felt the need: Ints. Betsey Wright, Feb. 15, 1993, and Dick Morris, Aug. 4, 1994.
428   She told Drew: Int. Roy Drew, April 22, 1994.
428   wanted to build a swimming pool: Int. Dick Morris, Aug. 4, 1994.
429   she would devote hours to courting: Int. Gloria Cabe, Sept. 13, 1994. Also *The New Yorker,* May 30, 1994: "Hillary the Pol," Connie Bruck.
429   "She's got to be out": Int. Dick Morris, Aug. 4, 1994.
429   During the 1986 gubernatorial race: *Arkansas Gazette,* Sept. 18, 1986: "White Says Clinton Lied About Rose Law."
429   The Clinton team's political response: Ints. Dick Morris, Aug. 4, 1994, and Betsey Wright, June 28, 1993.
429   Dan Lasater, the bond broker: *Newsweek,* Jan. 24, 1994.
430   she helped represent Jim McDougal: *NYT,* March 8, 1992.
430   According to McDougal and his wife: Ints. Susan McDougal, March 10, 1992, and Jim McDougal, April 22, 1994.
430   McDougal was feeling regret: *Ibid.*
431   Wright viewed the event: Int. Betsey Wright, Aug. 25, 1994.
431   They were discussing the works: Int. Don Jones, April 14, 1993.
432   "As a member of the British": Hillary Clinton gave speeches throughout Arkansas churches on why she was a Methodist. She included segments of the speech in her commencement address at Hendrix College, May 30, 1992.
432   Hillary's church in downtown Little Rock: Ints. Reverend Ed Matthews, July 13, 1993, and Clinton Burleson, July 13, 1993.
433   "One of her favorite thoughts": Int. Reverend Ed Matthews, July 13, 1993.

433 "not going to tote her Bible": *Ibid.*
433 "would get up there and act": Int. Mary Frances Vaught, May 1992.
433 Clinton did not go to church: The account of Clinton at Immanuel Baptist Church and his relationship with W. O. Vaught is drawn from interviews with Bill Clinton, May 14, 1992; Carl Vaught and Mary Frances Vaught, May 1992; Betsey Wright, May 1992; and Rudy Moore, June 10, 1993. Also *WP,* June 29, 1992: "Roots of Clinton's Faith Deep, Varied," David Maraniss, p. 1.

Twenty-four: Saying the Words

436 "The latest polls": *American Oxonian* (Winter 1986).
436 poor southern forebears: New England Historical Genealogical Society newsletter, Dec. 12, 1992.
437 one week after he turned forty: *Arkansas Gazette,* Aug. 27, 1986, p. 1.
437 "always standing, never sitting": Int. Harry Hughes, June 10, 1994.
438 "Nobody ever told me": Int. Gloria Cabe, Sept. 13, 1994.
438 After the election: Ints. Betsey Wright, Aug. 25, 1994, and Moril Harriman, July 15, 1993.
438 Early on the evening: *WP,* March 21, 1987.
438 Clinton had talked to friends: Int. Kit Ashby, Jan. 20, 1993.
439 Gloria Cabe ventured up: Int. Gloria Cabe, Sept. 13, 1994.
439 "Your willingness to help us": Letter to Charlie Daniels, May 20, 1987.
440 "a statute of limitations": Int. Bob Armstrong, Jan. 6, 1993.
440 Clinton "wanted to believe": Ints. Betsey Wright, Feb. 15 and June 28, 1993, Aug. 25, 1994.
440 "a tremendous terror": Int. Dick Morris, Aug. 4, 1994.
440 He traveled to Washington: Int. Steve Cohen, Feb. 3, 1994.
440 Their first choice was: Int. Betsey Wright, June 28, 1993.
440 A few days before the announcement: Ints. Betsey Wright, Feb. 15 and June 28, 1993, and Aug. 25, 1994.
441 Wagner was a generational cohort: Ints. Carl Wagner, June 28, 1993, Feb. 4, 1994.
441 "So what's the bottom line?": *Ibid.*
441 "this guy doesn't know": Int. Steve Cohen, Feb. 3, 1994.
442 Kantor took the lead: Int. Mickey Kantor, Sept. 14, 1994.
442 on a Sunday morning: Int. Paul Root, July 14, 1993.
443 "It was the turning point": Int. Mickey Kantor, Sept. 14, 1994.
443 Clinton faced the gathering: Ints. Gloria Cabe, Sept. 13, 1994; Betsey Wright, Aug. 25, 1994; Mickey Kantor, Sept. 14, 1994; Carl Wagner, Feb. 4, 1994; John Holum, June 1992; and Billie Carr, Dec. 15, 1992.
443 "I need some family time": Statement by Governor Bill Clinton on his decision not to seek the 1988 Democratic presidential nomination, July 15, 1987.
443 "this reminds me of the Fuhgawe": Int. David Leopoulos, June 9, 1993.
444 "the conflict between": Felix B. Arnold Lecture, University of Arkansas at Little Rock, Feb. 9, 1988.
444 Clinton had stayed up all night: Ints. Betsey Wright, July 1992, and Gloria Cabe, Sept. 13, 1994.
445 "No matter what happens": *Arkansas Gazette,* July 22, 1988.
445 Betsey Wright stood at the back: Ints. Betsey Wright, July 1992; Gloria Cabe, Sept. 13, 1994; and Harry Truman Moore, June 15, 1994. Also, *Arkansas Gazette,* July 21–22, 1988.
446 "God, Lindsey,": Int. Gloria Cabe, Sept. 13, 1994.
447 The Clintons tried to defuse: *Arkansas Gazette,* July 22, 1988: "I Just Fell On My Sword."
447 "We felt like we had made": Int. Gloria Cabe, Sept. 13, 1994.
447 Betsey Wright had flown back: Int. Betsey Wright, July 1992.

447   "So this is the guy": Int. Judy Trabulsi, Feb. 2, 1993.
447   Friends in Hollywood: Ints. Harry Thomason, July 16, 1992, and Mickey Kantor, Sept. 14, 1994.
448   Gloria Cabe said there were times: Int. Gloria Cabe, Sept. 13, 1994.
448   "He was upset that Dukakis": Int. Woody Bassett, June 21, 1993.
448   Not long after Dukakis lost: Rhodes class of 1968 annual letter, *American Oxonian* (Winter 1988).
448   White left the meeting: Int. Randy White, April 14, 1994.
449   "The Great Communicator in Washington": An Address to a Joint Session of the 77th General Assembly, Jan. 9, 1989.
450   Major Betsey: Int. Carol Willis, June 30, 1993.
450   Now she was exhausted: Ints. Betsey Wright, Aug. 25, 1994; Gloria Cabe, Sept. 13, 1994; and Dick Morris, Aug. 4, 1994.
450   They had argued over the death penalty: Int. Betsey Wright, Feb. 15, 1993.
450   He was into self-denial again: Ints. Betsey Wright, Feb. 15, 1993, Aug. 25, 1994. (Wright also confided contemporaneously in Gloria Cabe, although she and Cabe later had a falling out.)
451   Nearly every week: Ints. Mary Frances Vaught and Gary Vaught, May 1992.
452   He was getting strong advice: Ints. Betsey Wright, June 28, 1993, and Gloria Cabe, Sept. 13, 1994.
452   "dithering and depressed": Int. Dick Morris, Aug. 4, 1994.
452   On the day before the event: Int. Gloria Cabe, Sept. 13, 1994.
453   convinced that up to thirty minutes: Int. Betsey Wright, June 28, 1993.
453   "you could have knocked Hillary over": Int. David Leopoulos, June 9, 1993.
454   He was accepting free rides: *WP*, March 22, 1992: "In Arkansas, the Game Is Chicken," David Maraniss and Michael Weisskopf, p. 1.
454   called him "Pards": Int. John Jacoby, April 1994.
454   Many of his longtime county chairs: Ints. Gloria Cabe, Sept. 13, 1994, and Woody Bassett, June 21, 1993.
454   Wright felt that Cabe: Int. Betsey Wright, Aug. 25, 1994.
455   Cabe wanted nothing to do: Int. Gloria Cabe, Sept. 13, 1994.
455   Clinton suddenly lost control: Ints. Gloria Cabe, Sept. 13, 1994, and Betsey Wright, Feb. 15, 1993. Dick Morris would neither confirm nor deny the incident.
455   At a strategy meeting the day before: Int. Dick Morris, Aug. 4, 1994.
455   "If Sheffield Nelson called": Int. Randy White, April 11, 1994.
456   "You always wanted me to run": Int. Frank Greer, June 29, 1993.
456   Nichols was a familiar character: Associated Press Little Rock bureau chief Bill Simmons broke the story that led to Nichols's firing: "Arkansans Financed Contra Calls," Sept. 11, 1988.
456   workers at his campaign headquarters: Clinton press secretary Mike Gauldin kept a chronological diary of events related to the Nichols lawsuit. It mentions several times when Clinton campaign aides called Nelson's headquarters and were told about the suit.
456   they had taped a commercial: Int. Paula Unruh, December 1991.
457   Morris did not consider: Int. Dick Morris, Aug. 4, 1994.
457   Gloria Cabe recruited: Int. Gloria Cabe, Sept. 13, 1994.
457   "I stuck it up their ass": Gennifer Flowers tape-recorded four telephone conversations with Clinton between December 1990 and December 1991. When she revealed the existence of the tapes during the 1992 presidential campaign, certain questions were raised about whether they had been altered or edited, but Clinton did not deny their authenticity. Gloria Cabe, in an interview on Sept. 13, 1994, said she was in the kitchen of the Governor's Mansion and overheard Clinton talking to Flowers one night about Chuck Robb, a topic in one of the tapes.
458   As Ed Howard was moving: Ints. Ed Howard, July 19, 1993, Sept. 18, 1994.
458   As Clinton prepared to speak: Int. Bruce Reed, Sept. 21, 1994.

459 "We're here to save": Later transcript of Cleveland DLC speech, May 6, 1991.
459 Two days later: *WP,* May 4, 1994, Michael Isikoff, Charles E. Shepard, and Sharon LaFraniere, p. 1.
459 They had known Clinton and Rodham: Ints. Roy Spence, Feb. 8, 1993, and Garry Mauro, July 11, 1994.
460 Everywhere he went: Ints. Mike Gauldin, June 1992; Gloria Cabe, Sept. 13, 1994; and Betsey Wright, Aug. 25, 1994.
460 Kantor gingerly broached: Ints. Mickey Kantor, Sept. 14, 1994; Carl Wagner, Feb. 4, 1994; and Gloria Cabe, Sept. 13, 1994.
460 Greer had come to realize: Int. Frank Greer, June 29, 1993.
461 "Hell, I just had dinner": *Ibid.*
461 In the early morning: Ints. Frank Greer, June 29, 1993; Tom Caplan, Sept. 12, 1994; and Bruce Reed, Sept. 21, 1994.
462 As Diane Blair approached: Int. Diane Blair, Aug. 19, 1994.
462 Clinton gave a speech: Remarks of Governor Bill Clinton, Little Rock, Arkansas, Oct. 3, 1991.
462 His mother was there: Int. Virginia Kelley, Jan. 13, 1992. Also *Leading,* p. 272.
463 The two friends from Hot Springs: Ints. David Leopoulos, July 17, 1994, and Carolyn Yeldell Staley, July 17, 1994.
463 Tommy Caplan, Clinton's Georgetown: Int. Tom Caplan, Sept. 12, 1994.
463 Bob Reich had flown down: Int. Robert Reich, Sept. 16, 1994.
463 Here, finally, is the day: Int. Carl Wagner, Sept. 21, 1994.
463 Diane Blair looked up: Int. Diane Blair, Aug. 19, 1994.
463 Betsey Wright could not bring: Ints. Betsey Wright, Feb. 15, 1993, Aug. 25, 1994.
464 Cliff Jackson was also at home: Int. Cliff Jackson, Sept. 22, 1994.
464 Chelsea took a place: Int. Tom Caplan, Sept. 12, 1994.
464 Clinton stayed up: Ints. Carolyn Yeldell Staley, July 17, 1994, and Tom Caplan, Sept. 12, 1994.

BIBLIOGRAPHY

Ali, Tariq. *Street Fighting Years: An Autobiography of the Sixties.* Citadel Underground, 1991.

Allen, Charles Flynn. *Governor William Jefferson Clinton: A Biography with a Special Focus on His Educational Contributions.* University of Mississippi doctoral dissertation, 1991.

Becker, Ernest. *The Denial of Death.* Free Press, 1973.

Blair, Diane. *Arkansas Politics and Government.* University of Nebraska Press, 1988.

Breslin, Jimmy. *How the Good Guys Finally Won.* Viking, 1975.

Cash, W. J. *The Mind of the South.* Vintage, 1941.

Crawford, Ann, and Keefer, Jack. *John B. Connally: Portrait in Power.* Jenkins, 1973.

Didion, Joan. *Play It As It Lays.* Farrar, Straus and Giroux, 1970.

Dionne, E. J. *Why Americans Hate Politics.* Simon & Schuster, 1991.

Dumas, Ernest. *The Clintons of Arkansas.* University of Arkansas Press, 1993.

Fulbright, J. William. *The Arrogance of Power.* Random House, 1967.

Fulbright, J. William, and Tillman, Seth P. *The Price of Empire.* Pantheon, 1989.

Gallen, David. *Bill Clinton As They Know Him.* Gallen Publishing Group, 1994.

Gitlin, Todd. *The Sixties: Years of Hope, Days of Rage.* Bantam, 1987.

Green, V. H. H. *A History of Oxford University.* Batsford Ltd., 1974.

Hanson, Gerald T., and Moneyhon, Carl H. *Historical Atlas of Arkansas.* University of Oklahoma Press, 1989.

Hart, Gary. *Right from the Start.* Quadrangle, 1973.

Johnson, Haynes, and Gwertzman, Bernard M. *Fulbright: The Dissenter.* Doubleday, 1968.

Johnson, Rachel. *The Oxford Myth.* Weidenfeld Nicolson Ltd., 1988.

Johnston, Phyllis Finton. *Bill Clinton's Public Policy for Arkansas: 1979–1980.* August House, 1982.

Kelley, Virginia. *Leading with My Heart.* Simon & Schuster, 1994.

Kludas, Arnold. *Great Passenger Ships of the World.* Translated from German by Charles Hodges. Patrick Stephens, 1985.

Levin, Robert E. *Bill Clinton: The Inside Story.* S.P.I. Books, 1992.

McSorley, Richard, S. J. *Peace Eyes.* Center for Peace Studies, 1978.

Miller, William H., S.S. *United States.* Patrick Stephens, 1991.

Morris, Willie. *New York Days.* Little, Brown, 1993.

Nelson, Rex. *The Hillary Factor.* Gallen Publishing Group, 1993.

Osborne, David. *Laboratories of Democracy.* Harvard Business School Press, 1990.

Powell, Lee Riley. *J. William Fulbright and America's Lost Crusade.* Rose Publishing Company, 1984.

Radcliffe, Donnie. *Hillary Rodham Clinton: A First Lady for Our Time.* Warner Books, 1993.

Rennie, Eric. *From a Campaign Album: A Case Study of the New Politics.* Pilgrim Press, 1973.

Reston, James, Jr. *The Lone Star.* Harper & Row, 1989.

Schwartz, Marvin. *Tyson: From Farm to Market.* University of Arkansas Press, 1991.

Shapiro, Andrew O., and John M. Striker. *Mastering the Draft.* Little, Brown, 1970.
Snow, Peter. *Oxford Observed.* John Murray Ltd., 1991.
Starr, John Robert. *Yellow Dogs and Dark Horses.* August House, 1987.
Steel, Ronald. *Pax Americana.* Viking Press, 1967.
Thackrah, John R. *The University and Colleges at Oxford.* Terrance Dalton Ltd., 1981.
Thwaite, Ann. *My Oxford.* Robson Books, 1977.
Viorst, Milton. *Fire in the Streets.* Touchstone, 1979.
Warner, Judith. *Hillary Clinton: The Inside Story.* Signet, 1993.
Wolin, Steven J., and Sybil. *The Resilient Self.* Villard, 1993.

ACKNOWLEDGMENTS

The Washington Post, my professional home since 1977, has given me the freedom to develop my own style, and for that I thank the editors who set the paper's tone over the years: Ben Bradlee, the late Howard Simons, Leonard Downie, Richard Harwood, Bob Kaiser, and Bob Woodward. Harwood, Kaiser, and Woodward have been special colleagues, knowing when to protect me and when to push me. They did both during my work on this book, while also providing intelligent readings of the manuscript. Bill Hamilton was generous with his encouragement and made it easier for me to write the in-depth articles that inspired this book. Any writer would be lucky to have a colleague as supportive as Maralee Schwartz, who boosted my spirits countless times. Editors Steve Luxenberg, Karen DeYoung, Fred Barbash, Brian Kelly, and Bill Elsen also helped me along the way. I feel a special debt of gratitude to Michael Weisskopf, my longtime pal and colleague, who worked with me on several articles that informed this book, and to his wife Judith Katz, who put up with me, excessive use of towels and all, during my early reporting trips to Washington while I was still living in Austin, Texas.

Other *Post* journalists whose work educated me include David Broder, E. J. Dionne, Dan Balz, Tom Edsall, Ann Devroy, Mike Isikoff, Sharon LaFraniere, David Von Drehle, Ruth Marcus, Al Kamen, Martha Sherrill, Laura Blumenfeld, Lloyd Grove, Susan Schmidt, Howard Schneider, Gene Weingarten, Donnie Radcliff, and Chuck Babcock. I also learned more about my subject from other journalists: Mark Halperin of ABC, a good friend and invaluable source of information; Adam Nagourney and Bill Nichols of *USA Today;* Walter Shapiro of *Esquire;* Garry Wills of the *New York Review of Books;* Priscilla Painton of *Time;* Ron Brownstein, David Lauter, Cathleen Decker, and William Rempel of the *Los Angeles Times;* Gwen Ifill, Jeff Gerth, Alessandra Stanley, Maureen Dowd, and Michael Kelly of the *New York Times;* Matt Cooper and Donald Baer of *U.S. News;* Jeff Birnbaum of *The Wall Street Journal;* Curtis Wilkie of *The Boston Globe* and John Brummett of the *Arkansas Times.* Of Brummett, Ernest Dumas, Max

Brantley, and many of their colleagues in Arkansas journalism, I think it is time for an outsider to say that they did a fine job examining Clinton during his gubernatorial years. The notion that Clinton got an easy ride before the national press corps came along is a presumptuous canard of East Coast journalism.

During the course of this project, I was lucky to have the help of several brilliant young researchers: foremost Katherine McCarron in Washington, and also Jennifer Pitts in Washington, Sarah Maraniss in Austin, Dan Alexander in London, and Peter Green in Prague. Lucy Shackelford and Elizabeth Hudson of the *Post* were also generous with their research assistance, as was the entire *Post* library staff. Other helpful librarians were Jon K. Reynolds at Georgetown University's Lauinger Library; Ben Primer, archivist at Princeton's Seeley G. Mudd Manuscript Library; Betty Austin, Fulbright archivist at the University of Arkansas at Fayetteville; and Linda Pine, special collections librarian at the University of Arkansas-Little Rock. Thanks also to Mary Nell Turner, town historian of Hope, and Inez Cline, her counterpart in Hot Springs.

Alice Mayhew at Simon & Schuster, in guiding me through my first book, was everything I had hoped a book editor would be: encouraging, coaxing, intelligent, excited, and exacting. Her refined red pen, and the black pen of her calm deputy, Eric Steel, instructed me in the art of long-form narrative. Thanks also to Ann Adelman and Lydia Buechler, first-rate copy editors. Rafe Sagalyn, my agent, was always generous and supportive.

My work in England was made infinitely easier by the good-humored hospitality of the Harris branch of the Maraniss extended family: Pat Harris, Francis Harris, and Angela Harris. Special thanks to John Harris for paving the way for me at Oxford. Harry Walsh made it possible for a computer illiterate to write a book. Michael Norman, my old dear friend, pushed me to write and kept me going when I doubted myself, as did John Feinstein, Chip Brown, Neil Henry, Richard Cramer, Mike Connolly, Mike Tackett, Elsa Walsh, Steve Amos, Jon Kalb, Don McCarthy, Henry Bryan, Maddy Blais, John Katzenbach, Blaine Harden, and Frank Roloff.

Two great editors, my parents, Mary and Elliott Maraniss, came bursting out of retirement to devote themselves to this book. It was a joy to decipher my father's illegible brilliance and to see how my mother could snap a sentence into shape with one precise editor's mark. Maggie, our sweet old sheepdog, stayed home with me during my long year of writing, making it less lonely. And most of all my thanks go to Linda, who supported me through it all, reading and editing every word late at night on the computer screen, sitting in my wobbly, screws-loose chair. She and Andrew and Sarah are the reasons my wheels did not come off. They are not everything, as the old Packer coach would say, they are the only thing.

INDEX